STUDIES IN JEWISH RELIGIOUS AND INTELLECTUAL HISTORY

Photo courtesy Studio Alice Holz, Jerusalem

ALEXANDER ALTMANN

STUDIES IN JEWISH RELIGIOUS AND INTELLECTUAL HISTORY

Presented to
ALEXANDER ALTMANN

On The Occasion of His
Seventieth Birthday

EDITED BY
Siegfried Stein
AND
Raphael Loewe

Published in Association with
The Institute of Jewish Studies, London
by
THE UNIVERSITY OF ALABAMA PRESS
University, Alabama

Library of Congress Cataloging in Publication Data

Main entry under title:

Studies in Jewish religious and intellectual history.

"Bibliography of the published writings of Alexander Altmann": p.
1. Judaism—History—Addresses, essays, lectures.
2. Altmann, Alexander, 1906– –Addresses, essays, lectures. I. Altmann, Alexander, 1906– II. Stein, Siegfried, 1909– III. Loewe, Raphael.
BM42.S8 296'.09 77-7294
ISBN 0–8173–6925–2

CONTENTS

Subject-Matter of Articles in Hebrew

(for Hebrew titles see separate list of contents preceding the Hebrew section)

EDITORS' PREFACE

DEAR PROFESSOR ALTMANN,

The presentation of a scholarly tribute is not an occasion on which to dilate upon the significance of your own work and achievements: they are appreciated by all who have contributed to this volume and will be familiar to most of its readers, and indeed the bibliography of your publications set forth below speaks for itself. It may nonetheless be appropriate to take note of the fact that in spite of the very wide range of your interests, a common denominator is present. You yourself described it some forty years ago as the great theme of Philosophy and Revelation. It is this that has constituted the centre of gravity of your work even if, in the unending search for truth and the study of those who have likewise made it their goal, you have moved somewhat from the more rigid reasoning of Jewish philosophy influenced by Aristotle and the Kalam to the less inflexible method deriving from neoplatonism and holding converse with mysticism, on to the thought of the Enlightenment and modern philosophy.

There is something else that must also be put on record here. Throughout your career, whether you have occupied a rabbinic or an academic position, you have not only given yourself to scholarship, but you have devoted time and energy to fostering scholarly work and scholarly ideals in others. It was this sense of responsibility towards the scholarly address to Judaism, as an intellectual commitment with profound social implications, that led you to establish the Institute of Jewish Studies which you founded in Manchester and which has since your departure to Brandeis found a congenial home in University College London. And it is a matter of pride to us that the Institute has taken the initiative in organising in your honour this collection of studies, all of which in some way reflect facets of Jewish history and Judaism as an intellectual and spiritual entity in interaction with its environment.

It is in the confidence that the list of your manifold achievements is by no means closed that we wish you, on behalf of all who have contributed to this volume and all who have collaborated with us in making its publication possible, many more years of scholarly activity, of serenity, and of happiness.

SIEGFRIED STEIN
RAPHAEL LOEWE

STUDIES IN JEWISH RELIGIOUS AND INTELLECTUAL HISTORY

Bibliography of the Published Writings of Alexander Altmann

Abbreviations

EB	*Encyclopaedia Britannica* (1964 edition)
EI	*Ha-Encyclopedia Ha-ᶜIvrith*
EJ	*Encyclopaedia Judaica* (1972)
JC	*The Jewish Chronicle* (London)
JJS	*The Journal of Jewish Studies*
MGWJ	*Monatsschrift für Geschichte und Wissenschaft des Judentums*
YLB	*Yearbook of the Leo Baeck Institute*

Titles shown in CAPITALS indicate books and other independent publications

1927

1. Zum Wesen der jüdischen Aesthetik. *Jeschurun.* ed. Joseph Wohlgemuth, 14:5–6 (1927), pp. 209–26.

1930

2. Metaphysik und Religion. *Jeschurun*, 17:9–12 (1930), pp. 321–47.

1931

3. METAPHYSIK UND RELIGION: DAS PROBLEM DER ABSOLUTEN TRANSZENDENZ. Berlin: Reuther und Reichard Verlag, 1931, 27 p. [Identical with no. 2.]
4. DIE GRUNDLAGEN DER WERTETHIK: WESEN, WERT, PERSON. MAX SCHELERS ERKENNTNIS- UND SEINSLEHRE IN KRITISCHER ANALYSE. Berlin: Reuther & Reichard Verlag, 1931 [= Berlin Inaugural Dissertation, 1931], 113 p.

1933

5. WAS IST JÜDISCHE THEOLOGIE? BEITRÄGE ZUR JÜDISCHEN NEUORIENTIERUNG. Frankfurt am Main: Verlag des Israelit und Hermon, 1933. 38 p.
6. Zwischen Philosophie und Theologie. Drei Buchbesprechungen: Erich Przywara, *Analogia Entis* (1932); J. C. Franken, *Kritische Philosophie und dialektische Theologie* (1932); Ernst Bergmann, *Entsinkung ins Weiselose* (1932). *Der Israelit*, April 7, 1933.
7. Religion und Wirklichkeit: Zur Problematik der Gegenwart. *Bayerische Israelitische Gemeindezeitung*, 9:8 (April 15, 1933), pp. 113–18.

8. Bilanz der Emanzipation. Zwei Buchbesprechungen: Max Wiener, *Judentum im Zeitalter der Emanzipation* (1933); Joachim Prinz, *Wir Juden* (1934). *Der Israelit*, December 21, 1933.
9. Die religiöse Welt des Mittelalters. *Der Morgen*, 10:9 (December, 1934), pp. 390–96.

1935

10. Erneuerung des Sanhedrin. *Israelitisches Familienblatt*. Hamburg, February 7, 1935.
11. DES RABBI MOSCHE BEN MAIMON MORE NEWUCHIM (FÜHRER DER VERIRRTEN) IM GRUNDRISS. Auswahl, Übertragung und Nachwort. Berlin: Schocken Verlag, 1935. 88 p.
12. Rambam und die Halacha. *Mose ben Maimon 1135–1935. Festbeilage der C[entral]-V[ereins]-Zeitung,* March 30, 1935.
13. Der Sinn der Offenbarung in der Lehre des Rambam. *Gemeindeblatt der jüdischen Gemeinde zu Berlin,* 25:19 (March 31, 1935).
14. Die jüdische Mystik. *Der Israelit*, July 11, 1935. Reprinted in *Bayerische Israelitische Gemeindezeitung*, 11:15 (August 1, 1935).
15. Zur Auseindersetzung mit der dialektischen Theologie. *MGWJ*, 79 (N. F. 43) (1935), pp. 345–61.
16. Grundsätzliches zur Arbeitsmethode der Lehrhäuser. *Zion* (Berlin), 7:7–8 (August-October, 1935), pp. 46–49.

1936

17. Das Verhältnis Maimunis zur jüdischen Mystik. *MGWJ*, 80 (N. F. 44) (1936), pp. 305–30. See no. 135 (reprint).
18. Bildautorität und Wortautorität. *Bayerische Israelitische Gemeindezeitung* 12:11, (June 1, 1936.)

1937

19. Olam und Aion. Zum religionsgeschichtlichen Problem der jüdischen Olam haba-Lehre. *Festschrift zum siebzigsten Geburtstage von Jakob Freimann* (Berlin, 1937), pp. 1–14.
20. Joseph Wohlgemuth 70 Jahre. *Jüdische Rundschau* (Berlin), June 15, 1937.
21. Um das Erbe Franz Rosenzweigs. Zu zwei Büchern von Ignaz Maybaum. *Jüdische Rundschau*, September 3, 1937.
22. Dogmen im Judentum? *Der Morgen*, 13:6, (September, 1937), pp. 228–35.

1939

23. Gnostische Motive im rabbinischen Schrifttum. *MGWJ,* 83 (N. F. 47), (1939), [reprinted Tübingen, 1963], pp. 369–89.

1942

24. Gnostic Themes in Rabbinic Cosmology. *Essays in honour of the Very Rev. Dr. J. H. Hertz, Chief Rabbi . . . on the occasion of his Seventieth Birthday*, Ed. by I. Epstein, E. Levine and C. Roth. London, n.d., pp. 19–32.

1943

25. Saadya's Theory of Revelation: Its Origin and Background. *Saadya Studies*, Ed. by Erwin I. J. Rosenthal. Manchester: Manchester University Press, 1943, pp. 4–25. (Reprinted in no. 137).

1944

26. *Ḥaluqqath ha-Miṣwoth le-Rabbi Seᶜadyah Gaᵓon. Rav Seᶜadyah Gaᵓon.* Ed. by Yehuda L. Fishman. Jerusalem, 5703, pp. 659–73.

27. Saadya's Conception of the Law. *Bulletin of the John Rylands Library* (Manchester), 28:2 (December, 1944), pp. 3–24.

28. *Torath ha-aqlimim le-Rabbi Yehudah Ha-Levi. Melila.* Ed. by Edward Robertson and Meir Wallenstein. Manchester: Manchester University Press, 1, 1944, pp. 1–17.

29. Franz Rosenzweig and Eugen Rosenstock-Huessy: An Introduction to their "Letters on Judaism and Christianity." *The Journal of Religion*, 24:4 (1944), pp. 258–70. See no. 139 (reprint).

1945

30. Symbol and Myth. *Philosophy,* Ed. by Sydney E. Hooper, 20:76 (July, 1945), pp. 162–71.

31. The Gnostic Background of the Rabbinic Adam Legends. *Jewish Quarterly Review*, N.S. 25:4 (1945), pp. 371–91.

1946

32. SAADYA GAON. THE BOOK OF DOCTRINES AND BELIEFS. Abridged Edition. Translated from the Arabic with an Introduction and Notes. Oxford: East and West Library, 1946, 191 p. See nos. 91, 121, 138 (reprints).

33. *Shirey qedusshah be-sifruth ha-hekhaloth ha-qedumah. Melila*, Ed. by Edward Robertson and Meir Wallenstein, 2, Manchester: Manchester University Press, 1946, pp. 1–24.

34. Joseph Herman Hertz Memorial Address. *Essays and Addresses in Memory of J. H. Hertz*. Ed. by Wolf Gottlieb. London, 1946. pp. 1–6.

1948

35. William Wollaston (1659–1724): English Deist and Rabbinic Scholar. *Transactions of the Jewish Historical Society of England*, 16 (1948), pp. 185–211. (Reprinted in no. 137).

36. Leo Baeck: The Thinker. *Supplement to A[ssociation of] J[ewish] R[efugees] Information: Tribute to Leo Baeck on the Occasion of his 75th Birthday*. London, May 23, 1948.

1949

37. Review of Karl Kerényi, *Die antike Religion* (1941) and four other works of his (1941–1945). *Philosophy*, 24:91 (October, 1949), pp. 351–55.

38. Judaism and World Philosophy. *The Jews: Their History, Culture and Religion*, ed. by Louis Finkelstein, 2 (New York, 1949), pp. 624–79. Further editions: 1955; 1960 (pp. 954–1,009); see no. 145.

1950

39. Review of E. O. James, *The Concept of Deity: A Comparative and Historical Study* (1950). *JC*, April 14, 1950.

1951

40. Review of Samuel Rosenblatt, *Saadia Gaon, The Book of Beliefs and Opinions. Translated from the Arabic and the Hebrew* (1948). *Bibliotheca Orientalis*, 8:5 (1951), pp. 193–95.

41. Review of John Baillie, *The Belief in Progress* (1950). *JC*, January 19, 1951.

42. The Modern Analysis of Faith. *Addresses given at the Ninth Conference of Anglo-Jewish Preachers*, London, 1951, pp. 33–38.

1952

43. Notes on the Kedusha. *Chayenu*, 20:5–6, London (May/June 1952).

44. *Gishoth shonoth la-hisṭoriografiah ha-Yisreʾelith. Tarbuth,* 6:7–8, London, Nisan-Iyyar 5712/1952, pp. 31–34. (Abridged version of no. 49.)

45. Review of Walther Eichrodt, *Man in the Old Testament*. Translated by K. and R. Gregor Smith (1952). *JC*, March 28, 1952.

46. The Composition of the Berakah, *Chayenu*, 21:7–8, London, July/August, 1952.

1953

47. Jewish Philosophy. *History of Philosophy Eastern and Western,* ed. by Sarvepalli Radhakrishnan, 2, London, 1953, pp. 76–92. See no. 104.

48. Essence and Existence in Maimonides. *Bulletin of The John Rylands Library*, Manchester, 35:2 (1953), pp. 294–315. (Reprinted in no. 137).

49. *Gishoth shonoth la-hisṭoriah ha-Yisreʾelith. Yad Shaʾul. Sefer zikkaron ʿal shem ha-rav dr. Shaʾul Weingort*. Ed. by J. J. Weinberg

and Pinḥas Biberfeld. Tel-Aviv, 5713. pp. 133–41. See no. 44.

50. Review of Victor White, *God and the Unconscious* (1953). *JC*, March 6, 1953.

51. Review of Max Kadushin, *The Rabbinic Mind* (1953). *JC*, April 3, 1953.

52. Review of Morris Ginsberg, *The Idea of Progress: A Revaluation* (1953). *JC*, July 10, 1953.

53. *ʾArisṭo we-ha-Yahaduth. EI,* 5, 5713/1953, pp. 853–60.

1954

54. God and the Self in Jewish Mysticism. *Judaism*, 3:2 (Spring, 1954), pp. 1–5.

55. The Legacy of Maimonides. *JC*, July 2, 1954.

1955

56. Isaac Israeli. *The Manchester Review*, 7 (1955), pp. 246–47.

57–60. (Ed.), THE JOURNAL OF JEWISH STUDIES, Vols. 6–9 (1955–1958).

1956

61. Review of *Theologie als Glaubenswagnis: Festschrift Karl Heim. JJS*, 6:4 (1955–1956), pp. 253–54.

62. What is Judaism? *The Observer*, London, July 1, 1956.

63. Review of Arnold Toynbee, *An Historian's Approach to Religion* (1956). *JC*, November 30, 1956.

64. Tribute to Leo Baeck. *A*[*ssociation of*] *J*[*ewish*] *R*[*efugees*] *Supplement in Memory of Leo Baeck,* December, 1956.

65. Theology in Twentieth Century German Jewry. *YLB*, 1 (1956), pp. 193–216.

1957

66. In Memoriam—Leo Baeck. *JJS*, 7:1–2 (1956), pp. 1–2.

67. Isaac Israeli's "Chapter on the Elements" (MS Mantua). *JJS*, 7:1–2 (1956), pp. 31–57.

68. Isaac Israeli's *Book of Definitions*: Some Fragments of a Second Hebrew Translation. *Journal of Semitic Studies,* 2:3 (1957), pp. 232–42.

69. A Note on the Rabbinic Doctrine of Creation. *JJS*, 7:3–4 (1956), pp. 195–206, [reprinted in no. 137].

70. Review of Abraham J. Heschel, *God in Search of Man. A Philosophy of Judaism* (1956). *The Manchester Guardian*, March 6, 1957.

71. Review of Eric Voegelin, *Order and History. Volume I: Israel and Revelation* (1956). *The Manchester Guardian*, March 22, 1957.

72. Review of H. J. Schoeps, *Jüdische Geisteswelt, Zeugnisse aus zwei Jahrtausenden* (1953). *Journal of Semitic Studies*, 2:4 (1957), p. 407.

1958

73. *Ma'amar be-yiḥud ha-Bore*ᵓ. *Tarbiẕ*, 27:2–3 (1958). (Presented to Gershom G. Scholem in Honour of his Sixtieth Birthday), pp. 301–09.

74. ISAAC ISRAELI. A NEOPLATONIC PHILOSOPHER OF THE EARLY TENTH CENTURY. HIS WORKS TRANSLATED WITH COMMENTS AND AN OUTLINE OF HIS PHILOSOPHY (jointly with S. M. Stern). Oxford: Oxford University Press, 1958, 226 p.

75. (Ed.), BETWEEN EAST AND WEST. Essays dedicated to the Memory of Bela Horovitz. London: East and West Library, 1958. 214 p.

76. Franz Rosenzweig on History. *Between East and West*, (no. 75), pp. 194–214, [reprinted in no. 137].

77. TOLERANCE AND THE JEWISH TRADITION. Robert Waley Cohen Memorial Lecture 1957. London: The Council of Christians and Jews, 1958. 19 p.

78. JEWISH STUDIES: THEIR SCOPE AND MEANING TODAY. London: Hillel Foundation Annual Lecture, 1958. 16 p.

79. In Memoriam—Isaak Heinemann. *JJS*, 8:1–2 (1957), pp. 1–3.

80. Review of *Evangelium Veritatis Codex Jung*, ed. by M. Malinine, H.-C. Puesch, G. Quispel (1956). *JJS*, 8:3–4 (1957), p. 228.

81. Review of *Studia Patristica*, 1–2, ed. by K. Aland and F. L. Cross (1957). *JJS*, 8:3–4 (1957), pp. 232–34.

82. Review of Georges Vajda, *L'Amour de Dieu dans la théologie juive du moyen age* (1957). *JJS*, 8:3–4 (1957), pp. 236–37. See also no. 86.

83. Review of *The Oxford Dictionary of the Christian Church*, ed. by F. L. Cross (1957). *JJS*, 8:3–4 (1957), p. 249.

84. *Vorwort* to Siegmund Hurwitz, *Die Gestalt des sterbenden Messias*. Zürich and Stuttgart: Rascher Verlag, 1958, pp. 7–8.

85. *Be'ayoth be-meḥqar ha-neo-'aflaṭoniuth ha-Yehudith*. *Tarbiẕ*, 27:4 (1958), 501–507.

1959

86. Review of Georges Vajda, *L'Amour de Dieu . . .*, *Kiryat Sefer*, 34:1 (1959), pp. 52–54. See also no. 82.

87. Review of Leo Schaya, *L'homme et l'absolu selon la kabbale* (1958). *JJS*, 9:1–2 (1958), pp. 101–02.

88. The Motif of the "Shells" (*Qelippoth*) in ᶜAzriel of Gerona. *JJS*, 9:1–2 (1958), pp. 73–80. (Reprinted in no. 137).

1960

89. Chassidism Today. In commemoration of the bicentenary of the death of the Baal Shem Tov. *JC*, May 20, 1960.

90. Jewish Studies: Their Scope and Meaning today. *Reflections, 1960*, ed. by Jack Parnes. Toronto, 1960, pp. 5–12. (Reprinted from no. 78).

91. SAADYA GAON: BOOK OF DOCTRINES AND BELIEFS: *Three Jewish Philosophers.* Meridian Books and The Jewish Publication Society (1960), 191 p. (Reprinted from no. 32. See also nos. 121, 138).

92. Review of Else Freund, *Die Existenzphilosophie Franz Rosenzweigs*, Second revised edition (1959). *Historia Judaica*, 22:1 (1960), pp. 76–78.

1961

93. Eleazar of Worms' *Ḥokhmath Ha-ʾEgoz. JJS*, 11:3–4 (1960), pp. 101–112. (Reprinted in no. 137 under the title Eleazar of Worms' Symbol of the Merkava).

94. Review of Georges Vȧjda, *Isaac Albalag, averroïste juif, traducteur et annotateur d'Al Ghazālī* (1960). *Kirjat Sefer*, 37 (1961–1962), pp. 197–200. Also in *Bulletin of the School of Oriental and African Studies*, London, 25:1 (1962), pp. 167–68.

95. Zur Frühgeschichte der jüdischen Predigt in Deutschland: Leopold Zunz als Prediger. *YLB*, 6 (1961), pp. 3–59.

1962

96. Review of Max Scheler, *On the Eternal in Man*, tr. by Bernard Noble (1960). *Conservative Judaism*, 17:2 (1962), pp. 87–89.

97. Hermann Cohens Begriff der Korrelation. *In Zwei Welten. Siegfried Moses zum fünfundsiebzigsten Geburtstag*, ed. by Hans Tramer, Tel-Aviv, 1962, pp. 377–99.

98. *Hashgaḥah ba-filosofiah ha-Yehudith shel yemey ha-Beynayim. EI*, 15 (5722), pp. 478–83.

99. Wolfson, Ṣebi (Harry Austryn). *EI*, 15 (5722), pp. 919–20.

1963

100. (Ed.), BIBLICAL AND OTHER STUDIES. Philip W. Lown Institute of Advanced Judaic Studies, Brandeis University Studies and Texts, Volume 1. Cambridge, Mass.: Harvard University Press, 1963. 266 p.

101. The Delphic Maxim in Medieval Islam and Judaism. *Biblical and Other Studies* (see no. 100), pp. 196–232. (Reprinted in no. 137).

102. Nahum N. Glatzer: The Man and his Work. *Judaism*, 12:2 (1963), pp. 195–202.

103. An Unknown Letter by Abraham Geiger. *Living Legacy*. Dedicated to Hugo Hahn on the occasion of his 70th birthday. Ed. by Bernhard N. Cohn, New York, 1963, pp. 105–13.

104. Jewish Philosophy. *Philosophy A to Z*, ed. by James Gutmann, New York, 1963, pp. 89–104. (Reprinted from no. 47).

1964

105. Aristobulus of Paneas. *EB*, 2 (1964), p. 387.

106. Cabala. *EB*, 4 (1964), pp. 536–539.

107. (Ed.), STUDIES IN NINETEENTH-CENTURY JEWISH INTELLECTUAL HISTORY. Philip W. Lown Institute of Advanced Judaic Studies, Brandeis University Studies and Texts, Volume 2. Cambridge, Mass.: Harvard University Press, 1964. 215 p.

108. The New Style of Preaching in Nineteenth-Century German Jewry. *Studies in Nineteenth-Century Jewish Intellectual History* (see no. 107), pp. 65–116.

109. Review of Julius Guttmann, *Philosophies of Judaism*, tr. by David W. Silverman (1964). *Conservative Judaism*, 19:1 (1964), pp. 73–77.

110. Review of *The Guide of the Perplexed. By Moses Maimonides.* Translated with an Introduction and Notes by Shlomo Pines, with an introductory essay by Leo Strauss (1963). *The Journal of Religion,* 44:3 (1964), pp. 260–61.

111. Ahad Haam. *EB*, 1 (1964), p. 408.

112. Crescas, Hasdai. *EB*, 6 (1964), p. 726.

113. Gersonides. *EB*, 10 (1964), p. 367.

114. Ibn Falaquera. *EB*, 12 (1964), p. 34.

115. Ibn Gabirol. *EB*, 12 (1964), p. 34.

116. Israeli, Isaac ben Solomon. *EB*, 12 (1964), p. 732.

117. León, Moses ben Shem-Tob de. *EB*, 13 (1964), p. 932.

118. Maimonides. *EB*, 14 (1964), pp. 684–85.

119. Philo. *EB*, 17 (1964), p. 739–41.

1965

120. *Li-sheʾelath baʿalutho shel Sefer Ṭaʿamey Ha-Miṣwoth ha-meyuḥas le-rabbi Yiṣḥaq ibn Farḥi. Kirjat Sefer*, 40:2 (1965), pp. 256–76; 40:3 (1965), pp. 405–12.

121. SAADYA GAON: BOOK OF DOCTRINES AND BELIEFS. *Three Jewish Philosophers.* Harper Torchbooks (1965). (Reprinted from no. 32. See also nos. 91 and 138).

1966

122. Ibn Bājja on Man's Ultimate Felicity. *Harry Austryn Wolfson Jubilee Volume* (Jerusalem, 1965), pp. 47–87. (Reprinted in no. 157).

123. The Divine Attributes. An Historical Survey of the Jewish Discussion. *Judaism*, 15:1 (Winter, 1966), pp. 40–60. See no. 165.

124. (Ed.), BIBLICAL MOTIFS: ORIGINS AND TRANSFORMATIONS, Philip W. Lown Institute of Advanced Judaic Studies, Brandeis University Studies and Texts, Volume 3. Cambridge, Mass.: Harvard University Press, 1966. 251 p.

125. Moses Mendelssohn on Leibniz and Spinoza. *Studies in Rationalism Judaism and Universalism in Memory of Leon Roth.* Ed. by Raphael Loewe. London, 1966, pp. 13–45. (Reprinted in no. 137).

1967

126. *Midrash ʾallegori ʿal pi derekh "ha-Qabbalah ha-Penimith" ʿal Bereʾshith kaph-daleth. Sefer Ha-Yovel Tifʾereth Yisraʾel likhevod . . . Yisraʾel Brodie.* Ed. by Ṣevi Yaʾaqov Zimmels, Yosef Rabinovitz, Yisraʾel Shemuel Feinstein, London, 5727. Hebrew Part, pp. 57–65.

127. (Ed.), JEWISH MEDIEVAL AND RENAISSANCE STUDIES. Philip W. Lown Institute of Advanced Judaic Studies, Brandeis University Studies and Texts, Volume 4. Cambridge, Mass.: Harvard University Press, 1967. 384 p.

128. Moses Narboni's "Epistle on Shiʾur Qomā". A Critical Edition of the Hebrew Text with an Introduction and an Annotated English Translation. *Jewish Medieval and Renaissance Studies* (see no. 127), pp. 225–64. (Reprinted (with omission of the text) in no. 137).

129. An Ode to Professor Ṣevi (Harry Austryn) Wolfson on the occasion of his eightieth birthday (Hebrew). *Ha-Doʾar* (New York), 48:1, November 3, 1967.

130. An Ode to Professor Harry A. Wolfson Octogenarian. *Jewish Advocate* (Boston, Mass.), November 9, 1967.

1968

131. "The Ladder of Ascension." *Studies in Mysticism and Religion Presented to Gershom G. Scholem on his Seventieth Birthday by Pupils Colleagues and Friends.* Jerusalem, 1967, pp. 1–32. (Reprinted in no. 137).

132. *Homo Imago Dei* in Jewish and Christian Theology. *The Journal of Religion,* 48:3 (1968), pp. 235–59.

133. Eine neu aufgefundene Moses Mendelssohn-Korrespondenz zur Frage des Selbstmords. *Zeitschrift für Religions- und Geistesgeschichte,* 20:3 (1968), pp. 240–58.

134. Moses Mendelssohns Kindheit in Dessau. *Bulletin des Leo Baeck Instituts,* 10:40 (1967), pp. 237–75.

135. Das Verhältnis Maimunis zur jüdischen Mystik. *Wissenschaft des Judentums im deutschen Sprachbereich*, ed. by Kurt Wilhelm Tübingen, 1968, pp. 441–60. (Reprinted from no. 17).

136. *"Yerushalayim" shel Mendelssohn be-ʾispaqlaryah biografith ḥadashah. Zion,* 33:1–2 (5728), pp. 47–58.

1969

137. STUDIES IN RELIGIOUS PHILOSOPHY AND MYSTICISM. Ithaca: Cornell University Press, 1969, and London: Routledge & Kegan Paul, 1969. 309 p.

138. SAADYA GAON: BOOK OF DOCTRINES AND BELIEFS. *Three Jewish Philosophers.* A Temple Book. Atheneum, New York, 1969 (reprinted from no. 32. See also nos. 91, 121).

139. Franz Rosenzweig and Eugen Rosenstock-Huessy: An Introduction to their "Letters on Judaism and Christianity." *Judaism Despite Christianity,* ed. by Eugen Rosenstock-Huessy. University, Ala.: The University of Alabama Press, 1969, pp. 26–48. Reprinted, with minor revisions, from no. 29.

140. "Moses Mendelssohn's Gesammelte Schriften." Neuerschlossene Briefe zur Geschichte ihrer Herausgabe. *Bulletin des Leo Baeck Instituts,* 11:42 (1968), pp. 73–115.

141. MOSES MENDELSSOHNS FRÜHSCHRIFTEN ZUR METAPHYSIK UNTERSUCHT UND ERLÄUTERT. Tübingen: J. C. B. Mohr (Paul Siebeck), 1969, xii + 396 p.

142. Briefe Karl Gotthelf Lessings an Moses Mendelssohn. *Lessing Yearbook* 1 (Munich, 1969), pp. 9–59.

143. Die Entstehung von Moses Mendelssohns *Phaedon. Lessing Yearbook* 1 (Munich, 1969), pp. 200–33.

1971

144. Lessing und Jacobi: Das Gespräch über den Spinozismus. *Lessing Yearbook* 3 (Munich, 1971), pp. 25–70.

145. Judaism and World Philosophy: From Philo to Spinoza. *The Jews: Their Role in Civilization.* Ed. by Louis Finkelstein. New York: Schocken Books, 1971, pp. 65–115. (Reprinted, with the omission of the last section, from no. 38).

146. (Ed.), MOSES MENDELSSOHN GESAMMELTE SCHRIFTEN JUBILÄUMSAUSGABE, I, Stuttgart, 1971.

147. *Geleitwort* to no. 146, pp. v–viii.

148. Albo, Joseph. *EJ*, 2 (1971), pp. 535–37.

149. Angels. In Jewish Philosophy. *EJ*, 2 (1971), pp. 973–76.

150. Aristotle. Jewish Aristotelianism. *EJ*, 3 (1971), pp. 445–48.

151. Articles of Faith. *EJ*, 3 (1971), pp. 654–60.

152. Beatitude. *EJ*, 4 (1971), pp. 359–63.

153. Bible. Allegorical Interpretations. *EJ*, 4 (1971), pp. 895–99.

154. Commandments, Reasons for. *EJ*, 5 (1971), pp. 783–89.

155. God. Attributes of God. *EJ*, 7 (1971), pp. 664–69.

Israeli, Isaac ben Solomon. *EJ*, 9 (1971), pp. 1063–65.

157. Moses ben Joseph Ha-Levi. *EJ*, 12 (1971), pp. 421–22.

158. Providence. In Medieval Jewish Philosophy. *EJ*, 13 (1971), pp. 1282–84.

1972

159. Maimonides' "Four Perfections." *Israel Oriental Studies*, 2: In Memorian Samuel Miklós Stern. Tel-Aviv University, 1972, pp. 15–24.

160. Das Menschenbild und die Bildung des Menschen nach Moses Mendelssohn. *Mendelssohn Studien. Beiträge zur neueren deutschen*

Kultur- und Wirtschaftsgeschichte, 1. Ed. by Cecile Lowenthal-Hensel. Berlin, 1972, pp. 11–28.

161. *Miṣwah—ha-Sifruth ha-Yehudith ha-helenisṭith—bimey ha-Beynayim—ba-Zeman he-ḥadash. EI,* 24 (5732), pp. 116–19.

162–164. (Ed.), MOSES MENDELSSOHN GESAMMELTE SCHRIFTEN JUBILÄUMSAUSGABE, II; III. 1; XIV, Stuttgart, 1972.

1973

165. The Divine Attributes: A Survey of the Jewish Discussion. *Faith and Reason*, ed. by Robert Gordis and Ruth B. Waxman. New York, 1973, pp. 9–29. (Reprinted, with bibliographical additions, from no. 123).

166. *Malʾakh—ba-Sifruth ha-Yehudith ha-helenistith u-vimey ha-Beynayim. EI*, 23 (5733), pp. 518–20.

167. Isḥāq b. Sulaymān al-Israʾīlī. *Encyclopaedia of Islam*, 4 (1973), p. 111.

168. NEUERSCHLOSSENE BRIEFE MOSES MENDELSSOHNS AN FRIEDRICH NICOLAI. In Gemeinschaft mit Werner Vogel herausgegeben von Alexander Altmann. Stuttgart, 1973, 122 p. See also no. 172.

169. MOSES MENDELSSOHN: A BIOGRAPHICAL STUDY. University, Ala.: The University of Alabama Press, 1973; Philadelphia: The Jewish Publication Society of America, 5733: 1973; and London: Routledge & Kegan Paul (The Littman Library of Jewish Civilization), 1973. xvi + 900 p.

170. Eternality of Punishment: A Theological Controversy within the Amsterdam Rabbinate in the Thirties of the Seventeenth Century. *Proceedings of the American Academy for Jewish Research,* 40, 1972 (1973), pp. 1–88.

1974

171. LEO BAECK AND THE JEWISH MYSTICAL TRADITION. Leo Baeck Memorial Lecture 17. Leo Baeck Institute, New York, 1974, 28 p.

172. Neuerschlossene Briefe Moses Mendelssohns an Friedrich Nicolai. *Lessing Yearbook* 5, 1973 (appeared 1974), pp. 13–60. (A selection, with a revised preface, from no. 168.)

173. (Ed.), MOSES MENDELSSOHN GESAMMELTE SCHRIFTEN JUBILÄUMSAUSGABE, III. 2. Stuttgart, 1974.

174. "Vorbemerkung" to no. 173.

175. (Ed.), MOSES MENDELSSOHN GESAMMELTE SCHRIFTEN JUBILÄUMSAUSGABE, XI. MOSES MENDELSSOHN BRIEFWECHSEL I. Bearbeitet von Bruno Strauss. Mit Nachträgen von Alexander Altmann. Stuttgart-Bad Cannstatt, 1974.

176. The Religion of the Thinkers: Free Will and Predestination in

Saadia, Baḥya and Maimonides. *Religion in a Religious Age*, Ed. by S. D. Goitein. Cambridge, Mass. 1974, pp. 25–51.

1975

177. Letters from Dohm to Mendelssohn. *Salo Wittmayer Baron Jubilee Volume.* English Section, Volume 1, Jerusalem, 1975; New York and London, 1975, pp. 1–62.
178. A Tribute. *A Tribute in Appreciation of Professor Harry Austryn Wolfson.* Hebrew College, Brookline, Mass., 1974, pp. 3–7.
179. The German Rabbi: 1910–1939. *YLB* 19 (1974), pp. 31–49.
180. Moses Mendelssohn's Proofs for the Existence of God. *Mendelssohn Studien*, Ed. by Cecile Lowenthal-Hensel, 2, Berlin, 1975, pp. 9–29.
181. The Philosophical Roots of Mendelssohn's Plea for Emancipation. *Jewish Social Studies*, 26:3–4 (1974), pp. 191–202.
182. Leo Strauss—In Memoriam. *Proceedings of the American Academy for Jewish Research*, 41–42 (1975), pp. xxxiii–xxxvi.

1976

183. MOSES MENDELSSOHN GESAMMELTE SCHRIFTEN JUBILÄUMSAUSGABE, XII. 1. Briefwechsel 2:1. Bearbeitet von Alexander Altmann. Stuttgart-Bad Cannstatt, 1976, 332 p.
184. MOSES MENDELSSOHN GESAMMELTE SCHRIFTEN JUBILÄUMSAUSGABE, XII:2. Briefwechsel 2:2. Bearbeitet von Alexander Altmann. Stuttgart-Bad Cannstatt, 1976, 276 p.

1977

185. MOSES MENDELSSOHN GESAMMELTE SCHRIFTEN JUBILÄUMSAUSGABE, XIII. Briefwechsel 3. Bearbeitet von Alexander Altmann. Stuttgart-Bad Cannstatt, 1977. 436 p.
186. (Ed.), MOSES MENDELSSOHN GESAMMELTE SCHRIFTEN JUBILÄUMSAUSGABE, IV (Stuttgart-Bad Cannstatt, 1977).
187. Lessings Glaube an die Seelenwanderung. *Lessing Yearbook* 8 (1976), pp. 7–41.

1978

188. Maimonides and Thomas Aquinas: Natural or Divine Prophecy? *A*[*ssociation for*] *J*[*ewish*] *S*[*tudies*] *Review* 3 (1978), pp. 1–19.

The Crisis of Authority Within European Jewry in the Eighteenth Century*

C. ABRAMSKY

The definition of modern history has been the subject of intense debate among many historians of Europe since the middle of the nineteenth century. Various factors and causes have been advanced in the attempt to define the subject, the age, and the countries where the so-called modern age began, and there is certainly no general consensus as to what is meant by the term "modern history." Economic, political, religious, and scientific considerations have been put forward, and historians seem more and more divided on the issue. There are, however, some common denominators amongst the rival schools of interpretation, one of these being that at the eve of any new epoch there is a crisis of confidence in authority, it being irrelevant whether the authority is the state, the church, or any other established institution.

The same applies to Jewish history. The nineteenth-century leaders of *die Wissenschaft des Judentums* initiated the debate on Jewish historiography, some like Zunz, Steinschneider, and Abraham Geiger maintaining that the history of the Jewish people had reached its end and that the new age heralded the era of emancipation in which Jews would become Germans, Frenchmen, Englishmen, Dutchmen, Italians, Russians, and Poles, albeit "of the Mosaic Persuasion." Steinschneider even averred that all that remained to do was to construct a beautiful cemetery and arrange for a decent burial.[1]

The first serious historian to differ radically from the view of his seniors as pioneers in the science of Judaism was Graetz. For him the new age began with Moses Mendelssohn, and the new chapter of Jewish history inaugurated by the "sage of Dessau" would have to await some other historian, remoter in time and thus more detached than Graetz felt himself able to be.[2]

Surprisingly, it is but few historians who have dwelt on the problem of confidence in authority amongst the Jews of Europe during the eighteenth and nineteenth centuries, and those who have done so have dealt with the problem in an incidental manner[3]. One of the many gaps in specialized modern Jewish history is research into the rabbinate and its relation to the Jewish community—both its leadership and the rank and file—between 1650 and 1850. The late Professor Simha Assaf and Dr. S. A. Horodezky laid the foundations for this study, but their work suffered from an apologetic approach and a tendency to romanticize, avoiding difficult historical problems and generally lacking a critical attitude.[4] What has attracted me to the subject is a growing awareness of a sharp division between the writings of Moses Mendelssohn in Hebrew, which were directed at Jews, and those which he wrote in German for a small circle of his Jewish friends and a non-Jewish public. In Hebrew he appears as a moderate when he touches on Jewish institutions and self-government, whereas in his German writings he takes on the character of an opponent of a most militant kind. This study, which is part of a work in progress, is here nevertheless presented by way of tribute to Professor Altmann and particularly because of his own monumental biography of Mendelssohn.

One of the most characteristic features of the history of the Jews in eighteenth-century Europe is growing criticism of rabbis and communal leadership. The division between the leaders—whether elected or self-appointed—and the led seems to have been acute, with a wide gulf separating them. Ordinary Jews were accused of being disrespectful to the elders of the community and of hardly paying attention to the teachings of the rabbis. Already at the end of the seventeenth century, Judah Leib ben Moses of Selichow, a Polish Jew resident in Germany and in Amsterdam, complains that many Jews "indulge in gentile songs, drink wine and beer, and spend their time in jokes and jesting," and that these young Jews, once they attain the age of thirteen, "remove from themselves the yoke of the Torah and devote their time exclusively to commerce." He continues with accusations leveled at the common people: "I have seen an evil custom spread amongst us, and Satan has succeeded with his deeds, so that when a preacher (*darshan*) opens his mouth to preach in public it is impossible to hear his sermon because of the noise of the mob (*hamon*)."[5] Jews behave strangely in synagogue "jumping and turning somersaults," and "worshipping devils (*yizbeḥu le-shedim lo ʾeloahh*)," and "doing Satan's work *(maʿasey satan)*."

A similar note is struck in the well-known popular ethical treatise, *Qav ha-Yashar*, of Ṣevi Hirsch b. Aaron Samuel Kaidanower, of which over thirty editions appeared between 1705 and the middle of the nineteenth century,[6] and in the *Yesod Yosef* by Joseph Yuska of Dubno. In brief, the common people take a critical view of the rabbis and of communal leadership, the rulings of these—whether relating to matters of divorce, or to communal affairs—frequently being challenged. The prevalence of splits in communities in Europe right through the eighteenth century scarcely needs emphasis.[7] Rabbinical appointments often led to acute division, and it was common for the party opposed to an official rabbinical appointment to decide to proceed with the appointment of a candidate of its own whilst accusing the official side of appointing candidates of inadequate merit. Resort to the communal ban (*ḥerem*) by the established leadership against the dissidents to some extent lost its terror and power to deter, even though it remained for a time the most powerful weapon at the disposal of communal leadership against offenders. Frequent and unscrupulous invocation of the *ḥerem* produced a deep hostility towards it, and Jews who had felt its impact and had suffered in consequence took their revenge by resorting to non-Jewish courts of law, by laying information against other Jews, and occasionally even abandoning Judaism altogether by converting to Christianity. The number of Jewish converts in German cities grew rapidly during the eighteenth century, and sensing the dissatisfaction within the Jewish community, the Church opened a special mission aimed at conversion of the Jews with its headquarters in Halle.[8]

Many causes can be put forward for the decline in standing of Jewish authority in the eyes of the common people, *viz*., the sharp division between rich and poor; the contempt for the ignorant masses entertained by the learned talmudic scholars, who were often (through intermarriage) in close collaboration with the established lay leadership of the community; a decline in the number of *yeshivoth*, which had already commenced their downward path after the massacres of the Jews in the Ukraine in 1648–49; the large number of Jews in the rural areas of Poland, the German states, and Alsace-Lorraine. Others have pointed also to the rise of a small, powerful, and privileged class of Jews, the so-called court-Jews (*Hofjuden*), who were often a law unto themselves and paid hardly any attention to rabbinical injunctions. Moreover the court-Jews did not refrain from applying pressure to secure the appointment of their relations or nominees to rabbinical positions in various communities. The commonness of this occurrence in most countries of Europe (with the possible exception of Lithuania and Turkey) is such that on this point hardly any controversy prevails.[9] And a further cause in the decline of Jewish authority is the rivalry and division between the rabbis themselves, and their readiness to use the *ḥerem* against each other.

The most famous controversy of the eighteenth century among Jews is undoubtedly the "war" between Jonathan Eibeschütz and Jacob Emden —both of them scions of distinguished rabbinic families, both themselves rabbis, one of them a professional and the other, although technically a "layman," nevertheless distinguished as a leading rabbinical scholar in his own right. Eibeschütz was the foremost codifier of his age, the leading master of *pilpul*, a cabbalist and prolific sermon writer who had occupied leading rabbinic positions in the important Jewish communities of Metz and Hamburg-Altona-Wandsbeck ("*ʾAhu*"). Jacob Emden, his opponent, was the son of the famous Ashkenazi rabbi (Ṣevi ʾAshkenazi or Ḥakham Ṣevi) of Amsterdam, the great fighter against the Sabbataean heresy at the end of the seventeenth and beginning of the eighteenth century. His son not only inherited his father's immense rabbinic learning, but he was also endowed with exceptional polemical gifts, with a remarkable sense of a critical approach to history, and an almost uncanny ability to sniff out suspected secret adherents of the Sabbataean heresy. His suspicion lighted on none other than the widely acclaimed and highly respected rabbi of Hamburg, his own community, Jonathan Eibeschütz, and a storm broke out which literally split Ashkenazi Jewish communities in Europe into two camps, pro-Emden and pro-Eibeschütz. Both sides employed quite unscrupulous means of denouncing the other. The "war" lasted from 1750 to 1776, although already in 1726 Emden's campaign against the Sabbataeans had begun.[10] My concern here is not with the substance of the controversy itself, but with its profound influence on the decline of rabbinical and communal authority amongst Jews, and indirectly with the lowering of the standing of that authority amongst non-Jews as well.

The language utilized by both sides was extremely sharp, uncomplimentary, and was indeed almost unprecedented in Jewish polemic writing. Especially is this true of Jacob Emden, who omitted all rabbinic titles of courtesy when referring to his antagonist. He treated Eibeschütz as an outcast from Jewry—as one who ought to be completely ostracized and utterly excluded from the Jewish community.

In order to afford some understanding of the nature of such a controversy some examples are necessary, these shedding light on the style and manners of the respective opponents, particularly Emden. As is well-known, the latter accused Eibeschütz of being a secret adherent of the proscribed heresy of Shabbetai Ṣevi, of issuing amulets that contained the name of the false messiah in cypher, and—more important—of having composed a Sabbataean tract entitled *wa-ʾavoʾ ha-Yom ʾel ha-ʿayin.* He characterizes him thus: "Then along came Eibeschütz[er] and completed the evil in his writings; many drank his accursed waters and were persuaded to follow him, and they have thus died an eternal death. He has converted the synagogue (or house of learning: *u-veth ha-Waʿad di-klaus ha-Gadol*) that was founded by the illustrious Rabbi (*ha-Gaʾon*) Abraham Braudo into a house of ill fame (*la-hafokh beth waʿad li-zenuth*)." Emden also accused Eibeschütz of dishonesty in robbing innocent Jews of their money.[11] Many rabbis rallied to Eibeschütz' defense and threatened to put Emden under a ban.[12] Both sides attempted to mobilize the powerful Council of the Four Lands in support of their respective cases; in the end, despite the family connections that linked Emden with the leaders of the Council, it pronounced, in an ambivalent manner, for Eibeschütz.[13] Accusations were then made that the signatures in defense of Eibeschütz were forged.[14] Even before Eibeschütz' move to the rabbinical position in Altona-Hamburg-Wandsbeck, whilst he was still rabbi in Metz, his opponents had endeavored to employ the *ḥerem* against him, but "by an *arret* of the Parliament of Metz, passed in 1749, they were forbidden to pronounce sentence of excommunication, and the other Jews to submit to it."[15]

One need not be surprised to find that when Jacob Frank and his followers were engaged in attack on the rabbis, and particularly on Rabbi Ḥayyim Cohen Rapoport of Lvov, they became entirely unscrupulous in their means—resorting even to the most infamous slander ever alleged against the Jews, *viz.*, the blood-libel, on the pretext that they were thereby merely revenging themselves on the rabbis for the persecution suffered at their hands. One of Frank's associates, Eliezer of Jezierzany, turned on Rapoport, who was the leading rabbi of Galicia at the time, and addressed him in sarcastic tones, and without any honorific titles, as follows: "Ḥayyim, here is 'blood for blood.' You have spoken in a way that allows our blood to flow, so here is blood in return for blood."[16] To address a distinguished rabbi in such terms was unheard of in Poland in 1759, but as a model for such an outburst Emden's diatribe against Eibeschütz might well have served.

One of the most remarkable challenges to authority in the Jewish community was posed by the rise of the hasidic movement, with its successful disregard of all the various bans issued against it by the leading Jewish communities of Lithuania, Galicia, and Poland. Even bans inspired by Elijah the Gaᵓon of Vilna, the outstanding rabbinic authority of his day, although they did impose some hardship on the *ḥasidim*, failed to stop the spread of the movement itself. Eight years after the communities of Vilna, Brody, Grodno, Shklov, and others had publicly promulgated a strong *ḥerem* against the *ḥasidim*, threatening to cut them off from all intercourse with the Jewish community, the leading disciple of Israel Baᶜal Shem Ṭov, Jacob Joseph Cohen of Polonnoye, published (1780) the first hasidic book, the *Toledoth Yaᶜaqov Yosef*, which was issued without any rabbinic approbations—an unheard of thing in Poland at that time. In the body of the book he proceeded to criticize, in forthright language, the talmudic scholars of the age as arrogating to themselves power over the public and having no care for the spiritual needs of ordinary folk (*ᶜam ha-ᵓareṣ*). "There are three kinds of exile (*galuth*): one is the exile that separates Israel from the comity of nations, the second is the exile of the learned from the ignorant (*galuth ha-Lomedim me-ᶜammey ha-ᵓaraṣim* [*sic*]), and the third is that of honest scholars (*talmidey ḥakhamim*) from those scholars who are out to do evil—Jewish devils (*shedin yehudaᵓin*). And each exile is a consequence of the preceding." These so-called scholars he dubbed "people with strong arms and with the gift of the gab" (*we-gaveru baᶜaley zeroaᶜ u-baᶜaley lashon*).[17] The hasidic challenge to established institutions was in general so widespread and so far-reaching that a full study of it cannot be included here. It is a subject which has provoked many comments by historians and still awaits attention in a special monograph.[18]

Even after the community of Vilna had issued its famous ban against the *ḥasidim* with the full backing of the virtually undisputed authority of the Vilna Gaᵓon, there occurred the (almost unique) case of actual rebellion against the authority of the *Qahal.* It was led by Simeon b. Ze'ev Wolf, a self-taught man who had acquired some knowledge of Russian law. Despite this he was arrested by the communal leaders on 7 June 1786 and physically beaten. There is evidence that the opposition to the *Qahal* was inspired in part by the few *ḥasidim* left in Vilna. Four years after the issue of the *ḥerem* it did not deter the regrowth of opposition in the town, the movement thereby increasing its numbers by the people that it attracted.[19]

There are many other illuminating examples of defiance in the Jewish communities of eighteenth century Europe. Such opposition became part of a general malaise that touched France, Holland, and even some communities in Italy. These will be examined in the full study of which this is a preliminary version.

It is generally acknowledged that the main challenge to authority came *via* the "enlightenment" of Berlin from the circle of Moses Mendelssohn. He himself had a well-known argument with his close non-Jewish adviser, Christian Wilhelm Dohm, on whether to demand the retention of Jewish autonomy, or to ask, or even fight for its total abolition. Dohm was in favor of maintaining it, at least during the first transitional phase of the endeavor to achieve civil rights for the Jews. Mendelssohn, however, frequently reiterated (and indeed stressed in *Jerusalem*, his most important work) the need to get rid of internal Jewish government right away, insisting that the decision whether to belong to the Jewish community, or to be a member of any synagogue, must be a voluntary matter left to each individual Jew. The separation of church and state was for him, as a faithful disciple of Locke, paramount, and constituted a first priority. His militant attitude to this problem is well enough known for us to be able to dispense with extensive quotation; and yet, this categorical demand never once figures in Mendelssohn's Hebrew writings. Strangely enough, Mendelssohn scholars have not raised this question.[20] When writing in Hebrew, Mendelssohn had recourse to a very subtle style of argument and gave the outward appearance of being a man of very moderate views. Even the later, orthodox opponents of the reform movement failed to notice the discrepancy.[21]

In his (anonymous) commentary to *Ecclesiastes*, originally published in 1770, Mendelssohn advanced a new version of the concept of *Verbesserung der Juden*. Here he examines various methods of scriptural exegesis, probing into what is meant by the plain meaning (*peshaṭ*) and the homiletic (*derash*); and he has occasion to refer to *Gen.* 44:18, where the words *ki kamokha ke-farʿoh* are addressed by Judah to Joseph. The translation "you who are the equal of Pharaoh" itself embodies some commentary, but Mendelssohn adds an apologetic, almost timid gloss: "We see . . . from the prior and latter words that Judah did indeed intend to demand justice from the master of the land, but in terms of fearfulness and humility, as appropriate on ethical grounds and considerations of [prudential] wisdom for those who live in an alien country, so as not to speak in strident terms or stir his anger."[22] Jews should, when addressing royalty, adopt a pleading and not an aggressive tone, being aware of their inferior status as foreigners in their various countries of residence. Later he produces a purely mercantilist argument regarding the benefits that industrious people attract to the state, an argument possibly borrowed by him from Menasseh ben Israel and John Toland. On *Eccles.* 4:4[23] he advises his readers not to complain too forcefully of king or government should they feel themselves robbed, "and do not accuse the king" (cf. *Eccles*. 10:20), for everything is carefully supervised from above through a wide network of officialdom. What we have here is a plea for enlightened absolute monarchy.[24]

It took twelve years for Mendelssohn to adopt a very different note—timidity still being present but more subtle arguments appearing. The development of his thinking was assisted by the *Toleranzpatent* issued by Joseph II of Austria in January 1782, which was acclaimed by both Mendelssohn and his intimate friend and collaborator Naphtali Hertz Wessely. The latter's response was his tract entitled *Divrey shalom we-ʾemeth*, "Words of Peace and Truth." Mendelssohn published—once more anonymously—his introduction to the *Beʾur*, the commentary that he and his associates were preparing on the Hebrew Bible. Wessely outlined a comprehensive educational program for Jewish children with German as its linchpin. Science, geography, history, and civil law would be taught, and Hebrew would be treated as a compulsory classical language and a "must" for the understanding of the Bible. Hebrew no longer occupies the centre of the stage; a mere couple of hours a day would be required for its study, with more emphasis on grammar than on the Bible itself or Rashi's commentary thereto. In this scheme the holy quality of Hebrew is removed, and very little emphasis is placed on the study of Mishnah and Talmud—these to be reserved for the select few who would in due course become rabbis.[25] The treatise provoked a veritable storm. The leading rabbis of the time, Tevele of Lissa, Ezekiel Landau (author of *Nodaʿ biyhudah*) of Prague, and Phineas Ha-Levi Hurwitz (the *Baʿal haflaʾah*) of Frankfurt on the Main delivered fiery sermons against this educational program. But the strangest thing of all to behold is that no attempt whatsoever was made to invoke the *ḥerem* against Wessely and his group of associates, even though threats were implied.

Before essaying any answer to the question to which this gives rise, it is necessary to survey some of the arguments put forward by the opponents of enlightenment.

> "Evil is the day," thundered Rabbi Tevele from the pulpit, "that you have seen, because of the action of one person—a flatterer, poor in knowledge and indeed an utter ignoramus (*hedyoṭ she-Ba-hedyoṭim*), by the name of Hertz Wessely of the holy congregation of Berlin . . . he has come forward with impetuous advice to tender to scholars of discriminating understanding and perfection of character (*ḥakhamim u-nevonim u-themimim*) as if he were himself the outstanding luminary of his generation (*yaḥid be-doro*) . . . how did this evil fellow dare, as one himself lacking any outstanding wisdom save for his knowledge of Hebrew and the ordinary meaning of the Pentateuch . . . with no understanding of the depth of the Talmud or knowledge of the early codifiers of the oral law . . . how, I say, can he dare to say 'let us be wise, proffer advice to states of high degree that are full of learned hearts and of those who understand what scholarship and knowledge are' (*le-*

> *hashith ʿeṣah liphney medinoth yeqaroth meleʾoth ḥakhmey lev u-meviney maddaʿ we-yodeʿey daʿath*)? How shall a person who is lacking in all foundations of knowledge come forward to plan the order of study and teach God's way, instructing God's people of the deeds that they should do? . . . Move aside from him, declare him unclean, move away, touch him not! God almighty knows that it is for his sake and for the sake of the holy Torah that I have today come to cut down the horns of the one who tramples on the heads of the holy people, and to apprise you of this man's machinations (*baʾthi ha-Yom ha-Zeh le-gaddeaʿ qarney ha-Poseaʿ ʿal rashey ʿam ha-Qodesh*)."

Rabbi Tevele claimed that the rabbis were not opposed to the learning of German, and that they, too, were loyal subjects of the emperor or king; but

> "we Jews have been instructed by our masters, those who set in order the Babylonian Talmud, how to arrange for the teachings of the Torah and of our religion amongst our children from the age of five upwards. . . . For us, what is primary will remain primary, and what is marginal will remain of peripheral interest only. He is telling lies to the Jews in pretending that the emperor has ordained that a child should not enter the Jewish religious school until he has first completed his mastery of reading languages and is proficient in grammar. God forbid that we should entertain such ideas about the emperor, who is known for his love of people and as a leader of nations".

He proceeded to assert that Wessely is as good as a complete nonbeliever

> "who does not believe in the Torah; nay, he validates as truth strange notions, as do the naturalists (*she-ʾeyno ma'amin ba-Torah she-hu me-ʾammeth deʿoth zaroth min ha-Deʿoth kemo ha-Naṭuraliste*). But now there comes the inciter (*mesith u-maddiaḥ*) who would fain steal the heart of the people and trample on the glory of the Torah whilst flattering the emperor, in the hope that he will succeed in turning the hearts of the emperor's servants so that they will hasten to do what he tells them. How can we keep silent? . . . How comforted I felt when I heard from the true preachers of the holy congregation of Vilna how they [*sc.* the Jews] had burned the book in the street . . . although the emperor's name was mentioned there a number of times, and his praise frequently."[26]

Rabbi Tevele envied the Jews in Vilna who were still powerful enough to consign Wessely's "dangerous" booklet to public burning, whereas he himself could do no more than warn his congregants against following the writer's advice and limited himself to castigating Wessely as a miscreant and an ignoramus. Significantly, and indeed ironically, he was careful not to mention that seven years before he had himself written an eulogistic approbation to a well-known book by Wessely, in which he praised the latter's scholarship.[27]

Although a similar denunciation was uttered by Ezekiel Landau, the celebrated rabbi of Prague, not a single rabbi in Germany, Austria, or the province of Posen would have dared employ the *ḥerem* against the Berlin circle of enlightenment. The reason is simple and clear-cut. The *ḥerem* could not be pronounced unless the government, be it king, emperor, prince, or the authorities of a city-state, was prepared to lend its authority. The enlightened absolutist monarchy of the second half of the eighteenth century in Austria, Prussia, and France was primarily interested in circumscribing and diminishing the authority of rabbinical autonomy, and it would not have tolerated the application of the *ḥerem* as a sanction. Power had shifted from the rabbis to those of a new generation who stood close to court circles, and the traditional communal leadership remained hamstrung in regard to bringing rebels to book.

Mendelssohn, Wessely's friend and junior, was infinitely more learned and more sophisticated than Wessely himself. The course that he followed was a complicated one, his ideas being expressed in a very sharp and lucid manner in German, but in a subtle and disguised manner in Hebrew.

In 1772—that is, almost ten years before the *Toleranzpatent* of Joseph II—Mendelssohn addressed a letter to Rabbi Jacob Emden, discussing the question whether Jewish law would permit a post mortem and allow the postponement of burial for three days. He took as his starting point the circumstance that the king of Prussia had ordered this, and consequently there arose the question of whether the principle of *dina de-malkhutha dina* (the state law must be acknowledged) is applicable. His letter, addressed to the Jewish community of Schwerin on 8 Sivan 5532 (i.e., 18 May 1772), makes it clear that Mendelssohn was personally in favour of permitting post mortems. "What is the great fear that makes people anxious about this? In my humble opinion there is nothing in it involving the slightest contravention of religious law. . . . [Postponement of burial may be desirable] in case there is in fact some life still in the body, this making it impossible for it to be buried, since nothing can take precedence over concern for danger to life." He even argued that in Palestine during tannaitic times Jews used to place their dead in caves and keep watch over them for three days and nights, lest there was any life still left in the body. Medical science, he says, supports this procedure, since it is sometimes difficult to distinguish between fainting and actual death. He consequently advised the community of Schwerin to construct a cave or tunnel in the cemetery for the washing of the dead, and to keep bodies there for three days and thereafter inter them. "But," he says, "my advice to all holy congregations is not to deviate from the paths of the early codifiers (*mi-Darkhey ha-Qadmonim*) either to the right or the left, for their paths are the paths of pleasantness, and it is fitting for scholars of the generation to encourage them so to do. *Although I know they will not listen to me, as the hand of custom is mighty and powerful, and I might seem to them to be a trifler* (*ki-metaʿteaʿ*); *but I shall have saved myself*" [italics mine].[28]

The community of Schwerin had also invited the ruling of Rabbi Jacob Emden, who lived in the nearby Hamburg. Emden came out categorically against delayed burial. Mendelssohn then asked Emden how he justified his position, and Emden replied sharply, even rebuking Mendelssohn for daring to question a custom which had been adopted by Jewry as a whole, both Sephardim and Ashkenazim. Furthermore, Emden pointed out that preliminary cave burial had been discarded by rabbinic sages long since. Medical views cannot weigh against the stand of *halakhah*, and Mendelssohn had in any case misinterpreted the talmudic passages quoted by him. Although his reply to Emden has been lost, it can in part be reconstructed from Emden's second letter to him. Emden warned him that he would be doing himself an injury were he not to take Emden's advice, since already more and more people were expressing the opinion that he, Mendelssohn, was developing heretical views. With all his respect for Mendelssohn, the aged Emden told him bluntly that "in matters concerning the Torah I am not a respecter of persons, not even of famous ones."[29] Emden convinced himself too facilely that no one would pay attention to Mendelssohn's views on this matter when he wrote that "I am afraid that [Mendelssohn's opinion] will be treated as a matter of mockery."[30] Mendelssohn did not rise to the challenge of Emden's stern rebuke, and without changing his own mind quietly dropped the subject. Emden, like many other contemporary rabbis, did not believe and could not visualize that winds of change were blowing, and could not foresee that within one generation profound changes would occur within German Jewry, changes that would make even Mendelssohn's moderate conservatism look obsolete, indeed irrelevant, to his own followers. In a good old traditionalist way Emden failed to understand that even rabbinic institutions considered by him to be immutable would become subject to intense pressure and suffer major changes.

Mendelssohn revealed himself, in Hebrew, as a highly sophisticated thinker and a very astute polemicist, for the first time in his introduction, or prolegomenon, to his edition of the Bible with a German translation in Hebrew characters, together with a collectively written Hebrew commentary. He completed the booklet on 1 Kislev 5583 (December 1782), and it is not clear whether it was intended for sale to the public, since 300 copies only were printed;[31] possibly it was meant for a limited circle of friends, so that debate could proceed regarding the issues raised by the translation and commentary. What has hitherto attracted the attention of scholars are Mendelssohn's reasons for providing a translation in German and his penetrating criticism of earlier versions in Old Yiddish or, as he called it, *leshon ʾashkenaz*.[32] He outlined, briefly but in a very erudite way, the history of different translations of the Bible in Greek, Aramaic, Arabic, Spanish, and Old Yiddish, but he placed considerable stress on the weaknesses of earlier Old Yiddish versions, pointing to the weak grammatical structure and to the fact that some early translators, like Blitz, had misunderstood whole passages and could not fathom the meaning of a large number of words. Other considerations, regarding how the Bible came to be edited, and related matters, have somehow been left out of account by modern scholars.[33]

It would seem to me that parts of the booklet *ʾOr li-nethivah* contain very important views of Mendelssohn on institutional changes within the Bible that have their lessons for his own age; in other words, he held that some structural changes could take place within the Jewish community if only its leaders were willing, and daring enough, to carry through a reconstruction without resorting to the state as an extraneous authority. This is diametrically opposed to the view put forward by him in his *Jerusalem* and in his exchanges with Dohm, in which he emphasizes the need for the state to abolish Jewish internal autonomy and to deprive the rabbis of the power of exercising the *ḥerem* that could exclude Jews from their own community.

Mendelssohn proposed the following, very subtle arguments. All religious Jews believe that the Torah was given in its entirety to Moses, and he quotes, with seeming approval, that God spoke and Moses wrote down up to *Deut.* 31:26, and that from that point to the end of *Deuteronomy* God spoke and Moses wrote amid tears.[34] Even though one believes in the integrity of the Torah as a unit, it has nevertheless been subject to the vicissitudes of copying, scribes occasionally missing out or adding letters inadvertently. What we possess now is not the Bible as given by God to Moses, but as transmitted by Ezra the Scribe and his associates. There were serious differences between the masoretic schools of Ben Asher and Ben Naphtali, and furthermore the Masorah itself had been little studied, or even known at the time of Ezra. Spelling of Hebrew words was not fully systematized, and the most significant change took place when the ancient Hebrew script was dropped, and the Jews adopted a new alphabet of square Hebrew (*kethav ʾashuri*). Again, Mendelssohn quotes with approval the talmudic statement that mankind's original language was Hebrew, that being the language in which God addressed Adam, Cain, Noah, and the patriarchs and in which the tablets of the law were given. With his tongue in his cheek he proceeds to enumerate the appearance, quite early in history, of many other languages. Later on translations of the Torah came to be required in Aramaic, Greek, Judaeo-Arabic, Judaeo-Spanish, and Judaeo-German ("Old Yiddish"), which Jews had produced down the ages in order to meet a public demand. Although it is traditionally correct to say that Moses heard the whole Torah from God, complete with its vowel points and accents, these seem to have emerged much later. Even the talmudic sages were divided among themselves as to whether the Torah had been given in the ancient Hebrew script or in square, and in large, medium, or small letters.[35] Several times Mendelssohn underlines the circumstance that it was Ezra who was responsible for changing the Hebrew script to *kethav ʾashuri*, a profound and revolutionary change that had deeply affected the whole subsequent history of Hebrew literature.[36]

With some circumspectness, he began to quote from Christian scholars who had dealt with the Bible—a procedure quite unheard of amongst Ashkenazim, although in the Sephardi world he had been anticipated by Abravanel. Spinoza had, of course, done so, but he wrote in Latin, not Hebrew, he had been extruded from the Jewish community, and he was treated by Jews in general and by Mendelssohn himself as a "dead dog."[37]

The implications of all this were perfectly clear. What Mendelssohn was conveying was the message that in the past changes of a profound character had occurred in the Jewish religion, and that any opposition that they had elicited had been quickly silenced, the changes themselves being implemented and becoming standard practice. Were the leaders of the Jewish communities, both ecclesiastical and lay, to agree to the modest proposals that he had himself so carefully worked out for them, all, he believed, would be well. *Vis à vis* the non-Jewish world, he promoted the idea of *Verbesserung der Juden* along two lines: the Jews ought to master the German language, so that the resultant cultural assimilation would serve them as an "entrance ticket" to German society, whilst non-Jews should see to it that the autonomous institutions of Jewry—internal law courts (*battey din*), synagogal disciplinary powers, and the corollary right to punish recalcitrant Jewish individuals—be abolished, whilst securing the removal of all Jewish civil disabilities. Thus it was that Mendelssohn, although appearing to be a moderate conservative, was in many ways a forerunner—far more than his contemporaries realized—of revolutionary change of a profound character.

To coercion in any form he was opposed, irrespective of whether it sprang from church, synagogue, or state. When he suspected that Joseph II might resort to force in order to compel Jews to implement his proposals, conceivably with conversionist ends in view, Mendelssohn protested vigorously to his colleague Herz Homberg, pleading for genuine toleration: "as long as there is the danger of the 'Vereinigungs System,' it seems to me that this flattering toleration is more dangerous than open persecution."[38]

For many years before his death, Mendelssohn was out of range of attack from rabbinical quarters. No one assailed him in the crude manner in which Ezekiel Landau and Tevele had abused Wessely; he stood too close to non-Jews of influence and importance, and could be relied upon to act as a spokesman for Jews. His personal reputation was increasing, the gentile world adulated him. Already in 1763 he had been exempted from paying taxes to the community, and in 1771 he was, as a mark of signal distinction, elected a *Parnas*. Furthermore, his influence over court-Jews in important positions was enormous.[39]

Soon after Mendelssohn's death, new and very powerful winds began to blow across Europe, bringing with them most serious changes in western Jewish life. The French revolution more or less destroyed the structure of Jewish autonomy and converted the rabbis into servants of the state.[40]

Had Mendelssohn survived, he might well have shuddered at the far-reaching character of these cataclysmic events. As a result of the French revolution one of the most intimate members of Mendelssohn's circle, the redoubtable David Friedländer, blandly ignoring the spiritual legacy of his teacher, could pen the following sentence in a letter to a friend, Meyer Eger of Glogau. Writing in a mixture of Hebrew and German (in Hebrew characters) from Berlin on March 19, 1792, Friedländer addresses his correspondent—an ordinary business man—honorifically as "Mein lieber R. Meir." In the body of the letter Friendländer sneers at the well-known rabbis Raphael Cohen of Hamburg and Ezekiel Landau of Prague, the two most important rabbinical authorities in the German-speaking world, intimating that they are not concerned with living issues of importance in the contemporary world, being aloof from problems of ethics and those raised by natural religion or such great human events as the French revolution, being entirely preoccupied with trivialities: "Das von den Begriffen von Gott was die Rabbonim unter Religion verstehen, brauche ich Ihnen nicht zu sagen. 3000 Jahr *ʾahar qabolas ha-Tauroh* untersucht Ezekiel Yampoli ob man *ʿaḥar ʿakhilas maṣṣaus paḥaus mi-ke-zayis* noch eine *Brokhoh le-ʿaḥaronoh* [*sic*] machen muss oder nicht."[41] It would have given Mendelssohn much pain to see the figure of the distinguished rabbi of Prague referred to without the title of rabbi and with his regular surname of Landau replaced by the name of the little town in Galicia from which he originated.

Less than six years after Mendelssohn's death his own friends and disciples had largely eroded rabbinic and Jewish communal authority. The stormy events that succeeded, in the early part of the nineteenth century, constitute a chapter on their own.[42]

NOTES

* This study forms part of a larger work which the author has in preparation.

1. On the periodization of Jewish history cf. Simon Dubnow, *Divrey yemey ʿam ʿolam*, 8, Berlin, 1923, pp. 3–50; Benzion Dinur, *Be-mifneh ha-Doroth*, Jerusalem, 1955, pp. 19–68; Salo W. Baron, *A Social and Religious History of the Jews*, 1st ed., New York, ii, pp. 164–261; I. F. Baer, *Galuth*, New York, 1947, pp. 109–20; G. Scholem, *Devarim be-go*, Tel Aviv, 1975, pp. 385–403 (English translation in Scholem's *The Messianic Idea in Judaism*, London, 1972, pp. 304–13). Scholem had earlier advanced the daring thesis that modern Jewish history began with the antinomianism of the Sabbataean heresy; see his *Miṣwah ha-Baʾah ba-ʿaverah* (originally published in 1937, and included in his *Meḥqarim u-meqoroth le-toledoth ha-Shabbethaʾuth we-gilguleyha*, pp. 9f., especially 52–67 (English translation in *The Messianic Idea in Judaism*, pp. 78–141). A different view, with a quasi-marxist gloss, was put forward by Raphael Mahler in his four-volume (Hebrew) *History of the Jews in Modern Times*, Merhavia, 1952–56 (English abridgment, London, 1971).

2. On Graetz see S. Ettinger, "*Yahaduth we-toledoth ha-Yehudim bi-thefisatho shel Graetz*," in H. Graetz, *Darekhey ha-historiah ha-Yehudith*, Jerusalem, 1969, pp. 7–36.

3. Cf. Dinur, *op. cit.* (p. 25, n. 1), pp. 87 and 95; Scholem, *Meḥqarim*, pp. 116–18; I. Levitats, *The Jewish Community in Russia 1772–1844*, pp. 160ff.

4. S. Assaf, "*Le-qoroth ha-rabbanuth*", *Reshumoth* (ed. A. Druyanov) ii, Tel Aviv, 1921, pp. 259–300; S. A. Horodezky, *Le-qoroth ha-rabbanuth*, Warsaw, 1911.

5. Judah Leib b. Moses of Selichow, *Shirey yehudah* (Hebrew and Yiddish), Amsterdam, 1697, ff. 3–4, and especially f. 16a. The first to draw attention to this important source was David Kaufmann (*Yaʾir Ḥayyim Bachrach*, Budapest, 1894, p. 49). The booklet also contains valuable material regarding the spread of belief in Shabbetai Ṣevi, cf on this Scholem, *Shabbetai Sevi,* London, 1973, pp. 552–53.

6. Cf. *Dinur, op. cit.* (p. 25, n. 1), pp. 122–25, and E. Tcherikower, *"Di geshikhte fun a literarishn Plagiat,"* *Yivo Bletter*, iv, Vilna, 1932, pp. 159–67, and S. A. Horodezky, *"Zu der shalsheles ha-yichus fun Shimon Dubnow," Historishe Shriftn,* ii, Vilna, 1937, p. 9. A more detailed analysis of the *Qav Ha-Yashar* will be presented in the complete study.

7. Cf. the dispute in London concerning a divorce in 1706–07 (see Uri Phoebusch Hamburger, *ʾUrim we-thummim*, London, 1707; Yoḥanan Holleschau, *Maʿaseh Rav*, London, 1707). On the celebrated divorce controversy in Cleves, see Aaron Simeon b. Jacob Abraham of Copenhagen (ed.), *ʾOr ha-Yashar* (Amsterdam, 1769), and Israel b. Eliezer Lifshitz, *ʾOr yisraʾel* (Cleves, 1770), and F. Baer, *Das Protokollbuch der Landjudenschaft des Herzogtums Kleve*, Berlin, 1922, pp. 107–13. On the controversies in Hamburg see below, pp. 15f. On the split in the Vilna community see Israel Zinberg, *"Milḥemeth ha-Qahal be-ha-rav ha-ʾaḥaron be-wilno," He-ʿavar*, ii, Petrograd, 1918, pp. 45–74; *idem, "Di Makhloikes zwishn di roshei ha-kohol un dem rov in wilne in zweiter helft 18tn yorhundert," Historishe Shriftn*, ii, Vilna, 1937, pp. 291–321; Israel Klausner, *Wilno bi-thequfath ha-Gaʾon*, Jerusalem, 1942, pp. 50–292. The best introduction to the whole stormy period of the eighteenth century is Azriel Shoḥeṭ, *ʿIm ḥillufey tequfoth*, Jerusalem, 1961.

8. See Shoḥeṭ, *op. cit.* (previous note), pp. 174–97. Shoḥeṭ based his research primarily on the register maintained by the German Lutheran pastor Johann Heinrich Callenberg who was, from 1728, the principal of the mission to the Jews. His register and reports cover the years 1728–60, and contain a wealth of information relating to Jews. Scholem was the first to draw attention to them, and recovered thence a mass of material concerning secret Sabbataeans; see his (Hebrew) article on Contributions to knowledge about Sabbataeanism in the eighteenth century in *Zion*, ix, 1944, pp. 27–38 and 84–88.

9. See S. Dubnow, *Toledoth ha-ḥasiduth*, i, Tel Aviv, 1932, introduction, pp. 1–38. The classical studies on the court-Jews are by Selma Stern [Täubler]; *Jud Süss*, Berlin, 1929, *The Court Jew*, Philadelphia, 1950, and her outstanding *Der Preussische Staat und die Juden*, 6 vols., 1925–70.

10. The two studies available on Emden are far from satisfactory; Mortimer Cohen, *Jacob Emden, A Man of Controversy*, Philadelphia, 1937, and (in Hebrew) Abraham Bick, *Rabbi Yaʿaqov Emden*, Jerusalem, 1975. See Scholem's important and critical review of Cohen's book in *Kirjath Sefer*, xvi, Jerusalem, 1939–40, pp. 320–38. On the Emden-Eibeschütz controversy see M. A. Perlmutter, *R. Yonathan Eibeschütz we-yaḥaso le-shabbethaʾuth*, Jerusalem, 1947, and Scholem, *Liqquṭey margaliyyoth*, Jerusalem, 1941.

11. See Jacob Emden, *Hithʾabbequth*, 2nd ed. Lvov, 1877, ff. 1a, 3b. Examples

could be multiplied a hundredfold from Emden's many pamphlets, e.g., *Sefath ʾemeth we-lashon zehorith*, *Beth Yonathan ha-Sofer*, and particularly his book *Sefer shimmush*.

12. Eibeschütz assembled his defense in a book entitled *Luḥoth ʿeduth* (Altona, 1755; I have used the second edition, Lvov, 1877).

13. Cf, Israel Halperin, *Pinqas waʿad ʾarbaʿ ha-ʾarasoth*, Jerusalem, 1945, pp. 339–56, 368, 385.

14. See *Hithʾabbequth*, f. 18, and Halperin, p. 395.

15. See Abbé Grégoire, *An Essay on the Physical, Moral and Political Reformation of the Jews*, London, 1788, p. 194. Grégoire's comment is in line with his call for the abolition of Jewish autonomy: "If this right, however, be left them, confined to objects merely of a religious nature, it must have no relation with those of a political society, and must never brand a citizen with infamy, as the synagogue of Amsterdam branded Uriel Acosta. To obviate inconveniences, there must always be an appeal to our tribunals." It is interesting to note that in 1753 Eibeschütz felt it necessary to apprise Frederick V of Denmark that he proposed to sue Emden before the court of the Council of Four Lands; see Halperin, *op. cit.* (*supra*, n. 13), pp. 385–86. The decision by the parliament of Metz must surely be one of the earliest cases of interference by the government of a city or state in the internal affairs of the Jewish community, and it is of great significance. (The whole Emden–Eibeschütz controversy will be examined in greater detail in the full study).

16. See M. Balaban, *Le-tholedoth ha-Tenuʿah ha-Frankith,* ii, Tel Aviv, 1935, p. 265, and cf. the penetrating comment by Scholem in his study *Ha-Tenuʿah ha-Shabbethaʾith be-polen* (*Meḥqarim*, p. 118).

17. See *Toledoth Yaʿaqov Yosef*, 1st ed. Koretz, 1780, ff. 25b, 78a. For an even more extreme expression of opinion see f. 169b: "the worst of all is that exile suffered by scholars who are fearers of God at the hand of scholars who are Jewish devils that abuse true scholars (*talmidey ḥakhamim*) in the presence of ignorant folk, so that they suffer degradation in the eyes of the Gentiles" (see also f. 181b for another sharp passage). The phrase "Jewish devils" (*shedin yehudaʾin*) is first found in the *Zohar* and it was also used in the Spanish cabbalistic book *Sefer ha-Qanah* (see Scholem, *Kabbalah*, Jerusalem, 1974, p. 323), but not, of course, in the way that Jacob Joseph of Polonnoye used it. The taunt was applied by him a number of times, and the cases will be examined, as well as other antiauthoritarian passages, in the full study. No wonder that when the book appeared it provoked a storm of protest amongst opponents of hasidism; see Dubnow, *Toledoth ha-ḥasiduth*, pp. 138–43.

18. It has been partly covered by Dubnow (see last note); but see S. Ettinger, "The Hasidic Movement—Reality and Ideals", in "Social Life and Social Values of the Jewish People," *Journal of World History*, xi, 1–2, Neuchatel, pp. 251–66. Ettinger deals with the problem of authority, his article being a polemic against the views of B. Dinur and J. G. Weiss.

19. For the whole episode see I. Klausner, *op. cit.* (p. 26, n. 7), pp. 156–69, who deals with a mass of documents that have come to light since Zinberg wrote his well-known articles.

20. The latest biography of Mendelssohn is the monumental study by Professor A. Altmann, *Moses Mendelssohn, A Biographical Study*, Alabama and London, 1973; see pp. 449–61 and particularly pp. 470–71. Cf. J. Katz, *Out of the Ghetto*, Harvard, 1973, pp. 57–64, 161–62, and my critical review in *The New York Review of Books*, Dec. 12th, 1974, pp. 22–25.

21. Cf. *ʾEleh divrey ha-Berith*, Hamburg, 1819, p. iii, *Modaʿah*, second paragraph, beginning "through our sins . . ."

22. See Mendelssohn, *Gesammelte Schriften*, xiv, Stuttgart, 1972, p. 14:
שהיתה דעת יהודה באמת לדבר משפטים עם אדוני הארץ אבל באימה והכנעה כראוי מדרכי המוסר והחכמה לגר בארץ נכריה לא לדבר אתו קשות ולהקציפו

23. *Ibid.*, p. 173. On Mendelssohn's endebtedness to Menasseh b. Israel see Altmann, *op. cit.* (p. 27, n. 20), pp. 463–74.

24. *Gesammelte Schriften*, xiv, p. 176 and pp. 187–88.

25. N. H. Wessely, *Divrey shalom we-ʾemeth*, Part I, Berlin, 1782, particularly chapters i and v.

26. Tevele's sermon was delivered on *Shabbath ha-Gadol*, 1782 and first published by Louis Lewin in the *Jahrbuch der jüd. lit. Gesellschaft*, xii, Frankfurt, 1918; it was reprinted in an abridged form by S. Assaf in his *Meqoroth le-tholedoth ha-ḥinnukh be-yisraʾel*, i, Tel Aviv, 1925, pp. 236–38. For Landau's sermon cf. Assaf, *ibid.*, pp. 238–39; Landau's letter to the leaders of the Jewish community in Berlin, *ibid.*, pp. 239–40.

27. *Massekheth ʾavoth ʿim perush yeyn levanon*, Berlin [1775]. Others who wrote approbations included Saul Berlin, rabbi of Amsterdam, and Solomon Salem, of the Sephardi community there, and Ezekiel Landau. See M. Roest, *Catalog der Hebraica und Judaica aus der Rosenthalschen Bibliothek*, Amsterdam, 1875, p. 826.

28. Mendelssohn, *Gesammelte Schriften*, xix, Stuttgart, 1974, pp. 156–57.

29. *Ibid.*, p. 166 et sequ.

30. *Ibid.*

31. It was subsequently printed in every edition of the *Beʾur*; I have used *Gesammelte Schriften*, xiv, p. 267.

32. *Ibid.*, pp. 242, 255.

33. Cf. Altmann, *op. cit.* (p. 27, n. 20), pp. 369–83. The same thing applies to other Mendelssohn scholars.

34. See *Gesammelte Schriften*, xiv, pp. 211–13 (cf. T.B. *Bava Bathra* 15a and *Menaḥoth* 30a).

35. *Ibid.*, 213–21. The passage would have misled many an orthodox Jew because of its plethora of references to talmudic sources; but a thinly disguised irony lurks in the style, and one cannot be sure whether or not Mendelssohn is poking fun at early Jewish authorities. A similar situation occurs in Abraham ibn Ezra's biblical commentaries.

36. *Ibid.*, pp. 221–23, 224–26.

37. The expression is Mendelssohn's own (but cf. *Eccles.* 9:4).

38. Mendelssohn to Herz Homberg, letters dated October 4, 1783 and March 1, 1784; *Gesammelte Schriften*, Berlin, 1845, vol. v.

39. See *Gesammelte Schriften* xiv, pp. 384–85, quoting from the minutes of the Berlin Jewish community, where Mendelssohn is described as "his own people's proctor approaching each people in its own tongue, his own tongue uttering lofty sentiments" (*doresh le-ʿammo ʿam wa-ʿam ki-leshono lashon medabbereth gedoloth*).

40. This point will be treated more fully in my forthcoming study.

41. Cf. "*Brif fun Dovid Friedländer*," edited with an introduction by Joseph Meisl, *Historishe Shriftn*, ii, Vilna, 1937, pp. 404 and 390–94.

42. I have deliberately refrained here from analysis of the writings of Isaac Satanov, Mendel Lefin, Isaac Euchel, Aaron Wolfsohn-Halle, Saul Berlin, and others. These will be dealt with in a separate chapter in my forthcoming study, where more will also be said about David Friedländer.

Civil versus Political Emancipation*

S. W. BARON

Much has been written about Jewish emancipation. For the most part the main emphasis has been laid on the legal and political aspects of equality of rights for Jews. These developments were usually best dated according to the legal enactments guaranteeing such equality under the constitutions of the respective countries. The very term "emancipation" was deeply tinged with emotion. Emerging in the press and literature after the achievement of the "Catholic emancipation" in England in 1828, this term denoted, as its ancient Roman prototype, liberation from bondage. The normal tendency for the protagonists of emancipation was to overstress the existing or past "bondage" of the Jews and their discriminatory treatment by law and society, as against the forthcoming era of "freedom" in which Jews would be participants in the historic careers of the surrounding nations as citizens equal to all others in their rights and duties.

Out of this overemphasis upon the preemancipation status of discrimination and segregation grew not only the misconception of the meaning of medieval Jewish "serfdom," but also the long-prevailing "lacrymose conception" of Jewish history in the dispersion as being essentially a *Leidens- und Gelehrtengeschichte*. Ultimately, many people started talking of a "pariah" status of the preemancipation Jew. This term was supported by the great authority of Max Weber, who, in the introduction to his penetrating essay on the social ethics of ancient Judaism, had bluntly declared: "Sociologically speaking, what were the Jews? A pariah people. This meaning, as we know it from India, a guest people which is ritualistically segregated from its social environment either formally or actually." The forgetting of the qualifications suggested by Weber himself has meant that the Indian parallel has haunted many Jewish minds ever since. In fact, however, it has no justification whatsoever.[1]

I

This somewhat simplistic contrast between the modern Jew and his ghetto ancestor tended to overlook some basic lines of evolution which preceded and followed the American and French Revolutions. In the first place, the process of Jewish entry into general society depended much more on basic demographic, economic, and intellectual developments than on legal pronunciamentos. Very frequently legal enactments were merely a form of ratification of socioeconomic and cultural realities which had already taken place, sometimes over a period of generations. True, the law, once enacted, added new vigor and acceleration to those underlying trends. In some cases, however, when it was precipitately promulgated out of consideration for general principles, it proved quite ineffective in practice, because society was not prepared to follow its lead. We need but refer to the obvious dichotomy between the generally egalitarian constitutions of the Soviet Union or many Arab lands and the actual treatment of Jews by the existing regimes there.

Nonetheless, with the general penchant of the French revolutionary and post-Napoleonic generations up to World War I to attribute supreme importance to formal enactments and the belief in the sanctity of constitutional provisions as well as of international treaties, the struggle in the late eighteenth and most of the nineteenth century took the shape of political battles for the securing of such egalitarian pronouncements. Characteristically, the main driving forces in this struggle often were not the Jews, but rather the progressive forces in the various states, the spokesmen of which, often subconsciously, felt that Jewish emancipation was an even greater historic necessity for the modern state than it was for the Jews themselves.[2]

Most prolonged and widely debated was the struggle for Jewish equality in the German-speaking countries. The problems were aired from various angles in endless discussions, from the days of Mendelssohn, Lessing, and Dohm to the Congress of Vienna, through the basic constitution of the Germanic Confederation, the upheavals of 1848, and the numerous legal enactments in the various German states culminating in the Austro-Hungarian constitution of 1867 and that of the German Empire of 1871. These debates continued with great passion thereafter because of the unceasing anti-Semitic attacks on Jewish equality and the Jewish as well as general apologias in defence of it. One major item under dispute was whether Jewish emancipation was so intimately interwoven with Jewish assimilation that it formed a sort of contractual obligation on the part of Jews to become assimilated to German culture. Some Jew-baiters argued, therefore, that because Jews had not surrendered their ethnic identity, they had not kept their part of the contractual bargain, and hence emancipation ought to be revoked.[3]

At the same time Jews, and particularly spokesmen of the rising Jewish nationalist movement, not only argued that legal inequality of any segment of the population was incompatible with democracy but also that all ethnic minorities as such were entitled to enjoy both equality of rights as citizens and specific safeguards for the cultivation of their cultural heritage. They demanded, therefore, both equality and minority rights. These debates led up to international guarantees of both for the Jews living in the countries between the Baltic and the Aegean Sea, according to the Peace Treaties of 1919. Before long, however, these attainments were completely canceled out by the Nazi revolution which not only denied Jews legal equality but gainsaid their very right to existence.

During the two centuries of debate, the Germans emerged with a clearer conception of the distinction between what they called the *bürgerliche*

Gleichberechtigung and the *privatbürgerliche Gleichberechtigung*. The former implied complete equality in both political and civil rights and duties. The *privatbürgerliche Gleichberechtigung* was intended to grant Jews socio-economic equality, particularly in the occupational spheres, whilst denying them the political rights of public office, political franchise, and the like. This distinction underlay, for instance, the famous Prussian emancipatory decree of March 11, 1812. In Articles 7–9 it provided for full equality of Jewish *Einländer* with Christians, and even opened up to Jews all academic, teaching, and municipal posts. But it added: "We reserve for ourselves the right to provide in the future as to the extent to which Jews shall also be admitted to other state functions and offices."[4]

At times such limited equality also implied certain differentials in the duties of citizenship; for example, in military service. On the other hand, Jewish participation in the military forces was demanded in Austria and Russia even before the enactment of general legal equality. Remarkably enough, the Russia of Catherine the Great was ready to concede to the Jews electoral rights in municipal governments, rights formally granted in that period to the Jews of Tuscany only, where the Jewry of Leghorn had long played a noteworthy role in the grand duchy's affairs. Simultaneously, however, the Russian government imposed upon the Jews significant new residential and occupational disabilities to meet certain demands by powerful segments of society at large.[5]

II

In that entire evolution one must not overlook the fundamental fact that equality of rights for Jews was unthinkable in the general European corporate structure prevailing before the great eighteenth-century revolutions. There existed no equality of rights for other groups of the population. Each corporate body, such as the nobility and the clergy, the bourgeoisie and the peasantry, whether free or living in a state of villeinage, lived according to its own system of rights and duties. Very frequently the privileges granted to one city greatly differed from those granted to another in its immediate vicinity. In Poland some so-called *jurydiki* formed enclaves within the cities, the jurisdiction over which was in the hands of their private owners, especially nobles or churches, who independently regulated the rights of the respective groups in their domains. Even within individual cities the legal status of patricians often differed from that of the plebeians in both theory and practice. There even existed different regulations among members of various artisan guilds in accordance with their respective statutes. Under such a system Jews formed a corporate body apart, whose rights and duties were regulated by special privileges granted by monarchs or other masters, privileges which often varied from locality to locality and from period to period. It was the great historic accomplishment of the modern state to have swept away the cobwebs of these multifarious regulations which often came into direct conflict with one another and led to endless controversies, and even litigation, sometimes lasting for decades.

For Jews, this distinction between political and civil rights was of great importance. Civil rights, which primarily involved the removal of certain occupational disabilities, were of paramount concern to a people which was at that time rapidly increasing in numbers and badly needed an enlargement of its economic base. If my population estimates are at all correct, it appears that by the mid-seventeenth century the total world Jewish population had declined to less than 1,000,000, to rise to well over 2,000,000 at the beginning of the nineteenth century and to some 16,000,000 in 1939.[6]

With such a population explosion, Jews could not possibly live on the few limited occupations open to them under the restrictive legislation of the preemancipation period. Hence there was practical unanimity among their leaders about the desirability of the removal of the civil disabilities, although the admission of Jewish pupils to general schools—the public school system, started in Prussia in 1802, was rapidly gaining ground throughout the western world in the course of the nineteenth century—was not necessarily considered a blessing by the staunchly orthodox, who viewed their children's attendance at such schools as a threat to the survival of some of the most cherished elements in their intellectual heritage. But the threat to such survival on the part of political emancipation was infinitely greater. Among the new duties imposed upon the Jews loomed full participation in military service, which increasingly became subject to compulsory drafts of masses of young men in each country. Quite apart from such excesses as came to the fore in the Russian *recrutchina* of 1827–1855, such service often demanded from Jewish soldiers violation of the Sabbath and the neglect of the dietary laws.[7]

More generally, the integration of the Jews into the political structure of the respective countries usually presupposed the delimitation of Jewish self-government in communal affairs. In particular, authority of the Jewish courts of justice had now necessarily to give way to that of the general courts. Nor did the Jewish community function any longer in behalf of the state as the main tax collecting agency among Jews; it was happy to receive governmental guarantees for its right to impose limited taxation on its members in order to provide the greatly reduced communal services. Otherwise Jews as individuals were to be taxed directly, on a par with the other citizens, by the government's fiscal organs. The major political right, on the other hand, namely that of the franchise, was rather meaningless to the masses of Jews living in countries such as Russia and even Austria or Prussia before the proclamation of their more liberal constitutions. In absolutist states the diets possessed very limited legislative powers, and the right to vote in their elections meant very little in practice. Even the aforementioned right of the Russian or Tuscan Jews of the eighteenth century to elect, or to be elected, aldermen in their municipalities carried very little weight with them, since the municipal organs largely continued to be controlled by often hostile burghers.

For these reasons many traditional Jews were afraid of political emancipation even more than of a continuation of the existing discriminatory laws. Even in such western communities as those of Amsterdam in 1796 and the Grand Duchy of Baden in 1846 the conservative groups often strenuously objected to the sweeping declarations of complete equality of rights. Understandably, the opposition was more strenuous in the east-European mass settlements, where most Jews were able to live a full Jewish life and undisturbedly to cultivate their ancestral *mores*. In the Duchy of Warsaw, created by Napoleon I out of the eastern provinces of Prussia after the Battle of Austerlitz, the rumors spreading among the population about an impending enactment of a broad-gauged egalitarian constitution created consternation in the orthodox communities. Not surprisingly, some leading rabbis called upon the Jewries of the entire duchy to observe fast days and convoked special assemblies of worship to recite Hebrew prayers imploring the Deity to forestall the feared catastrophe. More practical elders instituted a large fund-raising campaign in order to dispatch a delegation to Warsaw to lobby there against the forthcoming legislation. As it turned out, however, the constitution proved to be far less egalitarian than expected. From a slightly different angle, half a century later Galician orthodoxy apprehended that the weakening of the traditional internal controls, resulting from the political egalitarianism proclaimed by the Austrian Constitution of 1867, would replace their own chosen leaders by outside authorities whom they had been accustomed to mistrust and fear. Popular Yiddish humor equated *Konstitutsie* with *konst du, tist du* (if you can, you do), meaning that the new individual liberties would replace the existing moral order by uncontrolled license and anarchical behavior. Nevertheless, in the long run, the political and civil rights became so intertwined, and the needs of both the Jewish people and the modern democratic states to establish a general system of equality of rights so imperative, that all such negativist attitudes on the part of the Jewish minority proved utterly futile.[8]

III

The governments and leaders of public opinion were not unaware of the Jews' reluctance to give up their accustomed way of life in return for some dubious benefits of political equality. Opponents of Jewish emancipation, such as Abbé Maury of the French National Assembly, harped on the theme of the Jews being a "state within the state." The abbot, and many of his successors in various lands, insisted that the Jews would always remain such a self-segregating entity within the body politic despite equality of rights. On the other hand, the proponents of an egalitarian system often outspokenly or tacitly presupposed that Jewish emancipation would automatically entail Jewish assimilation to the majority cultures. In his famous dictum at that assembly, the Girondist Count Clermont-Tonnerre emphasized that the new constitution ought to give "to Jewish individuals all rights, to the Jewish nation none," which was a clear call to the Jews to give up their separatism. To reinforce that nexus this protagonist in the struggle for Jewish equality added a most significant clause: If the Jews would accept this arrangement, well and good, but if not, "let them say so, and then let them be banished!" In other words, even Clermont-Tonnerre thus reverted to the old medieval intolerance of Jewish ethnic distinctiveness. In the middle ages total assimilation could be achieved only by the Jews' accepting conversion to the dominant faiths of their compatriots. Whereas since the Treaties of Westphalia of 1648, European nations had learned to live peacefully together with a variety of Christian sects, and assimilation to their secular cultures was deemed sufficient.[9]

Even more remarkably, when after considerable struggle the Congress of Vienna passed the basic constitutional Act of the newly formed Germanic Confederation under the guarantee of the Great Powers, it inserted into it the well-known Article 16 referring to the Jews, which read in part:

> The Confederate Diet will take under advisement . . . as to how the enjoyment of citizens' rights could be granted to the adherents of the Jewish faith in the Confederate States in return for their assumption of all the duties of citizens.

Evidently, even the sponsors of that resolution, including the chief defenders of Jewish rights at the Congress, the Prussian representatives, Chancellor Carl von Hardenberg and Wilhelm von Humboldt, wished to make sure that the Jews themselves would accept that condition.[10]

Yet, as it turned out, granting the Jews political rights encountered considerable resistance among the conservative groups in Prussia and the other Confederate States, and the promise of Article 16 was not to be implemented for several decades. For ideological even more than for practical reasons, many members of the ruling classes resented seeing Jews in public office and thus exerting political "domination" over Christians. As a small but irksome residuum of the medieval discrimination, German Jews, though obliged to serve in the army and navy along with their Christian compatriots, were kept out of the officers' corps and higher administrative posts from 1871 to 1914. At the same time, civil equality encountered even greater *practical* obstacles. Many Christians, entrenched in certain occupations, fiercely resisted the Jews' entry into them because they feared that their own sources of livelihood would thereby be subject to much stiffer competition. That is why the progress of civil equality was usually quite protracted and particular disabilities were removed step by step only, until society and government were ready to decree total equality by a sweeping declaration.

When, in the era of resettlement, Holland pioneered with the readmission of Jews and the extension to them of many civil rights, the eminent jurist Hugo Grotius realized that there were insurmountable obstacles to granting the Jews full equality in civil occupations. Although advocating in 1616 that Amsterdam admit Jews on the basis of fundamental equality subject only to specific disabilities, his famous *Remonstrantie* consisted of some 40 articles primarily devoted to the spelling out of such disabilities. Foremost among the proposed discriminatory provisions was to be a continued prohibition for Jews to engage in any retail trade, because increased competition in this field might undermine the livelihood of some Christian burghers. On the other hand, Jews were welcome to engage in banking, stock exchange transactions, membership of the East and West India Companies, the establishment of sugar mills and other factories, and in international trade—all desirable occupations from the standpoint of the Christian majority, because they thus helped to enlarge the occupational arena not only for themselves but also for the Dutch people as a whole.[11]

Similar considerations governed also the readmission of Jews by the city of Hamburg, as well as by that of Glückstadt then under Danish suzerainty. Most noteworthy was the law passed in England in 1697 with respect to the London Stock Exchange. So desirable appeared the presence of Jewish brokers, with their extensive international contacts and clientele in control of considerable capital, that the law provided for a total Stock Exchange membership of 124, of whom 100 were to be men enjoying the freedom of the city, 12 foreigners, and 12 Jews. Ironically, Jews were thus granted the privileged position of permanently holding nearly 10 percent of the total membership, at a time when they consisted of but an insignificant fraction of the inhabitants of the English capital and when the prevailing legal fiction still assumed that no Jews were allowed to live in the country.[12]

Another major obstacle to Jewish entry into various occupations stemmed from the existing guild monopolies. In many areas Jews were not only refused admission to the guilds which, incidentally, often were as much religious brotherhoods and social fraternities as occupational leagues, but were frequently prevented from competing with guild members in the production of their respective goods. At times, only crafts connected in some form with Jewish religious requirements, such as meat processing and tailoring (because of the biblical prohibition of mixing wool and linen) were exempted. In central and eastern Europe the perennial Jewish conflicts with existing artisan (and merchant) guilds formed a highly significant, often tragic chapter in the history of the Jewish people. On many occasions the guilds appeared in the forefront of the struggle entirely to eliminate Jews from a city or country. Only slowly did decisive economic factors prevail over such narrow class interests and largely under the pressure of other groups. Jews were allowed to form guilds of their own in Poland and Lithuania. To quote the English example again, such admission was gradual; for instance, Jews were allowed to become solicitors in 1770 and were admitted as barristers in 1833, long before the change of the oath of office of newly admitted members of Parliament in 1857 enabled Jews to be elected and subsequently to take their seats in the House of Commons.[13]

In Britain's North American colonies, however, Jews, like other white immigrants, were often considered welcome accretions to the much-needed manpower to populate and exploit the vast open spaces in the New World, and they could more readily overcome such economic disabilities. The saga of Asser Levy and his successful struggle in 1654–64 for permission to open a butcher's shop, to acquire real estate, and to stand guard instead of paying a special tax was a noteworthy example of how quickly such obstacles could be overcome. It was not surprising, therefore, that in the following century Myer Myers was not only admitted to membership in the Gold and Silversmiths Guild in New York but was even elected its president twice, once seemingly before the American Revolution.[14]

Most remarkably, the exercise by Jews of certain political rights, such as voting in elections for colonial legislatures—which were far more meaningful than municipal elections in most European countries of the period—caused hardly a ripple among the North American colonial public. Only once, when in 1737 a defeated candidate to the New York Assembly raised an objection to Jews having been allowed to vote in the election, did the New York Assembly declare that, as in the mother country, Jews ought not to enjoy political franchise. This declaration seems to have been subsequently disregarded, especially after the enactment, by Parliament in London, of the Naturalization Act for the North American colonies, in which special allowance was made for Jews' religious scruples, in order to facilitate their becoming naturalized citizens. Not long thereafter in 1774 Francis Salvador, a young English Jew who had but recently settled in South Carolina, was readily elected to the First and Second Provincial Congresses of that colony which in 1776 became the first general legislature of the state of South Carolina. Nor do we hear of any objections against the admission of Jewish volunteers to the Revolutionary forces, or to some of them serving as officers in command of predominantly Christian detachments.[15]

IV

Partly because of its legal disabilities and partly for other historic reasons, preemancipation Jewry in most countries had an economic stratification at variance with that of the majority of the population. This imbalance often served as a target for anti-Jewish attacks, Jews being called by their enemies usurers, unsavory merchants (*Schacherer*), and exploiters of the population. The Jewish minority of reformers and protagonists of equality were prepared to admit some of these charges and merely argued that it was not the Jews themselves, but the existing laws which were responsible for this awkward disparity.[16]

To remedy that disequilibrium progressive Jews, from the Mendelssohnian age on, were ready to cooperate with the governments in teaching Jewish youth to engage in "useful" and "productive" occupations and thus to make them better citizens for the countries concerned. In most western countries Jewish communities organized regular societies for retraining young Jews and for channeling their energies into "productive" work. Some governments, beginning with Joseph II of Austria and Alexander I of Russia, adopted large-scale programs for colonizing Jews on land so as to convert a people of petty traders and craftsmen into farmers and agricultural laborers.[17]

This idea of restratification ran, of course, counter to the prevailing economic trends which during the previous several generations had been driving untold multitudes of peasants into cities and constantly diminished the ratio of the farming population in all western lands. But such a reversal could appear, to quote a well-known Hegelian simile, as "placing history where it belongs, on its head." This ideal dominated Jewish thinking throughout the nineteenth and early twentieth centuries: it was the hallowed watchword of the *ᶜAm ᶜOlam* movement for the dispersion and of the Zionist *ḥaluṣiyyuth* for Palestine.

Yet such a defiance of prevailing economic tendencies is never easy or completely successful. We do not possess adequate Jewish occupational statistics, not even for the contemporary United States. Historically, even in countries where demographic data have been more readily available because recurrent governmental censuses have identified Jews as members of either a religious or an ethnic group, their occupational distribution is often inadequately known. However, on the basis of whatever information is now available, we may have to come to the amazing conclusion that if one compares the Jewish economic stratification along broad occupational lines as it existed in the year 1800 as against that of a hundred years later, one finds relatively little statistical change. Despite the gigantic efforts at rebuilding the Jewish economic structure and the opening to Jews of untold new economic opportunities in the rapidly expanding economies of the western world, the major occupational categories do not seem to have changed very greatly. According to the best available estimates, the Jewish people in 1800 comprised about 2 percent of households engaged in farming, some 30 percent derived their living from various crafts, while almost 50 percent lived from commerce, including moneylending, and allied occupations; only a small percentage consisted of professionals and public servants, many of them holding offices within the Jewish community itself. There was also a considerable residuum of so-called "*Luftmenschen*," who derived a meager income from occasional odd jobs, or lived on private or communal charities.

In 1900, notwithstanding the great colonizing schemes for Jewish immigrants in the United States, the efforts of the Jewish Colonization Association to settle East European Jews on the land in Argentina and other countries, and the protozionist scheme to develop the Palestinian *Yishuv* with an emphasis on agricultural colonies, the percentage of farmers in the Jewish world population seems not to have exceeded the 2 percent of a century before. Similarly, the industrial segment did not go beyond the one-third of Jews gainfully employed in the world. Perhaps the largest change consisted in the diminution of the ratio of *Luftmenschen* and the growth of the number of Jews in the liberal professions and other service industries. Some unfriendly critics could punningly claim that even at the beginning of this century—in fact, also nowadays—many Jewish and non-Jewish individuals make a living not from "the air" but from "hot air."

Needless to say, there is a qualitative difference between the large number of Jewish petty artisans and their apprentices who formed the majority of those engaged in industrial endeavors in the early 1800s and the legions of Jewish factory workers in eastern Europe or the United States a century later. Similarly, there is a qualitative difference between a mass of Jews owning small retail shops and the multitude of employees in or agents for large business corporations. Not to speak of the mercantile elite which controls large retail chains or department stores. The important role played by Jews in the arts, sciences, journalism, and other forms of communication may not be reflected in the occupational percentages to a sufficient extent, but from the point of view of economic well-being and sociopolitical influence, these differences are of basic importance.

Nevertheless, these transformations are not quite so radical as they appear on the surface. In short, what happened in the course of the nineteenth century was not so much that by securing wider civil rights the Jewish economic structure began to resemble that of the general population, but rather that because of the prevailing economic trends in recent generations—as I paradoxically contended as far back as 1937—"the world has become, so to speak, increasingly 'Jewish' in its economic stratification. Once more Jews may merely have anticipated the general developments."[18]

APPENDIX

A complete example of how not only the Jews, but also most German authorities in the post-Napoleonic era viewed the problems of Jewish emancipation is offered by the following document which is to the best of my knowledge published here for the first time. It stems from Württemberg, a medium-sized state with a relatively small Jewish population—the census of 1818 revealed the presence there of only 8,259 Jews, dispersed over 79 localities—living the life of most German Jews of the period. The regime was moderately conservative. Despite its membership over many years in the pro-French Rhenish Confederation, Württemberg had introduced but minor innovations in the status of its Jewry. It abolished, for example, the *Leibzoll* which was often resented by Jews as an especially degrading discriminatory tax.[19]

After the fall of Napoleon, the Diet of the newly formed Germanic

Confederation was expected to secure an amelioration of the Jews' legal status throughout Germany, in consonance with the pledge inserted into the Article 16 of the Confederate Act adopted by the Congress of Vienna (see above, p. 34). However, the nationalistic and conservative reaction which after 1815 dominated European, and particularly German public opinion, prevented the adoption of far-reaching egalitarian reforms; and the Diet spent years in largely futile debate. It was ultimately left to the discretion of the individual states what kind of new laws they wished to enact concerning their Jewish subjects.[20]

These debates received a new stimulus from the Vienna Ministerial Conferences of 1820. The Diet actually appointed a special Commission to assemble information about the existing legislation relating to Jews in the various member states. The Württemberg delegate, among others, was asked by the Commission to report about the status of Jews in his state. This inquiry forwarded by him to his foreign office prompted it to ask the Ministry of Interior about the progress of the deliberations on the Jewish question, then under way in the authoritative circles of Stuttgart. The resulting reply, here reproduced, showed that the ministry was still negotiating with some representative Jews about various important aspects of the new legislation under review. The ideas expressed therein are self-explanatory. They show that the main emphasis in these preliminary discussions was placed not upon the extent to which Jews were to be allowed to participate in the political affairs of the country but rather on various details affecting their civil and communal rights. Not surprisingly, even when after a passage of several years a new broad "Law Concerning the Public Status of the Adherents of the Israelite Faith" was promulgated on April 11, 1828, the large majority of its 62 articles was devoted to provisions relating to the Jews' civil rather than their political rights.[21]

MINISTERIUM DES INNERN
AN
MINISTERIUM DER AUSWÄRTIGEN ANGELEGENHEITEN.[22]

Stuttgart, den 16. August 1821.

Das Königliche Ministerium der auswärtigen Angelegenheiten hat in seiner verehrlichen Note vom 30. vorigen Monats die disseitige Auskunft über den Stand der angeordneten Revision der Gesetze über die bürgerlichen Verhältnisse der Juden und insbesondere darüber verlangt, ob die—für jene Revision getroffenen Einleitungen soweit vorgerückt seien, dass dem Königlichen Gesandten am Bundestage, für den Zweck des von einer Kommission der Bundes-Versammlung zu bearbeitenden Gutachtens über die bürgerlichen Verhältnisse der Juden in Deutschland die allgemeinen Grundsätze, von welchen man disseits ausgeht, zur Berücksichtigung bei seinen Arbeiten als Mitglied jener Bundestags-Versammlungs-Kommission mitgeteilt werden können.

Der Unterzeichnete hat die Ehre, hierauf zu erwidern, dass während der Dauer des letzten Landtags zu Beratung einer verbesserten Gesetzgebung über die bürgerlichen Verhältnisse der Juden eine zwischen der Regierung und den Ständen gemeinschaftliche Kommission niedergesetzt worden ist, welche, nachdem sie den Gegenstand im Einzelnen in Erwägung gezogen und erörtert hatte, mit besonders dazu berufenen Israeliten des Königreichs über die ganze Materie Besprechungen hielt, denselben ihre Ansichten mitteilte, und hierüber die schriftlichen Erklärungen der Israeliten vernahm.

Die Königlichen Kommissarien, welche auf die Grundlage dieser Beratungen einen Gesetzes Entwurf zu bearbeiten und vorzulegen haben, sind hieran durch die über einige Punkte noch ausstehende Erklärungen zur Zeit verhindert. Das Ministerium des Innern kann daher, da ihm die Akten über den Gegenstand noch nicht vorgelegt worden sind, eine Ansicht darüber noch nicht äussern und insofern kann also auch eine Mitteilung der allgemeinen Grundsätze, von welchen man disseits ausgeht, nicht statt finden.

Da es jedoch gleichwohl für den disseitigen Gesandten am Bundestage bei seinen Arbeiten als Mitglied der gedachten Bundestags-Kommission, und vielleicht auch für die Sache selbst von Interesse sein dürfte, von den Arbeiten der hier bestandenen gemeinschaftlichen Kommission und von deren Ansichten über die Grundsätze, von welchen der Gesetzgeber bei dem vorliegenden Gegenstand auszugehen habe, nähere Kenntnis zu erhalten, so gibt sich der Unterzeichnete die Ehre, dem Königlichen Ministerium der auswärtigen Angelegenheiten in der Anlage diejenigen Vorschläge für eine neue Gesetzgebung, über welche sich die Kommissarien der Regierung und der Stände vereinigten, und auf deren Grundlage sie ihre Beratungen mit den einberufenen Israeliten unternahmen, mit der Bemerkung mitzuteilen, dass die von den Königlichen Kommissarien zu Vollziehung ihres Auftrags noch zu erstattenden Anträge, in Folge der Verhandlungen mit den einberufenen Israeliten und der nachherigen weiteren Beratung, vielleicht noch in einzelnen jedoch nicht gerade wesentlichen Punkten von jenen Vorschlägen abweichen werden.

Zugleich schliesst der Unterzeichnete einen Auszug aus einem Gutachten des Ministeriums des Innern vom 1. Oktober 1820 welcher eine kurze Übersicht über den Gang der bisherigen Gesetzgebung in Betreff der Juden in Württemberg enthält, so wie das Gutachten eines disseitigen Kommissions-Mitgliedes über den vorliegenden Gegenstand, als dessen Privat-Ansicht, zum dienlichen Gebrauche des Bundestags Gesandten bei.

Der mit der Verwaltung des Ministeriums des Innern provisorisch beauftragte
Staatsrath: Schmidlin.

Vorschläge
zu
einem Gesetzes-Entwurf für die bürgerliche Verbesserung der Israelitischen Glaubensgenossen.

Eine neue Gesetzgebung über diesen Gegenstand möchte zu umfassen haben

I) den Kultus
II) die öffentliche Bildung
III) die bürgerlichen Rechtsverhältnisse der Israeliten

I) Kultus.

1) Den Israeliten im Königreich ist die öffentliche Ausübung ihres Gottesdienstes auf die ihren Religionsvorschriften angemessene Weise in ordentlichen vom Staate anerkannten Synagogen gestattet.

Die in einer Gemeinde oder in dem Bezirke mehrerer nahe gelegener Gemeinden ansässigen Israeliten vereinigen sich daher für den Zweck der gemeinschaftlichen Gottesverehrung zu einer eigenen kirchlichen Gemeinde, und errichten eine Synagoge.

Es ist Regel, dass jeder Israelite der nächstgelegenen Synagoge als Kirchengenosse angehöre. Doch findet, wo Israeliten vereinzelt und in zu grosser Entfernung von bestehenden Synagogen wohnen, kein Zwang zur Teilnahme an einer Synagoge oder Errichtung einer neuen statt.

2) Der Gottesdienst in der Synagoge muss unter der Aufsicht eines ordentlichen Rabbiners stehen.

Mehrere Israelitische Kirchengemeinden in einem Bezirke können jedoch einen gemeinschaftlichen Rabbiner haben.

3) Der Rabbiner hat an jedem Sabbat in einer Synagoge seines Bezirks Vormittags den Gottesdienst mit einem Vortrag über die Vorschriften der Religion und allgemeinen Moral zu halten, Nachmittags aber der jüdischen Jugend beiderlei Geschlechts katechetisch Religions Unterricht zu erteilen.

In den Synagogen, wo der Rabbiner den Gottesdienst nicht selbst besorgt, hat solchen der—bei der Synagoge angestellte geprüfte Vorsänger unter Benützung guter Erbauungsbücher auszuüben.

4) Die Errichtung einer Synagoge ist dem Erkenntnis und der Bestätigung der Staatsbehörde unterworfen, welche nur dann erteilt wird, wenn die Israelitische Kirchengemeinde entweder den Gehalt für einen eigenen Rabbiner—oder einen angemessenen Beitrag zu dem Gehalt eines für mehrere Synagogen gemeinschaftlichen Rabbiners ferner einen Gehalt für den Vorsänger aussetzt, und die Entrichtung hievon so wie die Bestreitung der übrigen Kultbedürfnisse auf zureichende Weise sicher stellt.

5) Die Wahl des Rabbiners steht den Judengemeinden des Rabbinats zu. Sie sind aber dabei auf solche Männer beschränkt, welche sich sowohl über ihren sittlichen Charakter, als darüber, dass sie Philosophie auf einer Universität und jüdische Gottesgelahrtheit auf einer jüdischen Hohen-Schule studiert, und von dieser das Befähigungszeugnis erhalten haben, ausweisen können.

Der gewählte Rabbiner unterliegt der Bestätigung der zuständigen Staatsbehörde, welche nur nach zureichend erstandener Dienstprüfung erfolgt.

6) Der bestätigte Rabbiner wird auf den Gehorsam gegen die Gesetze des Staats und die Verordnung der Regierung und dass er im Widerspruch mit denselben nichts lehren oder zulassen, auch in keine geheime Verbindungen mit auswärtigen Juden und Rabbinern treten wolle, verpflichtet.

7) Der bestätigte Rabbiner kann von der Judengemeinde nicht mehr willkürlich entlassen werden.

8) Der Wirkungskreis des Rabbiners beschränkt sich auf seine kirchlichen Verrichtungen.

Eine Gerichtsbarkeit darf sich derselbe unter keinem Vorwande anmassen. Doch ist ihm erlaubt zu Erhaltung der Kirchenzucht in Gemeinschaft mit den Kirchenvorstehern Ordnungsstrafen in Geld bis zum Betrag von 3 fl. zu erkennen, welche dem örtlichen Kirchenfonds zufliessen.

9) Die Wahl der Kirchenvorsteher ist dem Oberrat zur Bestätigung anzuzeigen.

10) Wo keine von der Regierung bestätigte Synagoge besteht, ist der Jude lediglich auf die einfache Hausandacht beschränkt.

10b) Vorstehende Bestimmungen werden auch auf die bereits bestehenden jüdischen Synagogen angewendet. Die angestellten Rabbiner werden innerhalb 1. Jahres vom Tage des neuen Gesetzes an zur Prüfung der Staatsbehörde einberufen, jedoch von dieser mit billiger Schonung behandelt.

11) An den jüdischen Fest- und Feiertagen ist der Jude nicht schuldig Staats- und Gemeinde-Frohnen zu leisten. Doch hat er entweder einen Ersatzmann selbst zu stellen oder den Wert der Frohnarbeiten von diesem Tag der betreffenden Kasse zu erstatten, um einen Ersatzmann für ihn stellen zu können.

12) Der Jude ist schuldig, auch an seinen Fest- oder Feiertagen vor der Obrigkeit zu erscheinen, doch soll er nur in dringenden Fallen an diesen Tagen vorgeladen werden.

13) Einer der Rabbiner im Königreich wird zum Ober-Rabbiner ernannt, welcher auf ähnliche Weise, wie ein christlicher Dekan die Aufsicht über das ganze Israelitische Kirchen- und Schulwesen führt, in Gemeinschaft mit einigen von den Judengemeinden dazu erwählten Israeliten, die obere entscheidende Behörde in Gegenständen, welche das Innere der jüdischen Religionsübungen betreffen, bildet.

14) Zu Bestreitung der allgemeinen Kirchen- und Schulbedürfnisse der Israeliten, wie z.B. des Aufwandes für die kirchliche Oberbehörde, sowie zu Unterstützung bedürftiger israelitischen Kirchengemeinden für die Kosten ihres Cultus oder ihrer Schule wird ein besonderer israelitischer Kirchen- und Schulfonds gebildet. Da es jedoch hiebei auf die Beiträge der Judenschaft ankommt, so muss der näheren Entwicklung dieses Punkts die Vernehmung von Notabeln der innländischen Israeliten vorangehen.

15) Die Verwaltung örtlicher Kirchen- Schul- und Armen-Stiftungen der Israeliten wird den betreffenden Israelitischen Kirchengemeinden überlassen. Sie sind jedoch dabei der Aufsicht der ördentlichen Staatsbehörde, welche insbesondere auf genaue Rechnungsablegung zu dringen und die abgelegten Rechnungen zu prüfen hat, unterworfen.

II) Öffentliche Bildung.

1) Die israelitischen Eltern sind bei Strafe verbunden, ihre Kinder vom 6.–14. Jahre in wohl eingerichteten Schulen unterrichten zu lassen.

Für die Vollziehung dieser Vorschrift ist der Gemeinde-Vorstand verantwortlich.

2) In Gemeinden, in welchen die Israeliten in zureichender Zahl vorhanden sind, ist es ihnen erlaubt, eine besondere Schule für Kinder ihrer Konfession zu errichten, wenn sie die nötigen Schulzimmer anschaffen und die Bezahlung des Gehalts für den Lehrer, sowie die Bestreitung der Schulbedürfnisse auf zureichende Weise sicher stellen.

3) Der Schullehrer wird in diesem Falle von der Judengemeinde aus der Zahl der inländischen gesetzmässig befähigten jüdischen Schulamts-Kandidaten gewählt. Er ist der Prüfung und Bestätigung der zuständigen Staatsbehörde unterworfen und kann, wenn er diese erhalten hat, nur aus einer hinlänglichen Ursache und nach vorgängigem Erkenntnis jener Staatsbehörde wieder entlassen werden.

Der Gehalt, welchen ihm die Judengemeinde auszusetzen hat, wird nach dem für die christlichen Schullehrer bestehenden gesetzlichen Maßstabe festgesetzt.

4) Den jüdischen Schulen wird von der Staatsbehörde ein bestimmter Lehrplan vorgeschrieben und dabei neben der formellen Bildung und den gewöhnlichen Real-

kenntnissen vorzüglich auf richtige Erlernung der deutschen Sprache, auf einen zweckmässigen Religionsunterricht und auf Unterweisung in den Pflichten des Menschen und des Bürgers Rücksicht genommen.

Der Unterricht in der hebräischen Sprache wird auf die Kenntnis und Erklärung der in den Synagogen üblichen Gebete beschränkt.

Die Schulgesetze und die Schulbücher werden von der Staatsbehörde vorgeschrieben.

5) Die nächste Aufsicht über die jüdische Schule haben der Rabbiner und der Judenvorsteher zu führen. In jedem Halbjahr wird die Schule einmal von dem Regierungskommissär visitiert.

6) Wo keine vom Staate bestätigte jüdische Schule besteht, da haben die jüdischen Eltern ihre Kinder in die christliche Schule ihres Wohnorts zu schicken, und die Schulbehörde hat in diesem Falle die Einrichtung zu treffen, dass der Religionsunterricht, an welchem die Judenkinder nicht teilnehmen, auf besondere Stunden verlegt werde. Auch sind die Judenkinder am Sonnabend vom Besuche der christlichen Schule befreit.

7) Das Schulgeld für die Kinder armer Juden wird von der gesammten Judenschaft, wie die notwendige Armen Unterstützung in andern Fällen, entrichtet.

8) Vorstehende Bestimmungen werden auch auf die bereits bestehenden jüdischen Schulen angewendet. Die bisherigen Schullehrer werden zur Prüfung der Staatsbehörde einberufen und wenn sie hier nicht zureichend bestehen, entlassen und die Schulkinder haben die christliche Ortsschule zu besuchen, bis sie in eine vom Staate anerkannte jüdische Schule aufgenommen sind.

9) Befähigten jüdischen Jünglingen, welche sich dem Schulfache widmen, kommen die gleichen Rechte und Vorzüge, welche die allgemeinen Gesetze den christlichen Schulamts-Incipienten und Kandidaten einräumen, zu.

III) Bürgerliche Rechtsverhältnisse.

A) Im Allgemeinen.

1) Alle im Königreich ansässigen Juden haben unter den in den nachstehenden Bestimmungen enthaltenen Modifikationen die Rechte und Pflichten der Staatsbürger. Sie sind allen bürgerlichen Gesetzen unterworfen, und haben alle Pflichten und Leistungen der Staatsbürger, namentlich die der Rekrutirungs-Pflicht zu erfüllen.

2) Jeder Juden Sohn hat daher nach zurückgelegtem 16. Jahr, wie der Sohn eines Christen den gesetzlich bestimmten Erbhuldigungseid abzulegen.

3) Jeder im Königreich ansässige Jude hat für sich und seine Nachkommen einen bestimmten Familien-Namen anzunehmen, welchen er in allen seinen Geschäften künftig führen muss.

Namen von bekannten Familien darf er nicht wählen. Juden, welche unter ihren bisherigen Namen eine Handlungsfirma führen, können den alten Namen als Handlungsfirma neben dem neuen beibehalten.

4) Die Juden haben sich künftig bei allen Urkunden, als Verträge, Verschreibungen, Testamente, Rechnungen, Zeugnisse, Handelsbücher, Ehe-Pakte usw. bei Strafe der Richtigkeit, der deutschen Sprache zu bedienen.

5) Den Juden Söhnen ist erlaubt, sich den Künsten und Wissenschaften zu widmen, und zu Erlernung der letzteren die Universität zu beziehen, sofern sie bei der gesetzlichen Vorprüfung die erforderliche Befähigung nachweisen.

Die der Wissenschaften oder der Künstebeflissenen sind unter den gleichen gesetzlichen Bestimmungen, wie christlichen Staatsgenossen, von der Rekrutierungspflicht befreit.

6) Es ist dem Juden, der die Heil- oder Wundarznei-Kunde studiert—und die gesetzliche Prüfungen erstanden hat, erlaubt, seine Wissenschaft auszuüben. Der Jude aber, der Rechtswissenschaft studiert hat, kann die Erlaubnis zur gerichtlichen Praxis nur mit besonderer königlichen Bewilligung erlangen.

7) Die Einwanderung und Niederlassung fremder Juden in dem Königreich ist verboten. Doch ist dem inländischen Juden die Verehlichung mit einer ausländischen Jüdin unter den allgemeinen gesetzlichen Bestimmungen wegen der Aufnahme in das Staatsbürgerrecht gestattet.

Die Annahme auswärtiger jüdischer Dienstboten, Schächter, Lehrer etc. ist verboten.

B) Rechtsverhältnisse der Juden zu den Gemeinden ihres bürgerlichen Aufenthalts.

1) Die in einer Gemeinde ansässigen Juden bilden in bürgerlicher Hinsicht keine eigene Verbindung, sondern sie schliessen sich an die andern Ortseinwohner an und bilden einen Teil der Ortsgemeinde.

2) Sie stehen daher in allen nicht namentlich ausgenommenen Fällen unter der gewöhnlichen Ortsobrigkeit und haben sowohl im Verkehr unter sich, als mit Christen, bei den ordentlichen Gerichtsstellen Recht zu nehmen.

3) Die in den blossen Landesschutz aufgenommenen Juden bleiben, so lange sie nicht in das Bürger- oder Beisitzrecht einer Gemeinde aufgenommen werden, in den bisherigen Verhältnissen zu den Gemeinden ihres Aufenthalts. Die Witwen der Schutzjuden haben das Recht des Aufenthalts in der Gemeinde, in welcher ihr gestorbener Gatte zur Zeit seines Todes den Schutz genoss. Eheliche Kinder haben das Recht des Aufenthalts in der Gemeinde, in welcher ihr Vater—unehliche Kinder in welcher ihre Mutter zur Zeit ihrer Geburt im Schutzverband stand.

4) Die Schutzjuden entrichten auch künftig die gesetzlich bestimmte Aufnahme- und die jährlichen Schutz- und Schirmgelder an die Staatskasse.

5) Wenn künftig ein Schutzjude seinen bisherigen Aufenthalt ändern und in einer andern Gemeinde nehmen will, so kann dies nur mit Zustimmung der letzteren geschehen.

6) Jeder im Königreich ansässige Jude, der weder den Hausier- und Schacherhandel, noch sonst ein wucherliches Geschäft- sondern ein ordentliches von ihm gesetzmässig erlerntes Gewerbe treibt, oder vom Landbau lebt, kann unter den gleichen gesetzlichen Bestimmungen, wie die christlichen Staatsbürger in jeder Gemeinde das Bürgerrecht erlangen.

Wenn er das Bürgerrecht in der Gemeinde seines bisherigen Schutzverbandes erhält, so ist er für sich, seine Gattin und seine Kinder nur die Hälfte der gewöhnlichen Bürger-Annahme-Gebühren—hingegen die vollen übrigen in jeden Ort herkömmlichen Leistungen zu entrichten schuldig.

7) Durch die Aufnahme in das Gemeindebürgerrecht erhält der Jude die Rechte und Pflichten eines Gemeindebürgers mit Ausnahme des Rechts, eine Stelle in der Gemeindeverwaltung zu bekleiden, doch kann er in den Bürgerausschuss gewählt werden. Er erlangt insbesondere auch den gesetzlichen Anteil an den persönlichen Gemeindenutzungen und das Stimmrecht bei Gemeinde Wahlen.

8) Jeder Schutzjude bezahlt an die Gemeinde seines Wohnorts die gesetzliche

Wohnsteuer. Auch entrichtet er neben der Staats-steuer alle auf dem Besitz von Gütern, oder auf dem Betrieb von Gewerben ruhende Stadt- Amts- und Kommun-Schäden und andere Leistungen, wie Quartier, Vorspann etc.

9) Die ganze Judenschaft hat, wie bisher, auch künftig die Verbindlichkeit die innländischen armen Juden im Notfalle zu ernähren.

C) Rechtsverhältnisse der Juden in Beziehung auf Gewerbe.

1) Den ansässigen Juden, sie mögen blosse Schutzgenossen oder Gemeindebürger sein, ist der Zutritt zu allen ordentlichen bürgerlichen Gewerben, insbesondere zu dem Ackerbau, den Handwerken, den Fabriken und Manufakturen und zu dem ordentlichen Handel gestattet, und sie sind hierin mit Ausnahme der hienach folgenden Modifikationen, nicht anders, als durch die allgemeine Gesetzgebung beschränkt. Nur sollen in Ansehung der Befähigung zum ordentlichen Handel noch Modifikationen stattfinden, über welche jedoch die Ansichten der Kommissarien noch verschieden sind. Im Betracht, dass wenn die Israeliten sich mit Vernachlässigung anderer Gewerbe bloss dem Handel widmen wollten, hieraus grosse Missverhältnisse entstehen müssten, kam vorläufig die Bestimmung in Antrag, dass der Israelite zu Errichtung einer Handlung mit offenem Laden besondere Konzession nötig haben solle,

a) wenn durch die Handlung, welche errichtet werden will, die Zahl der in dem Ort bereits bestehenden israelitischen Handlungen vermehrt werden würde, und

b) wenn in dem Ort in welchem jüdische Glaubensgenossen ansässig sind, bisher von keinem derselben ein offener Laden geführt worden ist.

2) Der Jude kann daher Häuser und liegende Güter zur eigenen Bewirtschaftung erkaufen oder pachten und dieselbe unter Beihilfe von jüdischen oder christlichen Dienstboten bearbeiten.

Der Erwerb liegender Güter zum Wiederverkauf ist demselben verboten. Er darf daher ein erkauftes Gut, ohne besondere Bewilligung nur, wenn er solches zuvor 3 Jahre lang selbst bewirtschaftet hat, wieder verkaufen. Ebenso darf er ein erkauftes Gut nur nach vorgängiger 2 jährigen Selbstbewirtschaftung verpachten. An Zahlungs Statt gerichtlich zuerkannte Güter kann er zwar sogleich, jedoch nur in öffentlichem Aufstreich und in Beisein einer obrigkeitlichen Person verkaufen oder verpachten.

Bei Käufen und Verkäufen liegender Güter unter Christen ist dem Juden jede Teilnahme als Unterhändler, Bevollmächtigter, Mäkler oder Bürge bei Gefängnisstrafe verboten, diese Bestimmung soll jedoch nur für die nächsten 15 Jahre gültig sein.

3) Wenn ein Israelite in den Besitz eines Guts kommt, mit welchem das Patronatrecht über eine christliche Kirche verbunden ist, so darf derselbe weder das Besetzungsrecht der Kirchenstelle ausüben, noch die Ehrenrechte des Patrons in Anspruch nehmen, obgleich er die auf dem Patronatrecht ruhenden dringlichen Verbindlichkeiten zu erfüllen hat.

Das Besetzungsrecht fällt in diesem Falle, für diejenige Zeit, während welcher ein Jude im Besitze des Guts ist, der Regierung anheim.

4) Dem Juden der ein adeliches Gut besitzt, ist die Ausübung der grundherrlichen Rechte, der Patrimonial Gerichtsbarkeit, der Orts Polizei oder Forst- und Jagdpolizei etc. selbst wenn er in den Adelstand des Königreichs aufgenommen wäre, verboten.

5) Jede Zunft oder Handwerksinnung ist verbunden jedem inländischen Juden auf sein Ansuchen, wenn er die dafür in der allgemeinen Gesetzgebung vorgeschrie-

benen Bedingungen erfüllt, die Aufnahme als Lehrling, Geselle oder Meister zu bewilligen.

6) Denjenigen Juden, welche bei Erscheinung des neuen Gesetzes das 20. Jahr noch nicht zurückgelegt haben, und kein ordentliches Gewerbe ergreifen, sondern auf dem Hausier- und Schacherhandel beharren, wird die Ansässigmachung und Verehlichung vor zurückgelegtem 35. Jahr nicht gestattet. Diese Bestimmung findet jedoch auf Judensöhne, die in den nächsten 5 Jahren nach Erscheinung des neuen Gesetzes zum Königlichen Militär ausgehoben werden, und nicht für sich einen Ersatzmann stellen, keine Anwendung.

7) In den Gemeinden, in welchen Judenfamilien ansässig sind, hat der Gemeindevorsteher die Eltern oder Pfleger derjenigen Judensöhne, welche 18 Jahre alt und noch zu keinem ordentlichen Erwerbszweig bestimmt sind, von Amtswegen aufzufordern, ihre Söhne oder Pfleglinge einem solchen Erwerbszweige zu widmen, und ihnen Lehrmeister aufzusuchen. Würde dieses innerhalb eines Jahres nicht geschehen, so hat der Oberbeamte die Eltern oder den Pfleger über die vorwaltenden Hindernisse zu hören, vermöglichen Eltern die ein Lehrgeld zu bezahlen im Stande sind, dringend zuzureden, und wenn das Hindernis in dem Mangel eines Lehrmeisters läge, durch amtliche Bekanntmachung einen zu suchen.

8) Der Rücktritt eines Juden von einem ordentlichen Gewerbe zu dem Schacherhandel wird unter keinem Vorwande mehr gestattet.

9) Den zur Zeit schon auf dem Schacher- und Hausierhandel ansässigen Juden wird die Ausübung desselben auch künftig gestattet. Auch soll den Judensöhnen, welche bei Erscheinung des neuen Gesetzes das 20. Jahr schon zurückgelegt haben, die Erlaubnis zur Ansässigmachung auf denselben nach erlangter Volljährigkeit nicht erschwert werden.

Hingegen wird zu Beschränkung der Nachteile dieses Handels verordnet, dass keine Privatschuldverschreibungen, welche für Rechnung eines Juden, der kein ordentliches Gewerbe treibt, nach Erlassung des neuen Gesetzes von einem nicht wechselfähigen Christen ausgestellt wurde, und keine von dem Christen an den Juden ausgestellte. Quittung oder Privatabrechnung, welche auf das Entstehen der Schuld Bezug haben sollen, Beweiskraft haben—sondern dass der Inhaber der Schuldverschreibung, er sei Christ oder Jude, gehalten sein soll, auf andere Weise den Beweis herzustellen, dass der Jude den Wert der Forderung vollständig geleistet habe.

10) Der Jude, der Landwirtschaft oder ein anderes ordentliches Gewerbe treibt, hat sich an den christlichen Sonn- und Festtagen aller Handlungen zu enthalten, wodurch der christliche Gottesdienst gestört werden könnte. Er darf daher während des christlichen Gottesdienstes kein Gewölbe oder Handwerksladen öffnen, noch Feldarbeiten vornehmen, noch viel weniger hausieren.

D) Rechte der Juden in Beziehung auf Familienverhältnisse.

1) Jeder Jude hat zu seiner Verehlichung die Erlaubnis seines Oberamts notwendig. Ohne diese Erlaubnis ist dem Rabbiner sowohl die Verkündigung, als die ehliche Verbindung bei Strafe verboten.

2) Die Heirat, die ein Jude ohne vorherige Erlaubnis im Auslande schliesst, unterliegt den allgemeinen gesetzlichen Bestimmungen.

3) Der priesterlichen Trauung eines Juden muss eine Verkündigung an 3 Sabbaten in der Synagoge vorangehen.

4) Die Ehehindernisse der Verwandtschaft und der Trauerzeit sind auch bei den

Israeliten nach den Landes gesetzen, wo nicht besondere Religionsgrundsätze derselben eine Ausnahme gebieten, zu beurteilen.

5) Während der geschlossenen Zeit darf der Jude nur stille Hochzeiten feiern.

6) Die Gerichtsbarkeit in Ehesachen der Juden kommt dem Königlichen Ehegericht zu, welches bei seinen Entscheidungen die religiösen Grundsätze und Förmlichkeiten der Juden zu berücksichtigen hat.

7) In Ansehung der Vermögens- und Errungenschaftsverhältnisse bei jüdischen Ehegatten sowie in Ansehung der Erbfolge gelten auch bei den Juden die allgemeinen Landesgesetze.

8) Das Ortswaisengericht ist die zuständige Stelle für Inventuren und Teilungen derselben. Es sorgt für die Bestellung der Pfleger bei Minderjährigen und hat die Aufsicht über die Verwaltung des Pflegschaftlichen-Vermögens von Juden. Die Pfleger werden zunächst aus den Israelitischen Glaubensgenossen genommen.

9) Bei der Vorschrift, dass keine Judenleiche vor Ablauf von 2 mal 24 Stunden begraben werden soll, verbleibt es auch künftig.

NOTES

* A paper read at the McGill Colloquium on Judaism and Human Rights held under the sponsorship of the American Jewish Committee and other organizations on April 21–23, 1974, at McGill University, Montreal, Canada, here revised and greatly enlarged.

1. See Max Weber's *Gesammelte Aufsätze zur Religionssoziologie*, 3 vols., Tübingen, 1920–21, Vol. iii: Das antike Judentum, pp. 2f.; and my remarks thereon in *A Social and Religious History of the Jews*, 2nd ed. rev., Vols. i–xvi, New York, 1952–76, esp. i, p. 297 n. 7. On the meaning of medieval Jewish serfdom, see *ibid.*, xi, pp. 4f., 289f. and the literature listed there. My rejection of Weber's thesis has by no means been weakened by its defense on the part of the English translators of Weber's *Ancient Judaism*, Glencoe, Ill., 1952, pp. xxivf.

2. This aspect has been more fully developed in my essay, "Newer Approaches to Jewish Emancipation," *Diogenes*, No. 29 (Spring, 1960), pp. 56–81 (also in its French and Spanish editions).

3. See Harry Sacher's succinct reply to these contentions in his *Jewish Emancipation—the Contract Myth*, London, 1917.

4. See the text and the discussions preceding its enactment in Ismar Freund's *Die Emanzipation der Juden in Preussen unter besonderer Berücksichtigung des Gesetzes vom 11. März 1812*, 2 vols., Berlin, 1912.

5. On the manifold vagaries in Catherine's Jewish legislation, see the brief summary in my *The Russian Jew under Tsars and Soviets*, New York, 1964, pp. 17f. or in the 1976 revised ed., pp. 15f.; and W. Bruce Lincoln, "The Russian State and its Cities: a Search for Effective Municipal Government, 1786–1842," *Jahrbücher für Geschichte Osteuropas*, xvii (1969), pp. 531–41.

6. See my *A Social and Religious History of the Jews*, 1st ed., 3 vols., New York, 1937, ii, p. 165f.; and my article on "Population" in the new English *Encyclopaedia Judaica*, xiii (1971), 866–903.

7. On the excesses of the Russian cantonist system, which left a permanent imprint on the Russian Jewish community, see esp. the graphic description by Saul Ginsburg in his *Historishe Verk*, 3 vols., New York, 1937–38, ii, 3–20, iii, pp. 3–135, 357–69.

8. E. N. Frenk, *Yehudey Polin biymey milḥamoth Napoleon* (Poland's Jews during the Napoleonic Wars), Warsaw, 1912, p. 23; Filip Friedmann, *Die galizischen Juden*

im Kampfe um ihre Gleichberechtigung (1848–1868), Frankfurt am Main, 1929.

9. See the text of Count Clermont-Tonnerre's oft-quoted address of December 23, 1789 (including the final threat of banishment), reproduced in the *Revue des grandes journées parlementaires*, ed. by Gaston Lebre and G. Labouchère, i (1897), p. 10. On "'A State within a State'—The History of an Antisemitic Slogan," see Jacob Katz's essay under this title in *Proceedings of the Israel Academy of Sciences and Humanities*, iv, 3 (1969). It may be noted that Katz himself admits that the same slogan was also used against such other disliked "separatist" groups as the Jesuits and the Freemasons.

10. Johann L. Klüber, ed., *Akten des Wiener Kongresses 1814 und 15*, 8 vols., Erlangen, 1815–19, esp. ii, pp. 456f., 590f.; and other data analyzed in my *Die Judenfrage auf dem Wiener Kongress auf Grund von zum Teil ungedruckten Quellen dargestellt*, Vienna, 1920.

11. See Hugo Grotius, *Remonstrantie nopende de ordre dije in de landen van Hollandt ende Westvieslandt dijent gestelt op de Joden,* reed. by Jacob Meijer, Amsterdam, 1949; Meijer's analysis of "Hugo Grotius' Remonstrantie," *Jewish Social Studies*, xvii (1955), pp. 91–104; Herbert I. Bloom, *The Economic Activities of the Jews of Amsterdam in the Seventeenth and Eighteenth Centuries*, Williamsport, Pa., 1937; and the additional sources quoted in my *Social and Religious History of the Jews*, xv, p. 390 n. 30.

12. Lucien Wolf, "The First Stage of Anglo-Jewish Emancipation," in his *Essays in Jewish History*, ed. by Cecil Roth, London, 1934, pp. 115–36.

13. H. S. Q. Henriques, *The Jews and the English Law*, Oxford, 1908, pp. 203f.

14. The sources cited in my "The Emancipation Movement and American Jewry," first published in Hebrew in *Eretz-Israel*, iv (1956), pp. 205–214 and subsequently reproduced in a revised English trans. in my *Steeled by Adversity: Essays and Addresses on American Jewish Life*, ed. by Jeannette M. Baron, Philadelphia, 1971, pp. 80–105, 592–98.

15. *Ibid.*, pp. 92f., 595f.

16. Characteristic of that approach was Christian Wilhelm Dohm's *Über die bürgerliche Verbesserung der Juden*, rev. ed., 2 vols., Berlin, 1783, partly written under Mendelssohn's inspiration and enthusiastically greeted by some Jewish contemporaries. On the "Dessau philosopher's" role in this enterprise and his own divergent views on some details, see now Alexander Altmann's comprehensive work, *Moses Mendelssohn: A Biographical Study*, Tuscaloosa, Ala., 1973, and his "Letters from Dohm to Mendelssohn" in *S. W. Baron Jubilee Volume*, Jerusalem, 1974; i, pp. 39–62.

17. See, for instance, J. M. Isler, *Rückkehr der Juden zur Landwirtschaft. Beitrag zur Geschichte der landwirtschaftlichen Kolonisation der Juden in verschiedenen Ländern*, Frankfurt am Main, 1929.

18. See my *A Social and Religious History of the Jews*, 1st ed., 1937, ii, 409. Certainly, the American farmers who, though they consist of but some 4 percent of persons gainfully employed in the United States and are yet able not only to meet the needs of their own society but also help to feed untold millions in other lands, statistically resemble much more closely the small minority of Jews living on agriculture in eastern Europe in 1800 or in the United States in 1900 than did the Christian farmers in those countries in either period.

19. Aron Tänzer, *Die Geschichte der Juden in Württemberg*, Frankfurt am Main, 1937, esp. pp. 10f., 24.

20. See the official *Protokolle der Deutschen Bundesversammlung*, Frankfurt am

Main, 1816f.; Johann Ludwig Klüber's early observations on *Öffentliches Recht des Deutschen Bundes und der Bundesstaaten*, Frankfurt am Main, 1817, esp. pp. 257f. No. 171, 624f. No. 379, 627f. No. 381c, 712f. No. 424; L. F. Ilse, *Geschichte der Deutschen Bundesversammlung*, Marburg, 1861, esp. i, p. 406; and the brief summary in my *Die Judenfrage* (see above, p. 48, n. 10), pp. 178f.

21. The intent of the 1828 law is defined in its preamble, as aiming at "bringing the public status of the adherents of the Israelite faith in the realm in consonance with the common welfare through timely legislation and at promoting the education and capacity of these members of the state towards their [ultimate] enjoyment of the rights of citizenship in return for their assuming the duties of citizenship." Yet in detail the legislators' major concern was to define more closely the restrictions imposed upon Jewish rights. See the summary in A. Tänzer's *Die Geschichte*, pp. 31f. On the Jewish role going back to the early discussions in 1821, see Isaak Marcus Jost, *Geschichte der Israeliten*, vol. x, Part 1, Berlin, 1846, pp. 158f. Most remarkably, Württemberg was then generally counted among the more progressive German states, and its long-reigning King William I (1816–64) was often admired in other parts of Germany as the "model constitutional king." See Karl Weller, *Württembergische Geschichte*, Leipzig, 1909, pp. 143f.

22. From the Württemberg State Archive, Fascicle Deutscher Bund No. 91. The orthography of the original has been retained.

The Structure of the Commandments of the Torah in the Thought of Maimonides[1]

L. V. BERMAN

One of the major early attempts at achieving the ordering of the subject matter of the law and related rabbinic material is the *Mishnah* of Judah the Prince. It is, of course, the *Mishnah* which represents an important expression of one major focus of pharisaic Jewry.[2] However, the literary form of the Babylonian and Palestinian amoraic commentaries on the *Mishnah*, along with the gaonic and other extra-talmudic materials, made a reordering of the law imperative. Maimonides' *Mishneh Torah* was just such an attempt to restructure the totality of the law. There had been various attempts at collecting the material together on specific topics, and one previous try at giving a brief but exhaustive account of all ordinances in a logical order,[3] but Maimonides eclipsed all previous efforts in this direction. In fact, no one had yet tried to embody all of the subjects included in the *Mishnah* in a new order, including materials dependent on the temple and actually inoperative.

As a preliminary to his code, Maimonides composed the *Book of Commandments* in order to identify exactly the composition of the 613 commandments mentioned in rabbinic literature[4] on the basis of fourteen general principles he had developed. The order of the commandments in the *Book of Commandments* differs from the order of the commandments in the *Mishneh Torah,* and in turn the order of the commandments in the *Mishneh Torah* differs from the order of the commandments laid down in Part III, Chapter 35, of the *Guide of the Perplexed.* In this paper, I propose to examine these three works in order to discover the principles, if any, underlying the different orders of the listing of the commandments, since none of them follows the order of the commandments blindly as given in the Pentateuch.

I

Upon opening the *Book of Commandments*[5] one is immediately struck by the fact that the commandments are divided into positive and negative. The point is that the primary division of the commandments here is not topical. Maimonides is following the traditional talmudic division of the biblical precepts into 248 positive and 365 negative commandments. In general, there are easily discernible groups of commandments, but it is difficult at times to grasp the relationship of the groups of commandments to one another. The structure of the commandments in both positive and negative categories has been a matter of some discussion.[6]

TABLE I*

The Commandments in the *Book of Commandments*

	Positive Commandments		*Negative Commandments*
I	God: 1–9	I	God: 1
II	Torah and prayer: 10–19	II	Idolatry: 2–66
III	Sanctuary and priests: 20–38	III	Sanctuary and priests: 67–88
IV	Offerings: 39–93	IV	Offerings: 89–154
V	Vows: 94–95	V	Vows: 155–157
VI	Purity and impurity: 96–113	VI	Impurity: 158–171
VII	Agricultural matters: 114–145	VII	Prohibited food: 172–209
VIII	Food regulations: 146–152	VIII	Cultivation of land: 210–231
IX	Holy days: 153–171	IX	Duties to fellowman: 232–272
X	State functions: 172–193	X	Administration of justice: 273–300
XI	Duties to fellowman: 194–208	XI	Public order: 301–319
XII	Family life: 209–223	XII	Holy days: 320–329
XIII	Punishments: 224–231	XIII	Sexual regulations: 330–361
XIV	Property regulations: 232–248	XIV	State affairs: 362–365

* To facilitate comparison, Tables I, II, and III are exhibited in parallel, *infra*, p. 62.

After examining both the positive and negative commandments, I divided them into fourteen groups, respectively (see Table I). Generally speaking both positive and negative commandments are divided into the man-God and man-man divisions based on the familiar rabbinic distinction.[7] Positive commandments 1–171 and negative commandments 1–231 fall into the man-God category, and the rest in each case fall into the man-man category. With regard to individual groups of commandments, I do not find a rigorous structuring of the material as is the case with the *Mishneh Torah* and the *Guide*. In comparing the groupings of the positive and negative commandments, one can see certain similarities but also clear differences. The first six groups correspond closely. Groups seven and eight in both the positive and negative lists are concerned with food. Group nine of the positive list has a correspondent only in group twelve of the negative. The other groups generally agree only in that they are concerned primarily with human relations.

In the *Book of Commandments,* Maimonides' primary interest is to determine the number of the commandments. He is only interested in a secondary way to group and structure them. One can see this inattention to structure in other areas as well, such as his enumeration of the *Tanna*ʾ*im* in his introduction to his *Commentary on the Mishnah,* which one would expect to be chronological but is not.[8] Here in the *Book of Commandments* we see Maimonides at work, making a preliminary attempt at ordering the unsystematic material of tradition.

It is remarkable that at the beginning of his *Mishneh Torah*[9] Maimonides lists the 613 commandments as given in the *Book of Commandments*. Immediately before bringing this list he states that the *Mishneh Torah* will be organized according to topic, not according to commandment, since in one topic there may be one commandment and in another many, everything depending on the material to be covered, "for this composition is divided according to topics, not according to the numbering of the commandments."[10] He then gives a general and a specific table of contents. In the specific table of contents he details those commandments to be included in each of the separate groups of laws in each of the fourteen books of the *Mishneh Torah*. He prefaces this detailed table of contents with a remark that "the division of the laws contained in this composition accords with the subjects of the books; the division of the commandments follows the subjects of the laws."[11]

It is clear that Maimonides is making a distinction between the order of the commandments in the *Book of Commandments* and the order of the commandments according to the subject categories of the law in general. There is a topical structure of the commandments which appears when one is trying to codify both the oral and written laws, which does not necessarily appear when studying the Pentateuch.

II

Upon examining the structure of the *Mishneh Torah* one perceives a general distinction between theoretical and practical commandments (see Table II).[12] The first book, the *Book of Knowledge*, deals essentially with those matters which are fundamental principles of belief, rather than practice, even though matters of practical import have been introduced by way of association.

The *Book of Knowledge* is composed of five subgroups. The first subgroup is mainly concerned with the basic principles of the Torah in Maimonides' view. Thus he sets forth elements of metaphysics and physics in Chapters 1–4, and in Chapters 7–10 he discusses prophecy. Chapters 5 and 6 concentrate on practical matters concerned with the sanctification of God's name and the destruction of the names of God taken up in connection with the discussion of God in Chapter 1. The section on prophecy also contains matters of practical import with respect, for example, to detecting true and false prophets, but the basic thrust is concerned with the principle of prophecy as a fundamental belief incumbent on the practitioner of the law.

The second subgroup, on "Ethical Qualities," is of course directly concerned with practical matters, but in a general way, much as in the Aristotelian corpus the *Nicomachean Ethics* is in part concerned with virtues and vices as types of behavior without being concerned with detailed legislation. Of course, the position of "Ethical Qualities" in a code of Jewish law makes Maimonides include matters which are concerned with specific commandments, not emphasized in Aristotle, such as slander and

TABLE II

Structure of the Commandments according to the *Mishneh Torah*

I	Knowledge (*Maddaʿ*)		
A.	Basic Principles (*Yesodey Ha-Torah*)		Theoretical
B.	Ethical Qualities (*Deʿoth*)		Theoretical
C.	Study of the Torah (*Talmud Torah*)		Theoretical
D.	Idolatry (*ʿAvodath Kokhavim*)		Theoretical
E.	Repentance (*Teshuvah*)		Theoretical
II	Love (*ʾAhavah*)	man-God	Practical
III	Times (*Zemannim*)	man-God	Practical
IV	Women (*Nashim*)	man-God	Practical
V	Sanctity (*Qedushshah*)	man-God	Practical
VI	"Expression" (*Haflaʾah*)	man-God	Practical
VII	Seeds (*Zeraʿim*)	man-God	Practical
VIII	"Service" (*ʿAvodah*)	man-God	Practical
IX	Sacrifices (*Qorbanoth*)	man-God	Practical
X	Purity (*Ṭohorah*)	man-God	Practical
XI	Damages (*Neziqin*)	man-man	Practical
XII	Acquisition (*Qinyan*)	man-man	Practical
XIII	Judgement (*Mishpaṭim*)	man-man	Practical
XIV	Judges (*Shofeṭim*)	man-man	Practical

talebearing. The inclusion of advice with respect to health is proper, it would seem, since preventive medicine is essentially based on temperance, an important moral virtue.

The laws concerning the study of the Torah are put next in order, I suggest, to justify the previous two subgroups, that is, the concern with theoretical and practical matters of a philosophic import and also to justify the study of the practical legislation of the Torah, for an important element in Maimonides' exposition is the definition of Talmud so as to include the investigation of philosophy, so that the study of Torah includes both the study of the oral and written laws as traditionally conceived and also matters ordinarily considered foreign to that study, namely, the study of philosophy.[13]

The fourth subgroup, Idolatry, is concerned with practical, legal matters, although there is a brief theoretical discussion at the beginning on the rise of idolatry. This subgroup is located here by association with the fundamental belief in the one incorporeal God, since the commandment not to believe in and worship idols forms a corollary of the fundamental principle. One ought also mention the fact that according to the *Guide*, the principle goal of the whole law is the extirpation of idolatry.[14]

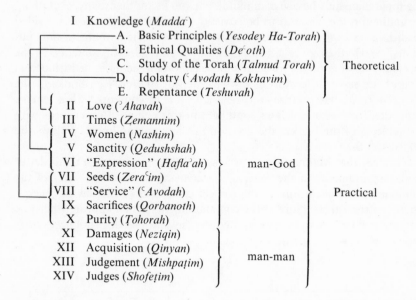

The fifth and last subgroup is Repentance which in essence is a religious rather than a philosophic concept. Without repentance there is no possibility for the believer to rid himself of his sense of guilt, but the mechanics of repentance from a rational point of view are absurd.[15]

The rest of the *Mishneh Torah* is concerned overwhelmingly with practical matters, what to do and what not to do. Within the practical part of the *Mishneh Torah*, one can distinguish between Books II through X, which are concerned with the relationship between man and God as the familiar rabbinic distinction has it and those concerned with the relationship between man and man, Books XI to XIV. Within the first group, I distinguish three subgroups: those concerned with prayer (Books II and III), those concerned with forbidden matters (Books IV through VI), and those dependent on the temple (Books VII through X). The order of the three groups would seem generally to be dependent on the order of the contents of the *Book of Knowledge*. *Love* and *Times* reinforce the belief in God essentially, since *Love* refers to the ways one expresses one's love of God through prayer and the festivals provide time for contemplation. The second subgroup, *Women*, *Sanctity*, and "*Expression*", is connected with the second major grouping in Book I, "Ethical Qualities," for it reinforces one's self-control and mastery over the passions concerned with sex and food primarily.

One might ask, of course, why women are listed in the man-God section of the *Mishneh Torah* and linked with "Ethical Qualities" and not with the group of laws concerning the relationship of man and his fellow, which is the case in the *Book of Commandments*.[16] It would seem that Maimonides' later thinking tends to the view that the function of marriage is to "bring about a decrease of sexual intercourse and to diminish the desire for mating as far as possible, so that it should not be taken as an end, as is done by the ignorant (or: the pagan) according to what we have explained in the *Commentary on the Tractate ʾAvoth*."[17] In the *Mishneh Torah* itself at the beginning of the "Laws concerning Marriage" the institution of marriage is looked upon as a restriction on the ways of sexual intercourse open to pagans.[18] Understood in this way, the laws concerning women contribute primarily to helping man control his appetites. The same thing is true of Book V, *Sanctity* which is concerned with forbidden foods and forbidden sexual relations. The idea of self-control is also the leading idea of Book VI, "*Expression*" (*Haflaʾah*). In large measure "*Expression*" (i.e. supererogatory utterance) is concerned with binding oneself to do or not to do certain actions. The regulations concerned with expressions of this nature are intended to strengthen one's resolve and firm one's will.[19]

The third subgroup deals primarily with matters concerned with the temple. It comes after matters concerned with forbidden things, since it is keyed to "Idolatry," which comes after "Ethical Qualities" in the *Book of Knowledge*. This third subgroup constitutes the positive answer of the Mosaic law to the defects of the idolatrous system according to Maimonides.[20] Book VII, *Seeds*, is primarily concerned with agricultural matters relating to the temple and the priesthood. Subsequently, the laws relating to the sanctuary are taken up, then the system of sacrifices in the sanctuary, and then the subject of ritual purity and impurity, both of these conditions being closely connected to the existence of the temple.

Finally, in the last major section of the *Mishneh Torah*, the laws dealing primarily with human relations are considered. Book XI deals with damages to property or person; Book XII deals with selling and acquisition; Book XIII deals with other matters of civil law; and Book XIV deals with matters assigned to the Sanhedrin and concludes with a treatment of the messianic age.

The logical basis for this general arrangement would seem to be a gradual descent from the theoretical to the practical. We descend from fundamental beliefs, to practices reinforcing those fundamental beliefs, that is, to use the rabbinic term, the commandments concerning the relationship of man and God, to commandments regulating man's relationship with his fellow-man. The structure of the *Mishneh Torah* in general can be conceived of as triangular with beliefs at the top, actions supporting those beliefs in the middle, and laws regulating the relations between citizens at the bottom.

III

In Chapter 35 of the Third Part of the *Guide*, Maimonides gives a general description of the fourteen categories into which he divides the commandments of the Torah, making some allusions to the divisions of his *Mishneh Torah*. In the next fourteen chapters he spells out each category in detail and advances some justification for their content. For a list of the categories of the commandments as laid down in the *Guide* and a schematic representation of their relationship, see Table III.

TABLE III

Structure of the Commandments according to the *Guide of the Perplexed.*

I	Fundamental opinions	Beliefs	Rational
II	Idolatry		
III	Ethical qualities	Ethics	Quasi-universal
IV	Giving of alms and bestowing of gifts		
V	Wrongdoing and aggression	Politics	
VI	Punishments		
VII	Mutual property transactions		
VIII	Days in which work is forbidden		Traditional
IX	Other general practices of worship		
X	Sanctuary		
XI	Sacrifices		
XII	Clean and unclean		
XIII	Forbidden food and related matters		
XIV	Prohibited sexual unions		

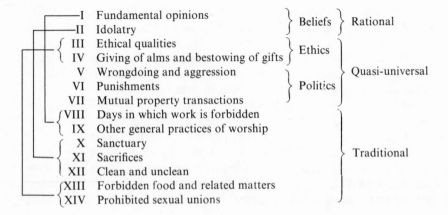

The first of the fourteen categories of the *Guide* is that of "Fundamental Opinions," which includes matter laid down in the *Mishneh Torah*'s "Laws of the Principles of the Torah," as well as "Laws concerning the Study of the Torah," oaths, commandments relating to calling on God in a calamity, "Repentance," and fasts. Here we see Maimonides taking three subgroups out of the *Book of Knowledge*, i.e., *Yesodey Ha-Torah*, *Talmud Torah*, and *Teshuvah*, and placing them prominently at the beginning of the categories of the *Guide*. It is interesting to note that Maimonides includes in this category both beliefs which are true and those which are necessary for political reasons.[21]

The second category is that of "Idolatry," which corresponds to the "Laws concerning Idolatry" in the *Book of Knowledge*, and other matters concerned with pagan practices, such as "Garments of Diverse Sorts," "First Products," and "Sowing the Vineyard with Diverse Seeds." Here we see a change in order with respect to the *Mishneh Torah*. In the *Mishneh Torah* the idolatry group comes after "Ethical Qualities." Here it is pushed up next to "Fundamental Opinions" and made a separate category of the fourteen, which of course emphasizes its importance vis-a-vis the other categories to a greater extent than in the *Mishneh Torah*. This is in line with the supreme importance of the laws regulating idolatry in Maimonides' mind in his understanding of the Mosaic code in the *Guide*.[22] Thus, in the total scheme of the *Guide* the place of beliefs, both positive and negative, is much more prominent than in the *Mishneh Torah*, since they occupy two categories instead of one.

Since the position of "Idolatry" has been changed, this has effected the place assigned to the group of commandments dependent on the temple. In the *Guide* matters dependent on the temple (categories X–XII) come after prayer (categories VIII–IX) and before forbidden matters (categories XIII–XIV), whereas in the *Mishneh Torah* matters dependent on the temple are placed after both prayer (Books II–III) and forbidden matters (Books IV–VI). The structural reason for the *Guide*'s different arrangement is that the categories dependent on the temple are keyed to idolatry, and the place of idolatry has changed.

The third category is that concerned with the improvement of ethical qualities, which corresponds to the second subgroup of *Mishneh Torah I, Knowledge*. Since the place of "Ethical Qualities" in the scheme of the *Guide* has been moved down after idolatry instead of following immediately after Fundamental Opinions, categories XIII and XIV of the *Guide*, "Forbidden Foods" and "Prohibited Sexual Unions," have been moved to the end of the list after matters dependent on the temple, since they are keyed to ethics.

The fourth category comprises those commandments which are concerned with the Giving of Alms and the Bestowal of Gifts. This particular category is made up of material taken from various parts of the *Mishneh Torah*. It is an innovation on Maimonides' part, and it constitutes a new category which does not appear separately in the *Mishneh Torah*, either as a book or a subgrouping, although it does include some subgroups of the *Mishneh Torah*. The purpose of this category is to instill "compassion for the weak and the wretched, giving strength in various ways to the poor, and inciting us not to press hard upon those in straits and not to afflict the hearts of individuals who are in a weak position."[23] Thus, this category is mainly devoted to developing the ethical quality of compassion, as well as brotherhood, love, extreme generosity, and humility.[24] In general, therefore, one can understand why this category comes after the third category since its object is one of instilling ethical qualities. More detailed consideration of the particular focus of Maimonides on this theme follows.

Maimonides states that "most of the evils that arise among people in the cities are due only to a furious desire for possessions and for increasing them and to the passion of acquisition."[25] A basic moral virtue underlying the political order, according to the common wisdom current in philosophical circles in Maimonides' time, was friendship, based on Book VIII, 1 of the *Nicomachean Ethics* and on general considerations. Without compassion and generosity there come to exist two opposing classes in society leading to its breakdown. Maimonides, as head of the Jewish community and in his personal life, might very well have become increasingly aware of the need for compassion in resolving conflict. As Maimonides states "love one another, help one another, and have pity on one another; and the attainment of these things is the greatest purpose of the law."[26]

Another possible factor might be that in Islam the giving of alms is a fundamental precept. In order, perhaps, to show that in the Jewish tradition the same position is taken and given equal importance, he has included the giving of alms under a separate heading.

The fifth category corresponds to *Mishneh Torah XI*, *Damages*; the sixth category, "Punishments," corresponds in the main to the last book of the *Mishneh Torah*, *Judges*; the seventh category concerns the laws of property and corresponds generally to *Mishneh Torah XII*, *Acquisition* and *Mishneh Torah XIII*, *Judgement*. In the *Guide*, the function of law seems to be repressive, and it is with categories related to restriction that Maimonides starts out. Only at the end does he deal with the more positive aspects of law.

With the enumeration of these seven categories, we come to the end of those laws which are the core of the law. The last seven categories are concerned with traditional legislation. I shall have occasion to discuss these two general groupings of law more fully later.

The eighth category of the *Guide* contains the laws of the days on which work is forbidden and corresponds to *Mishneh Torah III*, *Times*. The ninth category contains other general practices of worship and corresponds to *Mishneh Torah II*, *Love*. I take these two categories together since they are both clearly linked to the first category of the *Guide*, "Fundamental Opinions," reinforcing the love of the Deity and the idea, for instance, that the world was created in time. It is, however, curious that the order of the categories is the reverse of the *Mishneh Torah*. I suggest somewhat tentatively that the reason might lie in an emphasis on the possibility of contemplation, which is greater on days on which work is forbidden than in the course of the ordinary prayers.

The tenth, eleventh, and twelfth categories clearly concern the temple and correspond to Books Eight, Nine, and Ten of the *Mishneh Torah*. Here they are keyed to "Idolatry" and therefore follow categories VIII and IX, which are keyed to "Fundamental Opinions." As I have explained above, their place has changed with respect to the order of the *Mishneh Torah* because of the different place that "Idolatry" has in the *Guide* with respect to the *Mishneh Torah*.

Categories thirteen and fourteen include matters principally relating to forbidden foods and forbidden sexual relations. They correspond mainly to *Mishneh Torah V*, *Sanctity* and *Mishneh Torah IV*, *Women*. These regulations are intended to strengthen the self-control of the individual with regard to food and sexual relations. They therefore correspond to "Ethical Qualities" in the first group of seven, and come at the end of the second group of seven categories. Here again we have another change in the position of categories with respect to the *Mishneh Torah*. Perhaps Maimonides' marked aversion to the sense of touch which comes out so strongly in the *Guide* caused him to put the category concerned with sexual relations at the end.[27] It is curious, however, that the laws concerning marriage are put in the traditional group. We have met with a similar attitude in the *Mishneh Torah*, where the laws concerning marriage were classified with the man-God commandments rather than the man-man commandments. Perhaps the same reasoning is at work here, although the question is sharper, since in the *Guide* Maimonides has practically given up the rabbinic distinction between God-man and man-man commandments.[28] In any case, it is clear from the point of view of structure that Maimonides does not consider the laws regulating relations between the sexes to belong to the core of the law. In this connection, one might recall that in the *Republic* Plato does not consider permanent marriage essential for the proper working of the ideal state.

In conclusion, it seems quite clear that in the *Guide* we have a division of the categories of the commandments of the law into two groups of seven each, something which is clearly not true of the scheme of the *Mishneh Torah*. In the *Guide* we see that *Mishneh Torah I*, *Book of Knowledge* has been broken up into three component parts, each of which is given independent status as a category, in a different order. We also have seen the creation of a new category, "Giving of Alms and Bestowal of Gifts." The four books of the *Mishneh Torah* concerning man's relation with his fellow are condensed into three categories also in a different order. Finally, Books II through X of the *Mishneh Torah* are taken out of their central place and put towards the end, likewise in a different order and condensed into seven books. Thus in merely examining the external structure of the commandments of the law in the *Guide* over against the *Mishneh Torah*, one sees a radical change in the position of the categories.

IV

The fundamental difference between the *Guide* and the *Mishneh Torah* with respect to the structure of the commandments lies in the different place given to the traditional, ceremonial laws with respect to the other laws. How are we to explain this difference?

The explanation lies, it seems to me, in the different functions that Maimonides is fulfilling in these two works. In the *Mishneh Torah*, Maimonides is acting as jurisprudent, in the terminology of Alfarabi, whose task is to follow the guidelines laid down by the first legislator and interpreted by his followers, the rabbis.[29] The function of the Introduction to the *Mishneh Torah* is in fact to spell out the rabbinic ideology which Maimonides takes as his guiding principle in the *Mishneh Torah*. According to this ideology, there were two laws given to Moses on Mount Sinai, the written and the oral law, which were passed on to posterity by an unbroken chain of transmission. Although there is a difference between the oral law and the written law from a juridical point of view, there can be no essential difference between the commandments of the Torah, whether of a ceremonial or a nonceremonial nature. Therefore, in the *Mishneh Torah* the ceremonial commandments occupy a central position and are linked immediately to the various subgroupings of the *Book of Knowledge*. They are then followed by the last four books of the *Mishneh Torah*, which are concerned directly with human relations.

In the *Guide*, one of Maimonides' principal roles is that of the theologian (in the Alfarabian sense) who is interested in defending the Torah from attacks on it on the part of the philosophers. In order to defend the Torah, he has to make it philosophically viable, and therefore he is concerned with the principles of religion.[30] He is not concerned primarily with rabbinic ideology but rather with the law of Moses *per se*, for without a viable defense of the law of Moses the whole edifice of the law will crumble. Now from a philosophical point of view, the ceremonial law is of much less consequence than the laws which form the core of the legislation of the ideal city. Accordingly, I suggest that in Maimonides' view the first seven categories of the commandments in the *Guide* comprise those matters which constitute the core of legislation for the ideal city. The other seven categories are intended to reinforce the first seven and in fact directly follow the order of the topics of the first four categories, as pointed out.[31]

In examining the structure of the commandments in the *Guide*, the distinction between the first and second tiers is obvious. The assumption that all the commandments must be compatible with reason is also clear.[32] Are, then, the commandments in Maimonides' view essentially rational?

It would seem clear that in examining the essential nature of the commandments, Maimonides would say that the commandments as a whole fall into two groups: the rational in a strict sense and the other commandments which are not rational in a strict sense.[33] Those which are rational in a strict sense are those which are capable of apodeictic demonstration,[34] such as the belief in God and that He is one. These commandments are comprised in Categories I and II.[35] The other commandments are either quasi-universal[36] or traditional.[37] I would argue that Categories III through VII fall under the quasi-universal, and that Categories VIII through XIV belong to the traditional, in that they are peculiar to the Jewish people, proceeding as they do from the fiat of Moses as representing the divine wisdom, without having a clear correspondence with procedures in other societies.[38]

In light of the above, I conclude that the commandments in the *Guide* are ordered hierarchically according to a philosophical scale of values, which is not the case in the *Mishneh Torah*.

V

To sum up and conclude, the *Book of Commandments*, the *Mishneh Torah*, and the *Guide* seem to represent successive stages in refining Maimonides' understanding of the structure of the commandments of the Torah.

In the *Book of Commandments* one sees a first attempt at grouping and structuring the commandments of the law. The principal purpose of the *Book of Commandments* was simply to clarify exactly the identification of which commandments were to be recognised as constituting the 613 mentioned in the Talmud. The question of structure was consequently not uppermost in the mind of Maimonides.

In the *Mishneh Torah*, a more systematic structure of the commandments of the Torah was necessary, according to the materials of the oral and written laws which go far beyond the bare commandments of the Torah. Here the primary purpose was ordering the substance of the whole of the law, and the commandments of the Torah take on a structure in accordance with that purpose.

In the *Guide*, on the other hand, the structure of the commandments of the law is again considered but this time from the perspective of the theological apologist, in the course of Maimonides' defense of the law of Moses. It is important to point out here that the *Guide* is essentially concerned with defending the Mosaic world view in the understanding of Maimonides, and he is not interested primarily in defending the rabbis from attack. Consequently, in line with the insights of the *Guide* which I have mentioned above, it seemed necessary to Maimonides to rethink the structure of the commandments of the Torah, this time from the perspective of the philosophical theologian, without of course neglecting the insights derived from his work with the totality of the law as a jurisprudent in the *Mishneh Torah*.

TABLE I

The Commandments in the *Book of Commandments*

	Positive Commandments		*Negative Commandments*
I	God: 1–9	I	God: 1
II	Torah and prayer: 10–19	II	Idolatry: 2–66
III	Sanctuary and priests: 20–38	III	Sanctuary and priests: 67–88
IV	Offerings: 39–93	IV	Offerings: 89–154
V	Vows: 94–95	V	Vows: 155–157
VI	Purity and impurity: 96–113	VI	Impurity: 158–171
VII	Agricultural matters: 114–145	VII	Prohibited food: 172–209
VIII	Food regulations: 146–152	VIII	Cultivation of land: 210–231
IX	Holy days: 153–171	IX	Duties to fellowman: 232–272
X	State functions: 172–193	X	Administration of justice: 273–300
XI	Duties to fellowman: 194–208	XI	Public order: 301–319
XII	Family life: 209–223	XII	Holy days: 320–329
XIII	Punishments: 224–231	XIII	Sexual regulations: 330–361
XIV	Property regulations: 232–248	XIV	State affairs: 362–365

TABLE II

Structure of the Commandments according to the *Mishneh Torah*

I	Knowledge (*Maddaʿ*)		
	A. Basic Principles (*Yesodey Ha-Torah*)		Theoretical
	B. Ethical Qualities (*Deʿoth*)		Theoretical
	C. Study of the Torah (*Talmud Torah*)		Theoretical
	D. Idolatry (*ʿAvodath Kokhavim*)		Theoretical
	E. Repentance (*Teshuvah*)		Theoretical
II	Love (*ʾAhavah*)	man-God	Practical
III	Times (*Zemannim*)	man-God	Practical
IV	Women (*Nashim*)	man-God	Practical
V	Sanctity (*Qedushshah*)	man-God	Practical
VI	"Expression" (*Haflaʾah*)	man-God	Practical
VII	Seeds (*Zeraʿim*)	man-God	Practical
VIII	"Service" (*ʿAvodah*)	man-God	Practical
IX	Sacrifices (*Qorbanoth*)	man-God	Practical
X	Purity (*Ṭohorah*)	man-God	Practical
XI	Damages (*Neziqin*)	man-man	Practical
XII	Acquisition (*Qinyan*)	man-man	Practical
XIII	Judgement (*Mishpaṭim*)	man-man	Practical
XIV	Judges (*Shofeṭim*)	man-man	Practical

TABLE III

Structure of the Commandments according to the *Guide of the Perplexed*.

I	Fundamental opinions	Beliefs	Rational
II	Idolatry	Beliefs	Rational
III	Ethical qualities	Ethics	Quasi-universal
IV	Giving of alms and bestowing of gifts	Ethics	Quasi-universal
V	Wrongdoing and aggression	Politics	Quasi-universal
VI	Punishments	Politics	Quasi-universal
VII	Mutual property transactions	Politics	Quasi-universal
VIII	Days in which work is forbidden		Traditional
IX	Other general practices of worship		Traditional
X	Sanctuary		Traditional
XI	Sacrifices		Traditional
XII	Clean and unclean		Traditional
XIII	Forbidden food and related matters		Traditional
XIV	Prohibited sexual unions		Traditional

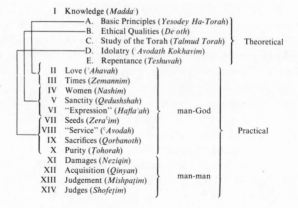

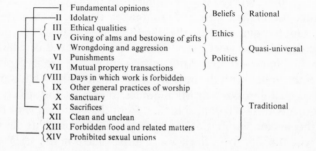

The very different results arrived at whilst wearing the cap of the theologian and whilst wearing the cap of the jurisprudent have become apparent in the course of our study.

We can only speculate how Maimonides might have structured the *Mishneh Torah* were he to have undertaken his work of theologian first, for he was always searching for a more exact expression of his thoughts as the various drafts of his works show. In fact, the *Book of Commandments*, the *Mishneh Torah*, and the scheme of Part III, Chapter 35 of the *Guide* may be considered closer and closer approximations to the deep structure of the commandments of the law.

Do the differences in structure which have been pointed out between the *Mishneh Torah* and the *Guide* represent substantive changes in Maimonides' general concept of the commandments and their relative value? Spinoza and Moses Mendelssohn would most probably have understood them as substantive changes; others of a more traditional mold as but tactical changes. In any event, the two different points of view which the *Mishneh Torah* and the *Guide* represent are clear enough. We do not, of course, have here two different authors as Jacob Emden claimed,[39] but we certainly do have two very different views on the nature of the commandments of the Torah.

NOTES

1. A preliminary version of this paper was read at the fifth annual conference of the Association for Jewish Studies at Harvard University on October 22, 1973. An abstract of the preliminary version was published in the *Association for Jewish Studies Newsletter*, No. 10, January, 1974, pp. 5–6.

2. See Isadore Twersky, "Religion and Law," in *Religion in a Religious Age*, ed. S. D. Goitein, Cambridge, Mass.: Association for Jewish Studies, 1974, pp. 69–74, for a good discussion of the concept of "halakocentricity" and its relationship to the pietistic, mystical, and philosophic trends within rabbinic Judaism.

3. See Ḥefeṣ ben Yaṣliaḥ, *A Volume of the Book of Precepts*, ed. by B. Halper, Philadelphia, 1915, p. 49.

4. T.B. *Makkoth* 23b and Halper, pp. 1–8. A. H. Rabbinowitz, *Taryag*, Jerusalem, 1967 provides a useful collection of material, but the level of analysis and approach leaves much room for improvement.

5. I have used the edition of the Arabic text by Joseph Kafiḥ, *Sefer ha-Miṣwoth*, Jerusalem: Mosad Ha-rav Kook, 1971, with his Hebrew translation. For an evaluation, see the review of Joshua Blau in *Leshonenu*, 37 (1973), pp. 291–302 (offprint). For an analysis of Maimonides' concept of positive and negative commandments, see Jacob Levinger, *Darekhey ha-Maḥashavah ha-hilkhathith shel ha-rambam*, Jerusalem: Magnes Press, 1965, pp. 66–87 (esp. 72–78). Levinger's three types of commandments relate to the juridical analysis of the commandments, not to their structure in the *Book of Commandments*.

6. The main bibliography on this question follows: Moritz Peritz, "Das Buch der Gesetze," in *Moses ben Maimon*, ed. W. Bacher *et al.*, Leipzig, 1908, I, pp. 445–49; Jacob L. Moinester, *Seder ha-Miṣwoth le-ha-rambam*, New York, 1945; A. Hillwitz, "*Seder ha-Miṣwoth be-minyano shel ha-rambam*," *Sinai*, 19 (1946), pp. 258–67; Israel

Porat, *Mevo' ha-Talmud le-masekheth sanhedrin*, St. Louis, Mo., 1951, pp. 243–46; Maimonides, *The Commandments*, translated and introduced by Charles B. Chavel, London: Soncino, 1967, I, pp. xi–xiv. In my own grouping of the commandments of the *Book of Commandments*, I have depended especially on Peritz, Moinester, and Chavel. In dividing the commandments into fourteen categories, I have followed a favorite tendency of Maimonides and tried to see whether it makes sense here. It is curious that the sums of 248 and 365, respectively, are fourteen. I hope to deal with the order of the commandments in the *Book of Commandments* in greater detail elsewhere. See also S. Rawidowicz, "*Sefer ha-Madda we-sefer ha-Miṣwoth la-rambam*," in his *ᶜIyyunim be-maḥasheveth yisraʾel*, ed. Benjamin C. I. Ravid, Jerusalem: Mass, 1969, I, pp. 346–80. My conclusions here accord with those of Rawidowicz and are supported by them.

7. See *Guide,* III, 35 end. All subsequent references are to Maimonides, *Guide of the Perplexed*, tr. S. Pines, University of Chicago Press, 1963. In parentheses, I have added references to the edition of the Munk text by I. Joel, *Dalālat al-ḥāʾirīn*, Jerusalem, 1931.

8. See Porat, p. 244; and Maimonides, *Commentary on the Mishnah*: *Order of Zeraᶜim*, ed. J. Kafiḥ, Jerusalem: Mosad Ha-rav Kook, 1963, pp. 50–52.

9. See *Mishneh Torah*: *The Book of Commandments*, ed. and tr. Moses Hyamson, Jerusalem, 1965. For the rest of the *Mishneh Torah*, I have used the Romm edition of Vilna (photographic reprint, New York, 1946).

10. See Hyamson edition, p. 5a.

11. *Ibid*., p. 19b.

12. The principal works dealing with the structure of the *Mishneh Torah* follow: B. Ziemlich, "Plan und Anlage der Mischne Thora," in *Moses ben Maimon*, I, pp. 248–318 (esp. 273–80, 308–18); A. Schwarz, "Der Mischneh Thorah," in *XII. Jahresbericht d. Israelitisch – Theologischen Lehranstalt in Wien*, Vienna, 1905 (not seen); I. H. Herzog, "*Seder ha-Sefarim be-mishneh torah le-ha-rambam*," in *Rabbenu Mosheh ben Maymon*, ed. J. L. Fishman (Maimon), Jerusalem: Mosad Ha-rav Kook, 1935, II, pp. 257–64. When I use the distinction between theoretical and practical, I do not mean to refer to the distinction between those commandments which are not applicable at "this time," and those which are applicable, as Ziemlich following Z. Frankel uses the term. On this point I agree with A. Schwarz as quoted by Ziemlich (pp. 308–18). S. Rawidowicz has devoted attention to the structure of Book One of the *Mishneh Torah*; see "*Sefer ha-Pethiḥah le-mishneh torah*," in his *ᶜIyyunim be-maḥasheveth yisraʾel*, I, 381–464. [Since preparing this article, I have received a copy of Schwarz, "Der Mischne Thorah." His remarks on the relationship of the *Mishneh Torah* to the *Mishnah* are quite good (pp. 8–11 and 17–18). Schwarz does not attempt to deal in any satisfactory way with the differences in the order of the classes of the commandments between the *Mishneh Torah* and the *Guide* (p. 12), merely noting the differences between them. In his general analysis of the relationship between the books of the *Mishneh Torah* (pp. 14–17), Schwarz has not realized the rigorous nature of Maimonides' structure, although his remarks are in themselves instructive. The rest of Schwarz' book is not directly germane to the inquiry pursued here.] Cf. also B. Cohen in *JQR*, New Series 25 (1935), pp. 519–40.

13. See L. V. Berman, "Maimonides, the Disciple of Alfarabi," *Israel Oriental Studies*, 4 (1974), p. 164, n. 31 with further references. See also H. A. Davidson, "The Study of Philosophy as a Religious Obligation," in *Religion in a Religious Age*, pp. 63–64 and I. Twersky, "Religion and Law," *ibid*., pp. 72–74.

14. See *Guide*, III, 37; Pines, p. 542 (Joel, p. 397. 5–6). But cf. n. 26, *infra*.

15. See Louis Jacobs, *A Jewish Theology*, New York: Behrman, 1973, pp. 247ff., 255ff.

16. See Table I.

17. *Guide*, III, 35; Pines, p. 538 (Joel, p. 393.28–394.1).

18. *Mishneh Torah IV. Nashim. Hilekhoth ᵓIshshuth* 1:1.

19. See *Mishneh Torah VI. Haflaᵓah. Hilekhoth Nedarim* 13:23 and Herzog, *Seder ha-Sefarim etc.*, p. 259; *Guide*, III, 35; Pines, p. 537 (Joel, p. 393.21–25); *ibid.*, III, 48; Pines, p. 600 (Joel, p. 441.1–18).

20. See Berman, "Maimonides, the Disciple of Alfarabi," p. 168 for references.

21. See *Guide*, III, 28, for "beliefs, belief in which is necessary for the sake of political welfare" (Pines, 512.20–21; Joel, p. 373.11–13). I have dealt with political myth in the thought of Maimonides and his contemporaries and predecessors in my *Ibn Bājjah and Maimonides*, Hebrew University Dissertation, 1959, pp. 134–185.

22. See n. 14 above, p. 64.

23. *Guide*, III, 39; Pines, p. 550 (Joel, p. 403.23–25) with Pines, p. 553.8 *infra.* (Joel, p. 405.26) and Pines, 4 *infra.* (Joel, p. 405.28) and *passim.*

24. See *Guide*, III, 39; Pines, p. 551.17 (Joel, p. 404.6); *ibid.*, pp. 551.24, 553.23 (Joel, pp. 404.10, 405.21) with *Nicomachean Ethics*, IV 2, 1122a28ff; Maimonides, *Commentary on the Mishnah. Neziqin. Introduction to ᵓAvoth*, ed. Kafiḥ, p. 381b16 *infra*, with p. 280b7; L. V. Berman in *Journal of Semitic Studies*, 12 (1967), pp. 268–72; *Guide*, III, 39; Pines, p. 551.2 *infra* (Joel, p. 404.14).

25. *Ibid.*, III, 39; Pines, p. 553.26–28 (Joel, p. 405.22–24).

26. *Guide*, III, 49 beginning. But cf. n. 14, *supra.*

27. See *Guide*, II, 36; Pines, p. 371 (Joel, p. 262.10–20).

28. See *Guide*, III, 35 end, with *Guide*, III, 54; Pines, p. 635 (Joel, p. 468.24–30) where moral perfection is understood politically.

29. See Berman, "Maimonides, the Disciple of Alfarabi," pp. 168–169. See also Levinger, *Darekhey ha-Maḥashavah ha-hilekhathith shel ha-rambam*, pp. 165 and 182–89, who emphasizes the dogmatic character of Maimonides' position in his *Mishneh Torah*, despite the "enlightened" tendencies of that work. See Levinger, p. 183 for Maimonides' distinction between the written and oral laws.

30. Berman, *ibid.*, p. 164, but see I. H. Herzog, "*Seder ha-Sefarim le-ha-rambam,*" pp. 261 ff. His conclusion betrays a certain apologetic tendency. One should keep in mind the difference between *uṣūl al-dīn* and *uṣūl al-fiqh*; see Levinger, p. 183.

31. See also *Guide*, III, 34; Pines, p. 535 (Joel, pp. 391.20–22), where Maimonides makes a distinction between those laws which are intended primarily and those intended secondarily. Laws intended primarily are not dependent on a particular time and place, e.g., the belief in correct opinions and the abolition of mutual wrong-doing. The prime example of matters intended secondarily is the temple cult (see *Guide*, III, 32; Pines, p. 531 (Joel, pp. 388.17–389.4).

32. See *Guide*, III, 25 and 26. The full-fledged understanding of Maimonides' concept of the will of God needs thoroughgoing treatment. See now A. Altmann, "The Religion of the Thinkers: Free Will and Predestination in Saadia, Baḥya, and Maimonides," in *Religion in a Religious Age*, pp. 35–51.

33. See *Guide*, II, 33 with *ibid.*, I, 2; *Book of Commandments*, Positive Commandment 1 and Negative Commandment 1; *Introduction to ᵓAvoth*, Chapter II; E. Schweid, *ᶜIyyunim bi-shemonah peraqim la-rambam*, Jerusalem, 1965, pp. 64–73; Alfarabi, *Risālat fi'l-ᶜaql*, ed. M. Bouyges, Beirut: Imprimerie Catholique, 1938, pp. 3–9; A. Altmann, "Saadya's Conception of the Law," *Bulletin of the John Rylands*

Library, 28 (1944), pp. 320–39; *idem*, "*Ḥaluqqath ha-Miṣwoth le-rabbenu Seʿadyah gaʾon*," in *Saadya Gaon*, ed. J. L. Fishman (Maimon), Jerusalem, 1943, pp. 658–73; *idem*, "Religion of the Thinkers etc.," pp. 26–29; George Hourani, *Islamic Rationalism*, Oxford University Press, 1972, Chapter VI.

34. See Maimonides, *Treatise on Logic*, Chapter VIII; for bibliographical details, see L. V. Berman in *Journal of the American Oriental Society*, 88 (1968), pp. 340–42.

35. See above at n. 21, p. 65, for beliefs necessary for political purposes. I hope to deal with these beliefs and their relationship to Maimonides' basic division of the commandments on another occasion.

36. *al-mashhūrāt*. See *Guide*, II, 33; Pines, p. 364 (Joel, p. 256.26); and *Treatise on Logic*, Chapter VIII; *Introduction to ʾAvoth*, ed. J. Kafiḥ, in *Mishnah ʿim perush rabbenu Mosheh ben Maymun. Seder Neziqin*, Jerusalem: Mosad Ha-rav Kook, 1964, p. 392.

37. *al-maqbūlāt*, *ibid*.

38. See further R. Lerner, "Moses Maimonides," in *History of Political Philosophy*, ed. by L. Strauss and J. Cropsey, Chicago, 1963, pp. 181–89 (esp. 196–99) and M. Fox, "Maimonides and Aquinas on Natural Law," in *Diney Yisraʾel* (Tel Aviv University, Faculty of Law), III (1972), pp. v–xxxvi. I hope to deal with the concept and authority of the commandments at greater length in a separate paper.

39. *Miṭpaḥath sefarim*, Jerusalem, 1969 (photographic reprint), p. 56, quoted by S. Rawidowicz, "Philosophy as a Duty," in his *Studies in Jewish Thought*, ed. N. N. Glatzer, Philadelphia: Jewish Publication Society, 1974, p. 305. Cf. A. Altmann, "Rambam und die Halacha," in *Festbeilage der Central-Verein-Zeitung*, March 30, 1935, beginning.

The Concept of Knowledge in the *Shi^cur Qomah*

J. DAN

In the last dozen years we have been witnessing a renewed discussion of the old problem of the gnostic element in the *heykhaloth* and *merkavah* literature. Since Graetz first raised the problem in the last century our knowledge of this early body of Hebrew mystical literature has increased considerably, and when Scholem put forward the thesis that this genre did in fact contain certain gnostic elements[1] he did so on the basis of a large corpus of new information and with penetrating analysis. Nevertheless, the thesis still remains controversial: D. Flusser put forward strong arguments against Scholem's thesis,[2] as did also I. Grünwald in a detailed study which analysed the concept of knowledge in the Bible, in apocalyptic literature, in the Dead Sea Scrolls and in the *heykhaloth* texts.[3]

There is a serious danger in discussing such a question as this that analysis of texts may deteriorate into a semantic argument; when such a thing occurs, the question "What does *heykhaloth* literature really mean?" is replaced by the question "What are the minimal characteristics of a gnostic concept of the world?" When we study the first question, we have a chance of approaching a better understanding of the material before us; when discussing the second, we become hopelessly entangled in a field of varying definitions, without achieving any progress in our attempt to understand the original meaning of the early mystics. It is therefore the purpose of this article to try to analyze some aspects of the basic text of this literature, the *Shi^cur Qomah,*[4] and the reader will judge for himself whether or not this analysis, if substantiated, brings this text closer to the usual connotation of the term "gnostic."

The *Shi^cur Qomah,* or "Dimensions of the [divine] stature," is one of the earliest works of the *heykhaloth* mystics. It was probably written in the second or third century C.E., although the fragments of it that have come down to us are of a much later date. Its contents can be divided into three basic elements, which are to be found in all the extant versions:

1. A list of the measurements of the divine "body," limb by limb, constituting a highly anthropomorphic text unparalleled in early Jewish literature.
2. A list of names attached to these limbs, often constituting long, unintelligible lists of letters.
3. A passage in which the alleged authors of the text, Rabbi Aqiba and Rabbi Ishmael, assure the student of the text that they will guarantee to any who study it the attainment of a high religious status.

The concept of knowledge is inherent in all three elements of this text, although it is in the third element that it comes especially to the foreground. Let us examine the type of knowledge that each section of the work seeks to impart to the reader.

As regards the first element, the list of dimensions, Scholem[5] has emphasized the fantastic nature of the astronomical figures given for these. Two examples will suffice to demonstrate this. "His neck—thirteen thousand times ten thousand, plus eight hundred parasangs is the height of His neck;" or "the black in his right eye is eleven thousand and five hundred parasangs."[6] In order to understand what precisely are the dimensions here indicated, we have to determine what is intended by the term "parasang." In normal usage this Persian measurement of distance means something over three miles, but not so in the *Shiʿur Qomah*, which itself includes a definition of the parasang as equal to ninety thousand times the width of the earth.[7] In various texts there are slight differences in these reckonings, but they all yield results of the same order of magnitude. Thus the data for the height of the divine neck give 11,700,072,000,000 units, i.e., nearly twelve trillion times the width of the earth. It thus seems to me that in such contexts the literal translation *parasang* can helpfully be replaced by the term *parsec* as used by astronomers to denote intergalactic distances. A parsec indicates a distance of about 20^{12} miles, being based on the distance of a star having a heliocentric parallax of one second.

If we now return from this brief mathematical example to the problem of the meaning of knowledge in the text, the question has to be formulated thus: "What is to be gained from the imparting of such detailed knowledge about the dimensions of the divine being as described here, since the figures are so far beyond the capacity of the human mind to comprehend? What difference does it make whether the exact measurement is the one stated, and not a few parsecs more or less? What is the disciple to gain from the knowledge of such meaningless figures regarding the various members and parts of the divine "body"?"

It would seem that we are not here dealing with "knowledge" in the usual sense. The text has no intention whatsoever of imparting facts. Rather the purpose is to prove that the divine "body" is beyond all knowledge, transcending comprehension, its understanding pertaining to the realm of mystical knowledge and not that of mathematical science. It is not intended that the disciple, after having studied the text, should "know"; the intention is that he should appreciate that the matter is a secret that he can never "know," even though some hint of the order of magnitude involved, and of the relative magnitude of the divine members is given. In other words, the disciple is given a veiled hint about the structure and outline of mystical truth which words and figures cannot convey. This is merely a further variation on the usual symbolic method of imparting mystical truths, a method that every school of mysticism had to develop in order to be able to communicate at all when dealing with matters that lie far beyond the realm of everyday speech. The astronomical numbers of the *Shiʿur Qomah* do not intend to convey knowledge, but to point to the existence of a mystical truth which transcends both mathematical expressions of magnitude and human speech itself.

It seems that when we examine the second element of the *Shiʿur Qomah*, i.e., the lists of the names of the various members, we encounter the same phenomenon. These names are unintelligible to us—a fact that has often been attributed to the corrupt state of the existing fragments of the text. I doubt whether this is an adequate explanation. If these names did originally intend to convey some systematic meaning, surely some of it would have been preserved by copyists who understood what the system was. More probably the names, like the numbers, were not given in order to impart definite knowledge but rather to convey the incomprehensibility of the realm of the divine.

Among the many hundreds of groups of letters which are in this work described as "names"—some of them comprising seventy Hebrew characters or more, and each limb having many different names—two groups can be clearly distinguished. One type—relatively infrequent—consists of names which are based on various permutations of the Tetragrammaton; the second, which is found far more often, consists in the grouping of letters which are not found so combined in Hebrew words. Since we may surmise that when copyists erred, their mistakes would tend towards creating recognizable words out of these jumbles of letters, we may assume that the original text of the *Shiʿur Qomah* will have been in this respect if anything even more chaotic than the texts which have come down to us. It seems safe to assume that these names were listed not in order to instruct, but rather in order to obstruct: to prove to the disciple how remote is the true nature of the divine being—a nature which is connected with the divine essence itself in most mystical and purely magical early texts—from all human comprehension, and how impatient it is of formulation in linguistically meaningful expressions. Once again some hint is furnished, in order to establish the possibility of communication; but no one was intended to mistake these lists of Hebrew letters for true knowledge about the divine being. It was intended that after having read the text the reader should become seized of his own essential ignorance and not suppose that divine truths had in fact been revealed to him.

These two lists, then—the list of names and the list of numbers—convey the same kind of negation of knowledge, of veiled hints at mystical truths that cannot be transmitted by words. In this context, therefore, the clear "facts" which appear to be given in this work—i.e., the assertion that the divine being is possessed of a neck, beard, eye, ankles, etc.—do not, after all, constitute "facts." Once it is appreciated that the dimensions and the names are alike beyond comprehension, the terms "neck," "eye," etc. likewise themselves recede from the realm of straightforward anthropomorphism into that of mystical symbolism. According to the structure of the work, it is from the knowledge of its name and its length that the meaning of "neck" in the description of the divine being is derived. When the disciple has become convinced of his ignorance of the two supporting factors, his understanding of the first term becomes obscured, and the "neck" is connected no longer with anthropomorphic realism but instead becomes obscured in incomprehensible symbolism. The truth can be attained by mystical means only and not by conventional, sensory ways of conveying "knowledge." This is not mere esotericism, but rather a concept of knowledge that is purely mystical.

The meaning of this relationship between the obscure figures and combinations of letters and "clear" anthropomorphic terms becomes obvious as soon as we compare the *Shiʿur Qomah* with its parent text, *viz.*, the anthropomorphically interpreted phrases describing the physical features of the lover in the *Song of Songs* (5:10f.). According to the traditionally accepted allegorical handling of the biblical text, the divine being is here described in highly anthropomorphic language; as against which, if the interpretation of the *Shiʿur Qomah* suggested in the foregoing be accepted, it must be conceded that the latter is in its mysticism relatively antianthropomorphic. It obscures the direct relationship between human and divine members and conveys the impression that these "members" have nothing to do with the ordinary terms for them as used both in the *Song of Songs* itself and in the *Shiʿur Qomah*. The true meaning of these seemingly anthropomorphic terms lies concealed in the same mystical realm where are hidden the meaning of the astronomical number of parsecs and that of the obscure groups of letters that constitute divine "names." It would seem that in the historical context of *heykhaloth* literature the *Shiʿur Qomah* represents a step away from the crude anthropomorphism of some interpreters of the *Song of Songs*, and that it constitutes a step towards awareness of the distinction between any rational knowledge of the Deity and the true, mystical knowledge of God which cannot be achieved so long as mundane terms, conventional mathematics, and the normal use of the alphabet are employed.

In the sections of the *Shiʿur Qomah* devoted to describing the dimensions and the names of the divine members the term "knowledge" does not itself appear, and we have here tried to reach an understanding of what kind of knowledge it is that the text is trying to convey through examining the information which it provides. But in the third element in the *Shiʿur Qomah*, the famous passage containing the promise by Rabbi Aqiba and Rabbi Ishmael, the term "knowledge" does occur, and in a context of a profundity deserving study. The passage is found several times, with some variants, in the available texts, and it was to be quoted times without number in subsequent Jewish literature. Parts of this passage have been translated by Scholem;[8] it is important for present purposes to study both the content and the structure.

> Rabbi Ishmael said, 'When I said this (*sc.* the text of the *Shiᶜur Qomah*) in the presence of Rabbi Aqiba, he said to me, Anyone who *knows these dimensions* of our *Creator*, and the *praise* of the Holy One, Blessed be He, who is hidden from all created beings, may be assured that he will participate in the world to come, everything will be good for him in this world as part of the next world, and he will live a long life in this world.'
>
> Rabbi Ishmael then said to him in the presence of his disciples: 'I and Rabbi Aqiba are pledges for this—that anyone who *knows* this *dimension-catalogue* of our *Creator* and the *praise* of the Holy One, Blessed be He, may be assured that he will participate in the world to come, so long as he studies it in the Mishnah every single day.'[9]

There are several revealing items in this short passage, some of them already noted by Scholem. The insistent use of the term *Creator* (*yoṣer*) throughout the *Shiᶜur Qomah* cannot be explained as an accident, and there is little doubt that the idea of the demiurge was prominent in the minds of these mystics. We may assume that the seemingly anthropomorphic divine being described in this text is in fact the demiurge. This is indicated in the passage here quoted by insistence on the connection between the terms *Creator* and *measure*. But we should not ignore the other fixed connection that is established here between the terms *praise* and the *Holy One*. Conceivably, whereas the disciple is being invited to "know" the mystical dimensions of the Creator, all that can be asserted regarding the "Holy One" is that He should be praised—probably with the mystical, esoteric hymns that constitute a great part of the *heykhaloth* literature. This juxtaposition of the Creator who can be "measured" with the "Holy One" who is simply to be praised is likewise to be found in a *heykhaloth* hymn identified by Scholem[10] which has become an integral feature of the Jewish liturgy, namely the prayer known from its first word as *ᶜAleynu*, the first two hemistichs of which run as follows:

> Upon us [rests the duty] to praise the Lord of all, to ascribe *greatness* to Him who *fashioned the work of creation*.

The Hebrew word *gedullah*, greatness, by its very nature denotes something which can at least notionally be measured. The relation between the "Holy One" and the Creator in the *Shiᶜur Qomah* is precisely that between the "Lord of all" and the Creator in *ᶜAleynu le-shabbeaḥ*.

It seems appropriate to note here that very often in talmudic literature when opposition is voiced to dualistic ideas, the dualism that is contraverted is one that asserts the existence of *two creators*[11] and not a dualism (if, indeed it may be styled dualism at all) of a Creator and a supreme Godhead. Thus the large body of rabbinic protests and admonitions against dualistic beliefs would not trouble one who chose to believe that above the Creator, who is one, there exists a supreme being who should be praised in mystical hymnody.

The implications of the term to "know" in this passage of the *Shiʿur Qomah* are perfectly clear. What is meant is redeeming knowledge that assures its possessor happiness in this world and a share in the next—the world of redemption. It is this redeeming function of the knowledge contained in the *Shiʿur Qomah*, the dimensions and the *nomina sacra*, that is guaranteed by the two most prominent Jewish halakhic authorities, whose teachings as assembled by their disciples constitute the Mishnah—the source of all Jewish religious law. No higher sanction could be imagined for so profound and far-reaching an assurance. "Knowledge" in this context is undoubtedly an object of supreme religious value, and it is for the reader to decide whether or not such an attitude towards mystical esoteric knowledge constitutes a gnostic element. For the *yoredey merkavah*, the "Descenders to the Chariot,"[12] such knowledge—both of the dimensions of the Creator and of the praises of the Holy One—without doubt meant the achievement of their ultimate religious goal.

A remark may be made in conclusion, not because the analysis of the text renders it necessary, but because some critics have felt unable to accept Scholem's application of the term *gnostic* in an orthodox context where there is no hint of heresy. According to this view gnosticism must, in order to justify its title, be heretical. The passage quoted above from the *Shiʿur Qomah* certainly could be interpreted in a heretical manner, but I am convinced that neither its authors nor readers ever dreamed of placing such an interpretation upon it. When it is the two most prominent teachers of Jewish law, based as it is on a very large number of precepts listed in the Mishnah, Talmud, and halakhic literature, who assert that all one has to do in order to attain supreme religious goals is to "know" the dimensions and praises of the Creator and of the Holy One, the question might be asked, "What, then, of the *miṣwoth* and the study of Torah?[13] What about ethical behavior? Are these things secondary, or even unimportant, when compared to mystical knowledge?" Here, indeed, we should have more than a hint of heresy; it would indicate that the two great halakhic authorities were being represented as lending their name to the replacement of the immense corpus of Jewish law, ethics, and study by mystical knowledge. Accepting such an interpretation, a scholar who insists that gnosticism is *ex hypothesi* heretical could find in this passage all that he wants. Nevertheless, such a procedure would seem to me to violate the first rule of textual analysis, namely that a historical text does not state the obvious. What this passage means is that after one has attained the required minimum of knowledge of the Jewish law—thereby achieving a minimal religious standard—one may proceed to higher spheres, making use of mystical knowledge as a vehicle. *Shiʿur Qomah*, being an esoteric text, has no need to advert to the well known requirements demanded of every Jew: its purpose is to point the way forward from these, and it is that assurance which is inherent in the words attributed to Rabbi Aqiba and Rabbi Ishmael.

NOTES

1. G. Scholem, *Major Trends in Jewish Mysticism,*[2] New York, 1954, pp. 63–5 *et passim*; *Jewish Gnosticism, Merkabah Mysticism and Talmudic Tradition*, New York, 1960; *Qabbalah*, Jerusalem, 1974, p. 17 *et passim.*

2. *Journal of Jewish Studies* xi, 1960, pp. 59–68.

3. *Israel Oriental Studies* iii, 1973, pp. 63–107.

4. I quote from the text most generally accessible to scholars, *viz.*, *Sefer Merkavah Shelemah* ed. by Solomon Musajoff, Jerusalem, 1921, f. 36f.

5. See especially *Major Trends* (*supra*, n. 1), pp. 63f.

6. *Merkavah Shelemah*, f. 37a: צוארו שלשה עשר אלפים רבבות ות״ת פרסאות גובה צוארו... שחור שבעין ימינו רבוא ואלף ות״ק פרסאות וכן של שמאל

7. *Merkavah Shelemah*, f. 38a: חשבון פרסאות כולן כמה שעורין כל פרסה ופרסה ג׳ מילין וכל מיל ומיל עשרת אלפים אמה וכל אמה ואמה שתי [שלש] זרתות בזרת שלו, וזרת שלו מלא כל העולם כולו, שנאמר מי מדד בשעלו מים ושמים בזרת תכן (ישע׳ מ׳ י״ב)

8. See *Major Trends* (*supra,* n. 1), p. 64, and cf. *Qabbalah,* pp. 17f.

9. *Merkavah Shelemah*, f. 38b: אמר רבי ישמעאל, כשאמרתי דבר זה לפני רבי עקיבא אמר לי, כל מי שהוא יודע שיעור זה של יוצרינו ושבחו של הקב״ה שהוא מכוסה מן הבריות מובטח לו שהוא בן עולם הבא, ייטב לו בעולם הזה מטוב העולם הבא ומאריך ימים הוא בעולם הזה.

אמר לו רבי ישמעאל לפני תלמידיו: אני ורבי עקיבא ערבים בדבר זה שכל מי שהוא יודע שיעור זה של יוצרינו ושבחו של הקב״ה מובטח לו שהוא בן העולם הבא ובלבד שהוא שונה אותו במשנה בכל יום ויום.

10. *Jewish Gnosticism* (*supra*, n. 1), p. 27.

11. See Grünwald (*supra*, n. 3), p. 102.

12. The question as to why those who ascend to the *merkavah* are consistently called "descenders to the Chariot" has not been satisfactorily explained. It appears to me that the phrase must be linked to the interpretation of a biblical passage, probably one from the *Song of Songs*; and following on the conclusion of the anthropomorphic passage 5:10–16 there occur in 6:2 and 11 two references to *descent* into the garden. That in v. 11 concerns descent to the *ginnath ha-ʾegoz*, or nut garden, which was identified with the holy Chariot. The question is when did that interpretation become accepted. I have considered this question in the *Journal of Jewish Studies,* xvii, 1966, pp. 73–82.

13. R. Loewe has suggested that the Targum to the *Song of Songs* is deliberately slanted so as to controvert any apparent downgrading in the *Shiʿur Qomah* of the study of the oral law, as constituting God's mystic gift to Israel; see "Apologetic Motifs in the Targum to the Song of Songs," in A. Altmann (ed.), *Studies and Texts*, iii, *Biblical Motifs*, Harvard, 1966, pp. 184f.

The Principle That a Finite Body Can Contain Only Finite Power

H. DAVIDSON

For the medieval philosophers, a demonstration of the existence of God must establish at least three things: the existence of a first cause; the incorporeality of that cause; and its unity.[1] Aristotle's demonstration from motion in *Physics* VIII and *Metaphysics* XII supplied argumentation for all three. The demonstration establishes a first cause for the universe, or more precisely a first cause of the motion of the universe. It establishes the incorporeality of the first mover. And it provides grounds for concluding that there can be only one first mover—grounds, however, which in the view of a number of modern scholars do not represent a consistent and considered position on the part of Aristotle.[2] Here we shall be interested in the argument for the incorporeality of the first mover which appears in *Physics* VIII, 10, and very briefly in *Metaphysics* XII, 7. I shall attempt to trace the modifications the argument for incorporeality underwent at the hands of Proclus, Simplicius, John Philoponus, Averroes, and Crescas.

§1. *Aristotle*. For Aristotle, it is to be remembered, motion can continue only as long as sustained by a motive factor.[3] Aristotle's demonstration of the existence of a first cause establishes a first mover that continually sustains the motion of the celestial spheres.[4] Aristotle's argument for incorporeality thereupon undertakes to show that the first cause of the motion of the spheres is an incorporeal being. The argument runs as follows: Nothing of infinite magnitude can conceivably exist; every object having magnitude, including the corporeal universe as a whole, must be finite. Whatever is of finite magnitude can contain only finite power. Finite power can produce motion for only a finite time. Motion, however, specifically the motion of the celestial spheres, is eternal and therefore dependent upon an infinite power. Consequently the ultimate cause of motion must be "without parts and without magnitude"; it cannot be the spheres themselves or any other part of the corporeal universe but must be an incorporeal being distinct from the universe.[5]

The argument contains four premises. Two of them—that nothing of infinite magnitude can conceivably exist and that motion is eternal—had been established by Aristotle before he approached the issue of the incorporeality of the first mover.[6] They are accordingly treated by him now as presuppositions. To complete the argument it remained to establish the other two[7] premises, to prove that a finite power can produce motion for only a finite time and to prove that a finite magnitude can contain only finite power.

Aristotle's proof of the principle that a finite power can produce motion for no more than a finite time has been interpreted by commentators on Aristotle in several ways. The interpretation to be given here is one offered by Averroes;[8] it is the only satisfactory interpretation that I have found.[9] Suppose, Aristotle begins, that a finite power A should indeed move a finite object B for an infinite time C. (Velocities, for the purpose of proving the present premise, are either ignored, or assumed to be fixed.) Let us take a portion of A which may be called D, and a portion of B, which may be called E, the unstated assumption being that D is a *smaller* fraction of A than E is of B.[10] Now a "greater [power produces motion] for a longer [time]"[11] and a lesser power for a shorter time. To be precise, the time over which a power can operate before exhausting itself is understood by Aristotle to be proportional to the power and inversely proportional to the object upon which it operates.[12] Since D is a smaller fraction of A than E is of B, D will suffice to move E for no more than time F, which is shorter than C. Inasmuch as anything less than the infinite is finite, F, being less than C, must be finite. D can now be multiplied until equal to the whole of A, and E can be multiplied until equal to the whole of B. On that calculation, the time over which all of A can maintain all of B in motion will be some definite multiple of F,[13] a multiple that again is finite. The original supposition that a finite power produces motion over an infinite time thus turns out to have been incorrect. Finite powers can produce motion for only finite spans of time.[14]

There remains the final premise needed for the argument, the principle that a finite magnitude can contain only finite power. Aristotle proves this not by considering the varying amounts of work performed by a greater and a lesser power, as he did in his proof of the previous principle. Here he considers velocities, which he ignored there; he compares the varying velocities at which greater and lesser powers perform a given amount of work.

The possibility that any power should perform a physical operation instantaneously is excluded by Aristotle without discussion.[15] And his contention is that no time span—which is equivalent to saying: no velocity—could be assigned for any operation of an infinite power contained within a finite magnitude; for no matter how brief a time span and how rapid a velocity we take, we shall always find a finite power performing the same operation in the same time span and at the same velocity. Aristotle explains: "Suppose Z to be the time required for the infinite power to perform [a given operation] . . . and Z plus Y the time required for a finite power to perform the same operation." The time required to complete a fixed amount of work is inversely proportional to the power applied.[16] Therefore, "by increasing the finite power . . . we can eventually reach the point[17] where it performs the operation in time Z. . . . The finite power would then require the same time that the infinite power was supposed to require." But it is "impossible" that a finite power and an infinite power should require the same time to perform the same work; it is impossible that they should operate at the same velocity. No time span or velocity whatsoever, then, can be assigned for the operation of the infinite power. If there is no time or velocity in which an infinite power contained within a finite magnitude can act, such a power simply does not act. But a power that does nothing is not a power. An infinite power, therefore, can in no way exist within a finite magnitude.[18]

There is an embarassing side to Aristotle's proof of this last principle. The proof appears to prove too much. It appears to show not merely that no infinite power in a finite magnitude could perform any operation, but more generally that no infinite power whatsoever could, hence that no infinite power whatsoever can exist. Such, of course, is not the conclusion Aristotle was aiming at. He wished to affirm, on the contrary, that an infinite power does exist, to wit, the infinite power maintaining the heavens in motion, and that such a power can have its source solely in an incorporeal being. To salvage Aristotle's proof that a finite magnitude cannot contain infinite power, some sort of distinction would have to be drawn. The inconceivability of finite and infinite powers' performing the same amount of work in the same time would have to be restricted in some way to powers in bodies, and more precisely, as Aristotle formulates his proof of the principle, to powers in finite bodies.[19] A power deriving from an incorporeal being could then be subject to different rules, so that it could, with no absurdity ensuing, be assumed infinite and yet able to mete out its activity at the same velocity as a finite power contained in a body. A distinction of the requisite sort, between powers in bodies and powers deriving from incorporeal beings, seems to be adumbrated by Simplicius, although not, as far as I could see, spelled out there;[20] and such a distinction was later worked out by Averroes.[21]

Perhaps because Aristotle's proof of the principle is problematical, another train of reasoning was offered by Alexander of Aphrodisias to show that a finite magnitude can contain only finite power. Alexander's reasoning is similar to that whereby Aristotle proved the previous premise, the principle that a finite power can produce motion for only a finite time.[22] And it relates specifically, as it should, to the nature of finite magnitudes. If, Alexander contends, a finite magnitude should be supposed to contain infinite power, any designated portion of that magnitude would have to contain a smaller, hence finite power. The power contained in the whole will be a multiple of that contained in the part. Since the whole magnitude is finite, since the power contained in the part is finite, and since the part has a definite ratio to the whole, the multiple representing the whole power will also be finite. The whole magnitude thus turns out to contain finite, not infinite power as originally supposed. A finite magnitude can consequently contain only finite power.[23] Alexander's reasoning reappears in Avicenna and certain of his medieval followers.[24]

In any event, problematical though Aristotle's proof of the present principle might be, his overall argument for the incorporeality of the first mover is straightforward. The object of the argument is to show that the first cause of the motion of the spheres is an incorporeal being. Two premises are presupposed: the eternity of motion and the impossibility of an infinite body. Two premises are proved: the principle that a finite power cannot produce eternal motion and the principle that infinite power cannot be present in a finite body. The infinite power required to maintain the spheres in eternal motion must, it follows, derive from an incorporeal being.

§2. *Proclus, Simplicius, and John Philoponus.*

Proclus. Aristotle's demonstration of the existence of God, ostensibly at least, seeks to establish a first incorporeal cause solely of the motion of the universe, not of the existence of the universe. For its existence, the universe would in Aristotle's system be self-sufficient, depending on no further cause outside itself. The Neo-Platonists subsequently did expound the conception of an incorporeal cause of the very existence of the universe. And Proclus was able to convert Aristotle's argument for the incorporeality of the first mover into a demonstration of the proposition that the corporeal universe must indeed depend on an incorporeal being for its very existence.

The contrast between a first cause of existence and a first cause of motion is employed by Proclus in the course of distinguishing Plato's position from the position of Aristotle and his followers. Plato, according to Proclus, had maintained that the entire universe must depend for its existence on an "efficient" cause, whereas Aristotle and his school failed to recognize a cause of the existence of the universe. Nevertheless, in Proclus' view, Aristotle and the Peripatetics would have approached the correct Platonic position had they only grasped the full significance of the argument for the incorporeality of the first mover. As we have seen, the principles that a finite power can operate for only a finite time and that a finite body can contain only finite power enabled Aristotle to infer that the power contained in the corporeal universe is insufficient to maintain eternal motion; and inasmuch as the heavens do move eternally, the cause of their motion must be an incorporeal being distinct from the body of the universe.[25] The same principles Proclus now postulates, also apply to existence: not only eternal motion but eternal existence as well requires infinite power in order to be sustained. Since the body of the universe is finite, it can contain only finite power. And yet it exists eternally. The corporeal universe must consequently depend for its existence, and not merely for its motion, on an incorporeal cause distinct from itself.[26] Proclus thus extracts from Aristotle the nerve of a proof for an incorporeal cause of the existence of the corporeal, although not of the incorporeal, universe.[27]

Simplicius. Simplicius—following as he says, a book by his teacher Ammonius, who, it happens, had at one time been a student of Proclus—states the issue in a similar fashion but with one addition. Simplicius too writes that according to such Peripatetics as Alexander of Aphrodisias, Aristotle established a "final and motive cause of the heavens, not an efficient cause [of their existence]."[28] Simplicius further contends that the principle that a body can contain only finite power is "clearly" not limited to "motive power." It applies as well to the power "constituting the being" of a corporeal object, and "therefore [the heavens] . . . must receive even their eternal corporeal being from an incorporeal [cause]."[29] Such was the account given by Proclus. But Simplicius had undertaken a general harmonization of Aristotle with Plato. Accordingly, he goes beyond Proclus and contends that it was not Aristotle but only his students who failed to see the implications of the argument for the incorporeality of the first mover. Aristotle himself "was in agreement with his master [Plato] in holding God to be . . . an efficient cause of the [existence of the] entire universe and the heavens," and Aristotle intended his argument for incorporeality to establish that thesis.[30] To support his reading of Aristotle, Simplicius has recourse to a subtle, though unconvincing, exegesis of the Aristotelian text.[31]

Philoponus. John Philoponus, a contemporary of Simplicius, hereupon gave a new turn to Aristotle's argument for the incorporeality of the first mover. Philoponus, who was a Christian, was led by religious considerations to refute the philosophic arguments for the eternity of the world and to draw up his own positive counterarguments for creation. He wrote one work, still extant, in which he refuted a set of arguments for eternity formulated by Proclus[32] and another work, no longer extant, in which he refuted the arguments for eternity found in the various writings of Aristotle.[33] In connection with his refutation of Aristotle and also, perhaps, independently thereof, Philoponus formulated positive counterarguments, wherein the philosophical principles of Aristotle himself are employed to reach the anti-Aristotelian conclusion that the world was created.[34] None other than Simplicius, as it happens, is our sole source of Philoponus' refutation of Aristotle, as well as of Philoponus' counterarguments for creation.

In the passages that interest us here, Philoponus undertook to develop Aristotle's principle that "no finite body possesses infinite power" into a proof of creation. Such is Simplicius' report.[35] In fact, Philoponus was reading Aristotle with the aid of Proclus' insight. He was in effect readapting Proclus' earlier adaptation of the Aristotelian argument for the incorporeality of the first mover. Proclus had contended that the corporeal universe cannot contain the infinite power required to sustain it in eternal existence; and therefore, the corporeal universe must depend for its very existence on an incorporeal being distinct from it. Philoponus too contends that the corporeal universe cannot contain the infinite power required to sustain it in eternal existence. The conclusion he will draw, however, is that the corporeal universe cannot exist eternally; it must have been created.

From Aristotle, according to Simplicius' report, Philoponus adduced the proposition that since "the body of the heavens and universe is finite, it contains [only] finite power." "What contains finite power," Philoponus continues, "is destructible."[36] That is to say, since the power contained in the corporeal universe is finite, the corporeal universe, considered in itself, is incapable of existing eternally and consequently is liable to destruction. But if the universe has the "*logos* (nature or ground) of destruction," then that *logos* must "sometime come to actuality" and the universe must someday actually be destroyed;[37] for over infinite time, every possibility is eventually realized.[38] Such is the extent of the preserved report, and it leaves us short of an explicit proof of creation. Undoubtedly, Philoponus also adduced or presupposed the well-known Aristotelian rule that "whatever is destructible must be generated,"[39] a rule which in its turn, again ultimately rests on the more general rule that every possibility is realized over an infinite time.[40] If the universe is destructible, if the universe has the possibility of not existing, then this possibility must have been realized at some point in infinite past time, just as it must be realized at some point in infinite future time. Just as a destructible universe must eventually become nonexistent in the future, so too must it once have been nonexistent in the past. Philoponus' reasoning, then, may be summarized as follows: The Aristotelian principle that a finite body contains only finite power shows the universe to be destructible; over an infinite time every possibility is realized; the corporeal universe cannot therefore exist forever in the future and also cannot have existed forever in the past. It must have had a beginning.

As was observed earlier, Aristotle's proof of the principle that a finite body can contain only finite power has a problematical side.[41] Philoponus, perhaps for that reason, was not satisfied merely to cite the principle from Aristotle. He offered a set of additional considerations to support it, thereby providing a firmer foundation for his proof of creation.

(a) He reasons "first" that "the heavens are [composed] of matter and form; what is [composed] of matter requires the matter for its existence; what requires something is not self-sufficient; what is not self-sufficient is not infinitely powerful."[42] From all this he concludes that "the heavens, considering their own nature, are not infinitely powerful and hence are destructible."[43] It remains for us to add that what is destructible must be generated, and, consequently, the heavens and the rest of the corporeal universe cannot have existed for all eternity but must have been generated.

(b) The heavens, Philoponus again contends, are "composed . . . of substratum . . . and form," the latter being "solar or lunar" form and the forms of the other heavenly bodies. Even should someone question the distinction of matter and form in the heavens, he will still have to acknowledge the presence in the heavens of "extension in three directions," and that too is a mode of composition. Whatever has the "*logos* (nature or ground) of composition" has the "*logos* of dissolution" and the "*logos* of destruction." And what has the "*logos* of destruction is not infinitely powerful." The heavens are therefore not infinitely powerful.[44]

The present inference, to the effect that the heavens are not infinitely powerful since they are destructible, is puzzling; for twice already we have found Philoponus proceeding in the opposite direction and reasoning from the finite power of the heavens to their destructibility. If, as appears here, Philoponus contemplated deriving the creation of the heavens and of the world as a whole from their finite power—contending, for example, that what has finite power contains the possibility of not existing—he had no need previously to introduce the destructibility of the heavens. If, by contrast, he thought he could derive the creation of the heavens solely from their destructibility, he has no need now to introduce the proposition that the heavens have finite power. Philoponus may have intended something more than Simplicius' report reveals. Perhaps his intention was simply to stress that destructibility and finite power are mutually implicative.

(c) Philoponus further adduces the empirical observation that a minimum quantity of matter is always required for the presence of any natural form; and when the quantity of matter is reduced beyond a certain critical point, the form disappears.[45] When, for example, we rub a drop of water on the tip of our finger, the matter soon becomes so attenuated that it can no longer retain the form of water. The matter then loses its form and the water disappears.[46] Now, Philoponus continues, all bodies are divisible. Even the body of the heavens, although it may not undergo actual division, is in principle (τῷ ἰδίῳ λόγῳ) divisible. The body of the heavens must then, like the rest of the corporeal universe, be such that if reduced below a certain minimum magnitude it would be unable to retain its form. But whatever can lose its form is destructible and consequently not infinitely powerful. The heavens and the rest of the universe thus cannot possess infinite power.[47]

(d) Philoponus finally contends that the heavens cannot contain infinite power since their several parts cannot. One reason why the parts of the heavens cannot contain infinite power is this: "what has infinite power is self-sufficient," whereas the parts of the heavens are not self-sufficient, inasmuch as "they depend for their existence upon one another and upon the totality [of the heavens]."[48] Now the power contained in any totality is the sum of the powers of the parts. If the whole is finite and if the power contained in each of the parts is finite, then the power contained in the whole must also be finite. The heavens, and the universe as a whole, are thus seen to contain only finite power.[49]

An alternative reason why the parts of the heavens cannot have infinite power is given by Philoponus and runs as follows: Since a whole is greater than any of its parts, the power contained in any part is clearly less than the power of the whole. But if the power contained in the part is less than, and exceeded by the power contained in the whole, it is finite; for nothing exceeded by something else is infinite.[50] The total power contained in the heavens and in the rest of the universe is, again, equal to the sum of the powers contained in their parts; and if these powers are finite, the total power also is. The power contained in the corporeal universe is thus once again seen to be finite. The argumentation here is virtually identical with that met earlier in Alexander.[51]

To summarize Philoponus' proof for creation: the Aristotelian principle that a finite body can contain only finite power shows that the corporeal universe is incapable of sustaining itself in existence over an infinite time. The corporeal universe, considered in itself, therefore has the possibility of being destroyed. But every possibility is realized over infinite time. The corporeal universe will consequently eventually be destroyed. Whatever is destructible must also be generated, the explanation again being that over an infinite time the possibility of nonexistence must be realized. The universe consequently must also have had a beginning. At certain points Philoponus apparently derived the generation of the universe from its finite power rather than from its destructibility, but his reasoning there very likely was similar. He very likely reasoned that what does not possess the infinite power required to sustain it in existence forever, has the possibility of not existing; and that possibility must be realized in both infinite past time and infinite future time.

As far as Simplicius' report goes, Philoponus' intention was not to establish creation *ex nihilo*. In each instance Philoponus contends that the heavens and the rest of the corporeal universe cannot maintain themselves in their present form over infinite time. He does not contend that even the underlying matter of the universe cannot maintain itself in existence over infinite time, although he might have done so.[52]

§3. *Averroes*. The proof of Philoponus' just discussed was considered by Averroes to be the strongest argument for creation,[53] its strength lying in the fact that it rested on genuine Aristotelian principles. As Averroes poses the issue, Aristotle himself had established in *Physics* VIII that a finite body can contain only finite power,[54] and in *De Caelo* II he had explicitly stated that the heavens possess only finite power since they are bodies.[55] These statements would seem, as Philoponus contended, to imply that the heavens can move and exist for only a finite time, not for all eternity. And yet Aristotle had demonstrated the eternity of the heavens and of the universe as a whole. A dilemma thus presented itself to Averroes. On the one hand, Aristotle had established that finite bodies, including the heavens, contain no more than finite power, and that would imply creation. On the other hand, Aristotle had demonstrated the eternity of the universe.

Averroes resolves the dilemma by distinguishing two senses of *finite power*, of which both apply to sublunar bodies but just one to celestial bodies. Finiteness of power, he writes, may be understood as finiteness in "intensity," which in the instance of motion means the capability to produce or undergo only a finite "velocity." It also may be understood as finiteness in "continuity" or "time."[56] Now every body that performs any operation whatsoever must do so at a finite velocity; for the nature of bodies is such they cannot act "instantaneously."[57] Because, then, of the very nature of bodies, irrespective of whether they are sublunar or celestial, their power of producing as well as of undergoing motion must be finite in respect to *intensity*. Aristotle's statement in *De Caelo* II regarding the finite power of the celestial spheres is interpreted by Averroes as affirming, in accordance with the present sense of finiteness, that the power to produce and undergo motion is, even in the case of the spheres, finite in intensity.[58]

Finiteness of power in the other sense, in the sense of *continuity* and *time*, is due, according to Averroes, not to the very nature of bodies but to the nature of a certain type of body. And only sublunar bodies are such that their power must be finite in respect to *continuity* and *time*. Averroes explains: Sublunar bodies are compounds of matter and form. The matter and form are fused and are dependent upon one another for their existence. The matter is brought to actuality only through the form, and the latter is a material form, capable of existing only in matter. The power through which a sublunar body continues to exist and move has its source in the form, and since the form must be present in the matter, the power too is present "within" the matter. It is divisible, just as matter is divisible, and for that reason, finite—finite not only in respect to its intensity, but also in respect to its continuity. Averroes discovers all of this in the argumentation of *Physics* VIII, 10; Aristotle's reasoning there for the principle that a finite body contains only finite power is understood by Averroes as turning on the presence of power within a material substratum.[59] Finiteness of power, then, in the second sense, that is in respect to continuity, follows from the nature of sublunar bodies, from their being compounds of matter and form.

The nature of celestial bodies, Averroes continues, is different from that of sublunar bodies. The substratum and the form of the spheres do not exist together in a compound. Each exists independently of, although in conjunction with, the other. The form of the spheres is not a material form present within a material substratum; and the substratum is not in a state of potentiality requiring a form to render it actual. The substratum accordingly does not exist through a power that is distinct from it, yet contained within it, and hence finite in respect to continuity. The substratum of the spheres does not exist through a power at all; and consequently the argument that a finite body can contain only finite power, and finite power can give rise only to finite existence, does not apply. In Averroes' most frequent formulation,[60] the substratum of the spheres exists "through itself," through its own simple nature, which contains "no contrary" able to bring about the destruction of the substratum. It thus has no possibility of not existing, and its continued existence is in no way subject to limitation. As for the motion of the sphere, that is indeed produced by a power, a power issuing from the immaterial form associated with the substratum. But since the form in question is immaterial, the power producing the motion of the substratum is not present "within" the finite substratum. Consequently, the power moving the sphere is not finite; and the ability to move continually through time is for the spheres—as it is not for sublunar bodies—unlimited.[61]

The difficulties occasioned by Aristotle's statements concerning the finiteness of power in a body are thus solved by Averroes in the following fashion: The statement in *De Caelo* II to the effect that the heavens contain only finite power refers to finiteness in intensity. It means that the heavens, like all other bodies, cannot possess a power infinite in intensity, which would produce motion of infinite velocity. By contrast, Aristotle's proof in *Physics* VIII, 10, of the principle that bodies contain only finite power, refers to finiteness in *continuity*; and the proof applies exclusively to sublunar bodies. It establishes that no body consisting in a compound of matter and form can contain a power infinite in continuity. The spheres, which do exist and move for an infinite time, are to be construed as a different type of body. On Averroes' interpretation, Philoponus' argument for creation from the finiteness of power in the sphere loses its *point d'appui* in the text of Aristotle, inasmuch as Aristotle is no longer understood to characterize the power of the spheres as finite in the significant sense of *continuity*.

The principle that a finite body cannot contain infinite power enabled Aristotle to conclude that the movement of the heavens must depend on an incorporeal first mover beyond the heavens.[62] Now that Averroes has given his own interpretation of the principle, he is led to recast Aristotle's argument for the incorporeality of the first mover. According to Averroes, the reason that the power moving the sphere must have an incorporeal source is not to be formulated as the principle that the power of bodies is unqualifiedly finite. It rather is to be formulated as the principle that a certain type of body, consisting in a true compound of matter and form, cannot possess power infinite in respect to continuity. The first formulation, which Averroes rejects, would imply that the celestial sphere consists in a compound of matter and material form and, considered as a whole, contains only a finite power of continued movement and existence. The sphere would thus have the possibility of both moving and of not moving, both existing and not existing; and since every possibility must eventually be realized, the spheres, it would follow, cannot exist or move forever. The second formulation, which has the benefit of Averroes' exegesis, leads to another result: Since bodies compounded of matter and form cannot possess power infinite in respect to continuity, and since the heavens do move for an infinite time, the heavens cannot be such a body. The heavens must instead be construed as a body of a completely different type, consisting in the association of a simple matter-like substratum in motion and an independently existing immaterial form moving the substratum. The matter-like substratum exists eternally by virtue of itself; and the form is a source of infinite power whereby the substratum is kept in eternal motion. Inasmuch as the form of the first sphere serves as the eternal mover of the entire universe,[63] Aristotle's proof, with Averroes' nuance, still arrives at an incorporeal first mover. But by denying that the substratum of the sphere contains a form within itself, and by construing the sole source of power for the sphere as an incorporeal form that is independent of—although associated with—the substratum of the sphere, Averroes is satisfied that he has avoided attributing to the sphere any power that is finite in respect to *continuity*. He thereby can retain Aristotle's argument for the incorporeality of the first cause, while deflecting Philoponus' proof for creation from the finite power of the sphere.[64]

§4. *Ḥasdai Crescas*. Crescas' design was to show that neither the existence, the unity, nor the incorporeality of a first cause—the three elements in a complete demonstration of the existence of God[65]—can be established through the Aristotelian proof from motion.[66] In connection with the incorporeality of the first cause, Crescas undertakes to refute the argument wherein Aristotle had traced eternal motion back to an incorporeal mover on the grounds that corporeal objects contain only finite power.[67]

The argument, as will be recalled, had four premises and ran thus: The universe and its motion are eternal; a finite power is incapable of producing eternal motion; a finite body can contain only finite power; and no infinite body exists. The conclusion drawn was that the motion of the universe must be due not to a power contained within the body of the universe but to an incorporeal being distinct from the corporeal universe.[68] Two of the four premises had been treated by Aristotle as presuppositions not requiring further proof in the course of the argument itself; these are the eternity of motion and the impossibility of the existence of an infinite body. Crescas rejects the first of the two, and he rejects the grounds adduced by Aristotle in support of the other. Rejecting the doctrine of eternity, Crescas explains, obviates the need to posit an infinite power as the source of the motion of the spheres. And rejecting the grounds for the proposition that no infinite body can exist, permits infinite power—if such should be assumed necessary for eternal motion—to be located in an infinite body.[69] Crescas' analysis of these two presupposed premises extends to considerable length and is not germane to our present subject.[70]

Here we are interested in the two premises remaining in the argument, namely the principle that a finite body can contain only finite power, and the principle that finite power cannot produce eternal motion. Crescas contends that Aristotle's attempt to prove the former of those two remaining principles fails; and, further, even granting the principle that a finite body can contain only finite power, that principle, when properly understood, cannot combine with the other premise to give the hoped for conclusion.

Aristotle's proof of the principle that a finite body cannot contain infinite power was, briefly, as follows: It is inconceivable that a physical operation should occur instantaneously; this is taken for granted and not even stated. If, now, a finite body should be supposed to contain infinite power, no time span and no velocity could be assigned for its operation. For whatever time span or velocity might be proposed, a finite power could be discovered which would perform the same operation at the same velocity; and for a finite power to operate as fast as an infinite power is impossible. Since the operation of an infinite power contained within a finite body cannot be assigned a velocity, no such power exists.[71]

The proof of the principle assumes that the time required for any operation is inversely proportional to the power applied. In response, Crescas revives an old, alternative hypothesis.[72] According to Crescas' hypothesis, each given object undergoing motion over a given distance requires a certain fixed minimum time (*zeman shorshi*) for its motion, a time that is irreducible no matter how large the moving force might be. The total time required to move a given object will not then be inversely proportional to the power applied. Only the increment over the minimum time will be inversely proportional to the power. The increment will of course decrease as the power increases but will never disappear as long as the power is finite. "The infinite [power] would accordingly require no time beyond the irreducible minimum in order to produce motion, whereas every finite [power] will require some increment over the minimum." On the present hypothesis, a time span and a velocity can be assigned for the operation of an infinite power contained within a finite body without the absurdity of a finite power's performing the same operation at the same velocity: The infinite power, and it alone, would complete its operation within the irreducible minimum time.[73]

But Aristotle's proof of the principle that a finite body cannot contain infinite power turned on the impossibility of assigning a velocity for the operation of the infinite power. By showing that a velocity can be assigned such a power, with no absurdity ensuing, Crescas renders Aristotle's proof of the principle invalid.[74] And without the principle, Aristotle's argument for incorporeality cannot reach its conclusion. The infinite power required for eternal motion no longer has to be traced to an incorporeal being; it may instead be located in the finite body of the universe.[75]

Crescas makes a further point regarding the principle that a finite body cannot contain infinite power: Even had Aristotle successfully proved the principle, his argument for the incorporeality of the first mover would still be invalid. For "the term *infinite* clearly may be used in two senses, both with respect to intensity and also with respect to time [or continuity]." Aristotle's principle—if his proof of it should be accepted—affirms merely that a finite body cannot contain power "infinite in respect to intensity." But a power finite in intensity might nevertheless be infinite in respect to continuity, hence sufficient to sustain the eternal motion of the heavens.[76] The principle that a finite body contains only finite power does not, therefore, permit the conclusion that the first cause of eternal motion is an incorporeal being.[77]

The same may be put in another way by stating that Aristotle was guilty of equivocation. Aristotle's principle affirms that a finite body cannot contain power infinite in respect to intensity.[78] The remaining of the four premises in Aristotle's argument for incorporeality[79] is the principle that finite power cannot produce eternal motion; all that this can mean, and all Aristotle established in proving the principle, is that power finite specifically in respect to continuity cannot produce eternal motion. In effect, then, Aristotle's argument for incorporeality reasons that the power of a finite body must be finite in respect to *intensity*; power finite in respect to *continuity* cannot produce eternal motion; therefore the power of a finite body cannot produce eternal motion. The conclusion, Crescas objects, is improper because it rests on an equivocation in the term *finite power*.

To summarize Crescas' critique of the Aristotelian argument for the incorporeality of the first mover: the argument is invalid in the first instance because three of its premises are unfounded. The two premises presupposed in the argument are rejected by Crescas on grounds not examined in the present paper. And the proof of the principle that a finite body cannot contain infinite power is refuted by him with the aid of the hypothesis that every object undergoing motion requires an irreducible minimum time. Furthermore, even conceding all the premises, the key principle that a finite body can contain only finite power, refers to finiteness in respect to intensity alone. The Aristotelian argument for incorporeality consequently again turns out to be invalid. For whereas a power finite in respect to continuity would undoubtedly not be able to produce eternal motion, a power finite in respect to intensity might very well do so. The body of the celestial sphere might contain a power finite in respect to intensity, yet infinite in respect to continuity, and such a power would suffice to move the sphere for all eternity.

Crescas' distinction between power finite in intensity and power finite in continuity deserves additional comment. The distinction certainly comes from Averroes, but Crescas applies it differently. Averroes, as will be recalled, construed the power both of bodies in the sublunar region and of bodies in the celestial region as finite in respect to intensity, finiteness in this respect being due to the nature of all corporeal entities. And he construed the power of bodies in the sublunar region alone as finite in respect to continuity. The celestial spheres, in contrast to sublunar bodies, do not, so Averroes explained, consist in a fusion of matter and form. The spheres consist, instead, in a material substratum and an incorporeal form existing independently of one another. The power maintaining the motion of the material substratum of the spheres is present not in the substratum but in the incorporeal form. For that reason it is indivisible, hence inexhaustible and infinite in respect to continuity.[80] Crescas for his part repeats neither Averroes' differentiation between the power of sublunar, and of celestial bodies, nor Averroes' justification for construing the power moving the spheres as infinite in respect to continuity. On the contrary, Crescas' contention is that the power moving the spheres may be located precisely within a finite body—within the body of the spheres—and still be construed as infinite in continuity. Crescas, that is to say, has adopted Averroes' distinction between two senses of infinite power, while ignoring Averroes' justification for applying the distinction.

Crescas' rationale is easily discovered. In proving the principle that a finite body contains only finite power, Aristotle had not put forth the considerations Averroes was to put forth; he had not reasoned that the power located in sublunar bodies is divisible, and consequently finite in respect to continuity.[81] Aristotle's reasoning was rather that no time span—in other words no velocity—could be assigned for an operation of an infinite power contained in a finite body without the absurdity of a finite power's performing the same operation at the same velocity.[82] The finiteness and infinity to which Aristotle's reasoning refers is clearly finiteness and infinity in respect to intensity, not in respect to continuity; for in Aristotelian physics the intensity, not the continuity, of a power determines velocity.[83] Very probably Aristotle regarded the intensity and the continuity of a power as translatable into one another, so that a finite power in one respect would be finite in the other as well. Still, he did not state, let alone defend, the proposition that the intensity and the continuity of a power are translatable into one another.

Crescas has thus adopted Averroes' distinction between two senses of finite power without applying the distinction as Averroes did. Instead he inspected Aristotle's proof of the principle that a finite body can contain only finite power. The proof, he discovered, can at most establish that the power contained in a finite body must be finite in respect to intensity. And that is not what the argument for incorporeality requires.

§5. *Summary and Conclusion.* Central to Aristotle's argument for the incorporeality of the first mover is the principle that a finite body cannot contain infinite power. The principle enabled Aristotle to conclude that the eternal motion of the spheres cannot be due to a power located within the body of the spheres but must be ascribed to an incorporeal being. Proclus extended the application of the principle. He reasoned that the very existence of the spheres cannot be due to a power within the body of the spheres but must also be ascribed to an incorporeal being. Philoponus then saw that Proclus' reasoning could be converted into a proof of creation. If the spheres and the rest of the physical universe cannot exist eternally through a power contained within themselves, so Philoponus contended, then the physical universe, considered in itself, has the possibility of not existing. That possibility must have been realized at some point in infinite past time; at some point in the past, the universe must therefore have been nonexistent.

Averroes, in his reply to Philoponus, defended the Aristotelian position on eternity with the aid of a distinction between power finite in respect to intensity and power finite in respect to continuity. This distinction was thereupon taken up by Crescas and employed as one of several grounds for refuting the original Aristotelian argument for the incorporeality of the first mover. The principle that a finite body can contain no more than finite power was central to the argument. And, Crescas observed, Aristotle's proof of the principle establishes only that a finite body must contain power finite in respect to intensity, not power finite in respect to continuity. When the principle is thus restricted, it no longer allows the tracing of the motion of the spheres to an incorporeal mover.

The historical development examined here reveals two ironic turns. Aristotle's argument for the incorporeality of the first mover suggested to Philoponus an anti-Aristotelian argument for creation. Then the distinction whereby Averroes answered Philoponus in defense of Aristotle provided Crescas with grounds for refuting the original Aristotelian argument for the incorporeality of the first mover.

A further irony is to be observed. In refuting the Aristotelian argument for the incorporeality of the first mover, Crescas intended merely to exhibit the inadequacy of Aristotelian method. For his own part, he wholeheartedly embraced the incorporeality of God, insisting only that the doctrine rests on Scripture and rabbinic tradition rather than on philosophic argumentation.[84] But it is, to say the least, questionable whether Scripture and rabbinic tradition do propound the incorporeality of God. The incorporeality of God is properly to be viewed as a Greek philosophical doctrine that infiltrated medieval Jewish philosophy and theology so successfully that a conservative thinker like Crescas no longer suspected foreign provenance.[85] Crescas' object was to defend Jewish theology against foreign influence by showing that the doctrine of divine incorporeality cannot be supported through the methods of Greek philosophy. He did not realize that acceptance of the doctrine was one of the prime instances of the influence of Greek philosophy on Jewish theology.

NOTES

1. Cf., for example, Maimonides, *Guide*, I, 71.

2. On the unity of the first mover in Aristotle, see *Physics* VIII, 6, 259a, 8–20; *Metaphysics* XII, 8,1074a, 35–38. On the question of Aristotle's final position, see the bibliography in D. Frede, "Theophrasts Kritik," *Phronesis*, XVI (1971), p. 65; also, H. Wolfson, "Immovable Movers in Aristotle and Averroes," *Harvard Studies in Classical Philology*, LXIII (1958), pp. 233–53.

3. Cf. *Physics* VII, 2. This is, of course, the contrary of Newton's first law of motion.

4. *Physics* VIII, 5–9.

5. *Physics* VIII, 10, 267b, 19–26.

6. *Physics* III, 5; VIII, 1.

7. W. D. Ross argues that there are not two, but only one premise here. See his commentary on the *Physics* (Oxford, 1936), p. 721.

8. *Middle Commentary on Physics* (Oxford, Bodleian Library, MS. Huntington 79) VIII, vi, 1.

9. Other interpretations are given by Simplicius, *Commentary on the Physics*, in *Commentaria in Aristotelem Graeca*, X, (Berlin, 1895), p. 1322; and by F. Cornford, *Classical Quarterly*, XXVI (1932), pp. 53–54, and also, Loeb edition of the *Physics* (Cambridge, 1934), vol. ii, pp. 406–410. Both interpretations are unacceptable since they have Aristotle proving the wrong proposition. They have Aristotle proving that no finite force requires an infinite time to move a finite object over a given distance; but Aristotle has undertaken to prove that no finite force can produce motion for an infinite time. See Ross's commentary on the *Physics*, p. 722, and T. Heath, *Mathematics in Aristotle* (Oxford, 1949), pp. 151–152.

10. The argument would have been simpler if Aristotle took a fraction of A and all of B. That is the way Averroes paraphrases the argument in the passage referred to above, p. 76, n. 8.

11. *Physics* VIII, 10, 266a, 18 (a particularly problematic passage).

12. If the velocity is unchanged, the time over which a power can operate will be exactly proportional to the power, and inversely proportional to the object moved. (I could not find this explicitly stated by Aristotle, but it is presupposed throughout his theory of motion; cf. for example, *Physics* VII, 2; VIII, 10, 266b, 28ff.) If, on the other hand, the time over which a power operates is fixed, the velocity will be exactly proportional to the power, and inversely proportional to the object moved; see *Physics* VII, 5. It remains now obscure when and why an increased power will express itself in increased time of operation or in increased velocity. As will appear in §4 of the present article, Crescas accused Aristotle of confusing the intensity of a power with its continuity.

13. If the velocity is fixed, the multiple will be $\frac{A}{D} \times \frac{E}{B} \times F$.

14. *Physics* VIII, 10, 266a, 10–23.

15. Cf. *Physics* VII, 5, 249b, 27–28.

16. *Physics* VII, 5. See above, p. 76, n. 12.

17. The point will be reached when the finite power is multiplied by $\frac{Z + Y}{Z}$.

18. *Physics* VIII, 10, 266a, 24—266b, 6.

19. For Aristotle has undertaken to prove that an infinite power cannot be contained in a *finite* magnitude.

20. Simplicius, *Commentary on Physics*, pp. 1321, 1339.

21. Averroes, *Long Commentary on Physics*, VIII, comm. 79; in *Aristotelis Opera cum Averrois Commentariis*, vol. IV (Venice, 1562), p. 427D.

22. That is to say, Alexander's reasoning turns on the proportionality of power to magnitude.

23. Alexander, cited by Simplicius, *Commentary on Physics*, p. 1326.

24. Avicenna, *Najāt* (Cairo, 1938), p. 130; Ghazali, *Maqāṣid al-Falāsifa* (Cairo, n.d.), p. 209; Ibn Ṭufayl, *Ḥayy b. Yaqẓān*, ed. and transl. L. Gauthier (Beirut, 1936), Arabic text, p. 84; French translation, p. 64; Shem Ṭob's commentary to Maimonides *Guide*, II, introd., prop. 12.

25. *Supra*, p. 75.

26. Proclus, *Commentary on Timaeus*, ed. E. Diehl, I (Leipzig, 1903), pp. 266, 295.

27. The principle that a finite body cannot contain infinite power says nothing about incorporeal beings.

28. Simplicius, *Commentary on Physics*, pp. 1362–1363.

29. *Ibid.*, p. 1363.

30. *Ibid.*, p. 1360.

31. *Ibid.*, pp. 1361–1362.

32. *De Aeternitate Mundi Contra Proclum*, ed. H. Rabe (Leipzig, 1909).

33. See H. Davidson, "John Philoponus as a Source of Medieval Islamic and Jewish Proofs of Creation," *Journal of the American Oriental Society*, 89 (1969), pp. 357–60.

34. *Ibid.*, pp. 358–59.

35. Simplicius, *Commentary on Physics*, p. 1327, lines 12–14.

36. *Ibid.*, lines 14–16.

37. *Ibid.*, p. 1333, lines 28–30. The report on p. 1331, lines 24–25, has to be harmonized with this.

38. Cf. Aristotle, *De Caelo* I, 12, 281b, 21–22; *Metaphysics* IX, 8, 1050b, 8–15.

39. *De Caelo* I, 12, 282b, 2.

40. Cf. *De Caelo* I, 12, 281b, 26—282a, 1.

41. *Supra*, p. 77.

42. The train of reasoning can be traced to Proclus, *Elements of Theology*, ed. E. Dodds (Oxford, 1963), §127.

43. Simplicius, *Commentary on Physics*, p. 1329, lines 19–24.

44. *Ibid.*, p. 1331.

45. Regarding this theory, cf. Aristotle, *Physics* I, 4, and A. Maier, *Die Vorläufer Galileis im 14. Jahrhundert* (Rome, 1949), pp. 179–80.

46. Simplicius, *Commentary on Physics*, p. 1332.

47. *Ibid.*, p. 1333.

48. *Ibid.*, p. 1335, lines 24–30.

49. *Ibid.*, p. 1336, lines 1–5.

50. *Ibid.*, p. 1335, lines 31–35.

51. *Supra*, p. 77.

52. He might have reasoned that any portion of matter contains only finite power, hence cannot exist eternally.

53. *Long Commentary on Physics*, VIII, comm. 79; *Middle Commentary on Metaphysics*, XIII (Casanatense Heb. MS. no. 3083) p. 140 (141)b; *De Substantia Orbis*, V.

54. Cf. *supra*, p. 76–77.

55. *De Caelo* II, 12, 293a, 10–11.

56. For other instances of the distinction, cf. S. Pines, "A Tenth Century Philosophical Correspondence," *Proceedings of the American Academy for Jewish Research*, XXIV (1955), p. 115; H. Wolfson, *Crescas' Critique of Aristotle* (Cambridge, Mass., 1929), pp. 612–613.

57. Cf. *supra*, p. 76, n. 15.

58. *Middle Commentary on De Caelo*, I (Vatican Hebrew MS. Urb. no. 40), pp. 49a–50a, and the other references *infra*, n. 61.

59. Averroes may have been thinking of Alexander's reasoning, *supra*, p. 77.

60. Another formulation is given by him in *De Substantia Orbis*, II.

61. *Long Commentary on Physics*, VIII, comm. 79; *Middle Commentary on De Caelo*, I (Urb. MS. no. 40), pp. 49b, 50b–51b; *Long Commentary on De Caelo* (Venice, 1562), II, comm. 71; *Middle Commentary on Methaphysics*, XIII (Casanatense MS. no. 3083) pp. 140 (141)b–141a; *De Substantia Orbis*, III.

62. *Supra*, p. 78.

63. The outer sphere, in the astronomical system known to Averroes, produces the daily movement of the heavens, to which the peculiar movement of each sphere is added.

64. *Middle Commentary on De Caelo*, I (Urb. MS. no. 40), pp. 51b–52b; *Middle*

Commentary on Metaphysics, XII (Casanatense MS. no. 3083), f. 141 (142)a; *Long Commentary on Metaphysics*, XII, comm. 41.

65. Cf. *supra*, p. 75, n. 1; Crescas, *ᵓOr ha-Shem* (Vienna, 1859), I, introduction; English translation: Wolfson, *Crescas*, p. 133.

66. *ᵓOr ha-Shem*, I, introduction; I, ii, 15.

67. Besides refuting Aristotle's argument, Crescas contends most generally that the argument can simply be dismissed by construing celestial motion as "natural" to the spheres, just as the rectilinear motion of the four elements towards their proper places is "natural to the elements." See *ᵓOr ha-Shem,* I, ii, 8; 15; Wolfson, *Crescas,* pp. 273, 535ff., 614.

68. *Supra,* p. 78, n. 25.

69. *ᵓOr ha-Shem,* I, ii, 15.

70. *ᵓOr ha-Shem,* I, ii, 1; Wolfson, *Crescas,* pp. 137–217; *ᵓOr ha-Shem,* III, i.

71. *Supra*, pp. 76f.

72. The hypothesis was apparently originated by Philoponus; see M. Clagett, *The Science of Mechanics in the Middle Ages* (Madison, 1959), pp. 433–34. It was espoused in the middle ages by Ibn Bajja, and came to Crescas through Averroes' critique of that philosopher; see Wolfson, *Crescas*, pp. 403–08.

73. *ᵓOr ha-Shem*, I, ii, 8; Wolfson, *Crescas*, p. 271.

74. Crescas, *ibid.*, also proposes a variation of the hypothesis just outlined. A finite power, he writes, may in some instances be conceded to require no increment above the minimum time. In other words, a finite power may be conceded to move some objects in the same minimum time and at the same velocity that an infinite power requires. Yet the finite power will not necessarily be as efficacious. For even acknowledging such instances, we may conceive of a larger object to be moved, an object of such magnitude that the finite power would no longer move it in the minimum time but would now require an increment. The infinite power would, by contrast, never require more than the minimum time to move its objects, no matter how great the latter might be. According to Crescas, this variation of the hypothesis again invalidates Aristotle's proof of the principle that a finite body cannot contain infinite power. The force of Aristotle's contention, as Crescas understands it, lies in the absurdity of a finite power's being fully as efficacious as an infinite power. On the present variation of the hypothesis, a velocity can again be assigned for the operation of the infinite power without that absurdity's ensuing. For although the finite power would in some instances operate as fast as the infinite power, it would not do so in all instances and hence would be less efficacious.

75. *ᵓOr ha-Shem*, I, ii, 8; 15.

76. *ᵓOr ha-Shem*, I, ii, 8; Wolfson, *Crescas*, p. 273.

77. *ᵓOr ha-Shem*, I, ii, 15.

78. See, further, immediately below.

79. See *supra*, p. 75.

80. See *supra*, pp. 83f.

81. Alexander had reasoned in this fashion; *supra*, p. 77.

82. *Supra*, p. 76.

83. The continuation of a power would merely sustain velocity. Cf. *supra*, p. 76, n. 12.

84. *ᵓOr ha-Shem*, I, iii, 6.

85. Judah Ha-Levi, whose outlook was similar to Crescas', had also unhesitatingly embraced the doctrine of incorporeality; cf. *Cuzari*, II, 1–2.

The Doctrine of the Mean in Aristotle and Maimonides: A Comparative Study

M. FOX

The scholarly literature dealing with the interpretation of the philosophy of Maimonides moves between two poles. There are those who insist that Maimonides was in all significant respects a true and faithful disciple of Aristotle, or of the Aristotelianism which he knew through the Arabic sources. At the other extreme there are those who argue that the Aristotelianism of Maimonides is only a surface appearance but that he is, in fact, not an Aristotelian at all in his actual philosophical and theological doctrines.

This difference of opinion is especially sharp in the discussions of Maimonides' ethics, particularly with respect to his doctrine of the mean. Many writers take the position that the Aristotelianism of Maimonides' doctrine of the mean is so obvious that it does not even require discussion or evidence. Writing about Shem Ṭov ben Joseph Palqera, Malter says that "the Aristotelian ethics of the golden mean found in Palquera a disciple scarcely less devoted than his master Maimonides."[1] Gorfinkle, in his edition of the *Eight Chapters of Maimonides* speaks of the chapter "in which the Aristotelian doctrine of the *Mean* . . . is applied to Jewish ethics." He adds that "Although Maimonides follows Aristotle in defining virtue as a state intermediate between two extremes, . . . he still remains on Jewish ground as there are biblical and talmudical passages expressing such a thought."[2] Harry S. Lewis speaks of "the famous attempt of Maimonides to equate Jewish ethics with the Aristotelian doctrine of the mean." He goes on to affirm that "Maimonides derived his doctrine of the Mean from Greek sources, but it was quite congenial to the native hebraic spirit."[3] Rosin, in his basic study of the ethics of Maimonides, sees the doctrine of the mean as essentially Aristotelian in origin and character, despite some of Maimonides' deviations from the Aristotelian pattern. "Handlungen, sagt M. in Übereinstimmung mit Aristoteles, sind gut, wenn sie angemessen sind indem sie in der Mitte zwischen zwei Extremen liegen . . ."[4] Even those writers, like Rosin, who seek also in rabbinic literature for the sources of Maimonides' doctrine of the mean, take the position that these are supports which legitimate the Jewishness of the doctrine, but they do not claim that they are the actual sources from which Maimonides derived his position.

Opposed to these writers are those who deny that Maimonides' ethics are Aristotelian in any significant respect. A typical voice from the traditional camp, that of Rabbi Yaʿakov Mosheh Harlap, affirms with the greatest passion that no non-Jewish source can make any contribution to Jewish doctrine. After having discussed at great length various aspects of Maimonides' doctrine of the mean, Harlap is concerned to protect his readers from the mistake of supposing that this doctrine has any non-Jewish origin. If it appears to be similar to the teachings of Aristotle, this is no more than an appearance, and we must understand it properly. Such a doctrine can enter Jewish teaching from the outside only if it is first thoroughly Judaized, only if, like the convert, it is reborn and acquires a new, specifically Jewish, nature. "Whatever is taught by others cannot be presented as Jewish teaching unless it has first undergone conversion (*geruth*). Just as it is possible to convert souls, so is it possible to convert doctrines."[5] Harlap claims that this is what happened with Maimonides' doctrine of the mean. It may appear to be similar to Aristotle's doctrine, but after having been converted, it is a totally new and uniquely Jewish creation.

Coming to the materials from a different background and perspective, Hermann Cohen also argues fiercely against the Aristotelianism of Maimonides' ethics. Cohen holds that for purposes of tactical effectiveness Maimonides chose to give the appearance that he was agreeing with Aristotle since otherwise he would open himself to endless attack.[6] In fact, says Cohen, his doctrine is not Aristotelian at all. It is independent of Aristotle and not in agreement with him. If we were forced to affirm that Maimonides derived his ethics from Aristotle and was in agreement with him, "so wäre die Ethik Maimunis nicht nur keine philosophische Ethik mit einem selbstständigen und einheitlichen Prinzip, sondern auch als religiöse Ethik wäre sie widerspruchsvoll in sich; auch als ein Anhang zum Moreh als eine Art von Homilie, würde sie sich nicht anpassen; und selbst als ein Glied in seinem System der Theologie wäre sie unorganisch und exoterisch."[7] Cohen goes on later to delineate carefully and in detail the ways in which Maimonides' doctrine of the mean differs from that of Aristotle.[8]

Our aim in the present paper is to present a fresh investigation of the question. We shall focus our attention specifically on the doctrine of the mean as it is treated by Maimonides in his various works. It is one of our main contentions, however, that no responsible treatment can be offered of the relationships between Maimonides' and Aristotle's doctrines unless we are first clear about what it was that Aristotle actually taught. In our view, conventional representations of the doctrine of the mean in Aristotle fail to grasp the fundamental philosophical ground on which that doctrine rests. We shall, therefore, attempt in this study to set forth a careful interpretation of the Aristotelian position as the basis on which to make the comparison. Our interpretation of Maimonides will then be directed to the double task of understanding him in his own right and of seeing him in comparison to Aristotle.

I

Although the doctrine of the mean is among the most familiar and popular of Aristotle's teachings, it has been widely misunderstood and misrepresented. This failure to grasp the essential elements in Aristotle's doctrine is evident in the standard criticisms to which it has been subjected, as a brief survey will reveal.

Some writers have argued that the mean is no more than Aristotle's adaptation of the long established Greek folk rule, *mēden agan*, nothing to excess. They deny that it is or is based on a philosophical principle but see instead in Aristotle's doctrine nothing but a restatement of the common sense of the ages. A related, but a more pointed and more serious charge, is that the Aristotelian mean is, in the last analysis, nothing more than an affirmation of the proprieties of social convention. Typical of this approach is the statement of Gomperz in which he charges that Aristotle's ethics rest on the view that "Current opinion, when purged or corroborated by the settlement of real or apparent contradictions, is identified with absolute truth so far as concerns questions relating to the conduct of life."[9] Hans Kelsen has expressed the criticism even more vigorously in charging that "Although the ethics of the *mesotēs* doctrine pretends to establish in an authoritative way the moral value, it leaves the solution of its very problem to another authority. . . . It is the authority of the positive morality and positive law—it is the established social order. By presupposing in its *mesotēs* formula the established social order, the ethics of Aristotle justifies the positive morality and the positive law. . . . In this justification of the established social order lies the true function of the tautology which a critical analysis of the *mesotēs* formula reveals."[10] This criticism gains support from Aristotle's admission that all judgment concerning the application of the doctrine of the mean to particular cases depends completely on the insight of the man of practical wisdom; but, the critics argue, that man has no standard to which he can appeal other than the accepted conventional attitudes and values of his society.

The absence of any objective standard appears to be underscored by the fact that the Aristotelian mean is not determined arithmetically and is thus not the same for all men. It is, rather, a rule which must be applied only with full cognizance of the particular circumstances and the characteristic peculiarities of the individual in question. It is *pros hēmas*, determined in relation to the individual moral agent. This compounds the difficulty, since it would now appear that in the doctrine of the mean we have merely social convention adjusted to individual differences—a far cry indeed, so it seems, from a serious philosophical principle.

Perhaps the most contemptuous of all the criticisms was made by Kant, when he wrote:

> The proposition that one should never do too much or do too little says nothing for it is tautological. What is it to do too much? Answer: More than is good. What is it to do too little? Answer: To do less than is good. What is meant by I ought (to do something or forbear doing something)? Answer: It is not good (contrary to duty) to do more or less than is good. If this is the wisdom we are to seek by returning to the ancients (Aristotle) as being precisely those who were nearer to the source of wisdom, then we have chosen badly to turn to their oracle. . . . For to be much too virtuous, i.e., to adhere too closely to one's duty, would be like making a circle much too round or a straight line much too straight.[11]

If these charges are justified, they are grave indeed, since they challenge what Aristotle himself claims explicitly. In his definition of moral virtue he includes the proviso that the choice in accordance with the mean is *hōrismenē logō*, determined by a *logos*, that is by a rule or principle of reason.[12] It is clear that in his view what he is offering is a principle of reason, not just the arbitrariness of convention.

Yet the charges against him do not appear to be totally without foundation. Does he not himself inform us early in the *Nicomachaean Ethics* that the actions which are the subject matter of ethical reflection and choice "admit of much variety and fluctuation of opinion, so that they may be thought to exist only by convention (*nomos*), and not by nature (*physis*)?"[13] Does he not, near the end of the same book, express the view that, "what all think to be good, that, we assert, is good?"[14] Moreover, he regularly invokes common opinion about moral matters and the good life as if it were clearly worthy of being considered authoritative. In all this he seems to be admitting the very criticisms that are thought by many to be fatal to his position. What can we make out of the doctrine of the mean in the light of these critical attacks? In what follows I seek to answer that question by offering an interpretation of the doctrine of the mean which takes account of and copes with the difficulties that have been raised.

To grasp the doctrine correctly it is extremely useful to take full account of the medical model which Aristotle uses repeatedly, the recurring comparison that he draws between the process of attaining moral virtue and the work of the physician who brings his patients to a state of physical health. At almost every important point in his exposition of the way to moral virtue, Aristotle employs the practice of medicine as a paradigm which illuminates and clarifies his basic points. The subject has been treated carefully and convincingly by Jaeger, who concludes on the basis of his study of the *Nicomachaean Ethics* that the appeal to the medical pattern is so deep and pervasive that "in the light of it Aristotle tries to justify almost every step he takes in his ethical philosophy."[15]

The essential elements in that medical model are easy to discern. The practice of medicine has as its end the attainment of health for the patient. That end is given in and defined by the physical nature of the human patient. There is nothing arbitrary about what physical health is in general. It is the proper excellence of the body which is gained when the body is brought to its highest degree of natural perfection. Insofar as it concerns the treatment of bodies in general, the practice of medicine involves a knowledge of principles that are fixed because they are the principles of a type of being which exists by nature and has its own nature. Yet, these general principles alone are insufficient for the practice of medicine. The physician's art requires him to deal with particular cases, to make practical decisions, and to offer practical guidance for each individual case. His prescriptions can be approximately correct only, at best, never absolutely precise. Even when he knows what foods are healthful, he is ineffective unless he is able to prescribe for each particular case a diet which is adjusted to the special needs and specific circumstances of the patient before him. It is here that his special art comes into play, for anyone who is modestly educated might be expected to know general rules of health, but only the skilled physician can be relied upon to diagnose individual cases and to apply the general rules to the particular needs of each patient. In his medical practice the doctor must use the rule of the mean as Aristotle repeatedly notes. As the work *On Ancient Medicine* (sometimes attributed to Hippocrates) expresses it, in the treatment of human ailments "it is necessary to aim at some measure."[16]

If we follow Aristotle in thinking about ethics on the model of medical practice, then we can solve most of the problems which his critics raise concerning the doctrine of the mean. Like medicine, ethics rests on a natural base. If there were not this base in the nature of man, a nature which is fixed, there could be no talk of ethics as a practical *science*. It would be at best a fairly sophisticated art, but even as an art it could not proceed successfully if it had no fixed points of reference. Like medicine, ethics is concerned not with knowledge for its own sake but for the sake of action. This is what makes it *practical*. This practical element is carried out primarily with respect to particular men in particular circumstances, as is the case with medicine. To achieve this, the moral teacher (the *phronimos*) cannot rely only on his knowledge of the nature of man in general. He must have the capacity to deal with particular cases, and that is done finally through *aisthēsis*, a kind of immediate perception of what is required in order to apply the general rules to the particular individual before him. In this situation he cannot expect to achieve demonstrative certainty. At best he can offer the kind of informed judgment which emerges from the total combination of his theoretical understanding, his practical experience, and the special intelligence of the practically wise man, which is a capacity to deliberate well about such moral issues. Finally, his judgment will depend, in some degree, on *nomos*, on the accepted patterns and attitudes of the society in which the individual lives. The doctor prescribes for his patient taking account both of his particular situation with respect to physical health and development and of his particular needs. Thus, when he prescribes for Milo, he must know not only that this patient has such and such specific complaints and that his physical condition is so and so, but also that he is a wrestler and wants to be restored to the state of health which is requisite for a successful wrestler. Similarly, the moral guide must know not only what the particular moral situation of his client is, but also what his place is in society and what the norms are of the society in which he must function. The norm of courage for a soldier at the battle front is likely to be different from that which is proper for a professional baby sitter.

Where the critics have gone wrong is in supposing that all Aristotle offers us is the social framework and the individual peculiarities of the moral agent. They have utterly ignored the crucial fact that his moral philosophy and his doctrine of the mean, in particular, are rooted in principles of nature. They have failed to see that Aristotle carefully introduces qualifications whenever he speaks of the conventional aspects of morality. The earliest passage in the *Nicomachaean Ethics* which deals with this topic is a case in point. Aristotle stresses that we must not expect in ethics the same kind of precision and the same degree of certainty that we expect in the demonstrative sciences. The subject matter of ethics and politics are *ta kala kai ta dikaia*, the fine or noble and the just, "but these conceptions involve much difference of opinion and uncertainty, so that they may be thought to exist only by convention and not by nature."[17] The stress is on the fact that "they may be *thought*" to be nothing more than convention, but those who think this are mistaken. For while they are, of course, in some measure dependent on convention, that is not the whole of the content or foundation of moral virtue. Let us, then, examine that natural foundation of moral virtue which has escaped the attention of Aristotle's critics.

Moral virtue, like any virtue (*aretē*), is concerned with the proper excellence of its subject, in this case man, and this is determined by his proper end as it is given in nature. This is standard doctrine for Aristotle, to be found consistently in those of his works which deal with the question in any way at all. The principle is stated in *Metaphysics* v, 1021b 21ff., where he says that virtue (*aretē*) is a *telos*, the perfection of a thing by achieving its proper end. "And excellence is a completion (*telos*); for each thing is complete and every substance is complete (*teleion*), when in respect of the form of its proper excellence it lacks no natural part of its excellence." Note that the *aretē*, the excellence of virtue, is natural, it is determined by the nature of the thing. The same point is made in *Physics* vii, 246a 10–247a 20. "Excellence (*aretē*, i.e., virtue) is a kind of perfection (*teleiōsis*), since a thing is said to be perfect (*teleion*) when it has acquired its proper excellence, for it is then in most complete conformity to its own nature. . . . Excellence and defect are in every case concerned with the influences whereby their possessor is, according to its natural constitution, liable to be modified. . . . The same is true of the moral habits (*tēs psychēs hexeōn*, the states of the soul), for they, too, consist in conditions determined by certain relations, and the virtues are perfections of nature, the vices departures from it." These passages speak for themselves and merely reinforce what is stated in the *N.E.* on the same subject. The stress is on the nature of a thing, since for all things that exist by nature there can be no knowledge of their virtue except in terms of their nature.

That ethics is closely tied to nature is eminently clear, since man's virtue is determined by his nature, and this, in turn, requires a knowledge of psychology, the principles of the human soul. Aristotle sets out some of these principles in *N.E.* as a first step in defining human virtue. Lest there be any doubt that psychology is a subject matter that is natural, one need only turn to the opening of *De Anima*, where Aristotle says explicitly that the knowledge of the soul admittedly contributes greatly to the advance of truth in general and, above all, to our understanding of nature. The particular problems of ethics arise because of the complex nature of man. To the extent that man is truly rational, it is easy for Aristotle to specify what his proper end is. Here the nature of rationality itself determines the end, namely, the use of reason for the knowledge and contemplation of that which is highest and most perfect. The most virtuous life for man would be one in which he would engage most completely in that supreme contemplative activity which is philosophical wisdom.

However, man is not a purely and perfectly rational being. He is a rational animal, an animal that has the capacity for being rational. This animal aspect of his nature must be given its due but must not be allowed to control him, otherwise man will be only animal and not rational at all. The problem then is to determine what it would be like for man's animal nature to be subject, to the fullest possible degree, to the rule of reason, and to discover the practical means by which this end might be achieved. True virtue for man will be the fullest realization of his *telos*, his proper end as a rational being, a life in which not only his contemplative powers, but also his actions and passions are directed and controlled by reason. But what exactly does it mean to say that action and passion are controlled by reason? Aristotle's answer is that formally such a state can be defined as that in which action and passion are directed in accordance with the rule of the mean, and this is what we call moral virtue.

The crucial question is, then, why should we consider the rule of the mean to be a rule of reason? Aristotle's answer is that the mean is the way in which nature and art normally achieve their goals of proper excellence, the realization of the proper end of each thing which exists by nature or is the product of art. To the extent that moral virtue has its foundations in nature, reason requires that it accord with nature. Otherwise it will not be virtue, i.e., the proper excellence of man (in this case). If the end is to fulfill our proper nature as men, then virtue will consist in the fullest completion of that nature. If the nature of all things is to find their proper completion, *qua* natural, in the mean or the middle way, then this is also the way which reason requires us to choose in order to achieve moral virtue.

For it is a rule, according to Aristotle, that a rational being acts always with an end in view, and that he must choose the means which are requisite to that end.[18]

The principle that all things that exist by nature tend toward the mean, or middle way, in order to attain their proper perfection is common to various areas of Aristotle's thought and is by no means peculiar to his ethics only. The simplest version of this point may be found in his discussions of the anatomical structure of animals. Over and over again he stresses that the middle is the best. "Eyes may be large or small, or medium-sized (*mesoi*). The medium-sized are the best."[19] "Ears may be smooth, or hairy, or intermediate; the last are the best for hearing. . . . They may stand well out, or not stand out at all, or intermediately. The last are a sign of the finest disposition."[20] "Now the tongue can be broad, or narrow, or intermediate; and the last is the best and gives the clearest perception."[21] The principle that nature always seeks the middle way is set forth in more complex cases as well. For example, Aristotle holds that all motions of sensation begin and end in the heart. This is as it should properly be he says, since reason requires that, if possible, there should be only a single source, "and the best of places in accordance with nature is the middle." (*euphuestatos de tōn topōn ho mesos*).[22] In this passage we see clearly how Aristotle ties together the way of reason with the normal way of nature, which tends always toward the mean.

He further expands and generalizes this doctrine when he propounds the view that nature always aims at the mean, always strives to overcome excess of every sort by counterbalancing it in such way that the mean is achieved. That is why the brain, which is cold, is continuous with the spinal marrow, which is hot. "Nature is always contriving to set next to anything that is excessive a reinforcement of the opposite substance, so that the one may level out (*anisazē*) the excess of the other."[23] Moreover, whatever comes into existence does so by way of the mean. In the process of generation opposites meet and are balanced, and in that way form new creatures by way of the mean. "It is thus, then, that in the first place the 'elements' are transformed; and that out of the 'elements' there come to be flesh and bones and the like—the hot becoming cold and the cold becoming hot when they have been brought to the mean (*pros to meson*). . . . Similarly, it is *qua* reduced to a mean condition that the dry and the moist produce flesh and bone and the remaining compounds."[24] This principle that nature always follows the middle way is explicitly viewed by Aristotle as a rule of reason. This might be expected in view of the relationship between *logos* and *ratio*, between reason and proportion or due measure. As Aristotle puts it, "Everything needs an opposite to counterbalance it so that it may hit at the mark of proper measure and the mean (*tou metriou kai tou mesou*). The mean, and not any of the extremes alone, has being (*ousia*) and reason (*logos*)."[25]

Since "art imitates nature," it is to be expected that the product of art will also conform with the rule of the mean. For art is defined by Aristotle as "concerned with making involving a true course of reasoning."[26] Consequently, it too must follow the rule of reason that all things achieve their proper realization when they have been formed in accordance with the right measure, that is, with the mean which stands at the proper point between excess and defect. The point is expressed charmingly by Aristotle in his discussion of the proper speed for narration in ceremonial oratory. "Nowadays it is said, absurdly enough, that the narration should be rapid. Remember what the man said to the baker who asked whether he was to make the cake hard or soft: 'What, can't you make it *right*?' Just so here. We are not to make long narrations, just as we are not to make long introductions or long arguments. Here, again, rightness does not consist either in rapidity or in conciseness, but in the happy mean."[27]

The principle is carried through consistently by Aristotle when he deals with what may be thought of as the highest products of art working in conjunction with nature, namely, virtuous men and good states. In his discussions of the various aspects of life in the city-state and of the constitution of such a state, he always considers the mean or the middle way to be the model which is most desirable. The structure and order of the state, which is, like the order of the life of the individual man, the combined work of art and nature, must be in accordance with the mean if it is to achieve its own proper perfection. Men would do well as individuals also to seek no more than moderate amounts of all desirable things. For since the mean is always best, "it is manifest that the middle amount of all of the good things of fortune is the best amount to possess. For this degree of wealth is the readiest to obey reason."[28]

We have now established clearly that Aristotle's doctrine of the mean is not peculiar to moral virtue. In his system of thought it is an over-arching principle that encompasses the operations of the world of nature and the world of art. One cannot properly understand his treatment of moral virtue without seeing the mean in this wider context. Given this context, we can now turn to a specific examination of the way in which the doctrine of the mean is conceived by Aristotle as the pattern in accordance with which moral virtue is brought about. As a first step, we must note that he is quite explicit about the fact that there is a natural foundation for moral virtue. We indicated this earlier in a general way when we noted that our knowledge of the proper end of man depends on the science of psychology. In introducing the discussion of moral virtue, Aristotle makes the point that it exists neither fully by nature nor fully contrary to nature but is a combination of nature and art. Virtue arises in us through habit as its efficient cause. This process of deliberate habituation, however, could not occur at all unless there were a natural medium in which it took place and to which it was adapted. "The virtues therefore are engendered in us neither by nature nor yet in violation of nature; nature gives us the capacity to receive them, and this capacity is brought to its proper completion by habit."[29]

In a later discussion in *N.E.* he expands his treatment of this topic. There he makes it clear that while all virtue is the product of a certain deliberate effort on man's part, nevertheless it has its origin and base in what is natural. For there is that which Aristotle calls natural virtue, and it is this natural virtue which is the initial source of all true moral virtue. Natural virtue is our inborn capacity for those states of character which become, when properly developed, the moral virtues. Without this inborn capacity we could not become morally virtuous. For it is that aspect alone of our nature which makes moral virtue possible. Just as cleverness is the natural base which, when developed properly, becomes practical wisdom, so, says Aristotle, is "natural virtue (*hē physikē aretē*) to true virtue (or virtue in the strict sense). It is generally agreed that the various kinds of character are present in man by nature, for we are just, and capable of temperance, and brave, or have the other virtues from the very moment of our birth. Nevertheless, we expect to find that true goodness is something different, and that the virtues in the true sense come to belong to us in another way."[30] There are, then, two types of virtue in us; natural virtue, which has a potentiality for development in a way which is appropriate to man, and true moral virtue, which is the actualization of that natural potentiality. The model for the development of that potentiality is the model which is followed by all natures seeking their own perfection, and that is, of course, the doctrine of the mean. Aristotle's insistence that moral virtue follows the rule of the mean is, thus, in no sense arbitrary. It is, following his own principles, a rule of reason. If the proper perfection of the moral part of our nature is specified by nature in accordance with its general rule that the middle is best and most complete, then reason requires that in seeking moral virtue we must employ as our guide and criterion that pattern which is the only appropriate instrument for attaining the end which we desire.

If this is so evident, how shall we understand all those criticisms which accuse Aristotle of offering us nothing more than a formalized approval of social convention? The answer, I believe, lies in the fact that the critics have ignored the natural foundations of moral virtue, despite the trouble Aristotle took to make his position clear. They have been further misled by two other considerations to which we must now turn our attention. The first is that there is, of course, a social-conventional aspect to moral virtue, as we already noted earlier. About this there can be no issue or difference of opinion. What is at issue is the question of how we should understand this dimension of moral virtue, what its nature is, what function it serves, and what weight we should put on it. Man is not an animal who ever achieves his goal of self-development in isolation or solitude. For Aristotle, man is a being whose development, whose excellence, whose true humanity, in fact, depends on society. By himself, detached from all social relations and structures, he is barely, if at all human. Man is by nature a political animal, a creature whose nature requires the association of community with other men of which the *polis* is a model. For this reason Aristotle considers the *polis*, or more widely the forms of human society, to exist by nature. Whatever the elements of human art that account for and cause the diversity of societies, society itself is natural, and only in society can man fulfill himself. Only in society, his natural setting, can he be humanly virtuous.

Aristotle is fully aware that, despite the natural basis on which human society rests, societies differ in their customs and value patterns. To the extent that there is such difference, moral virtue will always reflect the particular characteristics of the community in which a given man lives. Yet, this is not to say that moral virtue is only *nomos*, only convention and nothing more. Moral virtue is, rather, the result of the development of natural virtue toward its proper end in the context of a particular social setting. In fact, the existence of society is dependent on man's natural capacity for moral virtue. "For it is the special property of man, in distinction from the other animals, that he alone has the perception of good and bad and right and wrong and the other moral qualities, and it is partnership (community) in these things that makes a household and a city-state."[31] Without the natural capacity for morality there could be no human community at all. Given this capacity, there emerges a community in which moral virtue is possible for men. That virtue exhibits both the fixed elements which its nature determines and the varying elements which derive from the diverse characteristics of particular societies. When the man of practical wisdom deals with moral issues, he is guided by his knowledge of the natural character of moral virtue tempered by his knowledge of the standards of the society in which he lives. He is a model precisely because he has developed to its ideal level this combination of the natural and the socially conditioned. To understand Aristotle's conception of moral virtue one must give full weight both to the natural and the social elements. Those who say that morality is merely *nomos* are mistaken. Those who say that it is merely *physis* are equally mistaken.

The second factor which has led Aristotle's critics astray is the inescapable particularity of each moral situation. If the rule of the mean is to be applied to an individual with full cognizance of his own particular level of development and with equal cognizance of the circumstances in which he finds himself and of the special characteristics of his society, how can there be anything more than just individual and private judgments? To the extent to which this is a sound criticism it would appear to apply with equal force to any moral philosophy. The problem of moving from general moral principles to particular moral judgments is hardly peculiar to Aristotle. One need only think, as a classic example, of the agonies which interpreters of Kant suffer when they try to give an account of how he moves from the categorical imperative to particular moral judgments. The troubles that Kant's famous four examples have caused the commentators are sufficient to make the case.

Yet it seems that Aristotle is not without resources for dealing even with this aggravating problem. To begin with, let us note that he is fully aware of the problem. In the first chapter of *Book* vi of the *N.E.* he explicitly expresses his dissatisfaction with a moral rule which is general, unless one can show how to go about making it applicable to particular cases. In many places in the *N.E.* he repeats the same point, that judgments about conduct always deal with particular cases, and that it is especially difficult to apply the rule of the mean in an exact way to particular cases. Having laid down some procedural cautions for anyone who is trying to hit the mark of the mean, Aristotle recognizes that even if they are heeded, they offer no guarantee of success. One should aim at the mean, guided by these rules, "But no doubt it is a difficult thing to do, and especially in particular cases; for instance, it is not easy to define in what manner and with what people and on what sort of grounds and how long one ought to be angry."[32]

The difficulty of applying the rule to particular cases results in judgments which can never claim to be absolute or exact. They are, at best, approximations, guidelines for conduct leading to proper self-development, never demonstrated certainties. The lack of precision is compounded by the dependence on social circumstances as well as individual particularities. It is this that caused Aristotle to remark early in the *N.E.* that one should expect in ethics no more precision than the subject matter is capable of yielding. He stresses at several points that inquiry in this field can only be carried out successfully if one recognizes as a condition of the inquiry that he can expect conclusions which are far from certain or precise. "This must be agreed upon beforehand (i.e., before beginning to inquire into moral philosophy), that the whole account of matters of conduct must be given in outline and not precisely . . . matters concerned with conduct and questions of what is good for us have no fixity, any more than matters of health. The general account being of this nature, the account of particular cases is yet more lacking in exactness; for they do not fall under any art or set of rules, but the agents themselves must in each case consider what is appropriate to the occasion. . . ."[33] Nowhere does Aristotle claim that he is offering us a system which will result in precise and absolutely fixed and reliable moral judgments. In fact, he says exactly the contrary over and over again, so that it is difficult to understand why his critics think that they have discovered some secret dark failure in his treatment of these matters. Even general moral rules cannot be laid down, he believes, with precision, much less so judgments in particular cases.

Such judgments rest, according to him, with perception. The term used consistently is *aisthēsis*, which refers to a kind of immediate intuitive grasp of the particulars and a capacity to make a judgment concerning them. *Aisthēsis* is the only way in which we know particulars. It is one of the essential components of practical wisdom, which unlike scientific knowledge is concerned with particular cases. "Practical wisdom is concerned with the ultimate particular, which is the object not of scientific knowledge but of perception (*aisthēsis*)—not the perception of qualities peculiar to one sense but a perception akin to that by which we perceive that the particular figure before us is a triangle."[34] Here again Aristotle claims no certainty. On the contrary, he is fully aware of the fact that what he offers is both less than exact and less than certain. The development of the capacity of moral perception depends upon maturity and experience. There is no other source. Practical wisdom, though an intellectual virtue, is that part of the intellect that deals with opinion, not demonstrated knowledge. Its subject matter is not fixed but varies with individual and social circumstance. Yet it is capable of making judgments and offering guidance, precisely because it brings together the range of knowledge, experience, and perception out of which alone any reasonably sound moral judgment might emerge.

The problem which men face in their effort to attain moral virtue can now be readily formulated. Like all things that exist by nature, man has a fixed nature. This confers upon him certain fixed ends, the realization of which constitute his proper excellence. Unlike man, other things that exist by nature are without any independent power of choice and are moved by their internal principle of development in the direction of their proper ends only. It is outside forces or internal defects that prevent their attaining their end. The healthy acorn will become a full grown oak if nothing prevents it from the outside. Its nature, its internal principle of development, is fixed, and it can go only one way. Things are not nearly so simple for human beings. While they have a nature, they also have the capacity to choose their own actions. They can, by their choice, either advance or frustrate their development in accordance with their nature. If man had no fixed natural disposition toward moral virtue, such virtue would not be possible for him at all. If he had only a fixed natural disposition, moral virtue would be unnecessary; for he would achieve his end automatically. However, he is in the middle. He has a nature, but he must choose to bring it to its full actuality. He must develop his own character in accordance with his true nature, if he chooses to be a man in the full and proper meaning of the term. It is at this point that he must cope with the problem of knowing exactly what kind of action to choose. Nature specifies his end in a general way. It also specifies the criterion of virtuous character in a general way, namely, by the rule of the mean. However, this is insufficient as a guide to action in particular cases, and all action is particular. The components of the social framework, individual differences, and the special circumstances must all play a role in the decision. Here no precise rule can be specified. One can only appeal, within the context of a rule of reason determined by nature, to the perception and judgment of the man of practical wisdom.

Does it follow from all this that the doctrine of the mean is, as the critics claim, no more than an appeal to social convention, or that it is utterly useless as a guide to moral action, or that it is merely an empty tautology? I believe that we have shown otherwise. The doctrine of the mean is not a matter of social convention. It is a rational rule, which derives from nature and shows us the general way to actualize a deeply fixed principle of nature. It is not a fixed or precise rule, because it involves varying social circumstances and deals with a diversity of individuals, each of whom must be considered in the context of his special personal and social conditions. Even this is not arbitrary, however, since man is by nature a social animal, and action is by nature always particular.

Perhaps the matter can be made clear and the argument persuasive by returning to the medical model. The work of the physician, seeking the physical health of his patient, deals to a large extent with what is natural. No one wants to deny the natural aspect of the body and of bodily health. However, this is only part of the story. Health has to be achieved for each individual patient in the light of his special circumstances and conditions, and in the light of his particular constitution and its special possibilities. No diagnosis is foolproof. It can only claim to be probable, and it is never absolutely exact and absolutely certain. Similarly, no prescription is ever absolutely precise, nor is its anticipated effectiveness more than probable. All this is the case, just because medicine must take account of the particular. As Aristotle never tires of saying, a proper diet for Milo may be all wrong for the local chess champion. Despite its inexactness and uncertainty, we do not ordinarily condemn all medical practice as pointless. On the contrary, we see in it the very best we can achieve, considering the built-in limitations of the subject matter. Even if we doubt the soundness of a particular doctor's diagnosis, or if we fail to be helped by his prescriptions, we do not conclude that the practice of medicine is a fraud. We do know what good health is, and we do recognize that, with limitations, there are men of special knowledge and experience who can help us achieve that desirable goal. Similarly, Aristotle argues, we do know what a virtuous character is, for that is specified by our nature. Physicians of the soul may be harder to find than physicians of the body. It may also be more difficult for the former to lay out and justify their general principles and their rules of practice, to say nothing of their judgments in individual cases. It is our contention, nevertheless, that we have explained why Aristotle believes that this difficult task is not impossible and that his critics have misunderstood him.

II

As we reflect on the relationship of Maimonides' doctrine of the mean to Aristotle's, we are confronted by puzzles which demand resolution. Of all the areas concerning which Maimonides wrote, the ordering of human behavior should have presented him with the fewest problems. As an expositor of Jewish tradition and as a master of the law, he had a complete system of behavioral rules and norms ready-made for him in the *halakhah*. It would seem, then, that there should have been no need to seek beyond the *halakhah* itself for the principles and the specific patterns of virtue and the good life, all the more since Maimonides himself denied that there is any independent rational ground for morality. He rejected all claims that there is a natural moral law, holding rather that morality derives either from social convention or divine command. It is obvious that for Judaism the latter source only can be decisive.[35] Why, then, was it necessary for Maimonides to appeal to the doctrine of the mean at all? The elaborate and detailed principles and directions for the life of the Jew which he codified in his *Mishneh Torah* would seem to be sufficient to answer every need for guidance toward the virtuous life.

Furthermore, with respect to this subject matter in particular, an appeal to non-Jewish sources would seem to be singularly inappropriate. It might be argued plausibly that to the extent that his Jewish theology required principles of natural science or metaphysics as a foundation, these might appropriately have been drawn from non-Jewish sources, since the biblical and rabbinic literatures are relatively poor in these areas. This is surely not the case with regard to the area of human conduct. How strange, then, that in a treatise devoted to setting forth the principles and the end of the good life, Maimonides begins by telling us explicitly that he drew his materials from non-Jewish as well as Jewish sources. In his Foreword to *Shemonah Peraqim* he makes a special point of denying that the work contains any original ideas. All that is of consequence in the treatise has been gleaned, says Maimonides, "from the words of the wise occurring in the *Midrashim*, in the Talmud, and in other of their works, as well as from the words of the philosophers, ancient and recent, and also from the works of various authors." He immediately goes on to justify this procedure by invoking the principle that "one should accept the truth from whatever source it proceeds."[36]

The force of this open appeal to non-Jewish sources is even greater when we remember that these statements are contained in the introduction to a commentary on *ʾAvoth*, a treatise that takes great pains to establish its legitimacy (in its opening words) by associating itself with the tradition whose source is in the Torah which "Moses received at Sinai."[37] Our analysis of Maimonides' version of the doctrine of the mean will seek to resolve some of these puzzles. Our primary concern is to understand the doctrine precisely, to see it in relationship to the Aristotelian doctrine, and to determine how it fits into the Jewish tradition.

With respect to the general nature of ethical inquiry, Maimonides holds views which are similar to those of Aristotle. Like Aristotle, he makes clear at the very outset that he is concerned above all with the truly good life for man and that his interest in individual actions and states of character is primarily because they are instrumental to the realization of the ultimate good. In his foreword to *Shemonah Peraqim* he makes a point of explaining that the treatise on which he is commenting contains a rule of life which "leads to great perfection and true happiness." In fact, one who puts into practice the teachings of *ʾAvoth* can hope to be led even to prophecy. This ultimate human felicity comes to one who attains the knowledge of God "as far as it is possible for man to know Him" and the truly good life is that in which all of man's effort, thought and activity are directed toward the realization of that goal.[38] The same ideal is developed in *H. Deʿoth*, iii, and of course it constitutes a central theme which reaches its climax in the final chapters of the *Guide of the Perplexed.*

Maimonides also follows Aristotle in his view that the ultimate aim, the contemplative life, presupposes the achievement of moral virtue. Man is so constituted that he can only devote himself to the highest intellectual activity if he has first achieved that personal and social discipline which is included under the heading of moral virtue. The crucial question then emerges, namely, what specifically is the character and shape of the morally virtuous life. Here, too, in his initial approach Maimonides remains faithful to the Aristotelian pattern. His primary concern, like that of Aristotle, is with states of character, not with individual acts. Thus, in *Shemonah Peraqim* he introduces his discussion of the rule of the mean by distinguishing between good acts and good states of character. "Good deeds are such as are equibalanced, maintaining the mean between two equally bad extremes. . . . Virtues are psychic conditions and dispositions (*tekhunoth nafshiyyoth we-qinyanim)* which are midway between two reprehensible extremes. . . ."[39] The very title of the section of the *Mishneh Torah* which deals with the mean is *Deʿoth*, and it is beyond any question that the term is used to refer to states of character. This is obvious enough from the way the term is used in its context and is confirmed in a passage in which Maimonides explicitly distinguishes *deʿoth*, as states of character, from particular actions. In *H. Teshuvah*, vii, 3, Maimonides tells us that just as one must repent for those sins which involve a particular action, such as robbery or theft, so is one obligated "to search out his evil *deʿoth* and repent of them, i.e., from such states as anger, etc."

Aristotle had already defined virtue as a state of character, or, according to another translation, "a settled disposition of the mind" which observes the mean.[40] Maimonides follows him here, as he does with respect to his view that our actions follow from the fixed states of our character, so that what must concern us most is the development of the appropriate states of character, since that is the best assurance that our acts will also be virtuous. Finally, in what appears to be a thoroughly Aristotelian fashion, Maimonides also defines the good character as one which is determined by the mean and avoids the extremes. Given these general similarities, we must now ask just exactly what the main elements are of Maimonides' doctrine of the mean and how they compare with Aristotle's views as we set them forth above.

The most fundamental distinction of all is in the ground on which the mean rests. It is striking that both in *Shemonah Peraqim* and in the *Mishneh Torah* Maimonides introduces the rule of the mean without any discussion as to its origins or justification. He treats it rather as an established truth to which one need only refer but which does not require any evidence to support it. In both works he proceeds as if it were an established fact that good deeds and good states of character follow the mean between extremes. In the *Mishneh Torah* he opens the discussion with some empirical observations about the diversity of states of character that are to be found among men and then informs us that "the two extremes which are at the farthest distance from each other with respect to each state of character are not the good way . . . while the right way is the middle way."[41] Not only does he offer no defense of this claim, but he goes on to say that because it is the case that the mean is the right way, "therefore the early sages (*ḥakhamim ha-rishonim*) commanded that man should always make an estimate of his various states of character and direct them toward the middle way." If we accept the view of most commentators, that the reference is to the sages of Israel, a view which seems plausible enough in this context, then we have the remarkable situation that Maimonides appears to be telling us that the principle that the middle way is good is known as an independent truth and that because it is known to be true the Jewish religious authorities accepted it as their rule of conduct and character development. So far he would seem to be doing exactly what he says in his introduction to *Shemonah Peraqim*, namely, relying on established knowledge without regard to its source.

There is evidence to support the view that Maimonides was convinced that the rule of the mean was a well established basic principle of explanation in the sciences and in philosophy. In the *Guide of the Perplexed* he was explicit about this point. In thoroughly Aristotelian fashion, he strongly supports the view that the order of nature is such that all things achieve their proper excellence when they reach the mean which suffers from neither excess nor deficiency. The highest praise that he can pay to the divine creation of the world is that it has been formed in accordance with the mean, from which it follows that in the created world there can be no change in the fixed order of nature. "The thing that is changed, is changed because of a deficiency in it that should be made good or because of some excess that is not needed and should be got rid of. Now the works of the Deity are most perfect, and with regard to them there is no possibility of an excess or a deficiency. Accordingly, they are of necessity permanently established as they are, for there is no possibility of something calling for a change in them. . . . '*The Rock, his work is perfect*' . . . means that all his works . . . are most perfect, that no deficiency at all is commingled with them, that there is no superfluity in them and nothing that is not needed."[42]

Viewing the doctrine of the mean as a scientific principle, Maimonides treats it as fully established and needing no further evidence. He is explicit about the general rule that whatever is scientifically known, whatever is demonstrated, must command our assent. For such matters we do not need to look for confirmation in the official Jewish literature, nor should we be uneasy if on such matters the views of the sages of Israel are contradicted by our contemporary knowledge. Here the sages spoke not with the authority of the prophetic tradition but only as students of physics or metaphysics who were bound by the limits of their own knowledge and the general state of knowledge at their time.[43] It seems clear enough that this is one of the points that Maimonides had in mind when he informed his readers in the foreword to *Shemonah Peraqim* that he would seek the truth from whatever source it could be found. Even with respect to the standards and rules of virtuous behavior, good character, and the good life for the faithful Jew, we need certain general principles of explanation, a general theoretical framework, in order to give a philosophical account of the subject. We also need a sound psychology on which to base our understanding of human character and its development. Without these theoretical foundations, our account of moral virtue, even of specifically Jewish moral virtue, will be incomplete and will lack an essential dimension. Moreover, no practical guidance toward the achievement of good character and the performance of good acts is possible, unless we first have sound theoretical understanding of human nature and of the nature of the good in general. These are universal truths, in no way peculiar to the Jewish religious community, and for them we may, nay we must turn to the most reliable scientific authority that we can find. This is the point of Maimonides' elaborate announcement that he seeks guidance wherever he can find it.

So far we might say without hesitation that Maimonides has followed Aristotle or the Aristotelian tradition faithfully. However, when we move away from the general theoretical foundations to his specific way of understanding and applying the doctrine of the mean the differences emerge sharply and clearly. Perhaps the most significant single difference is that while Aristotle construes moral virtue as a case of art imitating nature, Maimonides has as his standard the imitation of God. The first of the eleven *miṣwoth* set forth in *H. Deʿoth* is *le-hiddamoth bi-derakhaw*, and it is to this commandment of *imitatio Dei* that the first five of the seven chapters of *H. Deʿoth* are devoted. The imitation of nature was for Aristotle nothing more than a general indication that the good life for man, like the pattern of all natural excellence, should be one of perfect measure. Nature does not itself give us specific norms or standards of behavior, nor does it tell us what a virtuous character is, apart from its general principle that the middle way is the best. Thus, given the imitation of nature as the only ideal, Aristotle has no choice but to fill out the specific details of the good life for man by appealing to the norms of society and to the judgment of the man of practical wisdom. Nature give us only the form, i.e., the mean but not the content. It does not, and cannot teach us what the rule of the mean is in concrete cases of human action or human character development.

In striking contrast, Maimonides works here fully inside the Jewish tradition. He readily adopts the outer form of the mean as his theoretical base and principle of explanation, but the specific contents of the good life are defined not by way of nature but by way of the imitation of God. Now, viewed as metaphysically ultimate, Maimonides' God is not truly knowable, except by way of negative attributes; however, Maimonides does permit us knowledge of God through the attributes of action. We can know Him indirectly through his works in the world, and in this way we can speak meaningfully of *imitatio Dei* as the human ideal. This is why Maimonides is so careful to formulate the commandment as *le-hiddamoth bi-derakhaw*, since strictly speaking we can imitate his ways only, but not his nature. The God who is represented as Creator, who continues in some manner to make his presence felt in history as well as in nature, is a being whom man can meaningfully hold before himself as an ideal to follow.

As in the case of Aristotle's prescription for the imitation of nature, the general rule is insufficient as a guide to man. It must be made specific and concrete. For Maimonides this is achieved simply enough. The commandments of the Torah are, in fact, according to his view, the specification of ideal behavior in accordance with the rule of the mean, and this is what is meant when we are told to imitate the ways of God. The structure of his argument is clear and unambiguous, though it has often been ignored or misunderstood. First he gives us the theoretical principle which is generally known and acknowledged. Good action and good states of character are those which follow the middle way. So far we are in accord with all men who follow the way of scientific knowledge. Next we face the question of what it means specifically to act in accordance with the mean, and here Maimonides answers, unlike Aristotle (for whom such an answer would have been meaningless), that we should imitate God. Finally, he faces the question of what divine behavior is like, so that we can have a concrete model for imitation; and he answers that it is the rule of the Torah that is the divine paradigm and therefore also the concretization of the middle way. Maimonides is absolutely consistent in his adherence to this principle that the rule of the Torah is in actual fact the rule of the mean, that is, whatever the Torah commands is the middle way. There is no external standard which measures the commandments in order to determine whether they accord with the mean. This is impossible, precisely because the only standard we have is that given by the commandments. In *Shemonah Peraqim* he writes that "The Law did not lay down its prohibitions, or enjoin its commandments, except for just this purpose, namely, that by its disciplinary effects we may persistently maintain the proper distance from either extreme."[44] He goes on to stress that since "*the Law of the Lord is perfect*", (*Ps.* 19:9) it is its injunctions and prohibitions alone that give us the proper standard. To impose upon ourselves ascetic practices or disciplines of self-denial that go beyond what the Torah commands is vice and not virtue.

The same principle is set forth in *H. De*ᶜ*oth*[45] and receives full expression in the *Guide*, where he argues that the Mosaic Law is absolutely perfect, the ideal and exact embodiment of true measure, the middle way in all regards. Thus, every law which deviates from it suffers from the fact that it moves away from the mean toward one of the extremes. "For when a thing is as perfect as it is possible to be within its species, it is impossible that within that species there should be found another thing that does not fall short of that perfection either because of excess or deficiency. . . . Things are similar with regard to this Law, as is clear from its equibalance. For it says: '*Just statutes and judgments*' (*Deut.* 4:8); now you know that the meaning of 'just' is equibalanced. For these are manners of worship in which there is no burden and excess . . . nor a deficiency. . . . When we shall speak in this treatise about the reasons accounting for the commandments, their equibalance and wisdom will be made clear to you insofar as this is necessary. For this reason it is said with reference to them: '*The Law of the Lord is perfect*'."[46] For the Aristotelian reliance on *nomos* as interpreted and applied by the *phronimos*, Maimonides has substituted the law of the Torah. The divine origin of this Law guarantees its perfection as a standard of behavior. All others fall short. Only the Torah "is called by us divine Law, whereas the other political regimens—such as the *nomoi* of the Greeks and the ravings of the Sabians and of others—are due, as I have explained several times, to the action of groups of rulers who were not prophets."[47] The Torah alone, according to Maimonides, can give us the true standard of the mean.

There is, however, more to be considered. We recall that the main interest in ethics is the development of virtuous states of character, not merely the performance of virtuous actions. The latter are derived from the former and are significant especially as outer evidences of a stable moral character. The passages we cited make the Torah the standard of the mean in action, but it is obvious that Maimonides must also provide for the Torah as the standard of the mean with respect to states of character. This is, in fact, precisely what he does in *H. De*ᶜ*oth*. The ideal of *imitatio Dei* is concerned primarily with states of character, and these are dispositions which are described as generally in accordance with the middle way. "We are commanded to follow these middle ways which are the paths that are good and right, as is written, '*And you shall walk in His ways.*' (*Deut.* 28:9). Thus have they taught with respect to this *miṣwah*: Just as He is called *ḥannun* (gracious), so shall you be *ḥannun*; just as He is called *raḥum* (merciful), so shall you be *raḥum*."[48]

In the case of states of character Maimonides does not simply make a rule that the Torah standard specifies the mean in every case, but rather that whatever standard the Torah sets is the standard that we are obligated to use as our norm, even in those cases where it clearly deviates from the mean toward one of the extremes. Thus, in the very discussion in which he takes the mean as the ideal Torah model of virtuous states of character, Maimonides proceeds to rule that "there are certain states of character with respect to which it is forbidden for a man to pursue the middle way."[49] Pride and anger are dispositions which should be avoided completely, as we have been specifically commanded. Aristotle also spoke of actions and passions for which the mean is an inappropriate rule. They are those, as he puts it, whose very names imply evil.[50] The problems which this passage has posed for the commentators are familiar, and this is not the place to review them. What is significant for our purposes is the fact that here again Maimonides has a different ground on which he rests his cases of deviation from the mean. Not the name itself, or some other self-evident ground, but the commandments of the Torah determine which are the cases in which we are required to abandon the mean. We know that there can be no proper moderation with respect to pride and anger, simply because we are so taught by various biblical verses and the explicit rulings of the rabbis.

With this background we can also appreciate the difference between the medical analogy which is used by Maimonides and that of Aristotle. On the surface both seem very similar, yet the foundations on which they rest differ very significantly. In his various ethical writings Maimonides, like Aristotle, recommends that those who are in need of moral guidance seek out physicians of the soul. Moral decay is viewed by him as a sickness of the soul, and those who treat it do so on the analogy of the therapy of the physicians of the sick body. So far all is similar to Aristotle. Yet here, too, we find very important differences that result from the basically distinct foundations on which the doctrine of the mean rests in each case.[51]

Both Aristotle and Maimonides require the physician of the soul to be one who knows how to take account of individual circumstances and to advise in accordance with those circumstances. Both require their physicians of the soul to have a sound understanding of human psychology, otherwise they will be incompetent to give guidance. Both agree on the practical rule that the morally sick soul is to be treated by being directed toward the extreme opposite of his present state; and both agree that the aim should be to arrive at a stable state of character determined by the mean. Both consider the true physician of the soul to be a wise man. For Aristotle, he is the *phronimos*, the man of practical wisdom, and for Maimonides he is the *ḥakham*, the model Jewish scholar-teacher-man of piety. He advises that the proper way for sick souls to be healed is to "go to the *ḥakhamim*, who are the healers of souls, and they will cure the illness by teaching them to achieve the proper states of character, thereby bringing them back to the virtuous way."[52] Despite all these similarities, the differences are of crucial importance. While Aristotle's *phronimos* has only shifting conventional standards to guide him, Maimonides' *ḥakham* has the fixed discipline of the Torah as his standard. Of course, he must take account of the special condition of each individual and must tailor his particular advice to fit the special needs and circumstances in which he finds himself. Nevertheless, he is bound not by a conventional *nomos* but by a fixed law, by commandments, and by principles which are held to be divine and thus unchanging. The divine-human ideal is set, and to be virtuous a man must direct himself to that ideal. Maimonides is fully aware of the variations and diversity of human temperament and of social conditions. Nevertheless, his physician of the soul carries out his function by adhering rigorously to the fixed Law. He only varies his advice for each individual in order to move that individual closer to the one common ideal. Aristotle's mean, even when viewed as a principle of nature, always reflects something of the attitudes and values of the particular society in which it is invoked as the principle of moral virtue. Maimonides' mean permits no such variation, because it is controlled by the ideal of *imitatio Dei*, and this, in turn, is concretized and fixed in the commandments and principles of the Torah.

It is revealing that this point, which is evident enough in the earlier works, comes out with striking force and clarity in the *Guide*. Here, where he deals with the law as a primary force for the ordering of society, Maimonides shows openly his deviation from the Aristotelian norm. He first argues that men differ from each other in their temperaments and moral habits far more than any other living creatures, yet man, being by nature a political animal, must live in society. He then goes on: "Now as the nature of the human species requires that there be those differences among the individuals belonging to it and as in addition society is a necessity for this nature, it is by no means possible that this society should be perfected except—and this is necessarily so—through a ruler who gauges the actions of the individuals, perfecting that which is deficient and reducing that which is excessive, and who prescribes actions and moral habits that all of them must always practice in the same way, so that the natural diversity is hidden through the multiple points of conventional accord and so that the community becomes well ordered."[53] With this background he subsequently goes on to distinguish the application of the Law from the model of medical treatment. The Law is, he says, a divine thing, a perfect ideal which is not necessarily actualized in the life of each individual. He argues, therefore, against Aristotle, that "in view of this consideration, it also will not be possible that the laws be dependent on changes in the circumstances of the individuals and of the times, *as is the case with regard to medical treatment*, which is particularized for every individual in conformity with his present temperament. On the contrary, governance of the Law ought to be absolute and universal, including everyone, even if it is suitable only for certain individuals and not suitable for others; for if it were to be made to fit individuals, the whole world would be corrupted 'and you would make out of it something that varies' (*we-nathatta devarekha le-shiʿurin*)."[54]

With all the seeming similarities between Aristotle's and Maimonides' doctrine of the mean, and with the especially striking similarity between the medical analogies of both thinkers, there is at the core a most fundamental difference. On these matters, Maimonides is finally controlled by the Jewish tradition, rather than by the principles of Greek philosophy. *Nomos* has about it an inescapable element of changing convention, while Torah has an equally inescapable element of fixity and permanence. For this reason Maimonides holds that a Jewish thinker may freely adopt general theoretical structures and principles of explanation which come to him from the world of Greek thought, if he finds them to be scientifically sound and useful in setting the foundations for his own doctrine. If, however, he is to remain loyal to his religious community, then he cannot substitute for the permanence of the Law and its divine-human ideal the shifting conventions of any society. (This is certainly true for Jewish thinkers of the middle ages, although it might well be challenged by our contemporaries.) Whatever the extent of Maimonides' possible deviation from orthodox Jewish theological norms, when he dealt with the world of practice, with the ordering of individual human life, and with the life of society, he was consistently faithful to Jewish law. At this point he is no longer an Aristotelian, but a Jew who stands fully inside the tradition.

The depth of this difference between Maimonides and Aristotle is underscored by the fact that even with respect to their understanding of psychology and the nature of man they diverge very significantly. For Aristotle, those faculties of the soul which man shares with other animals are essentially the same in man as in animals. Speaking of the nutritive faculty, Aristotle says that "The excellence of this faculty . . . appears to be common to all animate things and not peculiar to man." For this reason he concludes that in his discussion he "may omit from consideration the nutritive part of the soul, since it exhibits no specifically human excellence."[55] Maimonides categorically opposes this view. In his discussion of the faculties of the soul he makes a special point of emphasizing the fact that the human faculties, even when they carry the same name and exercise the same functions as the parallel animal faculties, are absolutely distinct and essentially different. As he puts it, "Our words concern themselves only with the human soul; for the nutritive faculty by which man is nourished is not the same, for instance, as that of the ass or the horse. . . . Although we apply the same term *nutrition* to all of them indiscriminately, nevertheless, its signification is by no means the same. In the same way, the term *sensation* is used homonymously for man and beast. . . . Mark this point well, for it is very important, as many so-called philosophers have fallen into error regarding it. . . ."[56] Little attention has been paid to this passage, but it seems to be of great importance. Maimonides is here saying explicitly that the standard psychology deriving from Aristotle (with whatever variations) is in error on a basic point. Man is not simply an animal, in all respects, with the addition of the faculty of reason. Man is absolutely distinct from animals, even with regard to those faculties that constitute what we usually call his animal nature. It is not our task here to take up the historical question of which "so-called philosophers" he had in mind.[57] We may wonder whether it was possible that Maimonides, with all his regard for Aristotle, should have included him among the "so-called philosophers."[58] However troubling it may be for Maimonides to have included Aristotle in this unflattering category of thinkers, it is certainly clear that he contradicts his great Greek predecessor directly and rejects his views. In the last analysis, it could not be otherwise; for if man is conceived as created in the image of God, he can no longer be understood as one more animal living in the order of nature. This affects the moral ideal and the medical analogy directly. In all respects man is now viewed as different from animals, and his ideal end, i.e., *imitatio Dei*, encompasses not only his reason, but all of his peculiarly human faculties. With such an understanding of man, the physician of the soul must be controlled by the divine norms. He is not training man on the analogy of training a dog or a horse. He is rather directing a human soul, in its totality, toward the divine ideal.

As a result of this difference we can understand why it is that Maimonides is so ready to deviate from the ideal of the middle way, while Aristotle holds to it firmly. Both acknowledge that moral virtue is only a propaedeutic to intellectual virtue and thus to the life of ultimate felicity. For Aristotle, however, the life of moral virtue, as he describes it in the *Nicomachaean Ethics*, is, with minor exceptions, a life in accordance with the mean. Maimonides, on the other hand, regularly invokes the rule of the mean but just as regularly deviates from it. In the foreword to his *Shemonah Peraqim* he reminds us that the treatise to which this is a commentary is concerned with *ḥasiduth*, with the life of special saintliness, and that such saintliness "paves the way to prophecy." If, therefore, one practises the teachings of *ʾAvoth*, one may hope to acquire prophecy. In short, the ultimate felicity is open to all who practise saintliness, and this is the subject under discussion in the treatise before us. Now saintliness is not simply a life in accordance with the mean but rather a deviation towards one of the extremes. Maimonides both recommends and defends this deviation at various points in those of his writings that deal with the good life in general and even in those that deal specifically with the mean. What is especially significant, however, is the fact that he sets forth an ideal which is, in principle, no longer in any way similar to the balanced life of the Aristotelian middle way. In *Shemonah Peraqim*, in *H. Deʿoth*, and in the *Guide* he repeats essentially the same line, namely, that all of a man's thought and activity, all of his striving, and all of his concern must be directed exclusively to the one single goal of the knowledge of God and fellowship with Him. It is especially revealing that Maimonides sets out this ideal immediately after having discussed the doctrine of the mean, as if to make clear that the mean is not the true ideal at all. He considers it man's proper duty to devote himself to one single goal only, namely, "the attainment of the knowledge of God as far as it is possible for man to know Him. Consequently one must so adjust all his actions, his whole conduct, and even his very words, that they lead to this goal. . . . So, his only design in eating, drinking, cohabiting, sleeping, waking, moving about, and resting should be . . . all to the end that man may reach the highest goal in his endeavors."[59]

It may well be that, as some scholars hold, Maimonides is here betraying Neo-Platonic influences on his thought. Our interest is not in tracing out the possible sources and lines of influence but in recognizing how far Maimonides has moved from the Aristotelian line. He has, in effect, rejected the mean as a guiding principle and criterion of the good life and has substituted for it a single controlling ideal; the good is that which leads to true knowledge and continuing contemplation of the divine being. Though Aristotle agrees, he does not counsel, as does Maimonides, that in ordering his life man should have this one concern only, that every activity, every choice, every state of character should be such as will move him effectively toward the ideal end. Maimonides holds that the mean may be a good general rule for this purpose, but it is not in and of itself the controlling consideration. In both *Shemonah Peraqim* and *H. Deᶜoth*, Maimonides cites in this connection the rule of the sages, "Let all your deeds be done for the sake of God," and the verse which teaches, "*In all thy ways know Him*." This, rather than the mean, is decisive. Unlike Aristotle, Maimonides wants this extreme to be the practical rule for all men.

* * *

We can now see that the extreme opinions on both sides of the question with which we have been dealing are equally mistaken. There are both Aristotelian and non-Aristotelian aspects to Maimonides' treatment of the doctrine of the mean. It is impossible to support the view that there is nothing whatsoever of Aristotle in him, since it is clear that the general form of his doctrine of the mean and much of his psychology are Aristotelian. It is just as impossible to defend the view that there is in Maimonides' version nothing more than a repetition of the Aristotelian teachings. As we have seen, there are deep and important differences. As heir, interpreter, and creative contributor to two traditions, Maimonides could not have been a pure Aristotelian in these matters. If Greek philosophy lived in him, and it did, the Jewish tradition and its Law never departed from the center of his concerns. In dealing with the nature of man, the ideal of human existence and the practical patterns by which human life should be ordered, Maimonides learned much from Aristotle but even more from the Torah.

NOTES

1. Henry Malter, "Shem Tob ben Joseph Palquera," *JQR*, N.S., 1 (1910–11), p. 160. See his extended footnote on pp. 160–161. See also Henry Malter, *Saadia Gaon: His Life and Works*, (New York, 1926), p. 257.

2. Joseph I. Gorfinkle (ed.), *The Eight Chapters of Maimonides on Ethics* (New York, 1966, Reprint of 1912 edition), p. 54.

3. Harry S. Lewis, "The 'Golden Mean' in Judaism," *Jewish Studies in Memory of Israel Abrahams*, (New York, 1927), p. 283.

4. David Rosin, *Die Ethik des Maimonides*, (Breslau, 1876), p. 79. Throughout the book, and particularly in his discussion of the mean, Rosin repeatedly cites the Aristotelian sources of Maimonides' doctrines. For similar views with respect to the mean see M. Wolff, *Musa Maimunis Acht Capitel*, (Leiden, 1903) pp. xiiif.

5. Yaᶜakov Mosheh Harlap, *Mey Marom: Mi-Saviv li-Shemonah Peraqim le-ha-Rambam*, (Jerusalem, 5705), pp. 85–86. An even stronger statement is made by Shem Ṭov ben Abraham ibn Gaʾon in his *Migdal ᶜOz*. Commenting on the passage in *H. Deᶜoth*, i, 4, in which Maimonides attributes the doctrine of the mean to the *ḥakhamim ha-rishonim* (presumably, though not necessarily the earlier rabbinic authorities), the *Migdal ᶜOz* makes the following observation: "All the moralists (*ḥakhmey ha-Musar*) have taught this principle, which they stole from the teachings of our sages (*genuvah hi ʾittam me-asher dareshu z"l*). Additional sources which make similar extreme attempts to find the doctrine of the mean in Jewish literature are cited in S. Rawidowicz, "*Sefer ha-Petiḥah le-Mishneh Torah*", in his *ᶜIyyunim be-maḥasheveth yisraʾel*, p. 429, n. 113. (Reprinted from *Metsudah*, 7 (1954). See also M. D. Rabinowitch (ed.), *Shemonah Peraqim le-ha-rambam* (Jerusalem, 1968), pp. 20–21, n. 9, and especially the quotation there from Holzberg.

6. Hermann Cohen, "Charakteristik der Ethik Maimunis," *Moses ben Maimon*, i, (Leipzig, 1908), p. 109. This important study by Cohen (reprinted in his *Jüdische Schriften*, iii) has as one of its main purposes the development of evidence that Maimonides was not an Aristotelian. In striking contrast is the view of Husik, who asserts without any qualification that in his ethics "Maimonides is an Aristotelian, and he endeavors to harmonize the intellectualism and theorism of the Stagirite with the diametrically opposed ethics and religion of the Hebrew Bible. And he is apparently unaware of the yawning gulf extending between them. . . . It is so absolutely clear and evident that one wonders how so clear-sighted a thinker like Maimonides could have been misled by the authority of Aristotle and the intellectual atmosphere of the days to imagine otherwise." Isaac Husik, *A History of Mediaeval Jewish Philosophy*, (Philadelphia, 1944), p. 300.

7. Cohen, *op. cit.*, p. 85.

8. *Ibid.*, especially pp. 113–115.

9. Theodor Gomperz, *Greek Thinkers*, (London, 1929), iv, p. 274.

10. "Aristotle's Doctrine of Justice," Walsh and Shapiro, *Aristotle's Ethics*, (Belmont, California, 1967), p. 109.

11. *Metaphysical Principles of Virtue*, (Indianapolis, 1968), p. 95, n. 10.

12. *Nicomachaean Ethics* (hereafter *N.E.*), 1107a 1.

13. *N.E.*, 1094b 15–17.

14. *N.E.*, 1173a 1f.

15. Werner Jaeger, "Aristotle's Use of Medicine as a Model of Method in his Ethics," *Journal of Hellenic Studies*, 77 (1952), p. 57.

16. *De Vet. Med.* ix.
17. *N.E.*, 1094a 16.
18. Cf., *N.E.* vi, 1139a 32f.
19. *Historia Animalium* i, 492a 7f.
20. *Ibid.*, 492a 33f.
21. *Ibid.*, 492b 31f.
22. *Part. Animalium*, iii, 666a 15.
23. *Ibid.* ii, 652a 31f.
24. *De Gen. et Corr.* ii, 334b 25–30.
25. *Part. Animalium*, ii, 652b 17–20.
26. *N.E.*, vi, 1140a 20.
27. *Rhet.* iii, 1416b 30ff.
28. *Pol.* iv, 1295b 3–7.
29. *N.E.* ii, 1103a 24.
30. *N.E.* vi, 1144b 1f.
31. *Pol.* i, 1253a 16–19.
32. *N.E.* ii, 1109b 13f.
33. *N.E.* ii, 1104a 1f.
34. *N.E.* vi, 1142a 25f.
35. For an extended discussion of this point see, M. Fox, "Maimonides and Aquinas on Natural Law," *Diney Yisra'el*, iii, 1972; Reprinted in J. I. Dienstag (ed.), *Maimonides and Aquinas*, (New York, 1975).
36. Joseph I. Gorfinkle (ed.), *The Eight Chapters* (see *supra*, p. 118, n. 2), pp. 35–36.
37. For the attitudes of traditional commentators who see this first mishnah as an attempt to underscore the independence of Jewish ethics from all external sources, see the comments of Bertinoro and *Tosefoth Yom Ṭov, ad loc.*
38. *Shemonah Peraqim*, v.
39. *Ibid.*, iv, Gorfinkle, pp. 54–55.
40. *N.E.*, ii, 6, 1106b 36f.
41. *H. Deᶜoth*, i, 3, 4.
42. *Guide of the Perplexed*, II, 28; ed. Pines, pp. 335–336.
43. For explicit comments on this point see *Guide*, II, 8 and III, 14; *Letter on Astrology*, ed. A. Marx, *HUCA* iii (1926), p. 356 and *Qobeṣ teshuvoth ha-rambam* (Leipzig, 1859), ii, f. 26a.
44. Gorfinkle, p. 64.
45. iii, 1.
46. *Guide*, II, 39, ed. Pines, p. 380.
47. *Ibid.*, p. 381.
48. *H. Deᶜoth* i, 5, 6. (From the manuscripts it seems clear that the end of i, 5, as we have cited it here from the printed versions, should really be the beginning of i, 6).
49. *Ibid.*, ii, 3.
50. *N.E.*, ii, 6, 1107a 9f.
51. The main sources for the moral-medical analogy in Maimonides are: *Shemonah Peraqim*, i, ed. Gorfinkle, p. 38, iii, iv, Gorfinkle, pp. 62f.; *H. Deᶜoth*, especially ii; *Guide*, III, 34.
52. *H. Deᶜoth*, ii, 1.
53. *Guide* II, 40; ed. Pines, p. 382.
54. *Guide* III, 34; ed. Pines, pp. 534–535 (my italics).

55. *N.E.*, i, 13, 1102b 2–12.

56. *Shemonah Peraqim*, i; ed. Gorfinkle, pp. 39–40.

57. An inadequate comment on this question is made by D. Rosin in *Die Ethik des Maimonides*, (Breslau, 1876), p. 48, n. 1.

58. The usual printed Hebrew texts read *harbeh min ha-Pilosofim*, but there is no doubt, as is evident from the Arabic text, that the reading should be *mithpalsefim*. On this point, see the editions of Gorfinkle and Kafiḥ.

59. *Shemonah Peraqim*, v, ed. Gorfinkle, p. 69ff; for almost identical language see *H. Deʿoth* iii, 2, 3; the very same idea is set forth elaborately in the *Guide*, III, 51.

Was Franz Rosenzweig a Mystic?

N. N. GLATZER

I

Some will consider the very question posed in the title irreverent, and, in view of Rosenzweig's reputation as an intellectual, inapposite. Yet the issue is quite complex and only a dispassionate review—however brief and sketchy—of some of Rosenzweig's arguments and disquisitions will permit an adequate answer.[1] It is a privilege to dedicate this essay to Professor Alexander Altmann who has contributed so much to the understanding of various aspects of Rosenzweig's life and thought.

Anent his antipathy to mysticism Rosenzweig was quite outspoken. He criticized the mystic's "irrationalist tendencies" (*K.S.* 392), noted that in his mouth "mystic" is a term of invective (*Br.* 411), suspected that Martin Buber's influence is due to his weakest quality, "the mystical bombast" (*Br.* 442), and he called *Ecstatic Confessions*, an anthology of mystical texts, a new edition of which appeared in 1921, "a dreadful book" (*Br.* 446). Later he observed that Buber was no longer "the mystic individualist such as whom people worship" but had "started to be a solid and rational human being" (*Br.* 461). Speaking of Rabbi N. A. Nobel of Frankfurt, he stated that "high-flown mysticism is hateful to me; I love Nobel not because of his mysticism but despite it," and that "in this rejection of mysticism I am in agreement with Buber" (Letter to Eugen Mayer; *Bulletin of the Leo Baeck Institute*, 1960, No. 9, p. 49).

On an ideological level, he devotes a subsection in Part Two, Book Three of the *Star of Redemption* to a critique of mysticism. The point which he makes is that the mystic's self, considering itself as the sole recipient of revelation, is closed to the world. Mysticism is objectively disastrous because it becomes a magic cloak of invisibility for the mystic. His soul is open to God, and to God only, but shut off from the world. In an act of arrogant confidence he is alone with "his" God and without communication with the world. For him, the sole road that exists connects him to God and God to him. He must deny the world, and since the world does not permit itself to be denied, he must repudiate it. The world is there, but the mystic will treat it as if it did not really exist, as if it had no essence, as if it were not created by the same God whose love the mystic himself claims to possess. This negative attitude to the world—and no other attitude is possible for the mystic—Rosenzweig terms "thoroughly immoral." Rather than coming to life as a speaking individual, ready to enter into dialogical relationships, the mystic is swallowed back into silent seclusion (*St.* 207f.).[2]

The Introduction to Part III ("On the Possibility of Entreating the Kingdom") offers a profound rejection of mystical, magical prayer, the plea of one who would attempt to coerce the coming of the kingdom. The mystic, acting as an individual, is always in danger of tempting God and hastening the advent of the kingdom. "But the kingdom of heaven will not be coerced: it grows"—a fact which is known to the man of faith only. "The fanatic [*der Schwärmer*], the sectarian, in short all the tyrants of the kingdom of heaven, far from hastening the advent of the kingdom, only delay it. In prayer everything comes down to this: is the future of the kingdom accelerated by it or delayed?" Only the community of the faithful is able, in prayer, to mediate between revelation, to anticipate the future into the moment, the eternity into a Today, and to hasten the coming of the kingdom. Here the prayer of the mystic falters; here mysticism fails.

Thus dismissing mysticism as a nebulous state of mind and as theologically misleading, Rosenzweig was ready to report on his own method in trying to describe the relationships between God, the world, and man, which result in creation, revelation, and redemption. He calls his approach "absolute empiricism" (a term suggested by the philosophy of Schelling): an attitude that claims "to know nothing more of the divine or of terrestrial matters than what it has experienced—but to know this really" (*K.S.* 398).

A little book on which Rosenzweig was working after the completion of the *Star*, and prior to the outbreak of his progressive paralysis, he called *Büchlein vom gesunden und kranken Menschenverstand*, indicating his belief in healthy common sense.[3] In this book the patient, a man paralyzed by philosophy and its search for "essence," is healed by common sense and its faith in the strength of reality. Common sense (not to be confused with Thomas Reid's "common sense") does not recognize preconceptions, prearranged "postulates." The sole stress is on actual experience. While working on the *Büchlein*, Rosenzweig wrote to his mother: "The chief thing is not whether a person 'believes' in the good Lord; what matters is that he open all his five senses and sees the facts—at the risk that even the good Lord may be found among the facts" (*Br.* 406). Rosenzweig's "New Thinking," grounded in common sense, traces the experience of the world back to the world, the experience of God back to God (*K.S.* 379). Furthermore, the "New Thinking" is dependent on time; only in due time will it be able to grasp and understand (*K.S.* 384). Rosenzweig takes time seriously (*K.S.* 387).

Yet the notion of time, real, irreversible, and as determining thought is one most readily understood by the mystic. The same is true of "experience" in the distinct sense in which Rosenzweig uses it.

Once only in his writings (at the end of the "germ cell" to the *Star*) does Rosenzweig assign mysticism a special place in the scheme of the things of the mind: "between real theology and real philosophy." This position, Rosenzweig feels, "offers an unforced [*ungezwungen*] solution for many historical difficulties, e.g., Plotinus, [the thought of] India and others" (*K.S.* 372). This rather suggestive notion of 1917 does not, however, have any sequel in Rosenzweig's work.

II

With our initial question in mind, let us now turn to Rosenzweig's discussion of love and of truth in his *Star of Redemption*, to the conclusion of this *magnum opus*, and then to the main motifs of his highly important and not yet sufficiently recognized annotations to the poetry of Judah Ha-Levi. It is understood that the central position of love was seen long before Rosenzweig, by philosophers and theologians, both in the middle ages and in modern times. Rosenzweig's emphasis on that motif is the first instance by a modern Jewish thinker. The motif of love in his thought appears first in the "germ cell" of the *Star of Redemption* (the letter to Rudolf Ehrenberg of November 18, 1917), to be most acutely elaborated in the *Star* (especially in Part II, Book II).[4]

In the "germ cell" he posits, in contradistinction to the "third person world" of Spinoza (he who loves God must not expect God to love him in return), the realm of revelation, where man may, yea must, demand that God respond to his love. Even more: he must demand that God love him first. He is silent, waiting for the redeeming word "thou" coming from God, the word to which he will respond with his timid "I" (*K.S.* 363f.).

This first formulation of love as the focal point of revelation is fully expanded in the *Star*, to wit, that although, theoretically, the concept of love implies want, and God is not in want, we have to say that his revelation is an act of love. For "God's love is not an attribute but an event." His love "is present, . . . ever wholly of the moment. . . . This love is the eternal victory over death" (*St.* 163f.). Man, the recipient of God's love, "knows himself borne by the love of the lover and sheltered in it. The beloved knows as eternal that which to the lover is a moment, ever to be renewed. . . . The love of the lover is a light which is ever kindled anew for him. . . . The love of the beloved sits quietly at the feet of the lover. . . ." The beloved "can only allow himself to be loved, nothing more. It is thus that the soul receives the love of God" (*St.* 168f.). This love is eternal. God will always love, the soul will always be loved. In the love of God, the soul "grows out of the rock of the self." And at this point man, previously without sense and speech, becomes the beloved soul (*St.* 169).[5]

The lover utters the commandment which is "the meaning and essence of all commandments:" "Thou shalt love thy God with all thy heart" (*Deut.* 6:5). "The commandment of love can issue only from the mouth of the lover" (*St.* 176).

What is the soul's response to the demand of love? The soul is ashamed to acknowledge to the lover its love without at the same time acknowledging its weakness; it responds to God's "Thou shalt love" with an "I have sinned" (*St.* 179). Yet out of the confession of sin springs the confession of faith: "Him, whom I have recognized as the lover in experiencing my being loved—He 'is.' The God of my love is truly God" (*St.* 181). In this connection Rosenzweig speaks of an "experience of love" which must imply that "he whom the soul experiences in its love really lives." In its being beloved the soul gains the certainty that "the God who loves it is truly God, is the true God." In love the soul awakes and begins to speak but it is only when it is loved that it attains being. "God, too, attains reality only here, in the testimony of the believing soul" (*St.* 182). And man—"the greatest gift presented to him in revelation is the ability to pray." What is the aim of prayer? The coming of the kingdom, the future repetition of the miracle in which God once descended and founded his kingdom (*St.* 184f.). Equally miraculous is the fact of man receiving his proper name; with it the word of revelation entered the real dialogue between God and man. "That which has a name of its own can no longer be a thing;" the rigid wall of thingness has been breached (*St.* 186). God's name, too, is revealed in revelation. The community of man lives its life "from the revealed name of God up to the present day, up to the present moment, and into the personal experience" (*St.* 188).

Thus revelation is the coming-of-age of the mute self, which, under the love of God, now emerges as the "Speaking Soul". "The analogue of love permeates, as analogue, all of revelation" (*St.* 198f.), a tenet that Rosenzweig finds expressed in the *Song of Songs* (*St.* 199–204), "the focal book of revelation" (*St.* 202). Love, "speech, wholly active, wholly personal, wholly living," strong as death, is victorious over death. "The living soul, loved by God, triumphs over all that is mortal" (*ibid.*). "From the miracle of divine love" man enters "the earthly world" and, recollecting what was "experienced in that magic circle" he carries love into the world. With a variation on a midrashic phrase, Rosenzweig concludes this book with the words "as He loves you, so shall you love" (*St.* 204).

In these sections of his book Rosenzweig raises some of the most profound issues of classical Jewish thought, issues which the period of emancipation considered outmoded or at least irrelevant. Liberals and traditionalists shared in this contempt for what lay beneath the surface of Jewish life and institutions. Rozenzweig boldly probes the depth. He speaks of the love of God as of an experience.[6] From the same source, so he posits, flows an awareness not only of the fact of this love but of the Lover Himself. In another connection he speaks of the "living experience" of the acts of God as the answer to the ultimate "mystical question concerning God's essence in the world above the world" (*St.* 390). His clear distinction between the mystical and the "living experience" must be respected, especially when we bear in mind his overt rejection of mysticism in other parts of his work. Yet to the simple reader who tries to understand Rosenzweig, "living experience" (such as the experience of divine love) will appear, however circumscribed, however technically incomplete, to be a mystical experience.

III

Part Three of the *Star* deals in its first book with Judaism ("the eternal life"), in its second with Christianity ("the eternal way"), and in the third with "the eternal truth." While the first two books are grounded in the historical realities of the two monotheistic religions, the main parts of the third book of Part Three rise high above and beyond of what can be perceived in human experience. We are confronted with a vision of the end. For "God is truth," and as truth He will be known "even when one day all has come to an end . . . in eternity"—both eternal life (Judaism) and eternal way (Christianity). In eternity there end both the way and the life. An ocean of light engulfs the way, and life dissolves in the light. "Life rallies in the silence of the transcendental world [*Überwelt*] and is transformed into light. God is light" (*St.* 380).

Revelation, in which God makes manifest his love, teaches us to trust in the Creator and to await the redeemer (*St.* 382). But redemption—man's loving response to the love experienced in revelation—is ultimately "the redemption of God Himself." He is being freed "from the work of creation, from his loving concern for the soul . . . and from all that is outside Himself." Even his revealed name is muted; "the end is nameless, it is above any name. Beyond the word there shines silence" (*St.* 383). We (i.e., Jews) refrain from pronouncing the name of God. This Rosenzweig explains as an anticipation "of the silence in which the name and we together will one day sink." "The very name of God itself falls silent on our lips . . . just as it will fall silent one day when he is al[l]-one—one in all the world." The ultimate silence points to the true depths of the Deity. "God Himself is there redeemed from his own word. He is silent" (*St.* 384).

In further discoursing on truth Rosenzweig maintains that it is only "in God" that the vision of the whole truth can be experienced. "This is the only thing which is seen in God." Here man does not sustain experience directly. "It is God who experiences, while man merely looks on." But even if man does experience God ("for what else is revelation?"), he "by no means experiences what God experiences." In a vision, however, he sees what God experiences. "He sees it in God. God himself experiences it" (*St.* 394f.; cf. also 416).

The conclusion of the third book harks back to the theme of its beginning. Revelation revealed divine love; here "the concealed had become manifest." "In the end this achievement" sinks back into the secret, ever-enduring beginning of creation. In a marginal revision Rosenzweig added: "The manifest becomes the concealed. And with revelation redemption too now merges back into creation." God alone remains, "the first and the last," and from eternity to eternity: Truth (*St.* 417).

The above condensation indicates the degree to which Rosenzweig allowed himself to be guided by a nonrational element of thought. The concepts of God as truth and God as eternal demanded that Rosenzweig be forced into the consequence, *viz.*, the exclusion of what is not perfect truth and what is not truly eternal. Scriptural phrases such as "I am the first and I am the last" (*Isaiah* 44:6), or "From eternity to eternity Thou wast God" (*Ps.* 90:2), helped him in the construction of a drama of a universe in which consciousness, purpose, love, concern, knowledge, speech awoke for a time a universe which, however, has to vanish before the impact of eternity and of truth. Such postulates are not the result of a poet's inflamed imagination but are a visionary perception usually associated with mysticism.

IV

In the section "Gate," which is the triumphant finale of the *Star*, all the limits on what can be expressed in words are eliminated, and the reader is invited to partake in what can only be called a vision. "The Eternal had become *Gestalt* in the truth. And the truth is none other than the countenance of this *Gestalt*" (*St.* 418). The Biblical assertion that (at Sinai) "you have seen no form, only heard speech" (*Deut.* 4:12) refers only to the realm of revelation, not the redeemed world, says Rosenzweig. The shining of the divine countenance—this alone is the truth. Man is allowed to know the truth as it is, namely as it is in God: as his countenance and part (*St.* 418).

The frenzy of paganism and its blind desire to see itself only collapses before truth. Points of view, philosophies of life, *isms* of every kind—all these vanish before this simple, constant sight of the truth. Views of the world and of life are absorbed into the one view of God. It is only when we appreciate the symbolism of the two superimposed triangles in the *Star of Redemption* and see the Star as countenance that we transcend the realm of mere possibilities and simply see (*St.* 421f.).

"In the innermost sanctuary of the divine truth . . . the Star of Redemption is become countenance which glances at me and out of which I glance . . . God, who is the last and the first—He opened to me the doors of the sanctuary . . . and allowed Himself to be seen. He led me to that border of life, where seeing is permitted, since 'no man shall see Me [Him] and remain in life'" (*Exod.* 33:20). On the margin of his manuscript Rosenzweig added: "That sanctuary had to be a portion of a world above the world [*Überwelt*] yet in the world, life beyond life. *What* He allowed me to see in this beyond of life, is what I was granted to perceive in the midst of life," in the realm of revelation. Now however "I could see it and not merely hear it. Only he who followed the words of the divine mouth [in revelation] is granted to walk in the light of the divine countenance" (*St.* 423f.).

Here Rosenzweig introduces Micah's threefold commandment addressed to man (*Micah* 6:8) and concentrates on the third part: "to walk humbly with thy God," a requirement that Rosenzweig explains in a marginal addition to the text: "Wholly today and thus wholly eternal as life and the way . . . and partaking of the eternal truth as do life and the way." And humility implies a wholly present trust [*Vertrauen*], a trust that is "the seed whence grow faith, hope, and love, and the fruit that ripens out of them."

After the aside on "trust," Rosenzweig returns to "to walk humbly . . . — the words that are written over the gate which leads out of the mysterious-miraculous shining of the divine sanctuary" into life. Wishing to make this concluding sentence of the *Star* more effective, he made several revisions, adding to "sanctuary" the phrase "in which no man can remain alive," prefacing "into life" by "whither, then, does the gate open?" correcting "the gate" into "the wings of the gate," then adding, "Thou knowest it not?" and not until this point concluding, "Into life" (*St.* 424).

"Life" refers here to the conduct of day to day affairs in all their simplicity, to simple speech and simple action, and to the discipline imposed on existence by religious tradition. But the fact that before stating his profession of humility and of "life" as that into which the gate opens, Rosenzweig had to reveal his vision of the divine countenance which "alone is the truth," of "the sanctuary of the divine truth," and the "border of life where seeing is permitted"—this fact should suffice to convince us that such a vision was, to Rosenzweig, a necessary precondition for the final insight of the *Star*. Once that position was reached, he could abandon what occupied his imagination on the road "to life." To Hans Ehrenberg, who in a review of the *Star* objected to its ending, the author wrote that this ending is "anti-mystical, not anti-intellectual" (*Br.* 413f.), for, we may understand, "life" sets itself in opposition to the (mystical) vision. In the sphere of "life" there is room for intellectual pursuits and for philosophy; mysticism would be out of place. Yet in the very private, very individual case of Rosenzweig—a situation which cannot be generalized—the serene acceptance of "life" did not take place until the vision of the sacred countenance was exhausted.

V

The *Star* was published in 1921. During the following two years, Rosenzweig was working on the first edition of his translation and annotation of selected poems by Judah Ha-Levi.[7] The annotations, while primarily intended to introduce the reader into the thought of the great poet, gave him the opportunity to express what occupied his own mind after the completion of the *Star*. He undertook the translation out of impatience with a bad rendition of Ha-Levi which he found in a prayer book (*Br.* 472), but, as the work progressed, he became increasingly aware of a kinship with the poet. In the last year of his life (in which he reviewed his past) he wrote to his mother that his correct Hebrew name should have been Judah (not Levi, as he had assumed) ben Samuel "which is exactly the name of the great man whose middle-sized reincarnation upon the road of *ʿibbur* [transmigration] I am: Judah Ha-Levi" (*Br.* 628).[8]

In his note on *yah shimekha*, the poem chosen for the opening of the volume, Rosenzweig has the poet approach the enigma of revelation. He knows "that all our knowledge, including prophetic knowledge is only a reflection [of the light]," yet he knows that this "only" is not a simple "only," but "man's share [in the truth]." "He is not wise, he is—nothing. Out of this ultimate and innermost experience of his nothingness he gazes upward to the greatness of his Lord. . . . Trembling in this feeling of the mystery above him he stammers words of prayer" (*J.H.* 172).

This "gazing upward" is intensified in the comment on *ye-ʿiruni.* "The poet sees God . . . and the experience of today confirms and repeats the historical revelation" (on Sinai). What happens in revelation? "God reveals *Himself*: this is the only content of revelation." The miracle of that vision "gives the poet the courage to bow down before the source of the miracle" (*J.H.* 174).

"Revelation is both (personal) experience and (historical) fact" and the two are interrelated. But how can the souls "endure in this fiery kernel of the mystery that is being revealed?" The strength to endure revelation "comes from revelation itself" (*geliley zevul*, *J.H.* 175).

It is notable that the cosmic nature of revelation, a process that fulfills the promise of creation—a basic notion in the *Star*—is here, in the comments to Ha-Levi, replaced by a revelation that comes closer to the Biblical concept. The personal aspect of revelation ("the experience") is affirmed in both the *Star* and the *Ha-Levi* commentary, but the place of the universal process is now filled by the event at Sinai ("the fact").

In the *Star*, revelation manifested the love of God to which man responded in love. The comments on love in the *Ha-Levi* commentary are more intimate and breathe greater simplicity and naturalness. "It is difficult to love, even to love God. . . . For the share of unhappy love that is in all love . . . is here increased *ad infinitum*." To love God spells happy and unhappy love simultaneously, "for God comes close to man and then again becomes distant." Man can overcome this antithesis "with the strength he can put into his entreaty that God respond to his love" (*yeḥallu peney ʾel ḥay*, *J.H.* 178f.).

Who, then, takes the first step, God or man? Conscious of his weakness man would seem to expect God to take the first step, yet clearly man hears that God demands this first step from him. On the Day of Atonement (for which this poem here commented on was written) this tension between God and man seems irreconcilable. The solution comes in the last minutes of the sacred day when man, in the ecstasy of his nearness to God, "anticipates this highest, this ultimate moment" of fulfillment of his "prayer of return, of homecoming" (*yeminekha noseʾ ʿavonay*, *J.H.* 180f.).

With growing intensity Rosenzweig describes the unconventional, nonconformist nature of Jewish religious thought, notions that defy all formal theology. Jewish rationalism, for example, may be very rational, yet "it will never be as rational as it is Jewish" (*J.H.* 183).[9] "We have to be aware of the limits of our knowledge, but also—and not less—of the limits of our ignorance. Beyond all our knowledge dwells God. But before our ignorance sets in, your God offers Himself to you, your plea, your readiness, your vision, your life" (*J.H.* 184). He goes so far as to justify the talmudic angelology in which he finds "genuine and great experiences of divine activity" that run parallel to "the genuine and great perceptions of science" (*J.H.* 187). The ultimate notion of human thinking is the first in Jewish thought, namely, "that the remote God is—at the same time—the near one, the unknown is the revealed, the Creator is none other than the redeemer." Man tries in vain to press God's ways into dogmas, to compose theological position papers on respectively, God's nearness and his distance and otherness. The truth is that "when God comes near us we do perceive that only which cannot be expressed," and "even at the very great distance, the burning gaze of God and man can fuse in such a way that the coldest abstractions grow warm" (*J.H.* 188f.). Yet, near or distant, "God is never absent, wherefore there is no concept of God" (*J.H.* 190). That this God knows man and loves man even before he enters life, "this the Jewish poet knew even without Platonism." "The knowledge that God knows man and loves man is a basis of human life" (*J.H.* 198f.)—life lived in "longing for the divine vision, in the knowledge of the heavenly origin of the soul and in the desire to return to the source" (*shem ʾelohim ʾodeh be-siḥi*, *J.H.* 217).

The biographical facts which constitute the background to the *Star* necessitated a debate with Christianity and called for a view of the world in which both Christianity and Judaism had a divinely ordained position. Thus the internal (religious, liturgical, sacral) life of both were presented in great detail in the *Star* and carefully compared with each other.[10] Once this dialogue with Christianity was concluded, Rosenzweig was free to devote himself entirely to Judaism; there was no need any more to be constantly considering the other side.

The desire to be able to concentrate on the mode of "the eternal life" is indeed indicated in the *Star*, especially between its lines. The simplicity Rosenzweig wanted to achieve was only possible through his immersing himself in the element that became more and more his own. At the conclusion of the *Star* the author saw inscribed over the gate of the sanctuary: . . . "to walk humbly with thy God." In the notes to *Judah Ha-Levi* we see the realization of this vision, a realization repeated over and over again in the author's life after the conclusion of the *Ha-Levi*.

Mystical terminology, mystical notions and symbolism which Rosenzweig had used so freely in the *Star* did not disappear from his thinking with the conclusion of that work. In his *Ha-Levi* he depicts the nature of the love of God, God's nearness, the enigma of revelation, the miracle of the vision of revelation, the experience of seeing God, and the feeling of mystery. Such notions were already firmly rooted in the thinker's mind when he wrote the *Star*. In his *Ha-Levi*, however, they appear in greater naturalness, greater freedom of movement. In addition, the *Ha-Levi* commentary contains explicit references to Jewish mysticism. Rosenzweig speaks of the "cabbalistic movements after Ha-Levi" (*J.H.* 173), and in a comment on the Sabbath, he mentions the Lurianic kabbalah (*J.H.* 212 and 213). It may incidentally be remarked that this mystic trend is mentioned already in the "germ cell" of the *Star*, anent a discussion of the reality of God (*K.S.* 360).

VI

Mystical imagery, symbolism, terminology (some of it vaguely, some incorrectly quoted and some borrowed from contemporaries) do not make Rosenzweig a mystic. His negative view of mysticism never changed and must be taken as an authentic repudiation of the *unio mystica*, the mystic's rejection of this world and of the discursive intellect, his ethical passivity, his defiance of expression, his disallowance of the law. What the use of mystical notions by Rosenzweig does show is that he was aware of the preeminent position of mysticism in the shaping of Jewish religious thought and of the viability of the mystical verb for the expression of his own (nonmystical) thinking.[11] His was a comprehensive, all-embracing view of Judaism. Torah "knows both the fire of the Sabbath candle and that of the martyr's stake;" it is the law "Akiba planted and the heretic ʾAḥer trampled under, the cradle Spinoza hailed from, the ladder on which the Baal Shem ascended" (*K.S.* 110). Equally, he was opposed to any one-sided definition of Israel, e.g., S. R. Hirsch's "pseudojuridical," Abraham Geiger's "pseudological," or "pseudoethical" theories. "A miracle does not constitute history" (*K.S.* 111f.)—and Judaism *is* a miracle. The description of a miracle requires a language unrestricted by theological conventions.

An entire complex of ideas, experiences, and insights presented by Rosenzweig is strangely related to the realm of mystical thought and traditions. Only within the mystical tradition can one speak of the meaning of the name, the meaning of prayer, or the meaning of redemption in the manner in which Rosenzweig discourses on them. It is no coincidence that he, who at the time had only a passing firsthand acquaintance with cabbalistic writings,[12] several times refers or alludes to Jewish mystical notions. He attributes the midrashic "if you are my witnesses, then I am God" to "the master of Kabbalah" (*St.* 171). He speaks of the *maʿaseh merkavah* as the bridge which Jewish mysticism erects between "the God of our fathers" and "the Law" and sees the world as "full of mysterious relations to the Law and the Law as the key to the enigma of the world" (*St.* 408f.). He refers to the mystical doctrine of the *Shekhinah* as the bridge between "the God of our fathers" and "the remnant of Israel" (*St.* 409), to "the sparks of divine light being scattered about the world," to "the dwelling-place of the exiled God," and to the fulfillment of the laws "for the sake of uniting the name of the Holy One, blessed be He, and his *Shekhinah*," to the preparation of the heart "in awe and love" (*St.* 410).

In answer to the question, "was Rosenzweig a mystic?" we must reply that although he was not a mystic, Rosenzweig did reach a position of "theistic mysticism," operating with "strictly mystical *theologoumena*."[13] A paradoxical position? Perhaps, but one resolved by the peculiar spiritual odyssey of the man himself.

NOTES

1. Sources and abbreviations: *St.*: *Star of Redemption*, quoted from the translation by William W. Hallo, New York, 1964, though at times a different rendition was required; *Br.*: *Briefe*, ed. Edith Rosenzweig and Ernst Simon, Berlin, 1935; *K.S.*: *Kleinere Schriften*, Berlin, 1937; *J.H.*: *Jehuda Halevi*, Berlin, 1927. *Paraleipomena* and the original version of the *Star of Redemption* are quoted from manuscripts in the Franz Rosenzweig Archives.

2. Cf. a different kind of criticism of mysticism in Rosenzweig's wartime diary called *Paraleipomena* (unpublished): "Mysticism outside of revelation does not know of 'the humility of God,' only the deification of man."

3. Rosenzweig withheld the book from publication. It appeared, posthumously, first in an English translation (*Understanding the Sick and the Healthy*, New York, 1953) and later in the German original (Düsseldorf, 1964).

4. An early reference to the subject appears in Rosenzweig's (unpublished) diary for August 23, 1906: "He [God] allows evil to exist in the world without regard to the curse hurled at Him by mankind. But individually his grace is 'endless:' his creatures may sin ever so much against Him, but He heaps upon them always acts of goodness. Why? Because He cannot otherwise, for He 'loves' them all. Not with the love of passion, but with the love of a close relationship, which is found also between creator and creature, as between children and parents."

5. Cf. the entry in *Paraleipomena*: "The god of Aristotle may 'love' the wise; what has this to do with the love of God who 'loves the stranger, the poor and the needy?"

6. Cf. the style of references to events in Rosenzweig's personal life: "I have felt upon my own body his rod as well as his gentle hands. . . ." (Letter to Edith Hahn, January 17, 1920; *Briefe*, 386) and "It is a great act of mercy that God once has uprooted me out of life during my life. It is extraordinary in us that God, in our case, has not only spoken to us through our lives; . . . on the empty stage He has spoken to us" (Letter to Margrit Rosenstock [Huessy], June 15, 1920; *Judaism Despite Christianity*, ed. Eugen Rosenstock-Huessy, University: The University of Alabama Press, 1969, p. 76).

7. The first edition, *Sechzig Hymnen und Gedichte des Jehuda Halevi, deutsch*, was published in Constance, 1924; the second (expanded) edition, *Jehuda Halevi, Zweiundneunzig Hymnen und Gedichte, deutsch*, appeared in Berlin, 1927.

8. Some of Ha-Levi's work was known to Rosenzweig long before he undertook the translation. He included the *Kuzari* in the curriculum of the two last years of the gymnasium (*Zeit ists* [1917], *K.S.* 66) and quoted Ha-Levi's parable of the seed and the fruit centrally in the *Star* (*St.* 379), after having alluded to it before (*St.* 335).

9. Cf. the entry in *Paraleipomena*: "The Jew is rational only for the sake of faith; . . . he is a rationalist who can be understood only out of his faith."

10. Already in an early entry in his diary (July 11, 1914) Rosenweig refers to Chris-

tianity as having a philosophical system (Christology), adding that analogous attempts with us (Jews) would constitute mysticism. "Would therefore a system of Judaism have to be mystical? Should there be one altogether?" The *Paraleipomena* show a close reading of Augustine and Kant and a small number of comparative references to Hebrew sources.

11. Cf. the cryptic entry in the diary (April 7, 1922): "Mysticism and anti-Mysticism."

12. In his diary (July 9, 1914) Rosenzweig gives a bibliographical reference to J. Abelson, *Jewish Mysticism*, London, 1913.

13. Gershom Scholem, "Rosenzweig's Star of Redemption," in his *The Messianic Idea in Judaism*, New York, 1971, pp. 320–23. *See also* Nathan Rotenstreich, *Jewish Philosophy in Modern Times*, New York, 1968, ch. vi.

Maimonides' *Guide of the Perplexed*: Towards a Critical Edition

M. H. GOSHEN-GOTTSTEIN

This paper is not only dedicated to Alexander Altmann. It has been written as a tribute to my first teacher of Judaic studies, linking up to an event long forgotten. To be sure, at this juncture of Altmann's distinguished career his attention is focussed on the "third" Moses, the master from Dessau. But for me Altmann remains the teacher who, four decades ago, was the first to acquaint me with the philosophy of the "second" Moses, the master from Fustat. Among the very few books in my library which have survived from my childhood days I cherish a little volume. This is the first prize I ever won, handed to me on the solemn occasion of my first examination in a tractate of the Mishnah—if I remember correctly. The instructor, then the rising star on the rabbinical sky of Berlin, was Alexander Altmann. The volume, which had then just been published, *Rabbi Mosche Ben Maimon—Ein systematischer Querschritt durch sein Werk* (Berlin, 1935).[1] If my path has taken me in directions different from Altmann's, my interest in the towering achievement of Maimonides has not subsided. It is therefore a welcome occasion to express my good wishes to my erstwhile teacher by returning, at least for a moment, to the field of medieval Jewish studies.[2]

Although the *Guide* is regarded as the central achievement of medieval Jewish thought, no critical edition has been attempted. Whereas some minor treatises of Maimonides are available in reasonable editions, the sheer quantity of work involved seems to have discouraged scholars from trying their hand at the master's *magnum opus*. This holds true both for Samuel ibn Tibbon's masterful rendering into Hebrew and for the Arabic original. To be more specific: the Arabic original did not pass through a series of printings, and no "vulgate" text existed. Hence it was edited and reedited from manuscripts which, on the whole, offered a fairly reliable text.[3] The Hebrew text, on the other hand, which served for centuries as

1. This volume was edited by N. N. Glatzer, who was also to become my colleague in later years, when I had the pleasure to serve as Visiting Professor at Brandeis University. Altmann prefaced his gift by a dedication which was perhaps not lost on the youngster: כל המרבה ללמד הרי זה משובח ויקבל הספר הזה לעדות ולתעודה

2. While Jewish and cognate studies tend to split into areas of specializations, each demanding its own skills, I should like to be permitted to regard my own work in light of the conviction that at least Hebrew philology should not be subdivided into mutually unintelligible subspecializations. We are coming dangerously near the point where the biblical philologist is unaware of the problems presented by talmudic and medieval texts and vice versa. The student whose special interest lies in what I have termed the "philology of translations" has much to learn from looking at the various aspects of what is a basic phenomenon of Hebrew literary history.

3. One has to study carefully the preface of Joel's edition (Jerusalem, 1930). Joel, with his usual modesty, did not take all the credit due for the work involved in reprinting Munk's

a major vehicle of Jewish philosophical tradition, was never edited critically. The best "edition" we possess is little more than a reissue of the "vulgate" prints, corrected at random on the basis of the Arabic original.[4]

The present article is intended as a philological exercise in the framework of my studies of *Medieval Translations and Translators*.[5] I am primarily interested in Ibn Tibbon's text; but the analysis of the Arabic original cannot be dispensed with. It is not more than an exercise analysing two small random samples, and I harbour no illusion that I shall ever have the time and the means to do for the *magnum opus* of Maimonides as a whole what I may do for a chapter or two. Our results are of necessity tentative, and all suggestions will have to be studied in light of the material as a whole.[6]

These exercises on the text of Ibn Tibbon's version were started in Oxford, a quarter of a century ago. This accounts for the preponderance of manuscripts from the Bodleian library. An *editio major*, based on many more manuscripts, might lead to stemmatic insights and to the discovery of additional facts. The readings for the present article have been recently rechecked.[7] For the sake of convenience the editions of Ibn Shmuel and Joel serve as basis for the collations, but the Hebrew orthography has not been rigidly kept. Remarks will be arranged according to the numbered readings,[8] but two points of a more general nature may not be out of place.

no. 3 (1830), pp. 93f.), that judgment seems to stand. J. Kafiḥ's edition (1972) adds practically edition and collating readings. However, he intended no more than to give a very general eclectic collation, the more so since he accepted the judgment of D. Z. H. Baneth that little of importance is to be gained. But for the possible emergence of additional fragments of a "proto-autograph" (cf. Hirschfeld *JQR* (Old Series) 15 (1903), pp. 677f., Yellin, *Tarbiẕ* 1, no. 3 (1930), pp. 93f.), that judgment seems to stand. J. Kafiḥ's edition (1972) adds practically nothing to our knowledge, and was not intended to be of textual value.

4. *Doctor Perplexorum* (Guide of the Perplexed) . . . revised . . . by Dr. Yehuda Ibn Shmuel (Jerusalem, 1946). As opposed to Munk and Joel, Ibn Shmuel had little interest in philological aspects. The list of readings appended to his (incomplete) annotated edition (Tel Aviv, 1935) is geared to the practical side of his "corrected" text, and cannot be taken as a basis for a critical edition of the Hebrew. Cf. p. lxxvi of his Introduction. On the whole his 1946 edition serves as a more trustworthy basis for collations, although a future edition should, of course, be worked around whatever manuscript should emerge from a pilot study as most suitable.

5. This is the sixth study in that series, and the first to appear in English. Previous papers were published as follows: 1) *Leshonenu* 15 (1947), pp. 173f. 2) *Tarbiẕ* 23 (1953), pp. 210f. 3) *ibid.* 26 (1957), pp. 185f., 335f. 4) *ibid.* 30 (1961), pp. 385f. 5) *Fourth World Congress of Jewish Studies* II (1968), pp. 109f. References to my *Medieval Hebrew Syntax and Vocabulary—as influenced by Arabic* (Jerusalem, 1951) will be indicated by *MHSV*.

6. Without extensive comparative notes as regards the linguistic usage of Samuel ibn Tibbon —preferably analytical concordances—no study will be complete. The problem of direct manuscript evidence, as opposed to quotations in commentators and to intentional improvements (as by Ibn Palqera), also remains to be studied. Because of the paramount importance of Maimonides' writings it is not surprising that the manuscripts point in the direction of repeated adaptation and revision of the Hebrew to the Arabic original. In a way, "Maimonidean philology" presents problems not dissimilar to those known from the study of Greek versions of the Bible.

7. As with much of my work, the credit for all the drudgery involved goes to my assistant, Mr. Shraga Assif, M. A. Thanks are also due my secretary, Mrs. Penina Firestone, who turned my hardly legible wriging into copy for the printer.

8. Remarks are confined to those readings which present a point of more general interest. Readings of Arabic orthography or (redundant) notation of cases have not been discussed.

a) The Arabic text emerges as very stable indeed. Even if we assume that further fragments of an earlier attempt at writing the *Guide* may emerge,[9] our manuscript tradition seems to derive from one archetype[10] and the preparation of a full scale critical edition may be expected to result in marginal improvements only. The Arabic apparatus will no doubt influence our judgment as regards the Hebrew tradition. But when we study in detail the MSS largely summed up as O[11] it seems doubtful indeed whether such an edition of the Arabic text, as was suggested by Joel (p. ט), would be worth the effort.

b) The Hebrew text, on the other hand, should certainly not be corrected according to the arbitrary procedure employed by Ibn Shmuel. Our exercise leaves no doubt that the Hebrew tradition underwent secondary adaptations to the Arabic—apart from "mechanical" changes, expansions, etc. Details will be discussed as regards some readings common to MSS נ and ע. No direct stemmatic connection seems obvious, and it is premature to speculate what final results will emerge. In any event, for the moment MSS נ and ע show a fair number of common deviations (aside from separate scribal changes) which are largely, though not exclusively, the result of an attempt to adapt Ibn Tibbon's rendering further to the Arabic.[12]

The following sigla are used for the manuscripts compared:[13]

Hebrew	*Arabic*
א — British Museum Add. 14763	1 — JTS mic. 2518
ב — Bodl. 1250	1* — JTS mic. 2513
ל — Bodl. 1251/2	2 — Berlin 105,1
מ — Bodl. 1253	3 — Leiden Or. 18
נ — Bodl. 1254	4 — Bodl. 1237,1
ט — Bodl. 1255	5 — Bodl. 1238
ע — Bodl. 1256	6 — Bodl. 1239
פ — Bodl. 1257	7 — Bodl. 1243
צ — Bodl. 1957,2	8 — Bodl. 1244
ק — Paris Heb. 691,1	9 — Bodl. 1245
	10 — Bodl. 2508
	11 — JTS mic. 2264
	12 — Bodl. 1247
	13 — Bodl. 1249
	14 — British Museum Or. 1423

9. Cf. above, n. 3. I do not wish to involve myself at present in a study of what these fragments really represent—in light of our present knowledge of Maimonidean autographs.

10. As far as I can judge, MS 4 of our Arabic apparatus offers little beyond scribal freaks.

11. cf. p. 474 of Joel's edition.

12. On the other hand ע and נ can be seen to have made revisions on "stylistic" grounds. It is needless to add that from a full scale apparatus additional MSS may emerge. The separate readings of MS ב should also be watched; note below reading 21/24, which could result from a rewording based on the Arabic.

13. Details of the MSS can easily be verified from the catalogues; they are all extant in the collection of microfilms at the National and University Library in Jerusalem, where readings were rechecked. Some unevenness in my collation could not be corrected. Some readings have been adduced from MSS not fully collated, and hence not enumerated in this list; these will be introduced as occasion arises.

SAMPLE TEXT A: II, 29

אעלם אן מן לם[1] יפהם לגה̈ אנסאן אדׄא[2]
סמעה יתכלם פהו בלא שך יערף[3] אנה יתכלם
גיר אנה לא ידרי[4] מקצדה ואשד מן הדׄא[5] אנה
קד יסמע מן[6] כלאמה כלמאת הי בחסב לגה̈ אל-
מתכלם תדל עלי מעני ויתפק באלערץׄ[7] אן
תכון תלך אלכלמה̈[8] פי לגה̈ אלסאמע תדל עלי
צׄד[9] דׄלך[10] אלמעני אלדׄי אראדה[11] אלמתכלם
פיטׄן[12] אלסאמע אן דלאלתהא ענד אלמתכלם
כדלאלתהא ענדה מתׄל לו סמע ערבי רגׄלא[13]
עבראניא[14] יקול אבה[15] פיטׄן[16] אלערבי אנה
יחכי[17] ען שכׄץ אנה[18] כרה אמרא[19] מא ואבאה[20]
ואלעבראני אנמא אראד אנה ארצׄאה דׄלך[21]
אלאמר ואראדה והכדׄא[22] יגׄרי ללגׄמהור[23] פי
כלאם אלאנביא סוא[24] בעץׄ[25] כלאמהם לא
יפהם אצלא בל כמא קאל ותהי לכם חזות הכל
כדברי הספר החתום[26] ובעצׄה יפהם מנה צׄדה
או נקיצׄה כמא קאל והפכתם את[27] דברי אלהים
חיים ואעלם אן לכל נבי[28] כלאמא[29] מא[30]
כׄציצא[31] בה[32] כאנה לגה̈ דׄלך[33] אלשכׄץ הכדׄא[34]
ינטקה אלוחי אלכׄציץ בה למן פהמה.
ובעד הדׄה אלמקדמה̈ פלתערף אן ישעיה[35]
ע״אס[36] אטרד פי כלאמה כתׄירא[37] גדׄא ופי
כלאם גירה קלילא[38] אנה[39] אדׄא[40] אכׄבר ען
אנתקאץׄ[41] דולה̈ או הלאך מלה̈ עטׄימה̈[42] יגׄיב
דׄלך[43] בלפטׄ[44] אן אלכואכב סקטת ואלסמא
כורת[45] ואלשמס אסודת[46] ואלארץׄ כׄרבת ו־

1) 6, 7, 8, 10: לא 2) 1, 10: אדׄי 3) 1: יעלם
4) 7: ידר 5) 10, 14: הדׄי 6) 4: מנה 7) 1: ב־
ערץׄ 8) 1: אלכמלה̈ 9) 10: > 10) 1, 10: דׄאלך
11) 1: אלדׄין אראדת 12) 1, 2, 10, 14: פיצׄן
13) 6: רגׄל 14) 1, 2, 10: עבראנייא; 6: עבראני
15) 2, 3, 4, 5, 6, 7, 8, 9: אבא 16) 1, 2, 10, 14:
פיצׄן 17) 6: חכי 18) 9: > 19) 1, 4, 5, 10: אמר
20) 1: > 21) 1, 10: דׄאלך 22) 1, 5, 6, 9, 14,10:
והכדׄי 23) 1: לאלגׄמהור 24) 8: סוי; 3: סוא
בסוא; 6: סוא הו 25) 6: פבעץׄ 26) 10, 14: >
27) 1, 2, 5, 6, 7, 8, 10, 14: > 28) 5, 6, 8: נביא
29) 1, 2, 3, 4, 5, 6, 7, 8, 9, 10, 14: כלאם 30) 3: >
31) 2, 3, 4, 7, 8, 9, 10, 14: כׄציץ;
1: מכׄצוץ; 5: מכׄצץ; 6: כׄצץ 32) 5: + כׄציץ
בה 33) 1, 10: דׄאלך 34) 10, 14: הכדׄי 35)
6: ישעיהו 36) 4: ע״ה; 5: עליה אלסלאם; 6:
על״ס 37) 1, 4, 5, 6, 7, 8, 9, 10, 14 כתׄיר; 2:
מתׄלאת כתׄיר 38) 1, 2, 3, 4, 5, 6, 7, 8, 9, 10,
14: קליל 39) 1: ואנה; 2: ודׄלך אנה 40) 6: >;
10, 14: אדׄי 41) 9: אנקראץׄ (?) 42) 2, 10:
עצׄימה̈ 43) 1, 10: דׄאלך 44) 1, 2, 10: בלפץׄ
45) 1, 2, 4, 5, 7, 8, 10: כוורת; 6: כוורה̈ 46)

דע כי[1] מי שלא יבין לשון אדם כשישמעהו
מדבר ידע[2] בלא[3] ספק[2] שהוא מדבר אלא שלא
ידע כוונתו ויותר גדול מזה שהוא ישמע מד־
בריו[4] מלות הם[5] כפי לשון[5*] המדבר[6] מורות על
עניין אחד ויזדמן במקרה שתהיה המלה ההיא
בלשון השומע מורה על[6*] הפך העניין ההוא[7]
אשר רצהו המדבר ויחשב השומע שהוראתה[8]
אצל המדבר כהוראתה[9] אצלו כאלו שמע ערבי
איש עברי[10] יאמר אבה[11] ויחשב הערבי[12] שהוא
מספר על איש שהוא[13] מאס עניין אחד ומאנו[14]
והעברי[15] אמנם ירצה שהוא[16] ישר[17] בעיניו
העניין[18] ורצהו וכן יקרה[19] להמון בדברי הנ־
ביאים שוה בשוה קצת דבריהם[20] לא יבין[21]
כלל אבל כמו שאמר ותהי לכם חזות הכל[22]
כדברי הספר החתום וקצתו[23] יבין[24] ממנו הפ־
כו[25] או סותרו כמו שאמר והפכתם[26] את[27] דברי
אלהים חיים ודע כי לכל נביא דבר אחד מיוחד
בו[28] כאלו הוא לשון האיש ההוא כן תביאהו[29]
לדבר הנבואה המיוחדת בו למי[30] שיבינהו[31].
ואחר זאת ההקדמה[32] תדע כי ישעיהו ע״ה נמ־
שך בדבריו הרבה מאד ובדברי זולתו מעט כי
כשהגיד[33] על[34] נתיצת[35] עם או אבדן[36] אמה[37]
גדולה יספרהו[38] בלשון[39] שהכוכבים[40] נפלו וה־
שמים[41] אבדו[42] ורגזו[43] והשמש קדרה והארץ
חרבה[44] ורעשה והרבה מכיוצא[45] באלו
השאלות[46] וזה כמו[47] שיאמר אצל הערב[48]
למי שימצאהו[49] פגע גדול נהפכו שמיו[50] על
ארצו וכן כשיספר בהתחדש[51] הצלחת אמה

1) **נ**: > 2–2) **נ,ע**: הוא בלא ספק ידע 3) **ל**:
בלי 4) **ע**: דבריו 5) **נ**: > 5*) **ל**: הלשון
6) **מ**: הדבר 6*) **א**: > 7) **ל**: > 8) **ל**:
שהוראתו 9) **ל**: כהוראתו 10) **נ,ס**: ערבי;
נ (שוליים): הערבי 11) **א,ל,מ,צ**: אִבא
12) **נ**: > 13) **ל**: > 14) **כ**: > 15) **מ**:
הערבי 16) **כ,ל,צ**: > 17) **ל,צ**: שישר
18 **כ**: > 19) **נ,ע**: ינהג 20) **נ**: דבריהן
21) **כ**: יובן 22) **ס**: כל 23) **כ**: מקצתו
24) **כ**: יובן 25) **כ**: והפכו 26) **מ**: והפכתים
27) **א,ל,מ,נ,ס,ע,פ,ק**: > 28) **א**: לו; **ל**: >
29) **כ**: + הנבואה 30) **כ**: כלמי 31) **צ**:
שיבנאהו 32) **מ**: הקדמה 33) **צ**: כשהוא
הגיד 34) **נ,ע**: > 35) **כ**: נפיצת; **מ**: נתיצב
36) **נ,ע**: מיתת 37) **צ**: > 38) **ל**: וספרהו
38–39) **נ,ע**: יסתיר זה במל(ו)ת 40) **ל,מ**:
הכוכבים 41) **ל**: ושמים; **צ**: מן השמים
42) **ל**: קדרו 42–43) **נ,ע**: רגזו 44) **מ,ס,פ,ק**:
אבדה 45) **נ**: כיוצא 46) **ל,נ,ע**: השא(י)לות
47) **מ,נ,ע**: כמה 48) **כ**: העדר 49) **א,ל,ע**:
שמצאהו 50) **א**: שמים 51–52) **נ**: הקדמת

תזלזלת[47] וכת̇יר מן אמת̇אל[48] הד̇ה אלאסת־
עאראת והד̇א[49] מת̇ל מא יקאל[50] ענד אלערב
למן[51] אצאבתה[52] מציבה̈ עט̇ימה̈[53] אקתלבת[54]
סמאוה[55] עלי ארצ̇ה וכד̇לך[56] אד̇א[57] וצף אק־
באל דולה̈ ותג̇דד סעאדה̈[58] כני[59] ען ד̇לך[60]
בזיאדה̈ נור אלשמס[61] ואלקמר ותג̇דד סמא
ותג̇דד ארץ̇[62] ונחו הד̇א[63] כמא[64] אנהם אד̇א[65]
וצפוא[66] הלאך שכ̇ץ או מלה̈ או מדינה̈[67] נס־
בוא[68] חאלאת גצ̇ב וסכ̇ט שדיד ללה[69] עליהם
ואד̇א[70] וצפוא[71] אקבאל קום נסבוא[72] ללה[73]
חאלאת פרח וסרור פיקולון[74] פי חאלאת אל־
גצ̇ב עליהם[75] יצא וירד ושאג והרעים ונתן קולו
וכת̇ירא[76] מת̇ל הד̇א[77] ויקולון איצ̇א צוה[78] ואמר
ופעל ועשה ונחו ד̇לך[79] כמא[80] סאצף[81] וכד̇לך[82]
אד̇א[83] אכ̇בר אלנבי[84] בהלאך אהל מוצ̇ע מא
קד יבדל[85] מכאן אהל ד̇לך[86] אלמוצ̇ע אלנוע[87]
כלה כמא[88] קאל ישעיה ע״אס[89] ורחק[90] ה׳ את
האדם[91] והו יעני[92] הלאך ישראל וקאל צפניה
פי ד̇לך[93] והכרתי את[94] האדם מעל[95] פני ה־
אדמה[96] ונטיתי ידי[97] על יהודה פאעלם הד̇א[98]
איצ̇א

4: אסוודת; 10: אסודה 47) 6: ותזלזל 48) 1:
< 49) 10, 14: והד̇י 50) 1: יקע 51) 4, 9: מן
52) 9: אצאבה 53) 1, 2, 10, 14: עצ̇ימה̈ 54)
6: אקתלב; 10: אקתלבה; 4: אנקלבת 55) 1, 2,
4, 5, 6, 7, 8, 9, 10: סמאה 56) 1, 10: וכד̇אלך
57) 10: אד̇י 58) 4: כעאדה 59) 1, 2, 4, 5, 6, 7,
8, 9: כנא 60) 1, 10: ד̇אלך 61) 6: שמס 62)
10, 14: אלארץ̇ 63) 10, 14: הד̇י; 6, 8, 14: הדה
64) 10: כמי 65) 10: אד̇י; 6:< 66) 1, 4, 10:
וצפו 67) 4, 9: מדינה̈ או מלה̈ 68) 1, 4, 9, 10:
נסבו 69) 4, 9,: ללאלאה 70) 10, 14: ואד̇י 71)
1, 4, 10, 14: וצפו 72) 1, 4, 9, 10:
נסבו 73) 4: ללאלה(?); 9: ללאלאה
74) 4: פליקולון 75) 1:< 76) 1, 2, 3, 4, 5, 6, 7,
8, 9, 10, 14: וכת̇יר 77) 10, 14: הד̇י 78) 1:<
79) 1, 10: ד̇אלך 80) 5: ממא 81) 9: אצף 82)
1, 10: וכד̇אלך 83) 10: אד̇י 84) 5, 6, 8: אלנביא
85) 6: יבדלך 86) 1, 10: ד̇אלך 87) 3: באלנוע
88) 10: כמי 89) 1, 3, 4, 5, 6, 7, 8, 9:< 90) 4,
5, 7: וריחק 91) 4: + וג׳ 92) 6: ועני 93) 1, 10:
ד̇אלך 94) 4:< 95) 5: אשר על 96) 1:<; 9:
+ וג׳ 97) 1:< 98) 10: הד̇י

יכנהו[52] בתוספת אור[53] השמש והירח[54]
והתחדש[55] שמים[55] והתחדש[56] ארץ[56] וכיוצא
בזה[57] כמו שהם[58] כשספרו[59] אבדן[60] איש או
אמה[61] או מדינה ייחסו ענייני[62] כעס וחרון[63]
גדול[64] לבורא עליהם וכשספרו[65] הצלחת[66] עם
ייחסו[67] לשם ענייני[68] שמחה וצהלה ויאמרו[69]
בענייני הכעס[70] עליהם יצא וירד ושאג והרעים
ונתן קולו והרבה כמו זה[71] ויאמרו[72] גם כן[73] צוה
ואמר ופעל ועשה וכיוצא בזה כמו שאספר וכן
כשיגיד[74] הנביא על[75] אבדן[75] אנשי מקום[76]
אחד[77] פעמים[78] יחליף מקום[79] אנשי המקום
ההוא[80] במין[81] כלו כמו שאמר[82] ישעיהו[83]
ע״ה[84] ורחק[85] ה׳ את האדם והוא[86] רוצה לומר
אבדת ישראל ואמר צפניהו[87] בזה והכרתי את
האדם מעל פני האדמה וגו׳[88] ונטיתי ידי על
יהודה ודע זה גם כן

(ד׳ מחוקה) אומה בהתחדש הצלחה יכנה;
ע: הקדמת אומה בהתחדש הצלחה יכנה זה;
צ: בהצלחת חדוש אומה יכנהו 53) **ע**:
+ מחדש 54 **נ,ע**:< 55–55) **א,מ,צ**:<
56–56) **ל**: וארץ 57) **כ,ל,מ**: בהם 58) **כ,נ**
(שוליים), **פ,צ**: + ר״ל הנביאים; **ל**: + כן
הנביאים 59) **א, כ, ל, מ, נ, ס, ע, פ, צ, ק**:
כשיספרו 60) **נ, ע**: מיתת 61) **מ,**
ס, ק: אשה 62–63) **צ**: כעס ועניני חרון 63) **פ**:
וחסרון 64) **ע**:< 65) **א, כ, מ, נ, ס, ע, פ, צ, ק**:
וכשיספרו; **ל**: וכשיהפכו 66) **נ**: הקדמת 67)
מ: ייחוסו 68) **ל**:< 69) **צ**: ויאמר 70) **ל**: כעס
71–73) **ל**:< 72) **ק**: ויאמר 74) **א, מ, נ, ס, ע, ק**:
כשהגיד 75–75) **א, כ, ל, מ, ס, פ, צ, ק**: באבדן;
נ, ע: באבדת 76) **מ, נ**: המקום 77) **נ, פ**:<
78) **א, ל, מ, נ, ס, ע, פ, ק**:< 79) **כ, צ**:< 80)
ע: + אנשי; **ק** (מעל השורה): + במקום 81) **א,**
כ, ל, מ, נ, ס, ע, פ, צ, ק: המין 82) **צ**: + הנביא
83) **ל, צ**: ישעיה 84) **א, כ, מ, נ, ס, ע, פ, ק**:<
85) **פ**: וריחק 86) **נ, ע**:< 87) **ע, צ**: צפניה
88) **א, כ, ל, מ, נ, ס, ע, פ, צ, ק**:<

NOTES ON HEBREW READINGS

2: The first case of an **נ, ע** reading is indicative of our problem. The Hebrew sentence ידע בלא ספק שהוא מדבר is correct; an imitation of the Arabic word order would result in . . . הוא בלא ספק ידע, which is what **נ, ע** read. In each instance of **נ, ע** deviations we have to ask ourselves whether **נ, ע** might possibly represent the original rendering while all other MSS have introduced a change. The overall evidence, however, precludes that model and נ, ע emerge as the revising MSS.[14]

14: The omission of ומאנו may be purely accidental, but it seems to illustrate textual dynamics. Maimonides had to use both *ʾabā* and a synonym to make his point. The only way in which Ibn Tibbon could match that was by using an equivalent for לא אבה, i.e. מאן. Thus an apparent redundancy resulted, which was resolved by omission.

16: The Hebrew of Ibn Tibbon attempted to imitate the double-faced position of Arabic *ʾamr* as subject and object. The construction *ʾarḍāhu l-ʾamru* is perhaps not quite classical, but its sense is obvious. The readings mirror attempts to smooth over, resulting in שהוא ישר בעיניו / שישר בעיניו העניין. To be sure, the attempt can result in conflation, as in MS כ (if our collation is correct). But, *e.g.* MS Harley 5507 (not collated here) reads אמנם ירצה שהוא ישר בעיניו.

19: The reading ינהג cannot result from יקרה. But it could result from a direct rendering of *yağri*.[15]

27: Both the Hebrew and Arabic manuscript evidence shows that Maimonides quoted *Jer.* xxiii, 36 without את, This is confirmed by Alḥarīzī's reading in Paris Heb 682. For "readings" in Maimonides' Bible quotations, cf. *e.g.* Yellin, *Tarbiẕ* i, 3 (1930), p. 94. There is, of course, no point in comparing other sources that omitted את, since this is the kind of reading which could arise again and again according to the "law of scribes".[16]

28: The Arabism מיוחד בו (cf. *MHSV*, p. 178) was often changed by scribes, who either substituted לו or omitted the preposition altogether.

36: The reading מיתת could not arise mechanically.

38: This case affords proof, if any were still needed. The Hebrew יספרהו is not an exact rendering of יגיב, but it fits the context. The revisors (נ, ע) offer יסתיר. I do not believe in any chain that changed יספרהו to יסתיר זה. I would rather submit that the reading results from taking the Arabic as יגיב instead of יג̇יב.[17]

42: The revising MSS may have attempted, among other things, to reduce redundancies. Arabic *kuwwirat* caused trouble to Ibn Tibbon, who tried to work in the root אבד as used by Maimonides in his explanation: *wa-maʿnā-ttakwir ʾibādatu-sammāʾ*.[18] The reviser cut out אבדו which seemed redundant.[19]

46: Unless a terminological study of the MSS shows otherwise, it seems that Ibn Tibbon used השאלה for *ʾistiʿārat(un)*.

14. Note the cases of secondary adaptations in the version of another treatise of Maimonides, which I have discussed in *Tarbiẕ* 26 (1957), pp. 186; 336. As a rule, the philology of medieval translations tends to confirm the experience gained from the philology of biblical translations, *viz.* that secondary adaptations tend to result in linguistically more awkward constructions.

15. Cf. *MHSV*, p. 202. Such an explanation runs counter to a basic point of method, that one should not assume a reviser to have worked blindly. One should assume that he tried to improve, not to spoil. But our MSS do not seem to follow that rule.

16. Cf. my *Text and Language in Bible and Qumran* (1960), index *s.v.* I wonder whether the reading with את (according to MT) as given in Kafiḥ's edition is in fact based on his MSS. In any event, his index to Bible verses in Maimonides (1972) does not hint at any textual deviation.

17. Again, we end up by accusing the corrector of not only lacking a proper sense of what he was trying to do, but also of attributing meanings to Arabic forms. It should be noted, at least, that אגאב is not attested in the dictionaries in any suitable sense; but it could easily have been construed as "make disappear".

18. Cf. the note in Munk's edition of the *Guide* II, p. 211.

19. On the other hand חרבה below was changed to אבדה under the impact of the parallelism.

51: The reading of נ, ע is another hapless attempt at verbatim rendering. הקדמה for *ʾiqbāl* in the sense of 'success' is not Ibn Tibbon's rendering; Cf. below, 66.

58: The additional ר"ל הנביאים may turn out to be of stemmatic value. It is also read by Harley 5507; 7586A.[20]

59: The MSS suggest that Ibn Tibbon rendered the tenses of the אדֿא-clause by Hebrew imperfect forms, hence כשיספרו. However, as regards no. 74 the situation is not identical, since the sentence deals with the description of a fact, not a general assumption.

74: The original reading seems to be ... כשהגיד הנביא באבדן (also MSS Harley 5507, 7586A). To be sure, הגיד without direct object is not found in classical Hebrew. Note הגיד על above, 34 (and נ,ע there). I do not know why the revisers favoured אבדה over אבדן.

78: This kind of reading may turn out to be of stemmatic importance for future study. The manuscript evidence (to which Harley 5507, 7586A can be added) is clearly against פעמים. Yet this is precisely the way in which Ibn Tibbon renders a *qad* construction (*MHSV* §9), and no Arabic MS omits *qad.* The manuscript evidence thus suggests a solution diametrically opposed to the idiomatic evidence. We should nevertheless operate at this stage with the assumption of hyparchetypal (?) omissions rather than further attempts at revision.

81: The manuscript evidence is clear: Arabic *ʾan-nawʿ* = Hebrew המין. Since the construction (with two objects) got a bit out of hand, the common החליף ב- got into the text. I cannot find evidence for a similar use of *ʾabdala* with two objects in classical Arabic.

86: This would illustrate the "stylistic" type of revision by MSS נ, ע. They must have assumed that והוא רוצה לומר is unusual—contrary to the Arabic.

NOTES ON ARABIC READINGS

The following notes deal mainly with aspects of the Arabic text which are connected with a problem in the Hebrew. They are not intended as a discussion of Judaeo-Arabic features.

1: Hebrew לא יבין does not tip the balance in favour of *lā yafham,* since Arabic *lam*-constructions are likewise regularly rendered by Hebrew לא (*MHSV* §287). Hence the judgment that *lā* is secondary can be arrived at only by tracing possible inner-Arabic developments of *man*-clauses.

15: Manuscript evidence shows that Maimonides used the Arabic *ʾabā*; the MSS in Hebrew n. 11 offer corroborative proof.

18: The omission of *ʾannahu* should be regarded as unintentional. The omission resulted in a *ṣifa*-clause; the syntactical parallel (Hebrew n. 13) should be regarded as coincidental, unless material is found to the contrary.

24: It stands to reason that scribes might vary adverbials slightly and interchange *sawāʾ* with *sawāʾ bisawāʾ*. The Arabic evidence clearly favours the simple adverbial. The opposite holds true for the Hebrew. According to the material collected in *MHSV* §125, I would assume that Hebrew שוה בשוה is directly dependent on its Arabic counterpart—contrary to the present evidence of Arabic MSS.

31: The overall judgment on the nature of a MS might be influenced by our observation of negligible variations such as the present one. It goes without saying that Maimonides intended the form *ḫaṣīṣ* (the problem of case endings does not concern us at the moment). The reading בׄצץ could easily arise mechanically. But מבׄצוץ/מבׄצץ are intentionally "easier" forms, which might connect up with similar

20. Kafiḥ is convinced (p. שסז, n. 10) that this is Ibn Tibbon's language.

changes in the MSS concerned. On the other hand, but for the force of manuscript evidence one might have thought of *ʾinqirāḍ* as the original form (no. 41, below), judging by suitability. But *ʾintiqāḍ* is what Maimonides wrote.[21]

54: We should not expect to find "easier" readings in one particular MS; the manuscript evidence shows that someone preferred *ʾinqalabat*. But Maimonides used *ʾiqtalabat*, which was certainly not standard usage.[22]

SAMPLE TEXT B: III, 34

ממא יג̇ב אן תעלמה איצ̇א אן אלשריעה̈
לא תלתפת ללשאד̇[1] ולא יכון אלתשריע בחסב
אלאמר אלאקל בל כל מא[2] יראד[3] תחצילה
מן ראי או כ̇לק או עמל נאפע אנמא[4] יקצד
בה אלאמור אלאכת̇ריה̈[5] ולא ילתפת ללאמר[6]
אלקליל אלוקוע או לאד̇יה̈[7] תקע לואחד מן
אלנאס מן אג̇ל ד̇לך[8] אלתקדיר ואלתדביר[9]
אלשרעי[10] לאן אלשריעה̈ הי אמר אלאהי
ולך אן תעתבר[11] באלאמור אלטביעיה̈[12] אלתי
תלך אלמנאפע אלעאמה̈ אלמוג̇ודה̈ פיהא פי
צ̇מנהא ולאזם ענהא אד̇יאת[13] שכ̇ציה̈[14] כמא
באן מן[15] כלאמנא וכלאם[16] ג̇ירנא ובחסב[17]
הד̇א[18] אלאעתבאר איצ̇א לא תעג̇ב מן כון
קצד אלשריעה̈ לא[19] יתם פי כל שכ̇ץ ושכ̇ץ בל
ילזם[20] צ̇רורה̈ וג̇וד אשכ̇אץ לא יכמלהם ד̇לך[21]
אלתדביר אלשרעי לאן אלצור[22] אלטביעיה̈[23]
אלנועיה̈[24] לא יחצל[25] כל מא ילזם ענהא[26]
פי כל שכ̇ץ ושכ̇ץ[27] לאן אלכל[28] מן אלאה[29]

מה[1] שצריך שתדעהו גם כן שהתורה[2] לא[3]
תביט [4] לדבר הזר[5] ולא תהיה התורה כפי
העניין המועט אבל כל מה[5*] שירצה ללמדו[6]
מדעת או[7] מדה[8] או מעשה[9] מועיל אמנם
יכוון בו העניינים שהם[10] על הרוב ולא[11]
יביט[12] לעניין הנמצא מעט ולא להזק[13] שיבוא
לאחד מבני אדם מפני השיעור ההוא
וההנהגה[14] ההיא התוריית[15] כי התורה היא[16]
עניין אלוהי ועליך לבחון העניינים הטבעיים
אשר התועלות ההם[17] הכוללות הנמצאות
בה[18] יש בכללם[19] ויתחיב[20] מהם[21] נזקים
פרטיים כמו שהתבאר מדברינו[22] ודברי[23]
זולתינו ולפי זאת הבחינה גם כן אין לתמוה
מהיות[24] כוונת[24*] התורה לא תשלם בכל[25] איש
ואיש[26] אבל יתחייב בהכרח[27] מציאות אנשים
לא תשלימם ההנהגה ההיא התוריית[28] כי
הצורות הטבעיות המיניות לא יתנו כל מה
שראוי בכל[29] איש ואיש[30] כי הכל מאל[31]

1) 1*: לאלשאד̇ 2) 12, 13: כלמא 3) 4:
ימכן 4) 1* 10, 11: אנמ̇י 5) 2, 10, 11: אלאכ־
ת̇רייה̈ 6) 1*, 10: לאלאמר 7) 2, 11: לאד̇ייה̈
8) 1*, 10, 11: ד̇אלך 9) 11: ואלתרתיב 10) 4:
או לתדביר אלשרט 11) 1*: תעבר 12) 1*,
2, 10, 11: אלטביעייה̈; 4: אלמודיה̈ ללטאעה̈
13) 2: אד̇ייאת 14) 1*, 2, 10, 11: שכ̇צייה 15) 4:
ולא יכני שכ̇ציה̈ באן פי 16) 3: וכלא 17) 4:
אד̇א 18) 4: בהד̇א 19) 4: לם 20) 3: לזם 21) 1*,
10, 11: ד̇אלך 22) 2, 10, 11: אלצוור 23) 1*,
2, 10, 11: אלטביעייה̈ 24) 1*, 2, 11: אלנועייה̈
25) 3: תחצל 26) 3: > 27) 11: > 28) 11: לאנהא
29) 6: אלאלאה 30) 1*, 2, 4, 5, 6, 10, 12, 13:

1) נ, צ: ממה 2) צ: > 3–4) מ: מפריש
5) ל: זר 5*) מ: > 6) פ: ללומדו 7) כ:
כל 8–9) ע: ממעשה 10) ל: אשר הם 11) כ:
לא 12) א, כ, ל, מ, נ, ס, ע, פ, צ, ק: יביטו 13) מ:
לחוזה; ק: לחוזק 14) ע: והנהגה 15) א, כ,
נ, ס, צ, ק: התוריים; מ, פ: התורייה; ל: התוריי
16) כ, ל: הוא; ע: > 17) כ: מהם; מ: הזה
18) א, כ, ל, מ, נ, ס, ע, פ, צ, ק: בהם 19) פ:
בכללן 20) ע: ותתחייב 21) פ: מהן 22) ל: >
23) ל: בדברי; כ: ומדברי (שתי האותיות
הראשונות תלויות) 24) ע: מלהיות 24*) ק:
כוונות 25) ל: > 26) ל: באיש; צ: > 27) מ:
בה כח 28) א, כ, ל, מ, נ, ס, ע, פ, ק: התורי(י)ה
29) ל, ע: לכל 30) ע: > 31) ע: מאד 32) א,

21. As noted above, internal idiomatic study will be decisive in this context. Note, for the present problem, the use of *ʾintiqāḍ* (ed. Joel, p. 236:14) as opposed to *ʾinqaraḍat* (p. 236:22). Yet there remains the problem of manuscript evidence; note Hirschfeld's collation (Joel, p. 483).

22. The only dictionary quotation known to me is from this very passage; cf. Friedländer, *Der Sprachgebrauch des Maimonides* (1902), p. 95. Cf. the idiom p. 236: 25 *was-samāʾ muntabiqat(un) ʿalayhi* which, surprisingly enough, was also rendered נהפכים by Ibn Tibbon.

ואחד ופאעל[30] ואחד נתנו[31] מרועה[32] אחד וכלאף הדא[33] ממתנע וקד בינא[34] אן ללממתנע[35] טביעה̈ תאבתה̈ לא תתגיר[36] אבדא ובחסב הדא[37] אלאעתבאר איצ̇א לא ימכן אן תכון אלשראיע מקידה̈[38] בחסב אכ̇תלאף חאלאת אלאשכ̇אץ ואלאזמאן שבה אלעלאג̇ אלטבי[39] אלד̇י יכ̇ץ עלאג̇ כל שכ̇ץ[40] בחסב מזאג̇ה אלחאצ̇ר[41] בל ינבגי אן יכון אלתדביר אלשרעי מטלקא עאמא ללכל[42] ואן כאן ד̇לך[43] לאזמא[44] פי חק אשכ̇אץ ופי חק אכ̇רין לא ילזם לאנה לו כאן בחסב אלאשכ̇אץ לוקע אלפסאד ללכל[45] ונתת[46] דבריך לשיעורין[47] ומן אג̇ל הד̇א[48] לא ינבגי אן תקיד[49] אלאמור אלמקצודה̈ קצדא אולא[50] מן אלשריעה̈ לא בזמאן ולא במכאן בל תכון אלאחכאם מטלקה̈ עאמה̈ כמא קאל[51] תעאלי הקהל[52] חקה אחת לכם[53] לכן[54] ילחט[55] פיהא[56] אלמצאלח[57] אלעאמה̈ אלאכת̇ריה̈[58] כמא בינא[59] ובעד תקדימי להד̇ה אלמקדמאת אכ̇ד̇ פי תביין מא קצדת תביינה

אחד ופוׄעל[32] אחד[33] נתנו[34] מרועה[35] אחד[36] וחלוף זה נמנע וכבר ביארנו שלנמנע[37] טבע קיים לא ישתנה[38] לעולם ולפי זאת הבחינה גם כן אי איפשר שיהיו התורות[39] נתונות[40] לפי עניני[41] האנשים[42] והזמנים המתחלפים כדמות[43] הרפואה אשר רפואת[44] כל איש מיוחדת לפי[45] מזגו הנמצא בשעתו אבל צריך שתהיה[46] ההנהגה התוריית[47] מוחלטת כוללת לכל[48] ואף על פי שהיא ראויה לקצת אנשים ולאחרים אינה ראויה כי[49] אלו היתה[50] לפי האנשים היה[51] נׄופל ההפסד בכל ונתת דבריך לשיעורין ומפני זה אין ראוי[52] שיקשרו העניינים המכוונים כוונה ראשונה מן התורה לא בזמן ולא במקום אבל יהיו[53] החקים[54] והמשפטים[55] מוחלטים סתם[56] וכוללים[57] כמו[58] שאמר ית׳ הקהל[59] חקה אחת לכם[60] ואמנם יכוון בהם התקנות הכוללות על הרוב כמו שבארנו ואחר הקדימי אלו ההקדמות אתחיל לבאר מה שכוונתי[61] לבארו

ופעל 31) 2, 3, 5, 10, 11: וכולם נתנו; 1*: וכלם נתנו 32) 1*, 11, 12: מרעה 33) 10: הד̇י 34) 1*, 2, 5, 10, 11, 12: ביינא; 4: בוננא 35) 1*: לאלממתנע 36) 2, 5, 6, 10, 11: תתגייר 37) 2, 10: הד̇י 38) 1*, 2, 4, 5, 6, 10, 11: מקיידה̈ 39) 4: אלטביי 40) 12: יכ̇ץ כל עלאג̇ שכ̇ץ 41) 6: אלחאט̇ר 42) 1*, 10: לאלכל 43) 1*, 10, 11: ד̇אלך 44) 1*, 2, 3, 4, 5, 6, 10, 11, 12, 13: לאזם 45) 1*: לאלכל 46) 1*, 2, 3, 4, 10, 11, 12, 13: ונתתה 47) 11: לשיעורים 48) 10: הד̇י 49) 1*, 2, 4, 5, 6, 10, 11: תקייד 50) 4: אלא 51) 2: בקולה; 10: בקו׳ 52) 11: בק׳ והקהל 53) 4, 6: + וג׳ 54) 3: < 55) 1*, 2, 6, 10, 11: ילחץ̇; 4: לחט̇ 56) 3: פי הד̇ה 57) 11: אלמצלחה̈ 58) 2, 10, 11: אלאכת̇רייה̈; 4: אלאכ̇ירה̈ 59) 1*, 2, 4, 5, 10, 11, 12: ביינא; 13: בוננא

ל, מ, נ, ס, ע, פ, צ, ק: ופע(ו)לה; כ: ופעלת 33) א, כ, ל, מ, נ, ס, ע, פ, צ, ק: אחת 34) א, כ, ל, מ, נ, פ, צ, ק: וכ(ו)לם נתנו; ס: בכלם נתנו; ע: והכל נתנו 35–36) ע: מחשבה אחת 37) מ, נ, ס, פ: של נמנע; ע: שכל נמנע 38) צ: תשתנה 39) ע: התוריות 40–41) א: נקשרות בעיני; כ, מ, ס, פ, צ, ק: נקשרות בעני(י)ני; נ: נקשרות מענייני (ה־מ׳ כתובה מעל ב׳ מחוקה; בשוליים: נתונות לפי); ע: נתונות לׄאׄ נקשרות 42) כ: האדם 43) ל, ע: בדמות 44) ע: רפואות 45) א, כ, מ, נ, ס, פ, צ, ק: כפי 46) ע: שתורה 47) א, כ, ל, מ, נ, ס, ע, פ, ק: התורייה 48) ל: < 49) א: כל; מ: בו 50) א, כ, ל, מ, נ, ס, ע, פ, צ, ק: היה 51) ע: ההם 52) א, כ, ל, מ, נ, ס, ע, פ, צ, ק: צריך 53) א: < 54–55) א, ל, מ, נ, ע, צ: המשפטים והח(ו)קים 56–57) ל: וכוללים סתם 58) ק: מה 59–60) ע: וכי יגור אתכם גר ועשה פסח לה׳ כחקת הפסח וכמשפטו כן יעשה חקה אחת יהיה לכם ולגר ולאזרח הארץ 61) ע: + בו

NOTES ON HEBREW READINGS

1: Construction of the type *mimmā..* would usually seem to have been rendered by Ibn Tibbon ... ממה. We have, as yet, no judgment as to the stemmatic position of MS **צ**; for MS **נ**, cf. above.

12: The reading יביטו is too strongly in evidence to be ignored. It might have originated through ילתפת being taken as passive (*yultafat*).

15: The possibility of התוריי׳ cannot be ignored. According to readings 28, 47 the feminine form is התורייה, but the syntax of a common attribute needs to be studied. This is the kind of case where the manuscript evidence *ad loc.* cannot be decisive.

18: This illustrates the problem of MSS *versus* emendation. Ibn Tibbon rendered *fīhā* by בהם. There is no evidence for בה. In fact, if such evidence were now to turn up, we might suspect the scribe. For the moment בה (as printed) is an emendation, not an attested reading.

30: Syntactically כל איש (ואיש) presents the same possibilities as *kull šaḫṣ* (*wašaḫṣ*). The omissions in both Arabic and Hebrew seem unconnected.

32: Again manuscript evidence clearly goes against פועל, as demanded by the sense. For the moment, ופועל remains an emendation. The Arabic evidence shows the widespread reading *wafiᶜl,* which may therefore have been in Ibn Tibbon's copy. Alḥarizi, however, reads ופועל.

34: The combined Hebrew and Arabic evidence decides in favour of ... וכלם נתנו. The omission of כלם stems from the (unwarranted) effort to quote the verse according to the biblical original.[23]

35: For the overall evaluation of ע one must take note of such a reading. I do not see how רועה could have been etymologized from √רעה = *think*.

40: It will by now be clear that in this second sample we hardly find cases of נ, ע revising the text. However, this instance is indeed striking. Ibn Tibbon rendered נקשרות. The revising MSS corrected to נתונות, which is the reading of our vulgate text. To be sure, the root נתן had been used by Ibn Tibbon in a similar context twice before. But in this case the reading is neither an adaptation to the Arabic nor a stylistic improvement.

51: Ibn Tibbon must have lost sight of the antecedent הנהגה; in any event the reading is היה.

53: Evidence is decisive that *lā yanbagī* was rendered אין צריך (cf. *MHSV,* p. 237).

59: The text intended is *Num.* XV: 15. In this case ע saw fit to revise the text to the point of substituting different biblical evidence (*Num.* IX: 14).

These two sample texts are no more than random exercises. We cannot expect that they will illustrate all the problems of textual development, nor can they guide us towards establishing clear outlines of stemmatic relationships. But they may suffice to illustrate that the major text of medieval Hebrew philosophy has had a more chequered history than we would have thought possible. It will be up to the students of Maimonides' *oeuvre* to decide whether a critical edition of the *Guide* in Hebrew (and in Arabic) remains a *desideratum* of medieval Jewish studies.

23. We may assume that Maimonides quoted the verse in the form he remembered from TB *Ḥagigah* 3b; cf. Munk III, p. 267.

Averroes on Causation

A. L. IVRY

The *locus classicus* for the subject of this article is found toward the end of the *Tahāfut al-Tahāfut*, beginning with the introduction to the first of Averroes' chapters on the "natural sciences."[1] This chapter is located after the sixteenth chapter (literally "question" or "problem," *masʾala*) of Averroes work and is a response to chapters sixteen and seventeen of al-Ghazālī's *Tahāfut al-Falāsifa*.[2] The centrality of the issue itself and the echoes of it throughout Islamic, Jewish, and scholastic philosophy and theology call for a detailed examination of these passages, and particularly of Averroes' position, which has perhaps not been fully appreciated hitherto.[3]

Ghazali (to use the westernized form of his name) begins his discussion of the "natural sciences" with a traditional division of the subject into "roots" and "branches."[4] The former class includes the sciences of terrestrial and celestial bodies, movement and types of change, elements, minerals, plants, animals, and soul; while the latter class, or subdivision of the principal classes, encompasses medicine, astrology, physiognomy, dream interpretation, the telesmatic art, incantation, and alchemy. Ghazali accepts with equanimity all these subjects as legitimate objects of inquiry, subject to the qualifications he is soon to express. To him they all qualify as sciences, to which the *sharīʿa*, or revealed law, is not necessarily opposed.

Averroes, on the other hand, accepts the roots above mentioned but rejects the branches. While he allegedly does this on Aristotelian grounds, his zeal is probably motivated by other considerations. At least formally, however, he wishes to maintain the traditional distinction between theoretical and applied, or practical pursuits; only the former are to be called the physical or "natural" ciences, *al-ṭabīʿiyyāt*. Medicine is, accordingly faulted for its practical orientation, and it is apparent that the same formal reason lies behind the rejection of the other branches. However, Averroes does not say this explicitly. Instead, astrology is considered to be "only a prognostication of future events," physiognomy a prognostication of present events, and the interpretation of dreams presumably a prognostication of both.

Yet Averroes cannot be objecting to prognostication (*ʿilm bi-taqaddumati l-maʿrifa*) as such, particularly if we think of it as mere prediction, the welcome benefit of knowledge in every science. The indictment of astrology, physiognomy, and dream interpretation as prognostic sciences must therefore be based (formally) on the political or personal uses made of such prognostications, the uses which are in effect the reason for which these subjects are pursued. All these "branch" disciplines are, after all, practically orientated and as such equally disqualified as physical *qua* "natural" sciences.

This formal distinction is, however, a convenient device within which Averroes can indicate his feelings on the substantive nature of these branch pursuits. Excluding medicine, they are not, he intimates, suitable subjects of scientific investigation; their subject matter either does not have the properties claimed for it (as is said explicitly of the telesmatic art), or it is not given to scientific analysis, being "occult" (*khafi*, literally, "hidden").

Interestingly, Averroes is most charitably disposed to alchemy, though he doubts that it works as normally construed, since "art can at most become similar to nature but cannot attain nature itself in reality" (p. 312). Alchemy may, however, be able to simulate nature, and this is something which prolonged experimentation can alone determine. That Averroes is explicit in deferring to empirical observation in alchemy only, may be taken as further proof that he does not think that the other subjects are disposed to scientific investigation.

The "branches" are thus not physical sciences for Averroes, being both not physically "natural," and either not composed of scientific data or not existent. He thus appears to be saying that for an object to be a scientific *datum*—to exist as an object of investigation, knowledge and prediction—it must be clearly visible, i.e., publicly knowable. As such, the object must have a recognizable identity, must be the sort of thing which can in some sense be reproduced and tested.

The opening issue between Ghazali and Averroes thus reduces to an acceptance or rejection of the data of these disciplines. If, then, astrology, physiognomy, dream interpretation, the telesmatic art, conjuring (i.e., incantation), and pure alchemy are rejected as "natural sciences" by Averroes on more than formal grounds, as seems likely, it must be because he does not believe that there is sufficient evidence to warrant even entertaining their claims. Surely Ghazali does not have more facts at his disposal than does Averroes; therefore Averroes must be rejecting the sorts of facts that Ghazali would advance in support of his claim that these are scientific pursuits. These activities do not lend themselves to scientific analysis, then, for Averroes, because he must consider them as specious.

To say this is not to doubt the existence of the raw data of these pursuits but of the interpretation put upon them, i.e., the molding of these data into the "facts" of a theory. For example, Averroes would agree that the heavens influence the earth and that dreams have some kind of relationship to their bearer. He would, however, deny that there is any evidence to show that stars or dreams have the influences claimed for them by astrologers and dream interpreters. It is this specific interpretation of the data, that which in effect constitutes the specific subject matter of the field, which Averroes rejects. He must, of course, be very circumspect in his remarks, for both popular tradition and religion sanction and even hallow most of these activities. That Averroes nevertheless casts doubt, however discreetly, upon their validity, is accordingly very significant.

Ghazali can take the position he does because for him, as we shall see, anything not self-contradictory is possible, there is no natural constraint upon objects, and thus it is in principle equally possible to predicate practically anything of a given subject. For Averroes, however, things have their own natures, objective existences which do not permit any but specifically defined actions, known by observation and generalized into laws of nature. The occurrences claimed by the occult sciences do not conform to these laws, i.e., they are not, for Averroes, borne out by universal experience and experimentation, alleged appearances notwithstanding; and this because they go beyond the natural limits of their subjects. One cannot be charitable to the occult, Averroes would say, for this would blur the distinction between that which exists and that which does not exist. Thus, in choosing to limit physical reality to the "roots" of the natural sciences only, Averroes is not arbitrarily deciding what is real but is trying to keep faith with a clearly defined, experientially based notion of "nature itself in reality," i.e., in truth, *fī l-ḥaqīqa*.

It is this notion of an essentially independent natural reality, of essences which function of necessity, that Ghazali next attacks (p. 312). The very first of the four points in which he dissents from the philosophers concerns the necessary nature of cause and effect relationships, and he contends that it is possible for what is usually (though wrongly) regarded as a "cause" to exist without an equally erroneously regarded "effect" and vice versa. Ghazali feels it is necessary to make this assertion in order to shatter the "usual course of nature," (*al-ʿāda*), and thus make room for the miraculous. Indeed, it is the existence of miracles which is taken as proof of the non-necessary relation of what is seen mistakenly as cause and effect in nature. While recognizing that the philosophers generally interpret scriptural miracles in a naturalistic manner, Ghazali feels he has found exceptions to the philosophers' stand on natural causation in certain of their attitudes to the imagination and intellect. They claim, he says, that individuals well endowed with one or the other (or both) of these faculties may either see into the future, comprehend difficult problems without the mediate steps of reasoning that are usually necessary, and/or effect material objects and events by psychic means alone. Ghazali would merely extend this category of the miraculous, he insists, and not impose any necessary conditions on it.

To this Averroes answers circumspectly (p. 315). Certainly he is not opposed to miracles *per se*; they are, he acknowledges, the sacrosanct "principles of the religions," (*mabādiʾul-sharāʾiʿ*), premises of faith similar to belief in the existence of God, blessedness (*saʿāda*), and "the virtues" (*al-faḍāʾil*). Belief is these principles is deemed necessary for performing virtuous acts, and virtue is regarded as a condition for attaining knowledge.[5] Hence belief in miracles, and the other tenets of faith, is seen by Averroes as a necessary condition for examining the nature of miracles. The paradoxical nature of this situation is regarded by Averroes as no greater than that which obtains in every science, each of which must initially posit certain assumptions and axioms.

This last argument has, of course, a certain weakness, which probably did not escape its author. Premises, after all, are necessary elements in the deductions of a given science and indeed determine its character; they do not, however, establish the truth, as opposed to the internal validity, of that science, something for which observation is also required. The laws of thought are another matter, but they are more universal than the religious or scientific principles to which Averroes is here alluding. Yet Averroes may well have something as basic as the law of thought in mind, thinking it logically contradictory to have knowledge without virtue and virtue without religious belief. If such claims are necessary truths, however, the grounds of this necessity are not immediately obvious. It may be for this reason that Averroes says that while the existence of the principles of religion cannot be doubted, the "mode of their existence" (*kayfiyyatu wujūdiha*) is beyond human comprehension, or, as he says on p. 322, "their causes are unknown."

Is this, however, completely so? Does not the Koran, like the Bible, posit a cause-and-effect relationship between man's actions and his state of virtue and blessedness? Are not miracles seen as responses caused by certain specific situations and agents? Is not God Himself intelligible to us mostly just as a causal principle? It would seem we do have a definite notion of the nature of the principles of religion *qua* final and efficient causes. Yet, on Averroes' own grounds this would not be regarded as sufficient for full knowledge of their natures, since we lack knowledge of the formal and material causes which, following Aristotle, would render their nature fully intelligible.

Our ignorance of the precise formal and material constituents of the principles of religion, however we may construe them, is thus responsible for our nonapprehension of the "mode" of their existence. "How" these principles exist is thus beyond us; and not knowing this, we do not really know how they function as efficient causes either. Our knowledge of the principles of religion is thus tantamount to knowledge of God as the final cause and to knowledge of miracles, virtue, and blessedness as imperfectly understood ideas and causes.

Yet it is belief in these very ideas which Averroes finds necessary to postulate for "human existence," i.e., for man's existence as a rational and similarly a social animal. The very universality of these notions, unblemished by specific descriptions, allows Averroes to speak of "the principles of the religions," i.e., principles not of one religion, not of *the* true religion, but of all valid religions, where validity is determined by the inclusion of these principles. Averroes is completely open on this point, and his stance allows him to appear at once orthodox and liberal, advocating death for nonbelievers (*al-zanādiqa*) on one line, and apparent acceptance of the legitimacy of other religions on the next.

Miracles, then, can be accommodated on the literal level, even as they can be really understood on the plane of universal truth only. There they may undoubtedly take their place beside "blessedness" and "virtues" as expressions of God's will, to be seen somehow as efficient, formal, and even material expressions of the final cause. This, however, must be deduced from Averroes remarks, since, citing the precedent of antiquity, he refuses to be drawn into an analysis of specific cases. The Koran itself is the "clearest of miracles" for him, its miraculous nature revealing itself not as an interruption of the course of nature but rather through observation and reflection (*ṭarīq al-ḥiss wal-ʾiʿtibār*). Now, when applied rigorously, these methods are the tools *par excellence* of the philosopher,[6] so that though the miracle of "God's Book" is ostensibly evident to all who ever live, as Averroes says, he must consider it as most fully and truly understood by those only who are suitably, i.e., philosophically trained.

Having thus presented a philosophical position on traditional miracles, Averroes is able with relative ease to dispose of Ghazali's examples of supposed philosophical concessions to the miraculous. He identifies and isolates Avicenna as the author of these views and attempts as much as possible to repudiate them by naturalizing the functions of the imagination and intellect. Prophecy is characterized mainly in political terms, as an ability to teach hidden things and to establish religious laws which accord with the truth and advance the happiness of all men.[7] Dreams and revelations are seen as proceeding immediately from the Active Intellect (identified, as is customary, with an angel) and ultimately from God; i.e., they are regarded as effects of the standard epistemological process,[8] even as miracles are viewed as explicable in theory within the realm of physics. For the prophet is regarded as acting in a way that is beyond the capacities of other men, but not beyond the limits of nature itself.

These limits are known, for Averroes, by a combination of logical and empirical means. No one, prophets included, can do that which is logically impossible, that which violates what is entailed in its own definition. Owing to their exceptional endowments, the prophets can, however, do that which is beyond the reach of other men and is usually therefore physically impossible. The nature of the prophets is thus different from that of other men, but both function according to nature, or rather, according to their natures. It is experience which has informed us of the limits of what is usually possible for all men other than prophets, and it will be experience which will also establish the actual, as opposed to theoretical attainments and capabilities of the prophets. Averroes thus recognizes again that things have their own natural limits and not any and every thing is physically possible, though the limits of the physically possible may exceed that to which we are accustomed. All effects do thus have a cause, for Averroes, and even the "miraculous" can be accomodated within a philosophical system.

Now in none of this has Averroes responded to Ghazali's direct challenge to the necessity of the causal relationship, contenting himself instead with explanations designed to show that in fact causality does occur in all those phenomena which we know to exist. If the prophets do work the miracles attributed to them, then, it would be due, for Averroes, to their unusual (but not unnatural) imaginative and intellectual faculties, and one could supposedly verify the existence of those faculties through observation. "Nature" for Averroes is thus not limited in principle to what we normally observe but is at least initially an open-ended term under which any claim to the existence of an unusual phenomenon may be entertained, so long as it is not self-contradictory and hence meaningless.

To entertain a claim is not, however, to grant it; and Averroes and Ghazali do differ on just what is entailed by the definition of a given natural object, and therefore what should be considered as self-contradictory. Ghazali at first takes a minimalist position on entailment, seeing, as we have noted, that nothing is necessarily related to anything else. This is brought out in the extended critique of causation which Ghazali next offers.[9] Actually he shifts his ground in the course of this exposition and modifies his position in a philosophical direction. Just as Averroes is sensitive to the theological implications of his remarks in the *Tahāfut al-Tahāfut*, so is Ghazali respectful of philosophical standards in the *Tahāfut al-Falāsifa*.

Ghazali begins by reiterating his view that there is no necessary connection between what is "usually (*fi l-ᶜāda*) believed to be a cause and what is believed to be an effect." Whatever is predicated of the one thing in this view entails nothing for the other. Neither does satiety entail eating, nor does burning entail contact with fire, or death decapitation, to give a few of the types of examples Ghazali mentions. It is rather God Himself, or, more specifically, His Power (*taqdīr*), which connects and orders things; He is the real "cause" of all, both of death without decapitation, and (what is more striking) of decapitation without death.

It is, to take Ghazali's major example, not fire, but God who is the "agent" of burning, and it is He or his intermediaries, the angels, who makes the cotton undergo change when burnt. Fire itself is called a "dead" (or solid, *jamād*) body, without action of its own. It is only the observation of fire occurring with burning that leads people to assume a causal relationship between the two; whereas for Ghazali this observation proves merely to be a concomitance in fact, a coexistence of factors, without establishing causal responsibility (*al-ḥuṣūl/al-wujūd ᶜinda, wa-lā al-ḥuṣūl bi*). True causation proceeds from God *via* his angels, expressed usually through "voluntary" acts of the heavenly bodies. Events are thus the product of choice and will, of God and his angelic messengers.

Now Ghazali recognizes that this negative view of nature, this picture of total dependency on God, could lead to what would normally be regarded as absurd consequences, both in nature itself and in our knowledge, or lack of knowledge of it. Anything could change into anything else, and we would never know what to expect or what might even be the present reality which, without God's assistance, we would be deprived of knowing. He therefore proceeds to modify his position significantly. Everything is indeed possible, we are still completely at God's mercy, and yet, thanks to Him, we know what to expect of things, what actually is the case, and what is not actually so, though theoretically possible. This knowledge may appear to us as necessary but is really a "fixed impression" which we are granted as a result of habitual occurrences of the phenomenon. When the situation changes, so that what was considered as not an actual possibility becomes actual, it is God again who causes us to realize it, removing from our hearts our former impression.

For all this, Ghazali is not ultimately prepared to say that absolutely anything is possible of an object and that God works in total indifference to nature. Miracles, he acknowledges, can have a physical explanation and as such may be considered as natural events. Thus resurrection or the changing of a stick into a serpent may be seen simply as vastly accelerated cycles of nature, no less improbable for our ignorance of their specific processes. All we need accept is the idea that matter can receive any form, that the disposition of a given matter to receive unusual forms is greater than we understand, and then all change becomes possible.

The only real limitation upon the possible, Ghazali concludes (p. 329), is a logical one, "the simultaneous affirmation and negation of a thing," i.e., the principle of contradiction, given in various formulations. Thus he says that black and white cannot both be identically predicated of an object, since it is assumed that black *is* nonwhite, by implication. Or, an individual is said to be in only one place at one time, since to be in place *x is* to be not in non-*x* (*nafhamu min kawnihi fi l-bayti ʿadama kawnihi fi ghayri l-bayt*). Objects thus have their own identity, which includes the exclusion of opposite identities. One must simply realize the logical, as opposed to physical entailments of identity and discern what is self-contradictory. Thus Will is seen as entailing the existence of an intelligent being which knows what it wills, so that an "unknowing will" is regarded as self-contradictory. So too knowledge is seen as entailing perception, which entails a living body capable of perception, such that "inorganic perception" is seen as an absurd term. Nor, for the same reason, can one genus change into another without the first ceasing to exist, which it does by a change of form. As for those things which do not share a common matter, change of one to another is considered completely impossible.

These examples, however, bring Ghazali close to Averroes' position, and seriously qualify his own. They mostly take him well beyond purely analytical self-contradictory propositions and embrace what we would call synthetic *a priori* ones. For there is nothing in the concept of "will" *per se* which necessitates knowledge, nor does the concept "knowledge" necessarily entail in itself a percipient, nor "perception" an organism which perceives. Each of these terms can be thought of without necessarily referring to another set of particular concepts, even as "black" can stand alone without "nonwhite." So too "change" as a concept does not necessarily imply formal or material change, such that generic change must be either one or the other. Consequently, in making the assertions that he does, Ghazali is using these terms in relations which pure logic does not dictate, but which are impressed upon us by experience or nature as somehow necessary, and which then become part of the definition of an entity.

It is surprising to find Ghazali resorting to the notion of a fixed nature for objects, which allows for certain relations within as well as between them. He had, after all, foresworn this approach as concerns the actions of an object, and the new set of properties, though related supposedly to the substance of an object, is not therefore more suited for permanence. The definition of an object should not, for Ghazali, imply anything at all about it other than to say that it is what it is, determined by ostensive means. It is probably the difficulty, if not impossibility of talking about objects without allowing them some necessary properties and relationships which leads Ghazali, as Averroes surmises, to modify his stance. In doing so, however, he deliberately rejects being limited to purely logical self-contradictions and accepts a *de facto* permanence of nature in objects. To brave the difficulty of his original position, Ghazali would have had to limit his knowledge to basic tautologous statements only, without even being able to define the substances which he would posit, since no such definition would be necessarily true. Ghazali would thus be in the anomolous position of making assertions about entities the identity of which was unknown.

There is, accordingly, no more reason to accept the substantiality of a particular object as necessary, than there is to accept the necessary nature of its active properties. Conversely, the particular properties of a thing, from which its acts derive, belong to the object as much as its substantial properties do. Indeed, it is difficult, if not impossible to talk about a thing without discussing it in terms of its properties, the actions of an object being integral to its nature.

Thus the conflict regarding causation between Ghazali and Averroes finally reduces, in Averroes' eyes, to what may be termed a difference of degree, more than one of kind. The philosophers, he says (p. 331), can accept with equanimity the fact that the actions of an agent need not always operate (due to external hindrance); and the theologians must yield on the existence of natural forms and matters. Averroes concedes that a (considerable) gap exists between what the philosopher and the theologian maintain is entailed by the existence of a particular object, but he feels that the theologian, at least he whom Ghazali represents, can no longer be seen as maintaining the extreme negative position on entailment originally stated. Moreover, as Ghazali has now accepted that objects have certain definite natures, it should no longer be possible to hold that any form can go with a particular matter, such that all manners of change are equally possible.

The principle of necessary entailment having thus been affirmed, Averroes can afford to be generous in admitting that there is a "certain latitude" (or "accidental factor," *ᶜaraḍ*) in determining the precise natures of objects, though not as much latitude as the theologians would wish. In fact, Averroes' list of entailments is quite exhaustive, including shape, quantity, quality and time, as well as the more remote and underlying properties of an object. These, as the manifestations of the four causes, with which they may be identified, actually circumscribe the natures of objects in a way that would be anything but agreeable to Ghazali, for all his compromises. Yet Averroes surely feels that the argument is his on principle and that both experience and logic would have forced Ghazali to yield.

Averroes has actually laid out the ground of his position in his initial response to Ghazali's presentation of the "First Discussion" (p. 318). There he begins with contempt for those who deny the existence of efficient causes, inasmuch as the existence of such causes is presumably self-evident and in no way obviates the need for more remote, final causes. Conversely, the existence of final causes, or of *a* final cause such as God, does not in itself sufficiently explain observed phenomena. For the actions of a thing are regarded as the expressions of its essential nature as much as is any other property, and to deny them is to deny the specific identity of the object itself. What then would be that upon which God would act? Without its own actions every being would become the same as the next, and even this same being could not be granted any distinguishing action and hence identity. The denial of active properties thus leads, in Averroes' view, to the rejection of separate natures and even to the denial of being itself. If Averroes wished to be very bold, he could even have said that substituting God for efficient causes becomes tantamount to pantheism.

It is similarly self-evident for Averroes, on this combination of both empirical observation and logical inference, that all four Aristotelian causes, the efficient, formal, material, and final, are necessary constituents of events; and, following Aristotle, Averroes insists that our knowledge of objects is nothing but knowledge of their causes, what makes them be what they are.[10] To deny causality is to deny knowledge, and thus to cast doubt even upon the truth of one's own denial. To talk about objects is, therefore, to talk about causes, and, Averroes points out, these causes are necessary for the existence of effects, indeed, they often form part of the effect. Cause and effect may thus be seen as two sides of the same coin, epistemologically and functionally distinguishable but ontologically identical.[11]

Granting the necessity for causation so understood, we may yet ask with Ghazali what compels us to regard any particular combination of cause and effect as necessary in itself? What, moreover, makes an object have just the particular cause that it has? To this there is really no answer except that nature so presents itself, or rather has always so presented itself. That fire has to cause burning is true of fire as we know it, that is as we always have experienced it, under normal circumstances. Our definition of fire incorporates this experience, but Ghazali is surely right in seeing this as based originally upon convention born of experience rather than upon necessary logical entailment. All we have to go on in causation, as Ghazali sees it, is a concomitance or succession of factors, from which we extract and identify relationships and assign priority to certain ones over others. It is inevitable that we do this in order to discuss objects and events at all, yet the particular selection and relation of causes is often more arbitrary than we should like to admit.

Fire is thus indeed the cause of burning, though why this must be so, beyond the possibly inexact description of how it is so, is something that we can never know. The "fact" *that* it must be so is, however, for Averroes, necessary for our understanding of fire and relation to it. There is no way of avoiding the absurdities which follow on the assumption that "the opposite of everything existing is equally possible," and that the particular possibility realized is solely the product of God's will. For this gives the various possibilities absolutely no identity of their own, and thus there is nothing objective to know about them. In that case, though, as Averroes says (p. 325), no permanent (*thābit*) knowledge of anything is possible, not even of the existence of a temporary natural order.

It follows, therefore, that it should be Ghazali's contention that there is no permanent knowledge, even as there is no permanent nature, but only temporarily valid knowledge of a nature that is liable to change at any moment. To this Averroes responds that any kind of true knowledge, even if it is of a temporary situation, must be based on a fundamentally permanent reality. It is senseless, therefore, for God to be taken as accustoming us to one set of totally contingent possibilities, which we call reality, until another set occurs. Indeed, as Ghazali suggests, we would in this scheme have to be "fixed" by God to believe in the reality of each set when it occurs and every moment that it occurs, without any chance of knowing the reality independently. Moreover, we could not know that it was possible for sets other than the one actually obtaining to obtain before they occurred, other than by God's informing us now of their future reality. As such, though, this "knowledge" would be part of our present impression, and God would presumably not have to actualize the possibility in the future after all.

Thus there is no way of knowing, in this scheme, what may be expected to occur in the future (beginning the very next moment), and which possibilities currently suppressed may be actualized. Practically all possibilities being equal for Ghazali, all future events are thus equally possible and impossible, and we can know nothing with certainty about any of them. It is for this reason that Averroes states that possibilities must be grounded in an actual, objective reality, limited to being the possibility of what actually exists. *What* actually exists may still be beyond our present knowledge, in any given case; but whatever we conceive as truly possible will have to be rooted finally in what is currently actual.

Averroes' conviction in the objective reality of nature is, moreover, buttressed by his religious and teleological view of the universe. Putting together his scattered remarks in this section, we could say for him that God in his infinite wisdom has determined that objects and events function as they do, and in this sense He *is* the cause of actions, *viz*., as the remote cause. He cannot, however, become the immediate cause without destroying the world in which He acts. The world, as an effect of God, moreover, testifies to the wisdom of its Agent by being a place in which wisdom, i.e., knowledge of the true nature of things, obtains. This knowledge can be had because objects do not change fundamentally, they have a permanent necessary nature. In this they reflect God's own unchanging self, in whom alteration is impossible (p. 320). Nor need God change the course of nature, for as a benevolent as well as omnipotent cause of the universe, He has "created" the best of possible worlds (p. 332). Theoretical possibilities notwithstanding, therefore, the phenomena of the universe must continue to be as we have come to know them, and thus we can be perfectly sanguine as to being able to know the precise natures of everything. This confidence can even encompass the occurrence of miracles, as we have seen, once we appreciate that they are not fundamental alterations in nature or real innovations on the part of God.

In this manner, in quoting *Sura* 35.43 of the Koran on Allah's unchanging "course" (*sunna*), and invoking an image of God that reflects both Islamic and Aristotelian values, a divine perfection of both an ethical and ontological sort, Averroes answers Ghazali. Ghazali's own image of God is unacceptable to Averroes, for it asserts his omnipotence at the expense of his goodness, his freedom at the expense of an order that alone renders that freedom intelligible. God becomes in this view, for Averroes, a "tyrranical prince" (or "King", *al-malik al-jāʾir*) who acts unilaterally and unpredictably, keeping his subjects in ignorance as to the nature of his actions. This follows necessarily for Averroes, since there would no longer be a standard by which to anticipate, judge, or even understand his actions, once these actions had no permanent natures of their own and all different possibilities were theoretically equal.

Yet this means that God's own actions would go unknown, i.e., would be indescribable, and all we could say would be that some event happened, but not what it was. Nor would we be able to speak with any certainty of the continuance of God's action, since the conditions for this continuance would also be solely within God's domain and "unknown by nature" (*majhūl bil-ṭabʿ*, p. 325). Ghazali's viewpoint, accordingly, obliges one to accept an extreme form of occasionalism in which God creates the universe anew totally every instant, and it is Averroes' insight that this very action, depriving the world of any significant permanence, prevents us from truly knowing it—and Him—whatsoever.

Ghazali's solution to this problem, that God habituates us to believe in the regularity—and, we could add, the identity—of a given phenomenon, by fixing its impression within us, until such time as He changes our impression, is also considered unworthy of the Deity by Averroes. Besides the philosophical problem of claiming that we could know that which was solely dependent for its existence upon God's will, which we have already discussed, this view also assumes a changing, habit-forming God, unlike the image of a perfect, unalterable Deity which alone, for Averroes, befits the God of faith and reason.[12] Judgments may indeed be formed by habit, Averroes concedes; but this may be merely the way our nature works.

On religious grounds, therefore, as well as philosophical grounds, it would seem that Averroes has a very strong case for advocating causality. In having its own identity, nature testifies to the greater glory of God. Man can rely on his intelligence and senses, firm in the conviction that a good God has vouched for their credibility. Ghazali's God is the totally unknown, incomparable, and indescribable Deity whose power (and presence) is all-encompassing, even as it is unintelligible, more so than Ghazali wishes to admit. Theological considerations aside, however, Ghazali has found a weakness in the case for necessary specific causation, which weakness Averroes cannot gainsay despite his convincing refutation of Ghazali's own proposed alternative. Averroes, on the other hand, has nobly upheld the scientific tradition by demonstrating again the necessity and even inevitability for human discourse and knowledge of assuming the existence of causal explanations and natural events.

NOTES

1. Cf. S. Van den Bergh's translation of this work, *Averroes' Tahafut al-Tahafut* (*The Incoherence of the Incoherence*), (London, 1954), i, p.311 f. Van den Bergh bases his translation upon M. Bouyges' edition of this work (Beirut, 1930), the pagination of which is referred to in the margins of Van den Bergh's work. We have utilized the more recent two-volume edition of S. Dunya (Cairo, 1965), ii, p. 767f., and future Arabic citations of this work will be taken from it. Page references in the text of this article are to the Van den Bergh translation.

2. Cf. the edition of S. Dunya (Cairo, 1955), pp. 220f.; used again instead of the earlier edition of Bouyges (Beirut, 1927). This work has been translated into English, after a fashion, by S. A. Kamali (Lahore, 1958); cf. pp. 180f.

3. Cf. the exposition of Averroes' view offered by M. Fakhry, *Islamic Occasionalism* (London, 1958), pp. 83f. Fakhry mistakenly believes that Maimonides was influenced in his critique of occasionalism by Averroes, and he also underestimates the religious component of Averroes' view of miracles, pp. 104f. See too the outline of this subject prepared by S. Gomez Nogales, "Teoria de la Causalidad en el Tahâfut de Averroes," *Acta del Primer Congreso De Estudios Arabes e Islamicos,* Cordova, 1962, ed. F. M. Pareja (Madrid, 1964), pp. 115–28. Ghazali's view on causality has been discussed by J. Obermann, *Der Philosophische und Religiöse Subjektivismus Ghazālīs* (Vienna and Leipzig, 1921), pp. 68f.; see also the recent attempt by M. Marmura to balance Ghazali's remarks in the *Tahāfut al-Falāsifa* against other writings of his, in which he apparently holds a more positive view toward science and nature, in "Ghazali and Demonstrative Science," *Journal of*

the History of Philosophy, iii (1965), pp. 183–204. We are concerned in this article solely with the views which Ghazali expresses in the *Tahāfut*. My own views on this subject have benefitted from the criticism and advice of my colleague, Professor Ivan Boh, whose assistance in reading a first draft of this article is particularly appreciated.

4. For the sources of this division in Greek and Islamic philosophy, cf. Van den Bergh's separate volume of notes to his translation, *Averroes Tahafut al-Tahafut,* ii, p. 171, nn. 311.1, 4.

5. These remarks are reinforced on p. 322, when Averroes brings out even more clearly that "miracles are the principles on which religion (literally, "religions," *al-sharāʾiʿ*) is based, and religion is the principle (again literally in the plural, religions) are the principles, (*wal-sharāʾiʿ mabādīʾ*) of the virtues." The virtues are in turn seen as necessary for man's existence, "insofar as he has knowledge" (*bi-mā huwa insān ʿālim*).

6. Cf. Averroes' opening statement in the *Kitāb Faṣl al-Maqāl*, ed. G. Hourani (Leiden, 1959), pp. 5f.; translated by Hourani in *Averroes on the Harmony of Religion and Philosophy* (London, 1967), pp. 44f.

7. Cf. *Averroes' Commentary on Plato's Republic*, ed. E. I. J. Rosenthal (Cambridge, 1969), p. 47, ll. 24–28; and compare R. Lerner's translation, *Averroes on Plato's Republic* (Ithaca and London, 1974), p. 48, and his comments in the introduction, pp. xvif.

8. Cf., for a description of this process, my article, "Averroes on Intellection and Conjunction," *Journal of the American Oriental Society*, 86, 2 (1966), pp. 76–85.

9. This is the seventeenth *masʾala* of Ghazali, the first solely devoted to the "natural sciences." Cf. p. 316, and p. 777 in the *Tahāfut al-Tahāfut* edition of Dunya.

10. Cf. *Posterior Analytics* I.2 71^{b}8f. and *Metaphysics* I.1 981^{b}27; and see too *Physics* II.3 194^{b}16 and *Met.* V.2 1013^{a}24.

11. Cf. the similarities with this position adduced in my article, "Towards a Unified View of Averroes' Philosophy," *The Philosophical Forum,* iv, 1 (1972), pp. 87–113, with corrections to the notes given in iv, 2.

12. M. Marmura has suggested (see *supra*, p. 154f., n. 3), p. 203, that Ghazali may be read as indicating in one place (the end of the excerpt on p. 324) that God creates in man advance knowledge of the provisional order of nature, *viz*., that it is subject to interruption at some future date. A consequence of this reading would be that when miracles occur they need not be regarded as entailing any change in God's will. Nature, moreover, as Marmura indicates, is on this reading constant and thus knowable, if for interrupted periods. Actually one could go further and say that miracles in this view are predictable and hence natural, even if all the facts about them—as the exact time and nature of their occurrence—are not known. The "orderly" course of nature can thus be expanded to include interruptions in that order, forming part of a greater order or nature which encompasses—and naturalizes—the miraculous. This resembles the position on miracles which Judah Ha-Levi and Maimonides, for example, take; see the *Cuzari* III, 73; the *Guide for the Perplexed*, II, 29, and Maimonides' *Commentary to ʾAvoth,* v, 6.

Yet it is doubtful if Ghazali would have adopted this view, for he would have felt that positing that miracles may in any way be prepared and known in advance defeats the claim to absolute freedom of God's will and action, to which miracles (as traditionally understood) attest. It would, moreover, be unthinkable for Ghazali that man could have a foreknowledge of miracles that could in any way be construed as compelling God's actions. For miracles or unnatural possibilities to be realized in the world they should, for Ghazali, be regarded as something spontaneous, unknown, and previously considered as totally impossible.

A charitable reading of Ghazali would thus have him implying at most only what Marmura has suggested, that God has made known the contingent order of nature, with assurances that it may be approached with certainty for the time being. Averroes has, however (p. 325), indicated the weakness in this argument, in challenging the grounds for accepting the notion of a provisional nature in the first place. For the same reasons which compel assigning natural causes to objects function against making these causes temporary and allowing certain possibilities to be realized only when a miracle occurs. If a given event or reality is to be limited to a certain duration, then there must be a true, i.e., permanent reason why this is so, a reason which is part of an eternal reality. Similarly, if miracles are to be posited, then one must know what is being talked about, i.e., its nature or objective reality. In either case a natural permanent order is assumed, and it is impossible to derive a fundamentally contingent reality from it.

Eating as an Act of Worship in Hasidic Thought

L. JACOBS

Three differing attitudes have obtained among religious people towards the gratification of the physical appetites where their indulgence involves no breach of the religious law. These may be called the ascetic, the puritanical, and that of thankful acceptance. The first considers abstinence to be a virtue. On this showing body and soul are in permanent conflict, so that to indulge one is to frustrate the growth of the other. The ideal is for man to reduce his physical needs to the bare minimum required for his existence. The state of holiness is to be achieved by means of fasting and a general mortification of the flesh. The puritan attitude, on the other hand, is not necessarily ascetic. It can be fully aware of the physical and spiritual perils which may result from ascetic exercises—ill-health, morbidity, rebellion, masochism, pride, and lack of charity. But it is as uncompromising as asceticism in rejecting any enjoyment of the physical as an end in itself. Macaulay was unfair to the Puritans when he accused them of objecting to bear-baiting not because it gave pain to the bear but because it gave pleasure to the spectators. After all, pleasure at the spectacle of animal suffering is an ugly emotion. But it seems to be true that the puritan mind considers pleasure to be somehow unworthy. The physical appetites, it seems to hold, were implanted by the Creator in order to guarantee the survival of the human species, but they are more in the nature of a necessary evil than a positive good or, in any event, are only good because they can serve higher things. The third attitude sees the physical appetites as a gift of the Creator. In this view physical pleasure is not the highest pursuit of man, but neither is it shameful or sinful or only of value as a means to an end.

Each of these attitudes has had its Jewish adherents. While there are undoubtedly to be found ascetic views among the talmudic rabbis,[1] the prevailing view in the rabbinic literature, if one can speak of such a thing as a prevailing view, is that of thankful acceptance.[2] The enjoyment of the sabbath and festivals, involving as it does eating as a religious obligation,[3] and the numerous benedictions in which thanks are given to God for food and drink,[4] all indicate a frank, at times joyous acceptance of physical pleasure as a divine gift to man. The ascetic attitude is to be found among some of the medieval Jewish philosophers (notably Saᶜadia[5] and Maimonides[6] with regard to sex), the *Ḥasidey ᵓAshkenaz*,[7] and the Lurianic cabbalists.[8] Puritanism is the attitude of many of the medieval Jewish moralists.[9]

Which is the attitude adopted by Hasidism? With few exceptions Hasidism is not ascetic. Indeed, the movement arose partly in opposition to Lurianic asceticism.[10] Nor, as Buber would evidently have it,[11] is the attitude of Hasidism that of thankful acceptance. As we shall endeavor to demonstrate, Hasidism is puritanical in essence but with certain subtle ideas of its own. We are concerned, however, not with the more general question of how Hasidism views physical pleasure but with the hasidic idea of eating as an act of worship. That the hasidic masters themselves thought this worthy of treatment as a separate and most important theme[12] is justification enough for us to do so.

Basically, the hasidic view is a development of the Lurianic doctrine of the "holy sparks." As *ʾEn Sof* (the Limitless), the Infinite Source of all being, emerges from concealment to become manifest in the finite universe, its infinite light has to become progressively coarsened so that the abyss between the infinite and the finite may be crossed. In the process the original light is split up into "lights" (*ʾoroth*) and "vessels" (*kelim*) in which the "lights" are to be contained. But at one stage of the process the "lights" become too powerful for the "vessels" to contain them, with the result that there takes place "the shattering of the vessels" (*shevirath ha-Kelim*). These "vessels" are later reconstituted in a form that enables them to hold the "lights." Yet the "breaking of the vessels" causes some of the light to be spilled over so as to provide cosmic energy. The over-spill from each world provides the divine force required to sustain the world immediately beneath it, until, eventually, there emerges this finite world. Even here there is an over-spill, and this provides the energy for the existence of the "shells" (*qelippoth*)—the demonic aspect of being. Thus in all things there are "holy sparks" of the divine light, the task of man being to elevate these by using the things of the world in a spirit of purity and as a means of serving God. In the Lurianic system all this is spelled out in intricate detail.[13] While the hasidic masters undoubtedly believed in the Lurianic kabbalah as revealed truth, their main interest was far less in its theoretical aspects than in the motivation which it provided for inwardness in their religious life.

Another Lurianic idea, used by the Ḥasidim, is that the letters of the Hebrew alphabet are not mere symbols, but the manifestations on earth of the various spiritual realities involved in God's creative processes. According to this "neo-platonic" idea, God actually "said," for example, "Let there be light," in the sense that He combined the letters *ʾalef*, *waw*, *resh* in their spiritual form on high, to produce the word *ʾor*, "light." Light continues to enjoy existence because these potencies continue to be combined by the divine fiat. Every kind of food, to give another illustration, exists as it does because of this type of divine combination of letters, the letters of that particular kind of food; and when man eats that food, he assimilates the energy it provides. Ideally, then, his mind should be directed to this divine force rather than be on the physical pleasure that he receives from the food itself.

Long before the rise of Hasidism the cabbalists had described the eating of food in a spirit of purity as an act of divine worship. Isaiah Horowitz (d. 1630), in his gigantic compendium of religious thought and practices, *Sheney Luḥoth ha-Berith* (the *Shelah*), writes:[14]

> Eating involves both the general and the particular. By this I mean that although it is carried out with the aid of particular organs of the body, namely the mouth and the gullet, yet in general it sustains the whole body. Similarly, with regard to the act of copulation, although it depends on that particular organ at the body's extremity, yet, since it is the cause of the birth of the child, it is a general cause. In my youth I studied the Torah at the feet of the great Rabbi, the illustrious and distinguished saint, our master Rabbi Solomon [Lebush of Cracow] of blessed memory. When I took leave of him to get married I said to him: 'Rabbi, give me your blessing and advise me how to conduct myself.' He replied in these words: 'Sanctify yourself in these two matters, in food and in copulation, and be exceedingly careful to keep at a distance of a thousand cubits from anything having to do with the illicit and be exceedingly strict in sanctifying them. For all the other precepts of the Torah make no physical impression. But with regard to these two, food sustains the body and copulation brings the body into existence so that theirs is a lasting impression.' Thus spake the holy mouth, may his memory be for a blessing for the world to come.

A verse quoted frequently in hasidic literature to convey this idea of eating as an act of worship is "And they saw God and they ate and drank" (*Ex.* 24:12). This application of the verse goes back in the first instance to Elijah of Smyrna (d. 1729) in his *Midrash Talpiyyoth*,[15] who quotes it from the 13th century teacher Baḥya Ibn Asher:[16]

> When a man needs to eat he should free his mind from other thoughts so that it can soar aloft to think of God while each mouthful is being swallowed. As Scripture says: 'And they saw God and they ate and drank'—this resembles the exposition of the rabbis[17] of blessed memory on the verse 'Let everything that hath breath praise the Lord' (*Psalm* 150:6)—'For every breath give praise to Him.' In this way man's eating is counted as true eating, like one of the acts of divine worship in the Temple or like the performance of one of the religious precepts. This is the main intention of a meal at table, the body being nourished, obtaining its bodily share from the physical act of eating, while the soul is sated, fattened and satisfied by means of this intention. The positive act of eating in this fashion is like fatness in the ways of the Lord and their pleasantness. It is in this connection that Scripture says: 'And that which is set on thy table is full of fatness' (*Job* 36:16).

In the same passage this author continues:

> Man's thoughts when he eats should be attached to God more than at any other time. The source of this idea is to be found in the verse: 'And

> they saw God and they ate and they drank,' which means, they had the intention of seeing the Glory in their hearts while they were eating and drinking.

In the writings of the early hasidic masters this idea of having holy thoughts whilst eating is repeatedly stressed. R. Jacob Joseph of Polonoyye observes[18] that for this reason it is preferable to eat in private rather than with a company at table, because only then can there be achieved adequate concentration on the divine without distractions. The same author speaks of two types of *ṣaddiqim*, those who eat frugally and those who enjoy good food and drink. The task of the latter is much more difficult, since the more enjoyable the meal the greater the effort required in order to concentrate on God without succumbing to the blandishments of the physical appetites that have been aroused.[19] Jacob Joseph[20] also remarks that there are two kinds of intention while eating. The simple intention is to eat in order to have strength for God's service. But the higher and more difficult intention is to elevate the "holy sparks" and raise in thought all the spiritual forces residing in the food, all in accordance with the cabbalistic mysteries. That is why God makes man experience hunger and thirst. The desire for food and drink is an inducement to man to eat and drink, so that he may elevate the "holy sparks" in that which he imbibes and digests. The spiritual aspect is concealed by the physical pleasure, just as an honest woman whose face is veiled may be mistaken for a harlot; but the *ṣaddiq* knows how to see the reality and his thoughts are exclusively on the "holy sparks" to be elevated.[21]

This theme is taken up by the grandson of the Baʿal Shem Ṭov, R. Moses Ḥayyim Ephraim of Sudlikov in his *Degel Maḥaneh ʾEfrayim*:[22] "When the *Ṣaddiq* eats, his sole intention is to sate his soul with the spiritual aspect of the food so that he may attach himself to the service of God. So it is with regard to all the material things with which he is engaged. He does not attach himself to the material side of that thing, but to its inward nature, the secret of God's portion within it. This is why there are to be found *ṣaddiqim* whose very body is also pure."

A number of hasidic authors develop the thought that this spiritual aspect of food is to be detected in its taste.[23] The tastiness of food is a very pale reflection, in this material world, of those spiritual forces which are responsible for the existence of the food. Man should allow his mind to move from his awareness of the physical pleasure of taste on to the source of taste in the divine realm.

A comprehensive account of the whole theory is to be found in R. Nahum of Tchernobil's *Meʾor ʿEynayim*.[24] The world was created by God's word, and it is this which keeps it in being. In every thing there is a "holy spark" which sustains it. It is this "spark" that becomes united with man's own essential being when he eats, to provide him with energy and vitality. This "spark" is spiritual food because the divine nature is therein contained but covered as though by a garment. When he eats, man should have this in mind, and he should use in God's service the fresh energy and vitality imparted to him by the "holy spark" once this has become assimilated. By so doing he unites the "spark" to its source in God and releases it from its "exile." The whole task of man is to rescue the "holy sparks" from their captivity among the *qelippoth.* All this is effected by the benediction over the food that is eaten and by the use of the fresh energy in God's service. Fasting is sinful,[25] because it is a refusal by man to engage in the task alloted to him. The Nazirite who denies himself wine sins against the soul,[26] in that he declines to free the soul-aspect of the wine. The Baᶜal Shem Ṭov is quoted as observing that even a Gentile can release the "holy sparks" when he eats and then uses the fresh energy he has acquired in order to help a Jew (!) who will then, in turn, serve God. But the Gentile himself is incapable of achieving the degree of elevation achieved by the Jew who eats his food with special intention. But what of that other saying of the rabbis,[27] that one who fasts is a holy man? This is perfectly true, but only a very few can serve God in this way. The easier way is to know God whilst enjoying food and drink. In this latter observation we have all the tensions between the more ascetic tendencies in earlier Jewish thought and the new way the hasidic masters sought to encourage.

R. Levi Isaac of Berditchev deals with the theme in his *Qedushath Levi.*[28] He likewise makes the distinction[29] between eating in order to have strength to serve God and having holy thoughts while eating. The former is also considered to be a form of divine worship, although, in reality, it is only a preparation for such. The second is an act of divine worship in itself. The rabbinic references to the great feast for the righteous in the world to come are to be understood both literally and metaphorically. Simple folk cannot be expected to have holy thoughts while eating, and for them the meal in the hereafter will be a real meal consisting of the best food and the finest wines. But the *Ṣaddiqim,* who, even in this life, find their delight not in the food itself but in their holy thoughts while eating, will be rewarded with a feast consisting of the divine mysteries which their souls will then be able to comprehend without let or hindrance.[30] R. Levi Isaac, too, makes the distinction between one who eats frugal meals and one who enjoys good food. True, it is more difficult to have holy thoughts in the latter instance, but the reward is greater. The former is called "bread without battle" the latter "bread with battle," constant struggle being the price one has to pay if the mind is to dwell on the divine without becoming distracted by the tasty dishes.[31] The Torah permits the clean animals and birds to be eaten so that the "holy sparks" that they contain can be elevated. The "holy sparks" which inhere in the unclean animals and birds can also be elevated, but this is achieved not by their direct assimilation, forbidden by the Torah, but by their rejection, i.e., when the Jew observes the dietary laws. By abstaining from forbidden food the Jew elevates the "holy sparks" in that food.[32]

These basic ideas are found in similar form in the reports regarding the teachings of the Maggid of Mezeritch,[33] who is said to have made the distinction between the simple intention of eating in order to serve God and that of having holy thoughts at the time of eating. The Maggid quotes the verse: "And they saw God . . . ," but adds that the word *ʾeth*, the sign of the direct object, represents the first and final letters of the Hebrew alphabet—*ʾalef* and *taw*—and thus the whole alphabet. The letters of the alphabet are the spiritual forces inherent in all things; they are the "holy sparks." The *Ṣaddiq* "sees God" when he eats; that is to say, his mind dwells constantly on the letters which are the ever-sustaining power of God in the food which he eats.[34] Moreover, by later using the fresh energy that he has acquired to speak words of Torah and prayer, the *Ṣaddiq* rescues God's word and restores it to Him. The *word* of God creates the food and is, as it were, *in* the food, ready to be rescued. When the food is consumed and man utters a holy *word* by the power given to him by the food he has eaten, it becomes *word* once again, and the task of restoring the "holy sparks" is continued. The *Ṣaddiq* serves God even when he goes to the privy, because there he expels the waste which the body cannot assimilate, and he thus repeats on earth the cosmic process in which that which can be used for the holy is so used, while the residue nourishes the *qelippoth*. The Maggid, too, refers to the taste of food as a faint reflection of the spiritual forces on high. He adds that the different tastes that man experiences when eating represent the various combinations of the spiritual forces on high. Thus, for example, sweet foods derive ultimately from the *Sefirah* of *Ḥesed* ('Lovingkindness'), while sour food derives from the *Sefirah* of *Gevurah*, God's sternness and judgement.

R. Menahem Mendel of Vitebsk[35] adds a further idea. Man embraces in his being the whole of creation since, according to the kabbalah, he is mirrored after the divine image and pattern. This is why the kabbalah speaks of the source of all things in terms of *ʾAdam Qadmon*, Primordial Man. It follows that in his "animal soul," i.e., the physical side of his nature, man has something not only of that which pertains to the clean beasts but also to the unclean ones. If man allows his animal soul to gain the mastery over him when he eats, so that his intention is solely for his own pleasure, and he has no holy thoughts, he then as it were converts the food into that which pertains to the animal, and this includes the unclean animals. Such a man is not allowed to eat meat and must be a vegetarian. The sole purpose for which the Torah permits man to eat meat is for the "holy sparks" in the meat to be elevated. But the gross person, far from elevating the "holy sparks" in the meat which he eats, drags them down, converting, in fact, the meat of the clean animal into that which pertains to the domain of the unclean.

The central idea in all these hasidic teachings is that of worship, not alone while praying or studying the Torah but even when enjoying food.

It is a moot point whether the early Ḥasidim would have agreed with a much later hasidic master[36] that to eat in a spirit of purity and with holy thoughts is *greater* than prayer. But they would all seem to agree with the sentiment expressed by R. Ḥayyim Haikel of Amdur,[37] who quotes the verse: "How fair and how pleasant is love in delights," (*Song of Songs* 7:7) to yield the thought that love of God is especially fair and pleasant when it is expressed whilst enjoying physical delights.

Some of the descriptions in the hasidic literature of the doctrine which we are considering are, it must be admitted, occult in nature, with the mythological elements strongly pronounced. Occasionally the doctrine is described in almost totemistic terms, suggesting a kind of eating of the divine by man. Adapting a scriptural verse for the purpose (*Deut.* 2:28) the Maggid is said to have noted that the desire for food can be "broken for the love of God" by abstaining from food one is enjoying in the middle of a meal. But his disciple, Issachar Dov of Zlotzhov, remarks that this method is for the majority of men. There can be found one who has been a *Ṣaddiq* from his youth, or one who has reached the highest rank in repenting of his sins, and he is not required to break his desire for food. On the contrary, he can eat without hindrance because all his thoughts are on the divine in the food. The Hebrew word for food referred to in the verse is *ᵓokhel*, and this (spelled *plene*) has the same numerical value (77) as the two divine names, the Tetragrammaton (26) + *ᵓEl* (51). Consequently, the thought that he is eating that which has so much holiness that it represents two divine names, is sufficient to enable such a *Ṣaddiq* to break his desire for the food itself without his having to stop in the middle of a meal as a lesser person is required to do.[38] There are references, too, in the hasidic literature to the idea that a wandering soul may have been condemned for its sins to become exiled in food. There it must remain until a good man eats, in a spirit of holiness, the food that is its prison, and so enables the lost soul to find its rectification (*tiqqun*). This is why eating at table without saying words of Torah is compared by the rabbis (*ᵓAvoth* 3, 3) to eating "sacrifices of the dead." The dead soul is "eaten" without its finding *tiqqun*.[39]

A more "rationalistic" and more realistic view of the whole doctrine is stated by R. Sheneᵓur Zalman of Liady.[40] The word for "bread," *leḥem*, is associated with the word for "war," *milḥamah*. At every meal battle is enjoined between the holy and the unholy. R. Sheneᵓur Zalman explains it in this way:

> We see that when a man eats in order to satisfy his greed for food and to fill his belly he becomes exceedingly coarse, so that he falls from his state of worship in holiness until he becomes really animal-like in gross insensitivity and the indulgence of the strange desires of the animal soul . . . But if man eats in order to become strong for the service of God and does not have in mind so much his own pleasure . . . then the food he eats in this manner

> strengthens his mind, his power of discernment, and his heart, to the extent that when he later contemplates the unity of God, and when he prays or studies the Torah, all his concentration in depth is due to the food that he has eaten . . . so that the evil in the food is converted into good . . .

Another hasidic author[41] acknowledges that man is incapable of fathoming the mystery of the elevation of the "holy sparks," yet he should eat, nonetheless, with this thought in mind, just as a faithful servant of the king will deliver a letter as instructed by his master, even though he is ignorant of its contents.

Associated in Hasidism with the doctrine of eating as an act of divine worship is the sacred meal[42] in which, especially on the sabbaths and festivals, and with particular emphasis on the third meal of the sabbath, the Ḥasidim sit around the table of the *Ṣaddiq* (the *'tisch'*). The *Ṣaddiq* who alone is able fully to have the proper holy thoughts, tastes a little of each dish, the remainder of which is then distributed among the Ḥasidim (*shirayim*). In this way the *Ṣaddiq* assists his followers in their much weaker efforts at elevating the "holy sparks." Moreover, the *Ṣaddiq* gives a hasidic exposition of texts read in the synagogue at that period of the year. This *torah* of the *Ṣaddiq* consecrates the meal. Most of the classical hasidic works are based on the *torah* originally delivered by the *Ṣaddiq* at the third meal of the sabbath.

NOTES

1. See e.g., *ʾAvoth* 6, 4; T. B. *Berakhoth* 63b, *Ḥagigah* 5b, *Nedarim* 20b.
2. See T. J. *Qiddushin* 4, 12 (66b).
3. *ʿoneg shabbath* and *simḥath yom ṭov*; for the details see T. B. *Shabbath* 118a–119b and *Beṣah* 15b.
4. See especially the whole of the sixth chapter of tractate *Berakhoth* in the Jerusalem and Babylonian Talmuds.
5. *ʾEmunoth we-deʿoth,* Book 10, chapter 6.
6. *Guide* II, 36; III, 49.
7. E.g., in the *Sefer Ḥasidim* and the *Roqeaḥ*; see J. Dan, *The Esoteric Theology of Ashkenazi Hasidism* (Heb.), Jerusalem, 1968.
8. See e.g., Schechter's essay on Safed in his *Studies in Judaism,* Second Series, Philadelphia, 1945, pp. 202–306.
9. E.g., in Baḥya Ibn Paquda's *Ḥovoth ha-Levavoth, Shaʿar ha-Perishuth*; M. H. Luzzatto's *Mesillath Yesharim,* chapters 13–15; Jonah of Gerona's Commentary to *ʾAvoth* 2, 10; *Ṭur, ʾOraḥ Ḥayyim* §231.
10. See *Sefer Baʿal Shem Ṭov*, Sotmar, 1943, vol. ii, to *mishpaṭim*, end, pp. 68–70, especially the quotation from R. Barukh, grandson of the Baʿal Shem Ṭov (*Buṣina Di-nehora*, p. 17), that the Baʿal Shem Ṭov introduced a new way, without mortification of the flesh, in which the three essentials are love of God, love of Israel, love of the Torah. Cf. the sources quoted here on the dangers of the ascetic life. However, ascetic tendencies are still to be observed among some of the hasidic masters such as Elimelech of Lizensk and Naḥman of Braslav. The latter (*Liqquṭey*

Moharan, No. 47) speaks especially of "breaking the desire for food," i.e., by eating frugally, though in this *derush* he also speaks of the *Ṣaddiq* eating well, but "for the sake of heaven." Cf. No. 39 for both food and sex. Even some of the recent hasidic masters have been ascetics, for instance R. Aaron Roqeaḥ of Belz (d. 1957), who is reported to have defended his ascetic life by declaring that one who serves God while eating does so during his meals only, but one who serves God by fasting does so all the time; see B. Landau and N. Urtner: *ha-Rav ha-Qadosh mi-Belza*, Jerusalem, 1967, p. 18.

11. Scholem's critique of Buber in this connection is very well founded; see his essay "Martin Buber's Interpretation of Hasidism" in *The Messianic Idea in Judaism*, New York, 1971, pp. 227–250; and R. Schatz-Uffenheimer: "Man's Relation to God and the World in Buber's Rendering of the Hasidic Teaching" in *The Philosophy of Martin Buber*, ed. Schilpp and Friedman, La Salle, 1967, pp. 403–434.

12. See *Leshon Ḥasidim* by Naḥman of Tcherin, Lemberg, 1876, new ed., Beney Beraq, n.d., *s.v. ʾakhilah*, pp. 18–19; his *Derekh Ḥasidim*, Lemberg, 1876, new ed. Jerusalem, 1962, *s.v. ʾakhilah*, pp. 27–34; *Qunṭeros ʿEth ha-ʾokhel* in *Peri Ṣaddiq* by Zadoq ha-Kohen of Lublin, Lublin, 1901, new ed., Israel n.p., 1960, pp. 235–240; R. Arele Roth, *Shulḥan ha-Ṭahor*, Jerusalem, 1966 (a huge book devoted entirely to this theme).

13. For a good account of the basic Lurianic doctrine see I. Tishby, *Torath ha-raʿ we-ha-Qelippah be-qabbalath ha-ʾAri*, Jerusalem, 1965.

14. *Shaʿar haʾothiyyoth, s.v. qedushah, be-feh u-ve-wesheṭ*, f. 53b.

15. Ed. Warsaw, 1875, *s.v. ʾakhilah*, ff. 50b–51a.

16. *Shulḥan Shel ʾArbaʿ* in Baḥya's writings, ed. B. Chavel, Jerusalem, 1969, pp. 496–497. The source of the quotation of *Ex.* 24:12 in this connection is *ʾAvoth de-rabbi Nathan* 1, 1 of the righteous in paradise; but there the meaning is not that of "seeing God" whilst eating, but of being sustained by the beatific vision. Cf. ʾOnqelos to Ex. 24:12, and *Lev. R.* 20, 10 (R. Joshua), *she-zanu ʿeyneyhem min ha-Shekhinah*.

17. *Gen. R.* 14, 9.

18. *Toledoth Yaʿaqov Yosef, Tazriʿa*, ed. Warsaw, 1881, p. 185; *ʾemor*, p. 235, in name of Samuel b. Isaac of Uceda (16th cent.) in his *Midrash Shemuel to ʾAvoth* 3, 3. It would appear that the institution of the hasidic 'Tisch', the communal meal with the *Ṣaddiq* surrounded by his followers, had not yet been developed in this early period of the movement.

19. *Toledoth*, *ʾemor*, pp. 221–22.

20. *Toledoth*, *ʾemor*, p. 225.

21. *Leshon Ḥasidim*, *s.v. ʾakhilah*, No. 6, pp. 18–19.

22. To *sidra toledoth, s.v. wa-yomer ʿesaw*, ed. Jerusalem, 1963, p. 36, following the thought of R. Naḥman of Horedenka.

23. See *Derekh Ḥasidim* on "Taste and see that the Lord is good" (*Ps.* 34:9), pp. 33–34; *Qedushath Levi*, Jerusalem, 1964, *Liqquṭim*, p. 287; R. Naḥman of Braslav, *Sefer ha-Middoth*, Warsaw, 1912, *s.v. ʾakhilah*, 2, 6, p. 24: "If one experiences no taste in his food he should know that God has departed from him." R. Elimelech of Lyzhansk (*Zettel Qaṭan*, printed at end of his *Noʿam ʾElimelekh*, No. 15) writes: "Before washing the hands to a meal, one should recite the penitential prayer of the ʾAri of blessed memory. After eating the piece of bread over which grace before meals has been recited, one should say the following: 'For the

sake of the unification of the Holy One, blessed be He, and His *Shekhinah*, I do not eat, God forbid, for my bodily pleasure, but only that my body be strong for God's service. Let not any sin, transgression, evil thought or physical pleasure prevent the unification of the Holy One, blessed be He, by means of the holy sparks in this food and drink.' Whenever he eats or drinks anything, he should have in mind that the taste he experiences in his mouth when he swallows the food or sips the drink is the inward part of the holy and the holy sparks which reside in that food or drink; and that by means of his eating, chewing with his teeth and digesting with his stomach, the inward part of the food becomes refined so that it does not become a surplus wherewith the outside ones are fed. His soul then benefits from the inward part of the food, the residue becoming waste to be expelled for the outside ones. He should then have in mind that as soon as he will experience a need to evacuate his bowels he will not, God forbid, keep the waste matter inside him to contaminate his mind and abominate his soul by retaining inside him the excrement and urine for even a single moment. And, as he eats, he should depict to himself the letters of the word *maᵓakhal* ('food') in their 'Assyrian' [i.e. square Hebrew] form, and should have in mind that numerically read they total 91, the numerical value of the Tetragrammaton plus *ᵓAdonay*."

24. To *sidra maṭṭoth*, quoted in *Derekh Ḥasidim*, pp. 27–29.
25. T.B. *Taᶜanith* 11a.
26. Against the *nefesh*, see *Num*. 6:11.
27. T.B. *Taᶜanith* 11a–b.
28. *Qedusshath Levi, wa-Yeshev,* ed. Jerusalem, p. 61.
29. *Qedusshath Levi*, *Liqquṭim*, p. 288.
30. *Qedusshath Levi*, *Liqquṭim*, p. 288.
31. *Qedusshath Levi*, *Liqquṭim*, p. 318.
32. *Qedusshath Levi*, *Liqquṭim*, p. 314.
33. *ᵓOr ha-Meᵓir* by Zeᵓev Wolf of Zabarazh, *derush sefirath ha-ᶜomer*, quoted in *Derekh Ḥasidim,* No. 8, p. 30. *Cf.* the quotations in *Torath ha-Maggid,* ed. Israel Klepholtz, Tel Aviv, 1969, pp. 149–51.
34. On this theme of the sustaining power of the letters and its significance for Hasidism see R. Sheneᵓur Zalman of Liady, in the name of the Baᶜal Shem Ṭov, in his *Tanya*, Vilna, 1930, *Shaᶜar ha-Yiḥud,* Chapter 1, p. 152.
35. *Peri ha-ᵓareṣ*, to *sidra be-har*, ed. Jerusalem, 1965, p. 44.
36. R. Zadoq ha-Kohen of Lublin, *Qunṭeros ᶜEth ha-ᵓokhel* (see *supra,* p. 165, n. 12), No. 6.
37. *Derekh Ḥasidim*, p. 31.
38. *Derekh Ḥasidim*, pp. 31–32, quoting *Mevasser Ṭov* to *sidra terumah.*
39. *Derekh Ḥasidim*, p. 34.
40. *Siddur ha-rav*, ed. New York, 1965, *Shaᶜar Neṭilath Yadayim Li-seᶜudah*, pp. 200–202.
41. *Derekh Ḥasidim*, p. 32.
42. See Dubnow, *Toledoth ha-ḥasiduth*, Tel-Aviv, 1967, pp. 362–364; S. A. Horodetsky, *Ha-ḥasiduth we-ha-ḥasidim,* iv, pp. 81–82; A. Wertheim, *Halakhoth we-halikhoth ba-ḥasiduth*, Jerusalem, 1960, pp. 165–169.

Mendelssohn und Lessing in ihrer Stellung zur Geschichte

H. LIEBESCHÜTZ

Der Verfasser ist am 29.10.1978 verstorben.

I

Es ist sicherlich ein Wagnis, dem Gelehrten, der in seiner Biographie Mendelssohns den Mann in Mitten seines Kreises umfassend und eindringend dargestellt hat, einen Aufsatz zu widmen, der einen begrenzten Ausschnitt aus diesen Beziehungen zum Thema hat. Ein solches Unternehmen lässt sich vielleicht vertreten auf Grund seiner Zielsetzung: Der Vergleich von zwei Denkern des achtzehnten Jahrhunderts mag Ausblicke erlauben, die unser Verständnis des ursprünglichen Verhältnisses von Judentum und Christentum zu einer charakteristischen Denkform moderner Kultur fördern können. Für solche Betrachtung ist es wichtig, daran zu erinnern, dass der Anteil der Aufklärung an der Entwicklung geschichtlichen Denkens sehr wesentlich durch ihre Kritik an der religiösen Überlieferung bestimmt gewesen ist. Im Zeitalter Spinozas und des englischen Deismus war die Idee einer göttlichen Offenbarung, die *einem* Volk eine besondere Rolle in der Heilsgeschichte der Menschheit zuwies, ein Stein des Anstosses geworden. Dabei handelte es sich nicht nur um den Widerspruch gegen die universelle Natur der Vernunft als Quelle wahrer Erkenntnis. In den religiösen Kämpfen des siebzehnten Jahrhunderts war in England und in der niederländischen Umwelt Spinozas das Alte Testament zur Quelle für die Autorität theokratischer Herrschaftsformen geworden. Puritaner und niederländische Prädikanten entliehen das Pathos ihrer Reden aus diesem Buch. Für die nach dem Zeitalter der Glaubenskämpfe einsetzende Reaktion galt daher die Bibel des hebräischen Volks als ein Lehrbuch der Unduldsamkeit. So kam es, dass die Bewegung, welche die Emanzipation der europäischen Judenheit aus dem Ghettodasein von Jahrhunderten möglich machen sollte, in ihrer Religionstheorie einen entschieden antijudaistischen Charakter zeigte. Buddha und vor allem Confucius sollten den Platz als Urheber höherer Kultur einnehmen, von dem man Moses verdrängen wollte. Wie verhielt sich Moses Mendelssohn zum Geschichtsbild seiner Epoche?

Thomas Abbt (1738–1766), ein junger Professor der Mathematik an der kleinen westphälischen Universität Rinteln, und schöngeistiger Freund geschichtlicher Betrachtungen, hatte den Auftrag erhalten, ein weltgeschichtliches Kompendium zu verfassen. Er hatte Mendelssohns Rat gesucht, aber zunächst keine Antwort von ihm erhalten. Nachträglich, im Februar 1765 gab ihm Mendelssohn die Erklärung für dies Versäumnis mit einer sehr weit reichenden Begründung. Er behauptet von sich, dass ihn nichts interessiere, was mit Geschichte zu tun habe. Weder die Entwicklung der Staaten noch die der Gelehrsamkeit könnte er ohne Langeweile studieren; dasselbe gelte von der Geologie und der Naturgeschichte. Keine Schrift über diese Themen würde ihn beim Lesen wirklich wach halten; es sei denn durch einen besonders anziehenden Stil.[1]

Aber gut zwei Jahre früher hatte Mendelssohn an Abbt berichtet, dass er Hume's *Geschichte Englands* gelesen und „unvergleichlich" gefunden habe.[2] Gewiss rühmt er in diesem Zusammenhang den Stil Hume's als anziehend; aber er erklärt sein Interesse wesentlich mit der Art, in der der schottische Philosoph die Wechselwirkung zwischen den Charakteren und den Ereignissen entwickelt. Daraus ergibt sich, dass die umfassende Ablehnung alles Historischen in dem späteren Brief als höfliche Einkleidung einer Weigerung gelten muss, an dem von Abbt beabsichtigten handbuchartigen Unternehmen ernstes Interesse zu nehmen. Als dieser später Mendelssohn den ersten fertigen Band dieser Arbeit, *Auszug der allgemeinen Weltgeschichte,* sandte, bestätigte der so Beschenkte den Empfang mit der Bemerkung, dass er das Buch nicht gelesen sondern nur durchgeblättert habe.[3] Abbt sei für eine derartige „Buchhändlerarbeit" zu fein. In der philosophischen Betrachtung der Geschichte würde er das rechte Feld finden. Von sich selbst sagt Mendelssohn, er habe bisher geglaubt, dass ein Mensch, der kein Vaterland hat, keinen Nutzen von historischen Studien haben könne. Jetzt aber sei er zu der Einsicht gekommen, dass auch die Geschichte der „bürgerlichen Verfassung", das heisst die Betrachtung eines begrenzten Kreises, untrennbar mit dem Ganzen der menschlichen Entwicklung zusammenfliesse. Schliesslich bittet er seinen Freund, ihn nun seinerseits bei universalhistorischer Lektüre zu beraten. Mendelssohns Definition historischer Studien als Beschäftigung mit der bürgerlichen Verfassung eines begrenzten Kreises erinnert uns an Abbts Freund Justus Moeser, den Geschichtsschreiber der Bauern- und Bürgerwelt von Osnabrück. Vielleicht hat Mendelssohn beim Gebrauch dieses Terminus wirklich in die dem Briefempfänger so wohlbekannte Richtung deuten wollen.

Er teilte mit seinen Zeitgenossen jenes Interesse an der Theorie der Geschichte, das von der kritischen Auseinandersetzung mit Rousseaus Lehre vom idealen Zustand der Menschheit in der Urzeit bestimmt war. Im Jahre 1767 hat Mendelssohn die Schrift des Schweizers Isaak Iselin, *Philosophische Mutmassungen über die Geschichte der Menschheit,* besprochen.[4] Bei diesem Buch handelt es sich um den Versuch, den optimistischen Glauben an die Vorsehung zu festigen. Mendelssohn betont, dass aus der Nähe gesehen die Wege des Schicksals oft einem Labyrinth gleichen. Aber ein umfassender Überblick, wie ihn Iselin biete, könne zu besserem Verständnis führen. Iselin hatte die Entwicklung der Kultur, die Erweiterung des Wissens, aus dem Wesen der menschlichen Natur abgeleitet. Fortschritt bedeutet für Iselin die Erfüllung eines natürlichen Triebes. Darum sieht er eine Verfassung wie die des Lykurg in Sparta, die auf das Festhalten eines bestimmten Zustands gerichtet ist, als dem Sinn der Geschichte zuwider, weil ein solches Grundgesetz jede Entwicklung von Geist, Kunst und Wissenschaft verneint. Mendelssohn rühmt das Buch, weil sein Verfasser es vermeide, die geschichtlichen Tatsachen einem vorher ausgedachten System als Beweisstücke anzupassen. Nur an einigen Stellen findet er Lücken der Überlieferung füllende Mutmassungen „hier und da mehr sinnreich als der Natur gemäss."[5] Mendelssohn bleibt offenbar skeptisch gegenüber dem Versuch, dem Ganzen der Geschichte eine klare Richtung zuzuweisen. Aber er zeigt Sympathie mit Iselins Idee, dass ein Fortschritt der Individuen in Bezug auf Tugend und Glückseligkeit irgendwie nachweisbar ist. 1782 kommt er auf das Thema Vorsehung zurück in einem Brief, den er an August Hennings, einen höheren Verwaltungsbeamten und Schwager des jüngeren Dr. Reimarus, geschrieben hat. Dort formuliert er die These, dass Rückschläge in Gesittung notwendig seien, weil ungebrochener Fortschritt die Ausbildung des Einzelnen schädigen würde: das Individuum braucht für die Steigerung seiner Kräfte Widerstand. Staatliche Tyrannei und selbst die Schikanen von Gerichtsbehörden können diesem Zwecke dienen, ebenso Kleinigkeiten des alltäglichen Lebens und Plackereien von Zollbeamten oder das Unverständnis eines Rezensenten gegenüber einem Schriftsteller. Eine utopische Vollkommenheit ohne Widerstand und Reibung würde den Anfang einer Degeneration bedeuten. Darum sind Zyklen von Aufstieg und Abstieg der Gesittung notwendig, um den Individuen die Möglichkeit der moralischen Ausbildung zu erhalten. Deren Vervollkommnung macht den Plan der Vorsehung aus, nicht der Fortschritt der Menschheit als Ganzes.[6]

Mendelssohns grösste Annäherung an die historische Fragestellung findet sich in einer apologetischen Bemerkung, mit der er das Alte Testament gegen die Bezweiflung seines religiösen Gehalts durch den älteren Reimarus verteidigt. Bei einem Aufenthalt in Wolfenbüttel hatte ihm Lessing die später so berühmt gewordenen „*Fragmente*" geliehen, vier Jahre vor deren erster Veröffentlichung. Nach der Lektüre tadelt Mendelssohn die Unbilligkeit des Ungenannten in seiner Charakterisierung biblischer Gestalten. Seine Art, alle Handlungen von bösen Absichten abzuleiten würde nicht einmal für einen Räuberhauptmann vollständig gültig sein; sogar bei einem Mann dieser Art verbinden sich stets gute und schlechte Motive. Bei diesem Versuch, das hebräische Altertum als ein rein menschliches Geschehen zu deuten, ist ein wesentlicher Gesichtspunkt übersehen worden: Diese fernen Zeiten besassen noch keineswegs die Begriffe von Völkerrecht und allgemeiner Menschenliebe, wie sie für die Gegenwart und den aufgeklärten Verfasser der Handschrift gültig sind. Die biblische Geschichte hat als Voraussetzung Kenntnisse und Sitten der Zeit, in der diese Menschen gelebt haben. Ohne Berücksichtigung solcher Vorbedingungen gibt es kein Verständnis, sondern nur Phantasiegebilde.[7]

Aber diese Wendung seines Denkens bleibt vereinzelt, vielleicht verständlich als eine momentane Anpassung an die Denkart seines Freundes und Korrespondenten. Bald darauf hat Mendelssohn die Formel gefunden, mit der er Glauben und Haltung des Juden vor der historischen Religionskritik der Aufklärung sicherstellen konnte: Die jüdische Lehre von Gott und Welt beruht auf der Tätigkeit des Verstandes, der allen Menschen gemeinsam ist. Dazu kommen als Sonderheit Gebote und Satzungen aus einem einmaligen Geschehen.[8]

II

Im Gegensatz zu dieser behutsam konservativen Haltung, mit der Mendelssohn die Tradition seines Volkes vor dem Kulturbewusstsein seiner Zeit zu rechtfertigen und gegen die Kritik der Aufklärung zu sichern versuchte, war Lessing schon früh ein Kritiker der Theologie. Für ihn bedeutete die kirchliche Tradition, in der er ebenso aufgewachsen war wie Mendelssohn in der jüdischen, eine Macht, gegenüber welcher er zunächst die Freiheit des Denkens wahren wollte. Schriftliche Überlieferungen als solche galten ihm nicht als Autorität für die Wahrheit religiöser Doktrin. Beschäftigung mit den Ursprüngen kirchlicher Überlieferung diente ihm zur Begründung dieser Haltung. Diese Tendenz führte ihn weit hinaus über das gelegentliche Interesse an dieser Fragestellung, wie es bei Mendelssohn vorkam. Lessing wollte zeigen, wie diese Traditionen, deren zeitlose Geltung er bestritt, aus bestimmten Umständen einer Periode entstanden waren. Lessings frühes Fragment über die Entstehung der geoffenbarten Religion umreisst das Problem im allgemeinen: Der einzelne Mensch ist in seiner Erkenntnis Gottes durch die individuelle Anlage seines Geistes bestimmt. Weil aber der Mensch auf das Leben im bürgerlichen Verband angewiesen ist, muss die so entstehende Mannigfaltigkeit überbrückt werden. Diesem Zweck dienen konventionelle Begriffe, welche den zufälligen Zuständen von Zeit und Ort ihrer Entstehung entsprechen, doch durch ihre Zurückführung auf Gott sanktioniert werden. Aus diesem Grunde hat jede positive Religion so viel relative Wahrheit wie die andere.[9] Als Lessing 1760, nach den Jahren, während derer in Berlin seine Verbindung mit Mendelssohn durch gemeinsame literarische Interessen und persönliche Sympathie entstanden war, nach Breslau ging, hat er sich dort sehr ernstlich mit patristischen und kirchengeschichtlichen Studien befasst. Er wollte fähig sein, die früheren Versuche mit konkretem Wissen zu unterbauen. Es ist vielleicht kein Zufall, dass am Ende dieser Breslauer Zeit Mendelssohn feststellt, dass seine Korrespondenz mit dem Freunde während der letzten Jahre zeitweise ins Stocken geraten ist.[10]

Als Lessing nach der Periode als Hamburger Dramaturg 1770 Bibliothekar in Wolfenbüttel wurde, hat ihn der *genius loci* der grossen Büchersammlung wieder religiösen und theologischen Problemen nahe gebracht. Er hat dabei die Fragestellung seiner Frühzeit fortgesetzt: Schriftliche Traditionen können keine ewige Autorität für die Wahrheitserkenntnis darstellen, weil ihre Gestalt von den besonderen Umständen ihrer Entstehung abhängig bleibt. In diesem Sinne hat er 1774 bis 77 die berühmte

Veröffentlichung aus den Papieren des Ungenannten unternommen. Der Hamburger Professor Hermann Samuel Reimarus, aus dessen Nachlass seine Kinder diese Schriften Lessing übergeben hatten, war ein radikaler Deist gewesen, der mit seiner Bibelkritik das Ganze des christlichen Glaubens widerlegen wollte.[11] Lessing war mit der kritischen Methode, aber nicht mit der Zielsetzung des Verstorbenen einverstanden. Er hatte das Gefühl, gegenüber der rationalistischen Theologie seiner eigenen Jugend positiver geworden zu sein. Schon bald nach seiner Ankunft in Wolfenbüttel hatte er an Mendelssohn geschrieben, es sei ihm, nicht erst kürzlich, klar geworden, dass er bei der Befreiung von Vorurteilen zu viel weggeworfen habe, was er wiederholen müsse.[12] Als im Kreise der Berliner Aufklärung gegen seine Kritiken an rationalistischen Theologen sich Bedenken regten, suchte er brieflich seinem Bruder Karl klar zu machen, dass er mit seiner Haltung keineswegs eine Rückwendung zum alten Glauben beabsichtige. Es handele sich für ihn durchaus nicht darum, die kirchlichen Dogmen wieder als Grundsätze des Weltverständnisses einzuführen; in ihrem Wortlaut blieben sie für ihn Zeugen einer vergangenen Zeit.[13] Lessing war damals zu der Überzeugung gekommen, dass hinter den kirchlichen Dogmen eine schöpferische Entwicklung erkennbar sein müsse, deren Richtung und Ganzheit wesentlicher blieb als die einzelnen Phasen traditioneller Lehrbildung. Er war sich bewusst, dass auch bei dieser Betrachtungsweise die Bibel als historischer Text den Anspruch auf Endgültigkeit verlor. Er war überzeugt auf diese Weise dem Fragmentisten den endgültigen Gegenstand seines Angriffs entzogen zu haben, ohne sich zu der Methode von dessen Kritik in Widerspruch zu setzen.[14] Er bezog damit eine Position, die im Gegensatz zum Bibelglauben des Protestantismus der katholischen Kirche benachbart erscheinen konnte. Gelegentlich hat er seinen Bruder darauf hingewiesen, dass ein solcher Eindruck für ihn von praktischem Vorteil sein würde, im Falle seine lutherischen Gegner eine Staatsaktion gegen ihn in Gang setzen sollten.[15] Aber er wusste genau, dass eine solche politische List nichts mit dieser Abwandlung seiner Religionstheorie zu tun hatte. Die neuere Forschung hat die Wendung hauptsächlich auf den Einfluss von Leibnitz zurückgeführt, in dessen Schriften Lessing gleichzeitig mit seinen kirchengeschichtlichen Studien gelesen hatte.[16] Es war nicht das System als Ganzes, was bei Lessing, wie überhaupt in der klassischen Literatur, zur Geltung kam, sondern charakteristische Einzelmotive.[17] Die Monadenlehre, nach der jedes der unendlich vielen Bestandteile das Ganze des Kosmos mit grösserer oder geringerer Bewusstheit spiegelt, bot ein formales Vorbild für die Rechtfertigung der Idee einer sich in Stufen enthüllenden Wahrheit. Es gab auch eine persönliche Verbindung; Leibnitz war neben seinen anderen Ämtern auch als Verwalter der grossen Büchersammlung in Wolfenbüttel ein Vorgänger Lessings gewesen. Der Übergang von der theoretischen Methode des Systems, durch den der Begriff des Kontinuums bestehende Gegensätze überwindet, in die Praxis der Religionspolitik, war schon bei Leibnitz vollzogen worden:

Alle Sekten haben einen charakteristischen Anteil an der Wahrheit; ihr Irrtum beginnt mit der Behauptung, dass alle ausser der einen als falsch zu verwerfen sind.[18]

Lessing benutzte die begriffliche Unterscheidung von geringerer oder grösserer Klarheit der Erkenntnis als Werkzeug für die Betrachtung der kirchlichen Doktrinen. Er sah auf diese Weise eine geistige Entwicklung zur Wahrheit, obwohl er die Zeitbedingtheit der einzelnen Stufen nach wie vor betonte. Das Einzelne empfängt durch den Zusammenhang eine Bedeutung, die die Umstände seiner Entstehung überschreitet.

Lessing hat gewusst, dass sein Interesse an Bibelkritik dem jüdischen Freund nicht sympathisch sein könnte. In seinem letzten Brief an Mendelssohn hat er dieses heikle Thema berührt. „Dass Ihnen nicht alles gefallen, was ich seit einiger Zeit geschrieben, das wundert mich garnicht. Ihnen hätte garnichts gefallen müssen; denn für Sie war garnichts geschrieben".[19] Diese Zeilen waren wenige Monate nach der vollständigen Veröffentlichung der Schrift über *Die Erziehung des Menschengeschlechts* formuliert worden. Dort hatte Lessing Theologie und Geschichtsanschauung in einem bestimmten Argument zusammengebracht. Zwei Jahre nach Lessings Tod hat Mendelssohn gegen diese Arbeit öffentlich Stellung genommen. Er wandte sich gegen die Idee, dass die Menschheit als Ganzes eine nachweisbare Entwicklung genommen habe. Sein verewigter Freund möge von irgendeinem Geschichtsschreiber eine solche These übernommen haben, die aber der Wirklichkeit nicht entspricht. In Wahrheit zeigt jede Epoche die verschiedenen Stufen, die Menschen erreichen können gleichzeitig nebeneinander. Die Vorsehung hat keine Vervollkommnung der Menschheit als Ganzes beabsichtigt; anderenfalls würde die Erreichbarkeit dieser Idee deutlicher sein.[20]

Wenn wir bedenken, welche Bedeutung die säkularisierte Gestalt der messianischen Hoffnung für den Glauben der Emanzipationszeit gehabt hat, so erscheint eine solche pessimistische Anschauung über den Gang der Welt fast paradox bei diesem Gründungsvater des modernen Judentums. Im neunzehnten Jahrhundert hat die jüdische Gemeinschaft in der prophetischen Kritik an der Gesellschaft ihrer Umwelt und in der Vision der Zukunft ein Programm politischen und sozialen Fortschritts gefunden; die allgemeine Herrschaft des Friedens im Völkerleben würde auch der Judenheit eine sichere Stätte bieten. Mendelssohn stand diesem Vorstellungskreis noch fern. In der damaligen Debatte über die Verbesserung der jüdischen Rechtslage war die messianische Erwartung zu einem Argument der Gegner geworden. Die Hoffnung auf den kommenden Erlöser wurde von ihnen als ein Anspruch auf die Herrschaft des jüdischen Volks gedeutet.[21]

Die Polemik Mendelssohns gegen Lessings Begriff einer religiösen Entwicklung entsprach dem Ganzen der Tendenz, welcher die Schrift *Jerusalem* dienen sollte. Der Verfasser wollte das Judentum und seinen Anspruch auf Geltung aus dem Fluss der Ereignisse und dem Wechsel der Erfahrungen herausnehmen. Für ihn ist der jüdische Glaube auf die Vernunft gegründet, die ihrer Natur nach überzeitlich ist. Die Lebensform, welche die Juden aneinander bindet, beruht auf dem göttlichen Gebot vom Sinai und ist daher ebenfalls unabhängig von dem Wandel menschlicher Dinge.[22] Mendelssohn wollte zeigen, dass seine strenge Loyalität gegenüber den ererbten Traditionen in keinerlei Widerspruch zu dem ebenso entschieden bekannten Grundsatz der Freiheit des Denkens stünde. Wenn der Dichter des *Nathan* dem Judentum eine frühere, das heisst niedrigere Stufe in der Entwicklung anwies, so bedeutete das mehr als eine vereinzelte Verschiedenheit persönlicher Stellungnahme. Die Einführung der Kategorie des Historischen, die der Schrift über *Die Erziehung des Menschengeschlechts* zugrunde lag, bedeutete trotz der Abwesenheit einer polemischen Absicht eine Erneuerung der alten Gegenüberstellung von Synagoge und Kirche. Beide Freunde vermieden mit gutem Grund eine Besprechung des sich so auftuenden Gegensatzes.[23]

Ein Blick auf die Motive und Quellen der strittigen Schrift wird diese Situation deutlicher machen. Es war Lessings Absicht, der radikalen Kritik des Reimarus, die jeden religiösen Wert der hebräischen Bibel geleugnet hatte, eine mehr positive Wendung zu geben, ohne dessen Methode zu verwerfen. So ergab sich die Aufgabe, zu zeigen, auf welche Weise das biblische Geschehen die ihrer Natur nach von Zeit und Umständen scheinbar unabhängige Vernunft in ihrer Entfaltung beschleunigt und zeitweise stossartig vorwärts getrieben hat.[24] Der Gegensatz zu der Fragestellung, mit der Mendelssohn das Verhältnis von Glaube und Tradition interpretiert hatte, ist offensichtlich. Es war kein Zufall, dass Lessing bei seiner Konstruktion Anschluss an die kirchliche Überlieferung fand. Die hierarchische Anordnung der beiden Testamente wurde zum Model für seinen Versuch. Er reihte sich damit ein in eine Geschichte, deren Ursprung auf die Anfänge des christlichen Glaubens zurückging. Der Apostel Paulus musste seine Vergangenheit, die ihn als Pharisäer an das jüdische Gesetz gebunden hatte, überwinden; aber er konnte sie nicht vergessen und wollte sie nicht verbergen. Im Kampfe um ihre geistige Selbsterhaltung hat die Kirche die Dialektik aufgenommen, mit der der Heidenapostel seiner Lebensgeschichte einen Sinn gegeben hatte. Was bei ihm eine Frage des persönlichen Daseins gewesen war, wird zu der kirchlichen Lehre von den zwei Perioden als Kern der Menschheitsgeschichte. Die religiöse Krise des zweiten Jahrhunderts, die Auseinandersetzung mit dem gnostischen Synkretismus, verstärkte die Bedeutung der Bibel des hebräischen Volkes. Damals wurde in der Kirche das Alte und das Neue Testament als Kanon der heiligen Schrift zusammengestellt. Damit war ein Dokument geschaffen, das in klarer Darstellung die Entstehung der Kirche mit der Schöpfung des Alls verband. Keine von den gnostischen Sekten konnte eine ähnliche Vorgeschichte ihrer Verkündung in der wirklichen Welt aufweisen. Die christlichen Theologen verlängerten die Verbindung, die im Pentateuch durch die Volksgeschichte zwischen Genesis und Sinai hergestellt ist, bis zur Menschwerdung. Aber gerade darum ist der weltgeschichtliche Einschnitt, der die so hergestellte Heilsgeschichte in zwei Teile zerlegt, von grosser Bedeutung: Die sinaitischen Gebote sind ihrem Inhalt nach zeitgebunden; ihr letzter Sinn bleibt den Juden, für die sie bestimmt waren, verhüllt. Ihre Nachkommen sind auf dieser überwundenen Stufe der Offenbarung stehen geblieben und haben so ihr eigenes Erbe verscherzt.

Diese patristische Lehre von der doppelschichtigen Wahrheit bot Lessing eine Denkform, wie er sie für seine Religionsphilosophie brauchen konnte. Dass sie im Mittelalter das Bild der Judenheit als des Volkes der verwirkten Sendung geschaffen und so dessen Schicksal für viele Jahrhunderte mitbestimmt hat, wird Lessing kaum bewusst gewesen sein. Aber es ist deutlich, dass die Wiederaufnahme dieser Betrachtungsweise, trotz abgewandelter Tendenz, das Verhältnis von Lessing und Mendelssohn belasten musste.

Für seinen Beweis, dass das hebräische Altertum den primitiven Anfang der religiösen Menschheitserziehung darstellt, braucht Lessing das Fehlen der Unsterblichkeitserwartung im Alten Testament. Erfüllung oder Nichterfüllung des mosaischen Gesetzes sind dort mit Glück oder Unglück auf Erden in Verbindung gebracht. Auf dieser Stufe würde eine weniger greifbare Vorstellung unverständlich sein und so ihren Zweck als pädagogisches Werkzeug verfehlen.[25]

Mit diesem Gedankengang hat Lessing eines der gebräuchlichsten Motive der mittelalterlichen Disputationen zum Thema Kirche und Synagoge aufgenommen. Die eindrucksvollste Parallele steht bei Augustin in *De civitate Dei:* Gott hat die Zerstörung von Jerusalem durch den Heiden Titus zugelassen, weil im Zeitalter des Neuen Testaments die irdische Stadt das Gottesreich nicht mehr vertreten durfte.[26] Lessing hat darüber hinaus die Primitivität der hebräischen Anfänge aufs äusserste gesteigert. Er bezeichnet dieses Volk als das ungeschliffenste und verwildertste und deutet an, dass es vor der sinaitischen Offenbarung möglicherweise gar keinen Gottesdienst gehabt hätte. Vielleicht haben die Ägypter diesen ihren Sklaven, denen der Gott ihrer Väter ganz unbekannt geworden war, Gottlosigkeit auferlegt, um ihrer eigenen Tyrannenart den Anschein der Billigkeit zu geben.[27] Dabei erinnert Lessing den Leser daran, dass Christen in der Gegenwart mit ihren Sklaven nicht anders verfahren. Auch wenn man diese Bemerkung als einen Versuch zu ausgleichender Gerechtigkeit ansieht, wird der heutige Leser etwas erstaunt sein, diese extreme Charakteristik bei dem Autor des *Nathan* vorzufinden; sie war sicherlich nicht für Mendelssohn geschrieben.

Andererseits haben solche Urteile nichts zu tun mit Lessings Stellungnahme zur zeitgenössischen Judenheit und zum Problem der religiösen Verständigung. Es kam ihm darauf an, jene Tendenz der Aufklärung zu überwinden, die allen Fortschritt auf zielbewusstes Denken und Tun vernünftiger Individuen zurückführte. Lessings *Skizze der Erziehungsgeschichte* soll demgegenüber den primitiven Schichten menschlichen Wesens Gerechtigkeit gewähren, indem er ihren Anteil am Werden der Kultur deutlich macht: Die Juden sind gerade dadurch zu tatkräftigen religiösen Erziehern der Menschheit geworden, weil ihre historische Situation sie aus geistiger Tiefe emporgetrieben hat.[28] Mit solcher positiven Wertung des Irrationalen rückt Lessing in die Nachbarschaft einer Richtung, die im letzten Drittel des achzehnten Jahrhunderts allgemeinere Bedeutung gewinnt. Wir brauchen nur daran zu erinnern, dass Herder, der im Februar 1770 in Hamburg mit Lessing zusammentraf, vier Jahre später mit seiner Kritik an Iselins psychologischer Geschichtstheorie neue Bahnen einschlug.[29] Lessing blieb in seinem Glauben an die Geschichte als den Weg, auf dem die Menschheit im Begriff ist, eine Annäherung an die Wahrheit zu erreichen, der Aufklärung näher als die vorromantischen Richtungen in seiner Umwelt. Aber er war skeptisch geworden gegenüber dem Glauben, dass seine Zeit das Ziel erreicht habe, die Welt endgültig zu erkennen und zu beschreiben.

Seine kirchengeschichtlichen Studien hatten Lessing den Eindruck gegeben, dass die rationalistische Auslese von Wahrheit und Wert zu geistiger Verengung führen müsse. Die Berücksichtigung des Triebhaften als positiven Faktor in der Kulturentwicklung, wie sie damals unter Hume's Einfluss in Schottland ausgebildet wurde, eröffnete ihm die Möglichkeit, traditionellen Lehren mit Verständnis zu begegnen, ohne sich ihnen zu unterwerfen.[30] Es war Mendelssohn, durch den er ein Exemplar von Adam Ferguson's *Versuch über die Geschichte der bürgerlichen Gesellschaft* erhielt. Als das Buch mit einiger Verzögerung von Berlin nach Wolfenbüttel gelangt war, deutet Lessing dem Freund an, warum er von dieser Schrift so viel erwarte: Menschliches Dasein vollzieht sich in einer Welt der Widersprüche; wir müssen mit diesem Nebeneinander des Gegensätzlichen leben.[31] Für diese Aufgabe hofft Lessing von dem Buch des Schotten orientierende Hilfe, weil dessen Thema die Entstehung der Bildung aus dem Primitiven, des Rationalen aus dem Triebhaften ist. Bei Ferguson entstehen weder Revolutionen noch Renaissancen aus bewusster Planung; ihre Vorbedingung liegt in der Situation, nicht im Gedanken. Der Verfasser dieser Betrachtungen lebte in Edinburg, ohne doch seine ursprüngliche Bindung an das stammhafte Dasein der Hochländer aufzugeben. Sein Gefühl für das Fortbestehen natürlich gewachsener Gesellschaften stammt aus dieser Erfahrung.[32] Die zeitgenössische Entdeckung des Irrationalen als historischer Triebkraft wurde für Lessing zum Anlass, die Primitivität der hebräischen Urzeit als Periode des Anfangs noch über die entsprechende Charakteristik in der kirchlichen Heilsgeschichte zu steigern.[33] Andererseits hatte er im Aufbau seines Arguments ein charakteristisches Motiv der Aufklärungshistorie benutzt. Es handelt sich um deren Tendenz, die Lehren der wahren Religion auch ausserhalb der biblischen Offenbarung anzuerkennen. Pierre Bayle hatte in dem Artikel *Zoroaster* seiner Enzyklopaedie dargelegt, dass die Lehre des persischen Weisen den Weg zum Monotheismus zeige.[34] Bei Lessing bringt das babylonische Exil die Begegnung der Juden mit den Persern als einem Volk, das durch Vernunft seinen Glauben vergeistigt hat. Durch diese Erfahrung haben die Juden gelernt, in Gott etwas anderes zu sehen als den einen, mächtigen Herrn ihres Volkes, dessen ziffernmässige Einheit nicht leicht festzuhalten war. Die Übernahme der Idee des „Einzigen," die auf der Ahnung der Unendlichkeit beruht, hat diese Gefahr der Abgötterei für immer gebannt. Der so gewonnene Standpunkt ermöglichte es den Juden, auch im Rückblick auf die eigene Tradition hinter der Oberfläche des Wortlauts die tiefere Wahrheit zu sehen; das „Elementarbuch" offenbarte einen Gehalt, der vorher verborgen geblieben war.[35] In dieser Weise hat Lessing den Doppelsinn religiöser Überlieferung, wie ihn die Kirche lehrte, für seinen Aufbau der Religionsgeschichte benutzt. Auch das zweite „Elementarbuch", in dem Christus als der zuverlässige Lehrer der Unsterblichkeit erscheint, besitzt für ihn einen tieferen Sinn, der nicht unmittelbar erreichbar ist und dessen Vorhandensein den Glauben an den weiteren Fortschritt durch ein „neues Evangelium" rechtfertigt.[36]

Lessing hat für diese Anschauung eine mittelalterliche Sekte als Zeuge angeführt. Joachim von Fiore und seine Schüler erwarteten nach dem Zeitalter des Alten und des Neuen Testaments ein Drittes, den drei Personen der Trinitätslehre entsprechend. In dem verkündeten Zeitalter würde spirituelle Erkenntnis die Macht der organisierten Priesterkirche als bindende und erlösende Kraft ersetzen. Auf Grund einer Berechnung der Generationenfolge in beiden Testamenten sah Joachim den Anbruch der neuen Periode in greifbarer Nähe. In solcher Hoffnung sah Lessing eine Übereilung; ein derartiger Wandel brauche Zeit in der Vorbereitung.[37] Diese Kritik an der mittelalterlichen Sekte lässt Lessings Abstand von der zeitgenössischen Aufklärung erkennen, die daran glaubte, einen Weg zur Wahrheit in Denken und Tun klar vor sich zu sehen. Lessing bestreitet diese Möglichkeit nicht nur für die Gegenwart, sondern für die Menschennatur überhaupt. Aber wir sehen aus dieser Auseinandersetzung mit der kirchlichen Tradition, wie sehr deren Macht in seinem Geist die Voraussetzung seiner Kritik bleibt.

III

Lessing hat diese mittelalterliche Anschauung der sich entfaltenden Offenbarung durch den Begriff der Erziehung in den Bereich des achtzehnten Jahrhunderts gebracht. Ereignisse können den Menschen in eine Lage bringen, in der aus Erfahrungen geistige Möglichkeiten in ihm sich entwickeln, wie sie ohne solche Wendung erst spät oder garnicht verwirklicht würden. Auf solche Weise wird die Leistung der Vernunft in die Kontingenz zeitlicher Abläufe einbezogen.

Lessing hat diesen Vorgang menschlichen Lernens in biblischer Sprache beschrieben. Die Offenbarung und ihre Weiterbildung gehen auf göttliche Vorsehung zurück. Solche Aussagen, im Wortsinn verstanden, scheinen eine Annäherung an den Standpunkt supranaturalistischer Transzendenz zu bedeuten, wie ihn Mendelssohn als Voraussetzung der Geltung der

Religionsgesetzes angenommen hat. Eine solche Deutung würde voraussetzen, dass Lessing in seinem letzten Jahrzehnt gegenüber seinen früheren Versuchen, Entstehung und Ausbreitung des Christentums zeitgeschichtlich zu erklären, einen Bruch vollzogen hat. Das *„Gespräch mit Jacobi über Spinoza"*, das kurz nach der vollständigen Veröffentlichung der zur Erörterung stehenden Schrift im Juli 1780 stattgefunden hat, macht eine solche Annahme zum mindesten schwierig. Die in Jacobis Bericht zitierten Worte über die Offenbarung, „dass er sich alles natürlich ausgebeten haben wolle", fassen die Tendenz seiner Äusserung zum Thema gut zusammen. Die faktische Richtigkeit der Erzählung ist weder von Mendelssohn noch von neueren Kritikern Jacobis bestritten worden.[38] Lessing hat die *Schrift über die Erziehung des Menschengeschlechts* als das Werk eines ungenannten Verfassers eingeführt, der seine individuelle Sicht der Allgemeinheit zur Prüfung anbietet. Die Übernahme des biblischen Sprachgebrauchs, die das Element des Exoterischen verstärkt, passt offenbar zu dieser persönlichen Zurückhaltung. Lessing hatte ein bedeutendes Vorbild für ein solches Verfahren in Spinozas *theologisch–politischem Traktat*.

Carl Gebhardt hat darauf hingewiesen, dass diese Schrift Lessings durch Urteile des jüdischen Bibelkritikers angeregt worden ist.[39] Wenn man die literarischen Zusammenhänge im Ganzen betrachtet, haben beide das kirchliche Schema der Heilsgeschichte benutzt. Während es sich bei Lessing um eine Auseinandersetzung mit der zeitgenössischen Theologie handelt, wollte Spinoza zeigen, dass das richtig verstandene Alte Testament keine Autorität sei, auf Grund derer man das öffentliche Wesen seiner Gegenwart im Sinne der calvinistischen Prädikanten beeinflussen dürfte. Bei ihm wurden die biblischen Berichte zu einer Art Verfassungsgeschichte. Dementsprechend beschränkt sich der Inhalt der sinaitischen Gesetze und Vorschriften auf die Errichtung und Erhaltung des hebräischen Staats in Palästina und das damit verbundene Wohlbefinden seiner Bürger. Daraus ergibt sich Spinozas These, dass die Bibel als Gesetzbuch einer vergangenen Epoche weder für die gegenwärtige Gesellschaft noch für die eigene Person des Philosophen Geltung beanspruchen könnte. Diese politische Interpretation der Bibel war schon bei Thomas von Aquino vorbereitet, der in den Untersuchungen seiner theologischen *Summa* über den Begriff des Gesetzes das mosaische Recht mit Hilfe der aristotelischen Staats- und Gesellschaftslehre interpretiert hatte.[40] Die hierarchische Abstufung, mit der das kirchliche Geschichtsschema Altes und Neues Testament zusammenordnete, wurde von Spinoza übernommen: Christus war als Erster im Stande, das göttliche Wesen angemessen, d. h. ohne Hilfe von Vorstellungen und Bildern, in denen sich die Vergänglichkeit der zeitgenössischen Welt spiegeln musste, zu denken.[41] Darum konnte der christliche Glaube der ganzen Menschheit gepredigt werden.

Wenn Bibelkritik bedeutet, die einzelnen Teile des kanonischen Schrifttums in ihrer Entstehung aus den Problemen der jeweiligen Umwelt zu verstehen, gehören sowohl Spinoza als Lessing in die Vorgeschichte dieser

Disziplin. Beide können als Vorläufer des Historismus gelten, der im neunzehnten Jahrhundert zu voller Geltung kam. Es fehlt in Spinozas *Traktat* nicht an Andeutungen, dass seine Gedankengänge den Pantheismus als Voraussetzung haben: Gottes Vorsehung wird definiert als Ausdruck für das Walten eines notwendigen und ewigen Gesetzes. Da der Mensch ein Teil der Natur ist, muss alles Geschehen, das ihm dient, auf göttlichen Ursprung zurückgeführt werden; von aussen her, wenn die Kräfte der Umwelt wirksam sind, und von innen her, wenn es sich um das eigene Tun der Individuen handelt.[42] Aber im Ganzen ist der Text Spinozas in der Sprache der Bibel gehalten, ebenso wie Lessings *Erziehungsgeschichte:* Die Juden haben ihre Verfassung durch Gottes Offenbarung an Moses erhalten, und die religiöse Erfahrung Christi wird ebenso auf das Einwirken Gottes zurückgeführt. Spinoza legte sich in seinem anonymen *Traktat* eine gewisse Zurückhaltung auf, weil die Schrift die Haltung der holländischen Regierung unter Jan de Witt unterstützen sollte; Lessing folgte seinem Beispiel exoterischer Darstellung, weil er sich nicht als Bestreiter der christlichen Tradition fühlte und nicht als solcher erscheinen wollte.

Die leidenschaftliche Erregung Mendelssohns über Jacobis Behauptung, dass Lessing ein folgerechter Anhänger Spinozas und als solcher ein bewusster Atheist gewesen sei, wurde ein wichtiger Antrieb für sein Denken und Schreiben während seiner letzten Jahre. Er hat die tatsächliche Richtigkeit der von Jacobi erzählten *Zwiegespräche* im Juli 1780 nicht eigentlich bestritten, aber in ihrer Bedeutung zu entkräften versucht. Er hat immer wieder die Neigung zum Spielerischen geschildert, mit der Lessings Dialektik zuweilen ein geistvolles Argument aufgebaut habe, um einer sinnlosen These für einen Augenblick Geltung zu verleihen.[43] Andererseits lag Mendelssohn viel an dem Nachweis, dass Lessing pantheistische Begriffe benutzt habe, um ein wesentlich theistisches Weltbild darzustellen; die *Erziehung des Menschengeschlechts* dient als Beleg solchen Verfahrens.[44] Jacobi hatte diese Abhandlung, deren vollständige Veröffentlichung kurz vor der Zusammenkunft mit Lessing erfolgt war, als Anlass bezeichnet, der sein Interesse an den Beziehungen Lessings und Spinoza erregt hatte. Die Rettung Lessings war für Mendelssohn auch gleichzeitig eine Rettung Spinozas, um die er sich seit vielen Jahren bemüht hatte. In einer Frühschrift hatte er die These aufgestellt, dass Leibnitz das Lehrstück der prästabilierten Harmonie von dem jüdischen Denker übernommen habe, eine Behauptung, die Lessing in einem Brief an ihn während seiner Breslauer Zeit als „Sophisterei" verspottet hatte.[45] Diese brüderliche Sympathie erreichte ihre grösste Wirkung in dem Spätwerk *Jerusalem,* mit dem Mendelssohn die fortdauernde Geltung der jüdischen Tradition in der Welt der Aufklärung nachweisen wollte. Julius Guttmann hat gezeigt, dass die zentrale Idee dieser Schrift, die Absonderung der Gotteserkenntnis von der sinaitischen Offenbarung an ein bestimmtes Volk, auf Spinozas *Traktat* zurückgeht.[46] Auch die Beschreibung des Gesetzes als eine nur während der israelitischen Periode erzwingbaren Ordnung der Gesellschaft, in der Gott das *politische* Haupt gewesen sei, findet sich hier und dort. Mendelssohn durfte überzeugt sein, dass er mit seinem Festhalten an der dauernden religiösen Geltung des Gesetzes die ihm wohl bewusste unjüdische Tendenz der Geschichtskonstruktion Spinozas beiseite gelassen habe. Nach Jacobis Mitteilung, dass Lessing sich als einen entschiedenen Spinozisten bezeichnet habe, richtete er durch Elise Reimarus die Anfrage an jenen, welches spinozistische System dabei vorausgesetzt sei. Er teilte das ganze Werk des Philosophen in drei Teile, und nannte den *Traktat* an erster Stelle. Mendelssohns letzte Schrift „*An die Freunde Lessings*" macht deutlich, was er mit seiner merkwürdig klingenden Unterscheidung gemeint hat. Dort erklärt er, „dass Spinoza seiner spekulativen Lehre ungeachtet ein orthodoxer Jude hätte bleiben können, wenn er nicht in anderen Schriften das echte Judentum bestritten und sich dadurch dem Gesetz entzogen hätte. Die Lehre des Spinoza kommt dem orthodoxen Judentum offenbar weit näher als die orthodoxe Lehre der Christen."[47] Dass Lessing, bei seiner Konstruktion der jüdischen Religionsgeschichte, die radikalste Tendenz Spinozas aufgenommen und damit das eigentliche Wesen seiner Einstellung ausgesprochen hätte, musste für Mendelssohn ein schwerer persönlicher Anstoss sein. Die Erfahrung war so schmerzlich, dass er nur in Andeutungen darüber schrieb.

Die Auseinandersetzung zwischen Judentum und Historismus, die von Abraham Geiger bis Franz Rosenzweig ein wichtiges Thema im Denken der Emanzipationszeit gebildet hat, begann mit Mendelssohn.[48] Sein Gegensatz zu Lessings Fragestellung, deren Bedeutung ihm am Ende seines Lebens fast gewaltsam zum Bewusstsein gebracht wurde, stammte nicht eigentlich aus dem Persönlichen. Er hatte als Ursache die weltgeschichtliche Stellung der beiden Traditionen, deren Deutung jeder der beiden Freunde sich zur Aufgabe gemacht hatte.

ANMERKUNGEN

1. Schriften und Briefe Mendelssohns sind, wenn nicht anders bemerkt, zitiert nach der Ausgabe B. G. Mendelssohn, *Moses Mendelssohn's gesammelte Schriften,* Leipzig, 1843f.; Lessing nach Karl Lachmann, *G. E. Lessing's sämmtliche Schriften,* Leipzig, 1853f. Brief v. 10. II. 1765, *Mendelssohn's Schrift.* V, S. 342. Zu Abbts Persönlichkeit: A. Altmann, *Mendelssohn*, Alabama, 1973, S. 100–112.
2. 2. XI. 1762, *Schrft.* V, S. 268.
3. 22. VII. 1766. *Schrft.* V, S. 368.
4. Aus der *Allgem. deutschen Biblioth.* IV Stück 2. 1767. *Schrift.* IV_2, Ss. 521–27.
5. Ebendort, S. 522.
6. 25. VI. 1782. *Schrft.* V, Ss. 597–600.
7. 29. XII. 1770. *Schrft.* V, Ss. 184–86; Lessings Antwort 9. I. 1771 ebendort S. 188f; vgl. dazu Mendelssohn an Dr. Obereit, 23. III. 1771 über moralische Veranlagung und kulturellen Fortschritt. V, S. 496f.
8. Brief an Elkan Herz 22. VII. 1771, bei F. Bamberger, „Mendelssohns Begriff vom Judentum" in K. Wilhelm, *Die Wissenschaft des Judentums*, Tübingen, 1969, II, S. 531.

9. *Über die Entstehung der geoffenbarten Religionen,* Lachmann, XI_2, S. 247f.

10. 26. III. 1765. *Schrft.* V, S. 346, an Abbt.

11. Über Reimarus und seinen Hamburger Kreis siehe Heinrich Sieveking, *Karl Sieveking, 1787–1847,* Hamburg 1923, I, Ss. 1–36.

12. 9. I. 1771. V, S. 188.

13. 2. II. 1774; dazu die Briefe 8. IV. 1773; 14. VII. 1773; 20. III. 1777; 25. II. 1778. Lachmann, XII, Ss. 469; 472; 577; 602f.

14. An den jüngeren Reimarus 6. IV. 1778. Lachmann, S. 606.

15. 23. VII. 1778. Lachmann, XII, S. 609.

16. H. E. Allison, *Lessing and the Enlightenment,* Ann Arbor 1966, Ss. 68; 75; 81f; 184f.

17. Ernst Cassirer, *Freiheit und Form,* Berlin, 1916, S. 63. erwähnt bei einer Besprechung von Leibnitz' Einfluss auf die literarische Bewegung einen Satz Friedrichs des Grossen, dass die Monadologie der „Roman eines genialen Mannes" gewesen sei. Das Urteil stammt aus Friedrichs Betrachtungen zur deutschen Literatur, *Werke* VIII, S. 90, Berlin, 1913. Ähnliche Kritik ebendort S. 41; VII, Ss. 95; 239.

18. Aus einem Brief an A. Arnauld von Porte Royal (1687), abgedruckt bei Allison (Anm. 16), S. 130f.

19. 19. 12. 1780. Lachmann, XII, S. 667.

20. *Schrft.* III, S. 317f.

21. So Schleiermacher in der anonymen Schrift: *Briefe bei Gelegenheit der politisch-theologischen Aufgabe und des Sendschreibens jüdischer Hausväter von einem Prediger ausserhalb Berlins,* 1799, in *Sämtliche Werke* I. Bd. 1846, S. 21. Schleiermacher sieht die Unterordnung des Ritualgesetzes unter die Staatsordnung und die förmliche Aufgabe der Messiasidee als Vorbedingung einer neuen Rechtsstellung.

22. *Schrft.* III, Ss. 319; 321; 350; 355.

23. In den *Morgenstunden* hat Mendelssohn auf diese Schrift als Beispiel für den mit dem Theismus vereinbaren Pantheismus Lessings hingewiesen, ohne die sonstigen Gegensätze der Auffassung zu berühren. Text bei H. Scholz, *Schriften zum Pantheismusstreit,* Berlin, 1916, S. 39.

24. *„Gegensätze des Herausgebers",* 1777. Lachmann, X, S. 31f. *Erziehung des Menschengeschlechts* §§4; 63; 77, ebendort Ss. 308; 320; 323.

25. §§16f; 23, ebendort S. 310f.

26. V, 18 ed. Dombart I, 227f.

27. §§8–11, S. 309.

28. §18, S. 310; vgl. die parallele Ausführung in den *„Gegensätzen".* Lachmann, X, S. 22 über das „unendlich mehr verachtete als verächtliche Volk".

29. Robert F. Clark jun. *Herder, his Life and Thought,* Berkeley, 1969, Ss. 110f; 188–196. Dazu Friedrich Meineke, *Die Enstehung des Historismus,* II, München–Berlin, 1936, Ss. 416–442.

30. Die ausführliche Behandlung von Hume als Historiker bei F. Meinecke, München, 1936, I, Ss. 208–247 ist aufschlussreich.

31. *An Essay on the History of Civil Society,* 1767; Correspondenz über Ferguson: Lessing an seinen Bruder Karl 11. XI. 1770. Lachman, XII, S. 322; Mendelssohn an Lessing 29. XI. 1770 *Schrft.* V, S. 186f.; Lessing bestätigt Empfang und definiert die Bedeutung des Buches 9. I. 1771, S. 188. Nachweis der Identität des nur mit dem Namen des Autors zitierten Buches bei A. Altmann, *Mendelssohn,* S. 252.

32. Duncan Forbes in der Einführung der Ausgabe 1966, Ss. xxxiv; xxxviii; dazu im Text Ss. 123; 170.

33. Allison hat in seinem wichtigen Buch (siehe oben, S. 180, Anm. 16), S. 130f. bestritten, dass Ferguson für Lessing wichtig gewesen sei. (gegen Karl Aner, *Theologie der Lessingzeit,* Halle, 1929, S. 351f). Die Übereinstimmung in Lessings Beschreibung, was ihm an Ferguson's Buch wichtig erscheine, mit der Tendenz der Erziehungsschrift, macht die ausschliessliche Zurückführung auf den Einfluss von Leibnitz unwahrscheinlich.

34. H. T. Mason, *Pierre Bayle and Voltaire,* Oxford, 1963, Ss. 76; 94.

35. *Erziehung* §§19–21 und 34–39. Lachmann X, S. 310f; 314f.

36. §86, S. 324.

37. §§86–90, S. 324f. Lessing hat offenbar ein Motiv im System Joachims nicht gekannt, das ihn wegen seiner mindestens formalen Ähnlichkeit mit seiner eigenen Absicht sicher interessiert hätte: In Joachims Lehre hatte jedes der drei Zeitalter einen Vorläufer unter der Oberfläche des vorhergehenden. Die Generationen Adam bis Abraham wirken in der Richtung auf das Gesetz; die Propheten bereiten das Evangelium vor, und das Mönchswesen das Kommen des Geistes.

38. Scholz, *Pantheismusstreit* S. 92. H. Thielicke, *Offenbarung, Vernunft und Existenz,* Gütersloh, 1957 hat den Nachweis versucht, für Lessings Begriff der Offenbarung einen transzendenten Sinn zu behaupten, obwohl er die tatsächliche Richtigkeit von Jacobis Erzählung anerkennt. Sein Argument beruht wesentlich auf Lessings Charakteristik der Offenbarung als einer Macht, die den Menschen gefangen nimmt. Aber Gedankengang und Stil der Schrift, sowie ihr Zusammenhang mit Lessings Studien scheinen dafür zu sprechen, dass es sich um eine pantheistisch gedachte Umschreibung des Geschichtsprozesses handelt, wenn er Völker und Individuen zu Einsichten führt, die ihre Vernunft ohne das Ereignis besonderer Erfahrungen nicht erreichen konnte.

39. B. de Spinoza, *Theologisch-politischer Traktat,* Hamburg, 1955, S. 369f.

40. Thomas hatte in seiner theologischen *Summa* II 1, *quaest.* 105 *art* 1. in der mosaischen Verfassung die Elemente von Monarchie, Aristokratie und Demokratie gefunden. Spinoza nimmt diese Charakteristik der biblischen Verfassung in seinem Kapital 16, vom Staate der Hebräer auf; dazu H. Liebeschütz, „Die politische Interpretation des Alten Testaments bei Thomas von Aquino und Spinoza" in *Antike u. Abendland,* IX, 1960, Ss. 39–62.

41. Kap. 1 §23; Kap. 4 §§32–34; Kap. 5 §§8–9, ed. C. H. Bruder, Leipzig, 1846, III Ss. 22; 69; 75. Die Erklärung Spinozas, dass diese Feststellungen keine Anerkennung der christologischen Lehren der Kirchen bedeuten, die er nicht verstehe, wird Lessing kaum Anstoss gegeben haben. Kap. 1 §24, S. 22.

42. Kap. 3 §§7–9. S. 49.

43. An die Geschwister Reimarus 18. XI. 1783, *Schrft.* V, S. 702; „Erinnerungen an Herrn Jacobi", 1784, Scholz, *Pantheismusstreit* S. 118. In diesen Charakteristiken spricht Mendelssohns verletztes Gefühl gegenüber Lessing, der ihm während eines Vierteljahrhunderts ihrer Freundschaft eine Richtung seines Denkens verborgen gehalten hat, um sie dann dem soviel jüngeren Jacobi ohne Zögern zu offenbaren. In diesem Sinne ist das abschliessende Urteil in *„An die Freunde Lessings"* zu verstehen. Scholz, S. 304. Lessing hat solchen Wechsel von Spott und Ernst in seinen dialektischen Argumenten durch die Worte *gymnastikōs kai dogmatikōs* bezeichnet. Der Charakter des Gegners bestimme die jeweilige Tendenz. Brief an d. Bruder 16. III. 1778. Lachmann, XII, S. 604.

44. *Morgenstunden,* Vorlesung XV. Scholz, S. 39. A. Altmann, „Lessing und Jacobi", *Lessingjahrbuch* III, Ss. 25–70, München, 1970, bietet eine kritisch Untersuchung der für die Deutung des Gesprächs einschlägigen Texte.

45. *Philosophische Gespräche,* I, Jubiläumsausgabe I, 1929, S. 11 „Sie waren damals . . . ein kleiner Sophist". Lessing an Mendelssohn 17. IV. 1763. *Schrft.* V, S. 169.

46. „Mendelssohns Jerusalem und Spinozas Theol.-Polit. Traktat," *Jahresbericht der Hochschule f. d. Wissenschaft d. Judentums,* 48, 1931, Ss. 33–61. *Jerusalem,* Abschnitt II. *Schrft.* III, Ss. 348; 350–357.

47. An Elise Reimarus 16. VIII. 1783. *Schrft.* V, S. 693. *An die Freunde Lessings,* Scholz S. 295.

48. Dazu vgl. A. Altmann, „Franz Rosenzweig on History," *Between East and West, Essays dedicated to the memory of Bela Horovitz,* 1958, Ss. 194–214.

Ibn Gabirol's Treatment of Sources in the *Kether Malkhuth*

R. LOEWE

In his great confessional poem, the *Kether Malkhuth*, Solomon ibn Gabirol sets out to correlate the human predicament of proclivity to sin with the psychology of Neo-Platonism and the cosmology of Ptolemy, the first being colored and the second elaborated by him so as to cohere with his specifically Jewish heritage. For his astronomical information he turned, as has been recognized since Haneberg's article[1] published in 1866, to the *Epistles of the Brethren of Purity (Rasāʾil ikhwān aṣ-ṣafāʾ)*, and whilst it is certainly true that these are his principal sources, this article sets out to show that they were not his only ones. The *Epistles* were compiled, perhaps in Basra and probably in Ismaili circles, in the late tenth or early eleventh century;[2] knowledge of them reached Spain through Maslama al-majrīṭī and Abulḥakīm al-kirmānī (d. 1065/6), the latter of whom was, like Gabirol's father, a native of Cordova and was also resident in Saragossa at the same period as Solomon ibn Gabirol himself.

In his recent book on the philosophy of ibn Gabirol[3] Schlanger, whilst adducing an impressive list of points of contact, concludes that the influence of the *Epistles* on Gabirol is on the whole limited to scientific detail rather than affecting his whole Neo-Platonic system. This assertion exposes itself to question as far as concerns the *Kether Malkhuth*, first because as will be shown below there is an additional source used for astronomical detail, and secondly because it seems hardly to appreciate adequately the significance of such parallels as the following, which despite some textual uncertainty may be accepted with Nasr as typical of the spirit of the *Epistles*:[4]

> [God] made these his works manifest, to the end that the intelligent might contemplate them; and he brought into view all that was in His invisible world, that the observant might behold it and acknowledge His Skill and Peerlessness, and Omnipotence, and Soleness, and not stand in need of demonstration. . . .

This at once recalls the structure of Gabirol's introductory section and that following it, as proclaimed in the heading of each successive paragraph (ii–ix, x–xxxii).[5] Nor should we underestimate the significance of their respective professions of universalism. The standpoint of the *Epistles* is summarized by A. L. Tibawi[6] as follows:

> The Brethren of Purity believe that the Truth is one without its being the private work of anyone. God has sent His Spirit to all men, to Christians as to Muslims, to blacks as to whites.

Next to this summary we may set Gabirol's avowal:[7]

All creatures are thy witnesses, in bond
Each to thy name with service to respond,
And each pays homage to thine honour so.
And though men worship other things, their act
Doth not from Thee detract
Since, in their striving, Thee they seek to find,
But lose the royal road. . . .

We have nevertheless to recognize that in the immediate sequel Gabirol makes it clear that it is the "clear-eyed servants," i.e., Jews, who in fact reach the king's palace, others merely enjoying the illusion of having done so. In this respect his universalism may fall short of that expressed in the *Epistles*.

Sections xiii–xxii describe the motions of the planets and their mansions in the Zodiac, repeatedly emphasizing that although influences flow through the planets to the sublunary sphere, this happens at the will of their Creator who assigns to each its duty. The stress laid here is upon the divine will (*raṣon*), a stress that is paralleled in the *Epistles*, which like Gabirol assign a particular influence to the Sun in effecting—always in subordination to God's will—political changes. The *Epistles* state that the intellect, with the permission of Allah, gives life to the Sun and Moon as representing respectively the first and male and second and female principles which, by their union, generate all things—a concept to which Gabirol is obviously alluding in a passage (xvii) which he handles with great poetical delicacy.

Finally, we may note how Gabirol has made use of the sufi idea of the attraction between God and the universe expressed in terms of passionate love (Arabic *ʿishq*), God being the only beloved (*maʿshuq*), and yearning (*shawq*) being the factor which causes things to come into being and governs the universe. "God is the first beloved of the universe," i.e., everything which is not God proceeds from God and desires to return to Him. This notion is taken up by Gabirol at the climax of his description of the tenth and outermost sphere that he postulates in addition to the Ptolemaic nine, *viz*., the Sphere of Intelligence which, he asserts, owes its existence to God and which, though separated from Him by the act of its creation, strives ever to return to Him (xxiv):[8]

. . . by Thee controlled
In orbit (for thy might caused it to be),
From Thee to Thee revolving, yearning aye for Thee.

The climactic words (*weʾeleykha teshuqatho*) are of course taken from God's comminatory conversation with Cain (*Gen*. 4:7) and are deftly applied by Gabirol in quite another sense colored by *Song of Songs* 7:11. The Hebrew word *teshuqah* strictly speaking means, as the modern scholars tell us, *impulse*: but as used in the Bible it means in effect *love* (*Song of Songs, loc. cit; Gen.* 3:16). Its root, we should note, (*shwq*) is probably to be regarded as distinct from the Arabic *shawq* = *yearning*. Hebrew *shwq* belongs with Arabic *saq* = *drive*. But since Hebrew root *shwq* and Arabic *shauq* are in effect homonyms, Gabirol himself, whose vernacular was Arabic, may well have assumed them to be synonyms rather than semantically discrete but easily fusible entities. We thus see him here picking up a biblical quotation with which he will have been familiar since his childhood and giving it (by dint of his own poetic insight) a new setting, in which the sinister "impulse" or "desire" of sin to overpower Cain is transmuted into not the self-assertive, possessive "desire," but rather the self-abnegating and quasi-passive "love" of creation for its Creator; and at the same time infusing into it a technical level of meaning that lifts the statement onto a plane where theologically sensitive readers could be expected to recognize in it not merely religious imagery, but a cardinal feature in the construction of a Neo-Platonic reading of Judaism.

Let us now consider Gabirol's use of technical astronomical data deriving ultimately from Ptolemy. Ptolemy's *Mathēmatikēs syntaxis*[9] was given the short title *megalē* or *megistē*, whence *almagest*, to distinguish it from minor astronomical works. It was first translated into Arabic from the Syriac version about the year 800 at the order of Hārūn al-Rashīd, but the version available to the compilers of the *Epistles* was an improved translation by Thābit ibn Qurra (d. 901). As it happens, the system of spheres is not mentioned in the *Almagest* at all, but it was dealt with by Ptolemy in one of his minor works entitled *Planetary Hypotheses.* The relevant portion of the Greek original of the *Hypotheses* is not extant, but an Arabic redaction by Thābit ibn Qurra has only recently been published, with an English translation.[10] From this Arabic version a Hebrew translation was made, but after Gabirol's time, in the fourteenth century. But the *Epistles* could also draw upon the introduction to astronomy—itself also naturally based upon Ptolemaic methods—of Aḥmad ibn Muḥammad ibn Kathīr al-Farghānī of Transoxania, known to the West as Alfraganus,[11] who died after 863. And Farghānī's figures for astronomical quantities are in some cases significant in comparison with those given by Gabirol.

I turn first to the figures given by Gabirol for the size of the planets (including, of course, the sun). They are here set out in a table alongside the Ptolemaic figures and also the latest ones available as determined by modern scientific method.[12] The standard of measurement is the size of the Earth (= 1), and it should be noted that Gabirol's figures relate to comparative volume and not to diameter. Despite his occasional references to width, the operative term is *guf* in every case except that of Mercury, where it is replaced by *middah* (xiii). Although Gabirol's sources provided information regarding both the volume and the diameter of the heavenly bodies, it would seem that his preference for statement of the volume only was due to the following aesthetic consideration. The Hebrew for diameter, *qoṭer*, is a loan-word from the Arabic *quṭr* first recorded by Ben Yehuda in Abraham bar Ḥiyya (i.e., Savasorda, d. *c.* 1136), although it was conceivably already naturalized in Hebrew by Gabirol's time. At an earlier period the Greek λόξον, *slanting*, had given the Hebrew loan-word *ʾalakhson[a]*, which is in one passage[13] used in the sense of the diameter—albeit of an urban area and not of a formally described circle. In Gabirol's poetry the vocabulary is severely restricted to roots occurring in the Hebrew Bible, with occasional license for postbiblical words familiar from the liturgy, and neither the rabbinic adoption *ʾalakhson* nor the hebraization of the Arabic *quṭr*, if already accepted by Gabirol's time, could have been admitted to the diction of the *Kether Malkhuth* without incongruity. True, the word *guf*, *body*, which he employs for volume, is also postbiblical, but the feminine *guphah* does occur twice[14] in the sense of *corpse*, and the vaguer *middah, measure,* which sometimes replaces it in Gabirol's data, is of course a common biblical word.

TABLE I

Comparative Volume of Planets Relative to Earth

	Gabirol	Ptolemy*	Recent Computation
Earth	1	1	1
Moon	$\frac{1}{39}$	$\frac{1}{40}$	0.02
Mercury	$\frac{1}{22,000}$	$\frac{1}{19,683}$	0.055
Venus	$\frac{1}{37}$	$\frac{1}{44}$	0.88
Sun	170 (variant 175):1	$166\frac{1}{3}$:1	1.3×10^6:1
Mars	$1\frac{5}{8}$:1	$1\frac{1}{2}$:1	0.15
Jupiter	75:1	$82\frac{1}{4} + \frac{1}{20}$:1	1,318:1
Saturn	91:1	$79\frac{1}{2}$:1	769:1
Fixed Stars	107 (variant 170):1	$94\frac{1}{6} + \frac{1}{8}$:1	—

* The values for Ptolemy are taken from Goldstein's *Planetary Hypotheses* (see p. 193, note 10), pp. 4, 11.

Professor Goldstein has been kind enough to comment on Gabirol's figures as follows:

> These numbers all follow the Ptolemaic system of planetary distances and sizes described by Ptolemy in his *Planetary Hypotheses.* There are many mediaeval versions of this system in which the numbers differ from those Ptolemy stated, but they are all computed according to the principles Ptolemy set forth. The numbers cited by ibn Gabirol all agree with those found in al-Farghānī's Elements of Astronomy (ed. J. Golius, Arabic text and Latin translation, Amsterdam, 1669: pp. 83–4 of both the Arabic and the Latin pagination, in the case of the fixed stars the Arabic supporting the reading 107: 1 in Gabirol), with the following exceptions.

For the Sun, al-Farghānī has 166:1, whereas Gabirol has 170:1 (the variant 175:1 being ignored). 170:1 is the very number that appears in the *Almagest.*[15] (see also below).

For Jupiter, al-Farghānī has 95:1 whereas ibn Gabirol has 75:1—a textual misreading of تسعون as سبعون The immediate source may well be the *Epistles of the Brethren of Purity* (which no doubt depended on al-Farghānī), for most of Gabirol's numbers also appear in *Epistle 2* of *Part II, The Heavens and the Universe,*[16] with these exceptions:

For Mercury, this Beirut edition has $\frac{1}{22}$ instead of the appropriate value of $\frac{1}{22,000}$ as in al-Farghānī, but this is just a textual corruption.

For Venus, it has $\frac{1}{47}$ instead of the appropriate $\frac{1}{37}$, again textual corruption.

For the Sun, 160 + a fraction (as against al-Farghānī's 166:1, see above).

For Jupiter, 95:1 as in al-Farghānī.

These *Epistles* have been printed many times in the last century, but none of the prints can be considered a modern critical edition. In particular, the numbers vary from one printed text to another. But it seems fair to conclude that ibn Gabirol probably used these *Epistles* for these astronomical parameters; it is also possible that he used some other text derived from al-Farghānī's treatise, or even al-Farghānī's treatise itself (it is, after all, an elementary introduction to astronomy that was widely read in the middle ages, both in Arabic and in Latin).

TABLE II

Periodicity of the Heavenly Bodies

	Gabirol	Recent Computation	
		Sidereal Period*	Synodic Period*
Moon	29 days (variant $29\frac{1}{2}$ + a further "known number of parts (*ḥalaqim yeduᶜim*)"	27.322 days	29.53 days
Mercury	10 days (variant 10 months)	87.969 days	115.88 days
Venus	11 months (variant 12 months)	224.7 days	583.92 days
Sun	1 year	—	—
Mars	18 months	686.98 days	779.94 days
Jupiter	12 years	4,332.59 days (11.89 years)	398.88 days
Saturn	30 years	10,759.2 days (29.89 years)	378.09 days
Fixed Stars	36,000 years (variant 36 (?) years)	—	—

* The distinction between these two periods has been formulated for me by Dr R. E. W. Maddison thus:

"*Sidereal period* expresses the time of revolution of the planet about the Sun with respect to some fixed star. *Synodic period* expresses the time for the planet to return to the same apparent position with respect to the Sun. In the case of the Moon, it is the period from new moon to new moon."

On these values Professor Goldstein comments thus:

> The periods cited present greater problems. Let us begin with those that can be explained easily.
>
> The periods for *Jupiter* and *Saturn* are their sidereal period (return to the position relative to the fixed stars). These figures occur in *Epistle 3* of Part I, Astronomy.[17] For the *Fixed Stars* the figure 36,000 years agrees with Ptolemy's value for precession, 1° per century, and this figure occurs in several places in these *Epistles,* e.g. *Epistle 3* of Part III, Periods and Epochs.[18] The figures for the *Moon* and the *Sun* present no difficulty and no specific source is needed. The figure for the Moon is well known and represents an approximate value (or, according to the variant reading, a very close approximation) for the length of the synodic month (return relative to the Sun).
>
> The remaining three numbers—for *Mercury, Venus,* and *Mars*—are meaningless and may be due to a corrupt manuscript on which Gabirol relied, or possibly reflect a misunderstanding by Gabirol of correct data. For *Mercury,* one would expect to find its synodic period, 116 days (cf. *Epistle 5* of Part III,[19] which may be translated thus: 'in every one hundred and six [and] ten days Mercury is in conjunction with the Sun'.) Perhaps the words *one hundred and six* were missing in the manuscript used by Gabirol.

Professor Goldstein's conjecture of a lacuna or corruption in the manuscript used by Gabirol may be supported by indirect evidence. (We may, of course, disregard the variant in Gabirol of 10 *months,* i.e., 295 days; it is perhaps due to a "corrector," who found 10 days an incredibly short period for Mercury). In citing the figure of 10 days (in no. xiii) Gabirol states that Mercury "makes the circuit of the sphere in ten days *by running* (*be-mereṣ*). *Mereṣ,* as a coinage from the common biblical root *rwṣ,* seems to be a neologism of Gabirol's own—at any rate Ben Yehuda can cite no earlier authority than the present passage. It would seem that Gabirol himself, like his subsequent improving "corrector," found 10 days a paradoxically short period, but that unlike his corrector he trusted the authority of his source in ignorance of the circumstance that his manuscript was in point of fact corrupt. He accordingly underscored the figure for his readers, by explicit reference to Mercury's "rushing past" as compared with the other planets. But the same paradoxical speed of course holds good even with 116 days (or 4 months) for Mercury, if the Moon is ignored (see table).

To revert to Professor Goldstein's remarks:

> For *Venus,* one would expect to find its synodic period, 584 days (cf. *Epistle 5* of Part III).[20] Perhaps "11 months" reflects a misunderstanding of a passage in *Epistle 3* of Part I:[21] 'If Venus is in conjunction [with the Sun] when it is retrograde, it will reappear after 5 days, rising in the east in the morning before sunrise, and *it is seen for eight months* rising at the end of the night, and it is called easterly; then it speeds up to overtake the Sun and

travels under its rays *and for three months it is not seen*; then it reappears in the evening in the west after sunset and it is seen for eight months; then it sets in the early part of the night and is called westerly. . . .' The italicised phrases may have misled Gabirol into thinking that the synodic period of Venus is 11 months.

For *Mars*, one would expect to find its sidereal period, 1.88 years (686.98 days),[22] stated in *Epistle 3* of Part I[23] to be 'about two years less one month.' The next phrase seems to have caused the confusion: 'staying in each zodiacal sign for 45 days more or less.' If we consider 45 days as a month and a half, twelve of them equal 18 months.

In sum, I hesitate to state the source for these periods; the correct values could be found in any number of sources (not, however, in al-Farghānī, for, as far as I could find, they do not appear there in this form), and the corrupt values may be accounted for in any number of ways.

If we leave on one side this factor of possible corruption in his sources, we have to conclude that, as previously accepted, Gabirol's source for his astronomical data was the *Epistles of the Brethren of Purity*, but that there are some pointers to his having used Al-Farghānī alongside the *Epistles* for information regarding the volume, but not the periodicity of the heavenly bodies. Furthermore, close comparison of his figures with the data in his sources leaves us with the picture of a scholar using them conscientiously (his treatment of the period of Mercury) but nevertheless occasionally getting them wrong (the period of Venus). The surviving portion of Gabirol's *Meqor Ḥayyim* gives no hint that he had any marked interest in the details of astronomical data, in spite of his feeling free to postulate, in the *Kether Malkhuth*, an outermost tenth sphere (distinct from the divine throne) that was unknown to earlier expositions of the Ptolemaic system. It would seem that in referring to an encyclopedic work for specialist information outside his own competence, as we all must, he neglected (as we so often do) to ask a specialist to check the use that he had made of it and thus failed to avoid some errors which must inevitably offend the eye of those in a position to control him, even though they in no way affect either the argument or the poetic force of their context.

Let us now examine an apparent inconsistency in Gabirol's use of rabbinic material, where he was not dependent on any specialist guidance. Since it concerns his psychological scheme, it is of considerable importance.[24]

There is recorded in the Babylonian Talmud[25] the statement of Rabbi Eliezer (b. Hyrqanos, 1st-2nd centuries C.E.) that the souls of the righteous are hidden beneath the throne of glory, *1 Samuel* 25:29 being adduced as a proof text ("but the soul of my lord [*sc.* David] shall be bound up in the bundle of life with the Lord thy God"). The biblical text itself refers, of course, in its setting to the continuation of terrestrial life with, perhaps, the implication of its perpetuation in the life of an individual's successors. As utilized by Rabbi Eliezer, it is applied to the situation of the souls of the righteous after death—survival being taken for granted—as is made clear by the reference of the subsequent words of the text to the fate of the wicked. Gabirol's poetic adaption of this (xxvii)[26] is straightforward, nothing being injected into it with reference to the point of origin of the souls of the righteous (and so of all other souls as well), as opposed to their ultimate destiny. It is when he is dealing with the origin of the soul that a discrepancy apparently occurs, but, as we shall suggest below, it is resolvable.

Two paragraphs earlier (xxv) Gabirol states[27] that it is from the effulgence of the sphere of intelligence, that is his tenth and outermost sphere, that God makes (*ba-ʿasothekha*) the brightness of the souls (*zohar ha-Neshamoth*) and "the exalted spirits", or souls (*we-ha-Nefashoth ha-ramoth*). It is probable that the *waw* is to be construed not as a simple copula introducing a second and parallel object, but rather as an explicative *waw*,[28] familiar in biblical usage, so that the *neshamoth* and the *nefashoth ramoth* will be identical, referring to the "psyches of highest rank." Since the sphere of intelligence (*sekhel*) in the *Kether Malkhuth* corresponds to what in the *Fons Vitae* Gabirol calls intelligence (the lost Arabic will have been *ʿaql*), what is said here is consistent with the statement of the *Fons Vitae*[29] that the soul is an emanation of intelligence. But in the immediate sequel in the *Kether Malkhuth* to the passage just quoted Gabirol explicitly identified[30] the [*neshamoth we-*]*ha-Nefashoth ha-ramoth* with the angels that fulfill the divine will. It is quite clear that, even allowing that the generality of human souls shares the radiative source from which the angels spring, that generality is here so far from the center of the picture as to be in effect ignored. It is on the angels themselves that attention is focussed, and a lengthy description of their functions follows, replete with vivid military imagery. He then leaves the sphere of intelligence behind and describes the throne of glory—which, for Gabirol, lies beyond the sphere of intelligence, and is to be identified with universal matter with its inseparable form—with (as noted above) beneath it the abode of the souls of the departed saints, and ranged beside it the storehouses of natural forces available to God for providential reward and punishment; and it is only when all this is dealt with that Gabirol returns (xxix) to the creation of the soul.

Here he asserts[31] that it is from the effulgence of the divine glory (*mi-Ziw kevodekha*), and not, as above, from the effulgence of the sphere of intelligence (*mi-Ziw galgal ha-Sekhel*) that God creates (*be-borʾakha*; not, as before, *ba-ʿasothekha*) "a pure bright appearance, quarried from the rock of the Rock." God also (and presumably as a second operation) imparts by emanation (*we-ʾaṣalta*) to the bright appearance thus quarried a spirit of wisdom (*we-ʾaṣalta ʿaleyha ruaḥ ḥokhmah*) and so gives it the name of "soul" (*we-qaratha shemahh neshamah*). "Thou didst [thus?] make the form (note no copulative here) from the flames of the fire of intelligence (*ʾasithahh mi-Lahavoth ʾesh ha-Sekhel ha-Ṣurah*) and didst despatch it into the body." The latter two expressions (*we-ʾaṣalta, ʿasithahh me-ha-Sekhel*) are consistent with the view expressed both in the *Fons Vitae* and at the earlier point of the *Kether Malkhuth* (xxv) that the soul is an emanation of the [sphere of the] intelligence: but it is problematic to find a consistency between this scheme and the explicit assertion that immediately precedes reference to emanation from intelligence, *viz.*, that it was from the divine radiance itself that God created the soul.

I suggest that Gabirol's apparent vacillation on this point may be due to his concern to do justice to another talmudic passage. In several places[32] the dictum occurs of the second century Rabbi Jose that "the Messiah will not come until all the souls in the 'Body' (*guf*) have been expended," i.e., have come to birth.[33] Rashi[34] explains that by *guf* is here meant a chamber or treasury, wherein all souls ever destined to be born are stored after their simultaneous primeval creation. It is only in the three talmudic passages[32] here listed that this repository is styled *guf*, but the notion itself—which owes something to the Stoics—is already reflected in earlier rabbinic texts;[35] and although Gabirol cannot have known the commentary of Rashi, at the most his younger contemporary, we may assume that he will have understood *guf* in this passage in the same way that Rashi did. Rabbi Jose found a proof text in *Isaiah* 57:16,[33] "for I will not contend for ever, neither will I always be wroth: for the spirit should fail before me, and the souls which I myself have made," which he understood eschatologically, tacitly elaborating thus: "*For* [it is] *not for ever* [that] *I will contend, nor evince wrath indefinitely* (i.e., I will not postpone messianic redemption because of anger). [But for the time being I do postpone it,] *because the spirit* [that is] *before me faints* (i.e., is dilatory about getting itself born), *and* [similarly] *the souls* [which] *I have made*" (*ᶜasithi*).[36] Talmudic psychology consequently makes two postulates: (a) a promptuary in which all as yet unborn souls must await the respective occasions of their terrestrial birth, and (b) a prior act, by which God created all souls that are destined ever to be born before the messianic age can commence. The two are here stated in that order, because Gabirol apparently links (a), the promptuary, with his tenth sphere of the intelligence, from which he states (xxv) that God "made" (*ᶜasothekha*) the brightness of the souls—all the souls, no doubt, but with attention so focussed on the high-grade psyches, i.e., the angels, as to identify in effect the *neshamoth* with these *nefashoth ramoth*. Because of this spotlighting he is free to speak, without logical inconsistency, in xxix of God having created (*borʾakha*) the soul from the refulgence of his own glory—this corresponding to postulate (b) in the Talmud. It is only thereafter that God proceeds to *instil* into the previously created soul (*we-ʾaṣalta*) the spirit of wisdom, *making* it (*ᶜasithahh*) in regard to its form out of the fire of the intelligence (*ᶜasithahh* in xxix apparently picking up *ᶜasothekha* in xxv, the picture of which is merely being filled out, and the spotlight being this time played not on the angelic souls, but on the generality of souls destined for sublunary birth). Not until this instillation-by-emanation of intelligence into the previously "created" soul has taken place, i.e., talmudic postulate (b) + (a) as applied by Gabirol, can the formation of the soul, quarried though it had been from the rock of the Rock (*mi-Ṣur ha-Ṣur nigzarah*) be said to be complete; and it is thus at this stage only that Gabirol asserts that "Thou didst give it the name of soul" (*we-qaratha shemahh neshamah)*. It could be argued that both stages are necessary equally in the case of angelic souls, about whose quarrying from the divine effulgence of glory Gabirol is inexplicit. Perhaps a contributory reason for his passing this over (apart from the fact that by xxix Gabirol is concerning himself specifically with the potentiality of the human soul, and its predicament during its sublunary existence) is that the "embryology," so to speak, of the human soul invites interest more so than does that of the angels. But the matter is a side issue. It is but notionally that the two stages, *creation* (b) and (a) *instillation-with-intelligence/formation*, can be dichotomized; and in the context of a metaphysical poem Gabirol is content to refer first to (a), then (b), and thereafter to revert elaboratively to (a) in a way that exposes the reader to assuming that such elaboration of (a) is subsumed within (b). A careful reading shows that such is not the case, and that there is neither internal inconsistency within the *Kether Malkhuth* on this point, nor any discrepancy between it and the *Fons Vitae,* once the bipartite equation *ʿaql = galgal ha-Sekhel = guf* has been appreciated.

Careful study of the structure of the *Kether Malkhuth* indicates that in it artistic, almost architectural symmetry was for Gabirol the dominant consideration. In that aesthetic situation, to be slightly inexplicit on a point of detail is no more relevant than, say, a sculptor's neglect to show more than the outline of the design of a warrior's shield within the context of the pediment of a Greek temple; provided always that there is no specific error to offend the attention of the sharp-eyed. In the case of his astronomical data, where he was dependent on scientific sources that he was not expert enough to control completely, he in fact did make some mistakes, but since the ptolemaic astronomy which they presuppose is now obsolete and as it were mellowed by its own patina, aesthetic appreciation is not impaired save for the historian of science, who corresponds (if we may sustain the comparison) to the archeologist. Perhaps even in Gabirol's own day few readers were fully equipped to spot mistakes in his use of Arabic scientific source material, and in his use of Jewish sources he can, as we have seen, not be faulted. Appropriately enough for its author, the *Kether Malkhuth* constitutes one of the supreme examples in Hebrew literature of the interpenetrative integration of matter and form.

NOTES

1. B. Haneberg, in *Sitzungsberichte der königlich-bayerischen Akademie der Wissenschaften*, Munich, 10, 1866, pp. 73–102.

2. For a recent exposition of the purpose, scope, and sources of the *Epistles* see S. H. Nasr, *An Introduction to Islamic Cosmological Doctrines*, Belknap Press,

Harvard, Cambridge, Mass., 1964, pp. 25–104, and the late S. M. Stern's article in *Islamic Studies* 3, Karachi, 1964, pp. 405–28.

3. J. Schlanger, *la Philosophie de Salomon ibn Gabirol*, Leiden, 1968, pp. 94–7. For Schlanger's translation of Gabirol's *Fons Vitae*, see below, p. 194, n. 29.

4. Nasr (see above, n. 2), p. 44, rather curiously quotes the passage as here printed from an English translation by J. Platts (ed. E. B. Eastwick), *Ikhwanu-s-ṣafa*, London, 1875, pp. 122f. That translation was made not from the Arabic but from an abridged and faulty Urdu translation thereof dated 1810; and the extract here printed does not correspond with the original, which he transcribes in Arabic from ed. Beirut, 1376/1957, ii, p. 232. F. Dieterici's text (*Thier und Mench vor dem Konig der Genien*,[2] 1881, p. 58), reads as follows, agreeing substantially with the Beirut text:

أظْهر مَصْنوعاتِه الى مشاهَدة الأبْصار وأَخْرج ما في مَكْنون غَيْبِه الى الكَشْفِ والاظْهار ليُدْرِكه العيانُ ويَسْتَغْنِي عن الدليل والبُرْهان

As will be seen, there is no mention here of the divine qualities of skill, omnipotence etc.

5. The paragraph numberings are those of I. Zangwill in his *Select religious Poems of Solomon ibn Gabirol*, Philadelphia, 1925, pp. 82–123, the Hebrew text of which was prepared by Israel Davidson. In my own forthcoming translation these numbers will be retained, with subdivision in some cases.

6. A. L. Tibawi, "Jāmaʿah Ikhwān aṣ-Ṣafā", *Journal of the American University of Beirut*, 1930–31, p. 60.

7. אתה אלוה, וכל היצורים עבדיך ועובדיך, ולא יחסר כבודך בגלל עובדי בלעדיך, כי כונת כלם להגיע עדיך. אבל הם כעורים מגמת פניהם דרך המלך, ותעו מן הדרך... אך עבדיך הם הפקחים ההולכים דרך נכוחה וכו׳ The translation is mine.

8. ומכחך מציאתו, וממך ועדיך מגמתו, ואליך תשוקתו

9. Study of this has to begin with O. Neugebauer's revised edition (Leipzig, 1936) of K. Manitius' annotated German translation, *Ptolemäus, Handbuch der Astronomie*. See also Neugebauer's Stern Lecture for 1955 (*Scripta Mathematica*, Yeshiva University, New York) entitled *Theories in Ancient and Mediaeval Astronomy*, especially pp. 6f., 11f.

10. Bernard R. Goldstein, "The Arabic Version of Ptolemy's Planetary Hypotheses", *Transactions of the American Philosophical Society*, New Series, 57, iv, 1967; see especially pp. 9, 11.

11. C. Brockelmann, *Geschichte der arabischen Literatur*, i, p. 249 (221), Supplement, i, pp. 392f.; H. Suter, "Die Mathematiker und Astronomen der Araben und ihre Werke", *Abhandlungen zur Geschichte der mathematischen Wissenschaften*, 10, Leipzig, 1900, p. 18; Francis J. Carmody, *Arabic Astronomical and Astrological Sciences in Latin Translation, A Critical Bibliography*, Berkeley and Los Angeles, 1956, pp. 113f. The most recent treatment is that by A. I. Sabba in the *Dictionary of Scientific Biography*, iv, 1971, New York, pp. 541–44. A Hebrew version was made from the Latin translation of Johannes Hispalensis but with reference to the original Arabic, by Jacob Anatoli: see Steinschneider, *Bodleian Catalogue*, 5499, 2 and 4753, 1; *Hebräische Übersetzungen*, pp. 554f., §343.

12. The modern computations are taken from C. W. Allen's *Astronomical Quantities*,[2] London, 1963, with occasional more recent corrections kindly supplied to me (2nd September, 1971) by Dr R. E. W. Maddison, F.S.A., Librarian of the Royal Astronomical Society.

13. T. B. ᶜ*Eruvin* 59a. S. Krauss, *Griechische und lateinische Lehnwörter im Talmud, Midrasch und Targum*, 1889, ii, pp. 54, 317.

14. Both instances in *1 Chron*. 10:12.

15. Ed. Manitius-Neugebauer (see *supra*, p. 193, n. 9), i, p. 313.

16. Ed. Beirut, 1376/1957, ii, p. 33.

17. *Op. cit.*, i, p. 130 (Saturn), p. 131 (Jupiter).

18. *Op. cit.*, iii, p. 251.

19. *Op. cit.*, iii, p. 252.

20. *Op. cit.*, iii, p. 263 (although correctly stated here, corruptions of this figure appear elsewhere in the text).

21. *Op. cit.*, i, p. 132.

22. Cf. W. M. Smart, *Textbook on Spherical Astronomy*,[5] Cambridge, 1962, p. 422.

23. *Op. cit.* (n. 16), i, p. 132.

24. For Gabirol's treatment of psychology see Schlanger, *op. cit.* (p. 193, n. 3), pp. 205–6, 209 etc (index, p. 328).

25. *Sabbath* 152b: תניא ר׳ אליעזר או׳ נשמתן של צדיקים גנוזות תחת כסא הכבוד שנא׳ והיתה נפש אדוני צרורה בצרור החיים ושל רשעים זוממות והולכות ומלאך אחד עומד בסוף העולם וכו׳.... ומקלעין נשמתן זה לזה שנא׳ ואת נפש אויביך יקלענה בתוך הקלע

26. מי יעשה כמעשיך בעשותך תחת כסא כבודך מעמד לנפשות חסידיך, ושם נוה הנשמות הטהורות, אשר בצרור החיים צרורות, ואשר ייגעו וייעפו, שם כח יחליפו, ושם ינוחו יגיעי כח, ואלה בני נח

27. מי יעמיק למחשבותיך בעשותך מזיו גלגל השכל זהר הנשמות והנפשות הרמות

28. Gesenius' *Hebrew Grammar*, ed. Kautzsch-Cowley, §154a footnote (b).

29. iii, 54; (incomplete) French translation by F. Brunner, Paris, 1950, pp. 199, 8–9 and 15–17; J. Schlanger's (complete) French translation, Paris, 1970, p. 208 (= C. Bäumker's Latin text, Munster, 1892f., p. 199).

30. הם מלאכי רצונך משרתי פניך, הם אדירי כח וגבורי ממלכת, בידם להט החרב המתהפכת, ועושי כל מלאכת, אל אשר יהיה שמה הרוח ללכת

31. מי יכיל עצמתך בבראך מזיו כבודך יפעה טהורה, מצור נגזרה, וממקבת בור נקרה, ואצלת עליה רוח חכמה, וקראת שמה נשמה. עשיתה מלהבות אש השכל הצורה, ונשפתה כאש בוערה, ושלחת בגוף וכו׳

32. T.B. ᶜ*Avodah Zarah* 5a, *Niddah* 13b, *Yevamoth* 62a, 63b.

33. א״ר יוסי אין בן דוד בא עד שיכלו נשמות שבגוף שנא׳ כי לא לעולם אריב ולא לנצח אקצוף כי רוח מלפני יעטף ונשמות אני עשיתי

34. On ᵓ*Avodah Zarah* 5a (similarly on *Niddah* 13b) - אוצר יש ושמו גוף ומבראשית נוצרו כל הנשמות העתידות להולד נתנם לשם

35. See L. Ginzberg's summary, *Legends of the Jews*, v, p. 75, n. 19.

36. Rashi on T.B. ᶜ*Avodah Zarah* 5a paraphrases thus: כי לא לעולם אריב לאחר זמן הגאולה ולא לנצח אקצוף מלגאול כי רוח אשר לפני נשמות בגוף הוא המאחר כמו העטופים ללבן ונשמות אני עשיתי

Die Geburtsgeschichte Moses

S. E. LOEWENSTAMM

Es ist seit langem Gemeingut der Forschung, dass die Geburtsgeschichte Moses zu der Kategorie der Wandersagen gehört, welche die Erstaunen erweckenden Umstände der Geburt einer berühmten historischen Persönlichkeit zum Gegenstande haben. Jedoch haben die sich hieraus ergebenden motivgeschichtlichen Fragestellungen erst durch die Arbeiten Ed. Meyers[1] und Gressmanns[2] ein schärferes Profil gewonnen. Insbesondere gebührt Gressmann das Verdienst, die Spannung klar herausgestellt zu haben, die zwischen der auf die Person Moses abgestellten Geburtsgeschichte in *Ex.* 2:1–10 und ihrer im Kapitel 1 enthaltenen nationalgeschichtlichen Einleitung besteht. Ein guter Überblick über die Weiterführung der hiermit eingeleiteten Diskussion ist in dem kürzlich erschienenen Kommentar zu *Exodus* von Childs[3] zu finden, der von wichtigeren neueren Arbeiten lediglich den Aufsatz von B. Jacob[4] unerwähnt lässt. Bei alledem ist jedoch die innere motivegeschichtliche Analyse der biblischen Geschichte etwas zu kurz gekommen, und insbesondere der sekundäre Charakter mancher ihrer Züge im Dunkeln geblieben.

I

Hierher gehört zunächst die Problematik der Gestalt des Vaters. Derselbe wird erstaunlicherweise ausschliesslich im ersten Verse erwähnt, wo in bündiger Kürze von seiner Heirat die Rede ist. Darnach verschwindet er aus dem Blickfelde, in dessen Mittelpunkt sogleich die Mutter tritt, von der wir nach Angabe ihrer Schwangerschaft und der Geburt ihres Kindes erfahren, dass sie das wohlgeratene Neugeborene betrachtet und zwei aufeinanderfolgende Tätigkeiten zu seiner Rettung entfaltet habe, deren letztere in höchst wundersamer Verkettung der Ereignisse am Ende dazu führte, dass keine andere als die Tochter des mörderischen Königs sie zur bezahlten Amme ihres eigenen Kindes bestellte. Des Vaters wird bei alledem mit keinem Worte gedacht. Es drängt sich somit der Eindruck auf, dass er der Geburt und dem Schicksal seines Kindes unbeteiligt gegenübergestanden habe.[5]

Es lässt sich dartun, dass die hellenistische Literatur diese Indolenz nicht hat wahr haben wollen. Getreu ihrer durchgängigen Tendenz, die Vorfahren Israels als beispielhafte Verkörperungen ethischer Ideale hinzustellen, verfehlte sie nämlich nicht, die getreue Sorge des Vaters Moses für seinen Sohn ins rechte Licht zu rücken.

Die Anfänge dieses Umformungsprozesses lassen sich bis in die Übersetzung der Septuaginta zurückverfolgen, die höchst bedeutsamerweise die Betrachtung des Neugeborenen und seine anfängliche Verbergung beiden Eltern zuschreibt, und erst von der Anfertigung des Kästchens an die Mutter allein handeln lässt. Diese verwunderliche Inkonsequenz liegt anscheinend in der Textgeschichte begründet. An Stelle der kurzen Lesart der Masora (V.3) findet sich nämlich nicht nur in der Septuaginta sondern auch in dem an der Singularform der Verben festhaltendem Samaritanus die längere Formulierung ותקח לו אמו , in welcher das Wort אמו einer Umwandlung von ותקח in den Plural entgegensteht, während bei den vorangehenden Verbformen ein derartiges Hemmnis nicht bestand. Im Gegenteil, scheint die Septuaginta (oder ihre Vorlage) in der ausdrücklichen Erwähnung der Mutter an dieser Stelle einen Anhaltspunkt für die willkommene Annahme gefunden zu haben, dass die vorangehenden Verben von beiden Eltern sprächen und demgemäss in Pluralformen umgewandelt werden müssten.

Philon (*Vita Mosis* I, 9–12) lässt es bei diesem schüchternen Versuch einer Ehrenrettung des Vaters nicht sein Bewenden haben, sondern berichtet eine gemeinsame Tätigkeit beider Eltern in sämtlichen Phasen der Rettung ihres Kindes.

Bei Josephus (*Ant.* II, ix, 3–4) wird der Vater sogar zur Hauptperson. Schon vor der Geburt des Knaben fleht er Gottes Hilfe an, der ihm im Traume die Erfüllung seiner Bitte versichert. Nach der Geburt handeln beide Eltern gemeinschaftlich. Überdies geht die Initiative zur Anfertigung des Kästchens von dem Vater aus. Zwar bleibt es der Mutter vorbehalten, der Tochter die Anweisung zur Beobachtung des Kästchens zu erteilen. Doch ändert dieser natürliche Vorrang der Mutter im Umgange mit der Tochter nichts an der führenden Stellung des Vaters als Haupt der Familie. Die Geschichte nimmt also bei Josephus einen durchaus erbaulichen Charakter an. Der Vater ist ein gottvertrauender Mann, der mit Umsicht und Tatkraft für seinen Sohn sorgt.

Dieser Ausweg freier Neuerzählung der Geschichte war natürlich derjenigen Richtung der späten jüdischen Bibelexegese verschlossen, die sich an den biblischen Text gebunden fühlte. Abarbanel erwähnt die Möglichkeit, dass der Vater vor der Geburt des Kindes verstorben sein möge, zieht aber die differenziertere psychologische Erklärung vor, dass er von lähmender Verzweiflung ergriffen gewesen sei.

Die freischwebende Exegese des biblischen Textes bei Abarbanel hat mit seinen Umbildungen in der hellenistischen Literatur das eine gemeinsam, dass sie ein strukturgeschichtliches Problem in helles Licht rückt, welches in der modernen Forschung vernachlässigt worden ist. Dies ist umso verwunderlicher, als die Lösung dieses Problems durch die Sargonsage[6] nahegelegt wird, welche seit dem im Jahre 1880 erschienenen Kommentar zu *Exodus* von Dillmann[7] in sämtlichen motivgeschichtlichen Untersuchungen der Sage eine wichtige Rolle spielt. Auch dort wird des Vaters nur flüchtig im ersten Satz gedacht, während alles weitere durch die Mutter geschieht. Doch ist der Sargonsage die Flüchtigkeit der Erwähnung des Vaters durchaus angemessen, weil Sargon offenbar ein uneheliches Kind war. Er erklärt nämlich eingangs, seinen Vater nicht zu kennen und berichtet von seiner Mutter, dass sie eine *enētu* gewesen sei. Die viel diskutierte Bedeutung dieses Wortes ist nun aber durch Lambert[8] endgültig klargestellt worden, der abschliessend bewiesen hat, dass das Wort eine hohe Klasse von Priesterinnen bezeichnet, denen das Gebären von Kindern untersagt war. All das lässt keinen Zweifel daran übrig, dass wir es mit einem unehelichen Kind zu tun haben, dessen Aussetzung durch die Mutter ja durchaus plausibel ist. Die Typologie dieses Motivs wird auch durch das indische *Mahabharata Epos*[9] illustriert, in dem von einer Königstochter die Rede ist, welche dem Sonnengotte einen Sohn geboren hat und aus Furcht vor ihrem Vater das Kind in einem wohlabgedichteten Kästchen im Flusse aussetzt, der es zu seinen Adoptiveltern hinabträgt. Im Lichte dieser verwandten Sagen wird deutlich, dass die Bibel die Sage der Aussetzung eines unehelichen Kindes aufgegriffen, sie jedoch durch die vorangeschickte ausdrückliche Erwähnung der Heirat der Eltern abgewandelt hat.[10] Diese Abweichung von dem Urtyp veranlasste nun zwar keine Schwierigkeiten in der Motivierung der Aussetzung, weil dem Grunde der unehelichen Geburt des Kindes das Bestreben der Mutter substituiert wird, das Kind vor der ihm drohenden Tötung durch die Ägypter zu retten. Doch bleibt hierbei die Unstimmigkeit zurück, dass der Vater des ehelichen Kindes einen nur bei dem Erzeuger eines unehelichen Kindes verständlichen Mangel an Fürsorge für das Kind zeigt. Das bei der Gestaltung der Erzählung benutzte Wandermotiv der Aussetzung eines unehelichen Kindes ist also in der Bibel nicht vollständig umgeformt worden. Erst die hellenistische Literatur glich die hierdurch entstandene Spannung aus, indem sie den ehelichen Vater so handeln liess, wie es einem solchen angemessen ist.

Dieser Sachverhalt verdient Berücksichtigung bei der Erörterung der Streitfrage, ob die Geburtsgeschichte Moses und Sargons als motivgeschichtlich verwandte Aussetzungssagen anzusetzen seien. Man hat dagegen unter anderem eingewandt, dass die Sargonsage von einer unehelichen Mutter spräche, die ihr unerwünschtes Kind loswerden wolle, während die Mosesage das Bemühen einer Ehefrau schildere, das bedrohte Leben ihres Kindes zu retten. Die eine handele im eigenen Interesse, die andere um ihres Kindes willen.[11] Hiergegen ist jedoch nicht nur zu sagen, dass die Antithese überscharf formuliert ist, da ja auch die Mutter Sargons für ihr Kind ein gegen Eindringen von Wasser wohlabgedichtetes Kästchen verfertigt, sondern vor allem, dass der verbleibende Unterschied zwischen beiden Erzählungen seine Relevanz für die Erforschung sagengeschichtlicher Zusammenhänge mit der Erkenntnis verliert, dass die biblische Form der Erzählung ihre Herkunft von der Sage der Aussetzung eines unehelichen Kindes verrät.

II

Ein weiterer, motivgeschichtlich sekundärer Zug der biblischen Erzählung tritt darin zu Tage, dass die Mutter das Kästchen in das Schilf am Ufer stellt. In der einfachen, gradlinig fortschreitenden Handlung der Sargonsage wirft die Mutter das wasserdichte Kästchen in den Fluss, der es davonträgt, bis es der Wasserschöpfer herauszieht. Fluss und Kästchen erfüllen also Aufgaben von ausschlaggebender Wichtigkeit, die sich ohne weiteres aus ihrer Natur ergeben. Anders liegt der Fall in der ungleich komplizierteren Erzählung der Bibel. Dem Fluss, der in der Sargonsage das Kästchen hinwegführt und den Hintergrund für die Auffindung des Kindes abgibt, bleibt in der Moseerzählung nur die zweite dieser Aufgaben, nämlich die Erklärung der Entdeckung des Kästchens durch die zum Baden herabsteigende Königstochter. Das Kästchen büsst seine ursprüngliche Hauptfunktion als eines das Kind wohlbehalten auf dem Wasser fortführenden Schiffchens vollständig ein, wenn auch in beiden Sagen die Anfertigung des Kästchens die Fürsorge der Mutter für ihr Kind veranschaulicht. Hierzu kommt in der biblischen Erzählung, dass das Kästchen dem Erzähler ermöglicht, die Szene der Auffindung des Kindes durch die Königstochter dramatischer und spannungsreicher zu gestalten. Bei alledem lässt sich kaum leugnen, dass das Kästchen seine eigentliche Aufgabe in der Bibel verloren hat, da ja die Königstochter das in das Schilf gelegte Kind auch dann hätte auffinden können, wenn es nicht in einem Kästchen gewesen wäre. Das Kästchen ist somit von einem den Fortgang der Handlung entscheidend bestimmenden Faktor zu einer blossen Ausschmückung der Erzählung geworden. Auch hier ist also die Umbildung eines Motivs erkennbar, das in seiner ursprünglichen Form in der Sargonsage vorliegt. Man mag sogar vielleicht noch einen Schritt weitergehen und statt von einem Urmotiv von einer Urfassung des hebräischen Textes sprechen. Hierfür liesse sich die Erklärung der Königstochter anführen, dass sie das Kind aus dem Wasser gezogen habe. Obendrein würde in einer solchen Version die Entsprechung zwischen dem Befehl des Königs, die Kinder in den Nil zu werfen und der Handlungsweise der Mutter weit schärfer hervortreten als in der gegenwärtigen Fassung[12]. Die Gründe der Umbildung des Urmotivs, bezw. der Urfassung sind offenbar in der Tendenz der Abschwächung der Aussetzung zu suchen, die ja durch ein Hineinwerfen des Kästchens in den Fluss eindringlich betont wird. Die Verharmlosung der Aussetzung ist nun aber ein Hauptanliegen des Erzählers, wie sich bereits daraus ergibt, dass er die Schwester in Sichtweite des Kästchens verbleiben lässt[13] und ihr am Ende die Aufgabe überträgt, der Mutter das Amt einer Amme ihres Kindes zu verschaffen[14]. All diese die Aussetzung mildernden Umstände verknüpfen sich aufs glücklichste, weil der feste Standort des Kästchens dem Bericht über die Schwester Natürlichkeit verleiht. Es ist weit leichter, einen feststehenden Gegenstand im Auge zu behalten, als einen der auf dem Flusse hinweggetragen wird. Das Eingreifen der Schwester ist aber seinerseits eine sekundäre Erweiterung des Grundmotivs, wenn man auch Zweifel an der Ansicht Gressmanns[15] und Noths[16] hegen mag, die soweit gehen, von einer literarisch sekundären Ausschmückung zu sprechen, d.h. eine vorbiblisch hebräische Version anzusetzen, die abweichend von dem Urmotiv bereits ein Niederlegen des Kästchens im Schilfe kannte, hingegen noch nicht die Gestalt der Schwester. Falls wir überhaupt eine ältere hebräische Urfassung postulieren, welche die Schwester nicht kannte, liegt es näher anzunehmen, dass in ihr die Mutter das Kästchen in den Fluss geworfen hat, aus dem es die Königstochter am Ende zog. Wie dem aber nun auch sei, bleibt es auf jeden Fall einleuchtend, dass die Bibel das Motiv eines auf dem Flusse schwimmenden Kästchens abwandelt.

Auch in diesem Punkte erweist sich ein Blick auf die nachbiblische Literatur als lehrreich. In dem Mosedrama des Ezechiel (Eusebius, *Praeparatio Evangelica* IX, 28, 2, hrg. K. Mras, 8, S. 525) berichtet Moses, dass ihn die Mutter am Ufer des Flusses in dichtbewachsenem Sumpfgelände niedergelegt habe. Ähnlich ist der Bericht Philons (*Vita Mosis* I, 10), dass beide Eltern das Kind am Ufer des Flusses ausgesetzt haben. Das in dem sonst so kurzen biblischen Bericht mit auffallender Ausführlichkeit behandelte Kästchen bleibt in beiden Versionen unerwähnt. Hiermit ziehen diese die Konsequenz daraus, dass das Kästchen in der biblischen Geschichte für die Entwicklung der Handlung entbehrlich geworden ist. Umgekehrt verfährt Josephus (*Ant.* II, ix, 4), der die Eltern das Kästchen in den Fluss werfen lässt, welcher es davonträgt. Diese Änderung der biblischen Erzählung zwang ihn zu weiteren Modifikationen. Die Schwester musste wohl oder übel bemüht werden, das den Fluss hinunterschwimmende Kästchen am Ufer gehend zu begleiten, bis es die Königstochter durch Schwimmer ans Ufer bringen liess.

Im Gegensatz zu den hellenistischen Quellen bietet der Midrasch keine fortlaufende, geschlossene Erzählung, sondern nur einzelne Erklärungen. Doch tritt auch hier manchmal die Auffassung zu Tage, dass das Kästchen sich im Wasser befunden habe, z.B. in der Erklärung von סוף als ים סוף (TB *Soṭa* 12a). Hierher gehört wahrscheinlich auch die Deutung der Worte ותשלח את אֲמָתָהּ nicht als "sie schickte ihre Leibzofe", sondern "sie streckte ihren Arm 'אַמָּתָהּ' aus" (*Soṭa* 12b), wobei dieser Arm die Länge von 60 Ellen angenommen habe (TB *Megilla* 15b), was doch wohl voraussetzt, dass das Kästchen aus dem Wasser herausgeholt werden musste. Ausdrücklich ist diese Auffassung in einem Midrasch erwähnt, demzufolge die Wahrsager den Tötungsbefehl aufgehoben haben, nachdem Mose in den Nil geworfen worden sei (*Soṭa* 12b).

Die in dem Berichte über den festen Standort eines zum Schwimmen hergerichteten Kästchens inhärente Spannung wird also in der späteren Literatur weitgehend aufgelöst. Das funktionsarme Kästchen wird entweder weggelassen oder seiner ursprünglichen Zweckbestimmung zurückgegeben. Auch hier bietet also die spätere Literatur eine indirekte Bestätigung des aus unmittelbarer Vergleichung des biblischen und des babylonischen Textes gewonnenen Ergebnisses, dass die Sargonsage die ältere Fassung darstellt. Die eindrückliche Schilderung der Herstellung eines Gegenstandes, der dazu bestimmt ist, ein in ihm geborgenes Kind unversehrt auf den Wassern eines Flusses zu tragen, verrät das Urmotiv, dass der

Gegenstand diese Aufgabe tatsächlich erfüllt hat. Auch hierin steht also die deutlich erkennbare Vorstufe der Mosesage der Sargonsage näher als der vorliegende biblische Text.

III

Bei alledem lässt sich nicht verkennen, dass das Grundmotiv der Sargonsage in der Geburtsgeschichte Moses dadurch eine tiefe Umformung erfahren hat, dass als Motivierung der Aussetzung der Mordbefehl Pharaos an die Stelle der unehelichen Abkunft des Kindes getreten ist. Die Bedeutsamkeit dieses Unterschiedes tritt darin zu Tage, dass er nicht als sekundäre Weiterentwicklung des Motivs der Sargonsage abgetan werden kann. Auch macht sich dieser Befehl in den Ausschmückungen des Fortgangs der Handlung geltend, d.h. zunächst in dem die Spannung erhöhenden, retardierenden Moment der dreimonatigen Verbergung des Kindes, vor allem aber in der Episode des Eingreifens der Schwester, welche mit der Bestellung der Mutter zur Amme ihres Kindes endet. Beide die Sage zu einer Kunsterzählung ausformenden Berichte spiegeln den Widerstand der Mutter gegen die durch den Befehl Pharaos aufgezwungene Trennung von ihrem Kinde wider.

Dieser Befehl ist also von Hause aus dem Motiv der Sargonsage durchaus fremd.

Es sei bereits hier vorangeschickt, dass das gleiche für eine im folgenden näher darzulegende nachbiblische Variante gilt, die den Befehl Pharaos auf die Weissagung der Geburt eines Kindes zurückführt, das—herangewachsen—die Stellung Pharaos bedrohen wird, da auch diese Fassung dem Typus der Sargonsage nicht weniger fernsteht[17]. Hieraus ergibt sich, dass eine Vergleichung beider Versionen mit der Sargonsage keine Antwort auf die viel diskutierte Frage zu geben vermag, welche von ihnen als die traditionsgeschichtlich ältere anzusehen sei. Das aber will besagen, dass die oben angewandte Methode der Bestimmung traditionsgeschichtlicher Sequenz sich in diesem Punkte als unanwendbar erweist und wir nach anderen Kriterien für die Lösung des Problems Umschau halten müssen.

Wir beginnen mit einer Analyse des biblischen Berichts, die in den Grundlinien Gressmann Folge leistet. Dieser Bericht erzählt bekanntlich, dass die starke Vermehrung der Hebräer in Pharao die Furcht erweckt habe, dass diese sich zu einer militärischen Gefahr für Ägypten entwickeln könnten und dass er deshalb auf Mittel zur Verringerung ihrer Zahl gesonnen habe. Nach dem Scheitern früherer Versuche habe er schliesslich angeordnet, ihre männlichen Neugeborenen in den Nil zu werfen. Nun lässt sich zunächst die Zweckmässigkeit dieses Befehls diskutieren. Der Midrasch (*Ex. Rabba* I 14; *Seder Elijahu Rabba* VIII) wendet hiergegen ein, dass ein Mann viele Frauen, eine Frau hingegen nur einen Mann heiraten könne und dass deshalb die Tötung der neugeborenen Mädchen mehr zur Minderung der Zahl der Hebräer beigetragen hätte, während Philon (*Vita Mosis* I, 8) die überlieferte Fassung des Befehls damit erläutert, dass nur von Männern eine militärische Gefahr drohe. Selbst diese an sich plausible Erwägung lässt jedoch die Frage offen, weshalb Pharao es lediglich auf die Neugeborenen abgesehen habe. Auch mag man mit gutem Grunde Zweifel daran hegen, ob das Werfen der Neugeborenen in den Nil die nächstliegende Form ihrer Tötung war. All diese Erwägungen machen es deutlich, dass die vorliegende Fassung des Befehls nur aus ihrer literarischen Funktion verständlich wird, als Einleitung für die folgende Geburtsgeschichte Moses zu dienen. Hierfür spricht auch ein weiteres, schlechterdings ausschlaggebendes Argument. Wir sollten nämlich erwarten, dass auf den Befehl die Schilderung seiner Ausführung folgt, da er ja notwendigerweise eine schicksalhafte Krise im Leben der Gesamtheit der Israeliten nach sich ziehen musste, deren physischer Weiterbestand aufs Schwerste gefährdet war. In Wirklichkeit jedoch sind die Folgen der Anordnung nur mittelbar aus der Geburtsgeschichte zu erschliessen, hingegen fehlt es durchaus an einer unmittelbaren Darstellung.[18] Dem entspricht es denn auch, dass der Erlass keine weiteren Spuren in der Bibel zurücklässt. Insbesondere wird der Auszug aus Ägypten nirgendwo mit dem naheliegenden Hinweise auf die systematische Tötung der männlichen Neugeborenen begründet, sondern lediglich mit der Fronarbeit, die doch ein unvergleichlich geringeres Übel war. *Deut.* 23:8 geht sogar so weit, den Israeliten die Pflicht der Dankbarkeit gegen die Ägypter aufzuerlegen, weil sie Gastsassen in deren Lande gewesen seien. Ein solches Gebot beweist, dass keine echte Tradition bestand, die den Ägyptern eine organisierte Ausrottungspolitik zuschrieb. Deshalb ist auch der Versuch Greenbergs[19] abzulehnen, die Historizität der Verbindung von Zwangsarbeit und Ausrottung durch einen Hinweis auf die Untaten des Hitler-Regimes zu illustrieren und glaubhaft zu machen. Diese Argumentation scheitert daran, dass es ausserhalb der Geburtsgeschichte Moses an jeder Erwähnung der Durchführung der Mordmassnahmen fehlt, während doch die Fronarbeit unter Anführung so mancher realistischer Einzelheiten ausgemalt wird und die Zahl der allgemeinen Hinweise auf sie Legion ist. Man muss demnach daran festhalten, dass der Erlass Pharaos literarische, nicht historische Wertung erfordert und dass seine einzige Aufgabe darin besteht, als Hintergrund für die Geburtsgeschichte Moses zu dienen.

Hiermit ist jedoch zugleich eine deutliche Spannung gekennzeichnet: seinem Inhalt und seiner Begründung nach bezieht sich der Befehl auf ein ganzes Volk und ist zeitlich unbegrenzt, seiner Zweckbestimmung nach auf das einmalige Ereignis der Geburt eines einzigen Kindes.

Es ist nun höchst verständlicherweise weitgehend beobachtet worden, dass diese Unebenheit in den Darstellungen des Josephus und des Midrasch ausgeglichen wird. Hierbei hat man sich allerdings im allgemeinen mit dem summarischen Hinweise darauf begnügt, dass bei Josephus der König seinen Befehl erlassen habe, weil die Weissager ihm die Geburt eines ihn gefährdenden Kindes verkündet hätten, und dass sich dergleichen später auch im Midrasch fände. Die Quellen verdienen aber eine eingehendere Darstellung. Zunächst sollte beachtet werden, dass auch Josephus (*Ant.* II, ix, 2) seine Schilderung mit dem missglückten Versuch der Ägypter einleitet, die Zahl der von ihnen gefürchteten Hebräer durch Fronarbeit zu dezimieren. Hierzu kam—berichtet Josephus—ein weiterer Grund, der den Vernichtungswillen der Ägypter bestärkte. Die Weissager Pharaos hätten ihm nämlich die bevorstehende Geburt eines hebräischen Knaben verkündigt, der das ägyptische Königtum demütigen und ewigen Ruhm erlangen würde. Diese Weissagung sei von dem Rate begleitet gewesen, die neugeborenen Kinder der Hebräer durch ägyptische(!)[20] Hebammen in den Nil werfen zu lassen. Die Tötung des einen Kindes war hiernach nicht der ausschliessliche Zweck der Aktion. Daher ist denn auch verständlich, dass bei Josephus die Hebräer bittere Klage über die Gefährdung der Existenz ihres Volkes führen. Das Problem der Begrenzung der Gültigkeitsdauer des Befehls bleibt bei Josephus ebenso ungelöst wie in der Bibel.

Reinere und sich von der Bibel weitergehend entfernende Fassungen des Weissagungsmotivs liegen im Midrasch vor. Nach einem Midrasch widerrufen die Wahrsager den Tötungserlass, nachdem ihnen—offenbar durch magische Künste—bekannt geworden war, dass man Mose in den Nil geworfen hätte, woraus sie irrtümlich entnommen hätten, dass es um ihn geschehen wäre. Sie sollen nämlich gewusst haben, dass Mose durch Wasser sein Ende finden werde, dies jedoch irrtümlicherweise nicht auf seine Sünde bei Massa und Meriba, sondern auf sein Werfen in den Nil bezogen haben (TB *Soṭa* 12b). Dieser Midrasch lässt also das Motiv einer beabsichtigten Vernichtung der Hebräer fallen. Auch bietet er eine—wenn auch recht gekünstelte—Begründung dafür, dass der Befehl binnen kurzem aufgehoben worden sei. Beachtlich ist ferner der Midrasch, der aus den Worten ויצו פרעה לכל עמו (*Ex.* 1:22) ableitet, dass der Tötungsbefehl auch die Erstgeborenen der Ägypter betroffen habe (*Soṭa* 12a). Schärfer lässt sich nicht sagen, dass hier keinerlei Absicht der Vernichtung des hebräischen Volkes im Spiele war. In seinem Kommentare zu diesem Midrasch führt Raschi den *Midrasch Tanḥuma* an, der besagt: "Am Tage, an dem Mose geboren wurde, sagten die Weissager: heute ist der Erlöser Israels geboren worden und wir wissen nicht, ob er ein Ägypter ist oder ein Jude. Da erhob er (d.h. Pharao) sich, versammelte sein gesamtes Volk und verlangte ihm die an jenem Tage Geborenen zu übergeben und legte diesen Befehl auch seinem Volke auf." Die Fassung des Midrasch kann also auf eine Aufhebung des Befehls verzichten, da dieser von vornherein auf die an einem bestimmten Tage Geborenen beschränkt ist. Hiermit ist eine einfache und natürlich anmutende Lösung des Problems der zeitlichen Begrenzung der Gültigkeit des Befehls erreicht.

IV

Die Ansetzung einer Geschichte dieses Typus als vorbiblisch hätte den unleugbaren Vorteil, eine ursprünglich enge Verbindung zwischen dem Befehle und der Geburtsgeschichte herzustellen und möchte obendrein eine höchst erwünschte Erklärung dafür bieten, dass der Befehl im Fortgange nicht mehr spürbar ist. Trotzdem stehen dieser von Gressmann befürworteten Lösung des Problems mannigfaltige Bedenken entgegen.

Zunächst lässt sich einwenden, dass die einzige zusätzliche Bezeugung dieses Sagentyps die Geburtssage Jesus in *Matthaeus* ist, die in ihrer Grundstruktur an den *Midrasch Tanḥuma* erinnert. Ältere Belege existieren nur für Erzählungen, in denen sich der durch die Weissagung veranlasste Tötungsbefehl auf die Person des gefahrdrohenden Kindes beschränkt, wie z.B. in der bei Herodot I, 108f. berichteten Geburtssage des Cyrus. Es fehlt also in den älteren Quellen das Motiv des Massenmordes der Neugeborenen, welche die nachbiblische Mosesage mit der Bibel gemeinsam hat. Dieser Sachverhalt lässt es von vornherein als wenig einleuchtend erscheinen, dass die nachbiblische Mosesage vorbiblische Tradition widerspiegeln solle. Vielmehr dürften wir eher zu der These Greenbergs[21] neigen, dass die späte Mosesage durch die Aufpfropfung klassischer Legenden wie der Geburtsgeschichte des Cyrus oder des Ödipus auf die biblische Geschichte entstanden sei. Dem wäre hinzuzufügen, dass das Ergebnis ein neuer Mischtyp war, in dem Gültigkeitsbereich und Zweck des Befehls auseinanderfallen, weil hier ein die Tötung einer unbeschränkten Zahl von Neugeborenen anordnender Befehl den ausschliesslichen Zweck der Beseitigung des einen einzigen gefahrdrohenden Kindes verfolgt. Unter dieser Voraussetzung liessen sich verschiedene Stadien des Mischungsprozesses verfolgen, da ja in der Fassung des Josephus die Absicht der Tötung des Mose noch die der Beseitigung sämtlicher hebräischer Kinder unberührt lässt, während es im Midrasch dem Pharao ausschliesslich auf Mose ankommt. Auch ist in der Midraschliteratur selbst ein Fortschritt von tastendem Versuch zu einfacher klarer Darstellung erkennbar. Während der ältere Midrasch Zuflucht bei ausgeklügelten Spekulationen sucht, um die Aufhebung des Befehls zu motivieren, hat der spätere Midrasch bereits das höchst wirksame faches Mittel gefunden die Gültigkeit des Erlasses von vornherein auf eine Zeitspanne zu begrenzen. Diese Entwicklung liesse sich leicht auf Grund der Annahme erklären, dass ein von aussen eindringendes Sagenmotiv zu einer schrittweisen Umbildung der biblischen Erzählung geführt habe.

Überdies begegnet ein Versuch der Ableitung des biblischen Textes von einer der nachbiblischen Erzählung verwandten Fassung grossen Schwierigkeiten. Gressmann[22] führt diese von ihm postulierte Umwandlung auf die Verdunkelung des Befehls unter dem Einfluss des Motivs der Knechtschaft zurück, die ja das gesamte Volk betroffen habe. Doch will das kaum überzeugen, da ja die Verknechtung ursprünglich nichts mit einer Tötungsabsicht zu schaffen hat und sie lediglich in *Ex.* 1 unter dem Einfluss der Tradition des Tötungsbefehls in einen Versuch der Verminderung der Zahl der Hebräer umgedeutet worden ist. Vollends hinfällig wird diese Erklärung, wenn wir die von Gressmann[23] selbst akzeptierte These Ed. Meyers[24] an-nehmen, dass in der Urfassung von Kap. 1. v. 15 unmittelbar auf v. 10 gefolgt sei, womit das Motiv der Knechtschaft in Kap. 1 als Zusatz gekennzeichnet wäre. Diese Annahme aber hat vieles für sich. Die von der Knechtschaft handelnden vv. 13–14 fallen offensichtlich aus dem Rahmen der Erzählung heraus und werden denn auch gemeinhin auf P abgeschoben. Die gleichfalls über die Knechtschaft sprechenden vv. 11–12 sind nun allerdings mit der Entwicklung der Handlung verknüpft, aber trotzdem nicht unverdächtig, weil die Äusserung Pharaos in v. 10 es an jeder Andeutung einer Anordnung der Verknechtung fehlen lässt und der dahingehende Erlass Pharaos nur indirekt aus der Schilderung seiner Durchführung in v. 11 erschlossen werden kann[25]. Diese Schwierigkeit entfällt, wenn wir v. 15 unmittelbar an v. 10 anschliessen, da dann der Darlegung der Absicht Pharaos, die Zahl der Hebräer zu mindern, sofort der Befehl an die Hebammen folgte, in dem sich diese Absicht konkretisierte. Sollte aber diese Beurteilung des Textes zutreffen, so entfiele jede auch noch so entfernte Möglichkeit, die Verdunkelung des ursprünglich die Tötung eines einzigen Kindes bezweckenden Befehls auf den Einfluss des Motivs der Verknechtung zurückzuführen.

Alle diese Erwägungen befürworten die zugegebenermassen wenig bestechende Annahme, dass die an inneren Spannungen reiche Version der Bibel auch motivgeschichtlich älter sei als die späteren, ausgeglicheneren Formen der Sage. Es gilt nun dieses an das Paradoxe grenzende Phänomen unmittelbar ins Auge zu fassen und die Frage nach den historiographischen Tendenzen zu stellen, die die biblische Fassung bestimmt haben mögen. Es sei hier der Versuch gewagt, die Deutung in einer allgemeinen Charakteristik des Inhalts des mit *Ex.* 1 einsetzenden Hauptteils der Erzählungen der Tora zu suchen. Zwei Themen sind hier unauflöslich miteinander verwoben, die Geschichte Israels von seiner Volkswerdung bis zum Ende der Wüstenwanderung und die Lebensgeschichte Moses. Unter diesem Gesichtspunkte gesehen ist es nun aber sinnvoll und die Thematik des gesamten Werkes einleitend, dass bereits die Geburtsgeschichte Moses in einen nationalgeschichtlichen Zusammenhang eingegliedert ist. Schon von seiner Geburt an wird das Schicksal Moses aufs engste mit dem seines Volkes verknüpft. Die Einfügung der Geburtsgeschichte Moses in einen volksgeschichtlichen Rahmen lässt sich also als gewollter und bewusster Ausdruck einer historiographischen Tendenz begreifen, die Geschichte des Volkes und seines Propheten und Erlösers von ihren ersten Anfängen an miteinander zu verbinden. Dieser Gesichtspunkt dominierte so stark, dass eine gewisse Gewaltsamkeit bei der Zusammenschweissung zunächst mit in Kauf genommen wurde. Doch wurde die hierdurch geschaffene Problematik später lebhaft empfunden und drängte zu neuen Lösungen.

Wir fassen zusammen: Die Erzählung der Geburt Moses verwendet als Rohstoff die Sage von der Aussetzung eines zu einer hohen Aufgabe vorbestimmten unehelichen Kindes, formt diesen Rohstoff jedoch mit souveräner Freiheit um. An Stelle des wegen seiner unehelichen Abkunft ausgesetzten Kindes tritt ein eheliches, dessen Aussetzung durch die Geschichte seines Volkes bedingt ist. Das aus der Aussetzungssage eliminierte individuelle Moment macht sich in der nachbiblischen Sage wieder geltend, wenn auch in der national gefärbten Fassung, dass es Pharao bei seinem allgemeinen Tötungsbefehl auf die Beseitigung des Erlösers Israels angekommen sei.

V

Wir haben bisher die Bemerkung Ed. Meyers[26] unberücksichtigt gelassen, dass die Königstochter, die Mose findet "ursprünglich gewiss auch tatsächlich seine Mutter gewesen ist". Das Auftreten eines Königs, dessen Versuch der Tötung eines Neugeborenen fehlschlägt, sowie der Tochter des Königs, erinnerte Meyer an das Sagenmotiv von dem König, dem geweissagt worden ist, dass der künftige Sohn seiner Tochter Unheil über ihn bringen werde, der dann vergeblich danach trachtete, den Neugeborenen zu töten und am Ende von seinem Schicksal ereilt wird[27]. Daher statuiert denn Meyer auch, dass in der Ursage Mose den Pharao des Tötungserlasses selbst geschlagen habe, nicht dessen Sohn. Der Mose der hiermit postulierten Ursage sei also ein Ägypter gewesen. Gegen diese von Rank[28] weiter entwickelte Hypothese hat Freud[29] mit Recht eingewandt, dass eine derartige Sage weder bei den Ägyptern noch bei den Israeliten im Umlauf gewesen sein könne, da eine Verherrlichung Moses durch die Ägypter ebenso unvorstellbar sei wie die Behauptung seiner ägyptischen Abkunft bei den Israeliten. Jedoch argumentiert Freud[30], dass im Unterschied zu dem Mose der Sage der historische Mose ein Ägypter gewesen sein müsse. In den Geburtssagen verwandelten sich nämlich stets die wahren Eltern in Adoptiveltern, während die als wirkliche Eltern geschilderten Figuren freie Erfindungen der Sage seien. Dem später zur Grösse aufgestiegenen Kinde werden hierbei im allgemeinen königliche Eltern angedichtet, während die dem einfachen Volke angehörigen Eltern in der Sage zu Adoptiveltern würden. Ähnlich läge der Fall in der Mosesage. Zwar sei hier die Adoptivmutter der Sage von weit höherem Range als die Eltern, doch bestimme in dem vorliegenden Sonderfall die Tendenz der Beilegung einer hebräischen Abkunft. Das Ergebnis dieser geistreichen Beweisführung dürfte kaum vor einer historischen Wahrscheinlichkeitsrechnung bestehen. Führer unterdrückter Völker pflegen ihrer eigenen Nation zu entstammen, und zwar deren höheren Schichten, die mit der Kultur des Herrschervolkes vertraut sind. Nehmen wir dies nun aber auch für Mose an, so konnte sich ein solcher Sachverhalt recht wohl in der Sage widerspiegeln, dass die Tochter des ägyptischen Königs ihn aufgezogen habe. Obendrein erzielt diese Version ja erzählungstechnisch den Überraschungseffekt, dass die eigene Tochter des mörderischen Königs zur Retterin des Kindes wird. Dieses Kunstmittel der Handlungsgestaltung ist jedoch der Mosegeschichte eigentümlich und ohne Analogie in anderen Sagen.

VI

Die vorangegangene motivgeschichtliche Analyse deutete bereits auf den Unterschied zwischen der einfachen Gradlinigkeit der babylonischen Sage und der kunstvoll ausgestalteten Form ihrer hebräischen Parallele. Im folgenden sei der Versuch unternommen, die höchst eigentümliche literarische Struktur des biblischen Textes näher zu beschreiben.

Bereits auf den ersten Blick wird klar, dass in der Sargonsage die Zahl der handelnden Personen auf das unerlässliche Mindestmass beschränkt ist, d.h. auf das Kind, die Mutter und den Adoptivvater. Zwar ist auch der Vater eingangs kurz erwähnt; jedoch gehört er nicht zu den Personen der Handlung, die erst nach der Geburt des Kindes beginnt. In der mit der Heirat der Eltern einsetzenden Geschichte der Bibel hingegen wird auch er einer der dramatis personae. Noch wesentlicher ist die Einführung der Gestalt der älteren Schwester, einer traditionsgeschichtlich offenbar sekundären Figur. Auch auf Seiten der Adoptivmutter erscheinen zusätzliche Handelnde, nämlich die נערות (Hofdamen?) und die אמה (Leibzofe?).

Hiermit hängt es denn auch zusammen, dass in den gezählten Worten von zehn Sätzen eine Fülle wechselnder Bilder den Leser fesseln und in rascher Folge an seinem Auge vorbeigleiten. Wir erfahren von der Heirat der Eltern, der Geburt des Kindes, der ihren Knaben mit Wohlgefallen betrachtenden Mutter, der zeitweiligen Verbergung des Neugeborenen, dem Herrichten eines Kästchens für das Kind, seiner Aussetzung im Schilf und von der in Sichtweite des Kästchens verbleibenden Schwester, deren spannungsvolle Erwartung sich auf den Leser überträgt. Und freilich werden seine Erwartungen nicht enttäuscht. Kein Geringerer als die Tochter des Königs steigt zum Flusse hinab, in ihm zu baden, und das Umhergehen ihrer Hofdamen am Ufer unterstreicht den königlichen Charakter ihres Auftretens, der auch in der Schilderung des Auffindens des Kästchens zum Ausdruck gelangt, das die Königstochter sich durch ihre Leibzofe bringen lässt. Hiermit erreicht die Erzählung einen Wendepunkt. Die Königstochter öffnet das Kästchen, wird von dem Anblick des weinenden Säuglings gerührt und bemerkt, dass es ein hebräisches Kind sei. Diese Worte leiten wie von ungefähr eine erstaunliche Fortsetzung ein, welche die Hörer beglückt und erheitert. Die Schwester erscheint, erbietet sich eine hebräische Amme zu beschaffen und ruft die Mutter, die von der Tochter des mörderischen Königs zur bezahlten Amme ihres eigenen Kindes bestellt wird. Selbst diese Überraschung wird durch eine zweite überboten. Die Königstochter verleiht dem ihr nach seiner Entwöhnung überantworteten Knaben den Namen Mose und offenbart damit am Schlusse der Erzählung die bisher durch die Verschweigung der Namen der Eltern verhüllte Tatsache, dass die vorangegangene Geschichte von der Geburt des Erlösers Israels handelte[31].

Der Stil der Erzählung zeichnet sich durch Gedrungenheit aus. Heirat der Eltern und Geburt des Kindes werden mit bündiger Kürze mitgeteilt. In der diesem nüchtern gehaltenen Referat folgenden kaleidoskopartigen Reihe von Bildern fällt die Weglassung mancher die Ereignisse verknüpfenden Umstände auf. So sieht die Erzählung von einem ausdrücklichen Bericht ab, dass die Schwester die Königstochter beobachtet und sich ihr genähert habe; vielmehr bleibt es der Vorstellungsgabe des Lesers überlassen, diese Lücke zu schliessen. Schwerer wiegt, dass manche den Fortgang der Handlung bestimmenden Momente unerwähnt bleiben. So wird die Frage übergangen, aus welchem Grunde nach drei Monaten die Mutter das Kind nicht länger verbergen konnte. Auch taucht die Schwester urplötzlich auf ihrem Beobachtungsposten auf. Hatte die Mutter sie mitgenommen und ihr aufgetragen, das Kästchen zu beobachten, war sie der Mutter aus eigenem Entschluss nachgeschlichen oder gar von ungefähr an den Platz gelangt? Auch fehlt es an jedem Hinweise darauf, woran die Königstochter die hebräische Abkunft des Kindes erkannt haben mag. Trotz dieser geradezu elliptischen Kürze bemerken wir hie und da einige Worte, die über das zur Entwicklung der Handlung unerlässliche Mindestmass hinausgehen. So wird die Herrichtung des Kästchens mit spürbarer Liebe geschildert. Die Erwähnung der am Ufer entlanggehenden Hofdamen ist offenbare Ausschmückung. Die Formulierung des Satzes: "Und sie öffnete und sah es das Kind und siehe ein weinender Knabe" ist vielfach als überfüllt angesehen worden.

Diese Längen der Erzählung haben nun allerdings erst die moderne Literaturforschung beschäftigt. Anders ist es um die Weglassungen verknüpfender Umstände bestellt. Insbesondere hat man sich seit jeher bemüht zu ergründen, weshalb nach drei Monaten eine weitere Verbergung des Kindes nicht länger möglich gewesen sei. Das *Jubiläenbuch* 43:3 berichtet in Kürze, dass die Mutter zu diesem Zeitpunkt ins Gerede gekommen sei. Philon (*Vita Mosis* I, 10) erklärt, dass manche die geheimen Winkel durchstöberten, um dem König Ohrenschmaus zu hinterbringen. Josephus (*Ant.* II, ix, 4) begnügt sich mit der einfachen Bemerkung, dass den Vater (!) nach dieser Zeit Furcht vor der Entdeckung befallen habe. Der Midrasch (TB *Soṭa* 12a) legt sogar dar, aus welchem Grunde eben nach dem Verstreichen von drei Monaten eine Erschwerung in der Lage eingetreten sei. Die nach seiner Annahme bereits früher mit dem Vater verheiratete, aber vorübergehend von ihm geschiedene Mutter sei nämlich bei ihrer Wiederverheiratung bereits drei Monate schwanger gewesen, wovon die Ägypter nichts wussten. Deshalb hätten sie erst drei Monate nach der Geburt des Kindes mit ihren Massnahmen zur Entdeckung des Neugeborenen begonnen, welche darin bestanden, dass sie einen schreienden ägyptischen Säugling an das Haus der Hebräer heranbrachten, damit der hebräische Säugling in sein Geschrei einstimme. Der Hinweis auf das verräterische Geschrei des Säuglings kehrt auch in der modernen Exegese wieder. S. D. Luzatto sucht in der Bezeichnung des Neugeborenen als טוב eine Andeutung, dass er anfangs nicht geschrieen hätte. Greenberg[32] erklärt ohne weitere Umschweife, dass das Geschrei des Kindes seine dauernde Verbergung unmöglich machte. Jedoch ist die Legitimität der Fragestellung vom Standpunkte der Literaturforschung nicht anzuerkennen. Diese hat nicht zu untersuchen, aus welchem Grunde nach drei Monaten die Möglichkeit der Verbergung des Kindes entfiel, vielmehr gilt es für sie zu prüfen, aus welchem Grunde der Erzähler davon abgesehen hat, uns hierüber zu unterrichten. Wir haben bereits oben dargelegt, dass die die Abneigung der Mutter gegen die Aussetzung ihres Kindes sinnfällig machende zeitweilige Verbergung des Kindes lediglich ein retardierendes Moment der Handlung darstellt. Die ins einzelne gehende Ausführung eines solchen Nebenmotivs aber hätte ihm unverhältnismässiges Gewicht verliehen und die Erzählung mit einer ihr wesensfremden schwerfälligen Pedanterie belastet. Auch das unvorbereitete Auftreten der einen Beobachtungsposten einnehmenden Schwester hat seinen guten literarischen Sinn. Kommt es doch als wirksame Überraschung, die auf eine Wendung in der Handlung hinweist. Der Ausruf der Königstochter, dass es sich um ein hebräisches Kind handele, leitet geschickt zu der Bestellung seiner Mutter als Amme über. Auch hier hätte eine nähere Begründung die bestrickende Anmut der Erzählung beeinträchtigt. Die mannigfachen zuletzt von Greenberg[33] diskutierten Erklärungen, woran die Königstochter die hebräische Abkunft des Kindes erkannt haben mag, haben mit einer literarischen Analyse des Textes nichts zu schaffen.

Die sparsam hinzugefügten, für die Entwicklung der Handlung entbehrlichen Worte erhöhen ihren Reiz. Die Schilderung der Anfertigung des Kästchens trägt einen recht anschaulichen Charakter. Das gleiche gilt für das Bild der am Ufer entlanggehenden Hofdamen, das den Eindruck des Erscheinens der Königstochter verstärkt und keineswegs die Analyse Fohrers[34] nahelegt, dass sich hier der Rest einer Version erhalten habe, nach der das Kästchen von eben diesen Hofdamen aufgefunden worden sei. Auch sollte der Unterschied zwischen der Formulierung על שפת היאר (v. 3) und על יד היאר (v. 5) nicht als Anhaltspunkt einer kritischen Analyse gewertet werden, da ein solcher Wechsel im Ausdruck durchaus *einem* Autor zugemutet werden kann. Selbst die viel bekrittelte lange Formulierung ותפתח ותראהו את הילד והנה נער בכה (v. 6) fordert zu keiner Textkritik, geschweige denn zu einer Literarkritik heraus und ist der anscheinend verkürzten Fassung der Septuaginta überlegen, die ותרא נער בוכה בתיבה bietet. Die proleptische Hinzufügung des Personalpronomens in ותראהו ist auch sonst in der Bibel bezeugt[35] und verlangsamt hier ein wenig das Tempo der Erzählung in einem Augenblicke, in dem der Leser mit angehaltenem Atem die Reaktion der Königstochter erwartet. Die Verzögerung trägt also zur Erhöhung der dramatischen Spannung bei. Auch die Verdoppelung der Schilderung des Anblicks des Kindes sollte nicht als eine durch die Verbindung von Paralleltexten entstandene Weitschweifigkeit gewertet werden. Die Worte "und sie sah es das Kind" sind in nüchternem Tone gehalten, während der Ausdruck "und siehe, ein weinender Knabe" den Leser an der Gemütsbewegung der Königstochter teilhaben lässt.

Gestufter Fortschritt verstärkt also auch hier den dramatischen Eindruck.

Zusammenfassend lässt sich sagen, dass Kürzen und Längen des Texts demselben Zwecke dienen, den Hörer in jedem Augenblicke in Bann zu schlagen.

Im Lichte dieses stark ausgeprägten Charakters der Erzählung ist denn wohl auch der berühmte Widerspruch zu verstehen, dass das Kind eingangs als Erstgeborener dargestellt wird, während im Fortgange der Erzählung eine ältere Schwester auftaucht. Der Eliminierung dieser Schwierigkeit dient bekanntlich der Midrasch (TB *Soṭa* 12a), welcher der in *Ex.* 2:1 erwähnten Ehe der Eltern eine frühere Ehe vorangehen lässt, in der Mirjam und obendrein der in der Geschichte nicht erwähnte Aron geboren sein sollen. Der Vater habe diese Ehe wegen des Befehls Pharaos aufgelöst, sei sie aber auf das Drängen seiner Tochter von neuem eingegangen[36]. In der modernen Exegese hat diese Schwierigkeit deshalb Unbehagen verursacht, weil man keinen Weg fand, sie mit den üblichen Mitteln der Quellenscheidung beizulegen. Insbesondere sei hervorgehoben, dass Wellhausen[37] eine Quellenanalyse hier als undurchführbar bezeichnet hat. Doch erwog er als Surrogat einer solchen die Möglichkeit, dass in den Hauptbericht ein anderer, quellenmässig nicht zu sondernder Bericht hineingearbeitet sein möge, der von der Schwester nichts wisse. Wie bereits oben dargelegt, kehren Gressmann und Noth den Vorschlag Wellhausens um, indem sie das Motiv der Schwester als eine später hinzugefügte Ausschmückung ansehen[38]. Doch bleibt diese Erklärung des Widerspruchs etwas lahm, da wir ja an die Konsistenz des Ausschmückens einer Erzählung höhere Anforderungen stellen dürfen als an die eines Redaktors, der ihm überlieferte Quellen aneinander fügt. Die Fragestellung spitzt sich noch mehr zu, falls die oben geäusserte Vermutung zutreffen sollte, dass die Urgeschichte nicht durch Ausscheiden des Motivs der Schwester rekonstruierbar sei, vielmehr in dieser die Mutter das Kästchen in den Fluss geworfen habe. Dies aber hiesse, dass die vorliegende Fassung der Geschichte auf einen einzigen Autor zurückginge.

Deshalb sei die Vermutung gewagt, dass der Gestalter der lebenssprühenden Geschichte den Widerspruch mit in Kauf genommen hat. Seine Vermeidung hätte wohl oder übel erfordert, eingangs eine Schilderung der Geburt der Schwester zu bieten, die sich höchst störend zwischen den Befehl Pharaos und die Geburt Moses eingeschoben hätte, was sich von der auffallend kurzen Notiz über die Heirat der Eltern nicht sagen lässt. Obendrein wäre der Überraschungseffekt des Auftretens der Schwester beeinträchtigt worden. Die logische Geschlossenheit der Erzählung wäre nur auf Kosten ihrer literarischen Wirksamkeit zu erreichen gewesen, welche durchgängig den Stil der Darstellung bestimmt. Der Erzähler hat sich anscheinend darauf verlassen, dass die Phantasie des Hörers durch die spannende Folge der schnell wechselnden Szenen so stark in Bann geschlagen war, dass er keine Musse, fand, über die Unstimmigkeit nachzusinnen. Es mag nicht unangemessen sein, hier die Worte anzuführen, mit denen Goethe[39] im Gespräch mit Eckermann seine Bemerkungen zu den Widersprüchen in den Stücken Shakespeares abschloss: "Er sah seine Stücke als etwas Bewegliches, Lebendiges an, das von den Brettern herab den Augen und Ohren rasch vorüberfliessen würde, das man nicht festhalten und bekritteln könnte, und wobei es bloss darauf ankam, immer nur im gegenwärtigen Moment wirksam und bedeutend zu sein." Ein Entsprechendes dürfte für die an Lebendigkeit und Beweglichkeit kaum überbietbare Erzählung von der Geburt Moses gelten. Die eng an den Tötungsbefehl angeschlossene Notiz von der Geburt Moses ist an ihrer Stelle ebenso wirksam und bedeutend wie das Auftreten der Schwester im Fortgang der Handlung, und ihre Bekrittelung verkennt die literarische Struktur des Textes[40].

P.S. Auch in dem samaritanischen Text *Memar Marqah* wird die Errettung Moses aus dem Fluss erwähnt. So sagt Gott zu ihm (I, 2, hrg. J. Macdonald, *BZAW* 84 (1963), i, S. 6) אף נטרת יתך לגו נהרה, 'Ich habe dich im Flusse behütet'. Ferner wird dort von Moses gesagt (V, 3, S. 124) לגו מימי נהרה הטלק 'in die Wasser des Flusses wurde er geworfen'.

ANMERKUNGEN

1. Die ungestüm vorwärtsdrängende Energie Ed. Meyers schiesst allerdings bei seiner Aufstellung von Grundformeln für "Wandersagen" offensichtlich über das Ziel hinaus und führt zu Vermischung verschiedener Typen. Vgl. seine unter vielen anderen und andersartigen auch die Geburtsgeschichte von Mose und Sargon einbeziehende Definition: "Dass ein mächtiger Herrscher dem neugeborenen Kinde, von dem, wie ein Schicksalsspruch verkündet, Gefahren drohen, nach dem Leben trachtet, dass dasselbe in einem Kasten im Wasser ausgesetzt, aber auf wunderbare Weise gerettet wird und nun heranwachsend das Schicksal erfüllt, das ist der Inhalt der Sage" (*Die Israeliten und ihre Nachbarstämme*, Halle 1906, s. 46). Es liegt nun aber auf der Hand, dass in der Sargonsage ein solcher Schicksalsspruch durchaus fehlt und dass die Mosesage ihn nur in ihren nachbiblischen Fassungen kennt. Zu allem Überflusse taucht in der Fortsetzung der Worte Ed. Mayers ebenda die kaum haltbare Theorie auf, dass in der Urfassung der Mosesage die Königstochter die Mutter des Kindes gewesen sei. Bei alledem hat die Kühnheit seiner Konzeption überaus anregend gewirkt.

2. H. Gressmann, *Mose und seine Zeit*, *FRLANT* 18 (1913), Ss. 1–16.

3. Brevard S. Childs, *Exodus* (*OTL*) 1974, S. 4.

4. B. Jacob, "The Childhood and Youth of Moses", *Essays in Honour of J. H. Hertz*, London 1946, Ss. 246f.

5. Im Buche der *Jubiläen* (47:1) setzt die Erzählung mit der Geburt des Kindes ein. Da der Vater überhaupt nicht erwähnt ist, tritt das Problem seiner Passivität weniger deutlich in das Bewusstsein des Lesers als in der biblischen Darstellung.

6. Siehe E. A. Speiser in *ANET*^{3} (1969), S. 119.

7. Au. Dillmann, *Exodus und Leviticus*, Leipzig 1880, S. 17.

8. W. G. Lambert und A. R. Millard, *Atraḫasis*, Oxford 1969, S. 102. Cf. C. Cohen, "The Legend of Sargon and the Birth of Moses", *JANES* 4 (1972), Ss. 72f.

9. Ausführlich erzählt bei Th. H. Gaster, *Myth, Legend and Custom*, London 1969, S. 226.

10. Ich verdanke diese Erkenntnis meiner früheren Studentin, Frau Yael Mishor, der hier mein Dank ausgesprochen sei.

11. Insbesondere B. Jacob, *loc. cit.* (S. 210, Anm. 4). Das Argument Jacobs ist von M. Greenberg, *Understanding Exodus*, New York 1969, Ss. 198f., aufgegriffen worden, der die Mosegeschichte im Anschluss an W. Helck, "Tkw und die Ramsesstadt", *VT* 15 (1965), S. 48, mit einem hellenistisch-ägyptischen Mythus zusammenstellt. Hiergegen siehe D. B. Redford, "The Literary Motif of the Exposed Child", *Numen* 14 (1967), Ss. 221–224, Cohen, *loc. cit.* (S. 210, Anm. 8), S. 50.

12. Diese selbst im gegenwärtigen Text erkennbare Entsprechung ist mit Recht von Jacob, *loc. cit.* (S. 210, Anm. 4) hervorgehoben worden.

13. Noch weiter geht in dieser Richtung das Buch der *Jubiläen* (47:4), das den Zeitraum zwischen Aussetzung und Auffindung zu einer liebevoll dargestellten Episode von sieben Tagen ausgestaltet, in welcher die Mutter das Kind nachts gesäugt habe, während tags die Schwester um das Verscheuchen der Vögel besorgt gewesen sei.

14. Auch die hier besprochene Abschwächung des Aussetzungsmotivs ist von Jacob, *loc. cit.* (S. 210, Anm. 4) gegen die Verwandtschaft der Geburtsgeschichte Moses mit der Sargons geltend gemacht worden. Hierbei geht er so weit, die Auffindung des Kindes durch die Königstochter als das beabsichtigte Ergebnis der Handlungsweise der Mutter darzustellen. Zur Bestärkung seiner Ansicht führt A. Cogan, "A Technical Term for Exposure", *JNES* 4 (1972), Ss. 46–51, an, dass dem in der Sargonsage verwandten akkadischen Aussetzungsterminus *nadû* im Hebräischen das Verb השליך entspräche, nicht hingegen das hier benutzte Verb שׂים. Ihre Argumentation ist von Greenberg, *op. cit.* (S. 211, Anm. 11), S. 199, angenommen worden. Hiergegen, insbesondere gegen Cogan, Cohen, *loc. cit.* (S. 210, Anm. 8), der sich für den Gebrauch von שׂים in unfreundlichem Sinne auf *Gen.* 40:15, *2 Chr.* 18:26 beruft. Doch ist all dies nicht ausschlaggebend. Das Aussetzungsmotiv ist trotz aller Milderung in der Mosegeschichte klar erkennbar, und ihre Analyse ergibt, dass motivgeschichtlich, wahrscheinlich sogar literaturgeschichtlich, ein Bericht voranging, in dem das Aussetzungsmotiv in ungeminderter Stärke existierte.

15. Gressmann, *op. cit.* (S. 210, Anm. 2), S. 1, Anm. 1.

16. M. Noth, *Exodus (OTL)* 1962, S. 25.

17. So mit Recht Childs, *op. cit.* (S. 210, Anm. 3), S. 10.

18. Die Verwunderung über das Fehlen eines Berichtes der Durchführung des Befehls veranlasste die Notiz des Buches der *Jubiläen* (42:2), dass man die Neugeborenen während eines mit der Geburt Moses endenden Zeitraumes von sieben Monaten in den Fluss geworfen hätte.

19. Greenberg, *op. cit.* (Anm. 11), S. 29, Anm. 2.

20. In der Fassung des Josephus ist also der Befehl, den Pharao an beide Hebammen erteilt hat mit dem Befehl an sein ganzes Volk zu einem zusammengeflossen, woraus sich leichtverständlicherweise ergibt, dass diese Hebammen Ägypterinnen waren. Für die Frage, ob der biblische Text hebräische oder ägyptische Hebammen im Auge hatte, lässt sich also aus den Worten des Josephus kein Argument ableiten.

21. Greenberg, *op. cit.* (Anm. 11), S. 30, Anm. 2.

22. Gressmann, *op. cit.* (S. 210, Anm. 2), S. 5.

23. *Ibid.* S. 1, Anm. 1.

24. Meyer, *op. cit.* (S. 210, Anm. 1), S. 41.

25. Dieses Argument scheint mir stärker als das gemeinhin angeführte, dass der Ausdruck הבה נתחכמה לו zu dem, vermutlich in aller Heimlichkeit, zwei Hebammen erteilten Befehle passe, nicht hingegen zu der in aller Öffentlichkeit durchge-

führten Verknechtung. Auch diese Massnahme liesse sich nämlich als besondere "Weisheit" verstehen, weil sie ja nur indirekt zu einer Verminderung der Hebräer führen sollte und obendrein Ägypten materiellen Vorteil brachte.

26. Meyer, *op. cit.* (S. 210, Anm. 1), S. 46.

27. Für eine Übersicht über diese Sagen vgl. Redford, *op. cit.* (S. 211, Anm. 11), Ss. 215–217.

28. O. Rank, *The Myth of the Birth of the Hero*, New York 1964, Ss. 173f. Zuerst erschienen unter dem Titel: *Der Mythus und die Geburt des Helden*, Schriften zur angewandten Seelenkunde, hrg. von S. Freud, Heft 5, Leipzig 1908.

29. S. Freud, *Der Mann Moses und die monotheistische Religion*, Amsterdam 1969, Ss. 19–21.

30. *Ibid.*, Ss. 22f.

31. Sowohl das Fehlen der Namen der Eltern wie die verspätete Namensgebung haben in der modernen Exegese Befremden erregt. Insbesondere hat man aus dem Nichterwähnen der Namen der Eltern folgern wollen, dass diese Namen erst einer späteren priesterlichen Tradition entstammen. Jedoch ist die Geburtsgeschichte als solche ein klarer Beweis für die Existenz einer hochentwickelten Tradition über Mose zur Zeit ihrer Abfassung, und es will nicht einleuchten, dass eine solche nichts über die Namen der Elteren berichtet haben solle.

Das schwierige, die namenlose Mutter determinierende את in *Ex.* 2:1 dürfte nach Analogie der für den bestimmten Artikel ה geltenden Regeln zu erklären sein. Dieser bezeichnet bekanntlich unter anderem ein lediglich durch die Umstände bestimmtes Substantiv, das in europäischen Sprachen durch den unbestimmten Artikel bezeichnet wird. Vgl. z.B. Gesenius-Kautzsch-Cowley, *Hebrew Grammar,* §126.4 (*q-t*). Das Gleiche dürfte hier für die Determination durch את zutreffen.

32. Greenberg, *op. cit.* (S. 211, Anm. 11), S. 39.

33. *Ibid.*, S. 41.

34. G. Fohrer, Überlieferung und Geschichte des Exodus", *BZAW* 91 (1964), S. 18.

35. P. Joüon, *Grammaire de l'Hébreu Biblique,* Rome 1947, §146 e 2.

36. D. Daube, *The New Testament and Rabbinic Judaism*, London 1956, S. 7 weist mit Recht auf einen inneren Widerspruch zwischen den beiden Midraschim hin, die von einer Unterbrechung der Ehe der Eltern Moses durch eine kurze Scheidung sprechen. Der die Existenz Mirjams erklärende Midrasch betone nämlich, dass der Befehl Pharaos den Vater zur Scheidung seiner Ehe bewogen habe. Dieses Argument aber gäbe keinen Sinn, falls die Mutter zur Zeit der Scheidung ohnehin schwanger war, die Scheidung also nicht mehr die Geburt eines Sohnes verhindern konnte. Hieraus folgert Daube, dass der Midrasch über die Schwangerschaft der Mutter zur Zeit der Scheidung sekundären Charakter trage. Als zusätzliches Argument führt er an, das der ursprüngliche, die Existenz Mirjams begründende Midrasch nicht nur in *Ex. Rabba* bezeugt sei, sondern auch in TB *Soṭa* 12a, während sich der sekundäre Midrasch über die Schwangerschaft nur in *Ex. Rabba* fände. Letzteres ist jedoch unzutreffend, vielmehr wird der Midrasch über die Schwangerschaft zweimal in *Soṭa* 12a vorgetragen. Obendrein werden dort beide Midraschim von demselben Rabbi Jehuda bar Zabida gegen Einwände verteidigt. Der von Daube hervorgehobene, innere Widerspruch hat offenbar niemanden angefochten. Ein jeder der beiden Midraschim löste eine Schwierigkeit des biblischen Textes auf, wenn man ihn für sich nahm, und das war offenbar alles, worauf es ankam.

37. J. Wellhausen, *Die Composition des Hexateuchs* etc., Berlin 1899, S. 69.

38. Allein steht die Ansicht Fohrers, *opt cit.* (*supra,* Anm. 34), Ss. 18f., der als

einziger von einer redaktionellen Zusammenarbeitung zweier Paralleltexte spricht, deren Sigel er allerdings nicht anzugeben vermag. Zu der einen Erzählung gehören nach ihm Vv. 1–3a, 5aβ, 6aβ, 10, der verbleibende Rest zu der andern. Ein klares Bild ergibt sich hierbei nicht.

39. J. P. Eckermann, *Gespräche mit Goethe*, den 18. April 1827, ed. L. Geiger, Leipzig 1902, S. 502.

40. Ein Problem für sich sind die sprachlichen Eigentümlichkeiten der Erzählung, d. h. lich die singulären Formen לדעה und ותתצב in V.4, sowie היליכי in V.9 Die Formen spiegeln wahrscheinlich einen vom Standardhebtäisch der Bibel abweichenden Dialekt wider. Die Ableitung der Form לדעה begegnet kaum Schwierigkeiten. Siehe Joüon, *op. cit.* (S. 212, Anm. 35), §75 m 3. Aber auch die Form ותתצב ist erklärbar. Siehe J. Blau, "Über die *t* Form des Hipʿil im Hebräischen", *VT* 7 (1957), S. 387. Es besteht also kein Grund, die Formen mit dem Samaritanus zu לדעת und ותתיצב zu nivellieren. Auch die Korrektur von היליכי zu הוליכי ist nicht unbedenklich. Bekanntlich wechselt in den Formen des Verbum הלך die Wurzel הלך mit der Wurzel ולך. Eine weitere Wurzelvariante ילך wäre deshalb leicht vorstellbar. Zur Semantik des Verbums in diesem Text vgl. Childs, *op. cit.* (S. 210, Anm. 3), S. 6, der einen ähnlichen Gebrauch des akkadischen Verbum (*w*)*abālu* anführt, und vgl. hierzu auch Targum Onkelos, der אובילי übersetzt. Syriacus הא לכי Samaritanischer Targum הא ליכי und die talmudische Erklärung הא שליכי (TB *Soṭa* 12b) beruhen auf aramäisierenden Volksetymologien. Auf die sprachlichen Eigentümlichkeiten der Geschichte hat zuletzt J. M. Grintz in *Leshonenu* 40 (1976), S. 157 hingewiesen. Neben den in underer Arbeit bereits besprochenen Abweichungen vom üblichen Bibelhebräisch zählt Grintz ירחים (statt חדשים) und על היאור (statt ביאור) auf. Nach der Ansicht von Grintz handelt es sich bei alledem um Kennzeichen eines episch-poetischen Stiles. Doch scheint uns die Annahme dialektischer Eigentümlichkeiten näherliegend.

The Jewish Religion after the Destruction of Temple and State: The Views of Bodin and Spinoza[1]

S. PINES

Jean Bodin's dialogue *Heptaplomeres*[2] produces, even at a first superficial reading, the impression of being an intricate work. It is also a disconcerting one, since the author's intentions, except as far as the final call for religious tolerance is concerned, are by no means perspicuous. For many years the work was regarded as dangerous and at a certain moment Leibniz[3] was opposed to its being published.[4] This opinion is also expressed by Gabriel Naudé in the following passage: "Compositum, sed nondum editum (atque utinam nunquam edatur) de rerum sublimium arcanis ingens volumen."[5]

The dialogue is supposed to have taken place in Venice[6] at the home of a Catholic, the other interlocutors being a Calvinist, another a Protestant who accepted the Augsburg confession, an adherent of the natural religion, a former Christian converted to Islam, an apologist for all religions including paganism, and a Jew named Salomo Barcassius. Salomo takes the leading part in the dialogue, more particularly in the latter part. What he says shows, as do other works of Bodin, that author's familiarity with various branches of Jewish learning, including philosophy, and a partiality for quotations gleaned from Hebrew works; it produces the impression that he had a predilection for Judaism. Because of this a rumour mentioned by Pierre Bayle[7] would have it that Bodin died a Jew. A later conjecture tried to account for his Jewish lore and sympathies by postulating that his mother was Jewish, a hypothesis which appears to have been disproved by Pasquier's researches concerning Bodin's family.[8] The present article, however, is concerned neither with Bodin's biography nor with his ancestry. On the other hand, the sources of some of Bodin's opinions pose a problem which may have a bearing on the main theme of this paper.

Before dealing with it directly, I shall refer to several related points, such as the question of the eternity of the world which is discussed in Book II of Noack's edition. Here Diego Toralba, an adherent of natural religion, is given the main role. On p. 20 he impugns Aristotle's notion of God, because the Greek philosopher, while attributing freedom to man regarded as *causa sui*,[9] considers that God's actions are governed by necessity.[10] On pp. 25 f. Toralba argues that since the *causa mundi effectrix et conservatrix* is not subject to the laws of the fates, and since its will is not identical with its essence, the world cannot be eternal: it must have been created in time and, contrary to Plato's opinion, it will perish. Noneternity has been affirmed by Avicenna,[11] who is designated as *princeps eruditione clarissimus*. Avicenna's argument, as given by Toralba, may be stated as follows: everything created is nothing; for in respect of its essence it derives from the First Cause. There could not, however, be a First Cause, if the world were eternal. The question of the eternity of the world is also dealt with in Bodin's *Methodus ad Facilem Historiarum Cognitionem,* Chapter viii, p. 229[12] where Bodin refers to the critique of Aristotle's arguments made by Maimonides[13] in the *Guide of the Perplexed,* II, 25. In speaking of the view that the world will have an end, Bodin mentions (p. 232) with approval Avicenna's thesis that the first sphere is not moved by God. According to Bodin, this thesis entails the conclusion that the world will necessarily come to an end, because the action of a finite mind *(mens)*—which the mover, if it is not God, must be—cannot but be finite. Avicenna's thesis is regarded by Bodin as correct, because it would be absurd to conjoin with a finite body, such as the world, an infinite mover. The high esteem in which Bodin held Avicenna may have been characteristic of the tradition to which he belonged at least in part. Pico de la Mirandola also praises Avicenna.[14]

A second point to which I wish to refer is the discussion found in *Heptaplomeres* (pp. 342 f.) concerning the eternality of punishment. Toralba and Salomo maintain, against some of the other interlocutors, that the punishment of sinners in the afterlife is not eternal. This contradicts a passage at the beginning of *Heptaplomeres* (pp. 3–4) in which reference is made to a preceding conversation that is not recorded, concerning the immortality of the soul. Salomo says on this occasion: (p. 4) "*Plus . . . quam satis est inter nos ipsos, quibus etiamsi nullae demonstrationes extarent, persuasa jam pridem est immortalitas animorum et sempiterna bonis praemia, supplicia sceleratis decreta.*"

As A. Altmann has shown,[15] the question of the eternality of punishment became an issue in the 17th century both in the Dutch Christian milieu (apparently under the impact of the Socinian teaching)[16] and in the Jewish Amsterdam community. The passage in *Heptaplomeres* antedates this development.

A third point which may be mentioned here is the praise of tolerance and the references to various cases of intolerance. They conclude *Heptaplomeres* (pp. 354–358) and are obviously regarded as odious. The impression is produced that everything in the dialogue is intended to lead up to this. Senamus, who has been described as an apologist for all religions, says: (p. 354) "I, for my part, . . . prefer to approve of all religions rather than incur the risk of excluding the religion which is perhaps the true one." Salomo observes (p. 356) that while the nation of Israel was ordered to exterminate and destroy the temples and the altars that were found in the promised land, the Israelites did not force the neighboring peoples to change their religion. Senamus, the Catholic Coronaeus, and the Moslem Octavius (p. 355) refer with approval to the tolerance which characterizes the Turkish empire. According to Senamus the Israelites believe, as do also he and

Octavius, that all prayers that come from a pure heart are agreeable and certainly not disagreeable to God. If all men were persuaded of this, people would be able to live everywhere upon the earth in friendship (*eadem concordia*) just as they do under the emperor of the Turks and the Persians. Coronaeus observes that the princes of that state tolerate the public performance of Jewish religious ceremonies, and that the adherents of other religions who do not enjoy this privilege are nevertheless allowed to make use of their freedom, if the latter does not trouble the tranquillity of the state. Nobody is forced either to be present at or to be absent from religious ceremonies. Octavius considers that this arrangement is wise, like all the institutions of the state in question, because of which it has flourished and will flourish for a very long time; nothing being more pernicious for a state than discord among its citizens. At this point Coronaeus is made to remark (p. 356) that "piety should be preferred to the public good (*utilitati tamen publicae pietas anteferri debet*)"; people should be forced, even against their will, to be present at public religious ceremonies; for this is laid down in the most holy ordinances of the Roman Church. In conclusion he quotes: *Compelle intrare,* i.e., the gospel verse (*Luke* 14:23) used by the exegetes in order to justify compulsory conversion.

A considerable portion of the last two pages of the printed edition of the dialogue (357–358) treats of Jews who in one way or another were victims of religious hostility and (sometimes simulated) intolerance. The Calvinist Curtius speaks about the banishment of Jews from Spain and subsequently of the Spanish exiles from Gallia Narbonensis, and also about the calamities which befell the Spanish exiles in Portugal. Three thousand of them were killed. The king crucified the agitator who incited the mob against the Jews. Salomo describes an incident in the Temple of Jerusalem, provoked by the sacrilegious demeanor of the (Roman) soldier, which led to the killing of twenty thousand people. He also refers to the use made of pious pretexts[17] by Ludovic of Hungary, Dagobert and Philippe Auguste of France, and Ferdinand of Aragon, with a view to confiscating the property of the Jews, a result which in fact ensued. In Cracow the Jews were killed—with the exception of the children, who were converted to Christianity—and their houses burnt.

Octavius the Moslem speaks of Ferdinand of Aragon who because of his inequitable piety (or rather his insatiable greed for money)[18] banished the Jews, and forced the Moslem Moors to renounce Muhammad. Afterwards informers were given the opportunity to bring about the confiscation of the property of new converts, accused of dissimulation in their practice of Christianity. All this was done at the instigation of the Cardinal Ximenes. Fridericus, an adherent of the Augsburg confession, praises Theodoric, king of the Romans and the Goths, (who, as we may add, was himself an Arian), for his reply to the Roman Senate. Having been asked to force the Arians to adopt the Catholic religion he answered: "religion cannot be commanded, for no one can be obliged to believe against his will."

Curtius, to whom the concluding remarks are assigned, regards the Emperor Jovian as superior even to Theodoric, because he called on Pagans, Christians, Manicheans, Jews, and about two hundred sects to live in concord.

A call for religious tolerance is thus the final message of *Heptaplomeres*. It may be added that the concluding pages of the dialogue appear to show that Bodin's views on the subject seem to have been greatly influenced by the plight of the Spanish and other Jews and of the Marranos. This is shown not only by the direct references to the persecutions of which they were the victims but also by the eulogy of the Turkish empire, in which exiles from Spain prospered. There is in these pages a certain animosity towards the Catholic Church, but no reference to the intolerance evinced by Protestants and Catholics towards each other, or to their mutual persecution which, for the better part of the century, determined the course of European and notably French history. The impression is conveyed that the Jews were the principal victims of religious intolerance.

The main theme of the present paper is related to Salomo's attempt to define and legitimate Judaism by referring to Natural Religion.[19] Thus, he speaks of "the best religion" which is "the most ancient," having been "transmitted by the best father of mankind" (*Heptaplomeres,* IV, pp. 141–142). It was observed by Abel and Cain[20] as well as by Enoch, Noah, and Abraham: "Four hundred years after God had made a covenant with Abraham, He took pity on his people and called upon Moses, through whom the observance of the natural religion, which God had implanted in the souls of men and which had been almost effaced in their souls, was restored."[21] A similar statement is made by Salomo in *Heptaplomeres* V (p. 190 f.): when Abraham is said to have observed the law of the Most High, he must have observed the law of nature. Philo observes that the precepts of the two tablets do not disagree in anything with nature. Salomo adds that since in the time of Moses the law of nature had been sullied by the crimes and shameful conduct of men and was nearly effaced in their souls, God wished to restore (*renovare*) it with his voice, to cause it to be contained in the tablets, particularly the prohibitions, by means of which we are forbidden to violate nature. "As men had become deaf to nature's laws, God's voice was needed, in order that those who had condemned nature, should hear the Father of nature as He makes his words resound." On p. 147 Abraham ibn Ezra is cited by Salomo in support of this opinion: according to him, as quoted in *Heptaplomeres,* the Decalogue is an epitome of the natural law which had been violated by the criminal and shameful conduct of men. God reconfirmed the natural commandments and prohibitions at a great assembly and . . . consecrated the eternal covenant of the Decalogue with the people by sprinkling the tablets with blood, since this was the usage with regard to covenants.[22] Toralba, too, considers that the Decalogue is the very law of nature (pp. 147 f.). He makes, however, one exception. Whereas the other (nine) commandments of the Decalogue are accepted by almost all peoples, which proves that the divine law is in complete accord with the laws of nature, this is not true of the fourth commandment, which concerns the Sabbath. This statement leads to an argument between Toralba and Salomo, who refers, *inter alia,* to the fact that Toralba's reasoning on this point had already been employed by Justin against Trypho the Jew.[23] He seems to refer to Toralba's assertion that something that is not just is not made just by the passage of time. In his rebuttal of this reasoning he elicits from Toralba the following noteworthy statement (p. 149): ". . . it is a law of nature that we obey a magistrate who gives orders. He who acts in a different way is regarded as unjust." Likewise in the course of this discussion Curtius refers to the following definition (p. 149): "The lawyers report that the main difference between the natural and the civil laws is constituted by the fact that the civil laws relate to matters that cannot be said to be just or unjust before they are ordered or forbidden. Justice, on the other hand, is a perpetual attribute of the natural laws[24]—without any orders or prohibitions."

The relation between the Decalogue and the Mosaic laws in general is alluded to by Salomo in a passage occurring on p. 143: "Nothing in the majesty of the Bible is more ancient and sacred than the divine law, which is divided into three parts. For, setting aside the historical books, the moral (*morales*) law is the principal (part), the ritual (*ritualis*) is the second and the political (*politica*) the third. Again the moral law is twofold, one part relating to the worship of God, the other to the reciprocal duties of men with respect to one another. The prescriptions with regard to the worship of God are contained in the four commandments[25] (which come) first, the other six relate to the safeguarding of faith and the social bond[26] which should subsist between men. The political part includes in a more detailed way that which is contained very briefly in the second tablet, namely judicial (*judiciales*) commandments and those relating to marriage and the administration of the state (*praetorias*), i.e., [the laws] by means of which the commonwealth (*res publica*) of the Hebrews was founded and constituted. [These are the laws] "without which a good man can achieve salvation in the most desolate solitude and anywhere on earth."[27]

As for the rites and sacrifices (*ritus et sacrificia*), they were instituted by God in order to make the Israelites renounce the worship of demons and statues of animals which was practised by the Egyptians and neighboring peoples; they would not have given up the habit of offering sacrifices to demons if they had not been ordered to offer them to God. Salomo does not in this connection cite Maimonides, who in the *Guide of the Perplexed,* III, 32 propounds the same explanation. He remarks that God does not delight in sacrifices and quotes in support of this opinion various prophetic texts. However, when the Moslem Octavius remarks that, in view of the fact that no animal sacrifices are offered anywhere by Jews, the laws relating to them are useless, Salomo retorts (p. 145 f.) that as Philo, Abraham ibn Ezra,[28] King Solomon, and Leo Hebraeus have remarked, all the sacrifices, the rites and the instruments of the holy ceremonies refer to hidden mysteries of nature.

An observation made by Salomo on p. 145 propounds the following classification of the commandments: "The 613 commandments[29] which are contained in the book of the law (*libro legis*) relate partly to judicial matters (*judicia*), partly to usages (*mores*), partly to rites (*ritus*), and partly to a more abundant explanation of the Decalogue."

At this point some historical observation may be in order. The identification of the Decalogue with the natural law attributed in the *Heptaplomeres* to Abraham ibn Ezra is also found in the Christian tradition;[30] the tripartite division of the Mosaic law propounded by Salomo on p. 143 is reminiscent of and practically identical with the likewise tripartite division of that law found in Thomas Aquinas' *Summa Theologica,* I, II, *qu.* XCIX, though the terminology is different; the three parts are *praecepta moralia, caerimonalia* and *iudicialia.* Aquinas' division of the Mosaic law is mentioned by Joseph Albo[31] when quoting a Christian opponent.

In the passages of *Heptaplomeres* cited above, Salomo seems to manifest a predominantly critical or even hostile attitude towards the laws concerning the sacrifices, i.e., laws which were no longer observed, but there is no suggestion of an opposition on his part to other commandments. Consequently the following interchange is rather unexpected (pp. 172–173): Toralba: "If the true religion consists in the pure worship of the eternal God, I firmly believe that the law of nature suffices for man's salvation. . . . When Marcus Tullius [Cicero] asked [an oracle] what rule of life he should adopt, he received the following answer: 'Nature ought to be followed.' Paul in writing to the Romans professes openly, without any obscurity or ambiguity, the same thing. He says: 'Gentiles,[32] who have not the law, live by nature in accordance with the law because, though they do not have the tablets of the laws, they nevertheless carry about the commandments sealed in their minds, while their conscience bears witness.' In these words he teaches that right reason and nature's law suffice for the salvation of men. This being so, what need is there of so many rites, which form an obligation for the Jews, the Christians, the Moslems (*Agareni*), and the pagans. (Accordingly) I firmly believe that this religion is the most ancient of all and the best."

"After Toralba had made these brief remarks, there was silence. For up till then, the sentiments of everyone concerning religion had not been brought into the open. Salomo,[33] relying on his public authority, finally [said] breaking the silence:

> My judgment (*mei sensus*), Toralba, is fully in accord with yours, for I hold that everything that pertains to salvation is contained in the laws of nature. It is by these laws of nature that Abel, Enoch, Noah, Abraham, Job,[34] Isaac, and Jacob lived. These are men who, according to the testimony of immortal God himself . . . have achieved the glory of supreme piety and integrity. For circumcision, which was given to Abraham and his descendants as a token of the covenant, is not necessary for salvation. We have been ordered to be

> circumcised mainly in order to seem to be chosen and separated from the other peoples. God himself however appears to refer to this law of nature when he says:[35] 'By the seed of Abraham all the peoples will be blessed, because he obeyed my voice and never transgressed my commandments and my laws.' But the law was only promulgated by Moses after four hundred and thirty years. The other[36] [commandments], however, which are included in the ritual and judicial laws have lost their validity[37] since the destruction of God's Temple and of the commonwealth of the Hebrews. For we are explicitly forbidden to sacrifice animals in any place other than the one that has been expressly marked out by God. But we keep[38] the Decalogue, and (in addition) circumcision together with the passover lamb with a view to an eternal remembrance of the favors we have received. I am, however, convinced that no religion whatever can subsist without rites and ceremonies."

At this point Bodin observes that for the first time in the course of the dialogue real views on religion have been disclosed by one of the interlocutors, i.e., Toralbo. The rejoinder of Salomo may likewise be assumed to express his true opinion; this suggests, of course, *inter alia,* that in his previous remarks he had not been perfectly frank. In fact, he had never before put forward the view that commandments other than those relating to sacrifices had lost their validity after the destruction of the Jewish state and Temple. It may be argued that the context of this statement and its exact significance are not quite clear: on the one hand, the meaning of *antiquata,* translated as "lost their validity," may be open to doubt; on the other, there is no perfect correspondence between the tripartite division of the Mosaic law to which the sentence appears to refer and the one Salomo had propounded before.[39] There the three parts were said to be: *lex moralis, lex ritualis,* and *lex politica,* which in turn was divided into *leges iudiciales, connubiales, praetoriae.* As against this, the sentence with which we are dealing speaks of *leges rituales* and *judiciariae* as having lost their validity; the *leges morales* are not mentioned in this context, for the obvious reason that they are still valid. On the basis of terminology alone, it could be argued that the *leges judiciariae,* which need no longer be observed, are but one subdivision of the *lex politica* and that its other subdivisions include laws which have still to be kept. However, on the face of it, this conjecture is highly unlikely, and it is put out of court by another sentence in Salomo's reply to Toralba's declaration, according to which the law of nature suffices for salvation. That sentence states clearly that only the Decalogue, circumcision and the rite of the passover lamb have still to be kept, the inference being that the other commandments have been discarded. As we have seen, the Decalogue is regarded by Salomo as corresponding to the law of nature: hence Judaism is, save for two commandments, identical with natural law and religion.

The question may be asked whether in this matter Salomo is merely a mouthpiece of Bodin, or whether to some extent at least he had a Jewish or Marrano prototype; is he to be compared to the Persian of *Lettres*

Persanes or to Lessing's *Nathan der Weise*? On the whole the second hypothesis seems to me to be somewhat more likely. In other words, the notion that most of the commandments are no longer valid and that Judaism is very close to the natural religion, may have originated in a Jewish or Marrano milieu.

However this may be, several decades after the writing of *Heptaplomeres* the problem is taken up in a very different spirit by two Marrano heretics. Both Uriel da Costa (*d.* 1640)[40] and Juan de Prado (*b.* 1614) praised the law of nature. The former describes it in his *Exemplar Humanae Vitae,*[41] written at the end of his life, as being common to and inborn in all men. It creates among them a bond of mutual love, teaches how to live well, and "distinguishes between right and wrong, between the foul and the fair."[42]Everything that is best in the religion of Moses and in all other religions is contained in the law of nature. The examples quoted by da Costa in order to prove the last assertion seem to refer to the Decalogue, although he does not expressly mention it. On the other hand, the religion of Moses and all other positive religions lead to actions contrary to nature, and indeed to crimes against nature, such as the killing or betraying of a father, a brother, a friend and so on. These false religions also cause men to lose hope of salvation, make them torture themselves and seek solitude. The argument that if there were no other law than the law of nature and if (in consequence) men were not persuaded by their religious faith that there is another life, they would all commit evil actions, does not hold water. It is possible to promulgate just and reasonable laws, rewarding the good and punishing the bad. If men had followed right reason and lived in accordance with human nature, all would have loved one another and have had compassion on one another.[43]

Our main source for the opinion of the Marrano Juan de Prado,[44] who settled in Amsterdam around 1655 and was for some time an associate of Spinoza, are the writings of Isaac Orobio de Castro, who polemized against him. The law of nature does not appear to play a considerable part in this debate;[45] but it was certainly contrasted by de Prado to Judaism, as may be seen from the full title of Orobio's *Epistola Invectiva*. The title reads:[46] *Epistola Invectiva contra Prado, un Philosopho Medico, que dudava o no creya la verdad de la Divina Escritura y pretendió encubrir su malicia con la afectada confession de Dios y la ley de Naturaleza*. Thus, as has already been suggested, the two Marrano heretics do not, in contradistinction to Bodin, attempt to achieve accord between an overriding belief in the law of nature and acceptance of Judaism, but rather use the former as a weapon against the latter.[47]

The position of Spinoza, who was likewise a radical critic of Judaism, is very different. As we shall see, on one point there is an unmistakable analogy between his view and that of Salomo in *Heptaplomeres*. Two passages in the *Tractatus Theologico-Politicus* are relevant in this connection. One occurs in Chapter V and follows references to various biblical passages which, according to Spinoza's interpretation, proclaim the universal divine law (*lex divina universalis*); a law that does not include sacrifices and ceremonial observances. The passage that interests us reads:[48] "That the Jews themselves were not bound to practise their ceremonial observances (*ceremonias*) after the destruction of their kingdom is evident from Jeremiah. For when the prophet saw and foretold that the desolation of the city was at hand, he said that God only delights in those who know and understand that He exercises loving kindness, judgment, and righteousness on earth and that such persons only are worthy of praise (*Jer.* 9:23). It was as though he had said that, after the desolation of the city, God would require nothing special from the Jews beyond the natural law by which all men are bound.[49]

"The New Testament also confirms this view, for moral doctrines only are taught therein, and the kingdom of heaven is promised as a reward, whereas ceremonial observances were not touched on by the Apostles after they began to preach the gospel to the Gentiles. The Pharisees certainly continued to practise these rites after the destruction of the kingdom, but more with a view to opposing the Christians than to pleasing God: for after the first destruction of the city, when they were led captive to Babylon, not being then, so far as I am aware, split up into sects, they straight away neglected their rites, bid farewell to the whole of the Mosaic law, buried their national customs in oblivion as being plainly superfluous and began to mingle with other nations, as we may abundantly learn from *Ezra* and *Nehemiah*. We cannot therefore doubt that they were no more bound by the law of Moses, after the destruction of their kingdom, than they had been before it had been begun, while they were still living among other peoples before the exodus from Egypt, and were subject to no special law beyond the natural right, and also, undoubtedly, the law of the state in which they were living, in so far as it was not opposed (*non repugnabat*) to the divine natural law."

The second relevant passage occurs in chapter XIX of the *Tractatus* and reads: "Lastly, for the same reason, after the destruction of the Hebrew dominion, revealed religion ceased to have the force of law; for we cannot doubt that as soon as the Jews transferred their right to the king of Babylon, the kingdom of God and the divine right forthwith ceased. For the covenant wherewith they promised to obey all the utterances of God was abrogated; God's kingdom, which was based thereupon, also ceased. The Hebrews could no longer abide thereby, inasmuch as their rights no longer belonged to them but the king of Babylon, whom (as we showed in chapter XVI) they were bound to obey in all things. *Jeremiah* (29:7) expressly admonishes them of this fact: "And seek the peace of the city, whither I have caused you to be carried away captives, and pray unto the Lord for it; for in the peace thereof shall ye have peace." Now they could not seek the peace of the city as having a share in its government, but only as slaves, being, as they were, captives; by obedience in all things, with a view to avoiding seditions, and by observing all the laws of the country, however different from their own. It is thus abundantly clear that religion among the Hebrews only acquired the force of law through the right of sovereign rule (*a solo imperii jure*); when that rule was destroyed, it could no longer be received as the law of a particular kingdom but only as the universal precept of reason. I say of reason, for the universal religion had not yet become known by revelation.[50] We may therefore draw the general conclusion that religion, whether revealed through our natural faculties or through prophets, receives the force of a command solely through the decrees of the holders of sovereign power;[51] and further, that God has no special kingdom among men, except in so far as he reigns through earthly potentates."

These two passages expound a conception a part of which can be summarized as follows: the Hebrew religion, with its rites and sacrifices, was bound up in the period of the first and of the second Temple with the existence of the Hebrew kingdom. After the destruction of the first kingdom,i.e., at the time of the Babylonian captivity, the Jews, because of this connection between the religion and the state, were released by Jeremiah from the obligation to perform ceremonial observances. "It was as though he had said that, after the desolation of the city, God would require nothing special from the Jews beyond the natural law by which all men are bound." In the light of other statements, this assertion has to be modified. The Jews were bound not only by the natural law but also by the laws of the Babylonian kingdom which had destroyed their state. In the books of *Ezra* and *Nehemiah* Spinoza finds evidence that at that time the Jews, having no state of their own, abandoned the Mosaic law and began to mingle with other nations. Like their ancestors who lived in Egypt before the exodus, they "were subject to no special law beyond the natural law, and, doubtless also, the law of the state in which they were living, in so far as it was consonant with the divine natural law."

The transformation of the Jewish religion which occurred after the first destruction of the Hebrew kingdom should, as Spinoza sets forth in Chapter V, have also taken place after the second destruction. The fact that this did not happen was due to the Pharisees, who thought more of "opposing the Christians than of pleasing God." In other words, Jews who live with no state of their own after the second destruction, ought, as were their ancestors after the first destruction, only to be bound by the natural law and the law of the state of which they are the inhabitants. This obviously can apply to the Jews who were Spinoza's contemporaries. The resemblance of these views with those set forth by Salomo in *Heptaplomeres* is evident, notwithstanding the fact that the latter appears as a representative and apologist of Judaism and Spinoza as its critic. For Salomo considers that after the destruction of the Jewish state (and of the Temple) the juridical commandments and those relative to ceremonial observances were no longer valid, and only the Decalogue, circumcision, and the passover lamb were left. Now the Decalogue is identified by Salomo with the natural law. In other words, he considers, as does also Spinoza, that the Jews of his time were first and foremost bound by the natural law. The fact that, unlike Spinoza, he enjoins the observance of two commandments which do not form a part of this law, does not seem to be of great importance in the context of our discussion: the similarity is indubitable and appears to call for an explanation.

At this point, an examination of some terms used by Spinoza seems to be required. In another passage, also to be found in chapter XIX, he asserts that religion after the first destruction of the Hebrew kingdom "could no longer be received as the law of a particular kingdom but only as *catholicum Rationis documentum* (i.e., as the universal precept of reason), I say of reason, for *catholica religio* (the universal religion) had not yet become known by revelation." Spinoza goes on to speak of "religion whether revealed through our natural faculties or through prophets." The passage appears to legitimate the conclusion that the context of *catholicum Rationis documentum*, cognized by human reason, is identical with that of *catholica religio* which, according to Spinoza, was revealed. The *catholica religio* plays a considerable part in the politicotheological system of the *Tractatus*.[52] As conceived by Spinoza, it would lend its sanction to the tolerant state whose institution he wishes to further. This religion has a certain number of dogmas or postulates which can be interpreted in such a way as to accord with practically all systems of belief; first and foremost it teaches moral duties; according to it: "we are bound to treat with piety (*pietas*) all men without exception and do no man harm." In Spinoza's interpretation this means *inter alia* regard for the public rather than for the private weal and obedience to the sovereign powers of the state.

In chapter XII, in which Spinoza wishes to defend himself against the attacks directed against him because of his critique of the Bible, he makes a number of statements about the origin and antecedents of this religion which, rather than the Bible, is to be regarded as the Word of God, "for not only reason (*ratio*), but the expressed opinions that are God's eternal Word (*verbum*) and covenant, no less than true religion, are divinely inscribed in human hearts, that is in the human mind, and that is the true original of God's covenant, stamped with his own seal, namely the idea of Himself, as it were with the image of his Godhead."[53]

Further on Spinoza asserts that according to *Isaiah* 1:10f. and comparable passages elsewhere, the way of life consists not in ceremonies but in charity and a true heart. He calls such religion God's law or God's word and refers to it as universal and catholic to the whole human race *(toti humano generi universalem sive catholicam)*.

Spinoza furthermore states—and this assertion appears to be, but need not necessarily be, in contradiction with the remark about *Isaiah*—that this religion was preached by the prophets before Christ "as a national law in virtue of the covenant entered into under Moses," while the Apostles who came after Christ, preached it to all men as a universal religion (*religio catholica*) solely in virtue of Christ's passion. In the same context, Spinoza denies that the *religio catholica, quae maxime naturalis est,* "was new (*nova*) except in relation to those men who had not known it; 'it was in the world,' as St. John the Evangelist says (*John* 1:10), 'and the world knew it not.' " In the same chapter this religion is equated with divine universal law (*Lex divina Universalis*).

In these statements Spinoza occasionally, and presumably deliberately, uses the terminology of the adherents of the doctrine of the natural religion and the natural law. Thus he uses in connection with it the phrases: *hominum . . . cordibus inscriptum*[54] and *quae maxime naturalis est.* The doctrine in question, however, generally postulates that natural religion and natural law were originally known to all men, including transgressors. Spinoza denies this in the same passage in which he quotes *John.* It may be conjectured that before this religion was "revealed," either by the prophets before Christ as a national law or by the Apostles as a universal religion, it was known and followed by those only who conducted their life in accordance with reason.[55]

The statements regarding *catholica religio,* quoted above from chapters XII and XIX, can thus by and large be brought into line with Spinoza's politicotheological system. This cannot be said of the remarks which, in Chapter V, refer to *lex naturalis.* These remarks read as follows: "It was as though [Jeremiah] had said that, after the desolation of the city, God would require nothing special from the Jews beyond the natural law by which all men were bound (*tenentur*)." The next sentence makes it clear that the natural law consists of moral precepts: "The New Testament also confirms this view, for only moral doctrines (*documenta tantum moralia*) are herein taught and the kingdom of heaven is promised as a reward, whereas ceremonial observances are not touched upon by the Apostles, after they began to preach the gospel to the Gentiles."

In Chapter V, Spinoza has a second reference to the natural law: "We cannot therefore doubt that they [the Hebrews] were no more bound by the law of Moses after the destruction of their kingdom than they had been before it had begun, while they were still living among other peoples before the exodus from Egypt, and were subject to no special law beyond the natural right, and also, undoubtedly, the law of the state in which they were living, in so far as it was not opposed to the divine natural law."

It may be inferred from these remarks of Spinoza's that (1) the natural law is a moral law of which all men are cognizant, and which is binding on all of them: and (2) that there may be a conflict between the divine natural law and the laws of the country in which one lives, and that in such a case the natural law has the superior claim. This conception cannot, as far as I can see, be explained on the basis of Spinoza's political philosophy, for it implies a different scheme of reference. The starting point of Spinoza's political philosophy is the state of nature which precedes, at least in theory, the social pact. Spinoza treats of this state in chapter XVI. He characterizes there, *inter alia,* natural right (*ius naturale*) as follows: "The natural right of the individual man is thus determined not by sound reason, but by desire (*cupiditate*) and power. All are not naturally conditioned so as to act according to the laws and rules of reason; nay on the contrary, all men are born ignorant, and before they can learn the right way and acquire the habit of virtue, the greater part of their life, even if they have been well brought up, has passed away. Nevertheless, they are in the meanwhile bound to live and preserve themselves as far as they can by the unaided impulses of desire. Nature has given them no other guide and has denied them the present power of living according to sound reason; so that they are no more bound to live by the dictates of an enlightened mind, than a cat is bound to live by the laws of the nature of a lion. Whatsoever, therefore, an individual (considered as under the sole sway of nature) thinks useful for himself, whether led by sound reason or impelled by the passions, he has a sovereign right to seek and to take for himself as he best can, whether by force, cunning, entreaty, or any other means."

Moral judgments and moral obligations came into existence merely in consequence of the social pact. As Spinoza says in chapter XIX: "For this reason we could not conceive sin to exist in the state of nature nor imagine God a judge punishing man's transgressions; but we supposed all things to happen according to the general laws of universal nature, there being no difference 'between the pious and the impious, between the pure and the impure'—as Solomon says in *Ecclesiastes* 9:2—because there was no possibility either of justice or charity. In order that the true doctrines of reason, that is . . . the true divine doctrines might obtain absolutely the force of law and right, it was necessary that each individual should cede his natural right and transfer it either to society or to one man. Then, and not till then, does it first dawn upon us what is justice and what is injustice, what is equity and what is iniquity. Justice, therefore, and absolutely all the precepts of reason, including love towards one's neighbour, receive the force of right and ordinance (*vim iuris et mandati*) solely through the right of dominion (*a solo imperii iure*), that is, . . . solely on the decree of those who possess the right to rule."[56]

The notion of natural law, referred to in chapter V, cannot be derived from the fundamental conceptions of Spinoza's political philosophy as set forth in chapters XVI and XIX. In fact, the two theories are incompatible for at least two reasons:

(1) The natural law in question is binding on all men, in other words it is a matter of indifference in respect of this obligation whether a man exercises his reason or not, apparently because *qua* man he is supposed to be cognizant of this law; and it is also a matter of indifference to what state or community he belongs. Contrary to the assertions of Spinoza in chapter

XIX, the law in question and the moral obligations which it imposes appear to be independent of the authorities constituted in virtue of the social pact, and presumably are anterior to that pact. This position is characteristic of the theoreticians of the doctrine of the natural law.
(2) In the passage from chapter V Spinoza appears to envisage the possibility of a conflict between the natural and the positive law and to consider that if such a conflict occurs, the dictates of natural law should be followed. This, too, is part of the classical doctrine of the natural law and is contrary to the view set forth in chapter XIX, according to which the laws laid down by the sovereign rulers of the state, i.e., the positive laws, have an overriding authority and legitimacy. In fact, primary religious and moral obligation consists in obedience to the laws and commands of these rulers.

It is not surprising that Spinoza contradicts himself. The *Tractatus* is full of such contradictions, many of which are doubtless deliberate. They both concealed and revealed the author's intentions and arrested the attention of the careful reader. In the case of the passage in chapter V, however, the contradiction may provide a pointer. As has been shown above, this passage calls to mind *Heptaplomeres,* by stating that after the destruction of their kingdom the Hebrews were bound by the natural law only and were released from the obligation to practise ceremonial observances. We have now discovered another circumstance pointing in the same direction. I refer to the fact that in chapter V Spinoza employs the term *lex naturalis* twice in a sense which is foreign to his political philosophy,[57] namely the sense in which the term is used in the treatises which expound the classical doctrine of natural law. *Heptaplomeres* was, of course, such a treatise. The questions arising from these considerations admit of several answers: (1) Spinoza may have read *Heptaplomeres* and have taken over from this work the view that, after the destruction of the Hebrew kingdom, the Jews were released from all religious obligations except the moral ones.[58] (2) The influence of *Heptaplomeres* on Spinoza may have been an indirect one, exercised through an intermediary of some sort. (3) The opinions set forth by Salomo in *Heptaplomeres,* and among them the view under discussion, may reflect notions which had originated in a Jewish and possibly a Marrano milieu. The thesis that the destruction of the Hebrew kingdom brought about the automatic abrogation of all the commandments except the moral ones may have been taught (as well as the classical doctrine of the natural law) in this hypothetical milieu; this could, of course, account for Spinoza's encountering it and for the coincidence (which, however, stops short of identity) between his view and that expounded by Salomo in *Heptaplomeres.* Whatever the correct answer may be, it seems certain that some of the ideas of Salomo or of Bodin on Judaism should be studied in the context of Marrano thought. It may be added that the view which has provided the main theme for our discussion may be regarded as an early attempt to conceive and to legitimate a reformed Judaism.

NOTES

1. I am indebted to Professor S. Stein for various valuable suggestions.

2. Bodin appears to have finished the work in 1593. On the meaning of the title, see R. Chauviré, *Colloque de Jean Bodin des Secrets Cachez des Choses Sublimes entre Sept Sçavans qui sont de Differens Sentimens* (traduction française du *Colloquium Heptaplomeres,*) Paris 1914, Introduction p.1, n. 1. It may refer, according to Chauviré, to the seven interlocutors who take part in the dialogue, and as each of them represents a different religion, to a sevenfold interpretation of the one natural religion. Chauviré also considers that this title may be reminiscent of Pico de la Mirandola's *Heptaplus.*

3. At the end of his life he changed his mind on this point.

4. It was not published in its entirety until 1857 (Schwerin, Paris and London) by L. Noack. This edition, which will be referred to in the present paper, is a very faulty one.

5. See Naudé, *Bibliographia Politica,* Venice 1633, p. 48, quoted by Chauviré, p. 4, n. 2.

6. According to a piece of information transmitted by Diecman (see Chauviré, *op. cit.,* p.2), this story is based on the fact that at a certain time four persons used to have regular meetings in Venice and that the well-known Christian cabbalist, Guillaume Postel, served as secretary at these gatherings. His papers are supposed to have been used by Bodin in *Heptaplomeres.* This story seems to be unverifiable. In considering Bodin's method of writing the fact should be taken into account that he sometimes uses the same Hebrew quotations and references both in *Heptaplomeres* and in earlier works. This similarity seems also to extend to certain passages embodying his own views. But the matter requires investigation.

7. See his entry on Bodin in *Dictionnaire historique et critique.* The article is reproduced in Pierre Mesnard's edition of *Oeuvres Philosophiques de Jean Bodin,* (Corpus Général de Philosophes Français, Auteurs Modernes, tome V, 3), Paris 1951; see p. xxiv. Bayle's phrase reads: "il y eut des gens qui le soupçonnèrent de Magie, ou qui assurèrent qu'il était mort Juif".

8. See P. Mesnard, *op cit.* (n. 7), pp. xi f. On Bodin's references to Jewish authors, see Jakob Guttmann, *Jean Bodin in seinen Beziehungen zum Judentum,* Breslau 1906. Cf. also J. Guttmann, "Der Einfluss der Maimonidischen Philosophie auf das Christliche Abendland", in *Moses Ben Maimon, Sein Leben, Seine Werke und Sein Einfluss,* ed. W. Bacher, M. Brann and D. Simonsen, Leipzig 1908, i, pp. 218–223. At the time of writing the present paper, I had not read G. Roellenbleck, *Offenbarung, Natur und jüdische Überlieferung bei Jean Bodin,* Gütersloh 1964. The point of view adopted in this scholarly work is somewhat different from the one taken up here.

9. Liberum, inquit, hominem diximus, quia causa sui est et quem aliena potestas cogere non potest. This appears to mean that man is endowed with free will.

10. He also criticizes Aristotle because he designates God as *animal.*

11. p. 24; Toralba refers to Averroes in the following terms: "Quod quidem Averroi adeo absurdum visum est, ut ab Aristotelis sententia discedens primam causam, quod esset infinita, segregaverit a coeli agitatione ac secundam causam orbi primo ac finito conjugarit, ne finita infinitis, sempiterna caducis necessaria connexionis serie copularet." The opinion summarized in this passage does not appear to accord with Averroes' views. The passage continues as follows: "Quae connexio necessaria eo absurdus est, quo mentes omnes ac formas a materia segre-

gatas simul ac semel a prima causa pendere scripsit Aristoteles, quam sententiam Avicenna et Averroes Academicos secuti repudiarunt, quia secundam causam a prima, tertiam a secunda certa serie derivari tradunt." This statement is correct with regard to Avicenna but may be inexact with regard to Averroes.

12. See P. Mesnard's edition of *Oeuvres Philosophiques de Jean Bodin,* I, pp. 228f.

13. Designated in this passage as Rabbi Moses Aegyptius. Bodin also occasionally calls him *Rambam.*

14. In *Heptaplomeres,* p. 170, Octavius the moslem contrasts Averroes and Avicenna. He quite clearly prefers the latter. The passage reads: Nihil mirum est, si Averroes Ismaelitarum religionem valere jussit, cum etiam Christianorum et Judaeorum leges foedissime proculcarit. Sed Avicenna, princeps in omni genere philosophiae et medicinae clarissimus, scribit legem Muhammedis miserias ac felicitatem summarum voluptatum corporis proposuisse, aliam tamen beatitatem lege praestabiliorem in animo habuisse.

15. In his paper: "Eternality of Punishment: a Theological Controversy within the Amsterdam Rabbinate in the Thirties of the Seventeenth Century," *Proceedings of the American Academy for Jewish Research,* 40 (1972), pp. 1–88. The paper includes the edition of Hebrew texts which are documents of a controversy concerning the eternality of punishment, whose main protagonists were Isaac Aboab de Fonseca and Saul Levi Morteira. The former takes up the position that no Jewish soul will undergo eternal punishment and claims that this view is derived from the teaching of the Kabbalah.

16. See Altmann, *op. cit.,* pp. 20f.

17. Pietatis speciem impie obtendunt.

18. Iniqua quadam pietate vel potius inexplebili pecuniarum aviditate.

19. Many of the relevant passages have been summarized in Jakob Guttmann's *Jean Bodin in seinen Beziehungen zum Judentum* (see above, p. 229, n. 8).

20. According to Philo, *De Opificio Mundi,* Loeb ed. i, pp. 137, 139f, 142f, 145f, Adam was not only "the first leader (of mankind)", but also "the first citizen of the world" whom God had endowed with a reasonable soul. Comparable statements on Enoch and Noah are to be found in *De Abrahamo,* Loeb ed., vi, pp. 3–6, 17–21; on Abraham, *ibid,* pp. 242f, 275f and in *De Migratione Abrahami,* iv, p. 128: "Walking in the track of right reason, his life was agreeable to Nature." On his wisdom, see Loeb ed., vol x, Index of Names, p. 278, note C. Naturally the predilection of *Heptaplomeres* for philosophising allegory left little room for midrashic exegesis of this kind. On rabbinic legends concerning Adam, see David Cassel, *Kuzari,* 2nd edition, Leipzig 1886, Book I, 95, pp. 62f. As for the references to Cain, some sympathy for him is expressed by Josephus, *Antiquities,* Loeb ed., i, pp. 57–59 and in greater detail in *Bereshith Rabba,* 22 towards the end: Cain had not received a specific warning and showed signs of genuine repentance (*Genesis,* 4:13f.)—hence the alleviation of his punishment. However, Judah Ha-Levi offers a still better key to the understanding of Salomo's statement: *Kuzari, locḤ cit.,* IV, 3, p. 302.

21. Deus igitur populi sui misertus quadringentos post annos, quam ictum foedus erat cum Abrahamo, Moysen excitavit, per quam naturalem et insitam animis hominum a Deo religionem ex animis hominum paene obliteratam ad usum revocavit. Toralba, the adherent of the natural religion approves of Salomo's statement. He also points out the connection of this religion with right reason (p. 142): "Constat igitur, optimam atque antiquissimam omnium religionem ab aeterno

Deo cum recta ratione mentibus humanis insitam, quae quidem Deum aeternum ac solum homini colendum proponit . . ."

22. In his commentary on the ten commandments ibn Ezra refers to them as implemented and acknowledged by all men of intelligence to whatever nation they may belong, but he does not refer to *dath ṭivᶜith,* a term which may have been introduced into Hebrew literature by Albo in his *ᶜIqqarim* I, ch. 7. The natural commandments and prohibitions of the Decalogue are seen by Philo as reconfirmation of God's covenant with Abraham, e.g., *De Abrahamo*, Loeb ed., vi, pp. 5f; *De Decalogo*, vii, 24, 154–178. Rabbinic, nonphilosophical examples on the subject have been enumerated by Bacher, *Tannaiten* i, pp. 392f., cf. *Ex. R.*, 46. Sprinkling of blood on the tablets of the law does not occur anywhere in biblical or midrashic literature. The passage clearly refers to the sprinkling of blood on the *altar* and on the people (*Exodus* 24:6–8).

23. No explicit statement to this effect appears to exist in Justin's *Dialogus cum Tryphone Judaeo*. This work does, however, contain several passages that refer to men, who having lived before the institution of the Mosaic law, did not keep the Sabbath nor observe various other commandments and nevertheless have to be regarded as righteous. It would, however, be ridiculous and stupid to suppose that God did not wish that men should always perform the same righteous actions. See *Dialogus,* 23, Migue, *PGL* 6, 525Df., cf. 19, (516–19), 27 (533Af.), 92 (696A).

24. Naturales vero justitiam perpetuo annexam habeant.

25. Capitibus.

26. Societas.

27. Sine quibus licet et viro bono in desertissima solitudine et ubique terrarum salutem adipisci. *Quibus* refers to *leges*. The text of the phrase is perhaps corrupt.

28. Philo's views on sacrifices are evaluated in Isaak Heinemann's *Philon's Grieschische und Jüdische Bildung,* Hildesheim, (repr., 1962), paragraph 2, Tempel und Opfer. Relevant general observations by Abraham ibn Ezra on sacrifices are to be found in his commentary on the first chapters of *Leviticus*. The mention of King Solomon and Leone Ebreo in this context seems to refer only to a few quotations from the *Dialoghi d'Amore,* which offer mystical interpretations of *Canticles,* but have no bearing on sacrifices or holy ceremonies.

29. One version of the text has *capita legum*.

30. For instance Irenaeus, see S. Pines, *La loi naturelle et la doctrine politico-théologique d'Ibn Zur'a, philosophe chrétien de Bagdad,* Scripta Hierosolymitana, ix, (Jerusalem 1961), p. 160, n. 18; cf. pp. 159f; R. W. Carlyle and A. J. Carlyle, *A History of Mediaeval Political Theory in the West,* London 1950, i, pp. 102f. Cf. also ii, p. 317, the Jurist Azo (*Summa Codicis* I, 18, 1711, where the expression *ius naturale decalogi* employed by the jurist Azo (*Summa Codicis,* I, 18, 11) is noted), *op. cit.*, ii, p. 31. In *Summa Theologica, qu.* XLIXa, 2, Thomas Aquinas discusses the relation between the law of the Old Testament (*lex vetus*) and the law of nature. He argues that moral precepts which according to certain opponents pertain to the law of nature only are also to be found in the Old Testament. He cites as examples of these moral precepts two commandments of the Decalogue. On the relation between the law of nature and the Decalogue, see also *qu.* C, a. 3. According to the *Summa Theologica,* the ceremonial and the judicial (commandments) lost their validity with the advent of Christ, see 4, 1, *qu.* 103 a.3. and 4, and *qu.* 104 a.3. See Beryl Smalley, "William of Auvergne, John of La Rochelle and St. Thomas Aquinas on the old

Law," *St. Thomas Aquinas* 1274–1974, *Commemorative Studies,* Toronto, 1974,ii, pp. 11–71. On Abraham ibn Ezra see also above, p. 231, n. 22. For a comparable, though again not identical concept cf. *Wisdom of Solomon,* ed. Charles, 18:4; *Testament of Levi, ibid.,* 14:4.

31. *ʿIqqarim,* III, 25, ed. I. Husik, Philadelphia 1946, iii, p. 218.

32. Cf. *Romans* 2:14–15.

33. The text may be slightly corrupt.

34. The natural order: Abraham, Isaac, and Jacob is interrupted by Job. Cf. Ginzberg, *Legends of the Jews,* v, pp. 381f.

35. Cf. *Gen.* 26:4f. See however, also 17:14.

36. Caetera vero, quae legibus ritualibus ac judiciariis continebantur, sublato Dei Templo et eversa republica Hebraeorum antiquata fuere. Nam diserte prohibemur usquam terrarum pecudes mactare nisi eo loco, quem nominatim Deus designarat. Decalogus tantum ac circumcisio cum agno paschali ad sempiternam acceptorum beneficiorum memoriam a nobis usurpatur. Sic autem persuasum habeo, nullam omnino religionem sine ritibus ac ceremoniis consistere posse. . . .

37. In the context this seems to be the only possible meaning which can be ascribed to *antiquata.* The same word is used in the comparable text of the Vulgate in *The Epistle to the Hebrews* 8:13. The preceding lines, 8–12, are to be understood in connection with *Jer.* 31:31–34. See, *inter alia,* Nestle, *Novum Testamentum Graece,* Stuttgart, 1956, pp. 559f. and Strack-Billerbeck, *Kommentar zum Neuen Testament aus Talmud und Midrasch,* Munich, 1926, vol. 3, p. 704.

38. Literally, make use of (*usurpatur*). The brief reference to the paschal lamb is obviously based on *Ex.* 12 and not on the customary domestic usage after the destruction on the Temple.

39. On p. 143; see above, pp. 219f.

40. Born, according to Gebhardt's hypothesis, in 1585.

41. See C. Gebhardt's edition of da Costa's works, *Die Schriften Uriel da Costa's.* Amsterdam-Heidelberg-London 1922, pp. 117f. The brief summary of da Costa's views here given poses some problems. To mention but one: his classification of the different kinds of laws does not conform to that of Albo, according to whom the Noachian commandments belong to the category of divine and not to natural law (cf. *ʿIqqarim* I, 7 and III, 14). Possibly (but admittedly the possibility is rather remote) da Costa's reference to the law of the sons of Noah is merely meant to make a point against the Pharisees, by calling to mind that they themselves admitted the existence of a true religion other than Judaism. On this reading, da Costa may not have intended to produce the impression that the commandments of the sons of Noah are identical with the law of nature, although such an identification was a matter of discussion in the 17th century Sephardic community of Amsterdam. Cf. I. S. Revah, *Spinoza et Juan de Prado,* Paris–The Hague 1959, p. 19, n. 2.

42. Discernit inter justum et injustum, inter foedum et pulchrum. It may or may not be relevant that according to Albo's *ʿIqqarim* (I, 7), it is the purpose of the natural religion to repress wrong (*ha-ʿawel*) and promote right (*ha-Yosher*), whereas the purpose of the conventional (*nimmusith*) is "to repress what is unbecoming (*ha-Megunneh*) and to promote what is becoming (*ha-Naʾeh*); Husik's translation. There is an exact correspondence between the two Hebrew antitheses *ʿawel* and *yosher* on the one hand and *megunneh* and *naʾeh* on the other, and the antitheses in da Costa's phrase.

43. Cf. *op. cit.,* (n. 41).

44. On him see I. S. Revah, *op. cit.*(*Supra,* p. 232, n. 41).

45. Revah, however, on whose edition this judgment is based, has not published Orobio's *Epistola Invectiva* in full.

46. See Revah, *op. cit.,* p. 86.

47. References to the laws of Noah may also be found at the end of the 16th and the first half of the 17th century in works by English authors or published in England. See S. Stein, "Philippus Ferdinandus Polonus", *Essays in honour of J. H. Hertz,* London 1942, pp. 405f.

48. In R. H. M. Elwes's translation. This translation is used in the present paper whenever passages of the *Tractatus* are quoted. Occasionally the wording has been slightly modified.

49. Praeter legem naturalem, qua omnes mortales tenentur.

50. Et eo destructo, non amplius tanquam jussum singularis imperii, sed catholicum Rationis documentum haberi potuisse; Rationis, inquam, nam Catholica Religio nondum ex revelatione innotuerat.

51. Absolute igitur concludimus, Religionem sive ea Lumine Naturali sive Prophetico revelata sit, vim mandati accipere ex solo eorum decreto, qui jus imperandi habent.

52. See S. Pines, "Spinoza's *Tractatus Theologico-Politicus,* Maimonides and Kant," *Scripta Hierosolymitana,* 20, (Jerusalem 1968), pp. 28f.

53. The last part of this passage reads in Latin: "Dei aeternum verbum et pactum, veramque religionem, hominum cordibus, hoc est humanae menti, divinitus inscriptam esse; eamque verum esse Dei syngraphum, quod ipse suo sigillo, nempe sui idea, tanquam imagine suae divinitatis consignavit."

54. Cf. *Jer.* 31:33 and *The Epistle to the Hebrews* 8:10. See also *Supra,* p. 232 note 37.

55. In his *Ethics,* Part IV, Proposition XXXV and the Corollaries and *scholium* attached to the proposition, Spinoza speaks of the men who *ex ductu rationis vivunt.* He observes in the *scholium* that such conduct is rare. Yet he remarks, in Corollary II, that for man to live *ex ductu rationis* is to act according to the laws of his nature (*ex suae naturae legibus*).

56. Cf. also Pines, *Tractatus Theologico-Politicus,* (*Supra,* n. 52), p. 30.

57. One of the sentences in which the term *lex naturalis* occurs may be self-contradictory. It refers to the Hebrews who lived in Egypt before the exodus and reads: "Dum enim inter alias nationes ante exitum ex Aegypto vixerunt, nullas leges peculiares habuerunt, nec ullo nisi *naturali jure,* et sine dubio etiam jure rei publicae in qua vivebant, quatenus *legi divinae naturali* non repugnabat, tenebantur". *Lex divina naturalis* is certainly identical with *lex naturalis,* by which, according to Spinoza's expression in the same passage, *omnes mortales tenentur*; as has been shown, it is the moral law. *Jus naturale,* on the other hand, is the technical term which Spinoza uses to designate the right of an individual to do—within the limits of his power—whatever he desires. The term is defined in chapter XVI, from which the following sentence may be quoted. "Jus itaque Naturale uniuscujusque hominis non sana Ratione, sed cupiditate et potentia determinatur", "the natural right of the individual man is thus determined not by sound reason, but by desire and power." If we assume, as we may legitimately do, that in the sentence quoted at the beginning of this note *jus naturale* has its usual meaning, the reference to *lex divina naturalis* makes no logical sense. It could, however, be supposed that Spinoza mentioned in this context *jus naturale* in order to hint to the careful reader that his use of the

notion of *lex divina naturalis* was mere window-dressing and was not to be taken seriously. In a way the contradiction is compounded by Spinoza's statement in chapter XVII, that "after [the Hebrews'] liberation from the intolerable bondage of the Egyptians, they were bound by no covenant to any man and therefore entered into their natural right that extended to whatever was in their power; and every man could deliberate whether to retain it or give it up, and transfer it to another" (*jus suum naturale ad omnia quae possent iterum adepti sunt . . .*) In chapter V, Spinoza describes the Hebrews when they left Egypt as being "unfit to frame a wise code of laws and to keep the sovereign power vested in the community; they were all uncultivated and sunk in a wretched slavery." This statement may have been influenced by Maimonides' *Guide for the Perplexed,* III, 32; Cf. S. Pines, *Tractatus Theologico-Politicus* (*supra,* p. 233, n. 52), pp. 23f.

58. The fact that Salomo mentions two other commandments which the Jews observe after the destruction of the Temple and the state does not, as has already been stated, seem to me to be of great significance in the context of our discussion. In two of his writings Hermann Cohen expressed surprise that Spinoza should not not have read *Heptaplomeres,* a work which in his time had a wide circulation and was known to Leibniz and Thomasius. He mentions in this connection Bodin's glorification of Judaism and his critique of the New rather than that of the Old Testament. The impression produced by these passages is that Cohen tended to believe that Spinoza was acquainted with *Heptaplomeres*; see Hermann Cohen, *Jüdische Schriften,* iii, p. 365 and *idem,* "Ein Ungedruckter Vortrag über Spinoza", *Festgabe zum Zehnjährigen Bestehen der Akademie für die Wissenschaft des Judentums,* 1919–1929, p. 53. In a reference to Cohen's remarks, Leo Strauss appears to take it for granted that Spinoza could not have known the contents of *Heptaplomeres* because it had not appeared in print at that time. See Leo Strauss, *Spinoza's Critique of Religion,* New York 1962, p. 25. This, of course, does not prove that Spinoza was not acquainted with the work. As we have seen, internal evidence suggests that he may have been. It should, however, be added that as Chauviré has shown (*op. cit.* p. 229, n. 2) pp. 4f.), the manuscripts of *Heptaplomeres* were not easily obtainable at the time of the writing of the *Tractatus,* i.e., in 1665–1669. In 1650–1651 Queen Christine of Sweden had had some difficulty in procuring a copy of the work. Similar conditions still seem to have prevailed in the early seventies. Later on the number of manuscripts increased. Eighty have been found in Germany alone. Reverting to an earlier period, we may add that a manuscript of *Heptaplomeres,* copied in 1630, which appears to have belonged to Grotius, is extant, and that reference is made to a manuscript which had been in the possession of John Milton.

Hebrew and Arabic in Medieval Jewish Philosophy

C. RABIN

The deep and lasting influence of Jewish philosophical works upon wide circles of Jewish readers in the middle ages and in modern times was achieved in their Hebrew form, either original or translated from the Arabic. The translations are almost all couched in an awkward, difficult style, that carries into the Hebrew many semantic and syntactical features of the Arabic original, and even the original Hebrew works affect for the most part a similar arabicizing idiom, whether their authors were speakers of Arabic or of European languages. Of one author, who wrote a work in the most obscure arabicized syntax, R. Levi ben Gerson, it is usually assumed that he could not read Arabic at all.[1] The present essay is an attempt to throw some light upon two questions: why the Jewish philosophers in Spain and the East wrote their works in Arabic, and why these Arabic works were translated into the particular form of Hebrew in which we know them. The suggestions offered are based upon the comparatively recent discipline of sociolinguistics, which investigates language in its role as one of the manifestations of human societies. It should be added that sociolinguistic research is mainly concerned with present-day linguistic problems, which it attacks with sophisticated methods of statistics, attitude research, and the like; such methods can, needless to say, not be applied to past periods, and therefore our remarks are in the nature of extrapolations from situations found and observed today, not of documented and measured direct observations. The facts which we shall seek to interpret are all well known, and need no elaborate documentation.

Except for a short eclipse from the third century C.E. onwards, the exact length of which has not yet been determined,[2] Hebrew was during the middel ages[3] a language alive in written, though not in spoken use. The use of the term "alive" may strike many readers as strange, especially since we speak—rightly—of the revival of Hebrew in the late nineteenth century, when the language began to be spoken once more. Of course, the application of terms like life and death to languages is merely metaphorical, and refers not to the language but to its use, i.e., to a state in the particular society which uses, or could be expected to use, that particular language. We may call a language dead when it is not used in the recognized social activities of any society whatsoever. Thus ancient Egyptian or Babylonian are dead languages. The fact that they are studied at universities and read by those who have mastered them does not make them alive, because neither Egyptologists nor Assyriologists are human societies in the accepted sense (though they may form "Societies"), nor are they to be considered living in virtue of the fact that menus of learned congresses in these disciplines have occasionally been couched in one of these languages. But if an existing national or religious group, or a part of this group with the knowledge and sanction of the whole group, uses a language for any purpose whatever, we shall have to call that language a living language. We may distinguish between a fully living language, meaning one in which a society carries on all activities for which it uses speech, writing, or reading, and a language of restricted life, or a language "alive in the activity (activities) *x*," where the society uses other languages for some of its activities. Fully-alive languages seem to be the exception rather than the rule, since many nations employ for some of their activities a language or languages other than that which they speak in informal communication. When an existing language adds to its fields of activity a new one of some importance, the term "revival" is often used.[4] The terminology suggested here conflicts with one employed frequently, by which those languages only that are spoken in everyday communication are granted the designation "living;" but such a usage is unable to account for the many situations intermediate between this and a language not used by anybody, or for cases in which spoken languages are not used for important cultural activities of the society in question. Widely used designations like "the revival of Irish" or "the revival of Lithuanian" show that this terminology is not taken seriously, since both these languages were spoken before the "revival," the former by a part of the Irish people, the latter by the entire Lithuanian nation. Besides, languages of restricted life, which according to this terminology should be called "dead," have in many cases exercized tremendous influence in the societies using them—a fact of which medieval Hebrew is one of the outstanding examples.

The areas in which a language of restricted life is used can best be defined by employing another concept of recent introduction, the terminology of *registers*. A register is a form of speech, distinguished by linguistic features, which is employed by members of a given society in given societal circumstances as a matter of habit or convention.[5] Examples of this are prayer, formal lectures, scientific articles, faculty club chitchat, adolescent slang, a doctor's way of talking to a patient, officialese, and journalese. The range of registers differs from society to society and from period to period, just as the sanctions differ which society imposes on those who willfully or out of ignorance use the wrong register, as Eliza Doolittle does in *Pygmalion*. When the linguistic features distinguishing registers are sufficiently pronounced to cause the speakers to relate to them as different languages, or for the outsider to gain that impression, we speak of *diglossia*.[6] The limits between the different languages in a diglossia situation may of course run at quite different levels of social life in different societies. However, every language of restricted life is part of such a diglossia situation, and its use—active or passive—is regulated by the social mechanism of registers.[7] This means, above all, that members of such a society do not have free choice in using the language in question, but are acting according to social habits and conventions, which they can only ignore at some risk. Owing to the way in which social conventions are internalized by members of society, it needs unusual individuals to effect a change in what they have been brought up to consider as natural and "right" and which they normally will justify by various rationalizations.

To these rationalizations belongs also the idea that the Hebrew language is poor in means of expression as compared with the richness of Arabic.[8] It is of course well known that there are no intrinsically "poor" or "rich" languages, but that every human language, by the very fact of being a language, contains within itself generative possibilities which enable it to deal with every field of human activity or thought, both grammatically and syntactically. What is more, the Hebrew language demonstrated the truth of that statement very shortly afterwards, by dealing effectively in translation with those very matters with which it is supposed to have been unable to deal during the golden age of Spanish Jewry. It is difficult to believe that men who could handle the Hebrew language as skillfully as did Ibn Gabirol and Judah Ha-Levi would not have been able to apply the generative processes carried out by the members of the Ibn Tibbon and Qimḥi families and others whose command of the language was—with the exception of al-Ḥarizi— probably much inferior to theirs. Ibn Gabirol showed himself quite adept at expressing philosophical ideas in his *Kether Malkhuth*, and that despite the double set of restrictions he imposed upon himself, by poetical form and a largely biblical language.[9] However, it should be noted that the term "richness" is in this statement applied in a curious manner: if Arabic is considered one of the richest of the languages of older times, this refers to the language of Arabic poetry and artistic prose. The language of philosophy and science, to which the statement refers, was not particularly rich; it was in fact Middle Arabic, a kind of poor relation of the Arabic of belles lettres.[10] Even within this Middle Arabic that written by Jewish authors held a special place and was probably considered even less elegant than that written by Moslem philosophers and scientists. On the other hand, in the very field that Arabic was without doubt rich—and the only field which the Arabs themselves considered worthy of attention from the linguistic point of view— Hebrew poets had no hesitation in competing with Arabic, and Jewish writers took care to point out that Hebrew was of greater nobility[11] and at least equal beauty. It seems, therefore, that what we have here is a conventional sentiment, and that the reason for the language behavior[12] of the Jews in Arabic-speaking countries during the middle ages is a different one. The suggestions offered in the following paragraphs are in the nature of a model, the justification of which depends on how well it fits both known facts and facts that may yet emerge in research owing to new material (e.g., from the Genizah), or to the model itself directing attention to details the significance of which it enhances.

Neither Hebrew nor Arabic were at the time simple monolithic linguistic entities. Each had varieties which served as registers, and these varieties were well differentiated by the Jewish intellectuals. In Hebrew we can distinguish the following registers, which in this particular case were contemporary reflections of the language of earlier periods:[13] biblical Hebrew,[14] which served poetry and artistic prose; mishnaic Hebrew, with an Aramaic admixture, which we find in halakhic literature,[15] although in that field Arabic was also used; paytanic Hebrew, used for liturgical poetry until the generation of Solomon ibn Gabirol, but abandoned by Ibn Ghayyāth and Isaac b. Reuben in the next generation although they still kept the form of the *piyyuṭ*;[16] subsequently this register was displaced in liturgical poetry by the biblical Hebrew one, having been denigrated by Abraham ibn Ezra.[17] The relative paucity of halakhic works in Hebrew and the ultimate rejection of paytanic Hebrew and of the *piyyuṭim* themselves from the synogogue rite show that the tendency was towards the restricting of the Hebrew registers to the biblical Hebrew one exclusively, even if this meant foregoing one Hebrew register altogether, since biblical Hebrew was felt to be unsuitable for halakhic discussion.[18]

The registers of Arabic were: the literary Arabic of poetry, carefully maintained in its purity by an array of grammarians and lexicographers; colloquial Arabic, rarely written and completely uncultivated; and a range of prose styles which differed by the concessions they made to the colloquial, and for the most part belong to Middle Arabic. It is probable that there was also a corresponding range of spoken semiliterary styles.[19] In addition there was colloquial Spanish, spoken in all probability by Moslems and Jews alike. It is not clear whether colloquial Arabic and colloquial Spanish were distinguished as registers for different social purposes, or coexisted as regional or class dialects.

If we consider the structure of registers in both these languages, it will be seen that the Jews shared most of the structure with the Moslems, except for the poetical register, which was Arabic in the case of the Moslem and Hebrew in the case of the Jew. Moreover, the attitude of the Jew towards the poetical register was the same as that which the Moslem had towards his: the use of biblical Hebrew in contemporary poetry was dominated by the opinions of grammarians and lexicographers, and the ruling opinion was that in accidence and vocabulary no addition to the established usage was allowed. Just as the Arab grammarians and lexicographers concerned themselves entirely with the language of poetry and neglected the language of prose, so the Hebrew grammarians and lexicographers restricted their efforts to biblical Hebrew.

The linguistic difference between Jews and Moslems is not exhausted by the above enumeration. Both groups also had several passive registers concerned with holy scripture, edificational literature, and prayer. These were of course Arabic for the Moslem (Koran, *Ḥadīth*, and prayer), while they were Hebrew for the Jew (Bible, Mishnah, and Midrash, the prayer book), although in the case of the Bible Hebrew was underpinned by the existence of written Arabic translations, by the system of teaching children Bible through word for word translation, and by the dictionaries and grammars, which were written in Arabic. The Jew in the Arab countries did not follow the example of the Christian in arabicizing also his religion. Moreover, the text of the Hebrew Bible filled two distinct social functions—that of sacred scripture for religious activities and that of classical poetry and linguistic source for imitation; in the Moslem sector these two functions were to a large extent divided between the Koran and the corpus of pre-Islamic poetry.

There is no doubt that there is much substance in L. Blau's explanation[20] that to learn Arabic to the degree of capability to write acceptable poetry necessitated an investment of time that Jews of the intellectual class preferred to devote to those studies which the Jewish religion demands; moreover, it seems unlikely that Jews would have been admitted to the educational institutions in which such knowledge could be obtained. There can nevertheless be little doubt that some Jews did learn to read and understand the works of Arab grammarians, lexicographers, and theoreticians of poetry, since these works are reflected in corresponding Hebrew treatises. The many details of Arabic poetical style which I. Goldziher was able to trace in Spanish Hebrew poetry[21] show that some poets at least were familiar with Arabic poetry, and such familiarity is also evidenced by the very adaptation of Arabic metres to Hebrew and by the expert way in which permitted alternatives in Arabic metrics were exploited in order to make it possible to use them for the Hebrew language with its very different statistical distribution of long and short (in Hebrew: reduced) vowels.

At the time when the Arabic metres were adapted to Hebrew, Hebrew possessed a lively poetical tradition of its own, the *piyyuṭ*, and there was no intrinsic need for making such a complicated adaptation of metres foreign to the language. Even if it was felt that Jewish society needed secular poetry, this could of course have been evolved out of the forms of the *piyyuṭ* with much less trouble. It appears, therefore, that the view expressed by several scholars is right, namely that the Arabic metres were introduced in order to prove the equality of Hebrew with Arabic in the artistic sphere, in other words, for ideological, or as we would today say nationalistic reasons. It is hardly accidental that the creation of a Hebrew poetry on the Arabic pattern followed closely upon Saʿadiah's revival of purist biblical Hebrew as a vehicle of artistic prose, both the type of prose and the use of highly-controlled language being innovations that had their model in Arabic literature of the time. The remarkable fact is that it was Saʿadiah himself who translated parts of the Bible into Arabic, wrote an Arabic commentary on them, wrote a book on philosophy in Arabic, and was the first to write on Halakhah in that language.[22]

This is a deliberate act of language revival, in the sense that the Hebrew language gained a sphere which it had not possessed before.[23] The model for this sphere was taken from the language behavior and cultural activities of the Arab society with which the Jews of the Arab countries had entered into a close symbiosis. In view of the great importance which poetry and rhetoric held in Arab society, the exercise of these two was a kind of entrance ticket to that civilization. Short of complete assimilation, this could only be achieved by imitation with one's own resources, by the kind of competition which in the writings of the period went under the name of *Shuʿūbiyya.* Several of the subject populations strove for it, but apart from the Jews, only the Persians achieved it in that period. Rudakī, the founder of Persian poetry, died almost at the same time as Saʿadiah (941/2). The creation of Arabic-style Hebrew poetry and rhymed prose completed the process initiated by Saʿadiah. It should be noted that the Jews living in Moslem countries did not extend their revival to include another prestige activity of Arab civilization, the writing of history. Oddly enough, this was achieved in areas lying just outside the territory of Islam, viz., in Italy, where *Sefer ha-Yashar* and *Yosippon* were written in that period, and in Christian Spain (Toledo), where at the very end of our period a contemporary of Maimonides, Abraham Ibn Da'ud, composed historical works. All these works were written in biblical Hebrew, just as in the Arab world histories were written in a highly rhetorical language close to that of poetry and at times in rhymed prose and parallelism.

With the establishment of prestige registers in a highly controlled language on the Arab pattern, it is only natural that Jewish society in Arab countries should also mirror the attitude of Moslem Arab society to other language uses. This was characterized by the dichotomy between the activities that required rhetoric and controlled language, such as poetry, essays, history, and official correspondence, and those that did not, in which a language with a certain colloquial coloring was in order. To these belonged not only philosophy and natural sciences but also the disciplines serving prestige and religious literature, for instance the writing of commentaries, grammars, and dictionaries. Among the Jews, the latter variety was carried on in an Arabic closely resembling that used by the Moslems, but written in Hebrew characters and with some specific Jewish traits,[24] reflecting probably the well-known phenomenon of separate Moslem, Jewish, and Christian dialects in colloquial Arabic in Arab countries.

The writing of treatises on medicine, natural sciences, and philosophy was not an activity for which there existed Hebrew works from before the period of Arab influence, in the way that there was an existing poetry in (paytanic) Hebrew, and there was consequently also no established register for dealing with these subjects. In a community in which attachment to and pride in the ethnic language had for centuries previously been concentrated upon scripture and poetry, and which had been accustomed to the use of two languages for written expression—mishnaic

Hebrew and Aramaic—there was no reason to embark upon creating a new register in Hebrew for this purpose; and the existing Arab custom, to write about these matters in a language related to the spoken idiom rather than the prestige language, was taken over without difficulty as an extension of the prevailing diglossia. In fact, as Blau has pointed out,[25] Arabic displaced Aramaic, not Hebrew, and entered into all activities in which Aramaic had previously been used. For the Jews of North Africa and Spain, Arabic similarly took over from Greek and Latin. We know nothing of any special attachment of Jews to any of these languages: they were purely functional vehicles of communication, and their use by Jews did not involve participation in the culture of the majority of speakers of these languages. Indeed, the use of Hebrew letters for writing Arabic may well have been transferred to that language from Jewish Aramaic,[26] but in the event it reinforced the nonparticipation of the Jews in the culture of the majority of speakers of Arabic. In the uses to which the Jewish community put written Arabic, it was as much a functional vehicle of communication as Aramaic and the other languages had been, all the more since this coincided with the view of the majority towards the type of Arabic registers which were in use among Jews. Only if the Jews had written poetry in Arabic would they have become involved actively in the culture of the majority group.

The use of Arabic for these purposes was not merely a matter of personal convenience. We may be inclined to imagine the Jewish intellectual of the time in the image of the modern Western European or American Jewish intellectual educated at school in the literary registers of the majority language[27] and finding it difficult to learn to read Hebrew discussions of intellectual problems. There was no education in the reading of contemporary intellectual discussion either for Jew or for Moslem, and the Jew was of course excluded from the Moslem *madrasa*, which transmitted traditional texts; nor were there texts of intellectual discussion of contemporary ideas in Hebrew to face the hypothetical Judaeo-Arab intellectual with the dilemma that faced, say, the German Jew before 1930 who was unable to read the books written in Hebrew in recent times. Yet, the ability to read the Arabic of scientific prose was not merely a question of knowing the Hebrew rather than the Arabic alphabet. Even though different from the elegant Arabic of artistic writing, literary Middle Arabic had forms and constructions not current in the colloquial language, not to mention an extensive vocabulary not found in everyday speech. If we consider that the Jewish intellectual would probably have had a fairly thorough Jewish education, based entirely on Hebrew texts both in biblical and mishnaic Hebrew, we may well ask ourselves whether the effort involved in acquiring scientific Arabic was really smaller than it would have been in the case of a scientific style evolved out of the style of the Mishnah or the Bible. The existence in European libraries of so many manuscripts of scientific works by non-Jews transcribed into Hebrew characters at least suggests that the hypothetical Jewish intellectual did not have such ready access to the works of non-Jews as to make it necessary for Jewish writers to accommodate themselves to reading habits acquired by their public before it might have become interested in Jewish writings.

To sum up: the dichotomy between artistic writing in biblical Hebrew and scientific writing in Arabic during the golden age of Spanish Jewry was a Jewish adaptation of the structure of language registers prevailing in the area and period in which they lived, with biblical Hebrew holding in the structure the place occupied elsewhere by classical Arabic; and Jewish Middle Arabic in Hebrew characters the place of Middle Arabic in the majority culture. These were fixed parts of a system of social conventions and habits that left no real choice to the individual.

The only areas of choice were grammar and *halakhah*. In the first-named field, there was extensive use of Hebrew in the debates of Menaḥem and Dunash and their respective disciples during the tenth century, but after that Arabic apparently became dominant; in the second, Arabic seems to have predominated from Saᶜadiah onwards, but some Hebrew was written. It is not clear whether the transition to Arabic for *halakhah* led to the cessation of the active use of mishnaic Hebrew in Spain, or whether the negative attitude to mishnaic Hebrew, proved by the lack of interest the grammarians showed in it, led to the adoption of Arabic as a vehicle of halakhic writing.

All that has been said refers to Jews in Moslem countries only. The sociolinguistic structure was quite different in Christian Europe. There was also diglossia, but the line between Hebrew and the spoken languages of the Jews ran exactly where it ran amongst most of Christian communities: at the point of writing. Thus there were much more variegated uses and registers of Hebrew than were available in Arabic-speaking Jewry.

As far as I can see, the beginning of the change in the system of registers in Sephardi Jewry came through contact with the Jews of Christian countries. Men like Abraham bar Ḥiyya (Savasorda) and Abraham Ibn Ezra wrote in Hebrew for Jews in Christian countries. Isaac b. Reuben of Barcelona (b. 1043) translated Hai Gaon's *Sefer ha-Miqqaḥ we-ha-Mimkar*[28] in an area which had been only for a very short time under Moslem rule and which in his own time was united with Provence. We may but assume that Moses Ibn Giqaṭilla, though he lived at Saragossa in Moslem Spain, translated two treatises of the grammarian Ḥayyuj not for his fellow citizens but for Jews in Christian lands. Whether translation of scientific literature began with Judah Ibn Tibbon, or before him, it was geared to Jews in Christian Europe, and it employed their type of Hebrew based on mishnaic language. The transition is marked in Maimonides, who in his *Code* not only returned to the use of Hebrew in halakhic writing but consciously chose mishnaic Hebrew;[29] he arranged for the translation of his *Guide of the Perplexed* into Hebrew and expressed his regret at having used Arabic in some of his works.[30] Although Maimonides' son still wrote a major work in Arabic, on the whole Spanish Jews, especially the exiles, from that time onwards begin to write in Hebrew.

This can be explained on romantic, "nationalist" grounds, and we do indeed find statements along such lines, e.g., in Profiaṭ Duran. However, there is a sociological explanation: the growing extremism and intolerance of Islam in Spain and the persecutions and expulsions loosened the cultural link between the Jewish and Moslem communities; and this made it easy for the Sephardi refugees to assimilate to the sociolinguistic habits of the Jewish communities in which they settled. Arabic ceased to be functional in communication, but for the Sephardi intellectual became part of a precious heritage, in which the differentiation between classical prestige Arabic and functional Middle Arabic was gradually blurred and the Arabic of scientific texts acquired something of the aura of the Arabic of poetry.

It is this phenomenon, which can be paralleled from other Jewish emigrant groups, that I would venture to suggest as the reason for the linguistic character of the translations made in southern France and in Italy from Arabic into Hebrew. Much has been written about the difficulties the translators encountered in rendering Arabic technical language into Hebrew. It is to be noted, however, that they generally solved their terminology problems in a satisfactory way by loan translation.[31] Where they failed—to our mind—was in clinging to imitations of Arabic syntactical constructions even where there was no difficulty in rendering them into idiomatic Hebrew, e.g., in putting the demonstrative pronouns in front of the noun instead of after it or in distinguishing between relative clauses with determinate antecedents and those with indeterminate ones. What is more remarkable is that over-faithfulness to Arabic syntax becomes more pronounced as time goes on, and, as stated at the beginning of this article, it becomes so much a hallmark of philosophical style that it is adopted also by authors of original Hebrew works.

In trying to explain this, we must once more remember that the translators introduced a new register into the system of Hebrew in the community for which they translated. As often in the case of the translation of other important works—e.g., in Bible translations—the translators took syntactical features of the source language to be features of the register (or of the individual style) of the original author, and they therefore transferred them to the translated text. This is the more likely to happen the higher the esteem in which the source language is held. In the discussion on the right way to translate literature of classical antiquity, which engaged many minds at the time of Goethe, this process was called "bringing the reader to the original." In the event the method adopted by the Sephardi translators was very effective, because it immediately created a well-defined register.

An interesting by-product of this was that this new register penetrated into European Jewry at the same time as the fashion of writing poetry in Spanish style in biblical Hebrew and with Arabic metres. Thus the former opposition in Spain between biblical Hebrew for artistic writing and Arabic for functional writing was now replaced by one in which biblical Hebrew still held the same position, but a development of mishnaic Hebrew took the place of Middle Arabic. For the first time two types of Hebrew from different periods came to be opposed to each other as registers. That system lasted for centuries until the mishnaic register was dropped in the East European *Haskalah*.

NOTES

1. His syntax has been analyzed by Jonathan Joel in an unpublished Jerusalem thesis.

2. The question depends on the date assigned to the beginning of paytanic poetry. While Zunz's dating in the 8th century will hardly be maintained by anyone today, it is difficult to decide between J. Schirmann's dating in the 3rd cent. (*JQR* xliv (1953), pp. 141 f.) and E. Fleischer's in the 5th–6th (*Tarbiẕ* xl (1970–71), pp. 41 f.).

3. I.e., the period beginning with the ʾAmoraim.

4. For discussion of the term "revival," see C. Rabin in *Language and Texts*, ed. H. H. Paper, Ann Arbor 1975, p. 149; *Leshonenu Laʿam* no. 258/9, Sivan-Tammuz 5735, pp. 227–233.

5. In actual cases the matter is often complicated by interaction with language varieties not bound to occasions, such as local dialect, social class, age, sex, etc.

6. Cf. C. Ferguson, "Diglossia", *Word* xv (1959), pp. 325–40.

7. Note that in many diglossia situations one or both languages involved live a "full" life somewhere else at the same time.

8. Cf. M. Steinschneider, *Hebräische Übersetzungen* etc., Berlin 1893, p. xvii, and A. S. Halkin, "The Medieval Jewish Attitude Toward Hebrew", in *Biblical and Other Studies*, ed. A. Altmann, Cambridge, Mass., 1963, pp. 233–48, especially p. 239. It is not clear whether the Hebrew phrase employed, *qoṣer ha-Lashon*, means insufficiency of the language or insufficient ability of the writer in it (cf. Ben-Yehudah, *Thesaurus*, p. 6118).

9. On Maimonides, see below.

10. Cf. Joshua Blau, *The Emergence and Linguistic Background of Judaeo-Arabic*, Oxford 1965; id. "The Status of Arabic as used by Jews in the Middle Ages", *JJS* x (1959), pp. 15–23.

11. This was expressed by calling Hebrew the "mistress" and Arabic the "handmaiden" (i.e., Sarah and Hagar).

12. This term is widely used to cover all the sociolinguistic aspects of language.

13. There seems to be no term in general linguistics for a contemporary style self-consciously reflecting a past period of the same language. In Hebrew the term is *roved*, "layer."

14. It is essential to realize that biblical Hebrew, as used at this period, was not a pastiche of any definite style or period of the Hebrew of the Bible but a mixture

from all of them, containing also some features conflicting with all biblical varieties.

15. E.g., by Isaac Ibn Ghayyath (d. 1089), possibly by Barukh Albalia (1035–94). However, the "Introduction to the Talmud" ascribed to Samuel ha-Nagid has been shown to be a translation from the Arabic, since its beginning was edited by A. Cowley in the *A. Harkavy Festschrift*, St. Petersburg 1908, pp. 161–3. There is no foundation, though, for Cowley's surmise that the Nagid was the translator.

16. Cf. S. Bernstein, *Tarbiẕ* xi (1939–40), p. 46; on Isaac b. Reuben, cf. Moses Ibn Ezra, *Kitāb al-muḥāḍara*, ed. A. S. Halkin, Jerusalem 1975, p. 74, line 88. Bernstein, *op. cit.*, p. 299 calls the abandonment of paytanic language "a public movement."

17. Commentary on *Eccles.* 5:1.

18. This is stated by Maimonides in his preface to *Sefer ha-Miṣwoth.*

19. Such a variety used today is described by Gustav Meisels, *Oral Literary Arabic*, unpublished Jerusalem thesis, 1975.

20. *Leshonenu* xxvi (1961–2), p. 283.

21. *JQR* xiv (1902), pp. 719–36.

22. Cf. Y. Ta-shma in *Hebrew Encycl.* xxvi (1973–4), col. 199.

23. Cf. literature cited above, p. 244, n. 4.

24. On this cf. Blau, *JJS* x, pp. 15–23.

25. *Leshonenu* xxvi, p. 282 middle.

26. Note that in the case of Aramaic the writing was taken over with the language, and the development of a special Jewish ductus happened in the natural way.

27. Blau, *JJS* x, p. 17 quotes a formulation of this view from I. Friedländer in the collective volume *Moses ben Maimon, Sein Leben*, etc., i, Leipzig (Gesellschaft zur Förderung der Wissenschaft des Judentums), 1908, p. 423.

28. Printed Vienna, 1800.

29. Cf. his preface to his *Sefer ha-Miṣwoth.*

30. Cf. Halkin, (*op. cit. supra*, p. 244, note 8), p. 238.

31. Cf. G. B. Sarfatti, *Mathematical Terminology in Hebrew Scientific Literature of the Middle Ages*, Jerusalem 1968 (in Hebrew).

Some Observations on Yoḥanan Alemanno's Political Ideas*

E. I. J. ROSENTHAL

Fulsome praise of Lorenzo de Medici and the city-state of Florence, its democratic institutions, the political education that its fathers impart to their sons and of "wisdom as the beginning for political administration," might lead the reader of Yoḥanan Alemanno's commentary on the *Song of Songs* to expect a renaissance approach to political philosophy.[1] And yet, while Yoḥanan learned wisdom from his observations and acquired a keen, genuine interest in the theory and practice of politics in Florence (as is evident from the first part of the commentary), his ideas are those of a well-educated, medieval Jewish scholar steeped in Greek and hellenistic philosophy as transmitted by the *Falāsifa*. Politics as understood by the medieval Muslim and Jewish thinkers are very important, but rather as a means to an end—the highest good, or ultimate, true happiness—than as an end in themselves. In Yoḥanan's case they form an integral part of Solomon's wisdom and perfection in all human virtues to which the first part of the commentary, called *Shir ha-Maʿaloth li-shelomoh*, is devoted. Solomon's kingship is therefore taken very seriously, but this part leads deliberately on to the interpretation of the *Song of Songs* under the title of *Ḥesheq shelomoh* (*1 Kings* 9:1, 19), which is directed towards *devequth*, i.e., attachment to God as the goal of ultimate perfection. In addition to philosophy, Yoḥanan has recourse to kabbalah and the occult sciences (astrology, magic) in order to bring out the deeper, esoteric meaning of the book and the true character of Solomon's wisdom and perfection. Taking his bearings from information furnished by the Bible and midrash concerning Solomon, he offers a literal as well as an inner—philosophical and mystical—interpretation of kingship as rule over Israel and as reaching the tenth sphere (*malkhuth*) of the *baʿaley ha-Sefirah*. While the mystical and pneumatic interpretation[2] must be left aside from our treatment, both are essential elements in the character and perfect wisdom credited to Solomon; and in Alemanno's description literal and cabbalistic meaning and significance are so closely linked that one has to be on one's guard in order to decide which one of them is intended and relevant. That he was not an original thinker is true,[3] insofar as new ideas are concerned. But his knowledge is extensive, and is skilfully employed in singing the praises of King Solomon, who was wiser than Moses because his wisdom was not confined to Israel but comprised other nations—even, indeed, the whole world. He is careful to distinguish between Solomon's three biblical books and the mystical and pneumatic writings attributed to him, e.g., the *Sefer Raziʾel* and the books with which Abu Aflaḥ credits *Sulaymān al-yahūd* in addition to those mentioned by Apollonius of Tyana. He nevertheless quotes extensively from Apollonius and particularly from Abu Aflaḥ in order to enhance the greatness of king Solomon, who in his perfect wisdom had a passionate longing to be joined to God. Yoḥanan's philosophical explanations are extensive and range from Plato and Aristotle over Fārābī, Avicenna, al-Ghazālī, Ibn Ṭufayl, al-Baṭalyawsī, and Averroes; Saʿadiah, Judah Ha-Levi, Maimonides, to Narboni, and Shem Ṭov ibn Palqera. Their writings are adduced as proof and justification of the biblical report, especially in *Kings* and *Chronicles*, of the ethical and intellectual virtues of a king loved by God and one whose wisdom was recognised by the kings of the world (including the queen of Sheba). Nor does he neglect rabbinic literature (*Targum sheni* to *Esther, Yelammedenu, ʾEkhah Rabbathi,* and *Pireqey de-Rabbi ʾEliʿezer.*[4]) Yoḥanan divides philosophy—as was usual—into the theoretical and the practical, the latter comprising ethics, economics, and politics; naturally he produces the adage "man is a citizen by nature," and he often refers to the *ḥakhmey ha-Medinah* in support of his description of political virtues and institutions. He praises the laws of the Florentines as being based on wisdom, insight, knowledge, and every art (f. 19b), and explicitly states that he wrote the commentary at the behest of Giovanni Pico della Mirandola, who listened to extracts from it (f. 20a) and was much impressed. Yet in describing the royal qualities of King Solomon he has recourse to Plato's four cardinal virtues and especially to Aristotle's *Nichomachaean Ethics*, and indirectly to both in his frequent references to Fārābī's *Six Principles*[5] and *Division of the Sciences*,[6] and to Abu Ḥamīd (i.e., al-Ghazālī's) *Moʾzeney ṣedeq.*[7] Just as the biblical *hod, tifʾereth* and *malkhuth*, for example, have their counterpart and equivalence in the corresponding spheres of the kabbalah, so the Biblical *ḥokhmah, gevurah, kavod, mishpaṭ,* and *yosher* find their correspondence in Plato and Aristotle and are explained as political virtues essential for good government. One of the key passages is *1 Kings* 3:9, with its implications regarding justice as the primary political virtue after wisdom.

Yoḥanan distinguishes between physical and spiritual goods, which are all contained in the highest good and subdivided systematically within the categories of internal (*penimi*) and external (*ḥiṣoni*).[8] The inner physical and especially the spiritual goods reflect the qualities of the soul. Thus, while beauty is the first of the external physical goods, God looks for the inner royal virtues suitable for rulers of states, as Plato declares in his "philosophical (i.e., philosophers') city-state" (Yoḥanan likewise quotes from the *Republic*[9] that the ruler (*manhig*) must have the nature of the dog). He censures Samuel the Seer for not recognizing that Saul's beauty was confined to his appearance, in contrast to the beauty of Moses, and he draws the interesting distinction between *yefi malki* and *yefi hamoni*. Saul possessed the latter alone, whereas beauty as the first royal good must engender love in the people complemented by fear. Saul, since he was lacking in this quality, was despised by the people, whereas Solomon possessed the combination and like Moses was both loved and feared as Yoḥanan shows from *Samuel, Kings,* and *Chronicles.*[10] Just as all the members of the body submit to the heart, so all the nations, not Israel alone, submitted to him who was king by nature (*ṭevaʿ*), not by effort (*melaʾkhah*),[11] unlike Saul and David who were kings by necessity. For Yoḥanan it is clear from *1 Kings* 1:47f. that the young Salomon governed when David was old.[12] Physical health is necessary so that man can bring his soul near to true happiness, *devequth,* together with intellectual and ethical perfection. Theoretical and practical reason constitute intellectual perfection, and the tending towards the mean between two extremes secures an ethical perfection characterized by equity and justice (*shiwwuy wa-yosher*). In both perfections King Solomon excelled. Yoḥanan again refers to the political philosophers in support of this, and stresses that it is only true wisdom that leads to ultimate happiness. Solomon's *Song of Songs, Proverbs,* and *Ecclesiastes* testify to the three parts of health:[13]

> "The *Song of Songs* teaches (or guides to) the perfection of his [*sc.* Solomon's] intellectual perception; *Proverbs* is all education of the intellect, pointing to the health of just desire and the will: *Ecclesiastes* shows his agreement with his times, the pleasures of his places, and the thoughts of many nations . . . for all this is full of knowledge to distinguish with understanding between good and evil . . . ."[14]

Next comes the natural faculty, which is illustrated from *Exod.* 18, where Jethro gives advice to Moses, his son-in-law, concerning the qualities of judges ruling the city-state—Jethro being "wise in the wisdom of government (or political administration)." Solomon possessed these necessary qualities to perfection, as is shown in his statesmanlike treatment of Bathsheba, Adonijah, Ebiathar, Joab, and Shimei, "and he was strong in natural power as it befits a royal person."[15] Furthermore, Solomon, as a king, enjoyed "length of days" more than had anyone who had lived before him, so that he could extract truth from all the sciences.[16]

Wealth is the first of the external physical goods; it guarantees its owner self-sufficiency (so that in this he resembles God), provided that he uses his reason properly and trains his theoretical intellect so that wealth becomes the crown of the wise. He to whom God has given this gift can concentrate on the *intelligibilia* and rejoice in all the desires of his heart to do good in his life to himself and others as political philosophers agree. Solomon possessed greater wealth and wisdom than all the kings of the earth.[17] Yoḥanan then treats of honour, concerning which the political philosophers know through the fourth and ninth books of the *Nicomachaean Ethics.*[18] He claims, basing himself on *Kings* and *Chronicles*, that all the kings of the earth brought Solomon a gift which is, according to Aristotle, the greatest honour. Solomon owed this to "the wisdom which God gave into his heart more than to any other man." Noble birth is another advantage in acquiring the external physical goods (this glances at Judah Ha-Levi's *Kuzari,* and the idea of the nation of Israel being the heart and the other nations the branches). Solomon's descent from David and Bathsheba is then related to government (or statecraft, *ha-hanhagah ha-Medinith*), and the need of relatives as helpers (*goʾalim*) is stressed, these being both members of the family and friends, since "man is a citizen by nature." Yoḥanan has an eye for *Realpolitik*: David left Solomon his conquests in the form of a pacified kingdom subject to princes, judges, and overseers, and admonished them to be loyal to Solomon "and commanded them to help him in his kingship, because he was only a boy."[19] Yoḥanan defends Solomon for having put away Joab and Shimei in the interests of the state at his father's behest. The culmination was the building of the Temple, which will be dealt with below.

Of special interest is Yoḥanan's claim that David made Solomon king with the help of Nathan the prophet, Zadok the priest, and all the people; that having thereafter assembled all the princes of Israel a second time, he kept them until they and the people had accepted him as king; that he then crowned him a second time before God, as a *nagid*; and Solomon thus sat on the throne and ruled under his father, in his time and in his presence, in the sight of all Israel.[20] He continues: "would that Solomon had made his son king in his lifetime . . . for this would have prevented the sin of Jeroboam." In discussing Solomon's helpers Yoḥanan is constrained to admit that his foreign wives were not among his proper helpers, for they made him build high places for worshipping their idols. He defends Solomon's compliance despite the explicit prohibition of the Torah by the ingenious claim that Solomon, in his insatiable thirst for knowledge of the highest powers of purity, wanted to know the forces of impurity as well: the idol-worship of his foreign wives helped him in this. Thus it constitutes part of Solomon's *ḥesheq*.[21] He also accepts the legendary account in the Aramaic Targum (*sheni*) to *Esther* of Solomon conversing with the animals as a sign of the king's superior wisdom.

Yoḥanan then proceeds to discuss the various kinds of inner spiritual good. The first is *haskel* (*cognition, discernment, understanding*), which is divided into four constituent elements. Here he leans heavily on Fārābī and Avicenna.[22] We can but mention his treatment of political science as part of *ḥokhmah*, which is one department of human knowledge and understanding (the other two being *melaʾkhah* and *yediʿah*) and is divided into political and natural science. Political science comprises ethics, economics, politics, and jurisprudence,[23] "which the ancients did not know nor value," but Fārābī did. Natural science is then discussed, its divisions and parts significantly including speculation about the future as revealed in dreams, magic, sorcery, or prophecies. It goes without saying that the sole purpose of the whole discussion is to highlight Solomon's wisdom, which was greater than that of any man. Naturally he possessed the five intellectual virtues which Aristotle enumerates in Book VI of his *Nico-*

machaean Ethics: *melaʾkhah, daʿath, tevunah, ḥokhmah, sekhel*, to which Yoḥanan adds *raʿayon* and *maḥashavah*—faculties that Aristotle had rejected.[24]

Another key passage which he quotes is *1 Kings* 5:9, *and God gave Solomon wisdom (ḥokhmah) and insight (tevunah) in abundance and a comprehensive spirit* (*roḥav lev*) *like the sand upon the shore of the sea*; he remarks that *ḥokhmah* corresponds to *yediʿah* among the philosophers of the peoples, comprising "the divine, prophetic and intuitional sciences:" *tevunah* corresponds to what they regard as *ḥokhmah*, for the philosophers equated it with physics, which is for them a greater root (principle) than political science. Nevertheless, the prophets made use of *tevunah* because with them political science is the greatest root (principle). Hence the prophet (i.e., the author of *Kings*) credited "insight in abundance" to Solomon, in whom it was very strong in respect of "the science of the laws" when he judged by *ʾamatla* and not with the formal processes of the Sanhedrin and witnesses (which will occupy us later.) This distinction between philosophers and prophets, with their different emphases on theoretical and practical philosophy, is a significant aspect of Yoḥanan's attitude to philosophy and religion. Finally, *roḥav lev* is, for the philosophers, *melaʾkhah* (= *technē*), which comprises theory and practice "as is clear from Aristotle, Plato, Abu Naṣr (i.e., al-Fārābī), Ibn Rushd (Averroes) and those who followed them."[25] And yet for the prophets *roḥav lev* is more comprehensive, comprising as it does intellect (*sekhel*), *raʿayon* (imagination), and power of judgement (*maḥashavah*). Intellect (or intelligence) is one of the five intellectual virtues mentioned by Aristotle (as we have seen) in Book VI of his *Nicomachaean Ethics* and defined in his *de Anima*. This faculty is the beginning for all virtues and perfections, for through it the first *intelligibilia* are recognized and understood.

The intellect in its perfection is called by the prophet *roḥav lev, breadth of heart*, because it widens the heart of man for all the *intelligibilia* if he is healthy and perfect (complete) at the beginning of his creation. It is the essential ground for bringing man to true happiness. But, as Fārābī wrote in his *Six Principles*, few only are worthy to reach ultimate perfection.[26] Solomon possessed this faculty to the utmost degree of perfection from the very womb (f. 42b). To say that he was "wiser than any man" means both in Israel and the other nations, even though it is clear from the words of the rabbis (in the Talmud, *Yelammedenu*, and *ʾEkhah Rabbathi*, f. 43b) that there were many in the Israelite nation who possessed the right power of judgement. Yoḥanan refers to Maimonides' *Guide*, II, 37 for the theory of prophecy, with the latter's requirement of perfect imagination and intellect, and he stresses the importance of the imaginative and rational faculties for political government.[27] He contrasts Avicenna and Ghazālī, and their ideas about men who excel in both faculties and who know and understand the sciences without training, with Averroes, who insists in his *Paraphrase* of *de Sensu et Sensibili* on the need of training in the sciences. He is very explicit in his concern to prove that Solomon was possessed of perfect imagination and intellect; that he was granted sudden, intuitive perception; and that he was complete master of political government and had knowledge of hidden and future things. He justifies his claim by recourse, apart from the ancient and medieval philosophers, to the biblical prophets and the rabbis, Naḥmanides, Narboni, Joseph ibn Caspi, and many *ḥakhamim*, to "prove" Solomon's expertise in agriculture and building (especially the Temple, palaces, gardens), in trade and commerce, and by appeal to his holy books: *Proverbs* exhibits his perfection in rhetoric as explained by Aristotle, whereas the *Song of Songs* is a model of Aristotle's exposition of poetics. Altogether, Solomon was accomplished in linguistic expression, of which Yoḥanan enumerates six kinds: grammar, rhetoric, poetics, logic, magic (*leḥashim*), and the combination of letters (*ṣērufim*, as practiced in kabbalah).[28] There follows a lengthy description of Solomon's accomplishment in all the practical and theoretical sciences, an accomplishment which testifies to his high intellectual stature as requisite in a king (and other rulers), in conformity with the requirements of political science and the art of government and administration. But it clearly goes beyond politics, which are but one aspect, albeit an essential one, of human life and thought. Mastery of the sciences means that comprehensive knowledge which alone enables man to attain the highest, ultimate perfection to which, to repeat, politics as the royal art are the indispensable guide. Knowledge includes mysticism and magic, which is why Yoḥanan pays so much attention to the world of the kabbalah and to the occult sciences in which, according to Apollonius and Abu Aflaḥ, Solomon was so proficient, and to which he allegedly contributed so many books. The paramountcy of knowledge is, of course, a commonplace in both medieval Judaism and in Islam, and it is therefore understandable that Yoḥanan should mention that Naḥmanides praised Solomon's distinction in astronomy and that the *Sefer Razi'el* was attributed to him; but above all there stands the circumstance that Solomon prayed for knowledge rather than for the scepter and throne. In astrology he surpassed its masters in Egypt. Again and again Yoḥanan stresses Solomon's perfection in political science and claims that *Proverbs* is the greatest book to deal with ethics: "all the ethical writings of Aristotle, Plato and Abu Ḥāmid and others did not reach to his ankles."[29] His political sagacity is attested by *1 Kings* 10:1–9. *2 Chron.* 1:10–12 shows that wisdom and knowledge were suddenly conferred upon him by God, as is clear from "the Aramaic book of *Esther*," not only that he might judge by his sudden intuition in truth and righteousness; it indicates further that God also granted him the knowledge of what was secret and hidden. Apollonius is deemed to confirm the *Targum sheni* to *Esther*. Yoḥanan defends himself against possible criticism that he quotes merely the opinion of the practitioners of pneumatology in regard to Solomon's sudden intuition, by pointing to Gersonides' *Milḥamoth Ha-Shem* as testimony drawn from amongst the practitioners of speculation. Moreover it is confirmed by the astrologers, as is evident from Abu Jaʿfar's commentary on the *Sefer ha-Peri* (wrongly attributed to Ptolemy). In further defense of his assertion that Solomon judged by *ʾamatla*, without witnesses and the formal cautioning of such, Yoḥanan quotes Fārābī's definition of "jurisprudence which is included in political science" from the latter's *Division of the Sciences*: "in the science of the laws (*fiqh*, jurisprudence) man can obtain judgement in a matter which the lawgiver had not explained" (f. 53b).[30] That is precisely what Solomon did, and "all Israel submitted to him and to his kingship more than to his father David, of whom it is said 'David executed judgment and justice.'"[31] Yoḥanan proceeds to contrast with this submissiveness of the people to their king the choice by Cato of suicide in order not to have to see the subjection of his own people, the Romans, to a tyrannical king, and he praises freedom-loving peoples. This is one of the few passages where one can detect the spirit of the renaissance in Yoḥanan.[32] Yet it is clear from the further discussion of Solomon's wisdom in relation to that of Abraham and Moses, both of whom he surpassed, that Yoḥanan attaches great importance to his kingship over Israel and in relation to the tenth sphere, the gateway to God.

Since happiness is the concern of political science resulting in good government, Alemanno stresses that the Torah of Moses repeatedly insists that the observance of the prohibitions and the commandments secures the happiness and the understanding of the Israelite nation, whom Moses desired to lead towards attachment (*devequth*) to God. Whereas Moses' concern was with Israel only, Balaam and Solomon were interested in the other nations as well. That Solomon exceeded Moses in wisdom we know, according to Yoḥanan, from e.g. Menahem of Recanati's commentary to the Pentateuch. Yoḥanan also refers to *Proverbs* for corroboration, as he had done earlier in regard to Solomon's perfection in ethics, as also to *Ecclesiastes*.

Another political virtue is meekness (or humility, *ʿanawah*), acquired by just desire, intellect, and (practical) insight. The political philosophers define *tevunah* (practical insight or intelligence) as the bringing into existence of human goods, which are purposes for the practical intellect, together with just desire, so that the resultant actions are all midway between two extremes.[33] It is thus both an ethical and an intellectual perfection. It belongs to the realm of practical reason, being found in abundance in the Torah. Solomon excelled therein by always treading the middle path in all his works. Humility is subdivided into fifteen elements, the first of which is moderation, like that shown by Solomon to Adonijah.[34] Order and arrangement of the kingdom fall under *ʿanawah* in the sense of equilibrium and balance, which appear in the appointment and equipment of Solomon's servants according to the plan of the highest spiritual divine beings: in the words of the *Pireqey de-Rabbi ʾEliʿezer,* Solomon ordered his earthly kingdom like the heavenly one.[35] The king comprehensively planned and arranged the administration of his kingdom in an order characterized by observance of the middle way and the avoidance of extremes. The same middle path applied to his building work, the most important of which was the Temple. He did not enslave the Israelites, who were already the servants of the Lord, but he used slave labour from the neighbouring countries. His prayers were also fixed in a certain order, as were his daily needs. "Oppression that occurs between a man and his fellow, which cannot be handed over to a court of law for judgement, he delivered to heaven in the bitterness of his heart through prayer."[36] The last of the eight orders of prayer concerns the time of the redemption.[37] Yoḥanan stresses the role of prayer in politics and the close connection between religion and politics. At the same time he underlines the uniqueness of King Solomon. The same order obtained in the economy, especially in the king's expenditure. Liberality and greatheartedness are royal, truly human virtues, which Solomon in his kindness displayed to all who came to ask something of him, and especially those who came to listen to his wisdom. Yet throughout all his worldly wisdom Solomon's motivation was his passionate desire of attaining attachment to God, as is clear from his *Song of Songs*—called by Yoḥanan *ḥesheq Shelomoh*—which teaches man "the happiness of passionate desire and attachment to Him, may He be exalted" (ff. 72b–73a). Man should "rejoice in his lot, and his soul should content itself with the good that it has . . . and this is truly found in King Solomon and in his whole people that are under his dominion."[38] He then stresses the importance of congenial company—as the rabbis said, "Acquire thyself a companion," since, unless he lives in solitude, man needs the help of others; and man does not isolate himself, being a citizen by nature.[39]

Next among the "inner spiritual goods" is courage, which consists of eight elements, the first being the faculty of patience, i.e. "the good and strong will that gives man knowledge and the power to bear everything that is difficult for the *anima vitalis* and causes pain to the flesh." This is reminiscent of Plato's *Republic*. Solomon evinced this quality in all his work, especially in his building activity, together with zeal and speed in the enormous labor required in order to translate his imagination into action. In a manner typical of the author, biblical quotations (from *Kings* and *Chronicles*) jostle with philosophical disquisitions and midrashic legend. "While it was from the *merkabah* that he conceived the pattern, revealed to his father David through the Holy Spirit (*1 Chron.* 28:18), he was the wisest of men in the whole art of *tavnith* because his imagination was divine and his thinking was that of a prophet: his practical and his theoretical reason were in harmony." Kabbalah is laid under contribution as well, Solomon's zeal, industry, and quickness being compared to the first *sephirah*. The Temple is proof of "the eternal existence of God, who is different from all other eternal and noneternal beings and has no connection with any being; yet there is a hidden connection with the perfect ones who observe his *miṣwoth*, with whom He made a covenant when our forefathers went out of Egypt"—this establishes the connection of Solomon's Temple with the Torah of Moses, the tent of meeting described in which was so much smaller. The great sanctuary is witness to *YHWH*, the God who in his goodness bestows all benefits on Israel, in particular peace: it is a sign of Providence and of Promise. "As long as the Temple stood, no innocent blood of the righteous was shed."[40] In building the Temple from his own resources and not from the treasure provided for the purpose by David, Solomon displayed great liberality—the hallmark of that greatness of soul for which he was prepared by nature. After the rabbis, it is the turn of the political philosophers to be adduced, reference being made to Aristotle.[41] Solomon's principal concern was right and justice as objects of his greatness of soul, as is clear from his "throne of judgement" like which nothing was made for all other kingdoms; no claim could be made in regard to his natural greatness of soul in connection with the furniture and appurtenances of the Temple, since it could be claimed that Solomon learned of these from Moses. "For (just) judgement is but to lead the people towards the virtues . . . ."[42] "Moses judged the people from morning till evening . . . to lead his people to human perfection in his right judgements." In Yoḥanan's view, in greatness of soul Solomon excelled Moses, who did not know about man's evil nature and needed the advice of his father-in-law. "Divine *mishpaṭ* encompasses all high and exalted virtues; it, and righteousness (*ṣedaqah*) likewise, . . . are the great and true virtues which are known through intellectual comprehension and knowledge of God, which is absolute good and absolute perfection: in this God takes delight. Consequently Solomon tended towards this perfection (arising) from the divine *mishpaṭ* . . ." (f. 86a). In support of the view that Solomon surpassed all those who went before him in just judgement, Yoḥanan tells the story—in default, he says, of any statement from "the prophet" (i.e., *Kings* and *Chronicles*)—"from the Aramaic translators of *Esther*, the Mishnah and *Baraita*", not, indeed, literally, but in a general way. And what a midrashic presentation it is, telling how Solomon the king dispenses justice from the throne of judgement surrounded by all the animals! Quoting *Ps* 119:32, he extols "the widening of the soul," equating *nefesh* with *lev*, "for the divine commandments, being great and mighty matters for those who understand that they bind together the physical and the spiritual world, widen the heart of men very greatly . . . . Thus Solomon after completing the temple widened his own soul and that of the priests and levites and of all Israel his people, so that the *Shekhinah* should rest upon them . . . ."[43] The eighth and final element of courage is "strength of heart", which enabled Solomon to carry out his work to the utmost perfection.

Justice (or equity: *yosher*) is next treated, in a strictly philosophical context as opposed to the midrashic exposition of the administration of justice which we have already noted. "Justice consists of three elements, the first of which is free choice or will (*beḥirah*): *viz*., that man chooses good and rejects evil because free will comes from that equity (fairness) which is to be found in mankind. God gave man the concupiscent faculty linked with the faculty of practical reason . . . which relies upon the straight desire to know whether its judgements are truth and equity."[44] "The political philosophers defined free choice as desire stemming from those things which exist for the sake of the purpose by which practical reason judges" (f. 92a). This judgement is necessary, since reason only can distinguish between the right desire, leading to *ʿoneg*, and the wrong desire for *taʿanug* (enjoyment of the senses). The second element is externally acquired good (wealth, honour etc), and the third is "the principal royal good—just desire" (f. 93a). King Solomon possessed all three, since he was born with the virtue of justice, and already as a young lad acted in accordance with it. "It is the first of all the goods, and necessary for political association; a great crown for the kings of the earth" (f. 92b). When asked by God what he wanted, he asked for "the principal royal good," because he was young, and thus did not ask for wisdom, the greatest of all goods which his father possessed, as well as the externally acquired good. He knew that he ruled over the wisest nation on earth, but one that was full of daily quarrels and strife. He needed most the concupiscent faculty, so that he could always listen to the power of practical reason and thus be able to judge with justice. But God granted him all three.[45] The order of the faculties of the soul from which there proceed wisdom, understanding, courage, and meekness finds its parallel in the order of the state, in the relation between king and people. Justice (equity) is the guiding principle and requirement: "when all have these qualities justice is the beloved order, be it in the virtues or in worldly affairs (literally, trade, and commerce) to take and give what is proper, or in the arrangement of the state whose order resembles the order of the parts of the soul."[46] In this sense Yoḥanan quotes and interprets *Psalm* 72—David's prayer on behalf of Solomon—to show that Solomon possessed the political virtue of justice to perfection, not only for the governing and judging of the people of Israel but also for his personal life, culminating in the perception of God (ff. 94b–95a). In perfecting himself Solomon endeavored to perfect the wise amongst the people, by attempting to lead them in the direction of understanding God. That is to be achieved through an intellect "bright as the sun"—which leads Yoḥanan to distinguish between the theoretical intellect that receives its light from the active intellect and the prophetic intellect the light of which is its own. The perception of God can be achieved only if two conditions are granted: tradition from generation to generation and intellectual understanding (perception) through emanation—neither is sufficient in itself. The light of the divine intellect (presumably identical with the prophetic intellect) is needed, and the order and justice of Solomon's kingdom extended over the remaining nations: these allude to the matter of the messiah and the good which is hoped for in his days, his name being Yinnon (based on *Ps.* 72:17). Yoḥanan then switches from this rabbinic conceit to philosophy and kabbalah—Solomon's *Sefer Raziʾel*—until he reaches a discussion of *ḥesheq* with a shortened quotation from Shem Ṭov ibn Palqera in the name of Plato which Steinschneider has traced to Fārābī's *Plato's Philosophy*.[47] Without the passionate desire for

God (*ḥesheq ʾeloqi*) man cannot attain ultimate perfection. The passage runs as follows: "man must be prepared to be a philosopher [omitting 'and citizen' (or statesman)], rule over himself, think about nothing else and be *shaṭuf* ("swamped", i.e., possessed, enthusiastic, ecstatic). And he said that ecstasy (*sheṭifah*) and strong love (*ʾahavah*) enter in the end[48] into the matter of *ḥesheq* . . . (which) is divine madness (or folly, frenzy, enthusiasm: *shiggaʿon ʾeloqi*) . . . . Philosophy and true perfection can only be attained if the soul of man is possessed by the ecstasy of passionate love and madness divine . . . . And the end of his words is that perfection is only to be found in the man who loves and passionately desires divine things. And such was King Solomon, for at the beginning he loved (*ʾahav*), and (only) afterwards did he passionately desire, for love is incomplete (imperfect), whereas passionate desire and *ha-ḥesheq* is perfected *ʾahavah.* This can be seen from what is said of him at the beginning of his kingship: "and Solomon loved the Lord to walk in the laws of his father David (*1 Kings* 3:3), for that was the most perfect of the three loves that are explained from the mouth of the political philosophers—*viz.*, the love of the good and the useful and the agreeable."[49] But the real perfection is the intellectual and spiritual longing (*ḥesheq*) for *devequth* to God, as Yoḥanan somewhat prolixly sets it out up to the end of the first part in praise of King Solomon. Philosophy, kabbalah, and pneumatology are now combined to bring out the inner, hidden meaning of Solomon's wisdom and perfection beyond his political achievements, the two most important of which were the building of the Temple and sitting on the throne of judgement. Solomon's life was the complete success that it was because God aided him; his happiness was a gift from God. Alemanno wavers between philosophy and religion. Divine guidance is necessary, the human intellect is inadequate, and yet he praises metaphysics pursued throught the active intellect under divine guidance. With this aspect we cannot deal here. Suffice it to say, in conclusion, that in his literal interpretation of Solomon's kingship[50] Alemanno shows considerable knowledge of Plato and Aristotle and of their Muslim and Jewish interpreters; and that whilst he has a flair for practical politics, he has no political theory of his own. But he is very conscious of the close link connecting religion with politics.

NOTES

* S. W. Baron, *A Social and Religious History of the Jews,*[2] xiii (1969), p. 143, n. 45 observes that Alemanno's political thought has not been properly examined. This remark gave me the idea to investigate the matter. Circumstances beyond my control have forced me to concentrate on the first part of Alemanno's commentary to the *Song of Songs* to the exclusion of his other works.

This paper is based on MS Oxford, Bodleian 1535.2(a), ff. 17–129. The (incomplete) printed edition of *Sefer shaʿar ha-ḥesheq,* Leghorn 1790, which begins from f. 41b, l. 16 of the MS, is not reliable. It is apparently based on another MS and contains some additional passages partly omitted in MS Bodl. through *homoioteleuton.* Word for word comparison shows the superiority of the Oxford MS, deviations in the printed ed. being insignificant and mostly faulty, e.g., "R. ibn Ezra" for Abu Naṣr (al-Fārābī). On Alemanno in general see U. Cassuto in the German *Encyclopaedia Judaica,* (Alemann, Johanan Ben Isaak), and his *Gli Ebrei a Firenze,* Florence, 1918, pp. 301f; C. Roth, *The Jews and the Renaissance*, Philadelphia, 1959, pp. 120f. Cf. also for some important details M. Steinschneider, *Hebräische Übersetzungen*, 1893, p. *s.v.* Alemanno. For the Latin text of the doctorate in Philosophy and Medicine conferred on Alemanno in Padua in 1470 see Daniel Carpi, "Notes on the Life of Rabbi Judah Messer Leon", *Studi sull' Ebraismo italiano in memoria di C. Roth*, Rome, 1974, pp. 56f. (this article had previously appeared in Hebrew in *Michael* [the Diaspora Research Institute, Tel Aviv], 1, 1972, pp. 227f).

1. Cf. ff. 8b–20a, first made available by F. Perles, "Les Savants juifs à Florence à l'époque de Laurent de Medicis", *REJ,* xii, 1886, pp. 244–57; Roth, *op. cit.* (see preliminary note).

2. He is influenced by Abraham Abulafia, and especially by the latter's disciple Joseph ibn Giqatilla (he spells the name Giqiṭila), Abraham ibn Ezra, Menahem de Recanati, Isaac ibn Laṭīf, and he often quotes the *Sepher yeṣirah.* Yoḥanan accepts that Solomon wrote many pneumatic books according to Apollonius of Tyana and Abu Aflaḥ, both of whom (especially the latter) he quotes. On the former see *infra*, p. 106, n. 28. I have dealt with the latter in a paper on "Yoḥanan Alemanno and the occult sciences" on the basis of his *Sefer ha-Tamar* (ed. G. Scholem, Jerusalem, 1926), see *infra,* p. 260, n. 29. He also quotes Ptolemy, the astronomer and author of the *Almagest,* although he may have mixed him up (as frequently happened) with al-Batlajauwsī in the guise of Bṭolomīyūs, author of *ʿAguloth raʿayaniyyoth* (e.g., f. 50a), which work he quotes (cf. *Enc. Islam*^{2} and David Kaufmann, *Die Spuren al-Batlajusis in der jüdischen Religionsphilosophie,* Budapest 1880 (reprinted, with an introduction by L. Jacobs, 1972), followed by an edition of the Hebrew version under the title just quoted, p. 28, n. 2. Yoḥanan certainly understood Ptolemy to be the author of the *Sefer ha-Peri,* e.g., f. 51a (Ṭolomiyʾus), and he is apparently also confused regarding the commentary of Abu Jafar (f. 53b), this astrological work being, however, wrongly attributed to Ptolemy (see *Enc. Islam*^{2}, *s.v.* Baṭlamīyūs, where this is stated by M. Plessner referring to the title *Karpós*, translated *Fructus* or *Centiloquium*). The *Sefer ha-Peri* is listed by Benjakob (*ʾOṣar ha-Sefarim,* Wilna, 1880, p. 494, n. 1101, and there described as "a hundred chapters on magic (*ʾiṣṭagninuth*) of Bṭolomīyūs with commentary by Abu Gāfīr Aḥmad ben Joseph ben Abraham . . . and it is also called *A Hundred Sayings*" (*Sefer ha-Peri = Fructus, A Hundred Sayings = Centiloquium*).

3. So. Cassuto in *Enc. Jud.* (see preliminary note, p. *supra*). That Alemanno was influenced by the platonist Ficino, whom he met in the company of Pico della Mirandola, does not appear from our text.

4. On f. 69b the author of the *Pireqey de-R. Eliezer* is said to hail from Worms, but not in the other passages quoted. I have been unable to establish whether Rabbi Eliezer ("the Great") b. Isaac of Worms was the author of a work entitled *Pireqey* . . . . Perhaps it is Eleazar of Worms who is intended, but which of his works I do not know. In J. D. Eisenstein's *ʾOṣar Yisraʾel,* ii, *s.v.* ʾElʿazar b. Yehudah mi-Garmayyezā (i.e., Worms), there is mention of a work (no. 17), p. 55, entitled *Shiʿur qomah u-fireqey de-R. Yishmaʿel*, which seems unlikely to be the work referred to here. On Eleazar see G. Scholem, *Major Trends in Jewish Mysticism*, especially chap. ii, and A. Altmann, "Eleazar of Worms' *Ḥokmath ha-ʾegoz*", *JJS,* xi (1960), pp. 101–13. Yoḥanan's use of rabbinic sources requires special investigation.

5. The usual Hebrew title of Fārābī's *Kitāb al-mabādi* (which are six in number) is *Sefer ha-hathḥaloth*, as in Filipowski's edition (in *Sefer ha-ʾasif*, ii, 1849), which I have used. Alemanno made frequent reference to the first, theoretical part of this important work, usually called *Kitāb al-siyāsāt al-madanīyah*. Cf. Filipowski, p. 35, for the five faculties of the soul, and pp. 40f. on *devequth* to the active intellect. Only such a man is a king fit to receive prophecy.

6. The Arabic original is called *Iḥṣā al-ʿulūm*. Chap. v, "on political science, jurisprudence and dialectical theology" (*siyāsah, fiqh, kalām*) is here used, and has been checked with the text reedited by M. Mahdi in his edition of Fārābī's *Kitāb al-millah*, Beirut, 1968, p. 75 (4).

7. In one passage it is called *Moʾzney ha-ʿiyyunim* (f. 50a), i.e., Arabic *Mīzān al-ʿamal*. The Hebrew translation was edited by J. Goldenthal, Leipsig, 1839. Cf., e.g., Alemanno, f. 27a and Goldenthal, pp. 29f.

8. Cf. ff. 22a–24b and references to Aristotle's *Nicomachaean Ethics*.

9. Plato, *Republic* ii, 375a, speaking of the guardians.

10. ff. 25b, 26a. The distinction between these two kinds of beauty seems to be Yoḥanan's own; he quotes David as an example and refers to *Ps.* 45:3–5. He remarks that in *2 Sam.* 12:24 the *qereʾ* (*wa-Tiqraʾ*) and the *kethiv* (*wa-Yiqraʾ*) show that father and mother were agreed in calling him Shelomoh, as a sign of his perfection. The next verse shows that the advice of astrologers needs to be supplemented by that of those who come in the spirit of prophecy, as is written in the *Sefer ha-Peri* (f. 26b). Nathan was sent by God because David needed interpreters possessed of the spirit of prophecy, not being himself sure whether love was particular or general. Hence Nathan called Solomon *Yedidyah*, meaning "[possessing] the love of heaven and the creatures" (f. 27a). Yoḥanan contrasts Saul with Moses, whose goodness includes beauty in government, because his beauty inspired fear.

11. f. 27b. Literally "work," or "art."

12. From *1 Kings* 1:35 "and he shall rule *under* me" (*taḥtay*: in place of, literally under me); Yoḥanan deduces this from the choice of the preposition *taḥath* rather than *ʾaḥaray* = after me.

13. Cf. ff. 28b, 29a–b, with comparisons from Galen and references to the political philosophers.

14. f. 29b. This is followed by praise of the fear of God and the fulfillment of the *miṣwoth*. Such traditionalism is nevertheless closely linked with philosophical intellectualism; and the whole of philosophy is the key to true happiness. The mystical ascent to the spheres is likewise an intellectual progression. For the relationship between philosophy and kabbalah see G. Vajda's important *Recherches sur la philosophie et la kabbale dans la pensée juive du moyen âge*, Paris 1962.

15. f. 31a. Yoḥanan significantly uses the term *takhsisey malkhuth* (approximately "strategy").

16. f. 32a, referring to Aristotle.

17. Translated literally in part, from ff. 32a–b. Yoḥanan quotes *1 Kings* 10:16, *2 Chron.* 9:22, and Rashi on *1 Kings, loc. cit.* for evidence of the amount of gold ducats that Solomon possessed, translating them into their equivalent value in the Italy of his own time.

18. ff. 33b–34a. The fourth book treats of liberality, greatness of heart, honor, and wealth; the ninth of friendship.

19. f. 36a. David follows this with the admonition to Solomon to be strong in kingship and to build the temple (*ha-Birah*) to the Lord, *1 Chron.* 29:1.

20. Cf. previous note, and f. 37a.

21. f. 37b; an ingenious justification (not to say whitewashing) of King Solomon.

22. f. 39b. "ʿAlī the Ishmaelite" is presumably Avicenna, who in other passages is indicated by the abbreviation ב"ס = ibn Sīnā. Yoḥanan uses both Fārābī's *Iḥṣā al-ʿulūm* and Avicenna's *Aqsām al-ʿulūm* in his enumeration and division of the sciences. His division cannot be reproduced here.

23. f. 40a; literally laws (*mishpaṭim,* = Fārābī's *fiqh*, cf. *supra*, p. 259, n. 6). This is a good example of Yoḥanan's dependence on Fārābī, and of his medievalism.

24. f. 41a; cf. Aristotle, *Nic. Ethics* VI, iii, 1 (*tevunah* renders *phronēsis*).

25. f. 41a–b. The whole passage *1 Kings* 5:9–14 is treated as a principal proof text of Solomon's surpassing wisdom. *ʾAmatla* is not to be understood here in its technical halakhic meaning, but for Yoḥanan signifies Solomon's own judgement based on his knowledge of human nature from acute observation and the effect of "sudden intuition" (*hashqafah pithʾomith*).

26. This is but the barest summary of a lengthy exposition based on Aristotle and Fārābī. Yoḥanan refers to Aristotle's *Nicomachaean Ethics, De Anima, Physica Auscultatio*, and *Posterior Analytics*, also stressing the faculty of divination (he quotes the Arabic term *qiyāfah*). As an example he cites Joseph's dealings with his brothers in Egypt and the incident of his cup.

27. f. 44b. Maimonides is quoted literally in regard to statesmen, lawgivers, diviners, and dreamers of true dreams.

28. f. 48a. *Leḥashim* are explained with the help of Apollonius, including an incantation prayer with theophoric and other names. Apollonius' work was translated into Hebrew under the title *Meleʾkheth muskeleth* by Solomon b. Nathan in Aix en Provence "a hundred years ago" (Steinschneider, *Hebr. Übers.* p. 848, gives the date as *c.* 1390; see also his "Apollonius von Tyana bei den Arabern", *ZDMG*, 45 (1895), pp. 439f., especially 444. Of the other five kinds of *dibbur* there explained, Yoḥanan adduces that only which is relevant to Solomon and his perfection in them.

29. ff. 51b–52a. This is a good example not only of Yoḥanan's exaggerated claims on behalf of King Solomon but also of his wide reading and uncritical evaluation on one level of the exact sciences and what we should consider the pseudosciences. It likewise illustrates his propensity to assign equal authority to Greek, Muslim, and Jewish philosophers and to writers on astrology and magic. Cf. my article "Yoḥanan Alemanno and the Occult Sciences" in the *Willy Hartner Festschrift* ΠΡΙΣΜΑΤΑ, ed. W. G. Saltzer and Y. Maeyama, Wiesbaden 1977, pp. 349f.

30. Cf. *iḥsā al-ʿulūm*, ed. M. Mahdi (*supra*, p. 259, n. 6), p. 75(4).

31. f. 54a. The quotation (approximate only) is from *2 Sam.* 8:15.

32. *Ibid.* There follows a long disquisition on Solomon's judgements as reported in the Bible in support of his great reputation for wisdom based on deep insight into human nature (e.g. the story of the claims of the two harlots to the same child, *1 Kings* 3:16f. Solomon carefully weighed both their words and their way of speech, ff. 54b–56b).

33. f. 68a. The text here is rather involved and obscure.

34. f. 69b, summarized with partial translation.

35. *Ibid*; literally "kingdom of the firmament." I am endebted to Dr Stefan Reif for tracing the statement to T.B. *Berakhoth* 58a, where it in fact occurs twice; the first time as such, the second with reference to God's establishing the earthly kingdom. L. Ginzberg's *Legends of the Jews* contains no evidence of the phrase being used of Solomon.

36. f. 70b, followed by a quotation from *1 Kings* 8:32.

37. f. 71a. This is Yoḥanan's interpretation of *1 Kings* 8:47–53.

38. f. 73a. His proof-text is *1 Kings* 5:5.

39. ff. 76b–77a. Cf. my *Political Thought in Mediaeval Islam*,[3] Cambridge, 1968, the chapters on Fārābī and Ibn Bājja.

40. A summary of ff. 77–83a. The name of God leads Yoḥanan to mention the oneness and uniqueness of God "as is clear from the *Book of the Stone of the Philosophers* of our R. Saᶜadiah Gaᵓon." G. Scholem states ("Alchemie und Kabbala", *MGWJ*, 1925, p. 28) that "Mose Botarel zitiert in seinem *Jezirah* Kommentar (*ca.* 1409) ein angeblich Saadianisches Buch 'der Stein der Philosophen' (zu *Jezirah* I, i). Der Inhalt des Zitats hat nichts mit Alchemie zu tun." This would bear out Yoḥanan's view of the genuineness of such a treatise by Saᶜadiah, who does in fact deal with this problem—the first principle of the *Muᶜtazilah*—in his *ᵓEmunoth we-deᶜoth.*

41. f. 85a. Aristotle treats of *megalopsychia* in *Nic. Ethics* II, vii, 7 and IV, iii; it shows in virtues which Solomon possessed through his greatness of soul. Cf. also Plato, *Republic* vi, 486a (*megaloprepeia*, as opposed to σμικρολογία ψυχῇ), and my *Averroes' Commentary on Plato's Republic*,[3] Cambridge (*ACR*), 1969, p. 179, n. 1.

42. Taking *mishpaṭ* in all three senses, Yoḥanan refers to "the philosophical state [of Plato], whose people are all wise, men of insight and knowledge of the right (*mishpaṭ*: or justice?), so that there is no need of physicians of the soul, i.e., the judges. For *mishpaṭ* brings all to perfection" (f. 85b).

43. ff. 89–90a. There follows a long description of Solomon's prayer and blessing based on *1 Kings* 8.

44. f. 91b; *yosher* stands for *dikaiosynē*. Cf. Plato, *Republic,* iv. 434c, and my *Averroes* (see *supra,* n. 41), p. 50 (I, xxiii, 4).

45. f. 93b; cf. *1 Kings* 3:5–14. According to Yoḥanan, Solomon refers to "concupiscent justice in order to judge the earth with righteousness (*ṣedeq*) and the nations with justice (*meysharim*)."

46. ff. 94b–95a (the well known Platonic-Aristotelian concept). Like Aristotle—and, based on Aristotle, Fārābī—Yoḥanan distinguishes between masters, servants, and those who serve and are served. Cf. my article "The place of politics in the philosophy of al-Fārābī" reprinted in my *Studia Semitica* ii, 1971, pp. 97f. from *Islamic Culture* 39, 3, July, 1955, pp. 157f.

47. Cf. M. Steinschneider, *Al-Farabi*, St Petersburgh, 1869, pp. 227f. G. Vajda (*L'Amour de Dieu dans la théologie juive du moyen âge*, Paris, 1957, pp. 280–285) discusses Alemanno succinctly and indeed in exemplary fashion. For our context cf. p. 282, with n. 2. The Arabic text is available with Latin translation and notes in Franz Rosenthal and R. Walzer, *Alfarabius de Platonis Philosophia*, London, 1943, §22(a), pp. 14f., 10f., and 23, where the editors trace the idea to Plato's *Phaedrus*, 22, 244d–245a. *ᶜishq* = *ḥesheq,* and *junūn* = *shiggaᶜon* (and probably also *sheṭifah*).

48. *be-sof* (f. 96a); Steinschneider (see previous note) reads *be-sug*.

49. f. 96a–b. There follow references to Galen, Hippocrates, Ptolemy (al-Baṭalyawsī) and Aristotle.

50. Cf. f. 150a, for *malkhuth*. Solomon's earthly kingdom is a replica, as it were, of the highest and final sphere as an aspect of the Deity—it is, as mentioned above, the gateway to heaven or to God. Of great importance, according to Yoḥanan, are the spheres *tifᵓereth*, *gevurah*, and *yesod* as stages in the progression towards the ultimate *malkhuth*: it is a political no less than a spiritual enterprise. From this final section of the first part of the commentary it becomes clear that in the title the word *ha-Maᶜaloth* means both virtues and stages in the upward journey of the soul towards *devequth*.

Enlightenment: Between Mendelssohn and Kant

NATHAN ROTENSTREICH

I

The subject of our investigation is related to two essays on the nature of "*Aufklärung*" or "*Aufklären*"—that by Moses Mendelssohn entitled *Über die Frage: Was heisst Aufklären?* and that of Kant entitled *Was ist Aufklärung?* Both of these essays appeared in the *Berlinische Monatsschrift* in 1784, Mendelssohn's preceding that of Kant by a few months. A few remarks on the terms used are here apposite.

The first term is *Aufklärung*, which is the German equivalent of *lumière*, enlightenment, or *siècle philosophique*. Although we do not suggest that the roots of words used necessarily prescribe their systematic meaning, one cannot be oblivious of the fact that the term *enlightenment* implies some relationship to the notion of light or *lumen*, and that it is, from this point of view, not totally alien to the tradition of philosophical thinking which used the metaphor of light or *lumen* and its equivalents in different versions. For some authors the age of *lux* or *lumen* was synonymous with the age of philosophy; this again reinforces the conjecture that the introduction of the term "enlightenment" into the philosophical dictionary represents a tendency to use metaphors in which *seeing* or the visual faculty predominate. This is the case, as is well known, with terms like *theōria* or *speculatio,* or even *intuitio* or *evidentia*. The accent on *lumen*, or on the light of the eye, represents an additional nuance in that same tradition of diverse metaphors, inasmuch as it points to the light of reason, or to what could perhaps be described as self-illumination.

The metaphor of light can be understood in two ways. First, as *light bestowed on* the individual concerned, as for example in *Ps.* 97:11, *ʾor zaruaʿ la-Ṣaddiq* (Vulgate *lux orta est justo*). But it can also be understood as the *emergence of light* out of the resources of the human being or of the person, or as *removing obstacles from the eye*, obstacles which prevent the light from being seen. As we shall see, different aspects of the notion of light appear in the two essays that concern us; and it has to be stated right at the beginning that "enlightenment" in the sense of *clearing up* or *elucidation* may have a more intellectual connotation, in the sense of making things known or conceived. This aspect of enlightenment appears, interestingly enough, in the Hebrew equivalent of *Aufklärung*, *haskalah*, which obviously derives from *sekhel* and *maskil* in the sense of reason and of one who, through application of reason, is in possession of knowledge. Whether or not Mendelssohn's interpretation of the term *Aufklärung* had its impact—because of Mendelssohn's special position in the movement—on the shaping of the Hebrew word, is a question of mere conjecture.

We turn now to the second term frequently used in the discussion, *viz.*, culture. That term, as is well-known, derives from *colere* and in this sense is rather akin to the aspect of *cultivation, training, improvement,* or *refinement.*[1] Thus the introduction of the term into the human or intellectual orbit initially points to the aspect of forming the human mind or behavior (Cicero's *cultura animi*), rather than to the aspect of emergence out of the internal resources of the eye or of reason. Formation or *Bildung*—the English term is perhaps less familiar in this sense than the parallel German—differs, of course, from reception; nevertheless, formation or cultivation is not a spontaneous outcome of one's own individual activity.

We thus find an affinity, at least *post factum*, between culture and *Bildung*. *Bildung*, as Mendelssohn comments, along with *Aufklärung* and *Kultur* are "in our language still newcomers" (*neue Ankömmlinge*). *Bildung* may have a religious background related to the notion of *Bild* or *imago* in the sense that God impressed his nature on human kind, or even on all things which, in virtue of being created, are "*gebildet*" or "*geformt.*" Eventually the notion of *Bildung* became synonymous with the formation of the intellect and the character, for instance in the sense of *shaping* (*Ausbildung*) of certain given predispositions in man, or in the sense that men are endowed with an urge towards *Bildung*, rendered into Latin as *nisus formativus*. Thus, in a sense, *Bildung* has two meanings, referring to the two ends of the consideration; at one end *Bildung* is related to the predispositions of human beings and at the other to the "formation" which ideas, or divine nature, bring about through the process of their absorption by individuals—or, to use a contemporary expression, through the process of internalization.

II

It is clear that Mendelssohn[2] sees the three terms *Bildung*, *Kultur*, and *Aufklärung* as interrelated. Moreover, as being trends that point to human social life in its various modifications, they comprise the result of human industry and endeavor to improve the social condition of mankind (*ihren geselligen Zustand zu verbessern*). Mendelssohn apparently uses, as a synonym for the social condition, the term "people" (*Volk*), and he takes it for granted that human destiny amounts to the achievement of living in harmony. That destiny is implemented through art and diligence, these two instruments increasing the *Bildung* of the people. This summary account leads to the conclusion that it is *Bildung* that is the broadest concept in Mendelssohn's presentation, whereas culture and enlightenment result from *Bildung*. Human destiny, which is not defined, serves here as an aim and criterion by which to measure all our aspirations and endeavors. Within the scope of human destiny a distinction has to be made between human destiny in terms of man as man (*Mensch als Mensch*) and human destiny in terms of men as citizens. Language plays an important role within the scope of *Bildung*, and is presented as the best indicator of the *Bildung* of a people. It is clear that Mendelssohn suggests an intrinsic connection between *Bildung* and the essence or destiny of man, but he is not at all specific as to what that destiny comprises or to what it points: for instance, whether it should be the discernment by the intellect of the essence of nature, or the realization of a moral imperative. Whether or not the concept of living in harmony has initially a moral or a practical connotation is doubtful, as we shall see, since Mendelssohn relegates the practical aspect of *Bildung* to culture; it would follow that he does not suggest an identity between *Bildung* and morality. This in turn shows that the nature of harmony, which certainly has a practical and a moral connotation, is bound to be understood in broader terms, even though Mendelssohn himself does not elaborate on the broader meaning of harmony.

Be this as it may, the two branches of *Bildung* are culture and enlightenment. Culture is directed rather towards the practical sphere and has as its objectives goodness, refinement, and beauty in artifacts as well as in objective social *mores* (*Geselligkeitssitten*). These are described as objectives because they are expressed in visible modes of behavior. And in this sense they differ from what Mendelssohn terms "subjective," referring thereby to urges and to habits. The subjective aspect of culture comes to the fore in diligence as well as in skills—again attitudes of the psyche or of the mind, which find their expression in behaviour as well as in artifacts. Culture, having a practical connotation and thus a social dimension, is not necessarily of a moral character. It has to do in general with social intercourse, and thus finds its expression also in poetry, eloquence, and courtly behavior. Eventually Mendelssohn wavers between praxis as morality (*Sittlichkeit*) and "praxis" in a broad sense as "virtuosity" (*Virtuosität*). Since "praxis" has as its orbit the social plane of human existence, and the social plane is limited, or does not correspond to the essence of man as man and to the universality of mankind, practical perfections have their value insofar only as human social life is concerned or if they correspond to the destiny of man as a member of society. Man as man does not stand in need of any culture, but he does stand in need of enlightenment (*Der Mensch als Mensch bedarf keiner Kultur aber er bedarf der Aufklärung*).

The notion of culture percolates to even deeper and more detailed levels of human social existence, to the status and vocation within social or civic life (*im bürgerlichen Leben*); notions or prescriptions such as duties and rights are encompassed within the concept of culture, since human beings take as their point of reference varying skills and accomplishments, inclinations, urges, sense of sociability, and habits, each according to his respective status and vocation, his duties and rights. Here culture and "polish" (*Kultur und Politur*) are interrelated. The culture of a nation eventually corresponds to the impact that *Kultur* and *Politur* make on the members of its society. This is in step with a Hebrew writer[3] who declares that every achievement has its corresponding perversion—the more noble it is in its flowering, the more aesthetically repellent its decomposition and degeneration: and in this sense the abuse of culture engenders gluttony, ostentation, laxity, superstition, and slavery.

III

Enlightenment may also be considered a theoretical parallel to culture. Since it refers to, indeed coincides with the theoretical approach, it comprises rational knowledge which is the objective aspect of enlightenment, as well as skill which is its subjective aspect, in the sense that it is man's rational faculty to be able to reflect. The subject matter of reflection is comprised by things related to human life, and that reflection is guided by the measure of the impact of those things upon the destiny of man. This is, to be sure, a description of enlightenment *qua* theoretical attitude. We find that enlightenment does have a predetermined focus, *viz.*, the destiny of man, since it is that destiny that is ultimately the measure and the objective of all our aspirations and endeavours. One could argue, of course, having in mind the Kantian notion of the destiny of man, that this notion is of a practical character, since it refers not to that which is given but to that which has to be or ought to be realized. But we have to be careful not to impose Kantian nuances on Mendelssohn, despite the fact that the notion of the destiny of man becomes rather vague for all its being the yardstick of enlightenment *qua* theory. We notice that Mendelssohn relates enlightenment to the sciences, to criticism, as juxtaposed to virtuosity or dexterity. Theory and practice, or enlightenment and *Bildung*, are objectively speaking interconnected, that is to say they both fall within the frame of reference of the destiny of man as being the broadest framework of reference; and yet they are separated subjectively, since each of these attitudes presupposes differing human capacities and approaches. Once Mendelssohn has introduced into his discourse or analysis the distinction between culture and enlightenment, he uses that distinction as a way of characterizing different groups or even different nations. To put it another way, he takes culture and enlightenment as focuses of group-characters in the sense of *Volksgeist* or *Volksseele*. Those who live in Nuremberg, says Mendelssohn, possess more culture, while the residents of Berlin possess more enlightenment, or again the French are characterized by greater culture, whilst in enlightenment the English have the advantage. Here the comment about Greece is of some significance. Mendelssohn states that the Greeks were possessed of both culture and enlightenment and in this sense were "*eine gebildete Nation*:" we might even add *gebildet stricto sensu*, since the concept of *Bildung* comprises both enlightenment and culture.

And yet, as we have already seen, there is a certain imbalance in Mendelssohn's description. If the destiny of man is something to be attained and therefore a human ideal, Mendelssohn sees enlightenment as characteristic of "man *qua* man," while he sees culture as characteristic of man *qua* citizen. It would follow from this description that human fulfillment lies by way of theory *qua Aufklärung*, and not by way of praxis *qua* culture. Nevertheless Mendelssohn probably thought of a kind of ultimately emerging identity or synonymity of enlightenment and the destiny of man, even though the historical model, namely the Greeks, were characterized by a synthesis of culture and enlightenment, or by civic virtue and universally human virtue. Insofar as enlightenment is a universal human attitude it applies to every human being, irrespective of social distinctions between individuals, even though insofar as enlightenment is to be realized as the possession of any specific human beings it is bound to be modified by their concrete and individual situations. In this sense there would be a difference between the situation and the profession of the human being here and now, and the destiny of man which is the objective and ultimate yardstick.

Mendelssohn is moreover aware of the fact that enlightenment in the universal sense and enlightenment insofar as it becomes absorbed by members of a given society—who are, as we now know, embraced by culture—may result in a clash between the level of universal humanity and the level of a particular civic polity. Certain truths which are useful to man as man can sometimes be harmful to him as a citizen. This is indeed a conflict of interests that has to be examined with care. Insofar as essential human characteristics go, they are indeed the *conditio sine qua non* of human existence, since without them man sinks to the level of the beasts. In just the same way there are certain essential characteristic features of man as citizen, without which the system of the state would cease to exist. Yet we do not find in Mendelssohn any listing of the different characteristic features pertaining to the different levels of human existence, either in the universal or in the civic sense. He says merely that a state is unhappy when it is unable to bring about a harmony of the essential features of the citizenry. Here, says Mendelssohn, philosophy has to keep silent—but he omits explaining the meaning of this far-reaching statement. Does he mean to imply that philosophy, as an analysis of human existence, has to restrain itself from even defining the distinction between enlightenment and culture, or does he wish to say that philosophy, in virtue of its own terms of reference, is closer to the universal aspect, i.e., to enlightenment and theory? If so, then in a case of conflict between the universal and the particular, or the theoretical and the practical, philosophy as standing closer to theory is expected to demand the primacy of theory; and yet, being itself involved in the predicament of the lack of harmony between the universal and the particular, philosophy is in the event constrained to keep silent, and thus, concretely or pragmatically, accords primacy to practice or the civic realm. This applies specifically to questions of religion and morality. In this context a new or different type of man of enlightenment appears—*der tugendliebende Aufklärer* ("the virtue-loving man of enlightenment.") He feels himself bound to deal with the situation circumspectly and to be prepared rather to suffer from prejudice than drive away that truth which is bound to him by such intimate ties. Indeed, long before, this maxim had been turned to use as a defensive weapon in the armoury of hypocrisy, with centuries of barbarity and superstition as the outcome. But in spite of this caution or awareness Mendelssohn does not propose an unequivocal attitude of enlightenment that would ignore the complexities of day to day human existence. He is aware of the fact that it is difficult, perhaps even impossible to find a line of demarcation between the proper use and the abuse of the tools of enlightenment, theory and analysis; and he seems to be satisfied with presenting the complexities rather than making any attempt to resolve them. Moreover, as he had done with regard to culture, he points out the shortcomings of enlightenment which amount to the misuse of it. Abuse of enlightenment weakens the moral sense, leads to stubbornness, egoism, irreligiosity, and anarchy. It seems to be clear that the deficiencies of enlightenment are connected with the conflict between theoretical and civic virtues, whereby enlightenment may cause harm to religion and morality. This is probably so, since the protagonists of enlightenment indulge in undue self-confidence and have regard for nothing but their own convictions, oblivious of actual human situations. In spite of the fact that philosophy seems to be, by definition, closer to enlightenment than to culture, and for all that theory seems to be more universal than practice, historical reality or *Bildung* leads to the reinstatement of the Greek synthesis, namely that of culture and enlightenment. A people that absorbs both these focuses of human activity is less exposed to corruption than a people which overaccentuates one only of the two lines of activity. All the same, a synthesis thus achieved is still exposed to the danger of an excess of national happiness and unjustifiable self-satisfaction, which ultimately lead to the disease of a body politic that ought to be kept entirely healthy. In this context Mendelssohn is concerned to emphasize that national self-indulgence is a barrier that prevents progress up the ladder of human achievement.

To sum up Mendelssohn's presentation of enlightenment and culture, we see that he placed the two pursuits of human destiny within the context of *Bildung*; although it is culture alone that is meant to have an immediate practical and historical impact, enlightenment also has a historical impact, at least insofar as it clashes with the expediencies of culture and civic life. Moreover, the ideal which coincides with human destiny is the synthesis of enlightenment and culture, despite the intrinsic affinity between enlightenment and philosophy. Our next task, therefore, will be to explore Kant's concept of enlightenment, in the context of his own definitions.[3a]

IV

It is appropriate to start our investigation with Kant's essay "What is Enlightenment?" which constitutes his response to the *enquête*—as we have already seen, he was anticipated by Mendelssohn who responded to it. Kant's point comes immediately to the fore: for him, enlightenment is the overriding concept, and not merely one line of activity alongside that of culture, both being embraced within the broader concept of *Bildung*. Secondly, Kant's presentation is rather polemical or at least antithetical, stressing that he addresses himself to a particular historical situation in which enlightenment can do nothing more than merely emerge; hence we do not live, as he puts it, in an *enlightened age* (*in einem aufgeklärten Zeitalter*), but rather in an *age of enlightenment* (*in einem Zeitalter der Aufklärung*).[4]

Since Kant interprets enlightenment as being a total human attitude, he actually identifies it with an attitude emerging from freedom, or rather from a freedom still to be restored, since man's fundamental freedom has somehow got lost *en route*. This loss of freedom is described by Kant as *selbstverschuldete Unmündigkeit*, a tutelage that is self-incurred and not imposed on man by oppressive and suppressive external forces. In this sense the motto of enlightenment is *sapere aude*—have the courage to use your *own* reason. At this point it may be appropriate to comment on the concept of tutelage, since Kant anticipates here the concept of self-alienation that did not become current until a generation later. Tutelage connotes man's subjugation to a reality which he has himself produced. The affinity between tutelage and self-alienation lies in the element of accepting direction from an external source: while self-alienation points to the very effect produced by the external source, tutelage points to the lack of courage which expresses itself in reliance upon it. Self-alienation connotes an outcome produced outside man, whilst self-incurred tutelage connotes a kind of withdrawal. Both concepts are meant to describe a situation in which human nature remains unrealized despite its potentiality for realization. Later on the concept of self-alienation gave birth to investigations into the causes of self-alienation, whereas Kant is in a sense content to point to laziness and cowardice as being the factors of character and psychology that lead to tutelage. It is easier, says Kant, where conscience is involved to be guided by a pastor, or by a physician where it is one's diet that is at stake, and not to take the trouble of making the proper judgements or decisions for oneself. Enlightenment therefore amounts to freedom, or to the realization of freedom, and more pointedly to the realization of freedom in the public domain. We shall presently see the relation obtaining between this description of enlightenment and some of the questions related to the critique of pure reason, and the affinity between reason proper and freedom. But at this juncture we have to look into an additional aspect of Kant's presentation, where he comes close to Mendelssohn's position even though he suggests a solution of the dilemma that differs from that of Mendelssohn.

Let us stress at the outset that Kant refers to the *age* of enlightenment, not to enlightenment as a perennial human activity. It is in this sense that he refers not only to a *Zeitgeist*, but also to the individual's dependence or reliance upon the self-emancipatory process of a given age, public, or society. For any single individual it is, according to Kant, very difficult to extricate himself from a life under tutelage that has almost become his nature. Very few have succeeded, by dint of their own exercise of mind, in freeing themselves from tutelage and yet achieving a steady pace (*einen sicheren Gang*). Kant is probably referring here, as in several of his writings, to the predicament in which individuals find themselves in social and political life, and even more to the problematics of being frank and upright in giving expression to these. He is aware of the pressures exercised by society and therefore shifts the onus from the individual to the public, since it is easier for the public to enlighten itself. Moreover, were freedom but granted to the public, enlightenment would almost certainly follow. This is not to say that the process of self-emancipation and the attainment of enlightenment is not a slow one. Yet Kant thought that political freedom in a sense to be delineated was, to be precise, a *conditio sine qua non* for enlightenment. Here, as in several other of his writings (for instance "*Perpetual Peace*"),[5] Kant conceives of the political regime as a necessary condition for the fulfillment of human capability; political freedom is the precondition of freedom and synonymous with the exercise of reason. If we view this statement of Kant in the context described by Mendelssohn, it has to be said that Mendelssohn distinguishes enlightenment from culture. That distinction coincides with the distinction between theory and practice and universality and particularity, the latter to be understood in the civic sense. Kant, in describing enlightenment as an overriding attitude, gives it a polemical import—emancipation from tutelage—but sees political and social existence as a primary condition for the exercise of enlightenment, as well as enlightenment being a primary step towards the realization of human freedom.

Kant's concern with problems that occupied Mendelssohn's attention becomes clear in an additional aspect of his presentation; and here, too, he and Mendelssohn diverge. He refers to the distinction between private and public use of reason. But he interprets the notion of "private" in a sense which differs from the common use of that word. He does not use *private* as a term referring to one's own self-enclosed personal realm, but rather to describe what one does in a particular civil post or office which one happens to hold. "Public," *per contra*, indicates the universal sphere, or to use Mendelssohn's phrase the sphere of man as man, which in this context is epitomized by the activity of the scholar. One cannot help observing that in Kant's sense the scholar is a person who actualizes theory. Thus Kant, in spite of his fundamentally different approach to enlightenment, comes back to at least one aspect of Mendelssohn's presentation. The scholar addresses the public through his writings, and he can argue about his activity as a private person without damaging those affairs for which he is in part responsible inasmuch as he is active in his particular civic post or office. Interestingly enough, Kant endeavors to resolve the dilemma between following the line prescribed by one's activity and yet remaining free on the level of scholarship, by describing the person involved in a civic post as a *passive* member, probably implying that the scholar, who expresses opinions whilst being detached from the activity entrusted to him, is an active partner and not a passive member. The examples illustrating the duality and coexistence of the different activities which Kant cites are rather telling ones: it would be calamitous, he says, for an officer on active service to debate the appropriateness or usefulness of a command given to him by his superior. The junior officer simply has to obey. But the right to make observations on errors committed in the military service and to lay them open to the public for judgement, cannot equitably (*billigermassen*) be denied him as a scholar. It is clear from the context that the term "scholar" here connotes the observer or the interpreter, and not necessarily the person concerned with the prosecution of scholarly business as generally understood. Another example which Kant gives is that of the clergyman who is bound to preach to his congregation in conformity with the symbols of the church that he serves. Kant is here referring to a kind of social contract between the clergyman and his congregation, whereby he has been accepted on condition that he acts in accordance with his congregation's religious doctrines. But as a scholar he has the freedom, even the calling or vocation (*Beruf*) to communicate to the public his carefully tested and well-intentioned thinking about what in those same symbols is erroneous, and to make suggestions for the better organization of the church. We note that Kant is rather cautious in describing the range of freedom, at least in the sense that he does not imply that, as a scholar, the clergyman is entitled to be an atheist. His scholarship may, after all, be expressed in limited criticism only of the symbols concerned and in making positive suggestions for a more appropriate organization of the religious body.

It is plausible to assume that Kant's main interest was in the political implications of enlightenment and the duality and coexistence between the private and public domain, or concomitantly between passivity and activity. The citizen cannot refuse to pay the taxes imposed on him; he can even be punished for failing to obey the rules. But the same person is not acting contrary to his duty as a citizen when, as a scholar, he gives public expression to his thoughts on the inappropriateness or even the injustice of the fiscal levies—and here, again, the term "scholar" indicates the position of the citizen as theoretically expressing his thought or speaking his mind.

To fail to draw distinctions between the legitimate right within one's private sphere of activity or responsibility and one's public performance amounts, for Kant, to an impossible or an intolerable form of social contract. An age cannot bind itself, in his view, and ordain that the succeeding age is to be put into such a condition that it cannot extend its knowledge, purify itself of errors, and make progress in general enlightenment. It is to be observed that the limitation imposed on the social contract which would nullify the distinction between the private and the public sphere is related here to what might be called historical responsibility, in the sense that no generation is entitled to block the ascent of a subsequent generation to progress, which clearly means freedom or progressive general enlightenment. Kant uses a very strong term—"a crime against human nature" (*ein Verbrechen wider die menschliche Natur*)—in asserting that it is the basic destiny of man to make progress. He thus tries to show the coalescence between freedom and progress, the process of enlightenment being a bridge between the initial freedom and the ideal goal of progress. Positively, Kant uses the term "the rights of mankind;" he allows the human individual the right to postpone in regard to himself, albeit for a short time only, the pursuit of enlightenment and of what he ought to know. But the renunciation of enlightenment for oneself more than temporarily, let alone to renounce it for posterity, is to injure the rights of mankind and indeed to trample upon them. Kant's political leanings become manifest when he examines the relationship obtaining between the spheres of religion and of politics, this examination pointing to the fact that whereas the rulers have no interest in playing guardian of the arts and sciences, they are definitely interested in doing so with respect to religion. Moreover tutelage in the religious sphere is not only the most damaging but also the most degrading form of tutelage. At this point Kant tries to bring together the polemical character of freedom and enlightenment and their overriding inclination, indeed vocation for free thinking. Any government will have to take this propensity and vocation into account, since government will find it essentially an advantage to treat men (who are not mere machines) with due regard for their dignity. It goes without saying that this last statement brings within the scope of Kant's presentation not only human freedom and the enlightenment that is anchored therein and conditions it, but also the destiny of man to which reference has already been made, and which now emerges as synonymous with the dignity of man.

To this analysis of Kant's essay on the nature of enlightenment we have now first to add some further comments from his various writings on the subject and then to consider the broader aspects of his presentation.

V

The political implications of Kant's concept of enlightenment and of the aspect of freedom which is both the origin of enlightenment and its hard core come to the fore in sundry statements. We shall here mention a few only of the more relevant points, in order to draw some conclusions as to the systematic meaning of Kant's basic notions. Freedom, he says, spreads by degrees. When the citizen is obstructed and has to seek his own welfare in his own way, the vitality of the entire enterprise is sapped, and therewith the power of the whole is diminished. There is but one proviso in this context: *viz.*, that the freedom of the individual citizen has to be consistent with the freedom of the remainder, and its gradual achievement amounts to the removal of limitations on personal actions—here, too, general religious freedom is the basic focus of achievement. Enlightenment, which is the atmosphere of freedom and, insofar as religious liberty is concerned, its very condition, emerges but gradually, with intermittent periods of folly and caprice. This achievement is regarded by Kant as a great goal which, once attained, must finally save men from the selfish aggrandizement of their masters; the concept of *master* probably being intended to refer to political and religious authorities. Eventually, step by step, enlightenment must ascend the throne and influence the principles of government.[6] It emerges clearly that Kant does not confine enlightenment to theory in Mendelssohn's sense, which construes it as one line of human activity parallel to that of culture. He assumes that enlightenment will gradually and ultimately permeate the actual behavior of mankind in the two most vulnerable areas, those of politics and of religion. Here theory has its practical impact. This is the case despite Kant's previously mentioned suggestion that there will be a kind of division of labour as between behavior in one's prescribed private sphere and one's attitude as a scholar or observer. When Kant suggests this sort of division of labor he is limiting enlightenment to what is in Mendelssohn's sense theory, even though he does not use Mendelssohn's terminology: this emerges in his *Streit der Fakultäten*. We may observe that Kant takes the same view in his essay on "*Perpetual Peace*," and it may be said that he suggests that freedom or liberty of expression is a self-contained liberty, without attributing to that liberty any "practical" consequences. Kant says, for example, that kings should not be expected to become philosophers nor philosophers kings.[7] Moreover, even if they did this would not be desirable, since the possession of power inevitably corrupts the untrammelled judgement of reason. Philosophers on becoming kings would therefore inevitably become exposed to the corruption of their judgement of reason, i.e., of their own competence and indeed their very *raison d'être*. Yet what he terms the class of kings, or king-like people, should not permit the class of philosophers to disappear or to be silenced but should let them speak openly. To be sure, there is a built-in proviso in terms of a *modus vivendi* current amongst kings and king-like people, *viz*., that their government shall be based upon laws of equality. Thus to allow philosophers to speak freely is indispensable to the enlightenment of the business of government. (The term that Kant uses here is not *Aufklärung* but *Beleuchtung*.)[8] One may venture the suggestion that this division of labor, as we have styled it, is Kant's adjustment to the situation of conflict between enlightenment as theory on the one hand and culture as a mode of behavior on the other, even though Kant's adjustment is not without a certain irony.

VI

When Kant emphasizes enlightenment as meaning emancipation from tutelage, he faces the question of how much freedom is to be attributed to thinking. His own well-known solution is that freedom of thought is the subjugation of reason to laws which are imposed by reason upon itself. In that context he does not posit the contradiction or opposition between the self-legislation of reason and subjugation to external laws. The opposition is between self-legislation and the employment of reason that is not governed by laws (*gesetzloser Gebrauch der Vernunft*). The latter situation is epitomized by the "genius" (*das Genie*), since the genius supposes himself to be more far-sighted than is possible under restriction by law. It is therefore interesting that Kant takes advantage of the notion of the self-discipline of pure reason in order to demonstrate that reason is essentially self-guided, and that consequently freedom or enlightenment does not amount to a total removal of restrictions or limitations. Reason, says Kant in the *Critique of Pure Reason*, depends upon this freedom for its very existence. "For reason has no dictatorial authority; its verdict is always simply the agreement of free citizens, of whom each one must be prepared to express, without let or hindrance, his objections or even his veto." We see that in the very presentation of the essence of reason Kant uses political similes or metaphors; there is a sort of interaction or parallelism between reason as spontaneity proper and the freedom of the citizen. Reason as freedom in its polemical application is basically directed against dogmatic counter-propositions. When Kant describes dogmatism as an employment of reason lacking the preceding critique of the capacity of reason, dogmatism can be understood as contradicting enlightenment: in the sense that it is the character of reason to subjugate itself to statements without exhibiting its freedom as expressed in critique or as expressed in the self-limitation of reason, as opposed to the imposed limitation that derives from statements or propositions that are accepted or are taken for granted. The justification of the freedom of reason lies not only in its exercise, which has to conform to the basic nature of freedom, but also "it is always best to grant reason complete liberty, both of enquiry and of criticism, so that it may not be hindered in attending to its own proper interests."[9] This is so because essentially the issue does not revolve around what in these enquiries is beneficial or detrimental to the best interests of mankind. The real question is how far reason can advance by means of speculation that are founded on the self-criticism of reason.

The extent to which all these considerations related to the nature of reason make use, to say the least, of political or philosophical parlance can be seen in the way Kant represents the situation of speculation in the absence of the critique of reason. He describes that situation as one similar to the state of nature, which is characterized (according to Hobbes' model quoted by Kant) as a situation in which reason can establish and secure its assertions and claims through nothing other than *war*, which is, of course, a metaphorical expression. As against the war of all against all, critique resembles resort to legal action: it is a situation in which all decision making is grounded in fundamental principles the authority of which no one can question. In this sense critique secures for us the peace of legal order. Under the order of law, as opposed to the state of nature, disputes have to be conducted solely by recognized methods of forensic procedure. There is legislation based on criticism, and such legislation is both intrinsically validated and vindicated by the nature of reason, as well as by the futility of endless disputes caused by a reason that is merely dogmatic. In this sense the critique of reason is a sort of refuge from the endless disputes described as the state of nature or as the situation of war. Again, this is the essence of reason and its original right, expressed in the context by employing socio-philosophical terminology, as being one of those rights of human reason that recognizes no other judge than that universal human reason in which everyone has his say. If we may exaggerate Kant's language somewhat we may say that he advocates, in addition to the enterprise of the critique of reason, a sort of republicanism of reason, since every human being has his share in universal human reason. That participation also has its practical and even political consequences, since the freedom at stake will carry with it the right to submit to open discussion those thoughts and doubts with which we find ourselves unable to deal. This will be done "without being decried as troublesome and dangerous citizens." In this statement Kant goes beyond the assertion of the right of the scholar to which we have referred above, since he emphasizes explicitly the grounding of the freedom of expression in the nature of reason. To put it differently, the nature of reason is not only the justification for the freedom of expression; it is also the protection of that freedom and of the individual who exercises his freedom by actualizing the basic freedom that is synonymous with universal human reason. Here again it has to be said that if we take *Aufklärung* in Mendelssohn's limited sense as theory, then the "theory" which leads to the expression of propositions and statements is imbued with a basic affinity to the very nature of reason, and thus it is to some extent not a parallel to culture but rather superior to it.

This last statement calls for some comments on Kant's own concept of culture and regarding a kind of inconsistency which is characteristic of his own use of the term.

VII

Whereas Mendelssohn tends to identify culture with practice and civility, Kant on the one hand employs the term in a rather broad sense; on the other, he distinguishes, within the scope of practice, between culture and aspects which do not come under its heading. We do not propose to analyze here all the divergent meanings of the notion of culture present in Kant's writings, and we shall limit ourselves to two or three aspects which are both relevant and terminologically significant.

As we have seen in our investigation up to this point, enlightenment as grounded in freedom absorbs into itself discipline in the strict sense as a restraining norm. Discipline, as Kant says, is distinguished from culture, since culture is intended solely to confer a certain kind of skill.[10] In that sense, culture does not invalidate any habitual mode of action already present. If we take this usage of the term culture literally, then culture lacks one significant element characteristic of practice and of morality in general, namely the element of restraint. Kant would rather be inclined (again following the root of the term culture as *colere*) to emphasize the positive direction of culture, namely fulfillment or achievement. And indeed he says that as factors conducive of development of a talent which as such contains in itself an impulse to self-manifestation, it is culture and doctrine that indicate the positive direction, while the negative or restraining direction is indicated by discipline. We should clearly understand that Kant, because he brings development or fulfillment under the heading of culture, lists culture and doctrine as belonging to the same class of activity. To cling to the literal meaning of that description would lead us to the conclusion that culture has a theoretical meaning rather than a practical one, and it is precisely that conclusion which the kinship between culture and doctrine is intended to convey. It is in this sense that we find even in Kant the far-reaching statement that metaphysics is the fulfillment of all culture of human reason—*die Vollendung aller Kultur*.[11] In this context metaphysics as a doctrine would mean the full realization of human reason, although critique and discipline lead us to the conclusion that such realization is unattainable. In this sense we may even conclude by saying that culture as akin to doctrine is an imaginary focus of the development of human reason; precisely in this sense it has to be lodged on a plane beyond that of practice.

To come now to the social and practical meaning of culture—which, to be sure, appears in Kant as well—we have to point in the first place to the contradistinction between barbarism and culture, or, in Kant's phrase, between roughness and culture; culture being related to the social worth of man. We see here a kind of merger of culture and enlightenment, since Kant refers in this context to progressively continuing enlightenment (*fortgesetzte Aufklärung*), in which human talents, taste, etc., gradually develop and become refined. This development, *qua* culture or enlightenment, is the precondition of a kind of substratum for the emergence of what Kant calls a moral whole (*ein moralisches Ganzes*). It is already clear from these hints or nuances in Kant's presentation that culture is not identical with morality, but it is, historically or anthropologically, the first step towards morality. Culture can mean here precisely a mode of discipline and not a mode of development or fulfillment, since in Kant's description it is related to the fruits of "unsociability" (*Früchte der Ungeselligkeit*); it thus leads to the overcoming of that very unsociability in order to develop a certain line of human activity which contains within itself the seeds of perfection—not, to be sure, the seeds of all activity natural to man, since some of these are, from the very outset, asocial. Culture proper would relate, then, solely to that basic human sociability which as such is but one amongst the various human potentialities and is by no means identical with their whole spectrum. Kant therefore distinguishes between three degrees or levels. We become cultured through art and science—and here again we see that practice is not the only level or arena of culture but that the impact of science is likewise directed towards making cultured individuals of us. Furthermore, in the present description Kant brings together art and science, but he does not particularly emphasize morality. Whereas Mendelssohn included under culture politeness and virtuosity, Kant suggests the distinction between being *cultured* and being *civilized*, the latter connoting all sorts of social graces and decorum—*Artigkeit und Anständigkeit*. He even adds parenthetically that we are, perhaps, too civilized for our own good, since for Kant the aspect of civilization connotes something that is superficial and external only. The third degree or level is that of morality. Morality belongs, he says, to culture, but is nevertheless different from it, for a reason that has to be explored. But (and this point calls for particular notice) in the context which we are here considering what Kant says is that although the idea of morality belongs to culture, to use that idea as a simulacrum in the love of honors and in connection with a purely outward decorum constitutes mere "civilization", or rather *Zivilisierung*.[12] Thus while on the one hand he distinguishes between morality and culture, on the other he points to the affinity between them, conceiving civilization, or the condition of being civilized, to be a sort of mere lip service to morality.

Kant employs the term culture in an even broader sense, when he says that there are two ends that must be present in man himself. One end must be of such a kind that man may be satisfied by nature and through its bountifulness. The other end is related to the aptitude and skill for which man may make use of nature in both the external and the internal senses. "The former end of nature would be the *happiness* of man, the latter his culture." Culture here connotes man's own achievement or that which man as a rational being produces out of his own choice; and culture is thus related to man's aptitude as a free being. The previous description of culture pointed to man's fulfillment in the theoretical domain, whereas the present connotation of it points to his fulfillment as a free being and therefore essentially as a moral being. To revert to the previous distinctions, culture in the broad sense is related to nature; it is a striving towards education (*nisus formativus*), since it is education that opens the door to higher ends than those which nature itself can afford. It is in this sense that culture is a higher vocation and a kind of end of nature. If culture connotes the higher vocation or the ultimate end and can to that extent be synonymous with morality, the position of the fine arts and of the sciences lies not on level of culture *qua* morality, since if the arts and sciences do not make man any morally better they do nevertheless make him civilized. This they achieve through conveying a pleasure that admits of universal communication and by introducing into society polish and refinement. In that sense civilization, or *Zivilisierung*, is not only a mode of adjustment to the norms of morality, but functions as a quasi-midwife in the process that leads to culture *qua* morality; since it helps to overcome the tyrannical propensities of the physical senses and so prepares man for a sovereignty that shall be exercised by reason alone.[13]

It is now clear that Kant uses the term culture in various contexts and uses it differently. It is from this point of view that we have to recognize not only a systematic difference between Mendelssohn and Kant insofar as concerns the anthropological and systematic position of morality, culture, and enlightenment, but terminological differences as well. The latter, in turn, are significant, since they point to a stage in the history of ideas and of philosophical terminology at which the four concepts of culture, enlightenment, civilization, and morality are conceived of as being both interrelated and yet distinct.

NOTES

1. Cicero, *Tusc. Disp.* ii, 5, 13 elaborates the connection; *ut agri non omnes frugiferi sunt . . . sic animi non omnes culti fructum ferunt . . . cultura autem animi philosophia est*, etc.

2. We refer to Mendelssohn's essay *Über der Frage: Was heisst Aufklären?* (*Moses Mendelssohn's Schriften zur Psychologie und Aesthetik*, ed. Moritz Brasch, Leipzig (Voss), ii, 1880, pp. 246f.)

3. The reference is obscure. Prof. E. E. Urbach suggests that the allusion is to Naḥmanides' statement regarding the destruction of Jerusalem—the holier the place, the more it is ravaged. Mendelssohn obviously has in mind the notion of *corruptio optimi pessima*.

3a. On the whole subject see A. Altmann, *Moses Mendelssohn,* 1973, especially pp. 660f. For the background to the controversy see Frieder Lötzsch, "Zur Genealogie der Frage 'Was ist Aufklärung': Mendelssohn, Kant und die Neologie", *Theokratia, Jahrbuch des Institutum Judaicum Delitzschianum,* 2 (1970–72) (K. H. Rengstorf Festschrift), Leiden, 1973, pp. 307f. On the notion of *Aufklärung* and the relevant sources see Giorgio Tonelli, " 'Lumières', 'Aufklärung', A Note on Semantics", *Studi Internazionali di Filosofia,* 6 (1974), pp. 166f.

4. We here follow in the main the English translation by Lewis White Beck in *Immanuel Kant on History*, edited and translated by L. W. Beck, Robert E. Anchor, and Emil L. Fackenheim (The Library of Liberal Arts, Indianapolis-New York, 1963), pp. 3f. See also "Was heisst: sich im Denken orientiren?" (1786), in Kant's *Kleinere Schriften zur Logik und Metaphysik,* 2nd ed. by Karl Vorländer, Leipsig (no date), part 2, p. 161.

5. See below, p. 273.

6. See *Idea for a Universal History from a Cosmopolitan Point of View* (*Kant on History* [see above, n. 4], pp. 22–3).

7. Cf. Plato, *Republic,* v, 473D; for a summary of the literary history of this quotation see the note on pp. 508f. of P. Shorey's translation (Loeb Classical Library, 1943).

8. *Perpetual Peace* (*Kant on History*, p. 116).

9. See *Kritik der reinen Vernunft*, B, pp. 766f; Norman Kemp Smith's English translation, New York-Toronto, 1965, pp. 593f.

10. *Kritik der reinen Vernunft*, B, pp. 737–8; English translation, p. 575.

11. *Ibid.*, B, p. 878; English translation, p. 665.

12. *Idea for a Universal History* (see above, notes 4, 6), pp. 17, 21.

13. Kant, *The Critique of Judgement*, translated by James Creed Meredith, Oxford, 1952. Part ii, Critique of Teleological Judgement, pp. 92, 94, 97.

The Psalm Superscriptions and the Guilds*

N. M. SARNA

I

The Priestly Code makes no provision for any recitative or musical component in the official cult.[1] This fact takes on significance in light of the wealth of detail that, by contrast, characterizes its descriptions of the ritual. The omission is extraordinary in that the ritual word and the ritual act are two interconnected and inseparable elements in the ancient near eastern cults. A. Leo Oppenheim has described the situation as follows: "Prayers in Mesopotamian religious practice are always linked to concomitant rituals. . . . Ritual activities and accompanying prayers are of like importance and constitute the religious act."[2] The lacuna in the Priestly Code fits in with the all but total silence in the superscriptions of the psalms concerning the cultic settings or associations of the individual compositions. Here again, Oppenheim's remarks about Mesopotamian practice are pertinent: "These rituals are carefully described in a section at the end of the prayer which addresses either the praying person or the officiating priest; . . . to interpret the prayers without regard to the rituals in order to obtain insight into the religious concepts they may reflect distorts the testimony."[3] The fact that Akkadian psalms generally furnish the requisite, self-identifying, typological, and cult-functional information merely serves to emphasize the extraordinary nature of the silence of the biblical psalms about their connections with the cult.

These two reciprocal peculiarities, that of the Priestly Code on the one hand, and of the psalms on the other, are augmented by yet a third puzzling phenomenon. The individual psalms are ascribed exclusively to nonpriests. The superscriptions feature the names of Moses, David, Solomon, and various Levites, but never that of Aaron or Aaronite priests, although several psalms are attributed to the sons of Aaron's archenemy, Korah.[4]

All this harmonizes with the consistent postexilic traditions that clearly differentiate between the two institutions of sacrifice and psalmody, the former being attributed to Moses, the latter to David (*2 Chron.* 23:18).[5] It is as though these sources are fully aware that the cultic situation in Israel was extraordinary in that the ritual act and the ritual word appear to have individually distinct and differentiated histories.

The classical critical reconstruction of the history of worship in Israel is best illustrated by R. H. Pfeiffer, who maintained that the Pentateuch achieved its final edition about the year 400 B.C.E. Since it ignores the whole institution of temple singing, although the contemporary ritual is described in great detail, it proves that the regular, organized liturgy was still unknown in Jerusalem in 400 B.C.E. It was between 400 and 250 B.C.E. that the guilds of temple singers, according to Pfeiffer, "were organized and provided with their hymnals." The bulk of the psalter, in fact, "probably originated at this period."[6]

Y. Kaufmann, on the other hand, who by and large ascribed the composition of the psalms to the preexilic period, suggested a different explanation for the nonmention of any recitative or musical element in the cult of the Priestly Code. To him, the first Temple was "the temple of silence", a distinctive innovation of the priests who deliberately set about fashioning a nonpagan, nonmagical religion by disengaging the spoken ritual from the cultic act, downgrading the former in terms of relative importance.[7]

II

As attractive as Kaufmann's theory is, it fails to take into account several important aspects of the problem. It is well known that all literature in the ancient world waged a constant struggle for survival.[8] If the psalms had been wholly separated from the cult, it would be difficult to conceive of another ambience in ancient Israel powerful enough to have ensured the preservation of the individual compositions and to have encouraged their assemblage into large collections. Moreover, there is abundant evidence to prove that the spoken word and vocal and instrumental music could not have been entirely absent from temple service in the period before the exile, the general silence of the pentateuchal sources notwithstanding.

In the first place, it should be pointed out that even though *Deuteronomy* repeatedly refers to the chosen "place" almost exclusively in relation to sacrifice, yet it is also a peculiar characteristic of this book that it prescribes the recitation of prayers and other formulae in connection with certain ritual ceremonies, namely, the expiation of an unsolved murder of an unidentified victim (*Deut.* 21:1–9), the bringing of the first fruits (26:2–10) and of the third-year tithe (vv. 12–15).[9] Furthermore, even the Priestly Code itself makes provision for verbal confession accompanying the offerings (*Lev.* 5:5; 16:21).[10] It also prescribes a verbal admonition by the priest to a suspected adultress (*Num.* 5:21–22) and an oral priestly blessing with a fixed formula (6:22–26). In another source, Hannah is engaged in prayer at the Temple of Shiloh when her family went there for an annual sacrifice (*1 Sam.* 1:3, 10–15) and it is hard to believe that such a form of religious expression was unique to her. The prophet Samuel is reported to have prayed aloud as he offered up a burnt offering (*ibid.*, 7:9), and it is quite apparent from the book of *Amos* that songs and music went together with animal sacrifice and oblation as a fixed and regular constituent of the rituals practised in the temple at Bethel (*Amos* 5:21–23).[11] There is absolutely no reason to think that this mode of worship was exclusive to this place. On the contrary, in his dedicatory invocation which he recited before the altar in the Temple at Jerusalem, Solomon envisages the institution essentially as a place of "prayer and supplication," and he begins and concludes his address with sacrifices (*1 Kings* 8:5, 12–64).[12] Isaiah similarly portrays the Temple as a house of prayer, and he denounces equally the multiplicity of prayers and sacrifices (*Isa.* 1:13–15). His contemporary King Hezekiah must surely be reflecting the reality of the first Temple when he speaks of offering music at the house of the Lord all the days of his life (38:20). Such a sentiment would hardly have been acceptable had not instrumental music constituted a fixed part of the service. Again, if the prophet of the Babylonian exile designates the Temple at Jerusalem the "House of prayer" (56:7), this, too, must faithfully reflect preexilic actuality.[13] The same conclusion is to be drawn from another exilic document, one most likely of Levite origin, in which a "Song of Zion" is identified as a "song of the Lord" (*Ps.* 137:3f.).[14] Finally, and perhaps the most decisive argument of all, is the presence of a vast amount of psalmodic language embedded in the prophetic orations.[15] This phenomenon testifies to a deep-rooted, well-formulated, and long-established tradition of public psalmody, one that could only have had its roots in and been sustained by the cult.

The cumulative effect of all the foregoing evidence adduced from the Biblical sources is the intensification of the twin problems of the general silence of the pentateuchal sources about any recitative or musical accompaniment to the sacrifices and the absence of any information in the superscriptions to the psalms about the cultic *Sitz im Leben* of these compositions. The conclusions would seem to be inescapable, firstly, that in the eyes of the priests psalmody was indeed extrinsic to the sacrificial rites, as Kaufmann observed, and, secondly, that the origins, cultivation and preservation of the psalms must be sought outside of priestly circles, though not necessarily beyond a temple ambience.[16] This state of affairs, however, presupposes the existence of independent nonpriestly musical guilds active within a temple complex. Can such an assertion be supported by the facts?

III

The only information that we have concerning temple singers and musicians derives from postexilic sources. As has already been mentioned, the Chronicler makes a sharp distinction between the institution of sacrifice, which he attributes to Moses, and that of psalmody, which he ascribes to David (*2 Chron.* 23:18). The same differentiation is made by the book of *Ezra* (3:2, 10), and the author of *Nehemiah* is likewise conscious of the fact that David had originally set up the musical guilds (*Neh.* 12:24, 45–46). The book of *Chronicles* purports to provide the historical background to this tradition. It describes how, when David moved the ark to Jerusalem thereby making the city the cultic center of Israel, he appointed Heman, Asaph, and Ethan, of the Levitical clans of Kohath, Gershom, and Merari respectively, to take charge of the vocal music (*1 Chron.* 6:16–34). This story is amplified in *1 Chron.* 15:16–24, and at the end of David's life there are supposedly no less than four thousand Levites whose responsibility it is to praise the Lord on musical instruments (23:5–6, 30). Further details of David's classification of the musicians are given in another passage (25:1–8) and no opportunity is lost by the Chronicler to emphasize the Davidic origin of the institution, whether the context deals with Solomon (*2 Chron.* 8:14), Jehoiada (23:18), Hezekiah (29:20, 25), or Josiah (35:15).

The obvious question is whether these traditions possess any historical kernel. Are they merely retrojections from the early second Temple into the first Temple? Admittedly, the genealogies of the biblical singers as recorded in the book of *Chronicles* leave much to be desired. They are often internally inconsistent, and they betray evidence of schematization and artificiality.[17] This, however, does not of itself discredit the claim of a preexilic origin for the guilds. In fact, a close examination of the various sources tends to support the basic proposition.

IV

Without doubt, the association of David with the institution of liturgical singing primarily arose from the fact that it was he who captured Jerusalem and who, by moving the ark there, transformed it into a great cultic center. There is no reason to doubt, and every reason to accept the authenticity of the traditions that stress David's ambition to build a temple (*2 Sam.* 7:2, 4 = *1 Chron.* 17:1, 4, *et al.*),[18] and if such be the case, why should he not have interested himself in the organization of its forms of worship? It is surely no accident that the biography of David depicts him as an accomplished harpist (*1 Sam.* 16:16–23; 19:9), a composer of dirges (*2 Sam.* 1:17; 3:33) and hymns, (22:1), and an inventor of musical instruments (*Amos* 6:5). This last-mentioned tradition is also prominent in the post-exilic sources (*Neh.* 12:36; *1 Chron.* 23:5; *2 Chron.* 7:6, 29, 26f.).[19]

Postbiblical lore has, of course, credited David with the authorship of the book of *Psalms*, even though seventy-three only of its one hundred and fifty compositions actually have the title *le-dawid.*[20] It has been shown that this tradition is but the late crystallization of a trend that gradually displaced earlier and variant traditions.[21] But the antiquity of the tradition associating David with psalm authorship is apparent from the fact that no less than sixty-five of the seventy-three Davidic psalms are contained in the first two divisions of the book. These are universally agreed to constitute the earliest collection, and this conclusion is supported by the colophon, "The prayers of David son of Jesse are ended" (72:20), which demonstrates that the editor was oblivious of the existence of the other eighteen Davidic psalms. The paucity of Davidic ascriptions in the rest of the psalter despite the increasing tendency to associate David with the composition of that work, as is evidenced by the Greek translation[22] and the colophon to the

Psalms scroll from Qumran,[23] proves that the canonical superscriptions were fossilized fairly early, and that scribes and editors did not feel free to add to them at will in the text tradition represented by the Masorah. An interesting case in point is provided by the Chronicles version of the removal of the ark to Jerusalem. At David's behest, the Levites, led by Asaph, chant *Pss.* 105, 96, 107, and 106 (*1 Chron.* 16). Nevertheless, none of these compositions appears in the canonical psalter with a Davidic or Asaphite ascription.[24] This is not to say, of course, that David is to be necessarily regarded as having been the author of all those psalms that bear the title *le-dawid.* It is to say that this ascription is very early and that it has its origin in an authentic tradition linking David with liturgical music.[25]

V

The question now arises as to whether the other names that appear in the superscriptions to psalms might not, in like manner, rest on ancient and genuine traditions. It is to be noted that Asaph, the Korahites, Heman and Ethan all appear as clan guilds[26] in the postexilic sources and that neither these nor the psalter contains the name of a guild that does not appear in the other. Are all these sources interdependent?

The fact of the matter is that of all the clan guilds the Asaphites alone are recorded in the lists of those returning from the Babylonian exile (*Ezra* 2:4 = *Neh.* 7:44), and they alone participate in the ceremony marking the founding of the second Temple (*Ezra* 3:10). Not one of the others is even mentioned in *Ezra-Nehemiah.*[27] There would be no reason for the Chronicler to have invented Heman, Ethan, and the Korahites had they never existed and no ground for the book of *Ezra-Nehemiah* to have suppressed the fact of their existence had they indeed been active in the restoration period. This line of reasoning receives added impetus from recent archaeological finds, for the name *bny qrḥ* appears on an inscribed bowl from the Arad temple, showing that the clan bearing this name was active in preexilic times.[28] Incidentally, this conclusion is reinforced by evidence from the same site for the presence of the Kerosites in this period, a family of the Nethinim the existence of which is otherwise known from *Ezra* 2:44 (=*Neh.* 7:47) only and is not recorded in any preexilic source.[29] It may be added that if the Levitical clan guilds, Asaph, Korah, Heman, and Ethan, be late inventions, it is strange that Books IV and V of *Psalms,* which by general consensus are the latest parts of the canonical psalter,[29a] do not ascribe any compositions to them. Nor do the Greek and Qumran versions add any but Davidic superscriptions.

Furthermore, it can be demonstrated that the clan guild names attached to some of the psalms cannot be connected with the Chronicles traditions, nor can the data of this work be a reflex of the psalms headings.

(a) Twelve psalms are attributed to Asaph[30] and eleven to the Korahites.[31] Clearly, there is little to choose between the two guilds in terms of their importance and roles in the history of psalmody as far as the evidence from the psalter is concerned. This picture, however, is in striking contrast to that reflected in the postexilic historiography. To the Chronicler, the Asaphites were by far the most prestigious of all the levitical clan guilds, and their association with the official cult is said to span the entire period from David to Josiah.[32] They participate in each of the great temple services and, as has already been noted, they are the sole remaining singers and musicians in the period of the restoration (*Ezra* 2:41; *Neh.* 7:44). The Korahites, on the other hand, are not mentioned among the levitical clans appointed by David to lead the recitative-musical side of the service. They play no role in any of the great national acts of public worship. Only once do they appear as participants in a cultic ceremony, and even then they share the honors with the Kohathites. This occurred in the days of King Jehoshaphat (873–849 B.C.E.) in connection with an Ammonite and Moabite attack at Eyn Gedi *(2 Chron.* 20:19). [33]Otherwise, the Chronicler depicts the Korahites as "guards of the threshold of the tabernacle" (*1 Chron.* 9:19), as "preparers of the wafers" (v. 31) and as "gate-keepers" (*1 Chron.* 26:1, 19).

(b) A similar discrepancy between the traditions of *Chronicles* and those of the book of *Psalms* emerges from an examination of the history of Heman. Only one psalm is associated with this name (*Ps.* 88), and this not exclusively so. Yet the postexilic historiographer accords Heman pride of place among the singers who are said to have officiated when David brought the ark to Jerusalem, and Asaph and Ethan acted as his assistants (*1 Chron.* 15:17, 19). Once the ark was in its resting place, Heman was appointed by David to lead the worship (6:18), and his precedence over Asaph is again demonstrated by his central position on that occasion, flanked as he was by Asaph on the right and Ethan on the left (vv. 24, 29). He bears the title "Heman the singer" (v. 18); he is connected with the Kohathites (*ibid.*), and is the grandson of none other than Samuel (*ibid.*). No less than twenty-one generations are listed back to Levi (vv. 18–23) in contrast with Asaph's fourteen (vv. 24–28) and, in addition, special mention is made of his fourteen sons and three daughters (*1 Chron.* 25:5). Moreover the Hemanites, like the Asaphites, took an active part in all the great occasions of public worship down to Josiah's time. Such is the Chronicler's picture; yet *Ezra-Nehemiah* ignores this guild and the psalter assigns it but a solitary composition.

There can be no doubt that in respect of Asaph, the Korahites, and Heman the data to be culled from the psalms, superscriptions are totally at variance with the traditions of postexilic biblical historiography. Neither source is a reflex of the other. Each is independent of the other and both, as was shown above, contrast strongly with the realities of the restoration period as recorded in *Ezra-Nehemiah. Psalms* and *Chronicles* must both represent genuine preexilic, if irreconcilable traditions.

VI

The antiquity of organized liturgical music in Israel should not be regarded as in any way surprising in light of the documented history of the institution in the ancient near east. Sumerian musicological traditions can be traced back to as early as the middle of the third millenium B.C.E. From this time come the Early Dynastic lists of professions which include singers and musicians. By the Old Babylonian period this tradition was very highly developed.[34] Vocalists and instrumentalists, both male and female,[35] were a staple feature of Mesopotamian temple personnel.[36] In Egypt, likewise, singers and musicians of both sexes occupied an important place in the temple cult.[37] One wisdom text declares "singing, dancing and incense" to be the "food" of the god,[38] i.e., they constitute the proper forms of divine service. The Ugaritic texts have yielded several references to *šrm*, vocalist-instrumentalists, in lists of people grouped together according to guilds.[39] In some of these *khnm* and *qdšm*, the two main priestly classes, are also mentioned in addition to craftsmen,[40] while in one text *mṣlm*, cymbalists, also appear.[41] The existence of identifiable, organized groups of professional musicians as temple personnel at Ugarit is firmly established.[42]

One of the characteristics of the guilds in general was the familial pattern adopted for their organization. A member might be designated a "son" of a trade or profession,[43] or the members of the same calling might trace their descent back to a common ancestor.[44] The longevity of such traditions is astonishing. In mid-second millenium Babylon there were scribal families that claimed to trace their ancestry back ten or more centuries.[45] In Assyria, from *c.* 900 B.C.E. to the fall of Nineveh in 612 B.C.E., a single family monopolized the office of Head of the Royal Chancery.[46] There are recorded instances of artisans who claimed descent from one who lived at least seven hundred years earlier, and the onomastic evidence from the guild lists in the early Achaemenid period shows that skills could stay in the same family generation after generation.[47]

The foregoing evidence makes it difficult to understand why the notion of the antiquity of liturgical music in Israel should have encountered such scholarly resistance. Nor is it clear why the various clans of professional singers could not have followed the familial pattern common to the guilds of Mesopotamia. Already in the period of the united monarchy, we can discern the beginnings of the concentration of skills and of bureaucratic positions within individual families, when Solomon appointed as "scribes" the two sons of David's "scribe" (*1 Kings* 4:3; *2 Sam.* 20:25).[48] Unfortunately, the onomastic data in the Hebrew Bible is too meagre to permit the kind of reconstruction that is possible from the Mesopotamian sources, but we can follow the history of a few professional families from the period of Josiah to the destruction of Judea, and the results are most revealing.[49]

Members of the Shaphan family were active during the reigns of three Judean kings in succession. Thus, Shaphan "the scribe", as well as his son, Ahikam, served King Josiah (*2 Kings* 22:3, 12; *2 Chron.* 34:8, 20; *Jer.* 26:24). Another son, Gemariah, was a high official during the reign of King Jehoiakim (*Jer.* 36:10, 12, 25) as was also Gemariah's son, Micaiah (v. 11). Elasah, another Shaphanid, served King Zedekiah (29:3), while Ahikam's son, Gedaliah, became governor of Judea after the destruction (*2 Kings* 25:22; *Jer.* 39:14; 40:5 *et al.*). Another family whose bureaucratic service also spans the reigns of the last kings of Judah is that of Achbor son of Micaiah (*2 Kings* 22:12; *2 Chron.* 34:20) who served Josiah. His son Elnathan was ambassador to Egypt for King Jehoiakim (*Jer.* 26:22; 36:12, 25) and his grandson is most likely the "Coniah son of Elnathan" mentioned in the Lachish letters as performing similar service for King Zedekiah.[50] A third instance is that of Neriah, whose son, Baruch, was Jeremiah's amanuensis (*Jer.* 32:12 *et al.*) and whose other son, Seraiah, was part of the diplomatic entourage of Zedekiah on his visit to Babylon (51:59)

These few examples, fortuitously preserved in biblical literature, may safely be understood to be representative of the general pattern, especially in Judah where the unbroken stability of the Davidic dynasty over a period of half a millenium would have fostered and sustained the growth of professional families who traditionally derived their livelihood from service to the state. The concentration of skills within these families, transmitted from father to son(s), would have been a natural concomitant of their status.[51] There seems to be no reason at all why the same situation should not have obtained in the cult centers of Judah and Israel. Conforming to widespread near eastern practice, these institutions may be expected to have nourished professional guilds modeled after the family pattern. There is no reason for skepticism either as to the first temple antiquity of the liturgical musical clan guilds in Israel, or as to the basic genuineness of the traditions which associate these groups with the names of Asaph, Ethan, Heman, and the Korahites. These guilds were attached to temples which were the source of their income, but because of their specialized skills, they would also have been highly mobile. When one cult center was destroyed or declined, the professionals could migrate to another. The narratives about Micah the Levite in the days of the Judges (*Judges* 17) and about the migration of Levites from north to south in the days of Rehoboam (*2 Chron.* 11:13f.) provide excellent examples of this type of mobility.

VII

If we look upon the psalms collections as the repertoires of musical guilds that operated in the various cult centers throughout Judah and Israel, then we can explain how the individual compositions came to be preserved and we are able to account for many puzzling phenomena. The fact of the multiplicity of shrines in Judah and Israel throughout most of the monarchy period hardly needs documentation,[52] but it is worth recalling that several existed for hundreds of years, apparently enjoying great prestige. Dan,[53] Bethel,[54] Beer Sheba,[55] Geba,[56] and Gilgal[57] receive special mention in the sources. Gibeon[58] is of particular interest, because David is said to have assigned Heman and Jeduthun to act as liturgical singers there (*1 Chron.* 16:39–42). The surprising discovery of the Arad temple, not referred to in any biblical source, amply illustrates the ramified nature of this network of cultic institutions.[59] All these places may be assumed to have maintained a cadre of professional personnel and to have provided opportunities of employment for the clan guilds. It would have been at such places that psalms would have been composed, recited, preserved, collected, and transmitted from generation to generation within the local guild.

The migration of professionals from guild to guild and the absorption or displacement of one guild by another[60] supplies a plausible explanation for the duplication of individual psalms or units within the psalter[61] and for the occasional attribution of one psalm to two personages.[62] By the same token, the presence of the name of the same singer in different genealogical lists[63] need not necessarily always be the product of scribal confusion but may sometimes authentically reflect different historical situations, in which a member of one clan guild passed over to another and was incorporated within it. Moreover, the otherwise inexplicable presence within the book of *Psalms* of compositions of undoubted northern Israelite provenance now finds a natural explanation. Psalms like 77, 80, and 81 in which Israel is referred to as "Joseph" could not have originated in Judah. They belonged to the northern shrines and must have been brought south by the remnants of the temple personnel who fled from the destruction of their shrines by the Assyrians.[64] At this time, much of the archives and literature of the north was brought to Jerusalem and was in this way preserved from oblivion.[65]

The severance of tradition about the meaning of the technical terminology of the psalms is another problem that can find its solution through the well-founded assumption that guilds were the bearers and tradents of liturgical poetry. The Greek translation shows that the terms were already alien to the scholars who worked on it early in the second century B.C.E. In other words, even during second Temple times, when the chanting of psalms constituted the core of the worship, the musicological terminology was no longer intelligible. The reason for this loss of understanding is that the terms belonged to the era of the first Temple when the different collections of psalms were still the actual repertoires of the various temple guilds who may be assumed to have carefully guarded their professional techniques. A curious parallel to such a state of affairs derives, indeed, from the second Temple. Tannaitic literature has preserved a tradition about a certain

Hygros b. Levi who was in charge of the temple singing and who earned the opprobrium of the sages for selfishly withholding his professional secrets from others.[66] At the other end of the chronological spectrum, Mesopotamian incantation and psalm literature provides us with another analogy, for the Akkadian scribes who inherited and copied the Sumerian texts were unable to understand the technical terms used therein.[67]

Another problem that can now be satisfactorily resolved is the discrepancy between the data that can be culled from the superscriptions to the psalms and that supplied by the book of *Chronicles*.[68] It is clear that the two sources reflect quite different perceptions of reality, the former having preserved the remnants of the guild repertoires, the latter the state of affairs in the Jerusalem cultus. If the Chronicler does not depict the Korahites as singers, it is because they did not function as such in Jerusalem. When the psalms headings disclose the importance of this guild in the composition and preservation of liturgical texts, they faithfully mirror the role of the Korahites in provincial shrines.[69]

VIII

It now remains to return to the problems with which this study opened, *viz*., why the Priestly Code has nothing to say about any vocal-instrumental component of the cult, and why the superscriptions of the psalms carry no cult-functional information.

The resolution of these enigmas must be sought in the contrast between the primary role of sacrifice and the undoubtedly secondary nature of liturgical music in the Israelite cult. Sacrifice lay within the exclusive domain of the established priesthood; the singers were minor clerics. Even outside Israel, where the cultic role of singers and musicians was highly important, their social status was not correspondingly so. In Egypt, it appears that in the oldest epochs these functionaries were of low rank, and it was in late times only that their prestige increased.[70] In Mesopotamia, the overseer of the musicians could not compare in social status and power with the overseers of other specialized crafts.[71] In Israel the separation of sacrifice from the vocal-musical side of the service, in emphasis of the nonmagical nature of the national religion,[72] meant that the singers would, merely in virtue of that fact, have assumed an inferior position in the temple hierarchy. The priestly texts are intended to be a manual of instruction for the levitical priesthood, and it should occasion no surprise that those aspects or forms of worship not entrusted to it should have been beyond their interest.[73]

As to the reason why the book of *Kings* ignores the singers, their lowly status in the first Temple and the additional fact that the main centers of psalmody were most likely the provincial shrines provide sufficient warrant.[74] But how to explain the absence from the superscriptions to the individual psalms of any information about an accompanying cultic act?

The possibility cannot be eliminated that such notices were once attached to the headings of individual compositions[75] and that in the course of time they fell out because they were rendered meaningless when the psalms came to be used for prayer independently of the temple service. However, the likelihood of this having happened is diminished by our inability to explain why, in the same circumstances, the information about the guilds and the technical musicological terminology was retained even though it, too, had become unintelligible. Accordingly, it will be prudent to assume that the psalms never did possess any such cult-functional notices.

In that case, when were the psalms recited? There is evidence to support the view that the times of the *tamid*, the regular daily burnt offering in early morning and late afternoon, were regarded as the most appropriate for intercession. The narrative in *2 Chron.* 29:27 shows that the levitical choir burst into song as the early sacrificial rite began (cf. v. 20). Other passages in the same book indicate that this was the usual practice in the early second Temple (*1 Chron.* 16:40–42; 23:30–31), and Ben Sira's description of the temple service at the beginning of the second century B.C.E. specifies the same procedure (*Ben Sira* 50:11–19). There is no doubt that this coordination of the vocal-musical recitation with the regular offering was rooted in first Temple usage. This finds clear expression in *Ps.* 92:2–4:

> It is good to praise the LORD,
> to sing hymns to your name O Most High,
> To proclaim your steadfast love at daybreak,
> Your faithfulness each night
> With the ten-stringed harp,
> With voice and lyre together.

The morning and late afternoon temple services naturally became the times for individual prayer. The morning occasion is attested in the psalter in several passages:

> Hear my voice, O LORD, at daybreak;
> at daybreak I plead before you, and wait.
>
> (*Ps.* 5:4)

> But I will sing of your strength,
> extol each morning your faithfulness;
> for you have been my haven,
> a refuge in time of trouble.
>
> (*Ps.* 59:17)

> As for me, I cry out to you;
> each morning my prayer greets you.
>
> (*Ps.* 88:14)

On the other hand, it was at the time for the regular evening (meal-?) offering *(minḥah)* that Elijah chose to submit his prayer *(1 Kings* 18:29, 36).

Daniel (9:3–19, 21) and Ezra (9:5) likewise selected the identical hour for the same purpose, and this would seem to reflect preexilic practice. One text, in particular, supports this and indicates that the custom of coordinating prayer with the evening temple service was well based:

> Take my prayer as an offering
> of incense,[76]
> my upraised hands as an
> evening sacrifice.[77]
>
> (*Ps.* 141:2)

This passage clearly belongs to a time when there was not only a close cultic connection between prayers and the late afternoon offerings but when prayer was itself achieving independent status. The psalm text, like all the preceding ones, does not mention animal sacrifice, although the burnt offering was prescribed for the evening as well as for the morning. The phrase used in each case is *minḥath ᶜerev*, "the evening (meal-) offering." It would appear that in the course of the monarchy period there were times when the animal sacrifices were suspended at the evening service.[78] Thus, the instructions of King Ahaz to the high priest concerning the use of his new "great altar," expressly distinguishes between the "morning burnt-offering" (*ᶜolah*) and the "evening (meal-) offering" (*minḥah*) (*2 Kings* 16:15). Similarly, Ezekiel mentions the morning sacrifice only and ignores completely that of the evening (*Ezek.* 46:13–15). In these circumstances, the evening service would comprise the incense-offering and the meal-offering, and it would be the smoke of the former that would be the signal for prayer. It cannot be accidental that in the great temple vision of Isaiah (*ch.* 6), the prophet observes the angels rhapsodizing God while the building kept filling with smoke (v. 4). This can be none other than the smoke of the incense,[79] since the visionary ritual takes place in the inner sanctuary which was the proper place for the altar of incense.[80] It must also be remembered that the incense had an expiatory function[81] that made it appropriate to the purposes of the ritual of *Isaiah* ch. 6.

This close association between the incense-offering and the prayers is of particular significance for the development of the Israelite liturgy in the cult places outside of Jerusalem. One of the intriguing questions relating to the religious history of Israel is the nature of the impact that the reformism of Hezekiah and of Josiah had on the type of worship carried on external to the Temple. Early in the eighth century B.C.E. widespread efforts were made under royal authority to restrict the practice of animal sacrifice.[82] The far-reaching and more thoroughgoing measures taken by Josiah about a hundred years later made the Temple in Jerusalem the exclusive cultic site.[83] The numerous cult centers that had existed for so long had clearly fulfilled a basic need for the individual and the community. What was the response to the centralizing measures of Hezekiah and Josiah? The fact that a precedent had already been set in the Jerusalem Temple for the possibility of a service without animal sacrifice but with incense offering, oblation, and psalmody, must have made the transition to new forms easier. It is possible, in fact, that archeology has supplied us with remarkable testimony to the reality of this development. If Aharoni's stratification and interpretation are correct, the temple at Arad remained in service for another hundred years after the altar of sacrifices had been removed in the time of Hezekiah, following two centuries in continuous use. In the subsequent intervening period there is evidence for the use of incense.[84] The proof is lacking, but it is reasonable to assume that prayer and psalmody became the core of the ritual.

A revealing narrative that supports the theory that incense and meal-offering developed independently of animal sacrifice is that of the eighty mourning men who set out for Jerusalem from Shechem, Shiloh, and Samaria. They carried with them "meal offering (*minḥah*) and frankincense" (*Jer.* 41:5) even though the temple was known to be in ruins. Nothing is mentioned of animal sacrifice.[85] The most decisive text of all comes from the Elephantine papyri. Here we have a petition (dated 408 B.C.E.) on behalf of the Jews of Yeb to Bigvai, the Persian governor of Judea, for permission to rebuild the temple in that place. It states that in the past "meal offerings [*minḥah*], frankincense, and animal sacrifices [*ᶜalawah*]" had been conducted there and it requests their reinstatement. It reports that an earlier appeal to the civil and ecclesiastical authorities in Jerusalem had gone unanswered. What is of crucial importance is that the affirmative reply of the governor permits only meal offering (*minḥatha*) and incense and that a further petition from the same source relating to this temple at Yeb emphatically excludes animal sacrifice. In other words, the priesthood in Jerusalem does not seem to have objected to this arrangement;[86] it already had a respectable history behind it.

It is worth noting that several texts from second Temple times, and beyond, have preserved mention of the practice of coordinating prayer with the incense-offering. Thus, it is related in the book of *Judith*:

". . . and the incense of the evening was now being offered at Jerusalem in the house of God and Judith cried unto the Lord with a loud voice. . . ." (*Judith* 9:1)[87] The *Testament of the Twelve Patriarchs* mentions "the archangels who minister and make propitiation to the Lord for all the sins of ignorance of the righteous, offering to the Lord sweet smelling savour, a reasonable and bloodless offering" (3:5–6).[88] A similar picture of angelic liturgy, which obviously is a reflex of terrestrial usage, comes from the *Book of Adam*: "And I beheld golden censers between your father and the chariot and all the angels with censers and frankincense came in haste to the incense-offering and blew upon it and the smoke of the incense veiled the firmaments. And the angels fell down and worshipped God, crying aloud and saying, JAEL, Holy One, have pardon, for he is thy image and the work of thy holy hands."[89]

Moving to the New Testament, we note a report that "the whole multitude of the people were praying outside at the hour of incense" (*Luke* 1:10). This close interplay of incense offering and prayer is explicitly and symbolically articulated in the book of *Revelation*, where "the golden bowls full of incense are the prayers of the saints" (5:8). A vision is described in which an "angel came and stood at the altar with a golden censer; and he was given much incense to mingle with the prayers of all the saints upon the golden altar before the throne; and the smoke of the incense rose with the prayers of the saints from the hand of the angel before God" (8:3f).[90]

In rabbinic literature of postdestruction times, the memory of the meal-offering incense-prayer association was well preserved:

R. Yose said: "the afternoon (*minḥah*) prayer does not correspond to the *tamid* of eventide, but to the incense. How so? 'Let my prayer be as an offering of incense before you, my upraised hands as the evening meal-offering'" (*minḥah*) (*Ps.* 141:2).[91]

A midrashic text interprets *Mal.* 1:11 as follows: R. Samuel bar Naḥman said, "what is the pure meal-offering which in every place is fragrantly (*muqṭar*) submitted for the name of the Holy One, blessed be He? It is the afternoon (*minḥah*) prayer. *Muqṭar* means none other than the afternoon prayer, as it is said, etc." (*Ps.* 141:2).[92] Another midrash which expounds *Ps.* 141:2 recognizes prayer as a substitute for the now defunct incense offering: "Thus said David, 'My Lord, when the Temple existed we used to offer incense before you. Now that we have neither altar nor high priest, accept my prayer, etc.'"[93]

IX

A wealth of evidence of a varied nature, stretching from rabbinic times back through the second Temple and well into the monarchy period, demonstrates an interaction of the daily *tamid* ceremonies with prayer and psalmody. In the Jerusalem center itself, there were times when the constituents of the late afternoon service were the meal-offering, the incense-offering, and psalmody. As a result of the movement toward centralization of worship, the provincial shrines dropped the sacrificing of animals and in most cases also the meal-offerings. In these circumstances, psalmody would assume ever greater importance and become increasingly divorced from the sacrificial cult. It achieved independent status as an act of worship, a situation reflected in *Ps.* 141:2. The musical guilds attached to different cult centers would thereby gain increasing prestige. The repertoires of the guilds would be carefully collected and edited. As the provincial centers were progressively destroyed by successive invasions and by the sweeping reforms of Josiah, two forces would be set in motion which would interact to preserve the psalms literature. The movement of guild survivors southward to Jerusalem and their incorporation into the temple cult enriched the repertoires of the choirs and in this way ensured the survival of provincial and northern compositions. The various smaller collections that can be isolated within the psalter owe their origin to the historical processes here described, and just as the proverbs literature was edited by Hezekiah's literati (*Prov.* 25:1), so the psalms must have undergone similar treatment. At the same time, the closing down of the cult centers, whether by force of the deuteronomistic movement or by enemy action, obviously left in its wake a spiritual void that had to be filled. It is absurd to believe that the designation of Jerusalem as the exclusive cult center was either intended to, or could actually succeed in depriving all votaries of the national religion not within easy reach of Jerusalem of all form of self-expression. The one constituent of the cult that was independent of both edifice and priesthood was psalmody, and it must have filled the breach. In this way, the transition from a sacrificial, priest-controlled, cult to a democratized cultless religion was effected, and the people of Israel was enabled to overcome with relative ease the great crisis that the destruction of Jerusalem by the Babylonians was to create.

NOTES

* The research for this paper was done during a sabbatical leave supported by a fellowship from the ACLS.

1. Rabbinic sensitivity to this peculiarity is reflected in eisegetical attempts to find pentateuchal "sources" for the institution of liturgical song; cf. T.B. *ᶜArakhin* 11a; *Num. Rabbah* 6, 10.

2. A. Leo Oppenheim, *Ancient Mesopotamia*, 1964, p. 175.

3. *Ibid.* Cf. S. Mowinckel, *The Psalms in Israel's Worship*, translated by D. Ap-Thomas, 1962, i, p. 20; cf. W. W. Hallo, *Actes de la XVIIe Rencontre Assyriologique Internationale*, 1969, pp. 116–134.

4. The consistent use of *beney* exclusively with Korah in the psalms superscription reflects the narrative of *Num.* 16; 26:1. The omission of a reference to Korah in *Ps.* 106:17 may well be out of deference to the prestigious guild of Korahites.

5. Cf. also *2 Chron.* 8:12–14.

6. R. H. Pfeiffer, *Introduction to the Old Testament*, 1948, pp. 624, 798, on which see the remarks of W. F. Albright, *JBL*, 61 (1942), p. 122.

7. Y. Kaufmann, *Toledoth Ha-ʾemunah Ha-Yisreʾelith*, ii, 1947, pp. 476–478; *The Religion of Israel*, translated and abridged by M. Greenberg, 1960, pp. 302–304.

8. For the situation in Greek literature, cf. M. I. Finley, *The World of Odysseus*, 1959, p. 9. For the underlying reasons, see the author's *Understanding Genesis*, 1970, pp. xviii–xix.

9. See M. Weinfeld, *Deuteronomy and the Deuteronomic School*, 1972, pp. 32, 42, 44, 213.

10. As noted by A. Rofé, *Kiryat Sefer*, 48 (1973), p. 86.

11. Pfeiffer's contention, *op. cit.* (*supra*, n. 6), p. 624, that Amos denounced liturgical music and song as such is simply untrue, nor is there any support for his assertion, p. 798, that the prophet found them to be "crude and noisy."

12. On Solomon's prayer, see Kaufmann, *op. cit.* (*supra*, n. 7), ii, pp. 361f., 367f.; Weinfeld, *op. cit.* (*supra*, n. 9), pp. 36, 195f. It should be noted that according to *1 Kings* 10:12 (=*2 Chron.* 9:11) Solomon makes provision for "harps

and lyres for the singers," but it is not clear whether the latter performed in the Temple or in his palace; cf. *Ezek.* 40:44 where, however, the text and context are uncertain, as v. 45 and the Greek show.

13. The same notice is reflected in *Isa.* 60:6–7.

14. Cf. *2 Chron.* 29:27 in which the "song of the Lord" is musical prayer accompanying the sacrifice.

15. On this subject, see Kaufmann, *Toledoth* (*supra,* p. 295, n. 7), ii pp. 646–727; iii, pp. 605–613.

16. Cf. M. Haran, *JBL*, 80 (1961), p. 158, n. 3.

17. The genealogies have been analyzed by J. Köberle, *Die Tempelsänger im alten Testament*, 1899; K. Möhlenbrink, *ZAW*, 52 (1934), pp. 184–231, esp. pp. 202f., 229–231; H. Gese, in *Abraham unser Vater . . . Festschrift Otto Michel* 1963, pp. 222–234 (drawn to my attention by Prof. M. J. Buss); J. Liver, *Chapters in the History of the Priests and Levites* [Hebrew], 1968, pp. 53–99, apart from the commentaries to *Chronicles.* For a rabbinic observation on the genealogies in the book of *Chronicles* in general, see *Lev. Rabba* (1,3); *Ruth Rabbathi* (2,1).

18. Cf. *1 Kings* 5:17; 8:17f. = *2 Chron.* 6:7f.; *2 Kings* 21:7 = *2 Chron.* 33:7.

19. Rabbinic tradition would even make David a singer before his birth; cf. T.B. *Ber.* 10a.

20. *Mid. Tehillim* 1, 2, ed. S. Buber, 1893, p. 3; T. B. *Bava Bathra* 14b.

21. B. Jacob, *ZAW*, 16 (1896), pp. 162f. As B. S. Childs has shown, *JSS,* 16 (1971), pp. 137–150, the thirteen superscriptions containing historical references to David are the product of exegetical activity and not a reflection of independent historical tradition.

22. This adds the Davidic title to *Pss.* 33, 43, 71, 91, 93–99, 104, and even 137 (!). Note that *Acts* 4:25–26 cites the anonymous *Ps.* 2 as Davidic.

23. J. A. Sanders, *The Psalms Scroll of Qumran Cave II* (*II Ps*[a]), 1965, col. XXVII, 4f., 9f., pp. 91f.; *The Dead Sea Psalms Scroll*, 1967, pp. 134–137.

24. It is to be noted that the Greek assigns *Ps.* 96 to David, even though it adds a superscription with a reference to postexilic history.

25. The genuineness of the tradition associating David with the founding of psalmody in Israel has merited increasing scholarly support in recent years; cf. W. F. Albright in *Alexander Marx Jubilee Volume* [English Section], 1950, p. 66; *Archaeology and the Religion of Israel,* 1969, pp. 121–125; *Yahweh and the Gods of Canaan,* 1968, pp. 250–253, 254 n. 134; R. de Vaux, *Ancient Israel,* 1961, pp. 382, 457; S. Mowinckel, *op. cit.* (*supra,* p. 295, n. 3), ii, pp. 80f.; R. North, *JBL,* 82 (1963), p. 374; 83 (1964), pp. 386f.; O. Eissfeldt, *Cambridge Ancient History*, 1965, ii, chap. XXXIV, fasc. 32, p. 49; H. H. Rowley, *Worship in Ancient Israel*, 1967, p. 206; I. Engnell, *A Rigid Scrutiny,* translated and edited by J. T. Willis, 1969, p. 74.

26. The use of the term "guild" in this study refers to the existence of recognizable cohesive groups of temple personnel. It should be noted that Jeduthun has been omitted for the following reasons: (i) he is not mentioned in the lists of *1 Chron.* 6 and 15. (ii) He appears as a singer only where Ethan is omitted, *viz., 1 Chron.* 16:41, 42; 25:1, 3, 6; *2 Chron.* 5:12; 29:14; 31:15. (iii) No ancestry of his is given. (iv) Although the name appears with *lamed auctoris* in *Ps.* 39:1, it features in *Pss.* 62:1; 77:1, extraordinarily, with *ʿal* (on which see Rashi and Ibn Ezra to 62:1). (v) His descendants are listed as gate-keepers, not as singers, in *1 Chron.* 16:38, 42.

27. *Neh.* 11:17 = *1 Chron.* 9:16 list a Levite (ʿAvda/Obadiah) of the fourth generation from Jeduthun, but he is not said to be a singer.

28. Y. Aharoni, *BA*, 31 (1968), p. 11; *Qadmoniyyoth*, 1, 3 (1968), p. 102, who assigns the artifact to stratum VII, which he dates to the age of Hezekiah (715–687 B.C.E.). This, of course, throws into question the attempt of G. Wanke, *BZAW*, 97, 1966, pp. 23–31, to show that the Korahites were postexilic.

29. Y. Aharoni, *IEJ*, 16 (1966), pp. 5–6, fig. 2; B. A. Levine, *JBL*, 82 (1963), pp. 207–212; *IEJ*, 19 (1969), pp. 49–51; *EJ*, 7, 552–554.

29a. Whatever the date of the individual psalms contained in them, *11Q Ps*[a] clearly shows that Books IV and V were edited late (*The Psalms Scroll of Qumrân Cave 11*, J. A. Sanders, 1965).

30. *Pss*. 50, 73–83.

31. *Pss*. 42, 44–49; 84, 85, 87, 88.

32. *1 Chron*. 6:16f., 24; 15:3, 17f., 16:5f.; *2 Chron*. 5:12; 29:13; 35:15.

33. On this event, see J. Liver, *The Military History of the Land of Israel in Biblical Times* [Hebrew], 1964, pp. 198f.; Z. Ilan, *Beth Miqra*, 53 (2), 1973, pp. 205–211: J. Maxwell-Miller, *CBQ*, 32 (1970), pp. 58–68.

34. A. Draffkorn Kilmer, *Pr. Am. Ph. Soc.*, 115, 2 (1971), pp. 147–181; *RA*, 68 (1974), pp. 69–82.

35. On the question of female singers in Israel, see Liver, *op. cit.* (*supra*, n. 33) p. 53, n. 1, as opposed to W. Eichrodt, *Theology of the O.T.*, i, 1961, p. 131, n. 3.

36. B. Meissner, *Babylonien und Assyrien*, ii, 1925, pp. 67, 71. On the existence in general of organized guilds in old and neo-Babylonia as well as in Assyria, see Meissner, i, 1920, p. 231; A. T. Olmstead, *History of Assyria*, 1923, pp. 538, 559; I. Mendelsohn, *JAOS*, 60 (1940), pp. 68–72; A. Leo Oppenheim, *op. cit.* (*supra*, p. 295, n. 2), pp. 79–82. For the Achaemenid period, see D. B. Weisberg, *Guild Structure and Political Allegiance in Early Achaemenid Mesopotamia*, 1967.

37. S. Sauneron, *The Priests of Ancient Egypt*, 1960, pp. 67, 69.

38. *ANET*, p. 420; A. Erman, *The Ancient Egyptians* (1966), p. 235. The text derives from a copy made in the Twenty-first or Twenty-second dynasty (11th–8th cents. B.C.E.), but it goes back in origin several centuries.

39. *UT* 80:1:10; 113:66; 169 (= 1026):11; 300: rev. 9; 1039:2; 1024: rev. 10; 2011:17. It should be noted that Hebrew *šarim*, = Ug. *šrm* is used in *2 Sam.* 19:36; *1 Kings* 10:12 = *2 Chron.* 9:11; *Ps.* 68:26; *Eccles.* 2:8; *2 Chron.* 35:25. (On *Ezek.* 40:44 see above p. 296, n. 12). Otherwise, *mšrrm* is uniformly used in the postexilic literature.

40. *UT* 113:66; 169:11.

41. *UT* 169: rev. 13.

42. *UT* 1107:4 refers to "singer(s) of Ashtoreth" (*šr ʿṯtrt*); 2011:37 mentions *šr ugrt* "singers of/at Ugarit." On the Ugaritic guilds, see C. H. Gordon in *The Aegean and the Near East*, ed. S. S. Weinberg, 1956, pp. 136–143; A. F. Rainey, *A Social Structure of Ugarit* [Hebrew], 1967, p. 72.

43. I. Mendelsohn, *JAOS*, 60 (1940), pp. 68–69. For a similar practice in Israel, cf. *Amos* 7:14; *2 Kings* 2:3, 5, 15 etc.; *Neh.* 3:8, 12, 15, 31 on which see *idem*, *BASOR*, 80 (1940), pp. 18f.; Z. W. Falk, *Hebrew Law in Biblical Times*, 1964, pp. 105f.; cf. J. S. Frick, *JBL*, 90 (1971), pp. 279–287. In the laws of Hammurabi, para. 188, *mâr ummânim*, lit. "son of an artisan," connotes a member of the guild; see G. R. Driver and J. C. Miles, *The Babylonian Laws*, ii, 1955, p. 246; Th. Meek in *ANET*, p. 174, n. 129. On the Ugaritic lists see A. Alt, *Kleine Schriften*, iii (1959), pp. 198–213. For a thorough study of the professional use of "son" in Hebrew and throughout the ancient near east, as well as for a theory of its origin, see G. Brin,

Lěšonénu, 31 (1967), pp. 5–20, 85–96. A Hebrew seal found at Lachish appears to read *bn h'mn* (Y. Aharoni, *IEJ*, 18 (1968), p. 166) which would be the exact equivalent of Akk. *mâr ummânim*. (But see now his *Lachish*, 1975, p. 21).

44. W. G. Lambert, *Babylonian Wisdom Literature*, 1960, p. 14.

45. D. J. Wiseman in *The Cambridge History of the Bible*, i, ed. P. R. Ackroyd and C. F. Evans, 1970, p. 36.

46. *Ibid.*

47. Weisberg, *op. cit.* (*supra*, p. 297, n. 36), pp. 1, 78, 103.

48. Without doubt, Shisha (*šyšʾ*) of *1 Kings* 4:3 is identical with Sheva (*šwʾ*) (*Kethib šyʾ*) of *2 Sam.* 20:25, as Shavsha (*šwšh*) in *1 Chron.* 18:17 shows. *2 Sam.* 8:17 reads Seraiah (*Sryh*).

49. See S. Yeivin, *Studies in the History of Israel and his* [*sic*] *Country* [Hebrew], 1960, pp. 269–278; *Encyclopaedia Miqraʾith*, 6, cols. 547f.

50. Lachish 3:15. The reading of the name is virtually, but not entirely certain; see H. Torczyner, *The Lachish Ostraca* [Hebrew], 1940, pp. 76f.; W. F. Albright, *ANET*, p. 322.

51. Cf. the remarks of F. M. Cross, *Canaanite Myth and Hebrew Epic*, 1973, p. 208.

52. For a list and discussion of local shrines, see R. Brinker, *The Influence of Sanctuaries in Early Israel*, 1946, pp. 136–178; M. Haran, *Encyclopaedia Miqraʾith*, vol. 5, cols. 322–328.

53. *Judges* 18:30; *Amos* 8:14.

54. *1 Kings* 12:28f.; *Amos* 4:6; 5:5; 7:13.

55. *2 Kings* 23:8; *Amos* 5:5; 8:14.

56. *2 Kings* 23:8.

57. *Hos.* 4:15; 9:15; 12:12; *Amos* 4:4; 5:5.

58. *1 Kings* 3:4–5; *1 Chron.* 21:29; *2 Chron.* 1:3, 13.

59. See above p. 297 nn. 28–29; Aharoni's discovery of the horned altar at Beer Sheba (*BA*, 37 (1974), pp. 1–6), which had been dismantled, apparently, during the reign of Hezekiah, should presage the unearthing of the temple there and shed further light on this phenomenon.

60. The guild of Ethan was perhaps absorbed or displaced by Jeduthun; see above, p. 296, n. 26.

61. *Ps.* 14 (Book I) = 53 (Book II); 31:2–4 (I) = 71:1–3 (II); 40:14–18 (I) = 70 (II); 57:8–12 (II) = 108:2–6 (V); 60:7–14 (II) = 108:7–14 (V). It is worthy of note that there are no duplications within the same book of the psalter.

62. Thus, *Ps.* 39 is ascribed to both David and Jeduthun, *Ps.* 77 to both Jeduthun and Asaph, and *Ps.* 88 to both the Korahites and Heman.

63. E.g. Mattaniah belongs to Heman in *1 Chron.* 25:4 but to Asaph in *1 Chron.* 9:15; *Neh.* 11:17, 22; 12:35.

64. J. P. Peters, *The Psalms as Liturgies*, 1922, esp. pp. 9f., 17f., 210, 273, 275, discerned that many psalms could not have originated in Jerusalem. In particular, he regarded books II and III as Israelite and traced the Korah and Asaph collections to shrines of the Northern Kingdom. *Pss.* 42–49 were assigned to the temple at Dan. M. H. Segal, *Mevoʾ Ha-Miqraʾ* iii, 1955, p. 541, conjectures that the Korahites were originally singers in the Ephraimite temples who later migrated to Jerusalem. M. J. Buss, *JBL*, 82 (1963), pp. 382–392 not only confirmed the view that the psalms of Asaph and Korah are homogeneous collections, but also showed that they have distinctive characteristics and that the bearers of the Asaph traditions must be

placed among preexilic and largely north Israelite Levites. Engnell, *op. cit.* (*supra*, p. 296, n. 25), pp. 79f., identifies Asaph, Heman and Ethan, and especially the psalms of the Korahites, as north Israelite in origin. On the other hand, J. M. Miller, *CBQ*, 32 (1970), pp. 58–68 located the Korahites in southern Judah. Wanke, *op. cit.* (*supra*, p. 297, n. 28) has greatly overestimated the importance of the references to Zion in the Korahite psalms. My student Steven B. Kaplan, in an unpublished paper, has shown that the Asaphite psalms are even more homogeneous than had been previously noticed, and that they share in common numerous unusual linguistic, stylistic and contextual features.

65. Cf. the remarks of J. A. Montgomery, *The Book of Kings* (ICC), 1951, p. 44, on the migration of Israelite literati to Jerusalem. Archaeological evidence for a population movement from Israel to Judah after 722 B.C.E. is now available; see M. Broshi, *IEJ*, 24 (1974), pp. 21–26; E. Stern, *BA*, 38 (1975), pp. 35f.

66. M. *Sheq.* 5, 1; *Yoma* 3, 11.

67. Engnell, *op. cit.* (*supra*, p. 296, n. 25), pp. 93f.

68. See the analysis above, section V, pp. 285–86.

69. More than a hint of this situation is contained in *2 Chron.* 20:19f., on which see above, p. 286, n. 33.

70. Sauneron, *op. cit.* (*supra*, p. 297, n. 37), p. 67.

71. Oppenheim, *op. cit.* (*supra*, p. 295, n. 2), p. 81.

72. See above, section I, pp. 281–82.

73. An analogous situation may perhaps exist in the Marseilles Tariff (*ANET*, p. 656). As M. Haran, *Encyclopaedia Miqraʾith*, 5, col. 883, has pointed out, the drink offering is ignored, since the inscription is concerned solely with payments to the priests.

74. No one would doubt the existence of Jeremiah on the grounds of his non-appearance in the book of *Kings*.

75. Cf. *Pss.* 92:1; 100:1. On the former and its title, see *JBL*, 81 (1962), pp. 155–168.

76. According to M. Haran, *VT*, 10 (1960), pp. 116f., *Keṭoreth* here refers to the meal-offering. The targum clearly took it as aromatic incense, and so did the Greek.

77. The raised hands as a symbol of prayer is widely diffused. See J. Ross, *HTR*, 63 (1970), p. 3. Akk. has *niš qātē* "prayer" and the verb *qāta năsû* (W. Von Soden, *Akkadisches Handwörterbuch*, 1972, iii, pp. 762, 797); Ugar. texts have *ša ydk šmm* (*Krt A*(*lk*) 2, 75f.) and *nša* (*y*)*dh šmmh* (*ibid.*, col. 4, 167f.); the eighth cent. B.C.E. Aram. inscription of Zakir reads: *wʾsʾ ydy ʾl bʿl š*[*myn*] (H. Donner and W. Röllig, *Kanaanäische und Aramäische Inschriften*, 1962, no. 202, A. 11), and Hebrew uses the verb *nsʾ* with both *yad* (*Ps.* 28:2; 134:2) and *kaf* (*Ps.* 63:5; 141:2; *Lam.* 2:19). G. Alon, *Studies in Jewish History* [Hebrew], i, 1967, pp. 181–184, has documented the prevalence of the custom of raising the hands in prayer during the period of the second Temple. See the writer's study of the chirotonic motif on the Lachish altar, in chapter 8 of Y. Aharoni's *Lachish*, 1975.

78. This was pointed out by M. Haran, *Encyclopaedia Miqraʾith*, 5, col. 29.

79. This was recognized by S. D. Luzzatto in his *Commentary* to *Isa.* 6:4 (Padua, 1867, p. 94) and has been noted also by de Vaux, *op. cit.*, p. 411 and M. Noth, *Exodus*, 1962, pp. 234f. One wonders whether the "cloud" that was filling the Temple, and that was the signal for Solomon to commence his dedicatory prayer (*1 Kings* 8:10–12), is not similarly to be identified with the smoke of the incense for which the same word *ʿanan* is used in both *Lev.* 16:13 and *Ezek.* 8:11. That the

incense altar of *Exod.* 30 is not secondary, but an integral part of the inner temple ritual complex, has been effectively demonstrated by M. Haran, *Tarbiẕ,* 26 (1957), pp. 115–125; *VT,* 10 (1960), pp. 113–129; *Yeḥezqʾel Kaufmann Jubilee Volume* [Hebrew], 1960, p. 23, para r; pp. 40–42, para. 20.

80. *Exod.* 30:6, 36; 40:5, 26, 27; *Lev.* 4:7.

81. *Lev.* 16: 12f., *Num.* 17: 11–13; cf. *Isa.* 6: 7. As J. Milgrom, *JBL,* 90 (1971), p. 151, n. 14, has pointed out, the juxtaposition of the incense altar pericope (*Exod.* 30:1–10) to that of the half-shekel (*ibid.,* vv. 11–16) is not accidental, since the latter, like the former, had an expiatory role; cf. T. B. *Yoma* 44a.

82. *2 Kings* 18:3f.; *2 Chron.* 30:14; 31:1. That the events recorded there are substantially correct, is clear from *2 Kings* 18:22 = *Isa.* 36:7 = *2 Chron.* 32:12.

83. *2 Kings* 22–23; *2 Chron.* 34–35.

84. See above, p. 297, n. 28. For a different view, see B. A. Levine, "Prolegomenon" to G. B. Gray, *Sacrifice in the Old Testament*, Ktav reprint, 1971, pp. xviii–xx. Decisive evidence may well be forthcoming when the temple at Beer Sheba is finally located, for the excavations to date show that the horned altar, now recovered, had been dismantled in Hezekiah's time; see Y. Aharoni, *BA*, 37 (1974), pp. 1–6; cf. *The Biblical Archaeology Review*, 1, 1 (1975), pp. 1, 8f., 15.

85. *Mal.* 1:11 probably mirrors the same cultic situation in that the prophet states that "in every place, *muqṭar* and pure meal-offering (*minḥah*)" are offered in God's honor. The *hapax legomenon muqṭar* might, admittedly, be a generic term for aromatic sacrifice, but it is far more likely to mean simple "incense-offering" in light of the parallelism *qeṭoreth–minḥah* in *Isa.* 1:13; *Ps.* 141:2 and the use of *minḥah* exclusively in the sense of "produce" in priestly texts; cf. *Tanḥuma,* ed. Buber, pp. 68f.; *Yalquṭ, Malachi,* para. 587.

86. A. Cowley, *Aramaic Papyri of the Fifth Century B.C.,* 1923, nos. 30, ll. 21, 25; 31, ll. 21, 24f.; 32, l. 9; 33, ll. 10–11 explicitly excludes animal sacrifice, the crucial negative being confidently restored from the surviving *ʾaleph* (א[ל]). See B. Porten, *Archives from Elephantine*, 1968, pp. 291f., 293, n. 29.

87. See the comments of Y. M. Grintz, *Sefer Yehudith*, 1957, pp. 139f.

88. R. H. Charles, *Pseudepigrapha*, 1913, p. 306.

89. *Ibid.*, p. 149, xxxiii, 4–5; K. von Tischendorf, *Apocalypses Apocryphae,* 1866, reprint 1966, p. 18, para. 33. On angelic liturgies, see J Strugnell, *VT Sup.* vii, 1960, pp. 318–345.

90. In *Acts* 3:1 mention is made of prayer offered in the Temple at the ninth hour; cf. 10:3, 30, Jos. *Ant.,* XIV, iv, 3 (Loeb ed., para. 65, pp. 480–481) describes the ninth hour as the hour of "sacred ceremonies at the altar." The references, of course, are to the *tamid* of the late afternoon of *Exod.* 29:38f.; *Num.* 28:3f., 8, and they correspond to the requirement of Mishnah, *Pesaḥim* 5, 1.

91. T. J. *Berakhoth* 4, 1 (7^{a}).

92. *Tanḥuma*, ed. Buber, p. 68f.; cf. *Yalquṭ Malachi*, para. 587.

93. *Mid. Pss.,* ed. Buber, p. 531; cf. *Tosafoth* to T. B. *Ber.* 26b s.v. *ad.* It is an interesting coincidence that the recitation of T.B. *Kerithoth* 6a, dealing with the composition of the incense, is immediately followed by M. *Tamid* 7, 4, listing the psalm for each day, in the closing liturgy of the sabbath additional service.

The Concept of the "Fence": Observations on its Origin and Development

S. STEIN

A. INTRODUCTION

It can safely be maintained that *seyag* has become one of the key concepts of rabbinic Judaism. Yet there is no systematic enquiry into its provenance in time and place, its original meaning, its relation to expressions like *mishmereth, geder, gezerah, taqqanah, ḥomah, gevul* and to comparable notions in Hellenistic-Jewish and Graeco-Roman Literature. Specialized studies on the Pharisees, medieval and modern commentators on the relevant passages in *Pireqey ʾAvoth* (henceforth P A) and *ʾAvoth de Rabbi Nathan* (henceforth *ARN* A or *ARN* B for versions I or II respectively) or on their targumic and midrashic counterparts offer only indirect help towards an answer to the questions involved. The same applies to otherwise competent dictionaries, concordances and encyclopaedias.

The noun *seyag* does not occur in the Bible[1] although it has its equivalents in other Semitic languages. In the first instance it signifies a natural fence or hedge, as for example in the Mishnah, *ʿOrlah,* I, 1: "He who plants something to use it as a fence . . . ." The root also appears as a verb in *piʿel* or *puʿal*. Thus a vineyard is *mesuyyag mi-Kol pinnothaw,* fenced on all its sides.[2] In a metaphorical sense, the noun occurs for the first time in the well-known maxim of *P A* i, 1, attributed to the men of the Great Assembly: "Be deliberate in judgement, raise up many disciples and make a fence round the Torah." The last part of the sentence: *wa-ʿasu seyag la-Torah* is generally interpreted to mean: make additional restrictions to the written law of the Torah to safeguard its kernel from neglect. According to this explanation, the term would owe its unfolding entirely to an internal Jewish evolution.

However, all modern scholars agree that neither the time to which the *ʾanshey keneseth ha-Gedolah* belonged nor the aims and organisational set-up of their circle can be determined with certainty,[3] especially since their above-quoted rule of conduct represents the only collective account that has come down to us from them. Moreover, *talmidim* are here mentioned for the first time in the sense of students of an educational institution[4] and it is still doubtful whether "*hewu methunim ba-Din*" refers exclusively to the decisions of a court of law.

Furthermore, the manifold meanings attached to *seyag* in other statements belonging to, or depending on, tannaitic literature call for a more thorough investigation of the whole problem. Without at present offering an analysis of all the passages under consideration, attention may be drawn to the fact that the concept is not only used in connection with ethical or ritual restrictions, added to the words of the Torah, but also with theological and apologetic considerations. Moreover, in *ARN* A and *ARN* B the original sense, implied by the imperative of the men of the Great Assembly to erect a fence around the Torah, has become blurred: God Himself, the Torah, the Prophets, the Hagiographa[5] and some of the famous men of old such as Adam, Moses and Job are described as each having made a *seyag round their words*, anticipating the much later ordinance of *ʾanshey keneseth ha-Gedolah*. The literary method employed is comparable to that of the *Book of Jubilees*, in which the observance of the festivals is traced back to patriarchal times. Rabbi Aqiba, on the other hand, connects the concept with *masoreth*, tithes, vows and silence, without adding biblical proof-texts (*PA* III, 13). His fences stand respectively for the punctilious observance of the written and the oral Law, for the prescribed use of wealth, for attaining ascetic standards of piety and for restraint in the transmission of "wisdom" to the uninitiated.[6]

In an attempt to outline the origin and development of the concept historically, it is natural to look for cognate terminology outside the Bible and the Mishnah. The nearest links between these two major legacies of normative Judaism are Hellenistic-Jewish, Greek and Roman literature. The reasons are obvious. Ever since the conquest of the Orient by Alexander the Great, Greek civilization began to strike deep roots not merely in Egypt, particularly in Alexandria with its growing and influential Jewish community, but also, if more gradually, in Palestine. Its specific impact on the latter manifests itself in thousands of Greek and, later on, though to a much lesser extent, in Roman loan-words. These do not only signify an adoption of an up-to-date military, legal, commercial and architectural terminology, but are also indicative of a sometimes unchanged, but more often substantially transformed penetration into the administrative and constitutional set-up of the Sanhedrin[7] and even into the celebrations of the Jewish festivals.[8] Similarly, the encounter of the two civilizations left its mark on the Rabbis' modification or avoidance of biblical anthropomorphism (*epikrypsis*) and unseemly expressions (*to aprepes*),[9] on their hermeneutical rules,[9a] on the policy of admission to their schools[10] and on the stoic colouring of their ethical teaching. Some hitherto unnoticed aspects, connected with the main subject of this paper, will be dealt with in the following pages.[11]

B. FENCES AND RELATED TERMS IN JEWISH-HELLENISTIC LITERATURE[12]

We meet the first comparable counterparts to the notion of *seyag* in the Greek pseudepigraph known as the *Letter of Aristeas* and generally assumed to have been written in Alexandria about the year 90 B.C.E. A translation of the relevant sentences runs as follows: "Now our Lawgiver (*nomothetēs*), being a wise man (*sofos ōn*) and especially endowed by God to understand all things, *took a comprehensive view of each particular detail* and *fenced us round (periefraxen)* with *impregnable ramparts* and *walls of iron,*[13] that we might not mingle at all with any of the other nations, but remain pure in body and soul, free from all vain imagination . . . *He (also) hedged us round on all sides . . . affecting alike what we eat or drink, or touch, or hear or see*" (139–142). The following sentences represent the first full allegorical explanation of the dietary laws and include exhortations to observe law-abiding relationships between man and man (168f). Although the sovereignty of God and the need to worship Him are never questioned, it is nevertheless Moses who is said to have "fenced" the Jewish people. Yet he never appears in the whole Bible as lawgiver[13a] and, wherever the root *ṣwh* is mentioned in connexion with him, it stands in close juxtaposition to a command of God. Even *Deut.* xxxiii: 3f cannot be adduced as permissible evidence for the identity of the faithful servant of the Lord or His prophet with the "lawgiver," particularly since the passage is generally recognised as being difficult. The same applies to the *meḥoqeq* in *Deut.* xxxiii:21. In spite of the fact that the *Sifrey in loc.*, the two Aramaic *Targumim*, the Vulgate and the *Peshiṭta* read into the line a reference to the burial place of Moses, the masoretic text does not lend itself to this interpretation, the Septuagint shows no trace of it and Ibn Ezra refutes the argument on solid philological grounds.[14]

There are likewise no biblical precedents for attributing wisdom to Moses. We are here confronted with Greek or Hellenistic-Jewish thought which found its way almost imperceptibly into tannaitic and midrashic literature. Thus, immediately before the diatribe on the *seyagim* in the first chapter of *ARN* A, Moses is described as *rabbenu, hakham gadol ba-Gedolim (we)-ʾav la-Neviʾim.*[15] In aggadic parlance he is called *ʾAvi-gedor*, the "father – of the fence."[16]

Midrash Rabbah on *Ct.* vii: 3, transmitted by R. Levi, one of the foremost Palestinian aggadists of the third century, also deals *inter alia* with the dietary laws. As in *ARN* A ch. 2 and *ARN* B ch. 3, his keywords are: "Thy belly is like a heap of wheat, *fenced* around with lilies." He comments on them as follows: "A dish of meat is brought before a man who is informed that some forbidden fat has fallen into it; he withholds his hand from it and does not taste it. *Who induced him not to taste it?* Did a serpent bite him? . . . Or did a scorpion sting him? . . . *Only the words of the Torah which are soft as lilies*, as it is written: You shall not eat any fat . . ." (*Lev.* iii: 17)

In the same context reference is made to a *seyag* to be observed between husband and wife during the period of her menses. "*What prevented him to come near to her? What kind of iron wall or a pillar of iron was there between them? . . . Only the words of the Torah.*" (*Lev.* xviii: 19) As in a number of other rabbinic examples to be given later on, there seems to be a connexion between the simile of the "iron wall" here and the above quotation from Pseudo-Aristeas. This is the more likely, since a midrashic association of ideas with *Jer.* i: 18 is neither mentioned nor are the two passages identical.

Numbers vi: 1–5 contains regulations about the vows a Nazirite has to take upon himself. An anonymous aggadist who deals with the passage in the *Midrash Bemidbar Rabbah*, about the middle of section 10, goes beyond the immediate requirements of his task and extends his halakhic comments to a lengthy denunciation of drunkenness. In the course of his exposition he asks: "*How can a man make a fence around his words in the way the Torah made a fence around her words?*" He concludes by saying that "*one should refrain from what is ugly and from what is similar to the ugly . . .*"[17] As in the case of *Ct. Rabbah,* these exhortations are linked to *Lev.* xviii: 19: "Thou shalt not approach a woman in the separation of her impurity . . .", followed here by a direct quotation from *ARN* A ch. 2 and *ARN* B ch. 3: "The Sages are pleased with a woman that makes herself ugly in the days of her separation, but displeased with one who adorns herself in the days of her impurity." Such formulation does not constitute a *mandatory mishmereth* nor a *gezerah* or *taqqanah.* Moreover, a warning is expressed against the excessive resort to *seyagim.*[18]

Syntactically too, there is little difference between the homily in *Ct. Rabbah*: *mi garam lo liṭʿom?* . . . and that in *Bemidbar Rabbah*: *keyṣad yaʿaseh ʾadam seyag li-devaraw?* . . . Furthermore, in *ARN* A, ch. 1, Adam adds to God's command not to *eat* from the tree of the garden by telling Eve not to *touch* it. The question in the Hebrew text runs as follows: "*mai garam la-Negiʿah zu? Seyag she-ʿasah ʾadam ha-riʾshon.*" *ARN* A, ch. 2 has this to say on the hedge of the Torah: "How so? A woman in her menses is alone with her husband at home. If he is so minded, he cohabits with her . . . *Can anyone see him . . . ? Nay, behold, he fears only Him who commanded against contact with a menstruant.*" (*Ha keyṣad?* . . . *We-khi ʾadam roʾehu?* . . . *Ha ʾeyno mithyareʾ ʾella mi-Mi she-Poqed ʾothan ʿal ha-Niddah* . . .)[19] In all these cases, one is struck by the number of interrogative sentences, so characteristic of the literary form of the diatribe, practised in Hellenistic literature long before its use can be traced in tannaitic or new testament writings.[19a]

In the pseudepigraphic fourth book of *Maccabees*, generally held to have been written in the first half of the first century C.E., the refusal of Eleazar and his seven sons to partake of forbidden food is the framework round which a philosophical address, not necessarily a synagogal sermon, is grouped. Of the former it is said that "*never did a city beleaguered by many and different engines put up such a resistance as did that perfect saint.*" (vii: 4). The fortitude of the latter in facing martyrdom is described as follows: "*Their seven-towered well-founded argument (heptapyrgos eulogistia)*[20] . . . *erected a bulwark (ochyrōsasa) round the haven of piety and overcame the unruliness of the emotions.*" (xiii: 7).[21] Under the title "On the Supremacy of Reason" (*Peri autokratoros logismou*) the book is quoted by Eusebius and Jerome, and this is perhaps the oldest title of the work. Its stoic mode of expression is obvious. Yet, it is ultimately Torah or pious reasonong (*eusebēs logismos*) which, in the author's view, determines what is right and wrong, leads to the conquest of the passions, frugality, and the observance of the dietary laws.

To understand his standpoint in its proper perspective, a comparable statement by Pseudo-Aristeas may here be quoted. "In general, all things are to the *natural reason (pros ton physikon logon)* similarly constituted, being all administered by a single power, and yet, *in each and every case there is a profound logic for our abstinence from the use of some things and our participation in the use of others*" (143).[22] This sentence follows immediately the one on Moses, "*hedging us about in matters of food and drink.*"

In contrast to *Aristeas, IV Maccabees* has no allegorical interpretations of the dietary laws, but both see in the Torah-legislation an equivalent to natural, universal law, or world-reason, which would allow and indeed, from their point of view, enjoin the Jews to uphold the tradition of their fathers.[23]

Although the rabbis of the tannaitic and amoraic periods steered altogether clear of philosophical exegesis, their acquaintance with, and often unqualified—albeit unacknowledged—acceptance of the ethical teaching of the Stoa is clearly noticeable in many of their maxims and parables. Yet, the generally brief and seemingly unsophisticated formulation of their faith may well imply a dissociation from, if not a deliberate challenge of the anthropocentric basis of Greek philosophy.[24]

Philo, who absorbed the legacy of early and late Greek and Hellenistic-Jewish thought, did not add much to the allegorical interpretation of the dietary laws,[25] but he has some philosophical comments which have a bearing on our main subject. I quote from his *Special Laws*, (Loeb, vol. viii, IV, 97–99). "Two things stand out in importance, food and drink; to neither of these did [Moses] give full liberty but *bridled* them with ordinances most conducive to *self restraint* and *humanity* and what is chief of all, *piety*. For he bids them to take samples of their corn, wine, oil and live-stock and the rest as first fruits, and apportion them for sacrifices and for gifts to the officiating priests: . . . . No one is permitted in any way to taste or take any part of his fruits until he has set apart the first fruits, a rule which also serves to give practice in the *self-restraint* which is most profitable to life. For he who has learned not to rush to seize the abundant gifts which the seasons of the year have brought but waits till the first fruits have been consecrated, clearly allays passion and thus curbs the restiveness of the appetites."

Before and after Philo, the juxtaposition of *egkrateia, philanthrōpia* and *eusebeia* in matters of food and drink, of sacrifices to the altar and gifts to the priests would probably have been considered unusual by the majority of Palestinian expositors of the Law.[26] On the other hand, Hellenistic-

Jewish authors would not employ prooftexts like *Cant.* vii: 3, nor would they include *seyagim* of the kind to be found in tannaitic, targumic or amoraic writings.[27] Hence, the use of *epiefraxen* in Pseudo-Aristeas and that of Philo's *epestomise* does not constitute an essential semantic difference since the two passages refer to pentateuchal law only. —

There is no such consistency in Hebrew source-material, although a few of the above-mentioned examples, culled from the fences of R. Aqiba,[28] *ARN* and some of the aggadic *midrashim*, show affinities with the approach of earlier environmental literature. Generally, however, rabbinic statements betray a gradual development towards additional restrictions. In the opposite direction, even the blowing of the *Shofar* on *Rosh ha-Shanah* or the taking of the *Lulav* on *Sukkoth* were annulled, if they happened to fall on a sabbath, because this might lead to carrying them on a public highway.[29]

Josephus undoubtedly spoke with greater inside-information than all other Jewish authors of our period who wrote in Greek. His *Contra Apionem* makes the following contribution to the subject under discussion: "Our legislator took great care to combine the two systems [of education, that of instruction by precept and that of practical training in the formation of character.][30] . . . He left nothing, however insignificant, to the discretion of the individual, what meats a man should abstain from and what he may enjoy; . . . what periods should be devoted respectively to strenuous labour and to rest. For all this he made the Law a limiting rule and norm . . . (*horon ethēken . . . kai kanōna ton nomon*)."[31]

Philosophical terminology, often in support of apologetic[31a] tendencies, is common to the quotations from *Aristeas*, the fourth book of *Maccabees*, Philo and Josephus. In the wider context of the next chapter, it will be shown in what sense they contribute to the understanding of the main topic of this paper. I am here referring to verbs, nouns or adjectives such as *perifrassein, ochyroun, epistomizein, adiakopon teichos, charax, chōrismos,*[32] *pyrgos, horos, kanōn* and, perhaps most important, *egkrateia.*

C. SOURCE MATERIAL ON FENCES AND RELATED CONCEPTS IN GREEK PHILOSOPHICAL LITERATURE FROM HERACLITUS TO THE LATE STOA

It is generally recognized that all Hellenistic-Jewish writings are strongly influenced by Greek philosophical literature. The first to relate *nomos* to a wall was Heraclitus of Ephesus, who flourished about 500 B.C.E. The brief fragment (44) which is of interest to us reads: *Machesthai chrē dēmon hyper tou nomou hokōsper teicheos,* "*The people must fight for the law as for their city wall.*" Another maxim of similar content is a little more explicit: "If one wishes to express oneself with reason and to act with reason, one has to arm oneself with what is common to all, as a city arms itself with law and still stronger, because it rules wherever it wills, is sufficient for all and remains victorious." (114) . . . To it man has to conform in his thinking and in his moral behaviour.[33]

"Heraclitus," to quote Herman Diels, the editor of these fragments,[34] "exerted a vast influence on later generations. Experts as well as laymen read his book right to the end of antiquity. Through the Stoa, the best of which is 'Heraclitism', his terminology became popular."

Democritus, a little later than Heraclitus, applies the idea of a wall to the principles of *education*: "One has to bring up children in soberness and to surround their possessions and bodies *with a wall and cover*."[35]

In note 20 of this paper reference has been made to Diogenes Laertius' enumeration of the varying possibilities of classifying the *ethical* branches of philosophy. Even more important for our deliberations is what he has to say about the tripartite division of philosophy itself: "They [the Stoics] liken philosophy to a fertile field, *logic being the encircling fence (peribeblēmenos fragmos)*, ethics the crop, physics the soil or the trees, or again to *a city strongly walled and governed by reason*."[36]

On the Jewish side, it is the author of the fourth book of *Maccabees* who clearly betrays acquaintance with the afore-mentioned comparison between philosophy or reason and an orchard or field. According to him, . . . "Reason, the universal gardener (*ho pangeōrgos logismos*), purges, prunes, binds up, waters and irrigates as it were the two trees, growing from body and soul by diverse devices and so tames the wild growth of inclinations and emotions, for reason is the leader of virtues and of emotions the sovereign." (*ho gar logismos tōn men aretōn estin hēgemōn, tōn de pathōn autokratōr*).[37] Referring to Noah, the man of the field who planted a vineyard, Philo offers a comparable simile: "The *lawgiver* . . . wished to bring out the truth that, just as a good husbandman does, the man of sound character in dealing with trees in a wild state cuts away all harmful shoots, grown from passions and vices . . . , leaving those which, though not fruit-bearing can serve as a *wall and be a most firm fence of the soul . . ." (fragmos psychēs ochyrōtatos)*.[38]

In a similar context, Philo speaks explicitly of the tripartite division of philosophy, suggested by the "men of old." It says in *Deut.* xx: 20: "Every tree whose fruit is not edible, you should cut down and make into a palisade to resist the city which shall make war against you . . ." Commenting on the passage, he describes logic as a fence and enclosure (*fragmos kai peribolos*) to physics and ethics. His formulation is almost identical with the one given by Diogenes Laertius, "*For even as the wall, built round the field serves to protect (esti phylaktērion) the fruit and the plants that grow in it, . . . the logical part of philosophy is, so to speak, a strongly fortified barrier* (*froura ochurōtatē*), guarding those other two parts, the ethical and the physical . . . It exposes fallacies, created by tricks of arguments (*sophismata*) . . . and makes the mind ready to receive . . . what aims at building character . . ."[39]

In his *De Fuga et Inventione* he continues his allegorical exegesis, retaining those metaphors employed by Heraclitus and his Stoic followers which, *mutatis mutandis,* would correspond to the rabbinic *geder ᶜerwah* and *seyag shethiqah.* His proof-text is *Lev.* xx: 18. "Whosoever shall have slept with a woman in her separation, has unclosed her spring and she has unclosed the flow of her blood; let them both be cut off . . ."[40] At such a time he has exposed himself *without covering or a wall of defence (astegos kai ateichistos)* . . . Moreover she, too, unclosed the flow of her blood . . . and is left destitute when widowed of an upright ruler (*chēreusasa hēgemonos orthou,* i.e. mind or reason), and *as it is the most grievous evil for a city to be without walls* so it is for a soul to be without a protector *(aphylaktos).* When then is it without a protector? Is it not when sight, wholly absorbed in objects of sight,[41] is left uncovered; . . . uncovered too the faculty of speech giving ill-timed utterance to *a thousand things that should have been kept secret* . . . ?" (*myria tōn aporrētōn* . . .) (Loeb, V, 188–191).[42]

One important aspect of Philo's writings thus lies in the fact that terms like *fragmos* and *teichos* which belong to Greek philosophy are linked to his exegesis of the Torah in an unmistakeable manner. The specific, though sometimes attenuated connotations of these concepts are also adumbrated by the other Jewish Hellenistic authors to whom we have referred above. The de-philosophized reappearance of these expressions in early rabbinic literature brought it about that they have not hitherto been recognized as part and parcel of the great Hellenistic transformation of biblical Judaism, although non-Jewish Greek and Roman authors continued to use the same terminology before and after Philo and Josephus.

Thus, Dio Chrysostom, a representative of the late Stoa and a contemporary of Domitian, still expresses himself as follows: "The law is for life a guide, for cities an impartial overseer, for the conduct of affairs a true canon (*tōn de pragmatōn kanōn dikaios*) . . . and so much more serviceable is it (for our cities) than their *walls* that many of them still remain unwalled, but without law no city can be administered."[43]

Epictetus lived about the same time as Dio. Attention has been drawn to affinities between his ethical teachings and those of early Christian and tannaitic literature. In this context it will suffice to quote one of his sentences: "Those who inhabit a strong city laugh at the besiegers . . .," "Our wall is safe, we have food for ever so long a time . . . . These are the things which make a city strong and secure against capture, but only firm principles (*dogmata*) make similarly secure the soul of man."[44]

D. LATIN LITERATURE ON FENCES

The philologist Marcus Terentius Varro, a friend of Cicero, who flourished about 60 B.C.E., was one of the first to introduce the classification of philosophy into Latin literature: "One part of the philosophy of the ancients," he says, "concerns itself with life and morals, i.e. ethics, the other with nature, i.e. physics . . . , the third with thorough discernment about what is true and what is false . . . and what in judgement calls for consent and what is repugnant, i.e. logic."[45]

Although the text does not mention a wall or a fence, it is clearly related to the afore-mentioned quotations. In view of the early identification of *Ḥokhmah* and Torah from *Sirach* onwards *via I Baruch, IV Maccabees,* Philo, Josephus[46] to a widely attested midrashic equation of the two terms,[47] we may, at this stage, submit the following tentative and extended paraphrase of *PA*, i, 1: "Be deliberate in judgement [by first clarifying your dialectical criteria], raise up many pupils and [thus] erect *a fence around the Torah*."

Internal philological support is lent to this rendering, since *din* in tannaitic literature stands not only for decisions in ritual, civil or capital cases, but also for the exegetical norms which include analogies, syllogisms or conclusions *a minori ad maius* that guided the rabbis in their deliberations.[48] The Stoics too used to say that "*without the study of dialectic the wise man will be unable to distinguish between truth and falsehood and to discriminate between what is merely plausible and what is ambigously expressed.*" He could also not "*methodically put questions and give answers.*"[49] The Torah-centred response of *PA*, v, 7 to the environmental stimulus runs as follows: ". . . *The wise man asks according to the subject matter (ka-ʿinyan) and answers according to the halakhah.*" *ARN* A, ch. 37 and *ARN* B, ch. 40 have approximately the same text as *PA*, although they add aggadic embellishments to their *Vorlage*. The phrase: "He (the *ḥakham*) is not hasty in giving an answer" (*ʾeyno nivhal le-hashiv*), also occurs in the three versions.[49a]

Seneca, who died in 65 C.E., offers a similar view in his *Moral Essays*[50]: [in cases of judgment] "*Reason gives time to both sides, then seeks to postpone action, even its own, in order that it may make use of the interval to sift out the truth. Impetuosity acts rashly*" (*ira festinat*).[51] On "*Questions and Answers*" Diogenes Laertius quotes altogether seven books *Peri erōtēseōs kai apokriseōs*, written by Antisthenes, Aristotle and Chrysippus.[52] The literary distinction of the platonic dialogues cemented and refined Socrates' inductive method of teaching logic and ethics.

On the Jewish side, Philo's *Quaestiones et Solutiones in Genesin et Exodum* resemble the Hellenistic commentaries on the Homeric epics.[53] As an independent technical term *shoʾel u-meshiv* occurs in *Qinyan Torah* only, i.e. in *PA* vi, 6, in the context of a list of 48 qualities by which the Torah can be acquired. At least ten of them could equally well be headed *Qinyan Ḥokhmah* and linked to stoic terminology of the same kind. I here refer to "*narrowing the limits of sleep, talk, pleasure, laughter and business.*"[54] These self-imposed restrictions are expressed in Hebrew by the construct *miʿuṭ*, prefixed to absolutes, and they appear to be loan-translations from Greek compounds like *oligohypnia, oligomythia, oligopragmosynē* or similar nouns such as *oligodeia* (contentment with little), *oligoposia* (moderation in drinking) and *oligositia* (moderation in eating.)[55]

The utilitarian motivation of the reproach against the sluggard who cannot arouse himself from his sleep, as given in *Prov.* vi: 10f., its parallel in xxiv: 33f. and, similarly, in x: 4 and xxvi: 13f. illustrates the general transformation from biblical to tannaitic wisdom literature. It is only in the case of the latter, and particularly in the text under discussion, that various subdivisions of *egkrateia* are placed side by side, including as they do indifference not only to pleasure but also to pain. The famous maxim of Epictetus *anechou kai apechou* comprises both aspects of the stoic discipline. *Endure* would stand for ready acceptance of suffering, corresponding to *qabbalath ha-yissurin in PA*, vi, 5 and *abstain* for the preceding *miʿuṭ shenah* etc. Yet, here again, formal similarity does not necessarily imply dependence on a traceable source nor unequivocal identity of thought: Graeco-Roman moral philosophy and rules of conduct remained within the framework of human reasoning, whilst Jewish ethics retained its adherence to the heteronomous, theocratic constitution of the Torah.

On the other hand, it is undeniable that the basic elements of the stoic doctrines and the way in which they were expressed left their mark on tannaitic literature. R. Aqiba, for instance, is quoted as the author of the saying in *PA*, iii, 13: "Laughter (*seḥoq*) and frivolity (*qalluth roʾsh*) accustom a man to lewdness (*la-ʿerwah*)." *ARN* A, ch. 26[56] and *ARN* B, ch. 33 read: "*A fence around honour is not to laugh.*" All three passages introduce (or are part of) R. Aqiba's four fences. As to *PA*, vi, 5, I am not aware of a direct Greek counterpart to *miʿuṭ seḥoq*, but the Hebrew wording seems somewhat strange in the context. On closer examination, it becomes clear that moderation in laughter or jesting also figures in those writings of the Stoics which contain long and varied lists of their recommendations for a life of self-restraint. Seneca, for instance, has a fairly extensive account of them: "Whatever command *the mind* gives to itself, holds its ground. *Some have reached the point of never laughing (ne umquam riderent), some have cut themselves off from wine, others from sexual pleasure, others from every kind of drink; another, satisfied by short sleep, prolongs his waking hours unwearied.*"[57]

Apart from the previously mentioned *shoʾel u-meshiv, PA*, vi, 6 lists other virtues required for the study of the Torah. Stated in the form of participles, they are, at least partly, amenable both to an *interpretatio Judaica* and to an *interpretatio Stoica* and include *inter alia*: "*One that recognises his place, rejoices in his lot, makes a fence around his words, shuns honour and loves mankind* (. . .*ʾeth ha-Beriyyoth*)." With the exception of the last sentence of the whole paragraph, no biblical proof-texts are given.

Among the demands on those who carry out their tasks on the religious or humanist-intellectual level, the phrase *ha-ʿoseh seyag li-devaraw* lends itself best to some observations relevant to the main topic of this paper. Used so frequently in the diatribe on the fences in *ARN*, it may simply be the equivalent to *miʿuṭ siḥah* of *PA*, vi, 5, but two passages in Philo invite comparison, even though his direct influence on the formulation of *PA*, vi, 6 is not to be assumed. In one of them he gives an allegorical interpretation of the dream which Pharaoh had, whilst he was "*standing on the edge (lip) of the river.*" (*Gen.* xli: 17): "*Nature has clearly provided men with lips for two most necessary purposes. One is to keep silence; for the lips form the strongest possible fence and barrier for confining sound (eryma kai . . . fragmos ochurōtatos phōnēs). The other is to give expression to thought.*" (*De Somniis*, II, Loeb, V, 262f).

In *De Confusione Linguarum*, (Loeb, IV, 33–36), the meeting between Pharaoh and Moses "*on the edge of the river*" (*Ex.* vii: 15) is similarly allegorized: "*The lips are the boundaries (perata) of the mouth and a kind of hedge to the tongue*" *(fragmos de tēs glōttēs)*. The paragraph includes an exhortation to oppose "contentious sophistry" and, at the same time, praise for the "holy choir which sang the anthem of victory "*at the edge of the sea*" (*Ex.* xiv: 30).

A comparable midrash, transmitted in the name of R. Jose b. Zimra, a Palestinian ʾ*Amora* of the first generation, is to be found in ʿ*Arakhin* 15b: "*The Holy One, blessed be He, said to the tongue: All parts of the body are standing, but you are lying; all parts of the human body are outside, but you are inside; and not only that, but I surrounded you with two walls (hiqqafti lekha shtey ḥomoth), one of bone and one of flesh. 'What else can He give, what else can He add to you, slanderous tongue?'* (*Ps.* cxx: 3)"

There are obvious differences between Philo and R. Jose b. Zimra. The proof-texts of the former are very far fetched and he himself is somewhat apologetic in referring to them, whilst the midrash of the latter is much nearer to its biblical *Vorlage*. Basing himself on *Ps.* cxx: 3, he interprets it as a warning against evil talk and calumny. Affinities between the two modes of approach lie in the use of *eryma . . . kai fragmos ochyrōtatos tēs phōnēs* or *glottēs* on the one hand, *seyag li-devarim* and *shtey ḥomoth* on the other. The quasi-military espressions in ʿ*Arakhin* and two similar, though not identical passages in *Lev. Rabbah*, section XVI and especially in *Midrash Shoḥer Ṭov* on *Ps.* lii: 3 (ed. Buber, p. 286) support the assumption of their oral, almost proverbial currency in both civilizations.[58]

It is also possible that the frequently occurring Homeric phrase *herkos odontōn*, the fence or wall which the teeth make round the tongue, forms the ultimate background of comparable figures of speech in Hebrew literature.[59]

The link between the legacy of classical antiquity and Jewish thought gains still greater plausibility if it is borne in mind that the traditional discipline of philosophical studies and its devotion to them tended to lose some of its force, to be gradually displaced by an intense moral earnestness and an almost religious enthusiasm. In view of the fact that many Stoics were not natives of Greece, a simultaneous development in a less restricted geographical area has to be reckoned with.[60] More than this should not be said before additional Latin evidence on fences, walls and the like has been listed.

It was Cicero who was mainly responsible for the transmission of Greek philosophy to the Roman world. The metaphor of the fence to be erected against the moral decay of man by a process of dialectical argument appears to play an important part in his world-view, as can be gauged from the following statement: "*When the mind, having attained to a knowledge and perception of the virtues, ... has put down pleasure as if it were a taint of dishonour, ... has taken up the worship of the gods and pure religion, ... so that it can choose the good and reject the opposite,*[61] ... *and further, when it has examined the heavens, the earth ... and the nature of all things, whence they came and wither they must return,*[62] *when and how they are destined to perish, what part of them is mortal and transient and what is divine and eternal, ... how well will it know itself, according to the precept of the Pythian Apollo! ... And in defence of all this, it will erect a fence of dialectic reasoning, of the science of distinguishing the true from the false ... and of understanding the consequences and opposites of every statement.*" (Loeb, *De Legibus,* I, xxiii, 60–xxiv, 62). Terms like *saepimentum, vallare, ratio disserendi* and *contrarium* are once again not used in a fortuitous manner, but belong to the technical language of stoicism and its sources.

This *Fachsprache* intrudes even into his personal communications. Thus he writes to a friend: *"Our Atticus, because he once noticed that I was upset by panic, always thinks the same of me and does not see, by what safeguards of philosophy I am fenced".*[63]

Another sentence taken from Cicero's writings reads as follows: "*There is no law which does not hedge itself in by trying to make repeal difficult.*"[64] *Seyag la-Torah* lends itself almost automatically to a comparison. Yet it comprises more and, at the same time, less than the philosophical and legal connotations of *saepimentum.*

Seneca, about a century after Cicero, continued the popularization of stoic concepts: "*Philosophy,*" he says, in one of his *Epistolae Morales,* "*must be enclosed with an impregnable wall. Though it be assaulted by many engines, Fortune can find no passage into it.*[65] *The soul should know whither it is going and whence it came; ... and what is that Reason which distinguishes between the desirable and the undesirable and thereby tames the madness of our desires and calms the violence of our fears.*" (Loeb II, 242f) ... Or, "*We need bulwarks, erected with all the greater care because of the greater power by which we are attacked.*" (*ibid.* III, 67). No comment is necessary on *inexpugnabilis murus, machinae* or *munimenta.* All of them are reminiscent of *adiakopon teichos, charax* and comparable metaphors, used in the *Letter of Aristeas,* the fourth book of *Maccabees,* in related, earlier or later sections of Graeco-Roman, Hellenistic-Jewish, and rabbinic literature.

Seneca also knew of the tripartite classification of philosophy, its theoretical varieties and intricacies, but his interests had shifted away from them and turned towards a semi-religious moralism: "Whatever phase of things human and divine you have apprehended, ... you will be wearied by the vast number of things to be answered and learned. Therefore you must remove all superfluous things. Virtue will not surrender itself to these narrow bounds of ours; a great subject needs wide space in which to move. Let all other things be driven out and let the breast be emptied ('from the useless furniture of learning') to receive virtue. *The desire to know more than is sufficient is a sort of impertinence.*"[66]

Acquaintance with the concept of the fence had spread to such an extent that historians like Livy (59 B.C.E.–17 C.E.) and Tacitus (55–120) could, in ordinary non-philosophical texts, refer to *women, fenced in by chastity (mulieres saeptae pudicitia)*.[67] Origin and development of a terminology of this kind make the appearance and evolution of their tannaitic counterparts intelligible, provided that some basic intellectual and religious disparity between the two civilisations is taken into account.

E. CONCLUSION

Earlier on, reference has been made to the environmental influence on the technical use of the diatribe in the relevant Hebrew source-material. Similarly, the general literary set-up of *PA* and *ARN* is comparable to a number of *Diadochoi* or *Bioi* which preceded Diogenes Laertius'[68] *Lives and Opinions of Eminent Philosophers* by centuries. These *Successions* or *Lives* either dealt with men of letters in general or were specially dedicated to a single, venerated founder of a school. Nevertheless, there is an essential difference between the Greek and Hebrew efforts to perpetuate the values of their respective legacies. The former restricted themselves to historically traceable and more or less accurate accounts of the development of *philosophical* thought, whilst the latter, in order to establish an unbroken chain of tradition and tradents, went back direct to Moses as the first recipient of God's *revelation* on Mount Sinai. Besides, *masar* and *masoreth* in *PA*, i, 1 and iii, 13, do not occur in the same sense in the Hebrew Bible and appear to correspond to to *paradounai* and *paradosis* in similar contexts of classical and Hellenistic literature.[68a]

The *terminus a quo* of these transformations cannot be fixed before the third century B.C.E., when the decisive encounter between Palestinian and Alexandrian Jewry, and that between both of them and the general impact of Greek civilization took place. Moreover, before and after oral traditions had been put into writing, their texts often gave rise to new interpretations and actual changes. The original meaning of *hewu methunim ba-Din* in *PA*, i, 1 has been tentatively suggested on p. 309 of this paper. It can now be maintained with certainty that, by the time of Hillel, at least some dialectical criteria in forming judgements, referred to in Greek and Latin writings on philosophy and law and in textbooks on rhetoric and grammar, had been adapted to serve as exegetical norms or canons of Torah-interpretation.[69] Yet, prior to the first century B.C.E., the first part of the maxim, ascribed to the men of the Great Assembly, was probably not understood to convey more than a general warning against overhastiness in assertion and precipitancy in legal proceedings. Apart from chapter 1 in *ARN* A and B such straightforward explanation is also reflected in the *Sifrey* on *Deut.* i: 16. "If you have to make a legal decision once, twice or thrice, do not say: 'I have made the same decision on three previous occasions', but be careful in your judgement, raise up many pupils and make a fence round the Torah."

As to *ᶜasu seyag la-Torah*, L. Finkelstein suggests to read instead *ᶜasu seyag le-divreykhem.*[69a] However, the proposed emendation does not seem to have any support in the unusually large number of extant variants in MSS. and scholarly editions.[70] Moreover, in view of the preceding observations, the attested traditional reading makes good sense, since Graeco-Roman and Jewish Hellenistic authors frequently used *fragmos* or *saepimentum* as metaphors for the fence which, as the logical part of philosophy, surrounds both the theoretical and the practical sciences, leads to their balanced application in life and ultimately to virtue. The transformation of these terms into *seyagim* is comparable to that of *ḥokhmah*, which came to be equated with *Torah*[71] or, *mutatis mutandis*, to that of Moses, the Prophet, whose biblical image was changed into Moses, the Lawgiver.[72] Hence, there is reasonable ground to assume that the final clause of the maxim of the men of the Great Assembly was originally meant to challenge the essentially rational connotation of *fragmos.* If, in the course of time, a considerable number of the ethical guidelines of the Stoa reappeared almost verbatim in the writings of *Tannaᵓim* and Palestinian *ᵓAmoraᵓim,* it has again to be borne in mind that the educational aims and methods of the rabbis as well as their authority over legal and ritual matters remained firmly based on, and fenced by, the laws of the Torah, however much was left for differences of opinion between individual scholars or between the houses of learning over which they presided.

An additional argument in favour of considering *seyag* as an early Aramaic calque of *fragmos* is to be found in *Midrash Rabbah* on *Lev.* i: 1. The translation of the homily reads as follows:[73] R. Eleazar (ben Pedat), a Palestinian *ᵓAmora* of the second generation, said: "Although the [whole] Torah had been given *as a fence* to the Israelites on Sinai, they were nevertheless not punished for (transgressing) it, until it was put before them officially *(ad she-nithpareshah)* in the Tent of Meeting, like an ordinance (*diatagma*) that had been written, sealed and then sent off to the province, but its citizens were not found guilty of [transgressing] it, until it was put up at the public administrative office (*dēmosia*) of the province." Now, *seyag* is indeed missing altogether in a parallel passage in *Midrash Rabbah* on *Cant.* vii: 3 and also in some MSS and printed texts of *Midrash Rabbah* on Lev. i: 1. Yet, the beginning of the latter seems to represent an original text, according to which the [whole] Torah was given to Israel *as a fence.*[74] *Lev. Rabbah* continues in the name of R. Yehoshua b. Levi: "If the nations of the world had known how useful the Tent of Meeting could have been for them, *they would have surrounded it with encampments and military fortifications . . .*"[75] A comparable figure of speech, again clearly reminiscent of Greek, Hellenistic-Jewish and Latin terminology in philosophical contexts, occurs in *Midrash Rabbah* on *Exod.* xv: 22. The key-word is *midbar shur*: "Before the giving of the Torah, the world was like a wilderness, but after Israel accepted it, *the world became a wall.*"[76]

In this connection, Philo's comments on Abraham's stay between *Kadesh* and *Shur* assume special significance, since they undoubtedly represent one of the earliest metaphorical interpretations of the passage in *Gen.* xx: 1.[77] Thus, in contrast to the literal rendering of these place-names by the Septuagint, the two Aramaic Targumim and the rabbinic commentaries of the middle ages, *Kadesh* is interpreted to stand for *sacred* and *Shur* for *wall*, "because within the borders of the two is the region of thoughts dear to God (*logismōn theophilōn*). There dwell those who are provided with, and surrounded by, virtues, as if by an *inexpugnable* and *indestructable wall*; *they are nourished by the sacred laws* and rejoice throughout the days of their life with God, the housemaster of wisdom (*oikodespotēs tēs sofias*)".

An evaluation of other passages which have a direct or indirect bearing on the origin and development of the concept of the fence, would go beyond the scope of this paper. Yet, the following results emerge from what has been said earlier on: R. Aqiba's four fences and their concomitant parts constitute, as far as we know, the first succinct, although by no means comprehensive summary of those aspects of the "new" term which he considered to be the most important ones. In addition, it was perhaps still during his life-time that *seyag* was made the special subject of a long, aggadic as well as halakhic Midrash.[78] Originally, it appears to have been a somewhat shorter diatribe on what by then had nevertheless come to exceed by far the extent of walls and hedges, surrounding law, reason, wisdom, ethics and education in earlier environmental literature.

It might be argued that the maxim of the men of the Great Assembly or the statements of Jewish-Hellenistic authors ought to have exerted at least as great an influence on R. Aqiba and his followers as those of their pagan antecedents. On the other hand, the *terminology* employed by Jews, whether they wrote in Greek, Hebrew or Aramaic, is so closely linked to the general intellectual history of the preceding centuries that no definite conclusion can be drawn on this point.

During the first half of the third century C.E., the creative employment of *seyagim* began to lose its force even among the Palestinian *ʾAmoraʾim* who previously had elaborated the legacy of their tannaitic predecessors in quite a few cases. This development is still more noticeable in the circles of their Babylonian colleagues. Because of their greater geographical distance from the main centres of Graeco-Roman civilisation, they had always been less able to adopt the "western approach" and to transform it into their own, almost exclusively halakhic methods of exegesis. Hence, the original concept of *seyag* and the variety of its extensions became more and more indistinct and, especially in the middle ages, identified with *mishmereth*, *gezerah*,[79] *taqqanah*, *geder* and *gevul*.[80]

Of these terms, only *taqqanoth* and *gezeroth*[81] could be enforced, whether, as in the case of *prosbul*, they were decreed by a single authority like Hillel (*Giṭṭin* 36b) or, subject to a majority of votes, by an assembly of scholars (*Shabbath* 13b).

NOTES

1. Cf. however, the passive participle *qal* of *sug*, to enclose (*sugah ba-Shoshannim, Cant.* vii: 3).

2. e.g. *Qoheleth Rabbah* on *Ecclesiastes* v, 14 and *sayyigu* in the Targum on *Cant.* vii: 3.

3. *PA* i, 1 refers only briefly to the transmission of the Torah by Moses to Joshua, the elders, the prophets and the men of the Great Assembly. *ARN* A and *ARN* B ch. I, ed. Schechter, add the names of (Eli), Haggai, Zechariah and Malachi, whilst the Targum on *Cant.* vii: 3 mentions also Ezra, Zerubbabel, Jeshua, Nehemiah, and Mordecai-Bilshan (i.e., *baʿal lashon*). *ARN* A, B, chs. 2, 3 have *sugah ba-Shoshannim* as one of their proof-texts for "*the fence the Torah made around her words*". Maimonides' *Introduction* to his *Mishneh Torah* has by far the largest list of tradents and their respective *battey din* up to the time of the *Geʾonim*: ". . . In every generation these sages, the prophets and the kings have promulgated ordinances (*gazeru*) *to make a fence round the Torah* . . . ." He bases his statement on the midrashic explanation of *Lev.* xviii: 30: *ʿasu mishmereth le-mishmarti*, which goes back to R. ʾAshi (*Moʿed Qaṭan* 5a) and to R. Kahana (*Yevamoth* 21a), two Babylonian *Amoraʾim* of the 6th generation. The earlier exposition of the same passage in the *Sifra, ad loc.*, is different and could not support his conclusion. In his *Shemonah Peraqim*, on the other hand, and to a lesser extent in his commentary on *PA*, he uses Aristotelian terminology and pays little attention to the chain of tradition. The same applies to the commentary on *PA* (*Sefer ha-Musar*, ed. Bacher, 1910) written by his favourite pupil, Joseph b. Yehudah ibn Aknin, and to other Jewish scholars of the middle ages who utilised their knowledge of Greek philosophy for the interpretation of biblical wisdom literature generally and of *PA* specifically. Of other medieval commentators on *PA*, only R. Menaḥem b. Solomon Meʾiri (*fl.* 1280: *Sefer beth ʾavoth*, ed. Salonika, 1921) offers a more succinct opinion on the origin of the concept of the fence, relating it to the period of Ezra: "*Before him there was no need to introduce a notion of this kind because originally God gave miṣwoth and ḥuqqim according to what man can bear in agreement with Nature.*" On *le-fi ha-Munaḥ ba-Ṭevaʿ* cf. *Moreh*, III, ch. 32.

4. In the Bible *talmid* occurs once only in *I Chronicles* xv: 8. There it refers to the training of apprentices by master-singers in the correct chanting of the liturgy.

5. At the end of *ARN* A, ch. 2 and *ARN* B, ch. 3 the last of these fences is assigned to the sages. It restricts the time for saying the evening-prayer to midnight "in order to prevent man from transgressing the words of the *ḥakhamim*." The preceding "sermon" or "diatribe" on a great variety of *seyagim*, which clearly meant to propagate the desirability of their general acceptance, was embellished by aggadic reconstructions of the past. This is not so in the case of the ruling of the sages. Cf. also the *Baraita*, quoted in *Berakhoth* 4b and the comparable prohibition to partake

of the paschal lamb after midnight in the *Mekhilta de-Rabbi Yishmaʾel* on *Ex.* xii: 8–10, ed. Lauterbach, vol. I pp. 45f. On the historical and halakhic background of the two passages in *ARN* A and B, see L. Finkelstein, *Mavoʾ le-masekhtoth ʾavoth we-ʾavoth de-Rabbi Nathan,* 1951, pp. 23–26.

6. Three of these *seyagim* have little, if anything to do with the protection of Torah legislation. The various kinds of tithes are at any rate commanded in *Lev.*, *Num.*, and *Deut.* Nevertheless, from the period of the Second Temple onward, an attempt at harmonisation between these pentateuchal sources and their adaptation to changed historical and economic circumstances had to take place, and R. Aqiba almost certainly meant to include halakhic modifications of the laws on *maʿaseroth*, current at his time. It was apparently only later that the traditional explanation comprising all of them: "Give your tithes so that you will become rich" was linked to *Deut.* xiv: 22 and transmitted in the name of R. Yishmaʾel b. Yose, a *Tannaʾ* of the fourth generation (*Shabbath* 119a), and also in the name of R. Yoḥanan b. Nappaḥa, a Palestinian *ʾAmora* of the second generation (*Taʿanith* 9a). Hence, Bacher, *Agada der Tannaiten*, II, p. 409, considers this interpretation as a later accretion to the original saying of R. Aqiba. A comparable, though not identical comment on *Deut.* xiv, 22, given by R. Levi, a contemporary of R. Yoḥanan b. Nappaḥa, is to be found in *Tanḥuma* Buber on *Reʾeh*, pp. 20f and in the *Pesiqta de-Rav Kahana*, ed. Mandelbaum, vol. I, 1962, pp. 161 f. It should be noted, however, that the reference to tithes is altogether missing in a few MSS of *PA* and in the parallel passages of *ARN* A, ch. 26 and *ARN* B, ch. 33. Yet in view of the terseness of R. Aqiba's statement and of its context, it is in all probability genuine, even if it does not lend itself to the above midrashic explanations. Thus, all four *seyagim* elude—at least at this stage—the effort to find a common denominator under which they could be grouped.

7. Cf. Y. F. Baer, *Yisraʾel ba-ʿammim*, 1955, pp. 62–70.

8. Cf. the present writer's "The Influence of Symposia Literature on the Literary Form of the Pesaḥ Haggadah," *JJS* VIII, Nos. 1 and 2, 1957, pp. 13–44.

9. See e.g. *ARN* A ch. 2 and *ARN* B ch. 3 about the fences the prophets made around their words, Bacher, *Exegetische Terminologie* . . . I, pp. 3f and A. Geiger, *Urschrift*, pp. 308–312 and 386–422.

9a. See note 69 *infra*.

10. In contrast to the School of Hillel, the School of Shammai was only prepared to admit a student who, apart from his moral and intellectual qualities, came from an aristocratic and rich family. In spite of essential differences in educational aims, *ben ḥakham we-ʿashir* under the heading *we-haʿamidu talmidim harbeh* seems to reflect the image of the young *eugenēs* who was brought up in one of the "public schools" of the Graeco-Macedonian period (*ARN* A, beginning of ch. 3). *ARN* B, ch. 4. has a slightly different, though not less interesting text (see Schechter *in loc.*, J. Levy, *Talmud. Wörterb. s.v. avginos,* and M. Hengel, *Judaism and Hellenism*, 1974, I, pp. 65f).

11. Hengel, *op. cit.* and S. Lieberman, *Yewanim wiywanuth be-ʾereṣ yisraʾel,* 1962 offer complementary and indeed indispensable information on the intellectual and historical background of the period under discussion.

12. With occasional modifications, translations from works written by Jewish-Hellenistic authors will usually be quoted from R. H. Charles, *The Apocrypha and Pseudepigrapha*, unless editions such as the one of the *Letter of Aristeas* by M. Hadas (1951) have been consulted. J. Goldin's translation of *The Fathers According To*

R. Nathan, 1974, has also been perused; all relevant *termini technici* have been italicised throughout. Other Greek or Latin texts will in most cases be cited from *The Loeb Classical Library.*

13. For *adiakopos charax* and *sidēron teichos* see *IV Maccabees* vii: 4f (ed. Hadas), Philo, Loeb, I, *Legum Allegoria,* II, 81 and Cohn-Wendland, *Philo,* vol. VI, index *s.v. adiakopos* as "*a principle of self-mastery*" and a "*rhetorical commonplace for determined resistance.*" Apart from Torah and Prophets, Ezra and Nehemiah had emphasized the necessity of Israel's separation from the nations, but only once, in *Lev.* xx: 25f, do we find a reference to the dietary laws as a means of attaining this religious-national isolation. The affinity between *Ezra* and *Nehemiah* on the one hand and *Pseudo-Aristeas* on the other is restricted to their common stand on mixed marriages. Even in this respect, the general tenor of the Hebrew and Greek arguments is by no means identical.

13a. *Torath mosheh* which occurs frequently from the book of *Joshua* to *II Chr.* does also not imply that Moses was considered the lawgiver.

14. In *The Zadokite Documents,* VI, 7–10, ed. C. Rabin, 1954, the *moreh ṣedeq* and "the nobles of the people" (*Num.* xxxi: 18) are considered the legitimate successors of Moses, the *meḥoqeq*, and their archetypes in the inspired searching of the Torah. Cf. also Philo, *De Ebrietate*, Loeb III, 112f. and *Targ. Ps. Jonathan* on *Num.* xxi: 18.

15. Ginzberg's *Legends*, V, p. 404 offers a long list of similar epithets e.g. *ḥakham ḥakhamim, gedol gedolim.* Lieberman, *l.c.* p. 212, recently added another: *nomiqah (nomikos)* i.e. learned in the Law. It has been preserved in the *Midrash ha-Gadol,* emanating from Yemen. Philo calls Moses all-wise (*pansophos*) (*De Agricultura,* Loeb, III, p. 118, 20). Josephus describes "our legislator" as "the most ancient of all in the records of the whole world." (Loeb, I, *Against Apion*, II, 154). Moses also appears as counsellor (*bouleutēs*) in *IV Maccabees* ix: 2).

16. "Many stood up to make a fence round Israel (*goderim*) but Moses was the father of all." This Midrash is based on *I Chr.* iv: 18 and transmitted by R. Huna b. ʾAḥa, a Palestinian *ʾAmora* of the third generation. Cf. also *Megillah* 13a.

17. *Harḥeq min ha-Kiʿur u-min ha-Domeh lo.* Cf. *ARN* A, B, ch. 2, *Bemidbar Rabbah, l.c., Ḥullin* 44b and, with slight variations, *Seder ʾEliyyahu Rabbah,* ed. M. Friedmann, 1960, pp 111f and 139. See also the *Apostolic Fathers,* vol. 1, *The Didache,* III, 1, ed. Kirsopp Lake, 1925: *pheuge apo pantos ponērou kai apo pantos homoiou autou.* Plutarch admires a similar exhortation from Empedocles: "refrain from evil *(nēsteussai kakotētos)*", himself "*applauding vows, made . . . to abstain from love and wine for a year, honouring God by self-control . . .*" (Loeb, *Moralia* VI, *De Cohibenda Ira*, pp. 156f). Under the influence of Pythagorean teachings, Seneca too abstained for a year from animal food (*Epistolae Morales*, CVIII, 22, as quoted by M. Stern, *Greek and Latin Authors on Jews and Judaism*, vol. I, 1976, pp. 433f). Without assuming a direct connection with these sources, R. Aqiba's maxim: *nedarim seyag la-Perishuth* comes to mind (*PA,* III, 13).

18. *ARN* A, ch. 1 on Adam, p. 4f and *ARN* B, ch. 1 on *ʿasu seyag la-Torah.* Additional evidence for the disparity of views on the appropriate extent of *seyagim* is to be found in *Niddah* 3b and 4b. In the course of the discussion on the first Mishnah of the tractate, a *Baraita* is quoted according to which Hillel asked Shammai: "What is the difference between your lenient decision in respect of menstrual uncleanness in *Lev.* xviii: 19 and all the other laws of the Torah around which we make a fence?" *(May shanē mi-kol ha-Torah kullah, de-khol ha-Torah ʿavdinan seyag)* Cf.

also the *Baraita,* quoted in *Shabbath* 153b, where two of the distinguished pupils of R. Yoḥanan ben Zakkai, R. Eliezer b. Hyrcanus and R. Joshua b. Ḥananiah argue about the same topic in comparable terms. It is equally difficult to determine by which norms judgements, passed on offenders against *seyagim* or, generally, against the words of the wise, were meant to be carried into effect. Thus there is apparently a denotational distinction between *ḥayyav mithah* in *ARN* A at the end of ch. 2. and *mithḥayyev be-nafsho* in *ARN* B at the end of ch. 3, although both passages deal with the fence, erected by the *ḥakhamim.* (See note 5 *supra*). Of the two versions only *ARN* B has *Eccl.* x: 8 as its proof-text: "He who digs a pit will fall into it, and he who pulls down a fence (*poreṣ geder*) will be bitten by a snake." Similarly, the Targum, the *Midrash Rabbah* and Rashi interpret the second stichos of this sentence as a reference to national or personal calamities and unusual forms of death, brought about "by the hands of Heaven." A technical term for this kind of divine intervention is *ḥiwya de-rabbanan de leyth leyh ʾasutha*, "*the snake of the rabbis for which there is no cure.*" (*Shabbath* 110a and *ᶜAvodah Zarah* 27b). On the other hand the following *Baraita* should be mentioned: R. Eliezer b. Jacob, a disciple of R. Aqiba, said: "I have heard, i.e., I have a reliable tradition, that a *beth din* may ordain flogging or the death penalty, not with the intent of transgressing the words of the Torah, but in order to make a fence round the Torah." The examples he quotes are restricted to the time of Greek rule when "the exigencies of the hour" required checking lawlessness. (*Migdar milta shanē.* Cf. *Yevamoth* 90b, *Sanhedrin* 45b, 46a and *Yer. Ḥagigah* 78a).

19. Apart from extensions of Torah-legislation on sexual relations between husband and wife, the passage also deals with some unfenced commandments of the Pentateuch, such as the required immersion after a night pollution, *qereh laylah*, (*Deut.* xxiii: 11), the privilege of priests to partake of loaves (*ḥalloth*), used for offerings on the altar (*Lev.* xxiv: 5–9) and their right to the first fleeces at the shearing of the flocks, *reʾshith gez ṣonekha* (*Deut.* xviii: 4). *ARN B,* ch. 3 reads instead: *mi mamḥeh be-yado,* adding untithed fruit which has been kept in one's house. "Perhaps one might come to eat it." *Shemma* is here, as often, used as a synonym for *seyag.*

19a. Cf. the article *Diatribe* in Klauser's *Reallexikon für Antike und Christentum*, 1957, and Marmorstein, *Studies in Jewish Theology*, 1950, *The Background of the Haggadah*, pp. 48–71.

20. *Heptapurgos logos* has been interpreted as a metaphor of cosmic significance, the adjective referring to the Babylonian planetary deities, to the seven pillars on which the world rests or simply to the usual architectural structure of palatial homes or temples. In the context of our passage, it is more plausible to connect it with the stoic classification of the ethical branches of philosophy, as given by Diogenes Laertius (Loeb II, VII, 84–131). Their number is shown to vary between eight and less elaborate divisions. An additional association with *Prov.* ix: 1 may well have prompted the author of *IV Maccabees* to choose the *seven-towered well-founded argument* as an appropriate simile for the moral excellence of Eleazar's sons. The relevant topics would at any rate include "life in agreement with nature" (as *ibid.* v: 25), virtue for its own sake, courage, self-control and *orthos logismos.* Ibn Ezra makes a similar comment on *Proverbs, in loc.* For the influence of the stoic definition of wisdom on Aristobulus' cosmological speculation about the "seven-fold logos," cf. Hengel, *op cit.* vol. I, pp. 167ff.

21. Cf. note 13 *supra.*

22. This translation follows again that of Hadas.

23. For an evaluation of natural or world-law on the one hand and of the Torah, exclusively communicated to Israel on the other, cf. Hengel, *op. cit.*, vol. I, pp. 160ff. As to the importance, attached to *patrika kai archaia nomima* see *inter alia* Plato's *Laws* 793 B and I. Heinemann, *Philo's Griechische und Jüdische Bildung*, 1962, pp. 470–487.

24. Cf. e.g. the dictum of R. Eleazar b. Azariah, president of the Sanhedrin and one of the official emissaries to Rome at the beginning of the second century: "How is one to know that one should not say: It is not my desire to wear a garment made of a mixture of wool and linen . . . to eat pork . . . or to have forbidden intercourse?" Rather should one say "It is my desire, but what can I do? Thus has my father in heaven decreed upon me. Therefore it says: I separated you from the nations, so that you should belong to Me (*Lev.* xx: 26). Hence, one abstains from sin and takes upon oneself the kingdom of Heaven." (End of *Sifra* on *Qedoshim*, ed. Schlossberg, 1862, f. 93d). For further statements of this kind, cf. the present writer's "The Dietary Laws in Rabbinic and Patristic Literature," *Studia Patristica,* II, 1957, pp. 141–154.

25. Cf. also I. Heinemann, *op. cit.* pp. 155–166.

26. A comparable association of ideas is to be found in *IV Mac.* I, 18–II, 9.

27. *ARN* B, ch. 3, for instance, read into *sugah ba-Shoshannim* a reference to the sages and their disciples who, through their prayers, guard the Jewish people from divine punishment. The comments of the Midrash and Targum *in loc.* link the same proof-text to the legislative and educational functions of the Sanhedrin. Moreover, in *ARN* A, ch. 2, also under the heading of the "fence erected by the Torah", a reward is promised to those who observe "*the minor commandments*," which will lead them to the life of the world to come. The division into *miṣwoth qalloth* and *ḥamuroth* represents another innovation *vis-à-vis* the biblical texts. Its origin is in keeping with the concept of making no gradations in error and corresponds to a well-known doctrine of the Stoics, traceable to Zeno. (See Townshend's note in Charles' *Pseudepigrapha* on *IV Mac.* v: 19ff). Hadas' objection to their interdependence in the light of later stoic developments misses an important point (*op. cit. in loc*): The teachers of the Mishnah were not full-time students of Greek philosophy, but accepted and/or transformed *termini technici* which had become popular and suited their purpose.

28. Variants to *PA* III, 1 occur in *ARN* A, ch. 26 and in *ARN* B, ch. 33.

29. *Rosh-ha-Shanah* 29b and *Sukkah* 42b, both in the name of Rabba, a Babylonian *ʾAmora* of the third generation. He no longer uses the term *seyag,* but *gezerah shemma* . . . .

30. On a comparable statement by Philo see n. 39 *infra.*

31. Loeb I, *Contra Apionem,* II, 171–174. In his *De Specialibus Legibus,* IV, 110 *(op. cit.),* Philo refers to the dietary laws as limitations *(choroi). See also* Lieberman, *Yewanim . . . , op. cit.*, pp. 210 and 213 on *kanōn*, *horos* and *gevul* and H. Oppel, *Die Bedeutungsgeschichte des Wortes Kanon . . . , Philologus*, Suppl. XXX, 1937.

31a. A different, hitherto unnoticed example of argumentative defence of Judaism occurs in *ARN* B, ch. 1 under the heading of "the fence, erected by the Holy One, blessed be He". The question is raised, how He could be supposed to do whatever He likes . . ., to drown the generation of the flood, to disperse the generation of the builders of the tower of Babel all over the world and to kill the people of

Sodom. What had they done? The answer uses *Deut.* xxix: 23–28 as prooftext implying that the Lord had forewarned all evildoers of the consequences of their transgressions, including those of pre-abrahamitic times. The reply can only be understood on the basis of one of the principles of R. Yishmaʾel, according to which there is no chronological order of "early or late" parts of the Torah. The passage is clearly directed against Marcion (*c.* 85–165 C.E.) or those gnostics who shared his dualistic world-view and levelled literally the same accusations against the biblical doctrine of God, the Omniscient and Omnipotent. In their eyes he was the *conditor malorum.* Cf., *inter alia,* Marmorstein's extensive and perceptive account of tannaitic and amoraic opposition to the teachings of Marcion in his *Studies in Jewish Theology, op. cit.,* pp. 1–47.

32. Cf. *III Mac.*, ch. 3, 4 in connexion with the dietary laws.

33. Antisthenes, a disciple of Socrates, makes a similar statement, quoted by Diogenes Laertius, Loeb, II, VI, 13.

34. *Herakleitos von Ephesus*[2], 1909, p. xii.

35. Cf. H. Diels, *Fragmente der Vorsokratiker*, p. 280.

36. Diogenes Laertius, Loeb II, VII, 32–41. The simile quoted represents one only of a number of given alternatives. For comparable divisions of logic, see *ibid.*, 42–83, of ethics, 84–131, of physics, 132–160.

37. Hadas, *IV Macc. , op . cit.*, ch. 1, 28–30. This passage and the two following quotations from Philo belong to a topic which compares husbandry in the literal sense with "*soul-gardening*" (*geōrgia psychikē*). In contrast to ordinary working on the soil for the sake of gain or pleasure, the latter "ministers to the mind and its aim is the fruit of virtue". To this Philo adds: "The trees . . . of licentiousness I will wholly cut down (*ekkopsō*). I will moreover extirpate the plants (*ta phyta*) . . . of desire, of anger and wrath and of like passions . . . and burn up their very roots . ." (Philo, *De Agricultura*, Loeb III, 17 and, in greater detail, *ibid.* 1–25). It is therefore possible that the much-debated expression *qiṣṣeṣ ba-Neṭiʿoth* corresponds to popular metaphors of this genre of literature. Subsequently, it was applied to Elisha b. Avuyah, the one-time companion of R. Aqiba and R. Meʾir who, after he had severed himself from the pharisaic way of life, *cut down the plants of the Torah instead of cultivating them.* In view of the preceding observations, "Reason, the universal gardener and leader of the virtues" or "husbandry, the most firm *fence of the soul*" could then be equated with the Torah. Thus, Scholem has tentatively suggested a connection between *neṭiʿoth* and those pentateuchal commandments, around which a *seyag* or *geder* had been erected by the sages. (Cf. his *Jewish Gnosticism . . . and Talmudic Tradition*, 1960, p. 16.) However, sources like *Ḥagigah*, 15a,b and their variants, in which the once-famous teacher is no longer called Elisha b. Avuyah but *ʾAḥer,* the "infidel", refer rather to his *complete* alienation from the teachings of the Torah. Even his tearing of a radish out of the ground and his riding on horseback on the Sabbath were not criticized as a transgression of this or that restrictive injunction of the rabbis. Instead, the change of his conduct was considered to be the result of his preoccupation with *ḥokhmath yewanith* or his leanings towards gnostic ideas. Ultimately, he was judged by most of his former colleagues to have acted out of moral deterioration and depravity (*yaṣaʾ le-tharbuth raʿah*).

38. *Quod Deterius Potiori Insidiari Solet,* Loeb, II, 105.

39. *De Agricultura, op. cit.,* 14–16. The next few sentences deal with "the whole

accomplishment of *general* education" (*hē sympasa tēs egkykliou mousikē*). Philo also links the story of the tree of life in the garden of Eden to the tripartite division of philosophy, indicating that "the complete moral victories . . . are the plants of the garden (*tou paradeisou ta phyta*). Now some of the arts and sciences are theoretical and not practical such as *astronomy* and *geometry*, some are practical, but not theoretical . . . , but virtue is both theoretical and practical . . . , since philosophy, the road that leads to it, involves conduct, for virtue is the art of the whole life . . ." (Loeb, I, *Legum Allegoria*, I, 56–60.) Elsewhere, Philo relates philosophy proper to "that practice of wisdom which is prescribed by the law of Moses." Cf. H. A. Wolfson, *Philo*: *Foundations of Religious Philosophy*, 1947, vol. 1, pp. 145–151. As to astronomy and geometry, the second clause of the statement of R. Eleazar Ḥisma, a contemporary of R. Aqiba and, like him, an expert in both fields, is of indirect relevance to the main subject of this paper. It reads as follows: . . ."*tequfoth we-gimmatreyaʾoth parperaʾoth la-ḥokhmah*" and is usually translated: . . ."Calculations of the equinoxes (or astronomy) and geometry are but the savoury dishes (or after-courses) of wisdom." (*PA*, III, 18.) However, A. Wasserstein has recently proposed to read *parpadiyyoth*, the hebraized plural of *propaideia*, i.e. the preliminary school-subjects, instead of *parperaʾoth* or *parperayoth*. The evidence he has assembled from the writings of Plato, Philo, the Greek and Latin Church Fathers, lends convincing support to his emendation. see *Tarbiẕ,* XLIII, 1973/74, pp. 53–57. There he also cites an assessment of the importance of *propaideia* for the defence of Christianity. It is taken from the *Strōmata* of Clement of Alexandria, ed. Stählin, I, XX, pp. 63f. According to him, these preparatory teachings or *egkyklia* "do not render Christian Truth more powerful . . . , but since they ward off the treacherous attacks of sophistry against it, one has properly called them the *fence* (*fragmos*) and *wall* (*trigkos*) of the vineyard. (Cf. *Isaiah* v: 1ff. and *Matthew* xxi: 33ff.) Now that Truth, compatible with Faith, (*hē kata tēn pistin alētheia*) is indispensable to life like bread, the *propaideumata* can be compared to a savoury dish (*prosopsēma*) or dessert (*tragēma*) to be eaten *together* with bread . . ." Although R. Eleazar Ḥisma was active in the first third of the second century C.E., and Clement of Alexandria lived from c. 150–220, both followed a much earlier classification of the preliminary studies which invariably included astronomy and geometry. Notwithstanding their different standards of knowledge in the field of Graeco-Roman civilisation, the main interest of the church father lay in the protection of faith, that of the Rabbi in securing the permanency of the written and oral law (*gufey halakhoth*). At any rate, the Greek loanwords of the Mishnah in *PA* clearly reflect in their emended and, for that matter, in their traditional form not only the cultural, but also the *historical* background to which they belong. Even *tequfah* does not mean calculation of the equinoxes or astronomy in biblical Hebrew. Cf. also *Shabbath* 75a. There, a few Palestinian *ʾAmoraʾim* otherwise known to have transmitted tannaitic traditions, present a view, reminiscent of, though not identical with the opinion held by Eleazar Ḥisma. In aggadic fashion, *Deut.* iv: 6, one of the two proof-texts of the passage, is entirely deprived of its plain sense. Instead, it is used to emphasize that it is man's duty (*miṣwah*) to calculate the eqinoxes and planetary courses (*ḥishshuv tequfoth u-mazzaloth*), because the conscientious observation of these natural phenomena displays Israel's "wisdom and understanding to the [other] nations."

40. Philo omits the end of the sentence, possibly to stress the universal importance of this commandment.

41. The example given under "the fence Job erected around his words" (*ARN* A, ch. 2 and *ARN* B, ch. 3) is, as to be expected, not allegorical, but based on *Job* xxxi: 1. Without referring to *seyag*, some earlier, comparable views are to be found in *Num.* xv: 39, *Sirach* ix: 1–9; sli: 20ff, *Testament of Issachar* vii: 2 and *Psalms of Solomon* iv: 4. Cf. also *Matth.* v: 28 and Strack-Billerbeck's extensive *Kommentar zum N.T. aus Talmud und Midrasch in loc.*

42. *Ta aporrēta* occurs in Plato's *Phaedo* 62b, where it refers to the esoteric teachings of the Pythagoreans. Students, admitted to their community, had to commit themselves not to divulge what they had heard or seen. Careful selection was also made, before they were allowed to participate in discussions on philosophical problems. O. Casel gives an historical survey of these ideas, ranging from Pythagoras via Plato, Aristotle and the Stoics to Clement of Alexandria. (Cf. his *De Philosophorum Graecorum silentio mystico, Religionsgeschichtliche Versuche und Vorarbeiten*, XVI, *Heft*, 2, 1919). Such restraint from transmitting speculative thought and ecstatic experiences to the unitiated, however transformed, also appears to be reflected in the *Mishnah Ḥagigah*, II, 1, the Palestinian and Babylonian *Gemaras* thereon, in related *Heykhaloth* texts and R. Aqiba's maxim "*A fence around wisdom is silence.*" This does not mean that he was sufficiently trained in the discipline of philosophical studies or interested in expounding them in the manner of the classical treatises on logic, physics or ethics. Nevertheless it is said of him in a *Baraita* at the end of *Soṭah* that, after his death "*the arms of the Torah became limp (baṭelu) and the foundations of wisdom were stopped up.*" On variants see Bacher, *Tannaiten* I, p. 275. He also refers to Aqiba's quotations from *Sirach, ibid.*, pp. 227 and 288. Moreover, R. Aqiba is known to have been an expert on calendrical calculations and, as a member of the *Beth Din* in Yavneh, he had to know Greek *ex officio*, although two of his colleagues, R. Eliezer b. Hyrcanus and R. Joshua b. Hananiah had achieved greater distinction in the persuit of "*ḥokhmath yewanith.*" (See Lieberman, *Yewanim . . . op. cit.*, pp. 14–21, and G. Allon's important review of his earlier book, *Greek in Jewish Palestine*, 1942. It appeared first in *QS*, XX, 1943, pp. 76–95 and is now also available in his *Meḥqarim be-toledoth yisraʾel . . .* , vol. II, 1970, pp. 248–277.) In a valuable article Kaminka has assembled a considerable number of aphorisms by R. Aqiba, his antecedents, contemporaries and successors and traced them back to early and late Greek sources. Yet it has again to be borne in mind that the rabbis never *quoted* them. Their sayings thus represented in fact only an adaptation to acceptable ethical ideas or rules of conduct which, during the first and second centuries, had attained wide-spread dissemination. (Cf. his *Meḥqarim . . . ba-Talmud u-va-Sifruth ha-rabbanith*, vol. II, 1957: *On Figures of Speech and Ethics in Judaea and Greece*, pp. 42–69 and on R. Aqiba, p. 135–158.)

43. Cf. Loeb V, 75th discourse, p. 240.

44. Cf. *Dissertationes*, Loeb II, book IV, v, 25; *ibid*, book III, vi, 15 and Oldfather's notes on both passages. See also A. Bonhöffer, *Epiktet und das Neue Testament*, 1911 and J. Bergmann, "Die Stoische Philosophie und die Jüdische Frömmigkeit" in *Festschrift für Hermann Cohen*, 1912.

45. . . . *Tertia de disserendo et quid verum sit, quid consentiens quid repugnans iudicando*. Cf. C. J. de Vogel, *Greek Philosophy*, *The Hellenistic-Roman Period*, vol. III, 1959, p. 50, note 897c on Varro. Some Greek texts will have to be quoted in this chapter in order to illustrate their connection with Latin sources.

46. Cf., *inter alia, Sirach* vi: 37, xxiv: 9, 23f; *I Baruch* iii: 9–iv: 1. For a detailed evaluation of relevant passages in *Ben Sira*, see Hengel, *op. cit.*, vol. I, pp. 131–162;

H. A. Wolfson, *Philo . . .*, vol. I, 1947, pp. 87–163; in Josephus, S. Rappaport, *Agada und Exegese bei Flavius Josephus*, 1930, pp. i-xxxvi (*passim*).

47. Cf. e.g. the homily of *Hoshaya Rabba*, a Palestinian *ʾAmora* of the first generation, at the beginning of *Bereshith Rabbah*, and large parts of the Midrash on *Proverbs*. The former has strong affinities with Philo's *De Opificio Mundi*, Loeb, I, 17–20, as already noted by Bacher, *Die Agada der Palästinensischen Amoräer*, 1892, vol. I, p. 107. The *Sifrey* on *ʿEqev* (37) expresses a similar thought and likewise has *Prov.* viii: 22 as its proof-text.

48. For an enumeration of the relevant *termini technici*, cf. Bacher, *Exegetische Terminologie der jüdischen Traditionsliteratur*, part I, 1899: *gezerah shawah, din, heqqesh*, and *qal wa-ḥomer*; (pp. 13–16, 20–23, 46, 172–174). Concerning the variety of meanings of *din* in tannaitic literature, a further point can be made with reference to *ARN* A and *ARN* B, ch. I. Both versions discuss the ultimate decision to include *Proverbs, Canticles* and *Ecclesiastes* in the biblical canon. *Proverbs* xxv: 1 is used as proof-text, the process of this development being supposed to have lasted from the time of Solomon to that of Hezekiah and, according to some, to the period of the men of the Great Assembly who received the chain of tradition from the last prophets. Hence, *hewu methunim ba-Din* "teaches us that man should be slow in giving his views and not angrily insist on them." (*yehē ʾadam mamtin bi-devaraw we-ʾal yehi maqpid ʿal devaraw.*) On a detailed interpretation of the *midrashic* procedure, employed in this passage, see Lieberman in the Hebrew part of the *Scholem Jubilee Volume*, 1967, pp. 166–169.

49. *Hodō erōtan kai apokrinesthai . . .* (Diogenes Laertius, on the Teachings the Stoics, Loeb. II, vii, 47f.) Cf. also *Sirach*, xi: 8f. (ed. M. Z. Segal, pp. 65 and 68.)

49a. Cf. *Apocrypha*, ed. Charles, *op. cit.*, p. 353 on *Sirach*, xi: 8 and the note thereon which draws attention to *Prov.* xviii: 13, and *Bava Bathra* 98b. These passages have some bearing on the first sentences of the Mishnah in *PA* and its parallels in *ARN*, but their wording is different and they lack the systematic presentation of the difference between the clod and the wise.

50. Loeb. I, *De Ira*, XVIII, 1, pp. 152f.

51. Cf. *ARN* A and *ARN* B ch. 1 in connection with *Numbers* xxxi: 14, where Moses is rebuked for having spoken in anger to the officers of the army.

52. As in Loeb II, p. 18, Loeb I, p. 466, Loeb II, p. 300. Other books in the two volumes deal with mathematics and astronomy as well as with those subjects which, in the early Alexandrian period, became basic elements of higher education in the arts and sciences, summarily known as *enkyklios paideia*. Cf. Hengel, *op. cit.*, I, p. 69.

53. Cf. Loeb, Supplement I and II and the Introduction of R. Marcus, pp. ixf.

54. I quote from Albeck's edition of *Mishnah ʾAvoth, Seder Neziqin* pp. 347–388, 493–502. His notes on the relevant passages and their variants in rabbinical literature are valuable, but have no bearing on our specific enquiry.

55. For the occurrence of these nouns, see Liddell & Scott. On the intellectual element in acquiring Stoic virtues, their enumeration and classification, cf. M. Pohlenz, *Die Stoa*, vol. 1, 1948, pp. 126 and 150 and his *Erläuterungen*, vol. 2, 1955, pp. 71f. and 80.

56. On the text of *ARN* A, ch. 26 and *ARN* B, ch. 33, see Schechter's notes *in loc.*

57. *Moral Essays*, Loeb, *De Ira*, II, 12, 4, pp. 192ff. Cf. also P. Smets, *Epiktet's Handbüchlein*, 1937, 33, pp. 46–60 on laughter and silence; *idem*, *Fragmente*, 24, p. 96. The nearest Greek equivalent to *miʿuṭ seḥoq* is to be found in the *Handbüchlein*, p. 48: "There should not be much laughter . . ." (*Gelōs mē polys estō . . .*)

58. Bacher, *Agada der Paläst. Amoräer,* I, p. 110 links Buber's reading *mangina-ʾoth* to Greek *maggana*, machines constructed for the defence of fortifications. *Ha-Sameaḥ be-ḥelqo* also belongs to the long list of virtues which are ment to lead to *qinyan ha-Torah.* Ben Zoma, the one-time colleague of R. Aqiba, expresses the same thought in a slightly different form (*PA*, iv, 1) "Who is rich? He that rejoices is his portion." His comment on his proof-text (Ps. cxxvii: 2), "Happy will you be in this world . . . and it will be well with you in the world to come" constitutes a not insignificant addition to what Epictetus says in his *Fragmente*, *op. cit.*, p. 172: "Who amongst men is rich? He that is content within himself (*ho autarkēs*)." Similarly, form and contents of Ben Zoma's aphorism in the same paragraph are to be linked to Stoic and Hellenistic-Jewish thought: "Who is mighty? He that subdues his (evil) impulse," as is written: "He that is slow to anger is better than the mighty and he that masters his temper better than he that takes a city." (*Prov.* xvi: 32). The second *stichos* of Ben Zoma's scriptural support for his statement is reminiscent of many examples in which law, reason or philosophy are considered more important for the defence of cities than their walls. It is therefore possible that the choice of his quotation from *Proverbs* was prompted by an association with current environmental similes of this kind. This is the more likely since, according to the additional explanation of *ARN* A, 23 *in loc.*, based on *Prov.*, xxi: 22 and *Ps.* ciii: 20, "the mighty are none other than the strong in Torah (*ʾeyn gibborim ʾella gibborey torah*)." Again, Epictetus has two almost identical formulations: "Who is unconquerable?" (*tis oun aēttētos*?) "He whom nothing outside the sphere of his moral purpose can dismay. He who passes all these tests is for me the invincible athlete (*ho anikētos athlētēs*)." (Loeb, *Discourses of Epictetus*, vol. I, Book, I, ch. 18 and, similarly, *ibid.* vol. II, Book III, p. 82: "Who is the man in training?" (*tis estin askētēs*?) "He who practises particularly in the things that are difficult to master." (For a shorter verion of *ARN A*, 23 cf. *PA*, iv, 1.). In other words: Only "the moral athlete" has control over his emotions and passions. Amongst these, anger and wrath had been the subject of special treatises in Greek and Roman literature. Thus, Chrysippus (3rd. cent. B.C.E.) split the four Platonic virtues into a great number of subdivisions, according to which self-control is part of bravery. (See Pohlenz, vol. II, *op. cit.*, as in note 55 *supra.*) Plutarch's *De Cohibenda Ira* and Seneca's *De Ira* have been mentioned before. In his *Moral Essays, op. cit.*, vol. I, xix, 3f., pp. 156f., the latter enumerates *inter alia* the following symptoms of unbridled rage: "the tearing of one's clothes, the hurling of cups on the floor and the pulling out of one's hair. Although there is no need to assume direct influence, it is hardly accidental that *ARN* A, ch. 3 and *ARN* B, ch. 4 transmit a practically identical Hebrew rendering of the first two concomitants of irascibility in the name of R. Aqiba. A *Baraita* in *Shabbath* 105b and the *Tosefta* at the end of *Bava Qamma*, ch. 9, have the same tradition in the name of R. Yoḥanan b. Nuri, a contemporary of R. Aqiba. Only the *Tosefta,* not infrequently retaining an older version, incorporates also the pulling of the hair. However, whilst, according to Seneca, actions of this kind contradict reason, the *Tannaʾim* consider them as ultimately leading to idolatry.

59. Loeb, *Iliad* IV, 350 and XIV, 83; *Odyssey* I, 64; III, 230; V, 22; XIX, 492; XXI, 68 and XXIII, 70. These passages are addressed to different people, but all of them censure aggressiveness in speech . . . "*What a word has escaped the barrier of your teeth*?" Elsewhere Homer uses *herkos* in the sense of a bulwark against missiles at the time of war or a fence around a vineyard. (Cf. Pendergast's concor-

dance to the *Iliad* and Dunbar's to the *Odyssey*). Lieberman, *Yewanim . . .*, pp. 110–123, enumerates comparable literary adoptions such as those taken by Petronius (first cent. C.E.) from Aristophanes (fifth cent. B.C.E.). The majority of cases refer to quotations from Greek or Roman authors which found their way into early rabbinic literature.

60. According to Norden, *Agnōstor Theos*, 1913, p. 112, "*ist die Orientalisierung des Hellenischen grösser gewesen als die Hellenisierung des Orients.*"

61. The end of the above quotation (. . . *ad bona seligenda et reicienda contraria*) also refers to the same topic and requires additional comment. An outline of early Greek speculative thought on pairs of opposites of various sorts and, from Plato onwards, its more precise use for establishing the validity of dialectical criteria must have been known to Cicero. Aristotle, Xenocrates and Chrysippus had written several books *Peri enantiōn* (Diogenes Laertius, IV, 12, 13, V, 22 and VII, 200). Generally, the Stoics held that "*good (traits of character) comprise the virtues of prudence, justice, courage, temperance, etc., while the opposites of these are evils (kaka de ta enantia)* namely *folly*, *injustice* etc. . . . *Others like life and death . . . health and disease . . . are morally indifferent (adiafora)*" (*ibid.* VII, 102–113). Such views follow substantially those of Plato (*ibid.* III, 102). For the history of the problem, see G. E. R. Lloyd's important book: *Polarity and Analogy. Two Types of Argumentation in early Greek Thought*, 1966, pp. 7f., 130f., 164f., 170f., 418f., 436–440. On the Jewish side, *PA*, v, 7 enumerates seven laudable characteristics of the wise . . . "*The opposites of these* are typical of the clod (*we-ḥillufeyhen ba-Golem*)." There is no linguistic and no connotative comparison between this paragraph and the very frequent, but dispersed passages on the differences between the wise and the fool in biblical wisdom literature, and there can be little, if any doubt that Greek or Roman influences have played their part in the *wording* of this Mishnah. The *Targum Pseudo-Jonathan* on *Deut.* xi: 26, 28, xxx: 1 and 19 offers a similar example, It has *birketha we-ḥillufah* instead of the masoretic *berakhah u-qelalah.* J. Levy, in his *Wörterbuch über die Targumim, s.v. ḥillufa,* considers the change as a euphemism, but in the light of modern scholarship his explanation has at least lost some of its relevance, since in *Pseudo-Jonathan* on *Deut.* xxx: 19 the literal Aramaic translation of Hebrew *ḥayyim u-maweth* precedes *birketha we-ḥillufah.* Some information about the logical significance of *termini technici* like *enantia* and *antikeimena, contraria* and *opposita* had also reached the rabbis of the tannaitic period, who availed themselves of it for their exegetical terminology. Generally the *piʿel* of *ḥlf* refers to the reverse of a given dialectical criterion. If a reasoning in the opposite direction is attempted, but turns out to be untenable, the initial one is to be accepted. The *Mekhilta* on *Exodus*, xxi: 28, (ed. Lauterbach, pp. 78f.) for instance, reads as follows: "*I advanced an argument and (then) tried to prove the opposite. It has been shown to be invalid, hence I was right in my (first) conclusion.*" *(Danti we-ḥillafti u-vaṭel ha-ḥilluf we-zakhiti ba-Din)*. For further examples see Bacher, *Exegetische Terminologie*, I, pp. 59f. In his *De Ira*, *op. cit.*, II, 12, 1–3, Seneca first gives a practical answer to the claim that neither wickedness nor anger can be eliminated from the scheme of nature. "One may", he says, "be protected against the inclemency of the season by a favourable place of residence or one may, by physical endurance, subdue the sensation of heat and cold." But then he continues: "*Verte istud*" (reverse this statement). "One must banish virtue from one's heart, before one can admit the violence of anger, since vices do not

consort with virtues, and a man can no more be angry and good at the same time than he can be sick and well." The *Mekhilta* argues on the basis of one of the then current norms of halakhic exegesis, Seneca on a philosophico-ethical level; but the *wording* of their statements indicates a connection with speculative thought which preceded both of them by centuries.

62. *". . . idemque cum caelum, terras . . . rerumque omnium naturam perspexerit, eaque unde generata, quo recursura, quando quomodo obitura, quid in iis mortale et caducum quid divinum aeternumque sit."* Similar phrases occur frequently in stoic and gnostic literature. Cf., e.g., Seneca's letter, quoted further on. Epictetus alone offers three versions (Loeb, Book III, XII, 15., XXIV, 95., Book IV, I, 34). The Jewish variant in *PA*, iii, 1 and in *ARN*, A and B, ch. 19 has a significant addition: *"Know whence you come and whither you are going and before whom you are about to give account and reckoning—before the King of Kings, the Holy One, Blessed be He."* See also A. Marmorstein, "Les enseignements d'Akabia b. Mahalalel," *REJ*, LXXXI, 1925, pp. 181–187.

63. *"Nec videt, quibus praesidiis philosophiae saeptus sum."* (Loeb, *Epistulae Familiares*, III, xvi, 23, 2).

64. *"Neque enim ulla lex est, quae non ipsa se saepiat difficultate abrogationis."* (Loeb, *Epistulae ad Atticum*, III, 23).

65. "*Philosophia circumdanda est, inexpugnabilis murus, quem fortuna multis machinis lacessitum non transit.*"

66. *Plus scire velle quam sit satis intemperantiae genus est.* For a summary on the subject, cf. Seneca's *Epistulae Morales*, Loeb II, pp. 363–395, especially pp. 370f.

67. Livy, Loeb, III, 44; Tacitus, *Germania*, 19, 1.

68. He lived in the earlier part of the third cent. C.E. R. D. Hicks (Loeb, vol. I, Introduction, 1966, pp. xxii–xxxii) gives a detailed account of his predecessors down to the second cent. C.E. Cf. also E. Bickermann, "La chaine de la tradition pharisienne," *Revue Biblique*, LIX, 1952, pp. 44–54.

68a. The article on *paradounai* and *paradosis* in G. Kittel, *Theologisches Wörterbuch*, II, 1935, offers a valuable historical assessment of the relevant material from Plato, Philo, Josephus and the mystery religions to the New Testament.

69. For a detailed account of the terminological development of the *middoth she-ha-Torah nidresheth bahen* cf. Lieberman, *Yewanim, op. cit.*, pp. 189–198.

69a. "Pharisiaism in the Making", *Selected Essays*, I, 1972, pp. 162f.

70. See Albeck's text of *PA, op. cit.*, Schechter's text of *ARN* and Finkelstein's *Mavoʾ le-massekhthoth ʾavoth we-ʾavoth de-rabbi Nathan*, 1951, pp. 23–26.

71. Cf. notes 46 and 47 *supra*, and midrashic and targumic comments on the relevant passage in *Proverbs* and *Ecclesiastes*.

72. *Nomothetēs* occurs also in Philo, *Quod omnis probus liber sit* (Loeb, IX, 43; cf. note 15 for other examples). It is still more significant that the same term for Moses was used by pagan philosophers or historians from *c.* 300 B.C.E. onwards. (Cf. e.g. Menahem Stern, *Greek and Latin Authors on Jews and Judaism*, 1976, pp. 26 and 237). Theophrastus, a disciple of Aristotle, described the Jews "as philosophers by race, who converse with each other about the deity". (See Stern, *ibid.*, p. 10).

73. Generally, I follow Lieberman whose version is based on a fusion of *Midrash Rabbah* on *Cant.* vii: 13 and on *Lev.* i: 1. His notes offer a thorough analysis of the

text in the light of Graeco-Roman juridical practice. Cf. his *Yevanim*, *op. cit.*, pp. 299f. I also made use of the edition of the *Midrash Rabbah* on *Lev.* by M. Margulies, 1972.

74. Margulies, *op. cit.*, pp. 24ff, gives a list of three MSS, the *ed. princeps* of *Lev. Rabbah* and the *ed. princ.* of another parallel text in *Yalquṭ Shimᶜoni* which have *seyag*. He ascribes its omission in some other MSS and editions to a lack of understanding on the part of the copyists. Liebermann decided apparently against the inclusion of *seyag*. See also n. 18 *supra*.

75. R. Yehoshua b. Levi was a Palestinian *ᵓAmora* of the first generation and a frequent tradent of his teacher Bar Kappara. Cf. Bacher, *Agada d. Tannaiten,* II, p. 506 and *Ag.d. Palästinensischen Amoräer,* I, p. 124.

76. The statement is assigned to R. Yehudah b. Simon, a Palestinian *ᵓAmora* of the fourth generation, He is known to have transmitted earlier aggadic and halakhic traditions, including those of the *Tannaᵓim*. In the *Midrash Rabbah* on *Cant.* viii: 8–10: . . . "I am a wall and my breasts are like towers", the text is *inter alia* referred to Abraha.n and, in almost identical terms, to the Jewish people as a whole. Similar to *sugah ba-Shoshannim* in *ARN* A, ch. 2 and *ARN* B, ch. 3, *ḥomah* stands here for the fulfilment of commandments and the performance of good deeds, *shaday ka-Migdaloth* for establishing different groups of *ṣaddiqim.* In a dialogue with the Master of the Universe, the patriarch pledges himself before Him: "I am (we are) the wall" etc. "Then" i.e. in messianic times, "I (we) shall be able to find peace in his eyes". The first part of this long homily is again transmitted in the name of R. Yehudah b. Simon.

77. *Questiones et Solutiones in Genesin,* Loeb, Suppl. I, Book IV, 59, pp. 339f. There are two observations of a similar kind on the story of Hagar who was found by an angel in the wilderness on the way to *Shur* (*Gen.* xvi: 7–9): a short one in Philo's *De Fuga et Inventione*, *op. cit.*, 203–206 and a long one in his *Quaestiones* . . . , *op. cit.*, Book III, 27–30, pp. 213–218. The contents of both passages can be summarized as follows: Hagar, the handmaid, symbolizes the preparatory school-studies, Sarah, her mistress, virtue. The former realizes the necessity to return to "a purer and more worthy spirit", to humble herself and to accept the implied censure of the questions, put to her "by the inward monitor of her soul": "Whence do you come and whither are you going?" In this context too, the allegory conveys the idea that *Shur* is to be interpreted as *wall* and that "the road towards discipline is all a highway, *thoroughly safe* and *most securely fenced* (*ochyrōtatē kai euherkestatē*)". With it goes the warning "not to use a trackless route, but to improve oneself by choosing the path that leads to virtue".

78. Like R. Aqiba, most of the sages referred to in this homily belonged to the second, a few others to the third or fourth generation of *Tannaᵓim*. In contrast, however, to his terse aphorisms, the relevant passages in *ARN* A and B begin with an interrogative sentence: "What was the fence he made around his words?" Or, respectively, "How do I know that he made a fence around his words?"

79. Cf. note 3 *supra*.

80. Cf. note 31 *supra*.

81. They too could be restricted to time and place and, under certain circumstances, annulled. There are also *taqqanoth* or *gezeroth* of an entirely aggadic character such as those supposed to have been enacted by King Solomon. His ordinances refer to the washing of hands before partaking of consecrated food, to the intro-

duction of additional restrictions regarding forbidden marriages (*sheniyyoth la-ʿarayoth*) and to the institution of the *ʿEruv*. (*Shabbath* 14b, 15a and parallel passages in *ʿEruvin* and *Yevamoth*.) *In loc.*, Rashi explains these enactments as *seyagim*. His grandson, Samuel b. Meir, equates the root *gadar* in another aggadic passage with *seyag la-Torah*. (*Bava Bathra* 91b).

Les Deux Théories de Maïmonide sur La Providence*

C. TOUATI

Dans son *Guide des Egarés*, Maïmonide offre deux théories dissemblables sur la Providence divine. Le grave problème posé par cette dualité de sa pensée sur un point fondamental de son système et ouvert avant même la mort du Maître en l'année 1204 n'a cessé d'intriguer commentateurs, philosophes et historiens des idées jusqu'à nos jours. Si les uns et les autres ont apporté une plus ou moins importante contribution à la solution de l'énigme—à l'exception des modernes comme Salomon Munk et Julius Guttman[1]—, il ne nous semble pas qu'ils aient entièrement résolu le problème, que nous voudrions reprendre dans cette étude.

Puisque les auteurs que nous citerons le plus souvent ont travaillé sur la version hébraïque de Salomon Ibn Tibbon, nous ne pouvons pas omettre de la citer; mais il est évident que nous nous appuierons constamment sur l'original arabe, qui seul nous donne un certain nombre de parallèles mettant sur la voie d'une solution. Nous essaierons d'exposer les idées de Maïmonide dans l'ordre où lui-même les a présentées en intervenant le moins possible dans l'exposé, de peur de fausser un mécanisme extrêmement délicat, mais en soulignant les détails importants, les allusions de l'auteur, ses appels à l'attention du lecteur, bref, tous les points sur lesquels se sont appesantis les exégètes ou sur lesquels nous comptons fonder nos propres interprétations. Certes, notre développement aura un air décousu; mais il ne fait que refléter celui du texte. On sait que l'agencement du *Guide* est assez singulier et que son désordre apparent est voulu par Maïmonide, qui n'entendait livrer sa pensée profonde qu'au lecteur cultivé, perspicace et subtil.[2]

I. EXPOSÉ DES IDÉES DE MAÏMONIDE

(a) Le Mal (*Guide*, III, chap. xii)

Maïmonide, après avoir combattu l'idée d'Al-Rāzī qui soutenait que dans le monde le mal est beaucoup plus abondant que le bien, répartit les maux en trois catégories, qui correspondent également à des fréquences de plus en plus grandes.

La première catégorie comprend les maux qui sont la conséquence inévitable de la génération et de la corruption: tares, infirmités ou tremblements de terre, effets de la foudre, ect. L'être, constitué de matière, qui prétendrait n'être pas susceptible de les subir, ressemblerait à quelqu'un qui voudrait concilier les contradictoires.[3]

A la deuxième catégorie appartiennent les maux que les hommes, parce qu'ils sont privés de la vraie science, se causent les uns aux autres: tyrannie, guerres, etc.[4]

Les maux de la troisième catégorie sont les plus fréquents: il s'agit là des maux que l'homme s'inflige à lui-même; et rares sont les individus qui ne sont pas les victimes d'eux-mêmes. Ces maux ont pour origines les défauts moraux et les désirs du superflu, tant dans le boire, le manger, la vêture et le sexe, lesquels sont infinis. Pourtant, dans le monde, l'indispensable se procure facilement, d'autant plus facilement qu'il est plus indispensable comme l'air et l'eau; et, par rapport à l'indispensable, tous les hommes sont égaux.[5]

Ce chapitre constitue une sorte de préambule aux chapitres sur la Providence. Il convient de signaler pourtant que ce chapitre xii est déjà la négation de toute Providence, au sens où l'entend le vulgaire. En effet, Maïmonide vient de prouver qu'aucun mal ne vient de Dieu mais d'un déterminisme rigoureux ou de la liberté humaine; or, Dieu est limité d'une part par l'impossible—ce n'est pas sans raison que Maïmonide a inséré au milieu des chapitres sur la Providence un chapitre, le chapitre xv, commençant par ces mots qui firent scandale: "L'impossible a une nature fixe et constante,"[6]—d'autre part, par la liberté humaine qu'il ne peut entraver.[7] Dieu ne peut donc sauver l'homme d'aucun des maux des trois catégories.

(b) Les Théories sur la Providence (*Guide*, III, chapitre xvii)

Maïmonide présente dans ce chapitre cinq théories sur la Providence; mais, en réalité, nous en trouverons six.

La *première* est celle d'Epicure, qui nie la Providence et voit en toute chose l'effet du pur hasard. Cette opinion a déjà été réfutée par Aristote.

La *seconde* estime que certaines choses sont bien ordonnées et agencées, tandis que d'autres sont abandonnées aux hasards. D'après Alexandre d'Aphrodise, le grand commentateur du Stagirite, celui-ci pensait que la Providence divine est fonction de la nature des êtres: elle se montre de plus en plus efficace au fur et à mesure qu'on gravit l'échelle ontologique. C'est ainsi qu'au-dessus de la sphère lunaire, elle accorde immutabilité et permanence aux corps célestes, tandis que dans le monde sublunaire elle n'a pour objet que les seules espèces mais non les individus; toutefois, plus la matière devient subtile, plus elle se trouve dotée de moyens de protection perfectionnés: faculté végétative, faculté sensitive, faculté intellective. Cependant, pour Aristote, la Providence n'accorderait aucun privilège à l'homme singulier: il ne voit aucune différence entre la mort d'un homme vertueux dans un bateau qui fait naufrage et la chute d'une feuille sous l'action du vent.[8]

La *troisième* thèse, soutenue par les Asharites, met l'accent sur la volonté absolue et inscrutable de Dieu qui a tout prédestiné, en sorte que le juste peut être voué à la Géhenne et l'impie au Paradis.[9]

La *quatrième* doctrine, celle des Mutazilites, voit partout la sagesse divine, pour qui le mal est destiné à procurer un plus grand bien, et qui accorde à tous ceux qui ont souffert—hommes et animaux—une compensation dans l'Au-Delà.

La *cinquième* opinion est la nôtre, dit Maïmonide qui immédiatement ajoute cette restriction: "je veux dire celle de notre Loi," à laquelle croit la *masse* (en arabe: *jumhūr*, en hébreu: *hamon*) de nos docteurs,[10] et il annonce qu'il développera ensuite ce que *lui* croit.

Le principe fondamental de notre Tora que personne n'a jamais nié au sein du judaïsme c'est l'existence d'une liberté humaine totale et voulue par Dieu. Selon la Tora, tout ce qui arrive à l'homme découle de *la justice* divine, selon ce qu'il a mérité (en arabe: *ᶜalā jihat al-istiḥqāq*, en hébreu: *ᶜal ṣad ha-din*).[11] Tout malheur est un châtiment; tout bonheur, une récompense. Cette doctrine a été exprimée par la *masse* des docteurs dans cette formule: "Pas de mort sans péché et pas de tourments sans iniquité."

Certains commentateurs de Maïmonide se sont étonnés de le voir adopter une opinion du *Talmud Babli*, *Šabbat* 55a, qui se trouve rejetée en fin de compte au profit de son opposé: "Il est des morts sans péché et des tourments sans iniquité." On pourra cependant faire observer que si l'opinion citée par Maïmonide n'est pas admise dans ce folio du Talmud, elle n'en est pas moins sous-jacente à maintes et maintes mises en équation opérées par la littérature talmudique entre tel péché et tel châtiment, entre telle pratique d'un précepte et tel bien, et qu'elle représente bien la pensée la plus constante des docteurs de la Loi.[12]

Maïmonide expose ensuite ce que *lui* croit. Ce n'est pas, dit-il, une démonstration qui l'a conduit à professer la théorie qu'on va lire, mais il lui a paru évident qu'elle traduit *l'intention profonde* (en arabe: *qaṣd*, en hébreu: *kawwana*) de la Tora divine et des livres prophétiques et qu'elle est, parmi toutes les thèses, celle qui se rapproche le plus de la raison.

La Providence divine, explique Maïmonide, a pour objet chacun des individus de l'espèce humaine. Ce sont eux qui sont traités *selon la justice* (en arabe: *istiḥqāq*; en hébreu: *din*), tandis que les autres êtres vivants sont livrés au hasard, comme le pensait Aristote. La Providence, selon l'auteur du *Guide*, dépend étroitement de l'intellect. Quand l'épanchement de l'Intellect a fait d'un homme un être intelligent à qui est révélé tout ce qui peut l'être à une telle personne, la Providence s'attache alors à cet homme-là; tout ce qui lui adviendra désormais sera ou récompense ou châtiment. Si le toit d'une maison qui l'abritait tombe, si le bateau où il avait embarqué fait naufrage, c'est l'effet d'un hasard, certes, mais la présence de l'homme sous ce toit ou dans ce bateau est un effet de la volonté de Dieu, conforme a sa *justice* (en arabe: *bi-ḥasab al-istiḥqāq*; en hébreu: *le-fi ha-din*) qui nous est totalement inaccessible.

En terminant, Maïmonide demande au lecteur de pénétrer sa pensée jusqu'au fond: à Dieu elle n'impute ni ignorance ni impuissance; elle énonce simplement que la Providence est fonction de l'intellect. Maïmonide répète que sa thèse est, de toutes, la plus proche de la raison et de l'Ecriture. Il conclut en affirmant que *toutes les autres* sont *erronées* et *nuisibles*.

(c) Les Personnages du Livre de Job (*Guide*, III, chapitre xxiii)

Pour Maimonide, le héros du Livre de *Job* et ses interlocuteurs développent tous des doctrines sur la Providence distinctes, malgré de communes opinions, des exhortations similaires etc. qui pourraient masquer leurs différences.

Plongé dans ses malheurs, Job estimait que tous les hommes sont confondus dans un même sort, bons et méchants, croyants ou impies (en arabe: *al-ṣāliḥ wa-l-ṭāliḥ*; en hébreu: *ṣaddiq we-rašaᶜ*). Cette opinion, il l'a exprimée quand il ne possédait pas encore *la science*, quand il ne connaissait Dieu que par *la tradition*, comme le connaît *la masse* (en arabe: *jumhūr*; en hébreu: *hamon*) des fidèles des religions révélées. Aussi bien d'ailleurs est-il qualifié par l'Ecriture d'*homme intègre et droit, craigant Dieu et s'écartant du mal* (*Job* 1:1), mais non pas d'homme *sage, intelligent* ou *savant* (en hébreu dans le texte: *ᵓiš ḥakham ᵓo mēbin ᵓo maskil*), selon une subtile remarque de Maïmonide.[13]

Mais, lorsque Job eut acquis une science réelle de Dieu, il confessa que la véritable félicité, *qui est précisément la connaissance de Dieu*, est accessible à tous les hommes et ne peut être troublée par quelque souffrance que ce soit. Alors il s'exclama: *Aussi mépriserai-je tout ce que j'avais désiré et me consolerai-je d'être dans la poussière et la cendre* (paraphrase de Maïmonide, en hébreu, de *Job* 42:6).[14] Incidemment, sans avoir l'air d'insister, Maïmonide observe que ces paroles de Job indiquent qu'il a véritablement perçu la vérité authentique (en arabe: *dālla ᶜalā l-idrāk al-ṣaḥīḥ*).[15]

Chacun des personnages du Livre de *Job* représente une doctrine sur la Providence que nous avons déjà rencontrée. Maïmonide identifie celle de Job avec celle d'Aristote, celle d'Eliphaz avec celle de "notre Loi;" Bildad est Mutazilite et Sophar Asharite.[16] N'oublions pas que plus haut Maïmonide a relevé que Dieu reproche aux *trois amis* de Job de n'avoir pas correctement parlé de Lui (cf. *Job* 42:8)[17]

Quand les amis de Job eurent gardé le silence, un nouvel interlocuteur intervint: Elihu. Ses propos semblent n'être pas très différents de ceux qu'avaient tenus Eliphaz, Bildad et Sophar. Ce qu'il ajoute cependant, c'est *le sens profond* (en arabe: *qaṣd*; en hébreu: *kawwana*) de la Tora (on n'a pas oublié que Maïmonide lui aussi a trouvé *le sens profond* de la Tora; voir ci-dessus). Mais le seul apport vraiment neuf d'Elihu est l'enseignement suivant lequel l'homme, même arrivé aux portes de la mort, sera sauvé s'il a un ange intercesseur, quel qu'il soit; il sera sauvé deux fois, trois fois; mais pas toujours. Maïmonide ajoute, encore une fois incidemment, qu'Elihu a prononcé également des paroles sur la prophétie.

Nous avions constaté que, celle d'Epicure étant évidemment exclue, les personnages du Livre de *Job* représentent chacun une des théories sur la Providence. Bien que Maïmonide ne le dise pas, il est clair que la conception d'Elihu et celle de Maïmonide interprétant le *sens profond* de la Tora coïncident. Enfin retenons dès maintenant qu'il y a un personnage auquel ne semble correspondre aucune théorie: c'est celui que nous appellerons le *Job régénéré*, l'homme qui a connu Dieu d'une science véritable.

(d) La Deuxième Théorie Maïmonidienne sur la Providence (*Guide*, III, chapitre li)

Au début de ce chapitre, Maïmonide avertit le lecteur que ce chapitre *n'ajoute rien à ce qui précède* et n'est rien d'autre qu'une espèce de conclusion. L'auteur va y brosser le portrait de l'*homme-qui-a-saisi-les-réalités* (*mudrik al-ḥaqāʾiq*, en arabe; l'hébreu: *massig ha-ʾamittot* deviendra comme un terme technique sous le plume des commentateurs),[18] et décrire le culte que cet homme rend à Dieu; ensuite il nous indiquera ce qu'est la Providence divine dans cette vie.

La vie du sage est faite d'esseulement et d'amour de Dieu. Un *corps* qui agit sur terre parmi les hommes, s'adonnant aux occupations habituelles des humains, et un *esprit* entièrement et constamment uni à Dieu et jamais distrait de cette union,[19] voilà ce qu'étaient les trois patriarches et Moïse, ces hommes accomplis qui sont parvenus à un sommet auquel Maïmonide lui-même n'espère pas atteindre.

Arrivé à ce point de sa méditation, Maïmonide constate qu'une merveilleuse spéculation vient de se présenter à lui, qui éliminera les difficultés et dévoilera des secrets. Elle lui enseigne que celui dont l'intellect ne se détache jamais de Dieu ne sera jamais abandonné par la Providence. Se détourne-t-il un instant de Dieu, la Providence s'écartera de lui pendant ce même instant. Quant à ceux qui n'ont jamais intelligé Dieu, ils sont plongés dans de perpétuelles ténèbres. Si certains prophètes ou certains hommes parfaits vertueux-et-pieux (en arabe: *al-fuḍalāʾ al-kāmilīn*;[20] en hébreu: *ha-ḥasidim ha-šelēmim*) subissent des malheurs, ceux-ci les atteignent dans les moments où ils oublient Dieu. Le mal est d'ailleurs proportionné à la durée de la période de l'oubli ou à la bassesse de l'objet qui alors remplissait la pensée.

Celui qui a appréhendé Dieu par les voies véritables et *a ressenti de la joie en raison de ce qu'il a saisi* ne peut être frappé par aucun mal. Mais que l'homme oublie Dieu, il devient vulnérable à n'importe quel malheur. L'homme pieux-et-vertueux peut donc être privé quelque temps du bien et l'homme imparfait peut ne jamais subir de malheur, si le hasard auquel il est livré ne lui en réserve pas.

Maïmonide trouve dans le *Psaume* 91 la description de cette extraordinaire Providence. Que la guerre fasse rage autour de la personne qui est l'objet de la Providence, qu'on en tue mille à sa gauche et dix mille à sa droite, aucun mal ne l'atteindra. *Car il te sauvera du piège de l'oiseleur, de la peste pernicieuse; tu ne craindras pas les terreurs de la nuit, la flèche qui vole de jour* (vv. 3 et 5).

Maïmonide présume que nous connaissons la différence entre *ʾōhēb* (celui qui aime, ami) et *ḥōšēq* (amant passionné); or, dans le *Psaume* 91, il s'agit précisément de l'homme passionnément et éperdûment amoureux (*ki bi ḥašaq*, v. 14).

Enfin, Maïmonide, reprenant un thème talmudique: la mort de Moïse et Aaron *sous le baiser divin*, qualifie cette mort de "libération de la mort elle-même" (en arabe: *al-salāma min al-mawt bi-l-ḥaqīqa*; en hébreu: *himmaleṭ min ha-māwet ʿal derekh ha-ʾemet*).[21]

Toutes ces réflexions maïmonidiennes reliées par un lien assez lâche, on les a prises pour des considérations *édifiantes* dont "l'auteur n'a pu croire qu'elles pouvaient servir a résoudre" le problème de la Providence;[22] ou bien on les a délibéremment négligées dans l'exposé de la pensée de Maïmonide en s'en tenant au seul chapitre xvii de la IIIe Partie.[23] Or rien n'est plus étranger à l'esprit du *Guide* que cette sorte d'édification; dans cet ouvrage, rien n'est superflu, ni incident, ni accessoire; tout y est signifiant et lourd de sous-entendus. Maïmonide nous a bien recommandé de ne point l'oublier.

Cependant, l'apparente naïveté et le "simplisme" désarmant de Maïmonide qui nous avait habitués à une plus grande hardiesse spéculative nous étonnent, et ils ont étonné maints commentateurs au Moyen Age qui ont proposé des interprétations et des solutions bien supérieures à celles des Modernes. Les ayant présentées ailleurs,[24] nous n'y reviendrons pas ici.[25] Ce que nous nous proposons de chercher ce sont les rapports véritables entre la doctrine du chapitre xvii et la doctrine du chapitre li, étant entendu que, pour nous, *l'un* comme *l'autre* chapitres expriment entièrement et totalement la pensée de Maïmonide.

II. ESSAI D'INTERPRETATION

(a) La Tora, Eliphaz et Elihu

D'emblée, il nous faut écarter des interprétations comme celles de Samuel ibn Tibbon, de son fils Moïse et de Shem Ṭob Palqera, selon lesquels la Providence dont il est question au chapitre 51 serait une grâce de Dieu qui, par un miracle, sauverait ses serviteurs, et qui estiment qu'elle n'est reconnue que par la foi mais non par la raison philosophique.[26] Une action providentielle qui découlerait d'une volonté particulière de Dieu en faveur d'un individu singulier est expressément niée par Maïmonide dans un texte capital qu'à notre connaissance on n'a pas relevé. Dans le chapitre x de la Iere Partie, il écrit en effet: ". . . lorsqu'il s'agit de l'arrivée d'une catastrophe dans une nation ou une contrée, en raison de l'*éternelle volonté* de Dieu,— où les livres prophétiques, avant de décrire cette calamité, disent d'abord que Dieu, après avoir visité les actions de ces gens, fit descendre sur eux le châtiment,—on emploie pour cela également l'expression *descendre*; car l'homme est trop peu de chose pour que ses actions soient visitées afin qu'il en subisse la peine, si ce n'est par *la volonté* [*éternelle*]."[27]

Il est exclu également que Maïmonide accepte l'interprétation vulgaire de la Tora (théorie n° 5a et théorie d'Eliphaz) selon laquelle Dieu rétribuerait l'homme selon ses actes singuliers conformément à la stricte justice. Comme l'a noté avec pertinence Moïse Narboni, le même mot essentiel revient dans la doctrine attribuée à "notre Tora" et dans celle de Maïmonide lui-même dégageant le sens profond de la Tora (doctrine n° 5b): c'est le mot *din* en hébreu (*istiḥqāq* en arabe) et Maïmonide est fondé à dire qu'Elihu (dont la doctrine correspond à la doctrine 5b) n'ajoute presque rien aux paroles d'Eliphaz.[28] Il s'agit en somme de deux variantes —mais combien différentes—d'une même thèse[29] qui met l'accent sur *ce qui est mérité véritablement par l'homme* (c'est bien le sens précis du terme *istiḥqāq*). Mais, tandis que pour Eliphaz, c'est Dieu qui proportionne exactement la rétribution méritée à ce que l'homme fait en bien ou en mal, pour Elihu-Maïmonide l'homme obtient ce qu'il mérite en proportion exacte du développement de son intellect qui l'unit à Dieu. En fait, pour reprendre les mots de Joseph Ibn Kaspi, *l'intellect est notre Providence,* c'est Dieu descendu en nous,[30] et la prophétie, qui est le suprême degré auquel un intellect humain peut parvenir, est aussi la Providence à son plus haut niveau: c'est pourquoi Elihu avait émaillé ses propos de considérations sur la prophétie. S'il a proclamé que "l'ange intercesseur", en qui la plupart des commentateurs médiévaux ont vu l'intellect,[31] sauve l'homme deux, trois fois, c'est-à-dire un certain nombre de fois, mais non pas à jamais, c'est que l'homme est voué à la mort, qui est inéluctable.

(b) Job Régénéré et la Doctrine du Chapitre li

Si, dans l'ensemble, les commentateurs médiévaux ont fort bien compris le chapitre li, ils n'ont pas posé trois questions qui nous semblent capitales: (1) si le chapitre li n'est qu'une conclusion qui n'apporte rien de vraiment nouveau, pourquoi Maïmonide écrit-il: "Et *maintenant* se présente à moi un aspect d'une très merveilleuse *spéculation* (*wa-qad ẓahar lī al-ān wajh naẓr gharīb jidd*^an^)?"[32] (2) A chaque personnage du Livre de *Job* correspond une doctrine sur la Providence; y en a-t-il un à qui corresponde la doctrine du chapitre li? (3) Pourquoi Maïmonide fait-il observer comme incidemment au chapitre li qu'il existe une différence entre *ʾōhēb* (celui qui aime, ami) et *ḥōšēq* (amant passionné)?

Il semble bien que le deuxième Job, celui que nous avons appelé Job régénéré, l'homme qui ne connaît plus Dieu par la seule tradition mais qui a vu Dieu, le connaît d'une science authentique, se console sur son fumier et devient totalement indifférent aux biens et aux maux "imaginaires" représente, dans l'ouvrage qui porte son nom, la doctrine du chapitre 51. Il suffit de disposer sur deux colonnes ce que Maïmonide dit du deuxième Job et ce qu'il expose au chapitre 51 pour qu'apparaissent en pleine lumière les ressemblances.[33]

פרק כ״ג, דף מ״ח, ע״ב - דף נ״א ע״ב

אמא ענד מא עלם אללה עלמא יקינא פאקר̈ אן אלסעאדה̇ אלחקיקיה̇ אלתי הי **מערפה̇ אללאה** הי מצ̇מונה̇ לכל מן ערפה ולא יכדרהא עלי אלאנסאן בליה̇ מן הד̇ה אלבלאיא כלהא ואנמא כאן איוב יתכ̇יל הד̇ה אלסעאדאת אלמט̇נונה̇ אנהא הי אלגאיה̇ כאלצחה̇ ואלת̇רוה̇ ואלאולאד טאלמא כאן יעלם אללה כ̇ברא לא בטריק אלנט̇ר פלד̇לך תחי̇ר תלך אלחיראת וקאל תלך אלאקאויל / (מט) והד̇א הו מעני קולה לשמע אזן שמעתיך ועתה עיני ראתך על כן אמאס ונחמתי על עפר ואפר תקדיר אלכלאם בחסב אלמעני על כן אמאס כל אשר הייתי מתאוה ונחמתי על היותי בתוך עפר ואפר כמא פרצ̇ת חאלה והוא יושב בתוך האפר ומן אג̇ל הד̇ה אלמקאלה̇ אלאכ̇ירה̇ אלדלה̇ עלי **אלאדראך אלצחיח** קיל פיה באת̇ר ד̇לך כי לא דברתם אלי נכונה כעבדי איוב.

(דף נ״א.)

פאד̇א עלם אלאנסאן ד̇לך סהל עליה כל מצאב ולא / (נא:) תזידה אלמצאיב שכוכא פי אללאה והל יעלם או לא יעלם או יעתני או יהמל בל **תזידה מחבה̇** כמא קאל פי כ̇אתמה̇ הד̇א אלוחי על כן אמאס ונחמתי על עפר ואפר.

Chap. 23, pp. 48b–51b

Mais dès que Job eut de Dieu une connaissance certaine, il reconnut que le véritable bonheur qui est la connaissance de Dieu est garanti à quiconque le connaît et qu'en l'homme aucune de toutes ces épreuves ne trouble ce bonheur. Or Job avait considéré comme le but un bonheur imaginaire comme la santé, la richesse et les enfants, aussi longtemps qu'il connaissait Dieu par tradition mais non d'une manière spéculative;

פרק נ״א, דף קכ״ח, ע״ב

תא̇מל שיר של פגעים תג̇דה יצף תלך אלענאיה̇ אלעט̇ימה̇ ואלוקאיה̇ ואלח־מאיה̇ מן גמיע אלאפאת אלג̇סמאניה̇ **אלעאמה̇ ואלכ̇אצה בשכץ דון שכץ** לא מא הו מנהא תאבע לטביעה̇ אלוג̇וד ולא מא הו מנהא מן מכאיד אלאנסאן קאל כי הוא יצילך וגו׳ ווצל לוצף אלחמאיה̇ מן מכאיד אלנאס אן קאל אנך לו את̇פק אן תעבר פי מערכה̇ חרב מנתשרה̇ ואנת פי חאל טריקך חתי לו קתל אלף קתיל ען שמאלך ועשרה̇ אלאף ען ימינך למא נדאך שר̇ בוג̇ה אלא̇ תנט̇ר ותרי בעינך חכם אללה ומכאפאתה לאולאיך אלשרירין אלד̇ין קתלוא ואנת סאלם וד̇לך קולה יפול מצדך וגו׳ ת̇ם תבע ד̇לך במא תבע מן אלציאנה̇ ת̇ם אעטי אלעלה̇ פי הד̇ה אלחמאיה̇ אלעט̇ימה̇ וקאל אן אלסבב פי הד̇ה אלענאיה̇ אלעט̇ימה̇ בהד̇א אלשכ̇ץ כי בי חשק וגו׳ וקד בינ̇א פי פצול תקד̇מת אן מעני ידיעת השם / (קכט.) הו **אדראכה** פכאנה יקול הד̇ה אלחמאיה̇ להד̇א אלשכ̇ץ למא **ערפני ועשקני** בעד ד̇לך וקד עלמת אלפרק בין אוהב וחושק לאן **אפראט אלמחבה̇** חתי לא יבקי פכר פי שי אכ̇ר גיר ד̇לך אלמחבוב הו אלעשק.

Chap. 51, p. 128b

Médite "le cantique des calamités"; tu y trouveras la description de cette extraordinaire Providence qui préserve et sauve de toutes les calamités corporelles, générales et particulières aux différents individus, aussi bien celles qui suivent la nature de l'être que celles qui viennent des artifices de l'homme. Il dit: "Car il te sauvera du piège de l'oiseleur . . ." (*Ps.* 91:3). Parlant de la protection contre les artifices des hommes, il en est venu jusqu'à déclarer que s'il advenait, pendant que tu es en route, de passer dans un champ de bataille déployé, en sorte qu'à ta gauche mille hommes et à ta droite dix mille seraient tués, il ne t'arriverait de mal d'aucune sorte, mais tu contemplerais et verrais de tes yeux le jugement de Dieu et la rétribution qu'Il a infligée à ces méchants qui ont été tués et toi tu serais préservé; c'est ce qu'il dit: "Il tombera à tes côtés . . ." (*Ibid.*, v. 7). Suit la conséquence de cette préservation puis la raison qui est donnée de cette protection extraordinaire. Il dit que cette extraordinaire Providence s'exerçant sur cet individu a pour cause qu' "il a un amour passionné de Moi . . . et connaît Mon nom" (*Ibid.*, v. 14). Or nous avons expliqué dans les chapitres précédents que la connaissance de Dieu signifie *son aperception* (*idrākhu*); c'est donc comme s'il disait que cet individu est ainsi protégé parce qu'il Me connaît et s'est ensuite pris de passion pour Moi. Tu connais la différence entre *ʾōhēb* et *ḥōšēq*: l'amour débordant au point que l'on ne pense plus à rien d'autre qu'à l'aimé c'est la passion. aussi était-il en proie à toutes ces perplexités et prononçait-il toutes ces paroles. C'est là le sens de ses mots: "Mon oreille avait entendu parler de Toi, mais maintenant mon œil T'a vu; c'est pourquoi je méprise . . . et me console sur la poussière et la cendre" (*Job* 42:5–6). Compte tenu du contexte, on doit entendre ainsi [le verset 6]: c'est pourquoi je méprise tout ce que je désirais et je me console d'être au milieu de la poussière et de la cendre; or c'est ainsi qu'on avait présenté sa situation: "Et il était assis au milieu de la cendre" (*Job* 2:8). C'est à cause de ce discours final qui prouve *l'authentique aperception* (*al-idrāk al-ṣaḥīḥ*) qu'il a été dit ensuite [des amis de Job]: "Car vous n'avez pas parlé correctement de Moi comme mon serviteur Job" (*Ibid.*, 42:7).

[P. 51a] Lorsque l'homme saura cela [i.e. qu'il n'y a aucune commune mesure entre la science et le gouvernement divins et la science et le gouvernement humains], tout malheur lui sera léger et les maux n'accroîtront pas ses doutes relatifs à Dieu, à savoir sait-Il ou ne sait-Il pas? exerce-t-il une Providence ou se montre-t-il insouciant? Au contraire, ils *accroîtront son amour*, comme il est dit en conclusion de cette révélation: "C'est pourquoi je méprise et je me consolerai sur la poussière et la cendre" (*Ibid.*, v. 6).

Au sujet du deuxième Job comme dans le chapitre li, Maïmonide parle de l'aperception philosophique de Dieu (*idrāk*) génératrice d'un amour débordant[34] qui débarrasse l'esprit de toute préoccupation mondaine et de tout problème relatif à la théodicée pour ne le remplir que de Dieu seul, au point que la souffrance elle-même cesse de tenailler l'homme et qu'il abandonne totalement la poursuite de biens "imaginaires."

Il est évident qu'on ne peut prendre au pied de la lettre le salut complet de l'homme plongé dans une bataille acharnée; il s'agit là d'une exégèse biblique et non d'une théorie philosophique qui ruinerait tout ce que Maïmonide nous a appris par ailleurs. Ainsi se trouve écartée la difficulté qui avait arrêté nombre de commentateurs.

Bien sûr le chapitre li ne comporte rien de neuf puisque le personnage que nous appelons le deuxième Job nous avait *déjà* été présenté au chapitre 23 (traduction Munk p. 176 et p. 186), mais Maïmonide n'avait *pas encore* dégagé *la théorie* qui lui correspond; aussi peut-il écrire d'une part que ce chapitre n'ajoute rien de nouveau et d'autre part qu'une extraordinaire spéculation se présente à lui.

* * *

L'action de la Providence se situe sur deux plans totalement différents: le premier est décrit par Elihu, le second nous est connu par le portrait du second Job. Elihu c'est le *ʾōhēb* (l'ami de Dieu), mais Job régénéré, c'est le *ḥōšēq* (l'amant passionné). Le niveau que représente ce personnage fictif[35] est très difficilement accessible: dans l'histoire, quatre hommes sont parvenus jusqu'à lui, Abraham, Isaac, Jacob et Moïse.

Elihu est encore *aristotélicien.* Souvenons-nous en effet de ce qu'écrit le Stagirite: ". . . l'homme heureux a . . . besoin, en sus du reste, des biens du corps, des biens extérieurs et des dons de la fortune, de façon que son activité ne soit pas entravée de ce côté-là.[36] Et ceux qui prétendent que l'homme attaché à la roue ou tombant dans les plus grandes infortunes est un homme heureux à la condition qu'il soit bon, profèrent, volontairement ou non, un non-sens."[37] Elihu a un minimum de biens physiques et matériels à demander, il veut échapper aux maux. Son ange intercesseur, l'Intellect, exaucera ses vœux deux, trois fois, mais ne pourra le sauver de la corruption qui est son lot.

Job, qui possède la vraie connaissance de Dieu, a dépassé ce stade. Dans son univers, toutes les contingences sont abolies, il est devenu indifférent aux biens "imaginaires" comme la santé, la richesse, les enfants. Il n'a plus rien à réclamer à Dieu, puisqu'il est comblé de Sa présence. Aucun malheur ne peut plus l'affecter. Il est semblable au sage de Plotin dans sa belle *Ennéade* I, iv: "Le sage est toujours serein; il jouit d'un calme et d'une satisfaction que n'ébranle aucun des prétendus maux, parce qu'il est sage. Et si l'on cherche un autre genre de plaisir dans la vie du sage, c'est qu'il n'est plus question de cette vie. . . . Il est un suprême objet de science (μεγιστον μάθημα), qu'il a toujours avec lui et toujours à sa disposition; il l'a plus encore que ne l'imaginent ceux qui disent: "je serai heureux, fussé-je dans le taureau de Phalaris." Il est vain de nommer plaisante une telle situation; le dirait-on mille fois, elle ne l'est pas. Qui dit cela en effet? C'est l'être plongé dans la souffrance; mais, chez le sage, la partie qui souffre est différente de son être qui reste en lui-même et qui aura, tant qu'il y reste, une contemplation indéfectible du bien."[38]

Au chapitre 51, Maïmonide formule un idéal qu'il ne croit pas pouvoir lui-même réaliser. Ni lui, ni beaucoup d'autres. C'est au niveau des patriarches et de Moïse, non pas de tous les prophètes comme disent certains commentateurs,[39] que les maux des trois catégories sont surmontés et même le Mal par excellence: la mort. Maïmonide n'a-t-il pas écrit que *la mort sous le baiser*, celle de Moïse par exemple, est la libération de la mort elle-même?

Ainsi entendue, la pensée de Maïmonide devient tout à fait cohérente, ses allusions prennent toutes un sens et les chapitres que nous avons exposés, s'éclairant l'un l'autre comme le voulait l'auteur, perdent leur décousu et leur disparité pour se fondre dans une harmonieuse synthèse.

On ne peut plus parler de *deux* théories de Maïmonide sur la Providence, mais de deux plans d'existence: dans le premier, se meut le philosophe aristotélicien; mais le second, contemplé de loin, est réservé à quelques êtres d'élite. Maïmonide n'a pas cru qu'il fût possible d'élargir l'accès à ce monde idéal.

NOTES

* Les ouvrages fréquemment utilisés pour cette étude sont les suivants:

Salomon Munk, *Le Guide des Egarés* par Moïse ben Maïmoun, original arabe et trad. française avec notes, 3 vol., Paris, 1856–1866;

Moses Maimonides, The Guide of the Perplexed, translated . . . by Shlomo Pines, The University of Chicago Press, 1963;

Rabbenu Mosheh ben Maïmon, *Morẹ ha-Nebukhim,* texte arabe et trad. en hébreu moderne par Joseph Kafiḥ, Jérusalem, 3 vo., 1972;

Rabbenu Mosheh ben Maïmon, *Sefer Morē ha-Nebukhim*, trad. en hébreu de Samuel Ibn Tibbon, avec les commentaires de Ephodi (Isaac ben Mosheh ha-Lévi), Asher Crescas, Shem Ṭob ben Shem Ṭob, Isaac Abrabanel, Varsovie, 1872;

Zevi Diesendruck, "Samuel and Moses ibn Tibbon on Maimonides' theory of Providence," dans *Hebrew Union College Annual*, xi (1936), pp. 341–366;

Shem Ṭob Palqera, *Morē ha-Morē*, éd. M. Bisseliches, Presbourg, 1837;

Nissim de Marseille, *Sefer ha-Nissim*, Bibliothèque Nationale, ms. hébreu n° 720;

Joseph Ibn Kaspi, *ᶜAmmūdē Kesef ū-maskiyōt Kesef* (Commentaires sur le Guide), éd. S. Werbluner, Francfort sur le Main, 1848; *Šulḥan Kesef* dans *ᶜAsārā Kelē Kesef*, éd. I. Last, Presbourg, 1903, tome I;

Moïse Narboni, *Commentaire sur le Guide*, Bibliothèque Nationale, ms. hébreu n° 699 (ce commentaire a été édité très médiocrement par J. Goldenthal, Vienne, 1852).

1. Voir *infra,* p. 343, les notes 22 et 23.
2. Voir *Guide,* I, Introduction, trad. Munk pp. 22 sq.
3. Voir *ibid.,* chap. lxxii, Munk pp. 368–369.
4. Voir tout le chapitre xi de la 3e Partie du *Guide.*
5. Cf. *Guide*, I, chap. lxxii, Munk p. 366 sq.

6. Voir le commentaire de Narboni au début de ce chapitre.

7. *Guide*, III, chap. xvii, Munk p. 123 *in fine*, p. 124; chap. xx, Munk pp. 151–153; chap. xxxii, Munk pp. 255–257.

8. Palqera est le premier à faire remarquer (*Morē ha-Morē*, p. 148) qu'un texte aristotélicien exprimant sur la Providence une doctrine proche de celle de Maïmonide a échappé à celui-ci: "L'homme qui exerce son intellect et le cultive semble être à la fois dans la plus parfaite disposition et le plus cher aux dieux . . . [qui] récompensent généreusement les hommes qui honorent le mieux cette partie . . . [Le sage] est donc l'homme le plus chéri des dieux. Et ce même homme est vraisemblablement aussi le plus heureux de tous" (*Ethique à Nicomaque*, X, 9, 1179a, 23 sq; trad. J. Tricot, Paris, 1959); Joseph Ibn Shem Ṭob fait la même observation (dans son *Kebod ᵓElohim*, éd. Ferrare, 1555, 13, et dans son commentaire manuscrit sur l'*Ethique à Nicomaque*, voir M. Steinschneider, *Gesammelte Schriften*, Berlin, 1925, p. 348). Son fils, Shem Ṭob, explique ainsi pourquoi Maïmonide n'a pas fait état de ce texte: ou bien il l'ignorait, ou bien l'auteur du *Guide* n'a pas cru devoir citer cette opinion populaire qui n'exprimerait pas la vraie pensée d'Aristote (*Sefer Morē Nebukhim*, III, 27b). Quoi qu'il en soit, pour Shem Ṭob, il est difficile d'admettre qu'Aristote ait soutenu la théorie "méprisable" que Maïmonide lui prête (*ibid.*). Joseph Ibn Kaspi avait le même sentiment: il écrit avec son humour habituel: "Puisque Aristote est d'accord avec notre Tora (*Šulḥan Kesef*, p. 141) . . .pourquoi pécherions-nous contre lui et le repousserions-nous s'il veut entrer dans la religion de Moïse?" (*ibid.*, p. 174).

9. Cf. *Guide*, III, chap. xvii, Munk p. 125: "C'est pourquoi il se pourrait . . . que Dieu condamnât pour toujours [l'homme vertueux] à ce feu qu'on dit être dans l'autre monde."

10. La traduction de Munk: "c'est aussi ce qu'ont admis en général nos auteurs" (III, p. 124) est un contresens. Dans le texte arabe éd. par Munk, *jumhūr* revient deux fois, p. 34b et p. 35a.

11. Dans le texte arabe, p. 34b–37a, le mot *istiḥqāq*, "*ce qui a été mérité selon la justice*", revient neuf fois.

12. Voir *Pirqē Abot*, v, 8–9; *Babli Šabbat*, 32b sq.; *Megilla*, 27b sq.; etc.

13. Texte arabe, p. 45b; trad. Munk p. 163.

14. Texte arabe, p. 49a; la trad. de Munk p. 177 n'est pas satisfaisante.

15. Texte arabe, *ibid.*

16. Trad. Munk, p. 180.

17. Texte arabe, p. 49a, lignes 5–7; trad. Munk p. 177.

18. Munk a fâcheusement traduit ainsi: "celui qui comprend les vrais devoirs qu'on doit pratiquer envers Dieu," p. 433, estompant totalement le terme technique, dont usent nombre de commentateurs de Maïmonide. S. Pines traduit beaucoup mieux: "one who has apprehended the true realities peculiar only to Him" (p. 618). Dans son *Introd. à Ḥeleq* (*Commentaire de la Mišna, Seder Neziqin*, ed. J. Kafiḥ, Jérusalem, 1964, p. 199) Maïmonide qualifie Antigonos Sokho de "*al-fāḍil al-kāmil al-mudrik al-ḥaqāᵓiq*", l'homme vertueux, parfait, qui a perçu les véritables realités (ligne 22).

19. Ce beau portrait a été repris par Naḥmanide, *Commentaire sur le Deutéronome* xi, 22 (éd. Chavel, ii, p. 395).

20. Texte arabe, p. 127b.

21. Texte arabe, p. 129b. La traduction de Munk: "cette espèce de mort, disent-ils, par laquelle l'homme échappe à la mort véritable" est franchement mauvaise.

S. Pines traduit fort bien: "this kind of death, which in true reality is salvation from death" (p. 628).

22. S. Munk, iii, p. 446, note 1.

23. Julius Guttmann, *Ha-Filosofia šel ha-Yahadût*, Jérusalem, 1951, p. 392, note 453; *Philosophies of Judaism*, New York, Chicago, San Francisco, 1964, pp. 432–433, note 99.

24. Voir Charles Touati, *Lévi ben Gershom, Les Guerres du Seigneur, . . .* Paris-La Haye, 1968, pp. 20–23.

25. Comme nous ne voulions présenter, *ibid.*, que les devanciers de Lévi ben Gershom, nous n'avons pu exposer les thèses et commentaires de Moïse Narboni; ce que nous ferons ici.

26. *Ibid.*

27. Trad. Munk, I, chap. x, p. 57. Les deux termes connotant la volonté divine chez Maïmonide ont été analysés par Abraham Nuriel, "La volonté divine dans *le Guide*" (en hébreu), *Tarbiż*, xxxix (1969), n° 1, pp. 39–61.

28. Ms., fol. 129^{r}; impression Goldenthal, p. 54a.

29. Joseph Ibn Kaspi, *Comm. Guide*, p. 128.

30. *Ibid.*, p. 98.

31. Voir Munk, iii, p. 183, note 1: l'ange peut être également une force naturelle.

32. Texte arabe, p. 127a.

33. Nous avons nous-même traduit les deux textes (l'éd. Kafiḥ n'a qu'une variante insignifiante par rapport à celle de Munk).

34. Voir les belles analyses de G. Vajda, *L'amour de Dieu . . .* , Paris, 1957, surtout p. 133 sq.

35. C'est très vraisemblablement l'opinion de Maïmonide, III, chap. xxii, Munk pp. 159–160.

36. Notons que ces traits caractérisent précisément l'ère messianique chez Maïmonide, *Mišné Tōrā, Hilkhōt Melākhim,* xii, 4–5. Cf. aussi *Guide,* III, chap. xi.

37 *Ethique à Nicomaque* VII, 14, 1153b, 17–21, trad. J. Tricot; voir aussi Aristote, *La Politique,* VII, 1, 1323b, 40 sq. et VII, 13, 1332a, 19 sq. et les notes de J. Tricot dans sa trad., Paris, 1970^{2}, p. 471 et p. 520.

38. I, iv, 12–13, trad. E. Bréhier; voir les belles pages de M. de Gandillac, *La sagesse de Plotin*, Paris, 1966^{2}, pp. 152–154.

39. Voir en particulier les commentaires de Narboni, ʾEphodi, Shem Ṭob sur *Guide*, I, chap. xxiii, *in fine*, sur les mots *heʿalot ha-šekhina*; voir aussi Shem Ṭob, *Commentaire sur le Guide*, III, chap. li, p. 67a, qui accentue d'ailleurs la note stoïcienne. En fait, Maïmonide lui-même envisage le cas où un *prophète* est frappé par un mal (III, chap. li, Munk p. 445).

Pour le Dossier de *Meṭaṭron*

GEORGES VAJDA

Au cours de deux de ses travaux, dans son étude consacrée à la théorie de la révélation chez Saadia[1] et dans son édition commentée de "l'Epître sur le *Shiʿûr Qômâh*" de Moïse de Narbonne,[2] notre jubilaire eut l'occasion d'évoquer les spéculations tendant à rationaliser, dans la pensée juive du moyen âge, la figure de *Meṭaṭron*, fort importante dans la mystique juive prékabbalistique, mais réduite à un rôle plus effacé à partir du surgissement de la Kabbale proprement dite. Nous voudrions apporter une modeste contribution à l'hommage offert au savant qui nous honore depuis bien des années de son amitié par la présentation de quelques textes non encore exploités, croyons-nous, se rapportant à ce thème.[3]

I

Traduisons, en premier lieu, deux passages du "Livre des Préceptes" (*Sêfer ha-Miṣwôt*), portant aussi le titre de *Gan ʿEden*, du Karaïte Aaron ben Elie, mort en 1369, qui composa cet ouvrage après 1353.[4]

Dans le premier texte, l'auteur impute aux Rabbanites l'idée que leurs prières (en fait, certains versets bibliques employés dans la liturgie) réfèrent à *Meṭaṭron*:

> C'est la doctrine des tenants de la tradition (*baʿaley ha-Qabbâlâh*)[5] qui s'exprime dans la liturgie qu'ils ont instituée. C'est qu'ils manifestent leur croyance en deux principes divins (*shtey reshuyyôt*) lorsqu'ils affirment: (nous prions ainsi) parce qu'il y a deux causes, (l'une) proche, (l'autre) éloignée. C'est là le mystère de *Meṭaṭron*, qu'ils dénomment aussi "Petit *YHWH*", (entité) qui dirige ce bas monde, qu'on appelle Intellect Agent (*sêkel ha-Pôʿêl*), lequel donne les formes (*she-Nôtên ha-Ṣûrôt*) à tout être existant dans le bas monde, celui de la génération et de la corruption.

Ce texte va donc d'une part dans le sens de la spéculation de la mystique juive archaïque qui assimile *Meṭaṭron* à "*YHWH* mineur," d'autre part il reflète l'identification excogitée dans les milieux touchés par la *falsafa*, la philosophie alfarabo-avicennienne en Islam, de *Meṭaṭron* avec l'Intellect Agent-Donateur des formes (*wâhib al-ṣuwar, dator formarum*), échelon inférieur de la hiérarchie des Intelligences séparées, préposé au monde sublunaire.

Le deuxième passage intervient à propos de la liturgie de la circoncision:

> En commençant son opération, le circonciseur récitera: 'Béni sois-tu Seigneur, notre Dieu, Roi de l'univers, qui nous a sanctifiés par ses commandements et nous a commandé de pratiquer la circoncision au huitième jour.[6]

Il faut comprendre que cette eulogie combine des verbes à la deuxième et à la troisième personne (*murkebet le-fânîm we-shellô le-fânîm*). Tu connais l'opinion[7] des tenants de la tradition au sujet de la cause proche et de la cause éloignée. C'est pourquoi ils disent:[8] 'béni sois-tu,' à la deuxième personne, (en référant cette tournure) à la cause proche, et 'qui nous a sanctifiés,' à la troisième, (par allusion) à la cause éloignée. La visée implicite de cette construction[9] est, affirment-ils, qu'il existe une cause proche et une cause éloignée. C'est là le mystère de *Meṭaṭron* par qui les formes ont été données; les philosophes le nomment 'Intellect Agent' et c'est par lui que prophétisent tous les prophètes. Voilà (selon eux) le sens symbolique de cette eulogie (*ʿal zeh ha-Ṭaʿam marmîz sôd zôt ha-Berâkâh*) qu'ils enseignent dans leurs livres.[10]

En revanche, nous autres qui croyons en l'unité véritable et rejetons tout médiateur entre Dieu et nous pour le don de sa Tora parfaite et digne de foi, nous n'acceptons pas la visée qui est la leur (*ʾeyn kawwânâtênû ke-khawwânâtâm*).

Par ailleurs, j'ai constaté que nos Docteurs ont admis cette eulogie dans la liturgie, notamment R. Aaron[11] et R. Judah ha-Abêl.[12] Ce dernier a cité l'opinion des tenants de la tradition au sujet de cette eulogie et il a démontré leur erreur.[13] Ajoutons que la rédaction de cette eulogie, avec le passage de la deuxième à la troisième personne, est de bonne langue.[14]

D'après l'enseignement que nous avons reçu (de nos maîtres) quant au sens de cette eulogie, (sa rédaction) vise à èrcarter (de Dieu) la corporéité. En effet, toute chose corporelle se trouve (nécessairement) en un lieu; l'on peut dès lors lui assigner une position spatiale qui lui soit particulière; par contre, ce qui n'est pas corporel n'est pas en un lieu; c'est pourquoi on est dans le vrai quand on en parle soit à la deuxième soit à la troisième personne puisqu'il n'est point entouré de limite.[15]

En plus de ce que le premier passage nous a appris sur l'identité imputée à *Meṭaṭron* par les philosophes, le second développement d'Aaron ben Elie rappelle le prétendu rôle de cette entité dans la vision prophétique.[16]

II

Le deuxième auteur dont nous rapporterons ici les textes qui nous ont été accessibles est Shemtôb ben Isaac Ibn Shaprûṭ de Tudèle (vers 1380–1400),[17] auteur de plusieurs ouvrages, entre autres d'un surcommentaire au commentaire d'Abraham Ibn Ezra sur le Pentateuque auquel nous emprunterons les passages intéressant notre sujet.[18]

Commentant la glose laconique et volontairement obscure dans la recension brève du commentaire d'Ibn Ezra sur *Ex.* 24:10:[19] "Le sens de *Dieu d'Israël est Auteur de l'oeuvre de la création* (*yôṣêr berêshît*) qui tient dans sa main l'âme de tout vivant. L'intelligent comprendra," Ibn Shaprûṭ s'exprime ainsi (fol. 143 r–v):

On peut admettre (*yittâkhên*) qu'il a voulu dire que les Anciens avaient appréhendé tout ce qu'il est au pouvoir de l'intelligence humaine d'appréhender, à savoir l'Intellect Agent, car ce dernier est l'Auteur de l'œuvre de la création, en tant qu'il confère ("donne") les âmes et les formes, et c'est lui qui tient dans sa main l'âme de tout vivant.

J'avais d'abord pensé (conformément aux opinions de ceux qui interprètent son opinion en un sens condamnable[20] que d'après lui "les notables des enfants d'Israël" (*ʾaṣîley beney yisrâʾêl, Ex.* 24:11) appréhendèrent la force souveraine de Dieu en tout ce qui est sous la sphère (de la Lune), et que c'est à cela que correspondrait l'expression *yôṣêr berêshît*). En effet, j'ai noté dans la péricope *Berêshît*[20bis] que (dans le récit de la Création) Moïse ne parle que du monde de la génération et de la corruption; c'est à cela que se rapporterait *qui tient en sa main l'âme de tout vivant*, les anges et même les sphères n'étant pas appelés *vivants* par homonymie complète,[21] puisque "vivant" se définit "se nourrissant, doué de sensation", ainsi que j'ai expliqué dans mon commentaire sur l'*Introduction* de Porphyre. (Les notables) appréhendèrent donc la force souveraine de Dieu en tant qu'Il est *Dieu d'Israël*, c'est-à-dire (l'entité qui) les gouverne dans ce monde-ci, mais ils n'appréhendèrent pas le Dieu des sphères et des anges (aspect sous lequel) Il est *Dieu des Dieux*,[22] autrement dit l'attribut en vertu duquel le Dieu béni gouverne le monde des sphères et des anges. Cependant quand j'ai vu ce qu'il écrit dans la péricope *Kî tissâʾ*,[23] je suis revenu [de cette interprétation de la phrase d'Ibn Ezra]. A Dieu ne plaise que ce dernier ait appelé l'Intellect Agent 'Dieu d'Israël' et 'Auteur de l'Oeuvre de la création' selon l'interprétation donnée (à son exégèse) par ceux qui l'entendent en un sens condamnable.[24]

Le sens de *fais-moi connaître Tes voies* est qu'il n'est au pouvoi r d'aucun être créé de connaître l'Auteur de l'œuvre de la création, si ce n'est etc.[25] Comme on peut voir dans l'autre recension, [les notables d'Israël] appréhendèrent par prophétie (quelque chose de) comparable à ce qu'appréhendèrent Isaïe et Ezéchiel.[26] C'est pourquoi je dis que les notables en question appréhendèrent le Dieu béni et le mystère de la connexion mutuelle des trois mondes (*sôd hitqashsherût 3 ʿôlâmôt zeh ba-Zeh*).

En effet les trois mondes s'associent tous à l'œuvre créatrice (*yeṣîrat berêshît*), puisque les deux supérieurs sont associés à la création de l'inférieur, (Ibn Ezra) le dit allusivement en interprétant 'à notre image' et aussi dans le mystère du Jardin d'Eden ainsi que je l'ai expliqué.[27] C'est pourquoi il a ajouté: 'celui dans la main de qui est l'âme de tout vivant.' faisant allusion à l'homme dont l'âme provient de l'esprit de Dieu. Et c'est la raison pour laquelle l'appréhension[28] [l'expérience visionnaire] des notables est désignée comme 'Dieu d'Israël' afin d'en souligner la haute qualité, puisqu'elle se réfère au '*Dieu des Dieux*' qui est en vérité le *Dieu d'Israël*, ainsi que nous lisons (dans *Deut.* 4:39 et 10:17): *Reconnais à présent et imprime-le dans ton cœur, que YHWH Seigneur seul est Dieu, dans le ciel en haut comme ici-bas sur la terre, qu'il n'en est point d'autres* (et) *YHWH votre Dieu, c'est le Dieu des Dieux et le Maître des maîtres.* J'ai vu d'autres qui ont interprété son opinion en un sens condamnable; mais tous leurs propos sont vanité, il est interdit de les évoquer; la vérité marquera sa voie.[29]

Il convient de joindre ici une autre page de Shemṭôb Ibn Shaprûṭ, dans l'appendice au *Ṣâfnat Paʿnêaḥ* où il glose, afin de les tirer dans le sens de la "philosophie," certaines *ʾaggadôt* dont la signification littérale avait de quoi heurter les "intellectuels" de l'époque. A propos de l'*aggada* haute en couleur concernant Léviathan et Behemôt (*Baba Batra* 74b) il écrit ce qui suit[30]:

> La *barayta* en question use de cette parabole afin de faire connaître l'enchaînement des facultés[31] corporelles et intellectuelles. Le Jourdain jaillit de l'*antre de Pamiyas.* Par *Jourdain* (l'aggadiste) désigne [*kinnah*] l'intellect émané, en raison du degré [qu'il occupe dans l'ordre de l'être], de sa pureté et de son abondance. *Il jaillit de l'antre de Pamiyas,* c'est-à-dire de la chose [entité] occulte et sublime, qui est le Dieu béni ou l'Intellect Agent, comme l'Ecriture le dit (*Gen.* 2:7): *Il insuffla dans ses narines un souffle de vie.* Et nos Docteurs ont dit: 'quiconque insuffle dans le nez de son prochain, met en lui [une parcelle] de son âme'.[32] La désignation *antre* exprime que la quiddité du désigné est occultée aux yeux de tout vivant, comme l'Ecriture le dit (*Ex.* 33:20): *car nul homme ne peut me voir et vivre* et (*Ps.* 18:12): *Des ténèbres Il fait sa retraite mystérieuse. Il traverse* (continue le texte du Talmud) *le lac de Tibériade*: (ce dernier) est (le symbole) du Second Intellect, qui porte chez nos Docteurs les noms de *Meṭaṭron* et de 'Prince Angélique de la Face' (*Sar ha-Pânîm*), car c'est lui qui épanche la forme des créatures du monde supérieur, et c'est pourquoi il est appelé[33] *Lac de Tibériade. De là* (poursuit le texte) *il roule ses flots jusqu'à l'océan,*[34] *le Dixième Intellect,* qui porte chez nos Docteurs le nom de Mikaʾel. Ce Dixième Intellect épanche la forme de toutes les créatures du bas monde, d'où son nom de 'Grande Mer.' *De là* [*le Jourdain*] *se déverse*[35] immédiatement *dans la gueule de Léviathan*, qui est l'Intellect matériel, et il fait passer ce dernier de la puissance à l'acte, (de sorte que l'intellect[36] matériel) se constitue en intellect subsistant à jamais. C'est pourquoi le dernier verbe est *il descend* et non *il roule.* Et pour cette raison (aussi) *Lac de Tibériade* désigne symboliquement la sphère de l'Intellect et *Grande Mer* l'Ame Universelle.

Dans la page qu'on vient de lire, Ibn Shaprûṭ jongle visiblement avec des spéculations déjà séculaires à son époque et vidées, à force de vulgarisations successives, du *tonus* philosophique qu'elles pouvaient avoir à l'origine. Les problèmes, vrais ou faux, peu importe, de l'identité de Dieu et de l'Intellect Premier, des fonctions de l'Intellect Agent dixième et dernier de la hiérarchie descendante et régent du monde sublunaire,[37] sont brouillés et la concordance laborieuse entre anges et "Intelligences" est encore compliquée par l'introduction de l'ange Mikaʾel (j'ignore s'il se voit attribuer ailleurs un rôle semblable).[38] *Meṭaṭron*, qui n'apparaissait pas dans le développement sur Abraham Ibn Ezra à *Ex.* 24:10, vient maintenant doubler en quelque sorte le *dator formarum* de la vision du monde avicennisante de manière à pourvoir les niveaux d'êtres intelligibles d'un "régent" homologue de celui du monde sublunaire, cette dernière fonction étant dévolue, cette fois-ci, à l'un des quatre anges de la *Merkaba.*

Le matériel comparatif dont j'ai disposé en écrivant ces pages est trop incomplet pour que je prétende déterminer dans quelle mesure Ibn Shaprûṭ est "original" tout au moins quant à l'agencement des éléments presque tous connus par ailleurs avec lesquels il a construit ses concordances entre les données de l'Aggada et celles de la philosophie. Mais peut-être n'est-il pas déplacé de rappeler ici brièvement les passages parallèles d'un autre glossateur d'Ibn Ezra, contemporain à peine plus âgé d'Ibn Shaprûṭ, à savoir Yôsêf Ṭôb ʿElem, et de référer aussi à quelques notations de Samuel Ibn Moṭoṭ.[39]

En glosant l'assertion dans le commentaire d'Ibn Ezra à *Gen.* 1:26[40] "Il [le prophète Ezéchiel] vit la Gloire de *YHWH* comme une apparence d'homme," Yôsêf Ṭôb ʿElem[41] ne se contente pas d'identifier *kâbôd* avec *shekînâh*, mais offre plusieurs autres équivalences: "Prince angélique de la Face," "Prince angélique du monde," "Auteur de l'œuvre de la création," "Ange rédempteur"[42] et il n'omet pas d'ajouter que cette entité est désignée par les "Sages de la Grèce" (*ḥakhmêy Yâwân*) sous l'appellation d'Intellect Agent.

Traitant du commentaire à *Ex.* 24:10, Yôsêf Ṭôb ʿElem soutient[43] que *Yôṣêr berêshît* introduit par Ibn Ezra dans son exégèse d'*Ex.* 33:12–13,[44] est l'Intellect Agent, créateur, de par la volonté de Dieu, du monde sublunaire; il rappelle à cette occasion que d'après Ibn Ezra, le récit de la création dans *Gen.* 1 ne concerne que le monde de la génération et de la corruption.[45] Cette même entité est également dénommée "Dieu d'Israël" en sa qualité de Prince angélique préposé à Israël (*ha-Sâr ha-memunneh ʿal yisrâʾêl*), qui épanche, toujours par "puissance divine" [*be-kôaḥ ha-Shêm*: c'est-à-dire en vertu d'un mandat reçu de Dieu], l'esprit de prophétie sur le peuple élu. "L'apparence humaine" dans la vision d'Ezéchiel est, derechef, l'Intellect Agent.

Tout cela ressemble fort, sans doute mitigé par des réserves, à la doctrine jugée condamnable dont Ibn Shaprûṭ cherche, nous l'avons vu, à innocenter Ibn Ezra.[46] Quoi qu'il en soit, Yôsêf Ṭôb ʿElem ne subodore, ou ne veut subodorer, aucune hétérodoxie dans les exégèses du Commentateur.

L'identification *sêkel ha-Pôʿêl* / *yôṣêr berêshît* revient encore dans la glose au commentaire à *Ex.* 33:12[47] où Yôsêf Ṭôb ʿElem s'étend assez longuement sur la connaissance que cette entité possède des niveaux d'être supérieurs à elle et à l'influx qu'elle en reçoit.

Quant à Samuel Ibn Moṭoṭ, il identifie sans hésiter "le Créateur du Tout" nommé par Ibn Ezra dans son commentaire à *Gen.* 1:26 (éd. Prijs p. 74, 20–21) avec *Meṭaṭron* "dont le nom est le même que celui de son Maître et qui est l'Intellect Agent Premier, l'Etre (produit) Premier, créateur du tout et aussi le Tout, suivant l'opinion [du Commentateur]."[48]

NOTES

1. "Saadya's Theory on Revelation" (*Essays on Saadya*) [page de titre *Saadya Studies*], ed. E. I. J. Rosenthal, Manchester 1943, en particulier pp. 18–19, 21–22 = *Studies in Religious Philosophy and Mysticism*, Londres 1969, pp. 154, 157.

2. "Moses Narboni's Epistle on *Shiʿur Qoma*" dans *Jewish Medieval and Renaissance Studies*, ed. A. Altmann, Cambridge, Mass. 1967, pp. 225–288 =

Studies . . . , pp. 180–205, sans le texte hébreu; cf. l'index de ces deux volumes au mot Meṭaṭron.

3. Bornons-nous ici à quelques références: R. Margulies, *Malʾakey ʿElyôn*, Jérusalem 1945, p. 79 *sq.*; Ephraim E. Urbach, *ḤZ"L Pirqey Emûnôt we-Dêʿôt* (The Sages. Their Concepts and Beliefs), Jérusalem 1969, pp. 118–119; Gershom G. Scholem, *Major Trends in Jewish Mysticism*, 2e éd., New York 1946, pp. 67–70 et index, *s. v.*; *Jewish Gnosticism* . . . , 2e éd., New York 1964, pp. 42–55, 131; article *Meṭaṭron* dans *Encyclopaedia Judaica*, 11, col. 1443–1446 (= *Kabbalah*, Jérusalem, 1972, pp. 377–381); *Von der mystischen Gestalt der Gottheit*, Zurich 1962, index, s. v. *Jozer Bereschith*, ajouter p. 293 (n. 60); *Ursprung und Anfänge der Kabbala*, Berlin 1962, pp. 184–188 et index s. v. *Joṣer Bereschith* = *les Origines de la Kabbale*, Paris 1966, pp. 244–228 (index *s. v. Yoṣer Bereshît*); G. Vajda, *Juda ben Nissim Ibn Malka*, Paris 1954, p. 78, n. 2; *Isaac Albalag*, Paris 1960, pp. 200, *sq.* (les passages de l'original hébreu. *Sefer Tiqqûn ha-Deʿôt*, éd. G. Vajda, Jérusalem 1973, pp. 58, 60); "Recherches sur la synthèse philosophico-kabbalistique de Samuel Ibn Moṭoṭ," *Archives d'histoire doctrinale et littéraire du Moyen Age*, 1960, en particulier pp. 35 *sq.*, 55, 58 *sq.*; *Recherches sur la philosophie et la Kabbale dans la pensée juive du Moyen Age*, Paris 1962, p. 402, n. 14; Johann Maier, *Geschichte der jüdischen Religion*, Berlin 1972, pp. 169 *sq.*

4. Cf. Zvi Ankori, *Karaites in Byzantium*, New York 1959, index, *s. v.* Aaron b. Elijah. Les deux morceaux qui nous occupent se lisent respectivement dans le texte imprimé à Gozlow 1866, fol. 72 b–c et 79 b–c.

5. Il s'agit, bien entendu, de la tradition rabbinique, non de la doctrine ésotérique, connotation actuellement prévalente du terme; *cf.* Ankori, *op. cit.*, p. 229.

6. Cette formule se trouve encore dans le rituel karaïte en usage: *Siddûr ha-Tefillôt ke-minhag ha-Yehûdim ha-Qarâʾîm*, réimpression (Israël, 1964) de l'édition d'Odessa 1870, IVe partie, p. 47. La formule rabbanite, différente quant à la finale, mais identique dans l'eulogie introductive (S. Baer, *ʿAbôdat Yisrâʾêl*, p. 582) est attestée dans la *Tosefta Berakôt* vi, 12 (et parallèles), éd. S. Lieberman, pp. 36–37, commentaire *Tosefta ki-fshuṭah* I, New York 1955, p. 114.

7. *daʿat*; on traduirait aussi bien "doctrine."

8. Les Karaïtes "disent" (récitent) de même, mais l'auteur saura trouver à cette façon de s'exprimer une justification théologique (voir ci-après) à l'opposé de la doctrine imputée aux Rabbanites.

9. C'est ainsi que j'interprète, sous réserve de correction, l'expression insolite (texte?) dans *zôt ha-Kawwânâh she-ʾemûnat ha-Berâkâh le-fânim we-shellô le-fânîm.* en mettant *ʾemûnâh* en rapport avec *ʾumân*, *ʾumânût.*

10. *ʾasher hôrû besifrêhem.* La clause est ambiguë: faut-il comprendre "la formule liturgique prescrite dans leurs livres" (mais elle est la même, pour la partie concernée ici, chez les Karaïtes, *cf.* l'avant-dernière note), ou bien l'interprétation symbolique du passage de la deuxième à la troisième personne qu'Aaron ben Elie leur attribue? La source de cette interprétation m'est demeurée inconnue: l'inconséquence apparente dans l'emploi des personnes dans la formulation des eulogies commençant par "béni sois-tu" et se poursuivant par une subordonnée relative a été certes remarquée par les commentateurs du rituel (cf. Judah b. Yaqar, *Pêrush ha-Tefillôt we-ha-Berâkôt*, éd. Samuel Yerushalmi, Jérusalem 5728/1968, p. 22; *Abudraham ha-Shâlêm*, éd. S. A. Wertheimer, Jérusalem 5719/1959, p. 33 *sq.* mais sans aucune référence *à Meṭaṭron*; *Siddur of R. Solomon ben Samson of Garmaise*, éd. M. Hershler, Jérusalem 5372/1971, p. 57 du texte. Les symbolismes "séfirotiques"

du pronom personnel de la deuxième personne, récapitulés par Joseph Ibn Waqâr dans son lexique kabbalistique inédit et par Moïse Cordovero dans *Pardês Rimmônîm*, l. xxiii (*ᶜArkhey ha-Kinnûyîm*) 1, *s. v.* *ᵓattâh* et, d'une manière générale, les spéculations ésotériques sur le changement de personne dans les "bénédictions" liturgiques (nombreuses références dans R. Margulies, *Shaᶜarey Zôhar*, Jérusalem 1956, à *Berâkôt* 33a, fol. 178 b–d) n'entrent pas en ligne de compte ici, puisque l'auteur karaïte les ignore ou les passe sous silence.

11. Aaron b. Joseph, "l'Ancien", vers 1260–1320, rédacteur du gros de la liturgie karaïte sous sa forme suivie jusqu'à nos jours; cf. P. Selvin Goldberg, *Karaite Liturgy and its Relation to Synagogue Worship*, Manchester 1957, p. 2.

12. L'auteur de l'encyclopédie *ᵓEshkôl ha-Kôfer*, première moitié du XIIe siècle; cf. Ankori, *op. cit.* (n. 4) pp. 28 sq. et l'index *s. v.* Yehudah Hadassi.

13. Je ne suis pas en mesure de préciser cette allusion. Hadassi a certes censuré les spéculations touchant *Meṭaṭron* = *YH qaṭan*, Alph. 105, 43 d, *cf.* Alph. 48, 26 b–c, mais sans les mettre en rapport avec le changement de la personne des verbes dans la formule liturgique dont il est question ici, pas plus qu'il ne mentionne l'équivalence "philosophique" *Meṭaṭron* = Intellect Agent.

14. *weᶜôd sêder zôt ha-Berâkâh huᵓ mah she-Yoṣᵓêt* (!) *mi-Tiqqûn ha-Lâshôn shehîᵓ murkebet le-fânîm we-shellôᵓ le-fânîm.* Si nous comprenons bien cette phrase, l'auteur a voulu dire: la rédaction de la formule liturgique dont il s'agit est tout à fait conforme à l'esprit du style hébraïque qui permet le passage de la deuxième à la troisième personne de verbes figurant dans la même phrase et se rapportant au même mot. Mais, derechef, *salvo meliori iudicio*!

15. Autrement dit, la deuxième personne désigne, "montre du doigt," situe dans l'espace ce à quoi elle réfère; en revanche la troisième marque que son sujet échappe à toute détermination (ou, ce qui revient au même, à toute limitation).

16. Voir A. Altmann, *Studies* (voir *supra*, p. 349, n. 1), pp. 154 et 157, et C. Sirat, *Les théories des visions surnaturelles dans la pensée juive du Moyen-Age*, Leyde 1969, pp. 103 et 121; Joseph Dan, *Tôrat ha-Sôd shel ḥasîdût ᵓAshkenaz* (The Esoteric Theology of Ashkenazi Hasidism), Jérusalem 1968, p. 223 *sq.* En fait, il n'est point assuré que notre auteur ait eu d'autres sources pour cette question que Hadassi et, peut-être, des adaptations hébraïques de commentaires bibliques (a-t-il lu aussi, c'est probable, Abraham Ibn Ezra?) ou de traités de *kalâm* en arabe.

17. Cf. M. Steinschneider, *Hebr. Üb.*, p. 689.

18. Intitulé *Ṣâfnat Paᶜnêaḥ*, à ne pas confondre avec le surcommentaire à Ibn Ezra portant le même titre, mais ayant pour auteur Yôsêf Ṭôb ᶜElem (Bonfils, vers 1330–1388), édité par David Herzog (1e partie Cracovie/Heidelberg 1911/12, 2e partie Berlin/Heidelberg 1930). Nous avons travaillé sur le manuscrit hébreu 852 de la B. N. de Paris.

19. Ed. J. L. Fleischer, *Sêfer Ibn ᶜEzra . . . le Sêfer Shemôt*, Vienne 1926 (réimpr. Jérusalem 1970), p. 215.

20. *le-khaf ḥôbâh*, autrement dit hétérodoxe.

20bis. En attribuant dans son commentaire à *Gen.* 1:1 au verbe *baraᵓ* le sens primitif de "trancher, découper" Abraham Ibn Ezra a-t-il voulu suggérer que la "création" décrite au premier chapitre de la Tora avait été effectuée à partir d'une matière première préexistante? Ibn Shaprûṭ entend défendre Ibn Ezra contre une telle imputation en s'aidant de l'opinion clairement soutenue par cet auteur (à *Gen.* 1:2) que le ciel et la terre dont il est question dans le récit de la création désignent uniquement le monde sublunaire (cf. B. N. - H. 852, fol. 41–42, 46 v, 53 v).

On peut lire à ce sujet les remarques de M. Leo Prijs, *Abraham Ibn Ezra's Kommentar zu Genesis Kapitel I*, Wiesbaden 1973, pp. 5–7, 12, 13, 16, 20–23.

Bonne discussion du problème dans Hermann Greive, *Studien zum jüdischen Neoplatonismus. Die Religionsphilosophie des Abraham Ibn Ezra*, Berlin 1973. pp. 53–59. Il importe peu pour notre sujet de décider si Ibn Ezra a professé l'existence d'une matière première terrestre en fait indépendante de Dieu (comme l'entendent ses "détracteurs" critiqués par Ibn Shaprûṭ, et M. Greive) ou si ses spéculations sont conciliables avec une doctrine créationniste sans faille (ce que semble admettre tout récemment encore, M. Prijs).

21. *Be-shittûf ha-Shêm ha-Gâmûr*, par univocité.

22. Désignation empruntée à *Deut.* 10:17.

23. A *Ex.* 33:13, interprétation qui sera appréciée dans la suite du morceau.

24. Donc, pour dire les choses d'une manière peut-être moins contournée et un peu plus claire, des glossateurs malavisés imputent injustement à Abraham Ibn Ezra une exégèse inspirée par la tendance à homologuer des concepts philosophiques (Intellect Agent, Donateur des formes) avec des données religieuses, avec le résultat d'introduire une sorte de dichotomie dans la notion de la divinité providente (*manhîg, hanhâgâh*), en répartissant certaines désignations bibliques ("Dieu des dieux", "Dieu d'Israël") ou traditionnelles ("Auteur de l'œuvre de la création") sur deux aspects distincts de la Déité, au risque d'en compromettre l'unité soit par un dualisme presque avoué, soit en divinisant en quelque manière une entité spirituelle de très haut rang, mais néanmoins créaturelle.

25. Citation du commentaire (recension brève) d'Ibn Ezra à *Ex.* 33:13; la phrase continue (éd. Fleischer, p. 315) "par Ses voies, et celui qui connaît Ses voies, Le connaît, car il est alors comme une forme."

26. Dans le texte de la "recension longue" (imprimée dans les éditions courantes) à *Ex.* 24 (c'est à ce passage qu'Ibn Shaprûṭ nous renvoie ici) on lit seulement que les notables furent gratifiés de "vision prophétique" (*be-marʾeh ha-Nebûʾâh*), aucun prophète n'étant nommé en particulier.

27. Cf. le deuxième et le troisième des passages cités du *Ṣâfnat Paʿnêaḥ*, dans la note 20bis pp. 351 *sq*.

28. C'est-à-dire l'objet de celle-ci.

29. En résumé, de la confrontation des exégèses d'Ibn Ezra touchant *Ex.* 24:10–11 et 33:13, Ibn Shaprûṭ conclut que selon le commentateur, les Anciens (notables) d'Israël furent favorisés de l'expérience prophétique (extatique) de la Divinité, sous son aspect d'auteur unique des trois mondes, à l'œuvre créatrice duquel collaborèrent cependant, une fois mis en existence, les deux mondes supérieurs, anges et sphères, sous le rapport de l'organisation et du gouvernement de ce bas monde. Ibn Ezra se trouve ainsi être lavé de tout soupçon d'hétérodoxie.

30. B. N. H. 952, fol. 306 v. Le passage parallèle de son commentaire sur les *ʾAggadôt (Pardês Rimmônîm*, Sabbioneta 1554 (reprod. photographique réduite, Jérusalem 1968), f. 10 a, lig. 1–11 représente une rédaction assez différente qui ne mentionne pas *Meṭaṭron*.

31. *sêder hishtalshelût*, l'échelonnement hiérarchique.

32. *Kol ha-Nôféaḥ beʾaf ḥavêrô mi-Nishmâtô nôtên bô*. On chercherait en vain cette sentence dans le Talmud et le Midrash. Il s'agit à l'origine de la formule prégnante par laquelle Isaac l'Aveugle avait illustré sa doctrine de la communication de l'âme divine à l'homme, créature privilégiée: *ha-Nôféaḥ ba-Nôd mamṣîʾ bô rûḥô*, "celui qui souffle dans l'outre y (re)produit son souffle," phrase citée (au nom du

Ḥasid) par Méir Ibn Abī Sahula dans son *Bê᾽ûr ᶜal Pêrûsh ha-RMBN,* Varsovie 1875, 5 b (cf. G. Scholem, *Ursprung,* p. 257/ *Origines,* p. 308, n. 162). La formule a été reprise, mais autrement stylisée (*ha-Nôféaḥ be-᾽appêy ᾽aḥêr mi-Nishmâtô yittên bô*) par Moïse ben Naḥman à *Gen.* 2:7 (éd. Chavel, p. 33, voir la note de l'éditeur *in loc.*), copiée ensuite par Menaḥem Recanati (commentaire sur le Pentateuque, dans *Sêfer Lebûshêy ᾽Or Yeqârôt,* Jérusalem 1961, 9 d.) et Josué Ibn Shuᶜayb, *Derâshôt ᶜal ha-Tôrâh,* facsimilé de l'édition de Cracovie 1573, Jérusalem 1969, 2 c. J'ignore si la rédaction que nous lisons chez Ibn Shaprûṭ est de son cru ou bien d'emprunt; sur cette sentence voir maintenant l'article de Mosheh Hallamish dans *Annual of Bar Ilan University* 13 (1965–6), pp. 211–223.

33. *niqrâ᾽îm* dans le manuscrit, mais *ym* est dittographie anticipée de *ym* (*yam*) qui suit.

34. La "Grande Mer" (*ha-Yâm ha-Gâdôl*).

35. Litt. "il descend" (*yôrêd*).

36. *we-yithawweh sêkhel ha-Nish᾽ar lâᶜad;* après *sêkhel* le manuscrit porte encore *nqbh*, mais ce mot est, semble-t-il, exponctué.

37. Voir *Juda ben Nissim* (*supra,* p. 350, n. 3), pp. 74 *sq.*

38. On trouve Mika᾽el dans les fonctions d'Intellect Agent "qui donne les formes aux matières" dans le *Mibḥar ma᾽amârîm* de Nathan ben Samuel (cf. U. Cassuto, *Codices Vaticani Hebraici,* n° 63, p. 92, Cité du Vatican 1958) à *Ex.* 23:20; mais il y est identifié (ms. hébreu Paris B.-N. 839, fol. 109 v) avec *Meṭaṭron* (Ibn Ezra *in loc.*, suivi par Baḥyé ben Asher, Chavel, p. 244, voit Mika᾽el dans l'ange dont il est question dans ce verset, sans cependant faire entrer en jeu *Meṭaṭron*); l'identification de *Meṭaṭron* et de Mika᾽el est attestée du reste déjà dans le *Sêfer Zerubbâbel* (cité par *Mal᾽akêy ᶜElyôn,* p. 110); en revanche, d'après Simon ben Ṣemaḥ Duran, *Magên ᾽Abôt* IIe partie, fol. 15a, Mika᾽el est le moteur de la sphère supérieure. N'insistons par ici sur la fin du morceau; elle ne contribue guère à clarifier la transposition en concepts "philosophiques" de l'imagerie mythique ou plutôt relevant du "folklore" savant que l'allégoriste Ibn Shaprûṭ fait subir au passage du Talmud. (Dans le *Megalleh ᶜamuqôt* de Salomon ben Ḥanok al-Qosṭanṭini, Vat. Hébreu 59 f. 20v, Gabriel est l'intellect hylique, tandis que Mika᾽el est *ha-Sêkhel ha-Ne᾽eṣal mê-ha-Sêkhel ha-Pô᾽êl ᶜal ha-Sêkhel ha-ḥomrî.)*

39. Indications bibliographiques, *supra,* pp. 351 et 350, notes 18 et 3.

40. Ed. Prijs (*supra,* p. 351 *sq.*, n. 20bis), pp. 74, 12.

41. Edition citée, (*supra,* p. 351, n. 18), p. 46, 24–47, 1.

42. *sar ha-Pânîm, sârô shel ᶜôlâm, yôṣêr berêshit, ha-Mal᾽âkh ha-Gô᾽êl;* ce dernier terme vient de *Gen.* 48:16 où Abraham Ibn Ezra renvoie à son commentaire sur *Ex.* 3:7 lequel relève de la question, hors de notre sujet, du nom de Dieu appliqué à l'ange, son mandataire occasionnel. Dans ses gloses à ces deux passages, Yôsêf Ṭôb ᶜElem (pages 171 et 195) ne revient pas sur l'identification mise en avant à *Gen.* 1:26; notons seulement en passant que dans le commentaire de Moïse ben Naḥman, repris et amplifié par Baḥyé ben Asher, l'ange rédempteur est bien identifié avec la "Présence", mais au sens kabbalistique (Xe *sefira*).

43. Edition citée, p. 273, 12 *sqq.*

44. Cf. *supra,* p. 352, n. 23

45. Cf. *supra,* p. 351 *sq.*, n. 20bis.

46. *Supra,* p. 352, notes 24 et 29.

47. Edition citée, p. 303.

48. Imprimé dans *Margaliyyût Ṭôbâh,* Amsterdam 1721, fol. 8 a. Dans son surcommentaire *Megillat Setârîm* (ms. Paris, B.N., Hébreu 186, fol. 13, à *Gen.* 1:26,

où le même auteur disserte sur la question de l'identité de la Première Cause et du Premier Moteur, il mentionne l'homologation opérée par les "Kabbalistes" (en fait les philosophes intéressés par la Kabbale comme Joseph Ibn Waqâr ou Moïse de Narbonne) de l'Intellect Agent (degré inférieur de la hiérarchie de ces entités) avec *Malkhût*: "Selon les Kabbalistes (*ha-Mequbbâlîm*), l'Etre intellectuel (*ha-Meṣîʾût ha-Siklî*) est (constitué par) trois *sefîrôt*, et (il y a) sept *sefîrôt* qui sont (elles) les moteurs (*ha-Menîʿîm*). . . . Le moteur de la sphère de la lune est, selon eux, le dixième (plus exactement la dixième *sefirâh*), *Malkhût* qui est l'Intellect Agent. J'ai trouvé, dans cet ordre d'idées, que certains Docteurs musulmans (*mâṣâʾtî ha-ḥakhâmîm* [*mi*]*yishmeʿêlîm*) appellent l'Intellect Agent Royauté et Présence (*malkhût u-shekînâh*) et ils enseignent que cette entité est la plus élevée des êtres spirituels (*rûḥânîm*), car ces derniers sont les anges dont la place (hiérarchique) est au-dessous de *Malkhût*". Sans nous arrêter autrement ici à ce texte remarquable surtout par l'amalgame de concepts hétéroclites, faisons seulement remarquer que *Malkhût* y est confondu, volontairement ou involontairement, avec *malʾakût*, "le monde invisible spécifié par (= peuplé de) les esprits et les âmes," selon les "Définitions" (*Taʿrîfât*) du Sharîf Jurjânî (que je cite seulement pour faire bref). Dans un autre passage (fol. 76, à *Ex.* 38), nous retrouvons sans surprise l'équivalence *yôṣêr berêshît/nôtên ha-Ṣûrôt*.

Dans *Ṣâfnat Paʿnêaḥ* à *Gen.* 1:26 (ms. cité, 46 v–47), Ibn Shaprûṭ se dérobe, mais dans l'appendice (fol. 305 *in fine*) il écrit à propos de *bôrêʾ ha-Kôl*: "(créateur) de l'Intellect Agent et des (Intellects) séparés au-dessus de lui et de ses parties (?)" (*ha-Sêkhel ha-Pôʿêl we-ha-Nivdâlîm sheʿâlâw wa-ḥalâqâw*); notation peu claire, mais qui semble aller dans le sens de la justification des formules téméraires qu'Ibn Ezra s'était permises (cf. *supra,* notes 24 et 29).

O Felix Culpa: A Cabbalistic Version*

R. J. Z. WERBLOWSKY

O Goodness infinite, Goodness immense,
That all this good of evil shall produce,
And evil turn to good—more wonderful
Than that which by creation first brought forth
Light out of darkness! Full of doubt I stand,
Whether I should repent me now of sin
By me done or occasioned, or rejoice
Much more that much more good thereof shall spring.

The rapturous meditation which John Milton[1] put into the mouth of Adam, the First Man and Sinner, is undoubtedly the most eloquent expression in the English language—and by a Puritan poet to boot—of the paradox of the Fortunate Fall, the latter being itself one of the most remarkable expressions of theological enthusiasm. But far from being just another seventeenth century "metaphysical conceit," the paradox can look back on a long and respectable ancestry.[2] In fact, it has been enshrined in one of the most glorious hymns in one of the most glorious liturgies: the *Exultet* (also known, more technically, as the *Praeconium Paschale*) of the Easter Vigil according to the Latin rite. Sin, it appears, is not only "behovely" (as T. S. Eliot put it in the *Four Quartets*), but in some mysterious way also "necessary" and even "fortunate:" *O certe necessarium est Adae peccatum, quod Christi morte deletum est. O felix culpa, quae talem ac tantum meruit habere redemptorem.*

Yet for all its apparent audacity, the traditional paradox carries no really serious antinomian implications.[3] The *Exultet* hymn is not an expression of latent antinomianism but a rapturous jubilation, overreaching itself to the point of deliberate paradox in its straining after adequate utterance of the surpassingly wondrous mystery of salvation. Theological writers, as Prof. Lovejoy pointed out,[4] may have been reluctant to dwell on paradoxes of this kind, yet paradox has "its own emotional appeal to many religious minds—partly, no doubt, because its very paradoxicality, its transcendence of the simple logic of common thought gave it a kind of mystical sublimity; between logical contradiction (or seeming contradiction) and certain forms of religious feeling there is a close relation, of which the historic manifestations have never been sufficiently studied."

In actual fact the Christian paradox is more apparent than real and hence relatively innocuous, since sin and reparation are not essentially related. Salvation is extrinsic to the Fall, no matter how *felix* the latter. Hence Lovejoy was right when he spoke of a "hint of antinomianism" only—and, we might add, a very faint one at that. The decisive act of salvation has no organic relation to the Fall, in regard to which it is both extrinsic and discontinuous. The Christian paradox differs significantly, in this respect, from the more radical and audacious versions to be found in certain strands of cabbalistic literature. It is one such strand that the present paper wishes to examine. We are not concerned here with presenting a general typology of the forms of antinomianism known to the student of religions (e.g., gnostic, tantric, mystical, messianic), or with describing the history of this motif in the kabbalah. The latter undertaking could do little more than summarize the relevant researches of G. Scholem and I. Tishby.[5] Instead, we shall deal here with the doctrine of one eminent post-Lurianic cabbalist, Rabbi Isaiah Horovitz (*ca.* 1565–1630), who, although a major figure in his own way, is nevertheless a lesser figure when compared to the great sixteenth century synthesizers and original system builders. It is surely unnecessary to add that the so-called lesser figures hold a very special interest for the historian, who frequently finds them no less significant than the great creative minds. In fact, the minor figures are very often more characteristic of an age and representative of its general mood. They may be less original, less exciting, and less impressive. Their tendency to gloss over many rough edges renders them less daring, revolutionary, and titanic, but all the more representative of their period, its modes of thinking and its spiritual temper. Isaiah Horovitz, better known as the *SHeLaH*,[6] is just such a representative figure, and I have described him advisedly as a post-Lurianic rather than a "Lurianic" cabbalist. No doubt Lurianic influence and terminology are in evidence throughout the *SHeLaH*, yet one can hardly describe this *magnum opus* as a Lurianic work. This fact merits emphasis, because it is precisely in the Lurianic kabbalah that latent antinomian tendencies—the same tendencies which subsequently found such explosive discharge in the Sabbatian mystical heresies—received theoretical and often audacious formulation. Both Scholem and Tishby, in their discussions of Lurianic as well as pre-Lurianic[7] and Sabbatian kabbalah, have been careful to distinguish between theoretical and practical antinomianism, the latter consummating the transition from heterodox ideas to heterodox reality. Another important distinction, that between antinomianism proper (e.g., that of Shabbethai Ṣevi) and what I would call "metanomism" (e.g., that of St. Paul) need not detain us at present. More relevant to our immediate subject is the distinction between "innocent" and less innocent forms of theoretical antinomianism. The suspicion that even the strictly theoretical antinomianism of many orthodox cabbalists is not really all that innocent is confirmed by their many hummings and hawings, the careful hedging in their formulations, their hesitations and verbal reservations. Evidently the specter of possible practical consequences was real enough to haunt them. Others, like Isaiah Horovitz, can be called innocent antinomians—so innocent, in fact, that it is doubtful whether the term 'antinomianism' is applicable at all. But Horovitz's theology and anthropology of original sin are of sufficient interest and originality to merit special treatment. Anticipating the results of our analysis and putting them in a nutshell, we might say that for Isaiah Horovitz, Adam's sin is the major and decisive mechanism of purification by precipitating and then ejecting the latent elements of evil. In other words, *SHeLaH* applies—albeit in a mitigated form—the Lurianic scheme of *qelippah*, evil and a cathartic process, to man's "original sin," rather than to a primordial event in the recesses of the creating godhead.[8]

It is not my intention here to go into the details of Horovitz's theology or to expatiate on the diluted and adulterated quality of his Lurianism. As has been noted above, the *SHeLaH* can hardly be called a "proper" Lurianist. He is a post-Lurianic cabbalist, who absorbed some of the more moderate (and in some ways less significant) features of Lurianism—eclectic Lurianism for that matter—and combined them with a great deal of Cordovero, Abraham Galante,[9] and the like. This view of the *SHeLaH* could be substantiated in detail by an analysis of his terminology, metaphors, and quotations. The Cordoverian elements are evident in the *SHeLaH*'s insistence on the connection between the coming into existence of the *qelippoth* on the one hand and the divine dispensation of reward and punishment on the other;[10] in the emanationist account of the emergence of the gross, crude, material and hence evil *qelippah* from the pure source of light and holiness,[11] and in his belief in a complete *restitutio in integrum*, i.e., the view that all *qelippoth* (and not only the *qelippath nogahh*) would be restored to holiness in the final *apokatastasis, viz., tiqqun.*

The Lurianic element appears firstly in the view that the original fall is ultimately a positive event and secondly in the dialectical conception of the relationship of fall and *tiqqun*. This is tantamount to saying that the ultimate restoration is not merely *in integrum* but actually *in melius et superius*. In a manner reminiscent of Milton's

> . . . evil turn to good—more wonderful
> Than that which by creation first brought forth
> Light out of darkness

SHeLaH never tires of quoting his favourite proof-text, a (mis)interpretation of *Ecclesiastes* 2:13 regarding the "excellence of the light that cometh from darkness" (as distinct from an originally simple and, as it were, non-dialectical light).[12] In fact, there is no dearth of "proof texts" to nourish and satisfy the cabbalist's appetite for paradox. Horovitz's favorites are, in addition to *Ecclesiastes* 2:13, *Judges* 14:14 ("out of the strong [i.e., the bad, the bitter] cometh forth sweetness"); *Jeremiah* 15:19 (taking forth "the precious from the vile"); and *Job* 14:4. The latter verse[13] had already been interpreted by the Midrash[14] in the sense of "Who can bring a clean thing out of an unclean? [Is it] not [The] One [i.e., God, the only one]?" According to the Midrash this principle is illustrated by Abraham issuing from Terah and similar instances drawn from Biblical history. Many other midrashic statements e.g., Eve's pressing of the grapes that ferment into wine,[15] or the strange "spelling" in the torah scroll of R. Meʾir (*kothᵉnoth ʾor*, "garments of light," instead of *kothᵉnoth ʿor*, "coats of skins") easily lent themselves to cabbalistic exploitation. As we shall see in due course, the play on the word *ʿor* in Genesis 3:21—although already used cabbalistically by Ḥayyim Vital and others—serves as a major symbolic "cipher" for Isaiah Horovitz. *ʾOr* ("light"), written with an *ʾaleph* (numerical value 1), also symbolizes original as well as ultimate unity, whereas *ʿor* ("skin") written with an *ʿayin* (numerical value 70) signifies gross matter (skin) as well as the principle of multiplicity and differentiation (seventy).

But whereas for Cordovero the *qelippah* and evil are, in good Neo-Platonic fashion, the almost inevitable result of the process of emanation, the Lurianists see things the other way round.[16] Evil is not due to the process of emanation, but the emanation takes place for the sake of producing, *viz.*, actualizing the latent "roots of *din*". It is not a matter of the divine light progressively materializing until, at the bottom of the chain of emanations, it becomes *qelippah*, but rather of the latent *qelippoth* becoming more actual, more material, and more grossly and crudely "real" and active as the process of emanation moves towards its ordained destiny. Hence the process leading to the first cataclysmic shattering and breaking of the vessels, and to the subsequent catastrophic events, has a purposive, teleological, and cathartic quality which compels us to view these events ambiguously, to say the least. Here "ambiguously" comes very near to serving as a euphemism for "positively." The breaking of the vessels and the diverse subsequent "descents" and "falls" of the divine sparks and of the souls, as well as the tragic descent of the *Shekhinah* together with Israel's parallel "descent" into exile—all these serve the cathartic purpose of purification, selection (*berur*), and restoration to perfection (*tiqqun*).[17] The attentive student of the vast corpus of Lurianic literature cannot fail to detect one glaring and very curious exception to this pattern. That exception is Adam's sin.

Adam's sin is never described as a cathartic, let alone a necessary event, as a teleologically "fortunate" fall, or (as might easily have fitted the overall pattern) as a repetition on the human level of the very same unwittingly purposive dialectic of breaking and *tiqqun* that had previously been enacted on the divine level of the *ʾAdam Qadmon*. One almost gets the impression that Lurianism takes very deliberate "anti-antinomian" precautionary measures when speaking of Adam's fall. Adam meant to further the *tiqqun* and did indeed intend a *miṣwah*, but the result was most unfortunate: not even a fall with ultimately "fortunate" results but rather an unmitigated disaster. It was a well-intentioned act that fatally miscarried, resulting in a catastrophic throw-back and actually reversing the process of *tiqqun* that had already been begun. Adam's failure (rather than "sin") deepened and aggravated the original fall and rendered the struggling ascent toward *berur* and *tiqqun* ever so much more difficult.

It is here that Isaiah Horovitz develops what appears to be a more strictly anthropological version of the teleological dialectic usually associated with the name of Luria. The theory, to which the author seems to attach the greatest importance, is expounded in several major (and almost identical) homilies.[18] Instead of quoting these extremely interesting texts *in extenso*, I shall try to summarize the main argument without troubling to point out in detail the many echoes of Cordovero (and Cordovero-type cabbalists), or the diverse points of contact with and divergence from Lurianic doctrines. The *SHeLaH* contends, in a Cordoverian manner, that some sort of coarsening and materializing process—including the possibility of actualizing evil—was necessary in the course of emanation, if the divine purpose of endowing man with perfection (i.e., freedom of choice and the reaping of just reward) was to be fulfilled. He also asserts, perhaps with dubious consistency, that ideally man could have reached the state of perfection by means of some positive, orderly, and "nondialectical" process. But something untoward happened. Adam sinned and fell, and his fall produced all manner of disastrous results. And yet, precisely because of this fall and its effects, man can struggle back to a state of perfection far superior to that which would have been his lot had he never fallen in the first place.

Like most cabbalistic expositions, that of the *SHeLaH* forces from the reader an admission, simultaneously admiring and grudging, that if this be madness, there is logic in it. The biblical proof texts, the puns on Hebrew words and letters, and the most fantastic homiletical combinations, all converge on a symbolic argument which, however abstruse and bizarre, cannot fail to impress by its curious profundity. Adam's sin turned the original *ʾaleph* of *ʾor* ("light") into the *ʿayin* of *ʿor* ("skin") i.e., base matter which is the very opposite of light, since the consonants of the word *ʿor* = *skin* can also be read as *ʿiwwer* ("blind"). This darkness is the doing of the serpent, that evil seducer of which *Proverbs* 16:28 says that "a whisperer separateth chief friends *(alluph)*." The whispering seducer had indeed separated the *ʾaleph* from its original wholeness, thereby leaving *ʾemeth* ("truth") shorn of its initial *ʾaleph* and truncated into *meth* ("dead"),[19] and similarly *ʾadam* = man without its initial *ʾaleph* reduced to *dam* ("blood"). The latter symbol easily leads, by way of what would be called by Freudians association and by Jungians amplification, to the idea of Eve's impurity through menstrual blood as a result of her contact with the serpent.[20] This weird accumulation of symbolic equations is but a series of variations on the one main theme: the excellence of the light that cometh from the darkness, or, in other words, of that light which is not the original *ʾor* (with *ʾaleph* = light) but a "light" that has passed, dialectically, through the stage of *ʿor* (with *ʿayin* = skin) and in which *Isaiah* 52:8 will be fulfilled "for they shall see eye to eye (*ʿayin be-ʿayin*)." It will be remembered that at the original fall the garments of *ʾor* (light) turned into garments of *ʿor* (skin) and blindness (*ʿiwwer*). But now the transfigured and perfected *ʿayin* = eye of Isaiah's prophecy (52:8) is none other than the vision of that which "no eye (*ʿayin*) hath seen, O God, beside thee" (*Isaiah* 64:3). Reverting again and again to the Biblical verses and midrashic texts mentioned before (e.g., bringing forth the precious from the vile, and a clean thing out of an unclean), Horovitz makes his meaning unmistakably clear: "The excellence of the light [that cometh forth] from the darkness . . . is not [simply] a reversion to the [original] intention of creation, but an increase of light . . . and then the light will be greater than that of the 'garments of light' before [Adam] sinned,"[21] much as the wine, after fermentation and sedimentation, is purer than the original grape juice and superior to it.[22] Of course God created man in a state of original perfection, and man could have kept himself and the world in that desirable state of original light. But God in his wisdom also provided for "two ways to the good" *(sic)*, one of them being the original *ʾor* = light, and the other leading, via the detour of the fall, from *ʾor* = light to *ʿor* = skin, as a result of which man and creation will ultimately find themselves in an increase of light.

The general tendency of the argument is that familiar to students of Lurianic kabbalah. But unlike Lurianism, which whilst concerning itself with dialectical mysteries and cathartic catastrophies in the very godhead, carefully refrains from applying any of these paradoxes to Adam's sin, the *SHeLaH* ignores the cataclysmic events shaking and affecting the sphere of the Deity, and squarely places his cabbalistic dialectic on the shoulders of man.[23] Whilst he is certainly not the only cabbalist to do so, I know of no other who has been so insistently explicit about it. It is Adam's freedom of choice that made him sin and thereby commit an ultimately fortunate fall. But perhaps the most striking feature of the *SHeLaH*'s doctrine is not its content but its style. Not even the sharpest ear can detect even the faintest echo of the kind of self-consciousness that usually goes with the awareness of teaching tremendous mysteries or awesomely audacious secrets. Horovitz expounds a doctrine that could easily be presented as a shockingly daring paradox, with the guileless innocence of simple piety. For the historian of religion, as distinct from the historian of theology, the almost naive and pious simplicity with which an eminent talmudic scholar and cabbalist can elaborate paradoxes bordering on antinomianism is even more fascinating than are the doctrines themselves.

NOTES

* The present paper was originally delivered as a public lecture at the Institute of Jewish Studies, University College London, on 23 January 1974. Having enjoyed the privilege of being associated with the founder of the Institute at its original

establishment and during its first period in Manchester, it is a particular pleasure to dedicate this paper to him.

1. *Paradise Lost*, Book xii, 11.469–76.

2. The history of this fascinating notion has been discussed by A. O. Lovejoy, "Milton and the Paradox of the Fortunate Fall", *Essays in the History of Ideas*, 1948, pp. 277–95.

3. As Lovejoy has correctly perceived, *op. cit.*, p. 295.

4. Lovejoy, *op. cit.*, (n. 2), p. 279.

5. Especially G. Scholem, *Shabbatai Sevi: The Mystical Messiah*, 1973, and I. Tisby, *Torath hara weha-Qelippah be-qabbalath ha-ʾAri*, 1942, as well as the many researches on *maḥashavoth zaroth* in later hasidic doctrine.

6. The abbreviation of the title of his major work *Sheney Luḥoth ha-Berith* ("The Two Tablets of the Covenant"). All references are to the 3rd ed., Amsterdam, 1698.

7. E.g., the *Qanah* and *Peliʾah*, and some later portions of the *Zohar*.

8. Cf. the accounts and interpretations of the "Breaking of the Vessels" given by Scholem, *op. cit.* (n. 5) and in *Major Trends in Jewish Mysticism*[2], 1946, ch. 7, and by Tishby, *op. cit.* (n. 5). In the Lurianic scheme the creation of man is a secondary act, intended as an attempt to heal the original, theo-cosmic fall.

9. Even in Abraham Galante's minor works (e.g., *Qol Bokhim*) many significant analogies to the *SHeLaH* can be found.

10. Cf. e.g., *Pardes, Shaʿar ha-Temuroth*, ch. 3.

11. *Ibid.*, chs. 1 and 6. Codovero is clearly aware of the fact that he is skating on thin ice and that the subject is an extremely delicate one; cf. *Shaʿar ha-Temuroth*, ch. 4.

12. The biblical text says that "wisdom excelleth folly as light excelleth darkness."

13. "Who can bring a clean thing out of an unclean? not one!" (מי יתן טהור מטמא לא אחד).

14. Cf. the homily in *Parah, Pesiqta de-Rav Kahana*, ed. Buber, f. 29b, and *Tanḥuma* ed. Buber on *Numbers* 19:2, f. 52a; also *Numbers R.* xix, 1, ed. Wilna f. 78a.

15. *Genesis Rabbah* xix, 5.

16. It is almost unnecessary to acknowledge that our brief summary of the Lurianic doctrine on the subject is indebted to Tishby's monograph, even though no page references are given.

17. It may not be inappropriate at this point to mention a somewhat unusual variation on the theme of the *berur* to be accomplished by Israel in (and through) their exile. According to the usual and better known version, Israel (representing the realm of holiness) is exiled among the nations (representing the realm of impurity and demonic evil) in order to discover, extract, and raise the holy "sparks" scattered there, and to liberate them from the defiling embrace in which they are held by the *qelippah*. One of the ways of accomplishing this was the making of converts; e.g., Ruth was such a spark of holiness snatched from the *qelippah* of Moab. That much was known even to nonspecialists in Lurianic Kabbalah—it was enough to have read Manasseh ben Israel (1604–1657), or for that matter any popular author. But the same notion could also be turned upside down, so as to serve as a *heilsgeschichtliche* interpretation of the fact that there also were cases of Jewish apostasy. *Tiqqun* also implies that the realm of holiness (Israel) be cleansed of any vestiges of *qelippah* that might adhere to it. Saul Levi Morteira of Amsterdam (1596–1660), in one of his homilies, expounds *Job* 14:4 by explaining that since dirt attracts dirt, the cleansing of an object is effected by exposing it to dirt. The impurities then attach themselves to the dirt outside, thus leaving the object completely pure. The purpose of exile,

therefore, is not so much the addition to Israel of righteous proselytes, as the cleansing and ridding Israel of all impurity. Being scattered among the gentiles and forced into close contact with the nations of the world, Israel can rid itself of the vestiges of *qelippah* still inhering in it (i.e., the impure souls that become apostates) and thus achieve the purity that leads to perfect *tiqqun* (Morteira, *Givʿath Shaʾul,* Amsterdam, 1645, fol. 62a).

18. E.g., foll. 19af. and 164bf.

19. The same pun played a considerable role in the *golem* legend: by erasing the *ʾaleph* from the word *ʾemeth* written on his forehead, the *golem* was turned again into a lifeless lump of clay.

20. The relentless logic of cabbalistic symbolism does not stop here. Blood is red, and hence the colour of *din* = strict justice; milk is white and therefore the colour of *ḥesed* = mercy. The theory current in medieval physiology according to which menstrual blood and mother's milk are transformations of the same essence—hence pregnant women and nursing mothers do not menstruate—made eminent symbolic sense to many cabbalists. It is interesting to note that the alchemists likewise juxtaposed *sanguis meretricis* and *lac virginis.* Cf. also T.B. *Niddah* 9b.

21. Foll. 21b and 164b.

22. *Ibid.*

23. Our brief account of Horovitz's doctrine of the "Fortunate Fall" does not pretend to present an exhaustive analysis of what can be found in the *SHeLaH* on the subject of antinomianism. Horovitz makes repeated reference to the aggadic theme of the distinction between the saintliness of David who mastered his evil *yeṣer* by destroying him, and, on the other hand, the superior perfection of Abraham, who succeeded in "mastering" his *yeṣer* by subjecting and using him. Clearly this *ʾaggadah* can be interpreted in a manner that has implications for the role of the *yeṣer ha-raʿ* in the life of the saint. The subject gains in interest if we bear in mind the indubitable influence which the *SHeLaH* exerted on the development of later hasidic doctrine.

והתקרבותם אל היהודים הולמים את דברי יצחק בער, ״תולדות היהודים בספרד הנוצרית״, מהדורה שניה (1959), עמ׳ 393–385, על תופעות אלו אחרי כיבוש קושטאנטינא (1452).

24. כן בדפוס הראשון, דף כח ע״ב, ובס׳ ״ליקוטי ש״ס״, דף נה, ע״א.

25. אמנם כדאי להזכיר כאן גם עדויות ידועות בספרות הקבלה העיונית הבאה להזהיר את התלמידים על שימושי השמות. וזה לשונו של ר׳ מתתיה דלקרוט בפירוש ל״ס׳ מערכת״ שנתחבר באמצע המאה הט״ז, על פי כ״י אוכספורד 1640 דף נו, ע״ב ״על כן האיש החרד על דברו ית׳ וחס על כבודו ועל עצמו ימשוך ידו מלפעול בשמותיו הקדושים וירחק ממנו מרחק רב. . . ולכן תראה כי כל שרדפו אחר אלו הפעולות ועסקו בשמות בדורות הללו לא כלו ימיהם בטוב ולא מתו מיתת עצמם או לא האריכו ימים, ולולא משום לזות שפתיים ושאין לדבר על שוכני עפר כדי להניחם במנוחתם כבוד הייתי מזכיר בשם קצתם אשר היו בדורות אתנו. לכן אם יפתוך בעלי השמות לאמור לכה אתנו ונראך פלאות פעולות נוראות אל תתן אזנך להם״; עיין גם דברי הרדב״ז בס׳ ״מגן דוד״, אמסטרדם תע״ג, דף טו ע״ב.

26. עיין ביחוד Ludwig Kiesewetter, *Faust in der Geschichte und Tradition* כרך ראשון (1894), עמ׳ 237 ואילך. אין כאן בסיפור יוסף דילה ריינה רמז היסטורי לקיום מלכות קושטא היונית אלא טשטוש של המוטיב המקשר את תורת השדים המזנים עם בני אדם (succubi בלע״ז) עם ההשכלה ההומאניסטית של המאה הט״ז.

27. וזה לשונו לפי ההעתקה בס׳ ״ליקוטי ש״ס״ דף נט ע״א: ״ואני המעתיק העתקתי אותו מכתבים ישנים בלויים מאד אשר מצאתי אותם בגניזות ספרים אשר בצפת תוב״ב בכאן וכתבתי המעשה הזה לאות ולזכרון למען אשר לא יקרב איש זר להביא הגאולה הגם שאפשר שיפציר הדבר בחכמתו. . . וגם שמזה יראה האדם כמה מתחזק ס״ם [סמאל] וסיעתו מעונותינו שבשביל דבר מועט כזה נתבטל כח קדושת השמות ונתגבר וחזר למקומו וגם יראה כמה גדול כח השמות הקדושים ובזה ילמד ליראה את השם הנכבד . . . כה דברי המעתיק שלמה נאוארו הירושלמי״.

28. א. יערי, ״שלוחי ארץ ישראל״ (1961), עמ׳ 282.

29. *Magna Bibliotheca Rabbinica*, כרך IV (1693), עמ׳ 526 ואילך. בספרו של Paul Drach, *De l'harmonie entre L'Église et la Synagogue* (פריס 1844), כרך 2, עמ׳ xxxiv, גליתי את הידיעה היקרה שתולדות חייו של נאוארו הכתובות בידי עצמו, עדיין היו קיימות בזמנו בספריית המוסד להפצת האמונה ברומא (בואטיקאן), בין עזבונו של Pastritius, ואני משער שאפשר למצוא אותה שם גם היום, עם שאר החיבורים שנאוארו חיבר אחרי התנצרותו, אך לפי שעה לא הצליחו נסיונותי לגילוים.

30. אולי אביו זהה לר׳ משה יהודה נאוארא שאגרות אליו משנת ת״ט (1649) נמצאו בכ״י שהוצע למכירה פומבית ברשימת ספרים וכתבי יד מאוסף ון־בימא (שנתחברה על־ידי שמואל (זיגמונד) זיליגמן), אמשטרדם 1904, עמ׳ 209, סי׳ 3579. כ״י זה הכיל גם אגרות אל חכם בשם ר׳ יוסף ראגינה משנת 1654, וקריאת השם לא היתה ודאית בעיני הרושם. ושמא מותר לשער שהשם הוא ראינה, והכוונה לר׳ יוסף דילה ראינה או ריינה בצפת שנזכר למעלה מס׳ ״קורא הדורות״ כבן־זמנו? וכוח הדמיון מפליג: אולי היו אלו אגרות משלמה נאוארו אל אביו באיטליה ואל חכם בצפת מצאצאי אותו מקובל שעליו עמד שלמה נאוארו לחבר סיפורו בירושלים? לצערי, לא ידעתי לאן נתגלגל כתב יד זה.

31. ס׳ ״ציצת נובל צבי״, מהדורת י. תשבי, 1954, עמ׳ 136.

32. אצל ברטולוצ׳י, עמ׳ 527. המומר לא עזב את הלך־רוחו האפוקאליפטי. לפי עדותו חיבר פירוש ל״נבואת הילד״ על כל חמשת פרקיו ופירוש בשם המופלא ״שובע שמחות״ למגילת איכה, שבו ניבא (או חישב?) את ביאת המשיח (בואו השני?) לשנת תל״ו (1676). ריח שבתאי חזק נודף מן השם ״שובע שמחות״, שכן לימד נתן העזתי שקינות איכה עתידות להתפרש כשירי שמחה על ביאת המשיח. (והלא כך פירש ר׳ בנימין הכהן ברג׳ו, ראש השבתאים באיטליה, את מגילת איכה בס׳ ״אלון בכות״, ויניציאה תע״ד (1712), ״לפרש אלו הקינות בלשון נחמה על הגאולה ועל התמורה״.)

33. ״מעשה ר׳ יוסף דילה ריינה במסורת השבתאית״, בספרו ״אורי דורות״ (1971), עמ׳ 95–75.

4. עיין במה שכתבתי ב״קרית ספר״ שנה ב׳, עמ׳ 271.
5. הערותי על זה בקיצור ב״קרית ספר״ שנה ז׳ עמ׳ 162, אבל טעיתי שם כאשר כתבתי שמדברי ר׳ אברהם ״ניכר שסיפור המעשה הנמצא בידינו נתחבר באמת כבר באותו זמן״ ואיפכא מסתברא כפי שאוכיח כאן. נתחלפה לי אז בזכרוני עדות הרח״ו בס׳ הגלגולים המתאימה באמת לסיפורו של ר׳ אברהם הלוי עם המעשה הנדפס השונה ממנו מכל וכל.
6. הקץ הידוע גם מספר הפליאה ושאר ספרים בסימן ״בר״ן יחד כוכבי בוקר״, עיין גם Silver, *A History of Messianic Speculation in Israel* (1927), עמ׳ 106.
7. כלומר בשמות קדושים לפי אבות דר׳ נתן פרק י״ב (מהדורת שעכטער עמ׳ 56).
8. במדרש שמות רבה, פר׳ ט, על הפסוק ישעיהו כד, כא: ״יפקוד ה׳ על צבא המרום במרום ועל מלכי האדמה באדמה״.
9. אין כאן זכר ל״תלמידים״ שבסיפור הנדפס.
10. על פי מס׳ גטין סח, ע״א.
11. מכאן שר׳ אברהם הלוי הכיר אישית את חברו של גיבור הסיפור, ויתכן שכוונתו לר׳ יוסף טאיטאצאק שפגש אותו בנדודיו באיטליה או בסאלוניקי.
12. גם מוטיב זה קיבל בסיפור הנדפס צורה אחרת לגמרי.
13. דבר זה מבואר מתוך השקפה מקבילה בס׳ ״כף הקטורת״ (על תהלים) שנתחבר אחרי הגירוש (אולי באיטליה) וקרוב מאד ברוחו המאגית והאפוקליפטית ל״ספר המשיב״ שידובר עליו למעלה. בכ״י פאריס 845, דף י״ג, ע״א נאמר: ״כשיתגלה מלכא משיחא, משיח בן דוד, סמאל יהיה קשור וחתוך כנפים, הוא גם המשנה שלו״, ר״ל אמון מנא. השיטה הדימונולוגית שבראשה סמאל ואמון מנוא מקורה בחוג בעלי הגילויים מסוגם של ר׳ יוסף דילה ריינה ור׳ יוסף טאיטאצאק. עיין גם למטה, הערה 17.
14. כתבתי על ספר זה בספרי ״כתבי יד בקבלה הנמצאים בבית הספרים הלאומי״ (1930), עמ׳ 85–89, אך נקטתי עמדה אחרת במאמרי ״המגיד״ של ר׳ יוסף טאיטאצאק והגילויים המיוחסים לו״, ב״ספונות״, ספר יא, עמ׳ 67–112, הכרך המוגמר בשנת תשל״א נגנז ולא ראה אור אלא בשנת תשל״ח.
15. ב״ספונות״ יא, עמ׳ קז–קי.
16. לעומת זה נזכר יוסף כחברו של הכותב ללא כל גנאי, שם, עמ׳ צ׳ וצ״ב.
17. תיאורי אמון מנוא בספרי קבלה מאוחרים לקוחים מ״ס׳ המשיב״. ר׳ אברהם הלוי דיבר עליו גם במקום אחר ב״אגרת סוד הגאולה״, עיין ״קרית ספר״ ז (1930), עמ׳ 164. שלושה ממקובלי פולין במאה הי״ז מדברים על תואר דמותו באופן אחר: ר׳ נתן שפירא בס׳ ״מגלה עמוקות״ (אופן קצג); ר׳ אריה לייב פרילוק בפירושו לזוהר (כ״י אוכספורד 1912, דף יד, ע״א); ר׳ בצלאל בן שלמה מלוצק בס׳ ״פלח הרמון״ (1659) המיוסד על אותו סעיף בס׳ ״מגלה עמוקות״. מקורם הוא בס׳ ״גלי רזיא״ שנתחבר בשנת 1552 או סמוך לו (כנראה בצפת); עיין בדפוס מוהילוב 1812, דף ל, ע״ג, ונראה שבעקבות ספר זה שינה גם ר׳ משה קורדובירו את תיאור ״השר הגדול ברקיע״ אמון מנוא בס׳ ״אלימה״ שלו, בחלק שלא נדפס, כפי שהעיד הרב חיד״א (אזולי), על פי ציטאטה שמצא בדרושים כ״י של ר׳ נתן שפירא ירושלמי, ועיין דברי חיד״א בס׳ ״יעיר אזן״ (ליוורנו 1793), דף קא, עא (= ס׳ ״מדב״ר קדמו״ת״, מערכת קוף, סי׳ יג).
18. כארבעים שנה אחרי הופעתו הראשונה של מאמרי שבו חשבתי את כה״י הזה לשייך אל אמצע המאה הט״ז, ייחד מ. בניהו מחקר מיוחד לקובץ זה וקבע שעיקרו הוא ס׳ ״שושן יסוד העולם״ לר׳ יוסף בן אליה תירשום. בניהו שיער שהחיבור נכתב בין 1510–1530 ונתן רק רמז לנימוקו ולא פירשו, עיין דבריו ב״טמירין״ כרך ראשון, ירושלים 1972, עמ׳ קפז–רסט, ובפרט עמ׳ קצט. בניהו הבטיח שם בכמה מקומות חיבור מיוחד על ר׳ יוסף דילה ריינה, ומי יתן ונראה אותו בקרוב.
19. ראה במאמרו של בניהו, עמ׳ ריב–ריח.
20. נראה כי ממקור זה שאב הרב ד״ר מ. גרונוואלד בוינה את הסיפור הזה בירחון *Menora* שנה ה׳ (1927), עמ׳ 361.
21. כן הועתק מכ״י ששון גם בכ״י ואטיקאן 456 שנכתב בשנת שי״ז (1557) באנגורה (היום אנקרה) ע״י יהודה רגוסי (בדף 110). חלק של כ״י נעתק מכ״י ששון.
22. ר׳ דוד קונפורטי, ס׳ ״קורא הדורות״, ויניציאה תק״ו (1746), דף מט, ע״ב.
23. ראה על כך במאמרי ב״ספונות״ יא, עמ׳ פ׳. תיאורי המחבר על התעוררות האנוסים

(בפיימונטי). אשתו הראשונה ילדה לו עשרה ילדים שרק בתו חוה נשארה בחיים. אחרי המצור על קאזאלי ושוד העיר בידי הספרדים (1630) עלה עם אשתו השניה Donnina ובתו לארץ ישראל דרך ויניציאה. בויניציאה נשאר שמונה חדשים, למד תורה וקבלה וקיבל סמיכה לרבנות מחכמי הישיבה. בארץ התישב בירושלים ובתו התחתנה שם. לדבריו, נשלח פעמים אחדות בשליחות ירושלים לגולה, ועל אחת מהן יש לנו עדות מפי ר׳ יעקב ששפורטש המספר שר׳ אלישע, אביו של נתן העזתי, היה בשליחות למארוקו ואלג׳יר עם ״חברו שלמה נאבארו שהיה חכם ומקובל וחסיד״. אבל ר׳ אלישע הפסיד כל כספי השליחות, ״ביען שחברו . . . בבואו לעיר ריג׳ו (Reggio) באיטליה, שם חשק גויה אחת ונשאה והמיר דתו.[31] גירסתו של נאווארו עצמו שונה לגמרי, כמובן. הוא מספר באריכות על חזיונות ונפתולים שהיו לו — חלק מסיפורו בסוגיא זו נדפס אצל ברטולוצ׳י — עד שהמיר ונטבל בריג׳ו ב־25 ביוני 1664. אשתו היהודיה לא נתרצתה בראשונה ללכת בעקבותיו עד שהתנצרה גם היא ב־6 באבגוסט 1664, ועוד אחרי הטבילה נולד לו בן־זקונים ממנה. האם שיקר נאוארו בסיפורו או האם השמועות שהגיעו אל ששפורטש לא היו אלא לזות־שפתיים להבאיש את ריחו של המומר? אין לעת עתה חומר מספיק ונאמן כדי להכריע בדבר. אבל דבר אחד ברור: באוטוביוגרפיה סיפר נאוארו־רוג׳יירי בפירוש כי הוא חיבר את סיפור התולדות של ר׳ יוסף דילה ריינה, כשם שחיבר גם ספר על תולדות ר׳ יוסף קארו וה״מגיד״ שלו.[32] את סיפור ר״י דילה ריינה חיבר בלי ספק בירושלים לפני המרתו, באופן שהסיפור הגיע למצרים לידי ר׳ יוסף סמבארי. ברטולוצ׳י לא ידע כלל שהסיפור העברי של נאוארו קיים ונכלל בינתיים בכרוניקה של סמבארי, ונפוץ בין יחידי סגולה וזכה לגלגול ספרותי־עממי חדש בעקבות כשלונו של שבתי צבי. נוסח חדש זה שהעביר את מקומו של ר׳ יוסף מצפת לחברון, נכתב אף הוא עברית ונשתמר לנו בתרגום ליידיש שנאמן הקהלה האשכנזית באמשטרדם, ר׳ ליב בן עוזר, כלל אותו בשנת 1718 בזכרונותיו על התנועה השבתאית ״באשרייבונג פון שבתי צבי״, על פי המקור שנמסר לו על ידי ר׳ שלמה איילון, רבם של הספרדים בעירו (ושבתאי נסתר מימי נעוריו), והלא גלגול אחרון זה של ״המעשה הנורא״ זכה להתפרסם ולהיחקר במסה מלאת עניין על־ידי נשיאנו המנוח זלמן שזר[33].

הערות

* זוהי נוסחה מורחבת ומתוקנת של מאמר קצר שנדפס לפני יותר מארבעים שנה במאסף השנתי ״ציון״ כרך ה׳ (תרצ״ג), קכ״ג–ק״ל; וכאן השתמשתי בחומר הרב החדש שהגיע לידי אחרי כן. במקום אחר אקווה לפרסם משרידי סודותיו של ר׳ יוסף שנשתמרו בכ״י ששון 290.

1. הסיפור בנוסח זה היה ידוע בהעתקה גם בשנת 1711 בפרנקפורט ע״נ מיין, על פי עדות בכ״י של בית המדרש לרבנים בניו־יורק, סי׳ 994. המיסיונרים ממוסדו של Callenberg בהאלי מזכירים בשנת 1735 (כרך י״ד של הדו״חות על מאמציהם (בגרמנית), עמ׳ 37), שראו תרגום הסיפור ליידיש שנדפס לדבריהם באמסטרדם: ״איינע שינע וונדרליכע מעשה פון יוסף דיל ריינה״. הדפוס הזה נעלם מעיני מאיר בניהו שרשם את כל החומר הביבליוגראפי והמהדורות השונות כמעט ארבעים שנה לאחר שהופיע מאמרי זה במהדורתו הקצרה הראשונה, עיין ״ארשת״, כרך א׳ (ירושלים 1972), עמ׳ 188–170, ובפרט עמ׳ 182.

2. בכתבי היד השונים ודפוסי ס׳ הגלגולים נכתב השם בצורות שונות, ומהן מסולפות כגון דולפינא וכיוצא בזה. אבל בכ״י רבים נשמרה הצורה הנכונה. בידי נמצא כ״י שגלגולים אלו באו בכותרת: ״גילגולי קצת אנשי דורינו״, וכן גם בסוף הפרק אחרי הזכרת יוסף, כאילו היה קרוב לזמנו.

3. איני יודע היכן נמצא כ״י זה כי רק מקצת כתבי יד אלו נקנה על ידי בית המדרש לרבנים בניו־יורק. כ״י 141 הכיל 238 דפים ובו חומר חשוב מקבלת האר״י, ו״נכתב בכתב ספרדי יפה מאד״.

יצחק אישיות היסטוריות הן. אין מדרכי ספרי הקבלה המעשית לברות שמות של אנשים מעיקרם. הם נהגו לתלות דברים שונים גם באנשים שלא היו כלל מבעלי הקבלה המעשית, אך במקרים רבים מסורת טובה היתה בידם על חכמים שבאמת ניסו כוחם בכך. גם הידיעה מכ״י ליידן שהבאתי למעלה ושנשמר בה שם המשפחה של ר׳ יוסף, מעידה על כך. מאידך גיסא, נמצאה גם משפחת דילה ריינה בין חכמי הספרדים ור׳ דוד קונפורטי מונה בין חכמי צפת סמוך לשנת 1630–1640 את שני האחים ר׳ יוסף ור׳ זרחיא די לה ריינא (!) ריינא.[22] עדותו של ר׳ אברהם הלוי שקבע את המעשה שהוא מספר עליו, כעשרים שנה לפני הגירוש, נראית לא רחוקה מן האמת שכן נכתבו גילויי ר׳ יוסף טאיטאצאק הקורא תגר על פעולתו, בשנות השמונים (בערך) של המאה הט״ו כאשר בעית האנוסים והליכותיהם בספרד העסיקו את הכותב[23]. הכשלון של נסיונו המאגי־משיחי נודע בחוץ לארץ לפני שידעו עליו בארץ ישראל עצמה. לאן גלה בנו ר׳ יצחק והיכן נפטר, עדיין טעון בירור ואולי ימים יגידו.

נחזור, איפוא, אל הסיפור הנדפס שהמעתיק הראשון, ר׳ שלמה נאוארו הירושלמי מצא אותו ״מקונטרס ישן נושן ומעושן אשר מצאו אותו בגנזי הספרים אשר בצפת תוב״ב מכתיבת יד הר׳ יהודה מאיר ז״ל תלמידו של ר׳ יוסף דילה ריינה כי שם היה עמו בשעת המעשה״.[24] לפי עצם הסיפור הנדפס וניתוח ענייניו, ניכר שהוא יצירה ספרותית מאוחרת: מחבר אחד שידע גם אגדות על מכשפים נוצרים ומעשיהם, עיבד את הסיפורים הישנים ושינה את כל תוכנם באופן חפשי לגמרי. המחבר המאוחר לא ידע עוד הרבה על אמון מנוא ושם במקומו את לילית בת זוגו של סמאל, שהיתה מתאמת יותר לסיפור ספרותי־עממי. הוא הוסיף מדעתו את התלמיד ר׳ יהודה בר מאיר שכאילו היה באותו מעמד, את כל סוף הסיפור על צאתו של ר׳ יוסף לתרבות רעה ומעשיו המופקרים. וכן רק הוא שהעביר את כל המעשה לצפת. בכל שינויי המוטיבים האלה ניכרת גם השפעה ברורה של סיפורי הנוצרים על מעשי מכשפים מפורסמים ועל מה שאירע להם בסופם (סיפורי תיאופילוס או פואסט).[25] דוגמא קטנה לכך הם גם דבריו (בסוף הסיפור) ״כה משפטו ימים רבים עד כי אהב מכל הנשים א ש ת מ ל ך י ו ן והיה מביא אות[ה] כמעט בכל לילה ובבקר היה מצווה להחזירה״ — מוטיב המזכיר מאוד את סיפורי המכשפים על אפשרות מעשים כאלה מצד אחד ואת הסיפור על השבעת מלכת הילינא על ידי ד״ר פאוסט הידוע כפי שבא בסיפורי פאוסט.[26] המחבר שמע דבר כזה אולי מפי השמועה והדברים נתערבבו וניטשטשו אצלו.

לא יוכל להיות כל ספק מי הוא מחבר הספר הקטן: דברי ה״מעתיק״ שלמה נאוארו הירושלמי שבסוף הסיפור מעידים בלשון די ברורה שהוא עצמו חבר אותו[27], וכן דרכם של מחברי ספרים כאלה לעשות את עצמם כמעתיקים מספר ישן נושן. והרי כאן היו למחבר באמת מקורות לעיבודו של הסיפור כיצירה עצמאית משלו.

אין כל הוכחה שהמחבר ישב בצפת (כפי שחשב אברהם יערי[28]). ומה שקבע את סיפור המעשה בצפת, יצא לו כנראה מדברי ר׳ חיים ויטאל ב״ס׳ הגלגולים״: הרי כל הנזכרים האחרים בפרק ס״ו היו מאנשי צפת. על היותו מחבר הסיפור יש לנו הודאת בעל־הדין עצמו והיא נתעלמה מעיני החוקרים וגם מעיני עד שעיינתי לא במקורות משניים המדברים עליו אלא במקור הראשון, בספרו של Julius Bartolocci שנפטר 1687. בכרך הרביעי של חיבורו הגדול על הביאו־ביבליוגרפיה של הספרות הרבנית נמצאת, בערך Prospero Ruggeri, ביוגרפיה של מומר מלומד זה המיוסדת על עזבונו הספרותי, כולל אוטוביוגרפיה, שהיה בידי יוהנס פַסטריציוס (חברו של ברטולוצ׳י ברומא).[29]

שלמה מאיר בן משה נאוארו[30] נולד בכ״ד בטבת שס״ו (1606) בקאזאלי

בין השאר מצאתי שם דברים המעידים עליו כמקבל גילוים מלמעלה והקרובים בחלקם לעיסוקו בענייני הגאולה.

א) "שאלה ששאל **ר' יוסף דלריינא** למשיב [מן השמים] על עניין שם בן מ"ב שב[תפילת] עלינו לשבח ולמנין המצות" (כ"י ששון סי' תיו).

ב) "שאלה שנית לו על חשבון הקץ ופתרון מלת זרזי"ר ומלת אלקו"ם וזוכר המשיב ענין ישו ומחמד י"ש" (שם, סי' תיז).

ג) "לזמן המגפה ב"מ [בר מינן] מקובל מהרב **ר' יוסף דלריינא ז"ל** שהיה משתמש בו" (סי' תשמג).

ד) "שאלה לר' יוסף דלריינא להשגת שאלה ולהרחיק רוח הטומאה ותשובתו על פי המשיב" (חסר עתה בכ"י ששון, אבל נזכר במפתח שבראש הקובץ, סי' תתשיז).

ה) "אלפביתא של ר' יוסף דלריינא" (והם ציורי חותמות, שם סי' א' תשכו).

ו) "שאלת ר' יוסף דלריינא על ענין הוראת הדרך על ידי [המלאך] סנדלפון" (שם, סי' א' תשמד). ואולי גם שני הסימנים שלאחריו הם משלו המזכירים את "המשיב" מן השמים.

ז) שאלת חלום לר' יוסף דילה רינה נמצאת בכ"י מיכל רבינוביץ (שוקן קב' 101), דף רנט ע"א, וכן בכ"י מאוחרים כגון ששון 788, ע' 159 (על פי הקטלוג "אוהל דוד", ע' 539) באותו כ"י, עמ' 158–155 נמצא גם "ספר השמות מהמקובל ר' יוסף דילא ראינא והוא דבר עמוק ומקובל לפני המלאך [המשיב?]".

ח) בכ"י אשכנזי מהמאה הי"ז שהועתק מתוך קובץ גדול של קבלה מעשית בכתב ספרדי ושרידיו נמצאו בזמנם בספרית הקהלה היהודית בוינה (סי' 52, VI) מצאתי בדף 23a: "זה הלוחות כתב החכם הר"ר יוסף דיליריינה ז"ל לשר אחד שבאו עליו גייסות להלחם עמו ותלה אותו בפתח העיר מבחוץ והניח הפתח פתוח כמצות ר' ז"ל ולא יכלו האויבים להכנס בעיר.... וילאו למצוא הפתח".[20]

אך לא זו בלבד, אלא גם בנו ר' יצחק דילה ריינה נזכר במקורות שונים של קבלה והנהגה, וברור שגם האב והבן מתו ביהדותם. אותו כ"י ששון 290 מזכיר בס' תקלח "נוסח קמיע של ר' יצחק דלריינא", ובמקום שלא השתמר סופר עליו כי ציוה להשים בקברו סיד על הארץ ויניחוהו כדי שיתעכל במהרה "ואמר שכך צוה אביו ר' יוסף דילה ריינה לעשות ולשים הדסים בין ירכיו, וכן עשה".[21] בהגהות בשולי הגליון של ספר הזוהר דפוס מנטובה שי"ט הנמצא בידי (בכתיבה ספרדית מזרחית יפה מסוף המאה הט"ז) באו בס' שמות, דף רח ע"ב דברים אלו אגב השמטות רבות: "ראיתי כתוב שהרב יצחק דילריינה נ"ע צוה לשים הדסים בין ירכיו אחרי פטירתו ושכן צוה לו אביו ז"ל". יתכן שבעל הגליון שהיה מקובל בקי מאוד בספרות זו השמיט את שמו של ר' יוסף בכוונה מפני הרינון אחריו בספרי מקובלי צפת. מדפוס הזוהר קושטא תצ"ו ואילך נכנסו דברי הגהה זו לגליונות שנתוספו מתוך העותק המוגה של ר' ישראל בנימין תלמיד הרח"ו אלא ששם המקובל נשתבש בדפוס (וכן בכל הדפוסים הבאים בעקבותיו): "מכאן טעם נכון שנמצא בשם ר"י דלא ריידה" וכו', ולא הכירו את זהותו. שיבושים מעין זה נמצאו גם במקורות אחרים כגון באותו קובץ של קבלה מעשית בספריית הקהלה בוינה דף ג, ע"ב: "שאלתי מר' יצחק די ליהיירי זלה"ה באיזה אצבע ישים הטבעת" (שנזכרה שם בסגולה לשאלת חלום והשיב", ובהעתקות אחרות נמצא על נכונה צורת השם: ר' יצחק דילה ריינה ז"ל. באותו כ"י, דף לז ע"א נמצא גם שיבוש קל אחר של השם: "זה העתקתי מכתיבת ר' יצחק דילא דיינא נ"ע שנמצא בידי ר' שלמה אלמשרי נ"ע מקונטרס כתיבה אשכנזית: קורא אני שמשיאל המלאך שאתה מן השרפים" וכו'.

מכל העדויות הנזכרות מתברר, איפוא, שאמנם כן ר' יוסף דילה ריינה ובנו ר'

לקונו ואשום אשם לה׳. והוא חטא רבים נשא כי **ראיתי אחד מבעלי ההשבעות אשר השיב לו המלאך הדובר בו כי זה היה סבה להאריך הגלות מ׳ שנה**״.

מכאן אנו למדים כמה דברים חשובים: (א) ר׳ אברהם הלוי ראה ״זמן רב״ לפני שנת רע״ט (1519) סיפור המעשה של ר׳ יוסף דילה ריינה כתוב באריכות ובסדר. מכיוון שר׳ אברהם בא לירושלים רק סביב לשנת רע״ה (1515), יוצא שראה את הסיפור בחוץ לארץ, בספרד, או בשנים הראשונות אחרי גירוש ספרד, ולכל המאוחר במצרים ששהה שם זמן רב לפני עלותו עם ר׳ יצחק שולאל לירושלים. הסיפור עצמו נכתב, איפוא, בצורתו המקורית כבר בשנים הראשונות של המאה השש־עשרה, לכל המאוחר. (ב) בסיפור זה **אין כל זכר לצפת או לארץ ישראל בכלל**, וברור שרק אחרי כן קבעוהו לסביבה מסויימת זו. (ג) הסיפור אינו יודע עדיין על יציאה לתרבות רעה, מכלל ישראל, ועל המוטיבים שבסוף המעשה הנדפס הלקוחים מן הפולקלור המאגי האירופי. גם העדים הנזכרים למעלה לא ידעו על כך ואפילו ר׳ חיים ויטאל הזכיר את יוסף דילה ריינה בתואר ״רבי״. אמנם נזהר ר׳ אברהם הלוי להזכיר שמו של ״בעל ההשבעה״, אבל אין ספק שכיון אליו. הרי בידינו עוד עדות אחרת ויותר קדומה בענין זה, ב״ספר המשיב״ שנתחבר, לכל הנראה, על ידי הרב המפורסם ר׳ יוסף טאיטאצאק (מפי ה״מגיד״ שהוא במקרה זה אינו אלא הקב״ה בכבודו ובעצמו), בעשר השנים **שקדמו** לגירוש, בהיותו עדיין בספרד.[14]

ספר זה, שחלק גדול ממנו נמצא בבריטיש מוזיאום (רשימת מרגוליות סי׳ 766) ובכתבי יד אחרים, יש בו פרקים ארוכים מאוד על שמות הטומאה והפעולות הקשורות בהם. את דברי ״המגיד״ (שהוא הקב״ה המדבר כאן תמיד בגוף ראשון) על דרכי העבודה וההשבעה לסמאל ומשנהו אמון מנוא פרסמתי בשלימותם מכ״י בריטיש מוזיאום דף מג, ע״ב — מה, ע״ב.[15] לבעל הספר היה חבר בפעולות מסוג זה בשם ר׳ יוסף הנזכר לפעמים לשבח ולפעמים לגנאי. דווקא בהמשך דבריו על שרי הטומאה הנ״ל, שבעזרתם אפשר להשיג גם זהב וכסף, נאמר: ״**והרשע מר׳ יוסף** אבד נפשו בו ועבד עבודתו **והביאו בצורה שראוהו אנשים** לא יאבה ה׳ סלוח לו ונתכעסתי עליו. ועוד כל ימי חייו לא יעשה אלא שמץ מנהו, והוא מצווה לאנשים שהוא הולך עמהם ולסוף סוף חרש יעלה בידו ואני אקח נקמתי ממנו ובי נשבעתי באשר חטא לי אמחנו מספרי ולא יכנס באור צדיקים״.[16]

מכאן מוכח שהמדובר במקובל נכבד שהיתה לו חבורה שהלכה עמו גם אחר המעשה שגרם לכעס ולפירוד בינו לבין הכותב מפי ה״מגיד״. התיאור של הופעת שליטי הסטרא אחרא כנחשים בכ״י של ״ס׳ המשיב״ קרוב מאוד לזה הנמצא במקור שממנו שאב ר׳ אברהם הלוי.[17] הקטרת קטורת לפני סמאל ואמון מנוא והבאתו בהקיץ ובצורה שראו גם אנשים אחרים הם החטא שלא יכופר. הרי בפירוש נאמר בסדרי ענייניו (בדף מד, ע״א): ״הוא אסור לכם להביאו בהקיץ כי לא תוכלו להביאו בלי קטורת״, וכל השבעה שיש בצדה הקטרת קטורת, הריהי בגדר עבודה זרה לדעת בעלי הקבלה. האם אין קרוב לשער וכמעט ודאי שאותו ר׳ יוסף ״הרשע״ הנזכר כאן אינו אלא ר׳ יוסף דילה ריינה, ורמז שני המקורות מכוון לאותו מעשה מאגי־משיחי? אבל גם ממקורות אחרים אנו שומעים על אודות ר׳ יוסף דילה ריינה ואפילו על בנו ר׳ יצחק דילה ריינה, ובפרט באוספים של קבלה מעשית מן המאה השש־עשרה ובכתבי יד מאוחרים יותר שהועתקו או ששאבו מהם. אזכיר כאן דברים שמצאתי בכ״י החשוב ביותר באוסף ששון סי׳ 290 שעיקרו נכתב כנראה במחצית הראשונה של המאה במזרח,[18] בכ״י גאסטר 177 שהועתק ממנו (ובמצבם היום הם עשירים במקום אחד ועניים במקום אחר, בשל חסרון דפים[19]), וכן בכ״י שנמצא בשנים 1940–1930 בידי מר מיכל רבינוביץ בירושלים והוא היום בספרית שוקן סי׳ קב 101, וכיוצא בהם.

מסגנון הדברים ניכר שהכותב לא ידע כלום על יציאתו של ר׳ יוסף לתרבות רעה כמו במעשה הנדפס, אלא קורא לו בתואר רבי וחכם ורואה בו בעל גילויים מן השמים, בשעה שהרמ״ק השמיט כל תואר־כבוד בהזכרת שמו. התפלה נדפסה **בעילום שם** בס׳ שערי ציון (1662), סמוך לתחלת שער ג׳: ״תפלה קדושה זו הובאה מארץ הקדושה מתוקנת לבעלי תשובה שנשאלה מן השמים על ידי החכם המקובל״ — והשם הושמט בכוונה, כפי שכבר הרגיש ד. כהנא. התפלה הועתקה גם בכתבי יד אחרים, כגון אדלר 1714 (עתה בבית המדרש לרבנים בניו יורק), דף י, ע״ב (שבא מן הגניזה בקהיר) ושם חסר רק השם יוסף בראש התפלה, אבל שאר חלקי השם נמצאים. ובכ״י אחר הנרשם ברשימת האוסף של ר׳ יצחק מאיר אלטר מגור (הנמצאת בידי בכתב־יד ולא נדפסה מעולם), ס׳ 141 דף קפג ע״ב,[3] מדבר המחבר בגוף ראשון: ״תפלה קדושה **אני הצעיר יוסף בן גבאי** שאלתי מאת ה׳ תפלה מסוגלת [לבעלי תשובה?]״.

אבל נוסף על אלו הידיעות יש לנו עוד אחרות ומתוכן אפשר לברר את הענין ביתר פירוט. הסיפור הנדפס הוא שונה לגמרי מפרטי הסיפור שהיה נפוץ במאה הט״ז. כבר רמיזתו הנזכרת של הרח״ו מוכיחה שהכיר נוסח אחר של הסיפור: הריהו אומר שר׳ יוסף הוריד את ״אמון מנוא״ בקבלתו המעשית ואילו בסיפור הנדפס אין זכר לאמון מנוא. אבל באגרת סוד הגאולה לר׳ אברהם בן אליעזר הלוי שנתחברה בירושלים בשנת רע״ט[4] נשאר (בכ״י אוכספורד 1743 דף 51) עוד נוסח אחר מסיפור המעשה[5] ואעתיקנו כאן כלשונו:

״ואלו זכינו שנת ר״ן היה סוף קץ לגלותנו[6] ולא זכינו יען כי בימים ההם כעשרים שנה בקירוב קודם שנת ר״ן היה איש אחד משתמש בתגא דמלכא[7] ונשאו לבו להוריד את סמאל ואת אמון מנוא משרתו למטה לארץ ולשבר כנפיו ולהחליש כחם ולעקור ממשלת אדום מן העולם כי בנפול שר שלהם יפלו גם המה[8] וקבץ האיש ההוא עמו עשרה חכמים[9] לפתח כדת עד [מקום?] א׳ בשדה כי כך היה צריך לפי סדר הקבלה ההיא וכאשר ירד סמאל היו צריכין ללכת אצלו כל אחד מהם ולתת בראשו כובע נחושת שהיה חקוק בו שם בן מ״ב ולומר לו: שמא דמארך עלך.[10] ובזה היה נקשר ונפל ולא יכול קום. וכבר האיש ההוא טבעת זהב באצבעו וחקוק בו שם הנז׳ עם שמות אחרים כלם קדושים והתחיל להשביע על סמאל ואמון מנוא משרתו ויהי בהשביעו והנה רוח גדולה חזק מאד וברד גדול וקול רעם. ובסוף נפלו לארץ סמאל ואמון מנוא בצורת נחשים צפעונים וכמדומה לי שראיתי כתוב בספר אשר מצאתי בו ספור הענין הזה כיצד היה סמאל בגודל גופו כמו קורה א׳ ואמון מנוא קטן ממנו. ואמרתי זה לפי שיש זמן רב שראיתי ספור המעשה הזה. אמנם הגיד לי איש אמונים כי הוא ראה בעצמו את אמון מנוע פעם אחרת שהכריחו לבוא האיש הנז׳[11] ולכתוב לו תשובת שאלה ששאל ממנו וגופו בדמות נחש, גבו ארכו כשני (!) אמות והיו לו ידים ורגלים וראשו כראש חתול ועיניו בוערות כלפידים כי כשמתלבשין אלו באויר לרדת למטה מתדמים בצורות כאלה, והנה כאשר ראו החכמים את המראה הגדול הזה רעדה אחזתם שם וינוסו על נפשם.[12] ואמנם נשאר האיש ההוא המשביע כי מלומד היה במעשים ההם, לבו כלב אריה ולא פחד ולא רגז הלך ונתן הכובע בראשו של סמאל ואמון מנוא משרתו כאשר ידבר איש אל רעהו ויאמרו לו עתה ידעת כי גם אנחנו קשורים אין הקשר אמיץ יען כי שאר החכמים היה להם לעשות כמעשיך ולא עשו ואמנם אנחנו מרוצים להיות קשורים תחת ידך והיינו לך לעבדים אם את הדבר הזה תעשה כי תכנס בבית הזה ותערוך שולחן ותקטיר עליו קטורת כך וכך ובכח הקטורת נהיה קשורים לעולם. לכן מרב מהירתו ופחיזתו [שכח] כי ידברו אליו דברי כזבים להנצל ממנו וכי זה המעשה יהיה ע״ז ויחלל קדושת הטבעת בבואו עמו בבית טומא׳ ע״ז ויעש להם כן: ומיד בעלות קיטור העשן קנו כנפיים[13] וחזרו ועלו והנה הוא חטא

למעשה ר׳ יוסף דילה ריינה*

ג. שלום

המוטיב של הבאת הגאולה בעזרת הזכרת שמות קדושים ופעולה מאגית ידוע בספרות הקבלה. כבר בדור גירוש ספרד הזהיר ר׳ יהודה אלבוטיני בס׳ סולם העליה (כ״י ירושלים, סוף פרק ט׳) מפני פעולה מסוג זה: ״אפילו לעורר ביאת המשיח שהוא גם כן ענין גדול ועצום והכרחי לכל העולמות כולם״ על ידי פעולה בשמות קדושים הוא איסור גמור, ״שלא יעוררו הענין הנזכר עד שידע שחפץ ורצון האל יתברך בכך״. ספר זה נכתב כנראה בראשית המאה הט״ז, ונשאלת השאלה אם זוהי סתם אזהרה בעלמא או שמא נרמז כאן למעשה שהיה.

הנה נודע הוא ה״מעשה נורא מר׳ יוסף דילה ריינה״ (Reyna), שדחק את הקץ וחשב להביא את הגאולה על ידי תחבולות של קבלה מעשית וביקש לאסור את סמאל ולילית ולשים קץ לשלטון הסיטרא אחרא בעולם על ידי מאסר וקישור זה, צעד שבעקבותיו תבוא הגאולה מאליה. חוט של חן נמשך על סיפור זה שנדפס פעמים רבות מאז ראה אור הדפוס בפעם הראשונה בקושטא בשנת נחל״ת (תפ״ח) בתוך ״ספור דברים המושכים את הלב מס׳ דברי יוסף״ (דף כח–לו). ספר זה כולו ליקוטים מס׳ דברי יוסף לר׳ יוסף סמברי, שנתחבר במצרים לא יאוחר מ־1672. כ״י אוכספורד (נייבאואר 2410, המכיל את הסיפור מדף טז–כא) כבר נגמר ב־ו׳ חשון תל״ג (שהוא סוף 1672), אם להאמין לקולופון[1]. אחר־כך חזר ונדפס עוד פעמיים במאה הי״ח, בס׳ מאורעות עולם (איזמיר תקט״ז) ובס׳ לקוטי ש״ס (ליוורנו תק״ן) ומשם ואילך כמה פעמים בקונטרס בפני עצמו, בעברית, יידיש ולאדינו.

מקור הסיפור ומחברו לא נחקרו לפני דורנו, ורק שטיינשניידר בספרו ״געשיכטסליטעראטור דער יודען״ (1905), סי׳ 130, ייחד לו הערות אחדות וקבע את ר׳ יוסף לצפת ולחברון במאה הט״ז. אחריו נמשך גם דוד כהנא ב״תולדות המקובלים, השבתאים והחסידים״ (תרע״ג, ח״א, עמ׳ 49).

מעטות היו העדויות על אודות ר׳ יוסף שהיו בידי חוקרים אלו:

(א). דברי ר׳ משה קורדובירו בס׳ פרדס רמונים שנתחבר בשנת ש״ח (1548) בצפת. בשער פרטי השמות פ״א התריס הרמ״ק נגד השימוש בקבלה מעשית, ואומר על סודותיה שהראשונים ״בעצמם לא רצו לגלותם לפי שראו אנשי חסד נאספים ונתמעטו אנשי מעשה וחששו שמא ישתמש בהם אדם שאינו הגון כמו שראינו כמה שהיו אחריהם הרבה **קרובים אלינו כמו יוסף דילה ריינ״ה** המחריבים בית אלהינו ומרבים את פרצותינו, ולטעם זה לא נחקור אחר שמוש השמות״. סתם הרמ״ק ולא פירש לאיזה סוג של שמוש בשמות כיוון.

(ב). ברורים יותר הם דברי ר׳ חיים ויטאל, אף הוא ממקובלי צפת, האומר בס׳ הגלגולים (בנוסח השלם, פרימישלא 1875, פרק ס״ו)[2] על רבו האר״י: ״גם ראה לר׳ יוסף דילא ריינה מגולגל בכלב אחד שחור על שנשתמש בקבלה מעשית והקטיר לע״ז [לעבודה זרה] **כנודע במעשה ההוא** (בגירסאות אחרות: במעשהו) **שהוריד לאמון מנוא**״. מכאן שהרח״ו לא נתכוון למעשה כפי שנדפס, שאין בו זכר לאמון מנוא. גם בסוף ס׳ שערי קדושה שלו (חלק ג׳ שער ו׳) באה אזהרה כמו בס׳ הפרדס ״קח ראיה מר׳ יוסף דילה ריינה ור׳ שלמה מולכו שנשתמשו בקבלה מעשית ונתאבדו מן העולם״.

(ג). על אישיות היסטורית רומזת גם התפלה בכ״י ליידן, ווארנר 24, אשר שטיינשניידר הזכיר אותה ברשימת כתבי היד העבריים בליידן, עמ׳ 92: ״תפלה קדושה מתוקנת לבעלי תשובה **שנשאלה מן השמים** מן החכם ר׳ יוסף גבאי דידיע [המכונה] דילה ריינה ז״ל. כ״י זה נכתב בין השנים 1542–1537״.

הכתובה ביד בנו ״תולדות יצחק״ (Jonas Spitz, *Biographische Skizze des . . . Rabbiners Isak* Spitz, Prag 1843). וייזל מכנה את מקבל המכתב ״אברך וכליל יופי״. המכתב חזר ונתפרסם מכתב יד ב״המליץ״, 1886 (26) עמ׳ 750. התאריך כאן הוא יום ג׳ ט״ו אלול תקנ״ו, אצל פלקלש, יום ג׳, ט״ז אלול, תקנ״ב (שני התאריכים מפוקפקים, כי שניהם לא חלו ביום ג׳).

86. ״עמק השוה״, כ״א ע״א — כב ע״א. על כונת המיזוג של קבלה ופילוסופיה שבדברי חורין כבר עמד לב, ״כתבים״ ח״ב, עמ׳ 272–274. לב גם הצביע על כך כי נסיונות של זיהוי הקבלה עם פילוסופיה נעשו גם בימי הבינים, אך אין זה גורע כמובן ממשמעות הדברים בהקשרם ההיסטורי החדש. למיזוג שני המקצועות מוקדש גם ספרו של יצחק הלוי סטנוב, ״אמרי בינה״, ברלין, תקמ״ב.

70. הדרשות מקובצות ב״אהבת דוד״ שלו.
71. שם, ג ע״א.
72. עיין בדברי ההקדמה ל״תשובה מאהבה״ ח״א, פראג, תקס״ט עמ׳ 4, 9–8.
73. ליבן במקום הנ״ל (הערה 64) עמ׳ 21, הערה 1, מצא סמוכין לכך שפלקלש המשיך במאבקו הפומבי נגד השבתאים עוד בשנת 1817.
74. חזקיה פייבל פלויט, ״לקוטי חבר בן חיים״ ח״ב, מונקטש, תרל״ט, הקדמה, א ע״ב.
75. עיין י. כ״ץ, ״קוים לביוגראפיה של החתם סופר״, ״מחקרים בקבלה ובתולדות הדתות מוגשים לגרשום שלום״, ירושלים, תשכ״ח עמ׳ קלא.
76. עובדה זו הודגשה על ידי שלום חזור והדגש, והיא התאמתה במחקרים שלו ושל הבאים אחריו.
77. ערעורו של רבי יעקב עמדן על אותנטיות הזוהר נבע מן המניע הזה. עיין י. תשבי, ״משנת הזוהר״ ח״א, עמ׳ 56–52. רבי יחזקאל לנדא העמיד אידיאל של הדורות הראשונים שהיו ״עמלים כל ימיהם בתורה ובמצות הכל עפ״י התורה ועפ״י הפוסקים אשר דבריהם ממקור מים חיים ים התלמוד״, כנגד ״דורינו הזה כי עזבו את תורת ה׳ ומקור מים חיים שני התלמודים בבלי וירושלמי לחצוב להם בורות בורות נשברים״, היינו ספרי קבלה (״נודע ביהודה״, מ״ק, י״ד, ס׳ צג). בחלק או״ח ס׳ ל״ה (מהדורת פראג, תקל״ו, כ פ״ג) מסדר הרב תיקון תשובה לחוטא שנכשל באשת איש. התמדה בלימוד תורה היא דרישה ראשונה, ״ולמוד תורה שיש בהם ממש משניות... ש״ס ופוסקים ותורה ונביאים כתובים וג״כ ספרי מוסר חובת הלבבות מן אחר שער היחוד עם גמירא ושל״ה במקום שאינו מדבר בנסתרות... וידבוק מאד בשירות ותשבחות של דוד המלך ע״ה... אבל שאר תפילות ותחנונים אשר חדשים מקרוב דורות מעוטים לפני דורינו ירחיק מהם״. ספר השל״ה הוא אחד הצנורות הראשיים דרכו נתפשטה הקבלה בציבור הרחב, והרב מבקש כאן לגנוז את החלק הנסתר שבו. רבי אלעזר פלקלש כמותו הביע את דעתו נגד לימוד הקבלה, הוא מצביע על דברי מורו הנ״ל (״תשובה מאהבה״, ס׳ א.) ובהקדמה לספרו (עמ׳ 9) הוא מאריך בדבר ומודיע על כונתו לחבר קונטרס מיוחד להראות את איסור העיסוק בקבלה מחוץ ליחידים יוצאים מן הכלל.
78. אין אני מונה את החתם סופר בין יוצרי חלל הריק, כי אמנם הסתייג אף הוא מן העיסוק בנסתרות, אך הוא כבר יצא ליצור שיטה חדשה לביצור המסורת. עיין במאמרי המובא בעמ׳ צח, הערה 60.
79. ״כל כתבי משה מנדלסון״, הוצאת היובל, כרך ט״ז, ברלין תרפ״ט, עמ׳ 114. המכתב לוקה בחסר, ולפי עדות המביא לבית הדפוס הראשון הכיל הקטע החסר דברי גינוי קשים לשבתאים. שנגדם מכוונים הדברים ברור גם מנוסח המכתב כפי שהוא לפנינו.
80. דברים מפורשים על כך מסר פרידריך ניקולאי מפיו של מנדלסון. הדברים מובאים אצל Hermann M.Z. Meyer, *Moses Mendelssohn, Bibliographie,* Berlin, 1965, p. 113. ועיין בספרו של א. אלטמאן *Moses Mendelssohn*, עמ׳ 866.
81. בחיבורו הקטן ״חיקור דין״ שנתפרסם תחילה ב״מאסף״ תקמ״ח ואחר כך בספר בפני עצמו. עיין ב״מאסף״, עמ׳ קד, קמז, קמ״ח.
82. הדברים נאמרים במכתב לאלמוני (עיין להלן, הערה 85) שנתפרסם ב״אהבת דוד״ של ר׳ אלעזר פלקלש, בעמודים שבין הפתיחה לגוף הספר. הגדרה דומה לעמדתו גם בחקור הדין, במקום הנ״ל (הערה 81) ב״מאסף״, עמ׳ צח–צט.
83. שם.
84. המצדדים בזכותו של אייבשיץ ביקשו להביא ראיה ממסורת זו כי לא היה שבתאי. כך כבר המחבר של ״שיחה בין שנת תק״ס ובין תקס״א״. עיין קסטנברג־גלדשטיין במקום הנ״ל (עמ׳ צו, הערה 5), עמ׳ 189–188, הערה 104. ואחר כך קלמפרר Gutmann Klemperer, *Rabbi Jonathan Eibeschütz*, Dessau, 1858, pp. 61–62.
85. ענינו של המכתב לא נתברר כל צרכו. המדובר על כל פנים בהמשך של התכתבות שבשלב הקודם שלה הביע וייזל דעה חיובית על הקבלה בקשר למאמר בשם ״מסודות הקבלה״ (שלא עלה בידי למצא את עקבותיו). הבעת דעה זו הפליאה את מקבל המכתב ואת חותנו, ועל תמיהתם הוא מגיב בהגדרת עמדתו. פלקלש אומר כי המכתב נשלח ״לאחד מתושבי עיר פראג״, וודאי שאין הוא זהה אתו (עיין קסטנברג־גלדשטיין, במקום הנ״ל, הערה 84). השערתי היא כי המתכתב עם וייזל הוא חתנו של פלקלש, רבי יצחק שפיץ, שישב כמה שנים בבית חותנו בפראג והוא היה ממעריציו של וייזל. עיין בביאוגראפיה

41. שם, עמ׳ 19.
42. שם. השאלה לא היתה איפוא כיצד יכול איש בעל השכלה פילוסופית להאמין בדברי הבל כאלה כניסוחה של קסטנברג־גלדשטיין (שם עמ׳ 186) כי אם, כיצד בגד האיש בעבר שלו.
43. סוף ״מצוה הבאה בעבירה״, ״מחקרים ומקורות״ עמ׳ 66.
44. תכנו של מסמך זה היה ידוע ממאמרו של V. Zacek, "Zwei Beiträge zur Geschichte des Frankismus in den böhmischen Ländern," *Jahrbuch für die Geschichte der Juden in den Tschechoslowakei*, ix (1938), pp. 385–387, אך רק עתה עם פירסומו על ידי גרשום שלום ב״ספר היובל של סלו בארון״ (למעלה עמ׳ קו, הערה 3) ניתן למצות את הכלול בו.
45. ״ספר בארון״, עמ׳ 810–811.
46. שם, עמ׳ 811.
47. ״שיחה בין שנת תק״ס ובין תקס״א״, עמ׳ 21–22.
48. שם, עמ׳ 23.
49. זצ׳ק, במאמרו הנ״ל, הערה 44. סברתו של זצ׳ק שלא עשה כן אלא להפסת דעת חותנו נדחתה כבר על ידי שלום, ״ספר בארון״, עמ׳ 788.
50. עיין למעלה, עמ׳ צז, הערה 39.
51. ״שיחה״, עמ׳ 21. שהמדובר באיש צעיר נאמר על ידי המחבר בפירוש. ״בעודני נער ורך בשנים, המוח עוד היה רך וענג ואין יכול לסבול דברים דקות מן הדקות כמו הדברים שלאחר הטבע״, שם, עמ׳ 21. מכאן ראיה מוחלטת שאין המדובר בוולי שהיה אז בגיל העמידה, ואילו הניג הוא בשעת כתיבת הדברים בן שלושים, והתפנית בחייו אירעה כמה שנים קודם לכן. זיהויו של הניג כמי שהתכתב עם מנדלסון בשנת 1784 (קסטנברג־גלדשטיין, ספרה הנ״ל, עמ׳ צו, הערה 5, עמ׳ 88) מופרך.
52. שם.
53. ״ספר בארון״, עמ׳ 811.
54. שם.
55. ראה הערתו של שלום שם, עמ׳ 812. הרמז הוא לזוהר ח״ב, קכ ע״ב, עיין י. תשבי, ״משנת הזוהר״, ח״ב עמ׳ רצא–רצב.
56. ראה שלום, ״ספר בארון״, עמ׳ 788–789.
57. אחת הקובלנות המרכזיות של הניג בכתב ההגנה שלו היא כי רדיפת הרבנים גורמת לו בידוד חברתי. אילו היתה זיקתו למשכילים משתמרת לו על אף מעברו לשבתאות, לא היה עולה לו כך.
58. במאמר "Die Metamorphose, usw." שנזכר למעלה, עמ׳ צו, הערה 3, עמ׳ 32.
59. ברוך קורצווייל טען וחזר וטען טענות אלה בלהט ובהפלגות האופיניות לו. את מאמריו שהופיעו תחילה בעתון ״הארץ״ קיבץ בספרו ״במאבק על ערכי היהדות״, ירושלים–תל אביב, תש״ל, עמ׳ 94–240. לגופם של דברים קרובות הערותיו של צבי ורבלובסקי (״מולד״, ט״ו, 1957 עמ׳ 539–546) להשגותיו של קורצווייל.
60. יעקב כ״ץ, ״הסטוריה סוביקטיבית ובקורת אוביקטיבית״, ״הארץ״, תרבות וספרות 28.5.1965.
61. עיין Jacob Katz, *Out of the Ghetto. The Social Background of Jewish Emancipation 1770–1870*, Cambridge, Mass. 1973, pp. 143–145; A. Altmann, *Moses Mendelssohn*, pp. 290–295.
62. ״דרושי הצל״ח״, ווארשא 1897, מ ע״א. תאריך הדרשה מוזכר בפנים, לט ע״א בסוף העמודה השניה.
63. שם, נג ע״ב.
64. על תולדות חייו ראה S.H. Lieben, "Rabbi Eleasar Fleckeles", *Jahrbuch der jüdisch-literarischen Gesellschaft*, 10 (1912), pp. 1–38
65. ״עולת ציבור״, פראג, תקמ״ו, לא ע״א. תאריך הדרשה שם, כט ע״ג.
66. ״אהבת דוד״, פראג, תק״ס, ב ע״ב — ג ע״א.
67. Lieben (עיין הערה 64), p. 18
68. ״עולת ציבור״, שם, פו ע״ב — פז ע״א.
69. שם, עמ׳ נב ע״ב — נו ע״א, פו ע״ב — פז ע״ב, צז ע״א.

17. Leopold Löw, *Gesammelte Schriften*, Szegedin, 1898. iv, p. 449.

18. שם, כרך ב, עמ' 172.

18*. עדות מפורשת על הזיקה בין השבתאות להשכלה חשב שלום למצוא בדבריו של המומר גוטפריד זליג בכתב העת שלו *Der Jude* משנת 1771, שמדבר על רדיפת היהודים את השבתאים ביחוד בפולין, בגלל נטיתם היתרה ל־Freigeisterei (*Eranos*, 1974, p. 49) וכבר קודם ב־*Zeugnisse* (למעלה דף צו, הע' 3), דף 31. המושג Freigeisterei נתפרש לשלום כשם נרדף ל־Aufklärung; אך אין זה משמעות הבטוי כפי שניתן להוכיח מכל ההבאות שבמילון הגרמני לאחים Grimm. Freigeist פירושו מופקר, פורץ גדר. זליג עצמו בכתב העת שלו בשנת 1780 עמ' 216 מגדיר את המושג בהקשר היהודי כך: "Freygeister, die sich von der Jüdischen Gemeinde dadurch absondern, dass sie nicht alle Gebraüche in den Synagogen als in den Lehrhaüsern mit beobachten wollen, im gleichen, die sogar in andern Religionen übertreten, und die מוסרים Mossrim d.i. Verräther .... alle diese werden von Gott gehasset".

19. *Major Trends*, p. 304.

20. הביאוגראפיה הופיעה תחילה ב־*Ben Chananya*, שנה רביעית 1861 תחת שם Dr. Weil, וחזרה ונדפסה בשנת 1863 ונכללה בכל כתבי לב כרך 2. יצוטט להלן על פי נוסח אחרון זה.

21. לב, שם, עמ' 254–255.

22. שם, חלק ה, עמ' 192–193.

23. דבריו של החתם סופר על חורין בשו"ת שלו חלק ששי פר–צו.

24. לב, כתבים ח"ב עמ' 276–281.

25. שם, עמ' 188.

26. לב, שם, עמ' 186–189, 260–269.

27. "עמק השוה" לט ע"א.

27*. בהפצת "מכתבי פלסתר" הכוונה לאגרת הפרנקיסטים. על ענינו של זה עיין שלום, "מחקרים ומקורות" עמ' 63–65.

28. "עמק השוה", לב ע"ב–לג ע"א.

29. ראה את מכתבו של מנדלסון להרץ הומברג Moses Mendelssohn, *Gesammelte Schriften*, Leipzig 1844, pp. 669–670; וראה Alexander Altmann, *Moses Mendelssohn, A Biographical Study*, Alabama 1973, p. 551.

30. "עמק השוה", לג, ע"ב.

31. ליאופולד לב הבחין בהבדל בין דרכו של חורין לבין דרכו ודרך עמיתיו הרפורמיים מן הדור השני שויתרו על הנסיון למצא סעד לתיקוניהם במקורות ההלכה. לב, "כתבים" ח"ב עמ' 345–347.

32. זהו כידוע פתגמו של החתם סופר. משמעותו נתבררה יפה יפה בעבודת הדוקטור של משה שרגא סמט, "הלכה ורפורמה", ירושלים 1967, עמ' 158, וחבל שחיבור זה לא זכה עד עתה לפירסום.

33. על אלה הצביע שלום במקומות המצוינים למעלה דף צו, הערות 3-4. את הפירוש להלל פרסם ב"ספר יובל ליצחק בער", ירושלים, תשכ"א עמ' 409–430 ונכלל עתה ב"מחקרים ומקורות". ועיין ב"ספר היובל לבארון", עמ' 789.

34. *Orient 1851, pp. 539*–540.

35. "קאריירה של פראנקיסט: משה דוברושקה וגלגוליו", "ציון", לה (תש"ל) עמ' 127–181. חזר ונדפס ב"מחקרים ומקורות", עמ' 141–209.

36. יעקב כ"ץ, "בונים חופשים ויהודים, קשריהם האמיתיים והמדומים", ירושלים, תשכ"ח עמ' 32–50.

37. Gershom Scholem, "Ein verschollener jüdischer Mystiker der Aufklärungszeit: E.J. Hirschfeld," *Leo Baeck Institute Year Book* vii (1962), pp. 247–278. ועיין ביחוד בעמודים האחרונים של המאמר.

38. Jacob Katz, "Moses Mendelssohn und E. Hirschfeld" *Bulletin des Leo Baeck Instituts* 7 (1954), pp. 295–311. ועיין במקום הנ"ל בספרי "בונים חופשים ויהודים".

39. החוברת נדפסה בפראג תק"ס. על בעית המחבר ראה רות קסטנברג־גלדשטיין, "קרית ספר" 40 (תשכ"ה), עמ' 569 ובספרה הנ"ל (עמ' צו, הערה 5), עמ' 189–190. ניתוח תוכן החוברת על ידי קסטנברג־גלדשטיין (שם, 184–191) מאלף, אך עיין להלן, הערה 42.

40. "שיחה בין שנת תק"ס ובין תשס"א", עמ' 16.

(Brünn, 1822–1823) לא ראה קשר ביניהן, ולא עוד אלא הקדים את תולדות החסידות (שם ח״ב עמ׳ 197–259) לתולדות השבתאות (שם עמ׳ 259--401). ולא בכדי, כי האחרונה היתה ידועה לו כתופעה חיה בעיר פראג (כפי שנשמע להלן) ואילו על הראשונה ידע לספר רק מפי זולתו. דוד כהנא (תולדות המקובלים, השבתאים והחסידים, תל־אביב תרפ״ז, ח״ב) מסמיך את החסידות לשבתאות רק מבחינה כרונולוגית (״בעת ההיא נתרבו בעלי כת החסידים החדשים בפולניא״ שם עמ׳ 88). גרטץ (*Geschichte der Juden*, Leipzig, 1900², ii) העניק לסמיכות משמעות סיבתית ומטעם כפול: (1) השבתאות יצרה אוירת מתח משיחית שהכשירה את הלבבות לפעילות הבעש״ט (שם עמ׳ 95); (2) חלק מחסידי יעקב פרנק שנרתעו מללכת אתו עד הסוף, ר״ל ההמרה לדת הקתולית, הצילו את נפשם מחרם המתנגדים ומחומרת הדת הרבנית כאחת על ידי הצטרפותם למחנהו של הבעש״ט (שם עמ׳ 98–97). דובנוב (תולדות החסידות, תל־אביב, תר״ץ עמ׳ 34) יצר את הקשר בדרך דיאלקטית: השבתאות הביאה את ״המסתוריות למצב של משבר״, העם הפשוט לא מצא סיפוק ״לא בפורמליות היבשה של לימוד התורה וקיום המצוות ולא בפרישות של בעלי הסוד״. נפתחה הדרך ״לאמונה פשוטה שהנפש מתחממת לאורה״. — את הקשר בין השבתאות וההשכלה העלה ליאופולד לב כפי שיתואר להלן בפנים. שלום עצמו ציין את ש״י איש הורוביץ ב״מאין לאן״, וז. רובשוב (שזר) במאמריו, ובייחוד בחוברתו ״על תלי בית פראנק״ (מחקרים, עמ׳ 15) כמי שקדמו לו בהערכת השבתאות כביטוי לרצון על התחדשות מבפנים.

2. המאמר הופיע בכנסת (תרצ״ז) וחזר ונדפס עתה בקובץ המאמרים של שלום, ״מחקרים לתולדות השבתאות וגלגולה״, ירושלים תשל״ד, ולפיו יצוטט להלן.

3. אציין כמה מאלה: "Zum Verstandniss des Sabbatianismus. Zugleich ein Beitrag zur Geschichte der 'Aufklärung'." *Almanach des Schocken Verlag* 5697 (1936/37), pp. 30–42. "A Sabbathaian Will from New York." *Miscellanies of the Jewish Historical Society of England* 5 (1948), pp. 193–211. "Die Metamorphose des häretischen Messianismus der Sabbatianer in religiösen Nihilismus im 18. Jahrhundert", *Zeugnisse. Theodor W. Adorno zum sechzigsten Geburtstag*. Frankfurt a/M 1963, pp. 21–32. פירוש פרנקיסטי ל״הלל״. ספר יובל ליצחק בער במלאת לו שבעים שנה, ירושלים תשכ״א, עמ׳ 409–430. "A Frankist Document from Prague", Salo Wittmayer Baron Jubilee Volume, Jerusalem 1974, ii, pp. 787–814. "Der Nihilismus als religiöses Phänomen", *Eranos Jahrbuch 1974* pp. 49–50 ועיין בהערה הבאה. וראה עתה

4. עיין בסוף ״מצוה הבאה בעבירה״, וביחוד ב־*Major Trends in Jewish Mysticism*, New York 1954, p. 304.

5. מאז הועלתה התיזה על ידי שלום נתפרסם מספר לא קטן של מחקרים בתולדות ההשכלה והרפורמה. ולא מצאתי מי שנזקק לשאלה זו אפילו דרך אגב. יוצאת מן הכלל היא Ruth Kestenberg-Gladstein, *Neuere Geschichte der Juden in den böhmischen Ländern*, Tübingen, 1969, pp. 173–191; אלא שבעוד אשר בדרך כלל הרי זה מחקר עצמאי מאלף, הרי בענין הנדון נכנעה המחברת לסמכותו של שלום ללא מאבק, וחזרה על דבריו ללא עמדה משלה.

6. *Major Trends*, pp. 330–331; הדגשה וביסוס נוספים במאמר ״שתי העדויות הראשונות על חבורות החסידים והבעש״ט״, תרביץ (תש״ט) עמ׳ 228–240.

7. *Major Trends* pp. 334–337.

8. *Major Trends*, pp. 331–334

9. "Devekuth, or Communion with God", *The Review of Religion* 14 (1949/50) p. 133.

10. ״מחקרים״, עמ׳ 66–67.

11. *Major Trends*, p. 304

12. שמות החתומים (ששים וששה במספר) על פרוטוקול היסוד מ־11 בדצמבר 1817 ב־*Festschrift zum hundertjährigen Bestehen des Israelitischen Tempels in Hamburg 1818–1918* (ed. D. Leindorfer), Hamburg 1918, pp. 16–17.

13. כך גם ניסוח הדברים של שלום עצמו במאמרו ב־*Encyclopaedia Judaica* 6, 1075, ערך Eybeschütz, Jonathan.

14. ״ליקוטי חבר בן חיים״, ח״ב, מונקטש, חרל״פ. הקדמה, עמ׳ א ע״ב. עיין להלן עמ׳ צט, הערה 74.

15. שלום, ״מחקרים ומקורות״ עמ׳ 144–145.

16. קסטנברג־גלדשטיין, שם, עמ׳ 105–108 וביחוד עמ׳ 107 הערה 62.

שנתמלא על ידי הנסתר. הם השאירו את תלמידיהם ושומעי לקחם מבחינה זו בידים ריקות.[78] באה ההשכלה ומלאה את החלל הריק שנוצר.

והנה השפעה זו שבדרך הרתיעה אינה רק סברה בעלמא, כי יש לה סמוכין בהלך המחשבה של אנשי המרכז שבתנועת ההשכלה. משה מנדלסון היה כידוע מעריצו של רבי יעקב עמדן, והמכתב הראשון אליו משנת תשכ״ז (1766) שנשתמר ממנו הוא הבעת הסכמה גמורה ליחסו השלילי לשבתאות.[79] בהרחקתו את הקבלה כמקור השראה אינטלקטואלי יכול הוא לראות במורו הרבני תנא דמסייע. אמנם שונה יחסו של מנדלסון לקבלה משל רבי יעקב עמדן. האחרון אם כי ביקש לטהר את המסורת הקבלית משיבושיה ולעצור בעד הסתאבותה, לא הפקיע את תקפה ואת משמעות מושגיה, והיא נשארה בעיניו כבעיני רוב שלומי אמוני הדורות הקודמים מסורת קדומה, המפתח האמיתי לפיענוח סודות האלהות והתורה. בעיני מנדלסון, לא היתה הקבלה אלא הסתעפות מעורפלת של הפילוסופיה הדתית שאפשר שלאחר הסרת המעטה המסתורי אפשר להעלות ממנו גרעיני מחשבה מסוימים.[80] מפנה כזה חל גם בדעתו של נפתלי הרץ ווייזל. ווייזל שילב בהסברת עיקר האמונה בשכר ועונש — תוך קיום המושגים הציוריים של גן עדן וגיהינום וכדומה — משפטים מדברי מקובלים כרבי משה די ליאון, ר׳ מאיר גבאי ואחרים.[81] דברי הקבלה לא זונחו איפוא ומכל מקום הוסר מעליהם מעטה המסתורין והופקעה סמכותם המתפיזית המוחלטת. כשנשאל על ידי מאן דהו לפשר יחסו לקבלה, הגדיר את עצמו ״איין גראסר פרעהרר דער קבלה״, היינו מכבד מאד את הקבלה, עמדה שעל פיה רשאי היה לקלוט ממנה מה שהתקשר לו עם ״תחושה ומושג״ (עמפינדונג אונד בגריף) כלשהו, ולהתעלם ממה שנשאר סתום לגביו.[82] למרבה הפלא יכול הוא להשען ביחסו הבררני הזה על הבעת דעתו של ר׳ יונתן אייבשיץ, שלפי דברי ווייזל אמר למפקפקים בדברי קבלה שהשמיעם בדרשותיו ״אם לא תאמינו אין בכך כלום כי אין אלו מעיקרי אמונתנו״.[83] אין כאן המקום לדון בהתאמת אמרה זו להשקפת עולמו ואישיותו של רבי יונתן.[84] יש לראותה על כל פנים כבטוי להסתגלות המופלגת שלו לדעת מי שעומד כנגדו.

עדים אנו בדבריו של ווייזל להתגבשות של יחס האופיני לכמה מן המשכילים המתונים, שמסגלים לעצמם ממערכת המושגים הקבלית מה שניתן לתרגום לשפת הפילוסופיה המקובלת עליהם. מבחינת הכוח המעמיד של הקבלה, הבלעת מושגיה בהשקפת עולם פילוסופית כמוה כגניזתה הגמורה מאימת הסתאבותה השבתאית. אין ספק ששתי המגמות האלה משתלבות ויונקות זו מזו, ולא לחנם מצא רבי אלעזר פלקלש לנכון לפרסם את מכתבו של נפתלי הרץ ווייזל בהקדמה לדרשותיו האנטי־פרנקיסטיות. אין זאת אלא שראה בהבעת דעתו של הפיטן המשכיל — שנגד דעותיו בעניני חנוך הוא יצא בשעתן בחריפות יתרה — תנא דמסייע בהשמטת הקרקע תחת רגלי השבתאים.[85] וצירוף דומה, היינו דחיית השבתאות וניטרול הקבלה על ידי הבלעתה במערכת מחשבה ראציונאליסטית, אנו מוצאים במחיצה אחת ב״עמק השוה״ של אהרון חורין. שכן נזקק חורין למושגי הקבלה בהרצאת הסבריו הפילוסופיים, אלא שאגב השימוש בהם מקפחים המושגים את משמעותם המקורית, מתרוקנים מתוכנם ומפסידים את משקלם.[86]

מכל מקום מתגלית כאן השפעת גומלין בין התמדת השבתאות וההשכלה — אגב הרתיעה מן הקבלה מצד מתנגדי השבתאות — ולא בצדי דרכים כי אם במרכזה של תנועת ההשכלה, בדעתם ובהלך רוחם של ראשיה ומעצבי דמותה.

הערות

1. ראשון ההיסטוריונים של שתי התנועות, פטר בר (Peter Beer, *Geschichte, Lehren und Meinungen aller... religiösen Sekten der Juden und der Geheimlehre der Kabbalah*, 1–2,

בשעה שתשומת לבו היתה מרותקת למשכילים. ידועות דרשותיו הנועזות בשנות תקנ"ט-תק"ס (1799) בגנות הפרנקיסטים[70] (שכנגדו בא כתב ההגנה של לב הניג), שבעקבות פירסומן נאסר על ידי השלטונות לכמה ימים. והנה גם בהזדמנות זו הדגיש את היותו עומד בשתי חזיתות, חזית "המינים והאפיקורסים" שאם כי "המה רעים וטמאים בנפשותם מאד . . . עכ"ז סוג השני קשה מהם והמה פגרי האנשים הרשעים, הנוטים אחר קבלת שוא וטפל משלשה רוח הטומאה, שבתי ברכי' יעקב" היינו שבתי צבי, ברכיה (מסלוניקי) ויעקב פרנק.[71] ונראה שבהערכה זו החזיק הוא עד סוף ימיו. הוא נפטר בשנת 1826, ואף כי במשך הדור הבא עברו על העדה היהודית באירופה מאורעות שעשויים היו לדחוק את ענין השבתאות לקרן זוית, עדיין ראה הוא צורך לחזור על אזהרתו נגדם בשנת 1809.[72] ויש רגלים לדבר שהמאבק נגד השבתאים נמשך גם עוד בעשור השנים הבא.[73] על כל פנים לא ניטשטשו הגבולות בין השבתאים והמשכילים, והם התייצבו נגד המחזיקים במסורת כשני מקורות סכנה נפרדים — וזו המסקנה המעניינת אותנו בהקשר דיוננו.

את האמור למעלה ניתן להחיל גם על אחרון המסתייגים מן השבתאות בפועל, הלא הוא רבי משה סופר, החתם סופר. חכם זה כבר היה נתון בראשו ורובו במאבק בלתי פשרני נגד הזרם החדש, ההשכלה והרפורמה, אולם בראשית דרכו נתקל עדיין גם הוא בשבתאים. תלמידו והביאוגראף הראשי שלו ר' חזקיה פייבל פלויט מספר, כי באי־רצון גדול התיישב רבי משה סופר בנעוריו בעיר פרוסניץ על פי מצות רבו, ר' נתן אדלר הנערץ, כי העיר היתה "מלאה מבני כת שבתי צבי".[74] ואמנם הכיר באחד מאלה על פי התנהגותו, במעשה בזיון בסידור התפלה של רבי יעקב עמדן, ודחק אותו מחבורתו. עוד בשנת תקס"א בהיותו כבר רבה של מטסדורף הביע את דעתו כיצד לנהוג במשפחת מי שרבק באמונת שבתי צבי, ומלהט הדברים ניכר שהנדון נגע לשאלה הלכה למעשה ואותו שבתאי לא משל היה.[75]

נתאמתה לנו איפוא גם מצד זה החפיפה הזמנית בין פעילות כת השבתאים ועלית תנועת ההשכלה. שתי תנועות הפועלות במסגרת חברתית צרה כעדת היהודים בתקופה זו, לא ייתכן שלא תמצאנה נקודות מגע גלויות וסמויות ביניהן. חשיבות החד־זמניות אינה מתמצית בהשפעת המוקדם על המאוחר, השבתאות על ההשכלה. פעילות שני הזרמים במחיצה אחת כששניהם מכוונים לאותה מטרה, לחתור תחת אשיות החברה המסורתית, עשויה היתה להוסיף על כוח המחץ המצורף של שניהם. לא לחנם ראו המתגוננים, שומרי החומות של החברה הישנה, את שתי התנועות כערוכות כנגדה, זו מעמדת חתירה בסתר וזו מזוית הסתערות גלויה. ויתכן כי יש להוסיף על דרך ההשפעה הישירה של השבתאות על ההשכלה השפעת עקיפין, אגב הרתיעה שנוצרה מכל סוגי המסתורין ותורת הנסתר לרגל פריצת הגדרים של הכתות הסוטות.

שהשבתאות היתה פרי גידול הקבלה היה גלוי לעין וידוע ומפורסם לכל. אולם הקבלה היתה המקור שממנו פינה ויתד לכל פירוש אקטואלי של היהדות זה כמה דורות, ברמה התיאולוגית הגבוהה כברמת הדרשנות העממית.[76] והנה בשעה שפרצה תנועת השבתאות — וביחוד כשספיחיה העלו גידולי פרא בתנועת הפרנקיסטים — לא על תנועה זו בלבד יצא הקצף, אלא נשמעו הרהורים נגד השפעת הקבלה בכללה. מחרימי השבתאות כר' יעקב עמדן, רבי יחזקאל לנדא, רבי אלעזר פלקלש ואחרים כיוצא בהם, קראו תגר על העיסוק בקבלה וביקשו לצמצמו ולהרחיקו. לא שהם כפרו באמיתותה של הקבלה אלא שראו את סכנת העיסוק בה גדולה מן התועלת הצפונה בו.[77] אולם הרחקה זו היתה פעולה שלילית בעלמא. הדרישה היתה להסתפק בעיסוק בתורה שבנגלה, מבלי להציע תחליף לתפקיד

השבתאות וההשכלה, שרויות היו בחברה היהודית זו בצד זו כימי שני דורות, הדורות האחרונים של המאה הי״ח ותחילת המאה הי״ט. רצוני להוסיף מימד חדש להבלטת החד־זמניות של שתי התנועות, מימד המתבטא בעובדה שקיימת היתה זהות אישית בין מתנגדיהן, שומרי החומות של היהדות המסורתית. דבר זה נפתח ברבי יעקב עמדן שעיקר מלחמתו היה בשבתאות, אך כידוע נקט עמדת דחיה גם כלפי ההשכלה כשנראית היתה לו פוגמת במסור ובמקובל, כגון בשאלת הקבורה המוקדמת.[61] שני לו לר׳ יעקב עמדן למלחמה בשתי התנועות הוא ר׳ יחזקאל לנדא רבה של פראג. אף מלחמתו של זה בשבתאות קדמה למלחמתו בהשכלה, הרי היה הוא מתנגד מושבע לכל סטייה מקו המסורת (לרבות הסטייה החסידית), אך הוא לא חדל להלחם בשבתאות גם בשעה שסימניה הראשונים של הכפירה הראציונאליסטית החלו מתגלים בתחום ראיתו, היינו בשנות ה־70. בדרשה משנת תק״ל (1770) מדבר הוא על ״שתי כתות ושכיחים בזמננו כתאי כת שבתי צבי שחיק טמיא אלו הם האומרים לרע טוב וכל העבירות אצלם מצוה... וכת השניה הפילוסופים בזמן הזה שאומרים על הבורא כי דרכיו גבהו מאד, רם ונשא למעלה ואינו משגיח בתחתונים ואצלם הכל ביד הטבע״, ואם כי את שתי הכתות דן הוא ברותחין, משפט השבתאים קשה משל הפילוסופים ״עכ״פ כת הפילוסופים עדיפא מכת ש״ץ״.[62] ונראה כי לא זז רבו של פראג ממשפטו זה גם בשעה שפעילות המשכילים משה מנדלסון ונפתלי הרץ וייזל עוררה אותו לצאת נגדם בתקיפות יתרה. אף בדרשתו המכוונת נגדם בשבת הגדול תקמ״ב (1782) חזר והזכיר את בני כת שבתי צבי: ״ובעוה״ר [=ובעוונותינו הרבים] יש בינינו כת השבתאי צבי. אלו עוברים על כל עבירות שבתורה״.[63] ובשיטת הרב הלך גם תלמידו המובהק רבי אלעזר פלקלש. ודבר זה רבותא גדולה יש בה: שהרי בין הרב והתלמיד הבדל של למעלה מדור וכן הבדל של מוצא. רבי יחזקאל לנדא נולד ב־1713 בפולין וראה בנעוריו את תעלולי השבתאים בפודוליה, ואפשר היה לתלות את קנאותו נגד השבתאות בחויית נעוריו. אולם ר׳ אלעזר פלקלש הוא יליד פראג משנת 1754.[64] את סמני המפנה הראשונים בכוון להשכלה יכול היה להרגיש מן הסתם בימי לימודיו בבית מדרשו של רבי יחזקאל לנדא. דרשותיו הראשונות שנשתמרו בידינו נאמרו אמנם לא בפראג כי אם בגויטיין שבמוראביה, שלשם נתקבל הוא כרב בשנת 1779. מובן שבעיירה זו לא היה מקום להטיף נגד ההשכלה. נושאי המוסר של דרשותיו הם העבירות השוטפות של החברה המסורתית שדרשני כל הקהילות היו למודים להזדקק להן. אך לא נעדרות הטפות המכוונות נגד השבתאות. בדרשה של ראש השנה תק״מ (1779) התריע נגד בעלי תקיעה שמביאים אתם תכריכי כתבים לכוון סודות,[65] וכפי שהמחבר בעצמו גילה לאחר זמן, כוונתו היתה נגד השבתאים.[66] ודבר זה מתאים למסורת שאמנם נתקל הוא בשבתאות בקהילתו או בקהילות הסמוכות לה.[67] אלא שעם בואו של ר׳ אלעזר פלקלש לפראג בשנת 1783 נדחקה לכאורה הדאגה לתעלולי השבתאים מפני אימת הפרצה בחיים המסורתיים בעקבות ההשכלה. פלקלש נכנס למערכה נגד המשכילים בכל מאודו, והדרשות של שנות שבתו הראשונות בפראג הן מאבק נמרץ אחד להגנת אורח החיים המקובל ומחאה נמרצת נגד כל נסיון של שנוי. ההטפה היא נגד דקדוק, נגד תרגומו של מנדלסון, נגד ההבחנה בין תורת אלהים ותורת האדם, ההבחנה הידועה של ר׳ נפתלי הרץ ווייזל ב״דברי שלום ואמת״ שלו, ועוד ועוד.[68] ר׳ אלעזר פלקלש הבחין בעצמו בשנוי התמטיקה של דרשותיו, עבירות ישנות מכאן ועבירות חדשות מכאן, הישנות שאמנם הכל דשים בהן כשם שרבים מטיפים נגדן, ולעומתן העבירות החדשות שמוטב שלא באו לעולם לא הן ולא ההטפה נגדן.[69]

גילוי זה של האויב החדש לחברה היהודית היה עשוי לכאורה להאפיל על קיום האויב הישן. אך לא כך היה הדבר. ר׳ אלעזר פלקלש הוסיף לרדות בשבתאים גם

החדש או יותר נכון נבלע בו.״[58] מבקריו של שלום טענו כי בתיאוריה זו ביקש הוא לנטוע את היהדות המודרנית לרבות את שלבה האחרון, הציונות החילונית, על מעינות המיסטיקה היהודית, שהפרנקיזם היה — על אף אופיו ההרסני — גידול פנימי וספונטאני שלה.[59] מן הדין להתעלם מן הנימה הפולמוסית שנתלותה לטענה בפי המערערים, ולבדוק אותה לגופה. ואמנם אמת ונכון שאגב הגדרותיו של שלום הוענקה לאירועים שבתחום התקופה המסורתית משמעות המקרבת אותם במהות לתהליכים מאוחרים, שחלו בתקופת הבתר־מסורתית — ההשכלה, הרפורמה והציונות. התפרקות היהדות המודרנית מעומס המסורת ביחוד בצביונה ההלכי־הנורמטיבי נמצא לה תקדים בהפקעת תוקף המסורת בתורה השבתאית. ואילו קיומה של חברה יהודית תוך ויתור על היסוד התיאולוגי המקראי־תלמודי, דוגמא לו בנסיון הפרנקיסטים להתקיים כקבוצה יהודית נפרדת על אף זניחת עיקרי היהדות המקובלים, וכל המשתמע מהם לגבי אורח החיים היהודי המסורתי. משוואה זו יצרה מעין יחס גומלין בין המוקדם למאוחר. מראית הכתות הסוטות שבתקופה המסורתית כמבשרות את התנועות המודרניות נפל גם עליהן מן ההארה החיובית הנועדה לאלה. ואמנם מתנוצצת בתיאוריו של שלום את האישים והמאורעות של הכתות הסוטות נימה של הבנה והערכה יחסיות, גם בשעה שבמישור האינטלקטואלי והמוסרי הגלוי מזדהה הוא עם השיפוט המקובל על עיוותי המחשבה ועקלקלות המעשים של הסוטים. מצד אחר מופיעים בתפיסתו של שלום שלבי ההתפתחות המודרנית, וביחוד זה של הציונות, לא כתגובת אונס כביכול להשפעות חוץ, כי אם כגידול טבעי שכוחות טמירים בתודעת האומה הצמיחום בבוא שעתם ההיסטורית. אין צורך לומר שהמדובר כאן לא בקביעת עובדות בדרך המחקר האמפירי, כי אם בקונצפציה היסטורית־פילוסופית המעוגנת בתפיסת עולמו של ההיסטוריון והמתגלית כרגיל בין השיטין של כל מפעל היסטוריוגראפי גדול. אולם טעות חסרת שחר היא להניח כי הקונצפציה שולטת כאן במחקר והיא הכתיבה את קביעת העובדות ותיאור המעשים. הנכון הוא שבמישור האישי של ההיסטוריון התפיסה הפילוסופית והמחקר האמפירי יונקים זה מזה. זיקתו של שלום למציאות, חיובה הקיומי של ציונות חילונית ועמדתו הבלתי־פשרנית כלפי האורטודוכסיה על כל גווניה, משתקפות בהצגת מחקריו, ומסתבר שהן שלובות בתודעתו בראיית תולדות ישראל על משמעותן והכוחות הפועלים בהן. שההתמסרות לחקר העבר ותפיסת מעמדו הקיומי של ההווה פירנסו ואף התנו זו את זו בהתפתחותן, היא עובדה ביאוגראפית גלויה לעין. טעותם של מבקרים שעמדו על הזיקה בין השקפת עולמו של ההיסטוריון לבין מניעי התמסרותו למחקר היתה, כפי שהסברתי במקום אחר, כי דיה בקביעת עובדה זו כדי לערער על התוקף המדעי של מסקנות המחבר, שלאמתו של דבר חייבות להבחן על פי כללי הבקורת המדעית שאין כגרשום שלום כופף עצמו להם בכל פינת עבודתו.[60]

VIII

תפקידו של מאמר זה היה לבדוק אחרי ממצאיו של שלום בתחום הנדון. הבדיקה המחודשת העלתה ספק בכמה מהוכחותיו והסבריו, אך היא השאירה את הממצא הבסיסי על כנו, שאמנם פעלו שתי התנועות השבתאות וההשכלה במחיצה זמנית ומקומית אחת, והתמדתה של הראשונה היתה גורם בהתפתחותה של האחרונה. שלום לא נלאה להדגיש את העובדה שפעילות השבתאים בחברה היהודית לא שקעה עם יציאת פרנק וסייעתו מן הכלל בשנת 1759, והוא חזר ואושש קביעה זו בראיות חותכות ונאמנות. משמעותה של קביעה זו היא כי שתי התנועות,

אחרות הותרו לו ביסודי הקבלה״.[52] אם דברים אלה נאמרו על יסוד מעקב מקרוב אחרי התפתלותו של האיש, או אינם אלא סברה ואמדן אין לדעת. יתכן כי אכזבה מכוח הפילוסופיה להשיב על שאלות מטרידות חלק לה בתהפוכה שעברה עליו. מכל מקום וידויו האוטוביואוגראפי רומז למניע נוסף, מתחום הדתי־החברתי.

כמשכיל היה הניג בקורתי לגבי מוריו הרבניים עוד מנעוריו. בקורתיות זו החריפה במשך הזמן, והיא קיבלה תוספת חיזוק בהשפעת העמדה השלילית של חותנו השבתאי. נתברר למשכיל הצעיר כי קיימת בקורת על הרבנות שהיא יסודית ומרחיקת לכת הרבה יותר משהוא העלה על דעתו. בקורת רדיקאלית זו אינה נאחזת במגרעות שהזמן גרמן, חוסר השכלה, קטנוניות, שיטת לימוד מעוותת, שהם גילויי הדורות האחרונים. מנהיגות היהדות הרבנית של כל דורות הגלות נדונה לשלילה, ״כי אנשי האותיות האלה, רוחם ולבבם, מתכתשים בקליפה ואינם מגיעים לעולם לגרעין״.[53] הוא מסתמך בבקורת זו על ספרים ש״מוכרים כספרים קדושים על ידי כל האומה״,[54] וכוונתו כפי שיוצא מהמשך הדברים לדברי ה״רעיא מהימנא״,[55] שקיטרוגו נגד ההנהגה הרבנית בשעתו — תהיה משמעותו המקורית אשר תהיה — נתפרש כאן פירוש קיצוני ספיריטואלי.

כתב ההגנה של לב חנוך הניג נכתב לשם הטית דעת השלטונות לטובת השבתאים בריבם עם רבני העיר, ורבי אלעזר פלקלש בראשם. נוסח הדברים הותאם לטעמם ולמושגיהם של זרים. השבתאים מוצגים כאן כמיעוט דתי נאור שבעלי השלטון הרבני האדוק יורדים לחייהם. הניג מעמיד את השבתאים בשורה אחת עם המשכילים — מנדלסון ווייזל שגם עליהם יצא הקצף — אולם תוך כדי דיבור מודה הוא שאם כי בנעוריו היה חוסה בצלם של אלה, הרי מאז נכנס תחת השפעתו של חותנו זכה הוא להארה חדשה שמשכילים סתם אינם נוטלים בה חלק. באשר אנו מכירים את טיבה של הארה זו, שכן נשתמרו מידו כתבים ברוח הפרנקיסטית המובהקת,[56] אנו מבינים את משמעות וידויו יתר על מה שהוא התכוון לגלות בו. צדק בלי ספק בעל ה״שיחה בין שנת תק״ס ובין תקס״א״ כי בהרכבת הרובד הקבלי על השכלתו הפילוסופית, הוא הוציא עצמו מכלל המשכילים מבחינה חברתית ואינטלקטואלית כאחד.[57] בתודעתו האישית נוצר קשר בין השבתאות וההשכלה, אך לא במתן השבתאות כרקע להשכלה כי אם בכיוון הפוך דווקא. הניג מצא אילן יחס למגמה האנטי־רבנית של ההשכלה בתסיסה המקבילה שהיתה רווחת בשבתאות ובחוגי המקובלים שקדמו לה. לולי דמסתפינא הייתי אומר כי הקדים משכיל־שבתאי זה בהשלכת מגמת ההשכלה לאחור את התיזה של ההיסטוריון המודרני שאנו מנסים כאן להתחקות אחריה.

VII

יציאת היהודים מן הגטו כמוה כגלגולה של החברה האירופאית מן הצביון המסורתי הנוצרי, אינה תהליך חד וחלק. בדרכה נוצרות דמויות בינים, שמתאחדות בהן מגמות הישן והחדש במזיגות משונות ומתמיהות. מכאן הקושי והבעיתיות הרובצים לפתחו של כל נסיון לקביעת הגבול בין התקופות, וגילוי הגורמים שפעלו בקידום התמורות. גרשום שלום נטה לראות בשבתאות בשורת התקופה החדשה לא רק על שום העתיד בהיותה מכשרת את הרקע להשכלה, כי אם בעצם הופעתה ביחוד בצביונה האחרון הפרנקיסט, כדבריו באחת הנוסחאות האחרונות של תיזה זו: ״ניתן לציין את הפרנקיסם כנסיון שבא קודם זמנו, לקבוע מקום ליהדות בצורת חיים אירופאית של ארציות תוך ויתור על תוכנה המיוחד אך לא תוך ויתור על יעודו מבלי להשגיח בכך מה ייותר ממנו. מכיון שנסיון זה נעשה קודם זמנו נשאר הוא תקוע במרד וירד לטמיון במדה שלא נכנס בשינוי צורה בעדן

ואומרים שיש בתוך המאמינים האלה איש אשר מקדם רודף חכמה היה יודע ספר ולשון, הלך בשבילי חקירת האנושי, מתפלסף ומבין בספרים, ועודנו אחד מן המקשי עורף לאמונת ההבלי הזאת״,[41] היינו שאיש מסוים זה היה משכיל מובהק והוא נתפס עתה לשבתאי עיקש. והשואלת תמהה ״היתכן, איש אשר אור החכמה נגה עליו רק רגעים, איש אשר ידיו לו אף מעט בידיעות דברים נשגבים להיות נלוה אל מעשה השגעון הזאת להשען על מקל קנה רצוץ כזה״,[41] כלומר אפילו משכיל מתחיל לא יכיר מקומו בין השבתאים, ולא כל שכן איש כזה שמדובר בו. ״איך נהיתה הדבר הזאת? ומה מעשה האיש ושיחו? כי כן נהפך״.[42] בהמשך הדברים מסבירה השנה היוצאת את פשר התופעה התמוהה, כפי שנשמע להלן. תיאור מעשה האיש ואופיו קוים ממשיים בו, והוא מהוה אתגר להסטוריון לגלות את זהותו. גרשום שלום חשב למצא אותו ביונס וולי ״מנהיגם הרוחני של השבתאים בפראג ומחנכם״.[43] אולם משמצוי בידינו כתב ההגנה של השבתאים מיד לב חנוך הניג וון הניגסברג, הוא חתנו של יונס וולי ובו נתונים ביאוגראפיים על עצמו ועל חותנו,[44] הרי אין כל ספק כי המדובר בו, ר״ל בהניג ולא בוולי. ״בנעורי דאגו הורי היקרים ללימודי במקרא, בדקדוק עברי, בתלמוד ובשפה הגרמנית ובכלל הגעתי לבקיאות מסוימת בספרות יהודית וגרמנית. הורי אף נתנו לי לעסוק בתורת ההגיון ובמטפיזיקה ורכשתי לי נטיה חזקה לפילוסופיה . . . מוקדם גם למדתי להכיר את הבורות ובערות (Unwissenheit und Dummheit) של רבני היום הרגילים שהייתי מצוי אצלם הרבה אך חשבתי אותם יראים ובעלי תמימות (religiös und von frommer Einfalt). צעיר צעיר מאד השיאו אותי לבתו של יונס בער וולי שנחשב לפנים בעיר כמופת לירא שמים, כתיאולוג גדול (היינו תלמיד חכם) ובקי בקבלה ובכלל בספרות היהודית״.[45] בהמשך הדברים מספר הניג כיצד הגיעו הם ללימודי גומלין, החתן קרא באזני חותנו ספרים פילוסופיים ואילו החותן, ״קרא והסביר לי כמה עקרונות תיאולוגיים וקבליים, מקומות סתומים־תמוהים (rätselhafte) בתלמוד ושיטות חכמינו ורוח היהדות״.[46] בין גילוי סודות אלה נכללה בלי ספק תורת השבתאות שיונס וולי היה אמון עליה.

הרי שוולי היה מוחזק תלמיד חכם מקובל והוא הוסיף לעצמו השכלה פילוסופית מסוימת לאחר זמן. ואילו החתן היה תחילה משכיל מושלם, והיה לאחר מכן למקובל שבתאי. מהלך חיים זה תואם בדיוק את מה שנאמר על ידי ״שנת תק״ס״ על האדם שהפך להיות איש אחר. ״ואח״ז כאשר נתקשר האיש הזה עם משפחת כת הקבליי הזאת בקשר אמיץ, והמה מרוח קבלתם האצילו עליו להביט באספקלריא מאירה, מראות זוה״ר והקבלה״,[47] הוא מערבב דברי קבלה ופילוסופיה, ״לקח מלמודי קאנ״ט החוקר וילבש אותם במלבושי זוהר וקבלת הר״י ויצא איש קשה אמונת ההבל, הולך ומתעתע בדברי רעיוני רוח אין בה ממש. אויל הנביא! איש האולת״.[48] במזיגת הפילוסופיה והקבלה ידה של האחרונה היתה כאן על העליונה. בהלך רוחו כבהתנהגותו, יצא הוא מכלל משכיל והיה לשבתאי לכל דבר. ואמנם ידוע על הניג כי הוא ביקר תכופות בחצר הפרנקיסטים באופנבך, ודבריו בכתב ההגנה על הכת הם כמאה עדים שעשה כן מתוך הכרה ולא כנגרר אחרי רצון בני משפחתו.[49]

הפיכת אחד מבני החבורה לשבתאי התמיהה את קהל המשכילים בפראג, ותמיהה זו היא שהניעה את אחד מראשי החבורה — לפי כל הסימנים ברוך ייטלס, כדעתה של רות קסטנברג־גלדשטיין[50] — להזדקק בצורה ספרותית לבעיה. ייטלס מציע הסבר למעשה התמהוני. לדעתו הלך המשכיל הצעיר בגדולות, ״נשא עיניו להררי אל, העמיד שאלה והגביה מעלה״,[51] דרש במופלא ממנו בביקוש פתרונות לבעיות פילוסופיות שהיו למעלה מהשגתו. כשהפילוסופיה לא נענתה לו נכנע הוא לקסם המסתורין ״וכל קושיות וספקות אשר נשארו לו בלתי מתורצות בחכמות

דהיתרא. אין כל סברה או הסבר שיאמר כיצד יכלה דבקות מקורית בשבתאות לשמש דחיפה להלך רוח ולהתנהגות מעין זו.

פקפוק כזה חל לאמתו של דבר לא רק על הבנת דרכו של חורין, אלא לגבי המקרים המעטים של שבתאים ודאיים שאנו מוצאים אותם לאחר זמן במחנה המשכילים. שיימצאו כאלה אינו אלא טבעי, ועדותו של ליאופולד לב על המעמד הנחות שלהם בחברה היהודית מכילה מעין הסבר סוציאולוגי למה עלה מספרם היחסי על סתם יהודים שנתפסו לדרך החדשה. שרפיון הזיקה למצוות המעשיות האופיני לשבתאים מצא את המשכו ביחס דומה של המשכילים ייתכן וייתכן. אולם שיתוף רעיונות או גלגול של נצוצות שבתאים ליסודות אידיאולוגיים של ההשכלה — כדרך שאירע כנראה בחסידות — לא הוכח. הכתבים השתבאים המראים על מגע של בעליהם עם הלך המחשבה של ההשכלה — כגון הדרשות שנתפרסמו על ידי וולפגאנג ווסלי ב־*Orient*, הפירוש הפרנקיסטי ל"הלל", והפירוש ל"עין יעקב" ששלום מייחס אותם לבני משפחת וולי בפראג[33] — מעידים על האפשרות של מזיגה סינקרטיסטית בין רעיונות הנובעים ממקורות שונים ומשונים זה מזה, אך לא על יניקת מערכת המחשבה של המשכילים ממעינות השבתאות. גם ההנחה ששאיפת הפרנקיסטים לשינוי סדרי עולם הכשירתם לקדם בברכה את פני התמורות שנתחוללו בעולם עקב המהפכה הצרפתית ואף לקחת בה חלק פעיל, אין לה סמוכין בעובדות. אם דרשן פרנקיסטי רואה בהפקעת נכסי הכנסיה סימן להגשמת צפיות הכת,[34] אין זה אלא הדרך האופינית לדרשני כל הדורות למצא אישור לדעותיהם במאורעות הימים. היחיד מבין הפרנקיסטים שנסחף לתוך מערבולת המהפכה ממש הוא משה דוברושקה, ששלום הקדיש לו תשומת לב רבה ובאחרונה הציג את תולדות חייו בתיאור מרתק.[35] אמנם המקורות שעליהם נשען תיאור זה מאכזבים, הם מרשים לעקוב אחרי דרכו בפיתוליו החצוניים, אך לא להציץ לנפשו פנימה, לא לדעת את מניעיו ולא לפענח את סוד אישיותו. מן התפקיד שמילא האיש לפני פרוץ המהפכה במסדר האחים האסיאתים, ומהתייחסות חברי המסדר אליו שעלה בידי לתאר בספרי "בונים חופשים ויהודים",[36] מצטיירת דמותו של הרפתקן חברתי וספיריטואלי המנצל כל שעת כושר לפעלתנות לשם פעלתנות, יותר מאשר אישיות בעלת שאיפה לתקון עולם מהפכני.

VI

תערובת של מערכות של מחשבה ממקורות מיסטיים וראציונאליסטיים, ביחוד אצל אינטלקטואליים ממדרגה שניה ושלישית, מצויות הרבה בתקופת המעבר. ספרות הבונים החופשים לדוגמה מלאה מהן, וודאי אין התופעה מיוחדת לפרנקיסטים אפילו במחנה היהודי. דוגמא מובהקת לכך נמצאת בדמותו של אפרים יוסף הירשפלד, ששלום ניתח את ספרו ***Biblisches Organon*** ונטה לייחס לו מוצא פרנקיסטי.[37] אולם לאחר מכן נתגלה כי האיש ישב תחילה כמה שנים במחיצתו של משה מנדלסון בברלין, ורק לאחר מכן נתפס לתיאוסופיה קבלית, נתבסם מתורת הפרנקיסטים ובא אתם גם במגע חברתי.[38] ואין הירשפלד היחיד שדרכו הובילה אותו מן ההשכלה למסתורין השבתאי ולא להפך. שני לו הדמות המרכזית בקרב השבתאים בפראג, כפי שהיא משתקפת בתיאורו של מחבר החוברת "שיחה בין שנת תק"ס ובין תקס"א".[39] השנה היוצאת מציגה את השבתאי הרגיל שכל מעיינו בלימוד הזוהר והקבלה והוא בוחל "בלימוד התלמוד, מאכלות אסורים, דיני נזיקין... הלא אין בם מועיל" ו"בספרי חצונים, חכמות ומדע כי המה מביאים לאפיקורסות והפקר אמונה".[40] על כך משיבה השנה הנכנסת, שנת תקס"א, שאינה בקיאה עדיין בהוואי העולם: "שמעתי שיחת אנשים הנושאים ונותנים בענין הזה

מיתת האדם... אבל כל זמן שיעמוד העולם ויהיו נמצאים אנשים ממין האדם בעולם דברי התורה הזאת לא ימושו מפינו כאשר הבטחנו הוא ית׳".[27]

הניתן ללמוד מקטע זה הוא שחורין הכיר את תורת השבתאים ועקב אחרי מעשיהם — בדבריו רמז לשיגור אגרת הפרנקיסטים משנת 1800[27*]. הוא ייחס לתורתם משקל מספיק שבספר אשר בא לסכם את עיקרי היהדות לפי השקפתו ייחד לה מקום על מנת לדחותה ובחריפות גדולה דוקא.

V

זיקה חיובית בין השבתאות לבין הרפורמה היתה מוטלת בספק לאמתו של דבר אפילו נתאמתת כי אמנם דבק חורין בשבתאים בנעוריו — אלא אם כן ניתן היה להראות כי המעבר מן השבתאות לרפורמה הוא השתלשלות פסיכולוגית סבירה — ובכך אנו מגיעים לבחינת הקשר בין השבתאות לבין ההשכלה והרפורמה מצד תוכנן הרעיוני. גרשום שלום משתמש בהקשר הנדון כאן בשני המושגים השכלה ורפורמה בערבוביה, כאילו הם היינו הך. אך מן הדין להבחין ביניהם בדרך כלל ובשאלת הזיקה לשבתאות בפרט. השכלה בחינת קבלת עקרונות הראציונאליזם תוך הסתלקות מעיקרי היהדות, או הענקת משמעות ראציונאליסטית להם, הוא דבר אחד; ונסיון למצא עקרון הבחנה שעל פיו ניתן לחדש את פני היהדות ולהתאימה לצרכי ההווה — הוא המטרה המוצהרת של הרפורמה על כל פלגיה — הוא דבר שני. המעבר לראשון יכול למצא עידוד ודחיפה מן הירושה השבתאית — כפי שהוסבר למעלה בעקבות דבריו של ליאופולד לב. בשבתאות כבהשכלה מדובר בערעור הסמכות הדתית הישנה, ולפיכך יכול הערעור האחרון לינוק ולהתחזק מכוח הערעור הראשון. ברפורמה מדובר בגילוי סמכות חדשה ליסודות שהוכרז עליהם על ידי המתקנים כעיקרי היהדות מני אז. בעיני המתנגדים היתה הרפורמה פעולה שלילית בעלמא, אולם יוזמיה וחסידיה ראוה כפעולה של חידוש ושיחזור, ואין להעלות על הדעת כיצד יכלו למצא לכך מניעים וסעד בתורת השבתאים או הלך רוחם. במקרה של חורין ידוע כי הגיע לפעילות הרפורמאטורית שלו רק צעד אחרי צעד. את השקפתו היסודית ינק הוא בלי ספק מקריאת ספריו של מנדלסון ושאר משכילי ברלין. הבעיה המרכזית העולה בספרו "עמק השוה" היא הבעיה שהעסיקה גם את מנדלסון, על שום מה יש צורך במערכת המצוות של היהדות אחרי שהרעיונות המתבטאים בהן הולכים ונעשים קנינם של האומות הנאורות.[28] אף תשובתו קרובה לזו של מנדלסון באחת מנוסחאותיה: כל עוד לא הגיע תהליך זה לקיצו, חייבים היהודים לשמור על מערכת הסמלים המיוחדת שלהם.[29] דומים היהודים בין העמים למעמד של כהנים בכל עם — במיצוי מלא של משל זה. אין הכהנים שומרים לעצמם ידיעות יתרות, הללו הן קנין הציבור כולו, אולם הכהנים מצטיינים באורח חיים מיוחד כדי להפגין את קיומן של הידיעות האלה.[30]

על יסוד השקפה כזו ניתן היה לחייב את קיומה של מערכת המצוות, אך לא להצדיק כמובן את פרטיה. חיוב הפרטים או הפיטור מהם היה מותנה בפסיקה של בעלי ההלכה, המופקדים על פי המקובל בעדה היהודית על הדרכת הציבור בספקות המתעוררים אגב שינוי תנאי החיים. בעלי הרפורמה המובהקים הפקיעו את תקפה של ההלכה אם במפורש אם בסמוי, והוא שהזקיק אותם לתור אחרי מקור סמכות חדש בהכרעותיהם. אולם חורין נשאר דבק בהלכה — אלא שהוא ניסה למצות את אפשרויותיה עד תומן,[31] ומתנגדיו — שהרחיקו לכת בכוון האחר והורו שחדש אסור מן התורה[32] — טענו שעבר גם את הגבול של כוחא

גם כאן אין איפוא יותר מאשר שאלות והשערות, וה״עד״ שבו מדובר בדברי ילינק אין בידו עדות כי אם ראיות שאינן חד־משמעיות אף לפי דברי ילינק עצמו.

לא היתה מסורת ממשית בידו של שום אדם בדבר שבתאותו של חורין, ואין המדובר אלא בספיקולאציות בעלמא. הדור הזה שלאחר אמצע המאה כבר צפה לאחור תוך נסיון להבין את תהליך ההתפרקות של החברה המסורתית. ליאופולד לב ראה בשבתאות, כפי ששמענו למעלה, גורם בין גורמי ההתפרקות, ובכך מצאנו את דבריו מבוססים על התבוננות ישירה במציאות החברתית. קרוב היה מעתה להעלות את ההשערה כי אם היה לחורין מגע עם השבתאים בפראג כדברי חבר נעוריו (והוא לא דיבר על יותר מזה) שמא גם הושפע מהם בנטיתו לרפורמה. משנתפרסמו דבריו של לב שנאמרו בזהירות הראויה לציון, באו אחרים וביקשו למצא להם סמך וסעד גם ממקום אחר, ומכאן חקירותיו והרהוריו של אדולף ילינק. השתלשלות הדברים בדרך זו סבירה ומתיישבת עם העובדות יותר מאשר ההנחה שמסורת סמויה מן העין צפה ועלתה על פני השטח. שיקולים כבדי משקל עומדים בדרכו של הסבר מעין זה.

אילו היתה שבתאותו של חורין עובדה, היא לא היתה נעלמת מאויביו־מנדיו שבראשם עומד ר׳ משה סופר, החתם סופר, שכפי שנשמע להלן היה עדיין ער לסכנת המינות השבתאית, אם כי עיקר תשומת לבו היתה כבר נתונה למלחמה במשכילים שואפי החדשות כדוגמתו של חורין. זה היה בעיניו עוכר ישראל, ראש המסיתים ומדיחים בעדת ישראל שבהונגריה.[23] בידו של החתם סופר ודאי שלא היתה ידיעה על שבתאותו של חורין, אלמלי כן לא היה נמנע מלהשתמש בנשק יעיל זה שהיה עשוי להפיל את יריבו במחי יד. והחתם סופר לא היה היחידי שבקש לרדת לחייו של חורין. קדמו להתנגשויותיו של חורין בגלל עמדתו הרפורמיסטית דברי ריבות בעניני הלכה עם רבי מרדכי בנט, רב המדינה של מוראביה, וסייעת מרעיו, ולאחר מכן בגלל פרסום ספרו ״עמק השוה״ שמתנגדיו חשבו למצא בו דעות הגובלות באפיקורסות.[24] אילו נפל חשד של שבתאות על חורין לא היו מתנגדיו — וביניהם היו מיוצאי מוראביה שהכירו מן הסתם את עברו[25] — נמנעים מלהזכירו. בריבו הראשון בשנת תקנ״ח (1798) בדבר התר של דג שהיה ספק בכשרותו נהנה הוא מתמיכת בית הדין של פראג שרבי אלעזר פלקלש היה חבר בו,[26] ומכאן שאותה שעה היתה לו חזקת כשרות בעיני חכמי פראג ולא נמצא בו פגם משום צד. ולהוכחת עקיפין להעדר פגם השבתאות בחורין יש להוסיף את דברי עצמו בסוגיה זו, שלא הושם להם לב עד עתה. בספרו ״עמק השוה״ (פראג תקס״ג) דן חורין ביחודו של עם ישראל שהוא לבדו נצטווה בקיום תרי״ג מצוות, ולפיכך אין זה מגרעת באופים של עמים אחרים אם אין הם נוהגים כמנהגי היהדות:

״אמנם ראוי שיגונה כל מי שהוא מזרע אברהם ומאנשי התורה ועזבו מקור מים חיים הקבלה אשר בידינו מאז מקדם איש מפי איש עד למשה מסיני, וחלפו חק הפרו ברית עולם אשר גבלו ראשונים ושעו לדברי שקר אשר נתחדשו זה איזה מאות שנה לגלות פנים בתורה שלא כהלכה מתוך ההפכה אשר הפכו משפט צדק לראש ולענה, האנשים האלה אשר מבקשים לחדש דת חדש, לא כתורתנו, ולא כתורת העמים שוכני אירופא, מהראוי שעל שער בת ברית תגל חרפתם ותראה ערותם, כי זה שנים העיזו הכת הזה בעזות מצח לחקוק חקקי און ומכתבי פלסתר בכל תפוצות ישראל (מבלי הגלות מקום הכתיבה) לדבר על תורת ה׳ תועה, ויאמרו כי מקרוב קם איש אחד ידוע להם מובחר מהאבות וגדול ממשה ומכל מניחו [צ״ל מניחי] הדתות עד עתה, ויעשו להם תורה חדשה, מוסיפים וגורעים מתורת משה, ואת דת העם אשר לפנים קבלו עליהם אינם עושים, יכירום כל רואיהם כי הם זרע — חולקים על עקרו, כל המודה בתורה יפרוש מהם ודע שמ״ש בנדה ס״א אר״י מצות בטלות לעתיד לבוא, ממקומו הוא מוכרע שמדבר בעולם הנשמות לאחר

על פי עקרונות ההשכלה. נטיה זו עברה גם לדור השני, אף אם נותקה שלשלת המסורת הרעיונית של הכת והבנים לא הוכנסו לסודות שפירנסו את עמדת אבותיהם. מכל מקום הועבר גם לאלה רפיון הזיקה למנהגי היהדות, המצוות המעשיות, המאפיין את שני הזרמים, השבתאות וההשכלה. הקשר המשוער הוא איפוא דו־מסלולי, מסלול סוציאולוגי ומסלול דתי, כשהמסלול הסוציאולוגי, העובדה של דחיקת החשודים לשולי החברה, הוא גלוי לעין, ואילו העתקת הרפיון בקיום המצוות הוא תהליך סמוי ומכל מקום אינו רחוק מן הדעת. ניתן איפוא לחזור על השערתו של שלום תוך מתון־מה של ניסוחה: במקום שההשכלה פגעה בציבור ששבתאים היו שרויים בתוכו, נתגלתה נטיה יתרה אצל השבתאים להגרר אחריה. תחום התגלות התופעה הוא קהילות בוהמיה ומוראביה כעדותו של ליאופולד לב, וביחוד שתי הערים הראשיות פרוסניץ ופראג[18]*.

IV

אם הבחינה הגיאוגראפית הגבילה את היקף התחום שבו עשויים היו להתגלות עקבות ההשפעה של השבתאות על ההשכלה, בחינת המישור האישי תצביע על צמצום ההשפעה מצד הרובד החברתי ששם נתגלו העקבות. מבין עשרות ואולי מאות פעילי ההשכלה והרפורמה מן השורה הראשונה והשניה, סופרים, הוגים, מורים ורבנים — השכבה המנהגת של שתי התנועות — לא נמצא אלא אחד, ר׳ אהרון חורין, שנפל עליו חשד שינק ממקורות שבתאים, וכפי שיתברר להלן חשד זה נשען על עדות מפוקפקת שקרוב לודאי שאין בה ממש. שלום ב־*Major Trends* שלו פותח את התיזה בדבר הזיקה בין השבתאות לרפורמה במשפט זה: ״סביב ל־1850 עדיין היתה חיה מודעות בדבר הקשר בין השבתאות לרפורמה בחוגים מסויימים״.[19] בהמשך הוא מדבר על ״מסורת שאין להטיל ספק באותנטיות שלה״, ואשר לפיה היה אהרון חורין, חלוץ היהדות הרפורמית בהונגריה, חבר של קבוצה שבתאית בפראג בנעוריו. שלום הניח איפוא כי קיימת היתה מסורת בדבר זיקת הרפורמה לשבתאות, והעדויות שבאמצע המאה — של ליאופולד לב ושל אדולף ילינק שמיד נשמע עליהן — הן שריד של מסורת כזו. אולם אין עקבות למסורת כזו לא בכתבי אנשי הרפורמה ולא בכתבי מתנגדיהם, ועיון מדוקדק בדבריו של לב ושל ילינק יוכיח שאף הם לא העלו אלא השערות וחשדות ולא התיימרו להשען על מסורת.

הענין נפתח בהערת אגב של ליאופולד לב תוך מסירת פרטים מתולדות חייו של חורין בביאוגראפיה שפירסמה בשנת 1861, שבע עשרה שנה לאחר מות חורין, בשם בדוי.[20] חבר נעורים של חורין, הירש בק, לימים רבה של סגדין, ״סיפר לא פעם כי חורין ישב בפראג זמן ניכר בבית שנחשד על שבתאות״, ועל כך מעיר לב ״ייתכן כי שם הוטל הגרעין הראשון למגמה הרפורמטורית העתידה בנפשו; אך ודאי שבנעוריו לא היה הוא מודע לדבר זה״.[21] לב עצמו לא ראה איפוא בידיעה שבידו יותר מאשר יסוד להשערה בדבר השפעה בלתי מודעת על הנער שבשובו מפראג ״לשבע הקהילות״ שבמערב הונגריה היה בן תשע עשרה שנה, ואותו זמן הלך בתלם המסורת ללא כל היסוס או סטיה. הענין צף ועולה שנית במכתב של אדולף ילינק ללב מ־27.4.1863 שוב בצורת השערה, ״האם היה חורין מעיקרו חבר השבתאים כפי שנאמר לי? לוא היה באמת (Wäre er es gewesen) הייתי מבין כיצד התעורר דוקא הוא כראשון באוסטריה לרפורמה. אם הנך רואה את הדבר כחשוב, מן הדין היה שתשיב על השאלה המוצגת בצורה פומבית.״ בהערה שבסוף המכתב מוסיף ילינק ״על השבתאות של חורין יש לי עד שנותן הוכחות משונות (der merkwürdige Beweise gibt). השאלה היא אם מן החכמה היא לדון עתה בנקודה זו.״[22]

מדיעות מסתוריות", אלא שהם מצאו ביוצאי הכתות המסטיות "אנשי צבא למלחמתם החדשה".[10] מכל מקום לחיזוק התיזה מן הצד הגיאוגראפי מציין שלום את שתי הערים פרוסניץ והמבורג כמקומות "שהיו במאה הי"ח מרכזי התעמולה השבתאית וזירה למאבקים מרים בין האורטודוכסים והכופרים או אוהדיהם", וערים אלה הן, בתחילת המאה הי"ט בין "המבצרים הראשיים של התנועה הרפורמית".[11] אולם מכיון שההשכלה והרפורמה פרצו גם במקומות שחסרו רקע שבתאי, אין בזימון זה כשהוא לעצמו כוח הוכחה של כלום. רק אילו ניתן להראות שיוזמי הרפורמה בהמבורג באו מחוגי השבתאים לשעבר היה לזימון הגיאוגראפי משקל ומשמעות, אולם זיהוי כזה לא הוצע מעולם והוא רחוק מן הדעת ומן המציאות. שמות המשפחות של מייסדי ה"היכל" בהמבורג ידועים והללו הותקפו והואשמו על ידי מתנגדיהם, אבל איש לא הטיל בהם את פגם השבתאות.[12] יתר על כן, לא הוכח ואף לא נטען מעולם שקהילת המבורג קני שבתאים היו שרויים בקרבה בדורות שקדמו לרפורמה. עם היות המבורג זירת המחלוקת הגדולה בין רבי יעקב עמדן ורבי יונתן אייבשיץ בגלל חשד של שבתאות, הרי תומכיו של רבי יונתן מבני קהילתו, רוב רובם אם לא כולם עמדו לימינו לא משום שהיו שבתאים כמותו, אלא משום שהאמינו לו כי אף הוא היה נקי מאותו עוון.[13]

שונה המצב בדבר קהילת פרוסניץ. עיר זו "היתה מלאה מבני כת שבתאי צבי אשר שתל שם ליבל פרויסטיץ שר"י (שם רשעים ירקב)" כדבריו של רבי חזקיה פייבל פלויט,[14] והעובדה ידועה ומוכחת ממקורות רבים ובלתי תלויים זה בזה.[15] אף נכון כי פרוסניץ היתה מן המתקדמות ביותר בין ערי הקיסרות האוסטרית, ורבו בה המשכילים ושוחרי החדשות בעניני דת בשנות התעוררות הרפורמה בתקופת הליברליזם משנות השלושים של המאה הי"ט. לכך אפשר לכאורה למצוא הסבר במעמדה הכללי של העיר, שכן זכתה פרוסניץ בהתפתחות כלכלית משגשגת יתר על ערי מוראביה האחרות, והקדימה את עיר הבירה ניקולשבורג בתהליך המודרניזאציה.[16] מכל מקום אם הוכשרה הקרקע להתפרקות מן המסורת על ידי התנאים הסוציאליים הכלליים, אין זאת אומרת שלא פעלו גם גורמים אחרים באותו כיוון. ליאופולד לב אף הוא היה מיוצאי מדינת מוראביה — ולו עינים להתבונן וחוש היסטורי מובהק לקשור נימה בנימה — חשב למצא גורם כזה ברקע השבתאי של אישים ומשפחות שלמות — ועדותו של לב שמשה משענת עיקרית לקביעתו של שלום לגבי השבתאות של אהרון חורין, ראש וראשון למנהיגי הריפורמה בהונגריה כפי שנראה עוד להלן. ליאופולד לב הוא איפוא מעין עד מלך בכל הפרשה הזאת, ומן הדין לבחון את דבריו בהקפדה. "במוראביה ובבוהמיה שמעתי עוד בעצמי שמות של אנשים משכילים (unterrichtete Männer) אשר זכו להערכה רבה בגלל ידיעותיהם והתנהגותם הישרה, אך אשר נמנע מהם מלזכות במשרה ציבורית כלשהי משום שפגם השבתאות דבק בהם. אחדים מאלה הכרתי באופן אישי. שבתאים אמיתיים או מדומים אלה קידמו בחוגיהם השכלה והוראה. השפעתם גברה ככל שהזקינו ככל שנזהרו במעשיהם וככל שפחת החשש מפני התפשטות השבתאות".[17] ועל העיר פרוסניץ הוא אומר במקום אחר כי "השבתאות השאירה אחריה יסודות אנטי־רבניים חשובים. אף יש מי שחושב להבחין כי בני השבתאים, אף כי אין הם יודעים את הזוהר אלא לפי שמו ואין הם בקיאים בעקרונות הכת הכפרנית כל עיקר, בכל זאת ירשו מאבותיהם רשלנות מסוימת בהקפדה על מנהגים רבניים. אומרים כי יש שהגיעו על ידי העיון בלסינג ובמנדלסון לאותן המסקנות שאבותיהם הגיעו אליהן על ידי העיון בזוהר".[18]

הגרעין הודאי שבהתבוננות זו במציאות ההיסטורית הוא קיומו של מיעוט נדחק ומורחק מפעילות ציבורית מחמת חשד של שבתאות, מצב שיש בו כדי להסביר את נטיתם היתרה של בני מיעוט זה להצטרף לחותרים לחידוש פני הקהילה היהודית

II

נדמה כי יש להעמיד את חוליות המגע בין השבתאות והחסידות שחוקרי שתי התנועות הצביעו עליהן על שלוש שהן ארבע. עיקרי הדברים מפורשים כבר בספרו הגדול של גרשום שלום *Major Trends in Jewish Mysticism* — התחום הגיאוגראפי ששם עלתה החסידות, פודוליה שבפולין, היה אחד המחוזות שתנועת השבתאות בגלגולה הפרנקיסטי נאחזה בו ביותר.[6] קהילות פודוליה היו מצוינות בקבוצות סתר בעלות מתח דתי ומשיחי, וכשבצדן עלתה תנועה דתית בעלת מגמה ציבורית גלויה, קרוב היה להניח כי האחרונה לא יצאה לאור עולם מבלי לספוג לתוכה גרעיני רעיונות והלכי רוח מן הכת שקדמה לה, וכמובן מתוך סיגול תכונותיה לצרכי הזרם החדש והמחודש. שנית, נמצא צד שוה לדפוסי ההתנהגות של בני הכתות ושל חברי התנועה וביחוד של טיפוס המנהיג השולט בכתות ובתנועה. בני הכת כבני התנועה מוצאים פורקן בהשגי שיאים בהתלהבות לעת מצוא — אם כי במדה שונה של שמירת הסייגים המוכתבים על ידי מסורת הדת היהודית. מנהיגי השבתאים החל משבתי צבי וגומר ביעקב פרנק ינקו את כוחם מהארה פנימית שהעניקה להם סמכות דתית כלפי עדתם, וכיוצא בהם נשענו ראשי התנועה החסידית, הבעש״ט ותלמידיו על סגולתם האישית החריסמטית — להבדיל מסמכות המנהיג המקובל עד אז, הרב התלמיד חכם שבקיאותו במסורת ויכולתו לפרשה העמידו אותו בראש עדתו.[7] כצנור לדעות השבתאים למחנה החסידים שמשו כתבי הכת עצמם שכמה מהם עברו לידי ראשוני החסידים, ובין אם עמדו אלה על טיבם ובין אם לא, ודאי ששאבו מהם השראה לביסוס תורתם ומגמתם.[8] דוגמא מובהקת לקליטתו של רעיון שבתאי תוך מיתון משמעותו נמצא בתורת ירידת הצדיק מגדולתו לעת מצוא. השבתאות פיתחה תיאוריה של צידוק החטא כהקדמה לתיקון האדם והעולם למען חפות על חטא ההמרה של המשיח וההולכים בעקבותיו ועושים כמעשיו. החסידות קלטה את הרעיון אך נטלה את עוקצו; ירידת הצדיק כתיקון הבא בעקבותיו היתה לאירועים פנים־נפשיים, ספיריטואליים, ואילו צידוק החטא כפועל אבד זכרו.[9]

סיכום זה של חקר תלות החסידות בשבתאות לא בא כאן לגופו, ודאי לא כדי לבחון את תקפו לפרטיו. הללו היו נושא לדיון בספרות המחקר, ואם כי יש שיצא ערעור על פרט זה או זה, עיקרי הדברים נראים כיום שרירים ומאוששים. לנו ישמשו מסלולי המחשבה של חקר היחס בין השבתאות לחסידות נקודות מוצא לשאל אם הקבלות כיוצא בה נמצאו פוריות ומנומקות גם בחקר היחס בין השבתאות לבין ההשכלה והרפורמה.

III

נפתח בשאלת התחום הגיאוגראפי ששתי התנועות מסוגלות היו להזדקק שם זו לזו. והנה שונה כאן המצב תכלית שינוי מאשר בפגישה בין השבתאות והחסידות. חפיפה גיאוגראפית של שתי התנועות נמצאת בבוהמיה ובמוראביה — בשני המחוזות האלה התנהלה פעילות שבתאית ערה כל ימות המאה הי״ח, והם היו מסוף המאה והלאה זירה רחבת ידים גם להשכלה ובמקצת אף לנסיונות רפורמה. אולם חפיפה גיאוגראפית זו חסרה לה החשיבות שיש ליחס לתופעה המקבילה שבפודוליה ששם עלתה החסידות במחיצת הכתות השבתאיות, ואילו בוהמיה ומוראביה אינן מקום עליית ההשכלה כי אם מקומות שהיא נקלטה שם בבואה מן המרכז הברלינאי, וברלין עצמה חסרה רקע שבתאי מכל וכל. עובדה זו לא נעלמה כמובן מעיניו של גרשום שלום, והוא נזהר שלא לתלות את עליית ההשכלה בגורם השבתאי שכן ״מנהיגי התנועה ה׳ברלינאית׳ לא היו שבתאים ולא הופשעו כלל

לשאלת הקשר בין השבתאות לבין ההשכלה והרפורמה

י. כ״ץ

I

חקר השבתאות משקל ומשמעות נתייחדו לו מעבר לקביעת העובדות הנוגעות לפרשה היסטורית זו לבדה. רק כמאה שנה מפרידה בין חייו של שבתי צבי לבין עלייתן של שתי התנועות: החסידות במזרח אירופה וההשכלה במערבה. ושתי תנועות אלה מהוות חידוש ומפנה בתולדות האומה, אליבא דכולי עלמא. קרוב היה איפוא לשאל אם סדר הזמנים הוא מקרה בעלמא או שמא קיים בין המוקדם — השבתאות — והמאוחר — החסידות וההשכלה — גם קשר סיבתי. ואם בימים הראשונים שתנועת השבתאות נדונה רק כלאחר יד לא עלתה מחשבה זו אלא פה ושם בדרך הברקה,[1] הרי מאז הפך השבתאות לאחד מנושאי המחקר הנכבדים הועלתה שאלת הקשר בין השבתאות לבין החסידות וההשכלה במכוון ובמלוא הכרה בחשיבותה. גרשום שלום קיבל את הזיקה בין השבתאות לחסידות כהשערה הראויה לעיון, וההשערה נתאמתה לו ולתלמידיו שהלכו בעקבותיו בנקודות לא מעטות. התיזה בדבר הקשר בין השבתאות וההשכלה הוא ניסח ניסוח פרוגראמאטי במסה ההיסטורית המזהירה שלו ״מצוה הבאה בעבירה״ משנת תרצ״ז (1937),[2] הוא חזר על ניסוחו זה פעמים אחדות[3] ואף ביקש לתת לו ביסוס לעת מצוא.[4]

שלא כהשערת העבודה בדבר הקשר בין השבתאות לחסידות שנשארה ענין לחוקרים לענות בה, לאמתה ולהעמידה על דיוקה, באה התיזה בדבר אבהות השבתאות לגבי ההשכלה למחלוקת הוגים וסופרים בעלי השקפה מנוגדת בדבר המעמד ההיסטורי־פילוסופי של ההווה. התיזה קסמה למי שביקש להעניק אילן יחס היסטורי ליהדות חילונית שגילגולה האחרון הוא הציונות. ואילו מי שההשכלה והציונות היו דומות עליו כהסתלקות מהפכנית מן היהדות הקלאסית ראה בנסיון לגשור על פני התהום שביניהן על ידי חולית הבינים של השבתאות המצאה מלאכותית ומחשבת שוא. ולא לחנם עלה לתיזה זו כפי שעלה, כי בעל התיזה עצמו פרץ בה את גדרי המחקר הפוזיטיבי. גרשום שלום עיטר את מחקריו בענין השבתאות בהערות אגב חוזרות ונשנות שהשתמע מהן כי הוא תופס את השבתאות כהתפתחות פנימית הרומזת לאפשרויות הסטוריות שעתידות היו להתקיים לאחר זמן — סברה ספקולטיבית שלא ניתן לאמתה או להפריכה. נשוב לצד זה של הענין בסוף דברינו. עיקר מטרתו של מאמר זה הוא לבחון את הבסיס העובדתי של התיזה, היינו אם אמנם היוותה השבתאות גורם בעליית ההשכלה והרפורמה הלכה למעשה — שאלה שבעלי הפלוגתא האמורים לא היו מעונינים ולא מוסמכים לדון בה. ואמנם מוטלת חובת הברור של שאלה זו על ההיסטוריונים העוסקים בתולדות ההשכלה והרפורמה, אך הם לא יצאו ידי חובתם זו, הם לא אישרו את ההשערה אך גם לא סתרו אותה.[5] מאמר זה בא למלא חסרון זה והוא ייעשה תוך נסיון להשוות את מצב הדברים בשני המישורים, הזיקה בין השבתאות לבין החסידות מכאן והזיקה בין השבתאות לבין ההשכלה והרפורמה מכאן.

ברורים ועקרונות משותפים והשואפת להשפעות תרבותיות־חינוכיות מסוימות.

ברור, כי לגבי עיבוד שיטתי של רעיונות יסודיים ותפיסות היסטוריות־פילוסופיות, נהא מצווים להפריד בין החיבורים במקום להתייחס אליהם כאל חטיבה ספרותית מאוחדת. עבודה זו הולכת ונעשית בקפדנות רבה ע״י מרק ספרשטיין הנ״ל.

נספח ב׳ (ע׳ דף עה, הערה 7)

יוסף פרלס בספרו הגרמני על הרשב״א, עמ׳ 74, הערה 100, מזכיר את דברי ר׳ יעקב ן׳ חביב, המאסף של עין יעקב, על אודות ספר חדש, פירוש לאגדות, מאת ר׳ יצחק בר׳ ידעיה. ן׳ חביב משער אח״כ שהמחבר הוא בנו של ידעיה הפניני. ״ובודאי שמעיד על גודל כחו בלשון הלציי כי אולי הוא בנו של הרב ידעיה שסדר מאמר בחינת העולם״. על ספר כזה לא ידענו ולא שמענו ואולי זהו הפירוש שאנו עוסקים בו — הרי כמה מפרשי אגדה איכא בשוקא במאה הי״ד? בכל אופן, דברי ן׳ חביב קולעים ומאפינים את פירושי הפניני וכדאי להביא משפטים מספר: ״הלא ראיתי ספר חדש מכונה לחכם פלוסוף הר׳ יצחק בר׳ ידעיה לפרש אגדות בקצת מסכתות... ורוב מה שכתב בפירושו הוא בדרך המשל לחומר וצורה. ובמקומות רבים אינו חושש אם סוגית הגמרא היא סותרת דבריו לגמרי. ובמאמרים הלציים הם ענינים ערבים אבל אינם מסכימים כלל דברי בעלי המאמרים להיות מבואר נגלה שלא כוונו כלל לפירושו״ (עין יעקב, ברכות נה ע״ב, ירושלים תשכ״ה, עמ׳ 172). ובסוף המסכת (עמ׳ 216) מביא ממנו ״פירוש נאה וערב בענין מדת הפרישות״... ״והתועלת המושג אצלי שכפי העיון הראשון הוא ענין ערב... אבל אינני מסכים אל אמתת כוונת המאמר... ועוד היתה לי כוונה שנית בכתיבתי פה דבריו למען יראו איך הוא מאריך בדברים... אבל אין בו ממש כל כך כי רוב מה שכתב הוא אריכות דברים בבלתי צורך. עוד היתה לי כוונה ג׳ להראות איך כוונתו לחלוק כנגד הכללים המאומתים לחז״ל כמו היזק עין הרע המאומת בדבריהם. וכוונתו לסתור סברת מציאות השדים...״ בהמשך דבריו הוא משווה את גישתו של ר׳ אברהם ביבאגו לר׳ יצחק בר׳ ידעיה. ״שניהם כתבו דרושים פילוסופיים אשר הוא עצמו יודה שלא כוון להם בעל המאמר״ (עמ׳ 217). הדברים מעמידים אותנו על עובדת הסלקציה, הסגנון הלצי (ר״ל ארוך ושוטף), וטיב הפירוש העושה את שלו על אף ההקשר הספרותי הברור, המגמה השכלתנית ידה על העליונה, וכבר אמר ר״ש אבן תבון, מאמר יקוו המים, עמ׳ 17: ״ואע״פ שאנו מוציאים לשון מאימתי נבראו המלאכים מפשוטו, לפי המפורסם ממנו להמון, טוב לדחוק הלשון מלדחוק המציאות״.

(הרבה דנתי עם תלמידי בפרשה זו, עוד לפני שניגשתי לבדוק את כה״י, וייזכרו כולם לטובה. פרופ׳ דב ספטימוס ופרופ׳ דב קופרמן אף כתבו עבודות סמינריוניות על הנושא.)

היסטורי עקום: "האמת היא כי אין להאשים החבר הנז' שפירש האגדה הזאת וגם לא החכם ר' ידעיה בשבחו אותו, כי הדעות האמתיות המקובלות לא נפוצו שם בארצותם ולא נתגלה להם מצפונם ועדיין לא יצאו לאורה ספרי הרב הגדול הנחמני ז"ל אשר בהם ירמוז דברי חכמים וחידותם".

80. כ"י לסנהדרין, עמ' 42.

81. הוריות, הוצאת גנחובסקי, עמ' י"ד. דוגמה ברורה למתיחות יש למצוא בפירושו למכות כב ע"ב: "כמה טפשי שאר אינשי. . . " הולך הוא ומדגיש את עליונות החכם המפרש על הספר המתפרש: "הספר ההוא הוא הקדוש והנכבד בעיניו ית' לא באה הצואה לעם שיקומו מפני הספר ולא הטריח על זה הגוי כלו . . .". בכל זאת, בסוף דבריו מוסיף: "ולא בא לגנות (!) האדם אשר יקום מפני ספר התורה חלילה, כי זה מחויב מכל איש ישראל לכבדה. . . " וע' רמב"ם, הלכות ספר תורה, פרק י, ט.

82. משנת רבי אליעזר או מדרש ל"ב מדות, הו"ל ה. ענעלאו, ניו יורק, תרצ"ד, עמ' 35 וההערה שם.

83. בכ"י למכות, עמ' 147 מהרהר הפניני אחר הדין של עדים זוממים — *topos* שכלתני ידוע: "ולא ירדתי לסוף דעתם ולא הבנותי כונתם ללכת בזה בהפך שאר העונשים הכתובים בספר תורת משה רבן של נביאים ודבריהם אלו דברי אלקים חיים כי הם הבינו כוונת התורה והשיגוה על בוריה ונתחדשה להם הלכה לדבר הזה מצד הקבלה ואין להרהר אחר דבריהם אלו . . .".

84. על דרכי הספירטואליזציה של הקבלה ויחסה ל"רוחניות המשתוללת" של הפילוסופים, ע' ג. שלום, ראשית הקבלה, עמ' 135–136.

85. ע' ספר האשכול, ב', עמ' 47. גם הלל מוירונה גם ר"מ המאירי מקיימים הבחנה זו.

86. מגן אבות, עמ' כ'. על דעת יחיד באגדה, ע' גם אגרת הרמב"ם לחכמי פרובנס, הוצאת א' מרקס, ב־*HUCA*, כרך ג', עמ' 356. וכן ר"י אברבנאל, הקדמה, ספר יהושע (ירושלים, תשט"ו), עמ' י"ג, "לא אמנע מהראות החולשה שבאה בדבריהם במקומות שהיו דבריהם על דרך הפירוש ולא היו מקובלים אצלם". ע' י. פולקר, עזר הדת, עמ' 27.

87. ויכוח ר' יחיאל מפריס, הו"ל ה. מרגליות, עמ' 13.

88. ויכוח הרמב"ן, הו"ל ח. שעוועל, כתבי הרמב"ן, א, עמ' ש"ח.

89. הלבנון ה' (1868), עמ' 472 הזכיר את הדברים הזכרה בעלמא. ה. ענעלאו, מנורת המאור, חלק ד, המבוא האנגלי, עמ' 16.

נספח א'

תלמידי מרק (מרדכי) ספרשטיין העוסק בפירושי האגדות לר"י הפניני מסר לי כי על יסוד בדיקה מדוקדקת של כה"י וניתוחם הרעיוני־סגנוני נוטה הוא להעלות השערה כי פירושי האגדות לתלמוד ופירושי האגדות למדרש רבה, תנחומא וכו'. . . אינם ממחבר אחד. סבור הוא, וטעמיו ונימוקיו עמו, כי פירושי האגדות למדרש רבה וכו' הם מעטו של ר"י הפניני וזהותו של המחבר השני מהווה לעת עתה חידה. כל הפרשה טעונה בירור וליבון. ברם, אם יש רגליים להשערה זו — והדברים נראים לי מכמה בחינות — אפשר להסתייע בה בכדי לסלק תמיהות אחדות ולברר שני עניינים חשובים.

(1) אסור להיחפז ולהיתלות בבוקי סרוקי — לייחס טעות או אי־דיוק לר' יעקב אבן חביב. מסתבר שהוא אמנם השתמש בפירוש אחר שלא היה מיוחס לר"י הפניני כלל. (2) אם נניח שר' יצחק, מחבר דנן (ע' למטה, נספח ב'), אינו בנו של הפניני אלא מחבר מהדור הקודם, אזי תיפתר הבעיה המסובכת של סדר הזמנים בתיאור המפורסם של ישיבתו של רבנו משולם. אם רבנו משולם נולד ב־1190 ור' ידעיה נולד בערך ב־1270 (ע' למשל אצל ש. אסף, מקורות לתולדות החינוך, כרך ב', עמ' לג, ורבות התלבטו החוקרים בענין זה) נמצאנו למדים שרבנו משולם היה זקן מופלג ובכל זאת עדיין יושב בישיבה, ולא נס לחו בשיבה כזאת. אם התיאור הזה נכתב בדור קודם, הכל על מקומו יבוא בשלום.

נדמה לי כי גופו של מאמרי, המנסה לאפין את הפרשנות הפילוסופית של האגדה, דרכיה ומגמותיה, ולעמוד על מקומה בפרשנות האגדה בכלל, נשאר עומד על כנו. שכן מוכח הדבר בעליל כי הצד השוה שבין כל הפירושים הוא גדול ואף מכריע. העובדה שדברי אבן חביב כחם יפה לגבי **כל הפירושים** מראה שהמדובר באסכולה פרשנית המושתתת על קווי־יסוד

לב בעם למים חיים נובעים אשר לא יכזבו בקיץ ובחורף... **כמו שבארנו בהרבה מקומות בחקירתנו זה**".

62. פלקירה, מורה המורה (פרעסבורג, 1837), עמ' 5. ביטוי מובהק לזה — שבכחו לשמש בנין אב לכל הנאמר בסוגיה זו על המרחק בין ההמון והחכמים — נמצא ברמב"ם, הלכות שבועות, ה, כ"ב.

63. ע' מאמרי "Religion and Law" בתוך הקובץ *Religion in a Religious Age* בעריכת ש.ד. גוייטיין, עמ' 83–69, ובפרט עמ' 77.

64. מאור עינים, אמרי בינה, פרק ט"ו. השוה גם דבריו האופיניים של רנ"ק, מורה נבוכי הזמן, הוצאת ש. ראבידוביץ, עמ' רמ"ו–רמ"ז. על עמדתו של ר' שמואל בן חפני גאון ביחס לפירוש האגדה, ע' מאמרו של מ. צוקר "לפתרון בעית ל"ב מדות ומשנת ר' אליעזר", ב־*PAAJR* כרך כ"ג (1954), עמ' 14–13.

65. הדברים רומזים להקדמת הרמב"ם למורה נבוכים.

66. מאמר על הדרשות, מהדורת ר. מרגליות, מלחמות השם, עמ' צ"ח.

67. ספר תגמולי הנפש, עמ' כ"ה.

68. צוואות גאוני ישראל, בעריכת י. אברהמס, כרך א', עמ' 155. הניסוח על "זרע אברהם אבינו" מזכיר את דברי הרמב"ם, הלכות איסורי ביאה, י"ט, י"ז. גם ספר הסוד של אבן כספי, הו"ל י. לאסט, ספר משנה כסף, א, עמ' 2.

69. מנחת קנאות, ל"ט (עמ' 86).

70. חידושי רשב"א לאגדות, ברכות, עמ' ל.

71. פרדס רמונים, הקדמה, ב.

72. ע' לעיל דף עו, הערה 18.

73. הדברים נתפרסמו באהל דוד, רשימת כתבי היד בספרית ששון, לונדון, עמ' 43–742. ציין את זה כדרכו הר"ש ליברמן, שקיעין, עמ' 82. ע' גם שו"ת הרדב"ז (ווארשא, 1882), חלק ג, ס' אלף–ס"ו (תרמ"א) המתרעם על הרד"ק שאמר כי דברי אגדה רחוקים מן השכל, "וטובה היתה לרב ז"ל השתיקה ולא יזכר דברי האגדה כיון שלא ידע ליישב אותם".

74. השגת הראב"ד, הלכות תשובה, ג, ז. השוה ספרי על הראב"ד, עמ' 282 ואילך.

75. מורה נבוכים, ג, ל"א; פירוש המשנה, הקדמה פרק חלק, מהדורת י. קאפח, עמ' ר"א.

76. צוואת גאוני ישראל (ע' למעלה, הע' 68), א, עמ' 152. ר"י אנטולי, מלמד התלמידים, פרשת ואתחנן כבר טבע את המטבע הזו: "אין ראוי לאמת שתהא ביישנית". והרי שוב ענין היוצא ללמד על פרשיות רבות בתולדות ישראל. מצד אחד, הפילוסופיה נפוצה ונדרשה בראש כל חוצות, מצב שהעלה את חמתם של ר' אבא מארי, הרשב"א וסיעתם. הללו צווחו כברוכיא נגד המשכילים הדורשים לפני עם ועדה, "כמו שעשו רבים מהדרשנים בזמנינו זה" (מנחת קנאות, פרק ד', עמ' 7). אפשר גם להצביע על עובדות ספרותיות מענינות: ספר הפסקים הגדול, ארחות חיים לר' אהרן הכהן מלוניל, מביא בראשית הספר מדברי אנטולי במלמד התלמידים. ברם, מאידך, לא שבעו הפילוסופים רצון, נדחפו והומרצו לפרסם דעותיהם ואמונותיהם בכדי לשמור על ייחודו הדתי של העם לפי רוחם וטעמם. כך, למשל, קובל גם אבן כספי על השפלת קרנה של החכמה (צוואות, עמ' 154) — במיוחד צר לו על הזנחת הלימוד בספר המורה — ובה בשעה התפשטה הפילוסופיה.

77. מורה נבוכים, הקדמה. מעניין כי גם הרמ"א הכין פירוש אגדות וכבשו — "מגלת סתרים שלי שהם פירוש האגדות" (ע' א. זיו, הרמ"א, עמ' 66) והשוה לשונו של אברבנאל, דף עה הערה 4 לעיל. ע' שו"ת חוות יאיר, ו.

78. ע' י. תשבי "אגדה וקבלה בפירושי האגדות של ר' עזרא ור' עזריאל מגירונה", מנחה ליהודה, ירושלים תש"י, עמ' 170 ואילך.

79. השאלה מתעוררת — אבל קשה להשיב עליה — עד כמה יש פה אפילו תגובה ותשובה לנסיון הקבלי להאחיז את תורת הסוד בדברי האגדה. באגרת ההתנצלות מציין הפניני כי אחת מתועלותיה של הפילוסופיה היא סתירת האמונה הנפסדת בתורת הגלגול — אמונה קבלית מובהקת (ולאו בכדי נטפל לזה באריכות ר' אביעד שר שלום בהקדמה לאמונת חכמים). בתיאורו של ישיבת ר' משולם אין כל ספק שהפניני משתמש ב"מעשה מרכבה", ככינוי לפילוסופיה ולא לקבלה. בכל זאת נראים הדברים שבדרום צרפת לא היוותה הקבלה אתגר חמור לפילוסופיה בתקופה זו, תקופת הפריחה בספרד. מעניין לציין כי ר' יחיאל מפיסא, מנחת קנאות, עמ' 15 הרגיש בבעיה והפגיש את הפילוסופיה והקבלה במראה

44. השוה מורה נבוכים, חלק ב, פרק לב.

45. שם, ג, מ״א. והשוה תשובות הרמב״ם, מהדורת י. בלאו, רי״ח (בענין קטלנית).

46. ר״י אבן כספי, תם הכסף, דרוש ה׳, עמ׳ 32, מפתח השקפה זו ״על דרך האמת אין בדבורו ממש ואינו סבה כלל בעצם, אבל עכ״פ יהיה סבה במקרה, רצונו מצד האמינם שאשר יאור יואר ויפעל זה המדמה ברובם״. התורה התייחסה לברכה ולקללה אעפ״י שאין להם ערך מציאותי משום שהאמונה ההמונית הנפוצה מייחסת להן ערך והשפעה. השוה, כנגד זה, ספר החינוך, מצוה רל״ט.

47. ר״י מפיסא, מנחת קנאות, עמ׳ 6 והרמ״א, תשובות, סי׳ ז׳, מניחים כי הפניני חבר את האגרת על דעת רבים, על דעת כל חכמי פרובנס. גרץ רוצה לשער כי האגרת היא פרי שיתוף פעולה ביניהם.

48. השוה אגרת הרמב״ם לר׳ יהונתן הכהן מלוניל, תשובות הרמב״ם, י. בלאו, כרך ג, עמ׳ 57: ״ואל יאמר הקורא בחבורי זה כי מה האדם שיבא אחרי המלך. אלא הרי הרשיתיו ויאמר המלך יבא״ (קהלת ב יב).

49. דוגמה אחת מובהקת: המאמר בסנהדרין (פז ע״א) ״מלמד שהמקום גורם״ נותן לידעיה הזדמנות וגירוי לסכם את תורת הרמב״ם בנוגע לקרבנות ולפרשה בצורה קיצונית. כל מגמתה של ההלכה וחכמתו של המחוקק היא ״למעט הקרבן״. ״גזרה חכמתו לצוות העם שלא יקריבוהו אם לא במקום אחד בכל גבול ישראל המיוחד להם לעשות כל קרבנם כדי למעט מהם הקרבן ולא יעשוהו יום יום... ועוד שהמקום ההוא היה קטן מהכיל רוב הקרבנות... וכל זה גזרה חכמתו ית׳ כדי למעט הקרבן מהם **ומי יתן את לבב העם שלא יקריבוהו אם מעט ואם הרבה**״. שוב לא נתקררה דעתו והוא ממשיך: ״המקום ההוא היה גבוה מכל שאר חלקי המיושב... והאויר זך מאד... ויזכך שכל הבאים שם שיבינו מצד עצמם על הקרבן שאינו מכוון ממנו ית׳..״ השוה, מורה נבוכים, ג ל״ב: ״כל זה הענין למעט זה המין מן העבודות ושלא יהיה ממנו אלא מה שלא גזרה חכמתו להניחו לגמרי״.

50. כ״י, עמ׳ 49.

51. ע׳ למשל כ״י, עמ׳ 5, 24, 56, ועוד. תורה־״חלק המיוחד ממנו״, ״ידיעת השם ומלאכיו הקדושים״, ״כוונת המצות אשר באו להמציא מציאות השם ומלאכיו הנבדלים מחומר״.

52. ע׳ ביאורים למדרש תהלים, עמ׳ 21; כ״י לאבות, עמ׳ 11 (קריאת שמע ותפלה הן מצוות שכליות ו״אם כוון לבו עליהם הוא יכיר את בוראו מתוכם ויחי עוד לפניו עד נצח״).

53. ביאורים למדרש תהלים, עמ׳ 26, 33, 39; כ״י, עמ׳ 66: כל האומר שירה בכל יום... שירה ״שהשתדל להכירו ולחקור עליו לתת כבוד לשמו להרחיק ממנו כל דבר הנמנע בחקו״.

54. כ״י, עמ׳ 9, 11, ועוד.

55. שם, עמ׳ 36.

56. שם, עמ׳ 37.

57. שם, עמ׳ 42.

58. שם, עמ׳ 14. בעמ׳ 148, בקשר למאמר חז״ל (מכות כב ע״ב) ״כמה טפשאי שאר אינשי דקיימי מקמי ספר תורה ולא קיימי מקמי גברא רבה״, מוסיף הפניני: ״ואמרם שאר אינשי דברו על ההמון ודלת עם הארץ שאינם בני תורה ואינם מכבדים לומדיה, ולהם לבדם באו להזהירם על זה. והמשכילים יזהירו למצוא דברי חפץ, אינם צריכים להזהר עוד... וההמון רבה קראו שאר אינשי על היותם נוצרים מהאדמה טמאה ומהחומר קורצו ואין בהם כי אם האנושות לבד ולא ראה לבם חכמה ודעת.. ועל מיטב העם אמרו לית בר אינש, להורות עליהם כי הם שכליים אלקיים אפילו בחייהם ואינם משתמשים בחומר אם לא בהכרח רב״.

59. ע׳ ספרי האנגלי על הראב״ד, עמ׳ 242 ומאמרי הנ״ל (דף עו, הע׳ 11), עמ׳ 186 הערה 3.

60. כ״י, עמ׳ 45. זהו עיקר גדול שהרבה תלוי בו. בעמ׳ 49 (בנוגע ל״עובד אדמתו ישבע לחם״) קובע שוב גישה עקרונית: ״ולא דברו הנה ז״ל לפי הנגלה מדבריהם אלו כי כבר נודע על שלמה ומפורסם הוא באומה עליו כי הוא דבר דבריו הטובים ברוח הקדש על שני פנים, גלוי ונסתר, והם ז״ל הלכו בדרכו ובאו לבאר דברו הטוב לפי הנסתר ממנו, לא לפי הנגלה לבד. כי מה באו ללמדנו על הנגלה מדבריהם אלו, אם באו להורות על עובד אדמה בזריזות וכל היום יחרוש לזרוע...״. אין כל קושי בנגלה אבל מוכרחים להתעמק ולגלות גם נסתר. לא הזרות הנראית ממריצה את הפרשן אלא הזכות הטמירה.

61. שים לב להערה זו (הוריות, הוצאת גנחובסקי, עמ׳ י״ד): ״המשילו הנביאים וכל חכם

29. שמונה פרקים, פרק ה׳. השוה ר״י הלוי, כוזרי, מאמר ג, פרקים סח–עג. וע׳ ר״ש ליברמן, שקיעין, עמ׳ 82. ויש להוסיף עוד למשל, ר״י אבן כספי, ספר הסוד, במשנה כסף, הוצאת י. לאסט, עמ׳ 2: ״חשבו שבכללו או יותר או קליפות או מילי דבדיחותא״.

30. אין לקבוע אם מאמרים אלה הובאו באקראי, בגלל היותם במס׳ ברכות, או שמא יש כאן נימה אנטי־קבלית, כפי שעוד נברר בסוף המאמר. השוה הרמב״ם, אגרת תחית המתים, עמ׳ ג. וכן פירוש המשנה, פרק חלק, מהדורת י. קאפח, עמ׳ ר״א (״דרשות ברכות ופרק חלק״). השוה גם א. הלקין, ״סנגוריה על משנה תורה״, תרביץ, כ״ה, עמ׳ 419.

31. משנה תורה, הלכות כלי המקדש, א י״ב.

32. ר״י אנטולי בפירושו לקהלת, פירושי שיר השירים של ר״מ אבן תבון ורלב״ג (וכן של עמנואל הרומי), ועוד כהנה. ע׳ רס״ג, פירוש תהלים, הקדמה, עמ׳ כ״ד–כ״ה: ״ודע . . . שספר זה מחמת גודל ערכו ולפי שהוא דבר ה׳ . . . לא נתנו ה׳ אלא בזמן שהיתה האומה בתכלית שלמות מצבה ותמות עניניה״. רלב״ג, בראשית, א:א (עמ׳ מ״ט): ״בימי משה רבינו . . היתה הפילוסופיה חסרה מאד״.

33. השוה פירוש הוריות, הוצאת גנחובסקי, עמ׳ י״ג: ״המשיחה ההיא באה לרכך ולהכניע לבבם אם הוא ערל . . . ואמרו ואותו שמן קיים לעתיד לבא ר״ל מה שהכוונה מן השמן שבא לרכך את לבבו להחיות את נפשו הוא קיים לעתיד לבא . . . המשיחה מן השמן היתה מרככת אותו לבלתי רום לבבו על אחיו . . . ועל הכונה ההיא באה המשיחה ההיא . . . לרכך לבבו אם הוא ערל כמו המשיחה מן השמן מרככת הבשר מבחוץ״.

34. ע׳ סוטה לד ע״א, קידושין עא ע״א, תענית טז ע״ב, ועוד.

35. ע׳ מורה נבוכים, חלק ג, פרק כ״ח.

36. ביאורים למדרש תהלים, עמ׳ 20.

37. שם, עמ׳ 35. ע׳ גם הפירוש לסנהדרין (עמ׳ 45) על ״הנסתרות . . . והנגלות לנו ולבנינו״.

38. הלכות סנהדרין, ב ו. וע׳ רש״י סנהדרין יז ע״א שמפרש בעלי קומה ״שתהא אימתן מוטלת על הבריות״, השוה מנחות סה ע״א, בכורות מה ע״ב.

39. ע׳ עוד הפירוש לאבות, עמ׳ 15 (בב״י) שם יש האדרת הנזירות כאמצעי בדוק וגם רצוי ״כדי שיכיר את בוראו מתוך הפרישות״. וכן עמ׳ 53 ״חסידי אומות העולם . . . קראום חסידים על ידי הפרישות״ . . . ״ענין הנזיר אשר בתורה על כל איש ישראל אם יפריש עצמו אף במה שמותר לו כי הוא הקדוש״. כדאי להדגיש פה כי בשעה שהפניני מותח בקורת קשה ומתמדת, ללא הפוגות, נגד החמרנות המופרזת שהיא בעוכריה של ההשגה השכלית, אין הוא נתפס לסגפנות או לפרישות קיצונית. דבריו בראש מסכת הוריות (״אין גוזרין גזרה על הצבור אלא אם יכולין רוב הצבור לקבלה״) חשובים לנידון: ״כי לא באו המצות לבני האדם שתכבד העבודה על האנשים חלילה אם לא שבאו להם על הדרך הממוצעת והבינונית שהיא תפארת לעושיה כמו שתמצא שלא באה הצואה בתורה ״פעמים שלש עם גבר״ (איוב, לג כט), לענות בצום נפשו יום ויום כמו שעושים **הנוצרים המתדמים בנו המתמידים רוב השנה לענות נפש** כאילו הוא מבוקש מהם על דברי הצומות וזעקתם, חלילה לאל . . . כי הוא ית׳ בחר בהם משאר כל אומה ונתן להם את תורתו הנותנת להם סדר ישר ולא הטריחם לעבור את הים או לשוט בארץ וללכת ארצות נשמות . . . ״. הרעיון שאין טורח בתורה נמצא במורה נבוכים, חלק ג, פרק ל, ופרק מ״ז. והשוה רד״ק, הושע, יא ג. ר׳ גם יהודה הלוי, הכוזרי ב, נ; אבן עזרא על קהלת ז ג. וע׳ עוד מורה נבוכים ב׳, ל״ט; הל׳ איסורי ביאה יג יד.

40. מורה נבוכים, חלק ג, סוף פרק נ״א. והשוה הקדמה לפירוש המשנה, מהדורת י. קאפח, עמ׳ ד ״והיה זה מותו ביחס אלינו שנפקד מאתנו, וחיים ביחס אליו במה שנתעלה . . . ״ ורלב״ג פירוש שיר השירים, א, ב (נשיקה=דבקות).

41. הלכות אבל, י״ג יא–יב. ר׳ בחיי בן אשר (כד הקמח, אבל) מטעים את ״פחיתות העוה״ז שכולו הבל גמור ודבר בטל״, אך זה מביאו להגדיל את ערך הלכות אבלות. מאידך, ע׳ רמב״ן, דברים י״ד, א.

42. הלכות שמטה ויובל, יג יג. והשוה פירוש הוריות, עמ׳ יד ע״ב.

*42. עבודה זרה יז ע״א, ופירושו על אתר.

43. השוה דב פלאטו, ״מלאכי עליון ושליחותם לדרי מטה״, אדר היקר, דביר, תש״ז, עמ׳ פ״א–פ״ז. על המנהג בפרובנס לקבל ברכה מזקנים וחסידים, ע׳ קלונימוס, אגרת המוסר, הו״ל מ. הברמן, עמ׳ 107; יוסף אבן כספי, תם הכסף, עמ׳ 32, ועוד.

מויכוח הרמב״ן ועד ״לעזר האמונה״ של ר׳ משה הכהן מטורסילה, הו״ל י. שמיר (פלורידה, 1972). ההקדמה למכלל יופי של ר׳ שמואל אבן סינה נתפרסמה באוצר הספרות, ב׳, מחלקה ג׳, עמ׳ 21 ואילך. השוה דברינו בסוף מאמר זה והציונים הביבליוגרפיים.

19. לשונו של הפניני, כ״י עמ׳ 66 על ״ולבני הפילגשים אשר לאברהם נתן אברהם מתנות״. פירושו מדגיש כי אברהם התאמץ להשפיע עליהם, להשלים ״נפשות בני דורו כפי יכלתן״.

20. השוה מש׳ במאמרי הנ״ל (דף עו, הערה 11), עמ׳ 202–204.

21. ע׳ לאחרונה Ch. Touati, "La Controverse de . . . 1303–1306", *REJ*, cxxvii (1968), pp. 21–37.

22. לית מאן דפליג כי לא האלגוריה מהווה בעיה אלא **טיב** האלגוריה. ר׳ יחיאל מפיסא, שירד לנבכי המחלוקת, העיר כי הכל מסכימים ש״לא נקח הדברים כפשוטן רק על צד ההסתר״ (מנחת קנאות עמ׳ 14). ברם יחסו של ר׳ משה תקו, בעל כתב תמים, ידוע, והשווה הר״ש משאנץ, כתאב אל רסאייל, עמ׳ קל״ו: ״ואיך יעלה על לב איש לומר שלא נקח דברי האגדה כפשטה״.

23. לאחר שסקר בטוב טעם את תולדות הפילוסופיה מרס״ג ואילך, הוא מפטיר על הרמב״ם: ״כללו של דבר עלה במעלות האמת בשלום ובמישור יותר מאשר שמענו על כל זולתו מחתימת התלמוד ועד הנה, והוא הבין באמת בפילוסופיא האמתית האנושית כל מה שהבין בה אריסטו וכל מפרשי ספריו, והבין בתשבורת והמספר והמצורף עליהם כל מה שהבין בה אקלידס וחבריו, וידע בתכונה כל מה שנודע מתעלומותיה לבטלמיוס הנקרא מגיסטא (ע׳ Steinschneider, *Heb. Übers.*, pp. 519f.) וסיעתו, ומצא במלאכת הרפואה כל מה שמצאו בה גאלינוס ואפוקראט וכותם, וכלל שכלו מקבלת התורה כל מה שנודע והתחדש עד זמנו, וחקק וצירף בסודותיה ובסתריה ובכלל באמתות הנבואה יותר ממה שנגלה לאחד מן המחברים הנמצאים עד יום צאתו״. אני השתמשתי באגרות הרשב״א עם אגרת הבדרש, הו״ל שמשון בלאך, ווארשא תרמ״ב, עמ׳ 52. השווה דבריו הידועים בסוף ספר בחינת עולם: ״סוף דבר תשמאיל לבי או תימין, תאמין בכל מה שהאמין בו אחרון הגאונים בזמן, **ראשם בחשיבות, הרב המורה הגדול הרמב״ם זצ״ל, אשר אין ערוך אליו בכל חכמי ישראל אחר חתימת התלמוד״. הדברים לא נאמרו לתפארת המליצה; הם משקפים תפיסה היסטורית ועמדה רוחנית.**

24. **אחת מ״תועלותיה הנפלאים״ של החכמה היא עקירת אמונת ההגשמה, ע׳ אגרות** הרשב״א, עמ׳ 53: ״וכמעט היתה ההגשמה מתפשט בקצוות רבות בתחלת צאת ספריו הקדושים בארצות, ובפי׳ ראינו בכתבים רבים בזמן המחלוקת הראשונה השלוחים כנגדו מכנפות הארץ שהם תופשים עליו ומגנים ספריו על אמרו שאין לבורא הכל שעור ותמונה, גם ראינו אגרת שלוחה מן החכם המופלא הרב המובהק רמב״ן ז״ל שלוח[ה] אל האיתנים רבינו (!) צרפת . . . טוען לפניהם . . . בהרחקת ההגשמה אשר האשימוה עליה כמדומה מפני שהיו מגשימים בפרהסיא בזמן ההוא . . . והנה היום ת״ל נעקרה אותה האמונה הרעה מעקרה מכל כתותינו . . . הנה אם לא יצא ולא יושג מן התפלספות רבנו הגדול תועלת בעיונו בלתי זה היה באמת מספיק והיינו מחוייבים להודות לפאר [ל]חכמתו הרחבה אשר הניעתהו אל האמת״. השווה ש. ראבידוביץ, ״בעית ההגשמה לרס״ג ולרמב״ם״, עיונים במחשבת ישראל, כרך א׳, עמ׳ 171 ואילך. ובפרט עמ׳ 230 ואילך. מאידך, השווה צבי וולפסון, "The Jewish Kalam", ספר היובל של *Jewish Quarterly Review*, 1967, pp. 569–573.

25. זהו עיקר גדול בכל הפולמוס הזה. ע׳ מורה נבוכים, חלק ג, פרק ט״ו. השוה י. אלבלג, תקון הדעות, הוצאת י. וידה, ירושלים תשל״ג, עמ׳ 12 ועמ׳ 24, שם מציע הסבר אחר לענין הנמנעות. דברי הפניני מובאים הרבה במרוצת הדורות; ע׳ למשל, מנחת קנאות לר״י מפיסא, עמ׳ 114; ישר׳ מקנדיא, מצרף לחכמה, עמ׳ 71; וכן דוד קונפורטי, קורא הדורות, עמ׳ 126.

26. שמירה קפדנית על סמכותם של בעלי המסורה היא נימה קבועה בספרותנו, ודברי הרמב״ם בהקדמה לפירוש המשניות, פרק חלק, משמשים בנין אב; ע׳ מהדורת י. קאפח, עמ׳ ר״א. השוה המובא בכרם חמד, ה׳, עמ׳ 13: ״אם נעלמו פירושיהם, זה מקוצר דעתנו והבנתנו, ולא ממיעוט חכמת אומריהם, וכמה הזהיר הרב ז״ל בחיבורו על זה שלא להוציא לעז בהגדות ולא על האומרים אותם״.

27. השוה רמב״ם, אגרת תחית המתים, הוצאת פינקל, עמ׳ ו.

28. ע׳ הקדמה לפירוש מגלת איכה. גם לוי בן אברהם, בתי הנפש והלחשים, ידיעות המכון לחקר השירה, כרך ה׳, עמ׳ 37.

9. לשונו של קרשקש, פירוש מורה נבוכים, חלק ב, פרק ל.

10. ע׳ ח. שירמן, השירה העברית בספרד ובפרובנס, ב׳, עמ׳ 489 ואילך. על המהדורות המרובות של בחינת עולם, תפוצתו ותהודתו ע׳ י. ריבקינד, קרית ספר, י״ג (תרצ״ו), עמ׳ 236 ואילך.

11. ע׳ במיוחד ש. פינס ״הצורות האישיות במשנתו של ידעיה בדרשי״: ספר היובל לצבי וולפסון, ירושלים תשכ״ה, עמ׳ קפ״ז–ר״א. וכן מאמרו הגדול ״הסכולאסטיקה שאחרי תומאס אקווינאס ומשנתם של חסדאי קרשקש ושל קודמיו״, דברי האקדמיה הלאומית הישראלית למדעים, ירושלים, תשכ״ו, במיוחד עמ׳ 3 ואילך. פרופ׳ פינס תורם להבהרת יצירתו העצמאית של הפניני בתחום הפילוסופיה המקצועית, פרט להישגיו בתרגום, עיבוד ופרשנות (כה״י תוארו ע״י ש. מונק, *Archives Israelites*, כרך viii (1847), עמ׳ 72–67). הוא מנסה להוכיח כי הפניני שלט בסכולאסטיקה הנוצרית בזה שיש הקבלות בין דעותיו ובין דעות סכולאסטיקאים כגון דונס סקוטוס. הוכחתו מושתתת על השערה לגמרי סמויה מן העין, כי הוגי הדעות בפרובנס השתמשו במקורות נוצריים אבל נמנעו מלהזכיר את שמותיהם בשעה שהזכירו במפורש את מקורותיהם היווניים והערביים. והרי המגע בין יהודים ונוצרים לא היה סמוי מן העין. ר״י אנטולי מדבר על מיכאל סקוטוס לעתים תכופות ב״מלמד התלמידים״. על רלב״ג ועמיתיו הנוצרים בחכמת התכונה, ע׳ ב. גולדשטיין, ״על תרומתו של רלב״ג לאסטרונומיה״, דברי האקדמיה הלאומית הישראלית למדעים, ירושלים תש״ל, עמ׳ 4. על ר׳ שמואל בן יהודה, מסיעת המתרגמים הפילוסופיים בפרובנס בראשית המאה הי״ד, ע׳ ל. ברמן, בקובץ *Jewish Medieval and Renaissance Studies* בעריכת א. אלטמאן, עמ׳ 295 ואילך. וע׳ מאמרי ב־*Journal of World History*, xi (1968), עמ׳ 190 ועמ׳ 205. הפניני (כ״י אסקוריאל, עמ׳ 80) מזכיר ״מה שהשיבותי לאחד מחכמי הנוצרים בענין משיח״, בעמ׳ 16 נאמר ״שיתחכם מכל אדם יהודי או ארמאי כפי יכלתו״. ב.צ. דינור, ישראל בגולה, ב, כרך ו׳, עמ׳ 220, מביא קטע מהקדמתו של הפניני לפירוש על ספר הקאנון של אבן סינה. עיסוקו הרב בספרי רפואות מהווה תחום־משנה עצמאי ביצירתו הפילוסופית.

12. ע׳ ש. הלקין, ״החרם על לימוד הפילוסופיה״, פרקים, א (תשכ״ז), עמ׳ 55–35. סופרים, מתנגדי הפילוסופיה, מכוונים את חציהם נגד הפניני אבל מזדקקים רק לאגרת ההתנצלות. כך, למשל, ר׳ יחיאל מפיסא, מנחת קנאות, הו״ל ד. קויפמאן (ברלין, תרנ״ח; צלום ירושלים, תש״ל), וכן ר׳ אביעד שר שלום, אמונת חכמים (ווארשא, תרמ״ח).

13. ע׳ A. Toynbee, *A Study of History*, xii, *Reconsiderations* (1961), p. 8: “The study of human affairs is really one and indivisible. The conventional academic dismemberment of the vast subject into “disciplines” is a convenient, and perhaps unavoidable, educational device, but it is an arbitrary surgical operation, and this makes it a serious impediment to the gaining of knowledge and understanding.”

14. למרבה הפליאה ישנם חוקרים שאינם מזכירים אפילו את מציאותם של פירושי האגדות; למשל, הברמן, צינברג, שירמן כנ״ל למעלה, דף עה, בהערה 1.

15. אזכיר למשל את תיאורו של הפרנס, איש החצר, רב ההשפעה (פירוש לאבות, כ״י, עמ׳ 8); פולמוס משיחי (עמ׳ 80); השתתפותם של יהודים נושאי ספר תורה בטקס הכתרת המלך (עמ׳ 148); הלואה ברבית (עמ׳ 152) ותיאור הישיבה בקטע שנתפרסם ע״י נויבואר. בראש מסכת הוריות הוא מתפלמס גם עם הסגפנות הנוצרית.

16. בני דורו, כידוע, שם טוב פלקירה (ספר המבקש) וקלונימוס בן קלונימוס (אבן בחן) מנמקים את סבות פרישתם מהשירה לאחר שהתמכרו לה ללא הסתייגות בראשית ימיהם. דבריהם של אלו ומעשיו של הפניני משתלבים.

17. ע׳ למשל, ביאורים על מדרש תהלים, הוצאת ש. באבער, עמ׳ 34; רמב״ם, מורה נבוכים, חלק ג, פרק מ״ג. ובדעתי אי״ה לדון בנושא זה והשלכותיו במאמר נפרד.

18. נזכיר רק את משה אבן תבון (ע׳ גרץ, דברי ימי ישראל, ה׳, עמ׳ 109 — ספר הפאה נמצא בכ״י אוקספורד [939/1] והוא רב ענין); הרשב״א — ע׳ עדיין הנספח העיקרי ל־J. Perles, *R. Salomo B. Abraham B. Adereth* (Breslau 1863), עמ׳ כ״ד ואילך, נוסח כ״י ותיקן ההולך ומתפרסם ע״י ש.מ. וינברגר ובעיקר דבריו של א. פלדמן, שנתון בר־אילן, כרך ז–ח (תש״ל), עמ׳ 138 ואילך; שם טוב ן׳ שפרוט, פרדס רמונים; הקדמות לפירושי התורה של הרמב״ן ור׳ בחיי בן אשר (והשווה הקדמת ר״י אברבנאל ליהושע) והקדמת הרלב״ג לפירוש שיר השירים; ר״מ המאירי, בית הבחירה, הקדמה, עמ׳ 15, ומגן אבות, עמ׳ כ; ספרות הפולמוס

נשמע הד הדעה הרגילה על כל הבעיתיות של פרשנות האגדה ויחס המשכיל אליה. ברם, פירושו צווח ואומר: האגדה בכללותה נאה וחסודה, וסופר מהיר אשר חש את הסכנה הכפולה של "ישיבת בתי כנסת של עמי הארץ" וגם "במחשכים הושיבני כמתי עולם", ישכיל לדלות ממנה פנינות יקרות.

* מוקדש בחיבה ובהערצה לידידי פרופ׳ אלטמאן שתרם גם להבנת הדרשנות החדישה באשכנז במאמרו הגדול "Zur Frühgeschichte der jüdischen Predigt in Deutschland", *Leo Baeck Year Book* vi (1961)

1. מבין הספרים והמאמרים כדאי להזכיר H. Gross, *Gallia Judaica*, pp. 101–103; Renan-Neubauer, *Les Ecrivains juifs français du XIVme Siècle*, pp. 359–402; S. Munk, *Archives Israelites*, vii (1847), pp. 67–72; D. Kaufmann, *Gesammelte Schriften*, iii, pp. 470–77; גרץ, דברי ימי ישראל, ה, עמ׳ 229–232; א״מ הברמן, תולדות הפיוט והשירה (1972), עמ׳ 139; צינברג, ספרות ישראל, ב, עמ׳ 84 ואילך; שירמן, פינס והלקין כדלקמן, הערות 10–12.

2. למשל, ר״י אברבנאל, פירוש התורה, פרשת תצוה (כח, א) בבואו "לבאר הרמז אשר ירמזו אליו [בגדי הכהנים]" דוחה בחריפות את שיטת הראב״ע והרלב״ג ואילו את פירושו האלגורי של אנבוניט הוא מקבל בסבר פנים יפות. "הדרך הזה ברמוז הבגדים הוא נכון כפי התורה וכפי הסברה המיושרת". ראוי לציין כי פירושו של אבן עזרא חותר לביסוס טבעי (אסטרונומי-אסטרולוגי) לרמזי הבגדים ואילו פירושו של הפניני הוא רוחני-פילוסופי.

3. למשל, ר״י עראמה, עקדת יצחק, פרשת וישב (פרעסבורג, צילום ירושלים, תשכ״א, עמ׳ רי״ז: "וכבר ביאר אותו החכם ן׳ בונט ז״ל . . . ואין סמך לדבריו אלו לא מן הכתובים ולא מן הסברא". הפירוש משבח את העיון הפילוסופי וההשגה השכלית, לא לפי טעמו של ר״י עראמה.

4. אברבנאל, ישועות משיחו (קעניגסבערג, 1861), עמ׳ ה: "ומפרשי התלמוד לא פירשו ההגדות ולבד התעסקו בפירוש המצות . . . אולי שהניחום לפרשם אחרי כן במגילת סתרים כמו שחשב הרב המורה . . . אבל ישלם ה׳ פעלו להרשב״א סיני ועוקר הרים וגם לאנבוניט ז״ל **כי התחילו מלאכת ה׳** זאת לבאר ההגדות . . ."

5. שם טוב ן׳ שפרוט, ספר פרדס רמונים (סביוניטה, צלום ירושלים, תשכ״ח) מזכיר את "הרב הגדול הרשב״א [אשר] נתעורר לבאר קצת הגדות בענין נכבד". ומסיים כי הוא בעצמו ילך בעקבות "רבינו הגדול הרמב״ם ז״ל והראב״ע ז״ל" ואילו הפניני — מאן דכר שמיה.

6. מ. בניהו רשם את כתבי היד בנספח למאמרו החשוב על "רבי שמואל יפה אשכנזי", תרביץ, מ״ב (תשל״ג), עמ׳ 419 ואילך; ע׳ במיוחד עמ׳ 457 והערה 3. ע׳ גם מיכל, אור החיים, עמ׳ 436. עבודתי מבוססת בעיקר על כ״י אסקוריאל — לתלמוד ולמדרש רבה; תצלומו במכון לכ״י בירושלים. תודתי נתונה למר בנימין ריצלר, מעובדי המכון; תלמידי מרק ספרשטיין מכין עבודת-מחקר מקיפה על הפניני ופירושיו.

7. צונץ, הדרשות בישראל, עמ׳ 504, הערה 202, יוצא ידי חובתו בציון לאגרת ההתנצלות ואלבק הוסיף "שהוא מחלק את ההגדות לארבעה חלקים". ש׳ באבר (ע׳ ההערה הבאה) לא העריך את הפירוש כראוי ודבריו שם הם שיגרתיים ושחוקים. ע׳ הנספח למאמר זה (למטה, דף פב), על אודות הערותיו הספרותיות-ענייניות של ר״י אבן חביב, בעל עין יעקב.

8. הפירוש על מדרש תהלים נדפס בויניציאה, שנ״ט וחזר והדפיסו ש׳ באבער (קראקא, תרנ״א; צלום ירושלים, תשכ״ז); דבריו על "תכונת הספר" בעמ׳ 8 הם דברים בעלמא. הפירוש לאבות נדפס בספר "פירושי ראשונים לאבות" בעריכת מ.ש. כשר וי.י. בלכרוביץ, (ירושלים, תשל״ג), עמ׳ מ״ט–ע״ד. ההוצאה היא שרירותית ומגמתית והעורכים עשו בפירושי הפניני כבתוך שלהם, ברצותם מקצרים וברצותם מטשטשים. הפירוש להוריות נכלל באוצר הפירושים: הוריות, הו״ל א.מ. גנחובסקי, תל אביב, תשכ״ט, עמ׳ י״ב–ט״ז. וזכור א. נויבואר לטובה שהדפיס קטע חשוב מפירוש זה להוריות ב-*REJ*, כרך כ׳, עמ׳ 245 ואילך וחזר והדפיסו ש. אסף, מקורות לתולדות החינוך, ב׳, עמ׳ ל״ג. גם ח. בראדי הדפיסו במבוא לספר השלמה, ברכות, עמ׳ xiv (ללא הוספת נופך כל שהוא). על מדרש רבה, בראשית, דפוס רדלהיים, תרי״ד האומר לכלול פירוש הפניני, ראה מ. בניהו, תרביץ, מ״ב, עמ׳ 457, הערה 3.

עליהם האיש הכסיל... ואז תמשך ותנצר ותכונן מלכותו לעד... ולא באו ז״ל להורות הנה לפי הנגלה מדבריהם אלו שצוו את העם שימשחו המלך על שפת היאור אשר יבחרו בו ואז תמשך מלכותו לו ולזרעו לדורותיו, ואם לא ימש[ח]ו אותו על המים שלא תמשך לו המלוכה **כי זה נראה בעיני כל משכיל דברי מהתלות ומעשי תעתועים והבלי התפלות וחלילה מהם להתעסק בדברים יגעים אלו.** כי איך תמשך המלכות למלך הנמשח על הנחל ההולך אל הים, מה הסגולה הנמצאת במעיין להמשך המלכות למלך הנמשח שם אם לא על הדרך שביארנו ולא זולת זה.״[81] הפניני, שנתחנך בבית מדרשו של ר׳ משולם והעיד על גירסא דינקותא שלו, קובע במפורש את מרכזיותה של ההלכה: התלמוד עומד בטיבורה של היהדות והכל מתמקד סביבו. הוא מהווה את התשתית מבחינה מעשית, למודית, ורוחנית. התכלית אליה שאף הפניני בהפצת רעיונותיו חייבה אותו לא להצטמצם בדברי אגדה אלא להזדקק גם לדברי הלכה. וכאן נתפס הוא לספיריטואליזציה מרחיקת־לכת. אינו דורש טעמי המצוות — התכליות של תקון הגוף ותקון הנפש אינן מבטלות את המעשה, כידוע, והדברים יגעים — אלא מפתח את סמליותה של ההלכה. כבר קבעו בעלי המדות והכללים: ״משל — מדה זו נוהגת רק בדברי קבלה אבל בדברי תורה ומצות אין אתה יכול לדורשן בלשון הזה.״[82] הפילוסופיה במובן עממי ובנטיתה הרוחנית היתה בקרבו כאש בוערת ויצרה מתיחות רבה, רווית אתגרים וסתירות.[83] יש בפירושיו גיבוש מיוחד של המגמה הספיריטואליסטית. בכשרון רב, לעתים בתוקף או באונס, מטה הוא את תוכן ההלכה וקביעותיה המעשיות לאפיק לגמרי רוחני.[84] שוב מובן למה רוחניותו הסעירה את הרוחות.

לאור כל הנאמר, יש להבין גם את העובדה שאין זכר אצלו להבחנה הקבועה ועומדת מאז רב האי גאון[85] בין אגדות הנמצאות בתלמוד ואגדות הנמצאות בספרות המדרשית מחוץ לתלמוד — הבחנה האומרת שלאגדות התלמוד יש זכות בכורה ואדם חייב להתאמץ ככל האפשר ולרדת לסוף דעתן, ואילו אגדות שמחוץ לתלמוד אם נראין, טוב, ואם לאו אפשר ללא יסורי מצפון ובכנות גמורה להזניחן ולדחותן. ממילא מובן שפטור הפניני מ״בקורת״ כלשהי נגד דברי אגדה. לא יצטרך לדחות מאמרים מוקשים כדעות יחיד וכדומה. תפקידו לפרש על מנת לפרסם והוא הולך ובורר מה שניתן להתפרש ומה שמשקף את עמדתו הרוחנית.

בכלל, התקיימו שתי אפשרויות או התרוצצו שתי מגמות לגבי פירוש האגדה הקשה והזרה; הנחה משותפת לכל הפרשנים היא שאין לקבלה פשוטה כמשמעה אלא יש להתמודד עם תעלומותיה ופליאותיה: (1) לנסות ולפענח אותה ולקרבה אל השכל. (2) להזניחה כחוות דעת שאינה מובנת ואינה מחייבת — או כדעת יחיד (הרמב״ם באגרת לחכמי מרסיליה), או כמילתא דבדיחותא או סתם כמימרה בלתי־נורמטיבית. לגבי המגמה הכפולה שראינו לעיל — פולמוס והגנה — שתי האפשרויות שרירות ויעילות וכל אחת, לפי דרכה, תשיג את מבוקשה. אם הענין אינו ניתן לפירוש המניח את הדעת, אז רשות נתונה לכל אדם להסתייג ממנו ולדחותו. במלים אחרות, הזלזול הוא דרך של התגוננות ותשובת המינים. ר״מ המאירי מסכם לגבי המדרשות: ״אלא יוכל לקבלו מי שירצה ומי שאינו רוצה אין בו הכרח.״[86] הדברים אמורים לגבי קביעת הלכה, אבל משנה לא זזה ממקומה. אלה ממש דברי ר׳ יחיאל מפריס: ״עוד יש בהם דברי אגדה למשוך לב האדם, אם תרצה תאמין אותם ואם לא תרצה לא תאמין אותם.״[87] הרמב״ן החזיק אחריו: ״עוד יש לנו ספר שלישי הנקרא מדרש... וזה הספר מי שיאמין בו טוב ומי שלא יאמין בו לא יזיק.״[88] מובן מאליו, פילוג כזה לא ישמש את מטרתו החינוכית־הסברתית של הפניני כפי שהיא מצטיירת לעינינו. נדמה כי אפשר אפילו להתחקות אחר גלגולי דעתו של הפניני. בספר הפרדס, אותו חיבור־נעורים מופלא, אומר הפניני על האגדה: ״מצד התמימות נאמין בהגדות, ומצד אחר נכזיבם.״[89] בפתגם זה עדיין

במשנתו־פרשנותו של הפניני. הוא אינו חרד מהתמוטטות האמונה ואינו נחלץ להגן על אגדות חז״ל מפני התקפות והשמצות. אין פירושו נועד ״להשיב על המלגלגים״ על אף שלעתים התפלמס עם ״חכמים נוצרים״. הוא נתן את דעתו כנראה לביצור עמדתה הרופפת של ההשכלה הפילוסופית, לתעמולה והטפה בתוך העם. אין בפירושו ענין של התמודדות עם פיסקאות מופלאות התובעות ליבון שכלי אלא הבלטת סממנים שכלתניים המתנוצצים לפי דעתו בתוך נבכי האגדה וההלכה גם יחד. משום כך נאלץ הוא גם לפנות עורף לפשטה של אגדה אפילו כשהיא מתקבלת על הדעת ולהפליג למרחקים דרשניים־אלגוריים. הפניני מופיע ככח המעמיד ומחזק את העמדה הפילוסופית התוקפנית שאינה מתגוננת ומתנצלת אלא מתקיפה ומאשימה. יכול הוא לדגול בסיסמתו של יוסף אבן כספי: ״אין ראוי לאמת שתהיה לא פחדנית ולא ביישנית.״[76]

משום כך מובן גם למה לא נרתע הפניני מפני המשימה הקשה הזו. הרי הרמב״ם נתלבט לבטים גדולים עד שלבסוף חזר בו מכוונתו לחבר פירוש לאגדות חז״ל: ״וכבר יעדנו בפירוש המשנה שאנחנו נבאר ענינים זרים בספר הנבואה וספר ההשואה, והוא ספר יעדנו שנבאר בו ספיקות הדרשות כולם אשר הנראה מהם מרוחק מאד מן האמת, יוצא מדרך המושכל, והם כולם משלים. וכאשר החילותי זה שנים רבים בספרים ההם וחברתי מהם מעט, לא ישר בעינינו מה שנכנסנו בבאורו על הדרך ההיא, מפני שראינו שאם נעמוד על ההמשל וההעלם למה שצריך העלמתו, לא נהיה יוצאים מן הדרך הראשון . . . ואם נבאר מה שצריך לבאר יהיה זה השתדלותנו בלתי נאות בהמון העם . . . וראינו עוד שהדרשות ההם אם יעיין בם סכל מהמון הרבנים לא יקשה עליו מהם מאומה . . . .״[77] הרמב״ם מעיד על עצמו כי ישב על מדוכה זו, התחבט הרבה ולבסוף ביקש לקבל שכר על הפרישה ולא על הפירוש, ואילו הפניני התגבר על כל המכשולים והמעצורים והסתירות. ברם, הרמב״ם נטפל בעיקר לחומר ה״יוצא מדרך המושכל״ והגיע בעל כרחו למבוא סתום. הפנינו נטפל בעיקר לחומר הניתן להתפרש באופן פילוסופי. אין הוא חושש למבוכת ההמון או ה״סכל מהמון הרבנים״ אלא לחינוכו ולהעלאתו. הוא מבקש יתד להיתלות בו והאגדה נענית לו.

כאן, נדמה, אפשר לדרוש סמוכין בין מפעלו ובין מפעלם הפרשני של מקובלי גירונה לפניו, היינו פירוש האגדות של רבי עזרא ורבי עזריאל. אלה, לפי סיכומו המאוזן של המהדיר, הופכים והופכים במאמרי התלמוד והמדרשים ומוצאים בהם אוצר בלום של השקפות, מושגים וסמלים קבליים.[78] מגמתם ברורה: לשבץ את מסורת הקבלה לתוך מקורות חז״ל עד שיתאחדו אחדות גמורה. בדומה לכך, בא הפניני לחפש מקורות והקבלות, אסמכתות ורמזים — שם רמז ואין מספר — לדעותיו השכליות ואמונותיו הפילוסופיות בתוך דברי חז״ל, כולל הלכה, ולקבוע זהות מוחלטת ביניהם. הוא מפגין כי רעיונותיו מעוגנים בחז״ל ונעוצים בהשקפת עולמם המסורתי.[79]

יש להתעכב פורתא על פירושיו הרוחניים־שכלתניים לענייני הלכה. קודם כל, הם מראים שהוא טשטש בכוונה את הגבולים בין הלכה ואגדה שהם, בלאו הכי, אינם ברורים כל צרכם. יתר מיכן, פירושי הלכה המעלים על נס את הפן הרוחני־פילוסופי הצפון במצוות מסויימות, טומנים בחובם אפשרויות אנטינומיסטיות — כאילו הותרה הרצועה. ההלכה של ״מלך לא ירבה לו נשים״ אינה בעיתית כלל וכלל, ובכל זאת מעיר הפניני: ״דברו ז״ל על המלך **בדרך הסתר** וקראו המלך המושל ברוחו ובחמר שלו.״[80] מי שמדייק בדברים הבאים על משיחת מלך יכול על נקלה לשלול את עצם מעשה המשיחה פשוטו כמשמעו: ״אמרו ז״ל בדרך הסתר ועל דרך משל שימשחו מלכיהם על המעיין להורות להם שלא ימליכו

בני מחלוקות של אברהם אבינו, ואם על כל פנים ירצה אחד מרבותיך התלמודיים שקצת ההגדות אין להם תוך אבל הם כפשוטם עם היותם אומרים דברים נמנעים או מיחסים גשמות או דבר מרוחק אצל הי״ת... לא תאבה לו ולא תשמע אל דברי המאמר ההוא ולאומרו כי יחידאה הוא...."[68] גם פה יוצא כספי להדריך את בנו להתמודד עם אגדות זרות ולהוציאן מפשוטן, אלא שכאן הפולמוס בעיקר כלפי פנים: אסור להכנע לאותם מרבותינו התלמודיים המתנגדים לאלגוריזציה. ר׳ יעקב בן מכיר כותב באגרת אחת הנכללת בספר מנחת קנאות: "כאשר יש באגדות רבות זרות רחוקה בפשטיהן, גם האומות מלעיגות עליהן. ואם ימצא איש מתקן אותם, להיותם ישרות בעיני או בעיניהן, צריכים אנו להחזיק טובה עליהן."[69] הרשב״א מתודה: "והוצרכתי לכתוב כאן פירושן של הגדות אלו מפני שהן מלקטין עלינו הגדות התלמוד כדי להגדיל הלשון ולטעון על חכמי האמת ז״ל דברים בטלים חלילה להם. וכן אצטרך בהגדות הבאות בתלמוד ורואה אני בעסקיהן לשקוד בהם כדי שנשיב את החולק על מלאכת שמים."[70] תלמידו ר׳ שם טוב בן שפרוט מזדהה עם מגמת הרשב״א שהמריצה גם אותו לחבר ספרו פרדס רמונים: "קנאתי בהוללים מלעיגים על דברי חז״ל, חברו ספרים לקטו בהם ההגדות. וידרשו בהם כהגדות של דופי". ברם מסתייג הוא מגישתו של הרשב״א, אשר פילוסופיה וקבלה משמשות בה בערבוביה, ובורר לעצמו דרך אחרת: "אשתדל בכל נפשי ובכל מאדי כפי אשר תשיג ידי לבאר ולפרש דברי ההגדות אשר יראו לי שצריכין פי׳ כפי דעות תוריות המפורסמות לנו מדברי רבינו הגדול הרמב״ם ז״ל והראב״ע ז״ל לפי שהם סברות קרובות לפילוסופיא ויכול אדם לדבר בהם לעיני כל האומות בשווקים וברחובות."[71] הדברים מזכירים את מטרת ר׳ משה אבן תבון בספר הפאה שלו "להשיב על הנוצרים המלגלגים על ספורי ההגדה."[72] נביא עוד את דברי ר׳ ישעי׳ דטראני האחרון, בן דור ממש של הפניני, הכותב בספר הפסקים שלו לסנהדרין: "ולפי שראיתי מבני פריצי עמנו המלגלגין ובוזין דברי חכמים ומלמדים המדרשים [לכומרי] אומות העולם לתעתע ולהלעיג על תורתנו באתי לבאר עניין המדרשין ומה היתה כוונת חכמי תורתנו בהם...". לאחר שמונה שלשה סוגי מדרש — (**א**) יש מהן שהן דרך גוזמא, כמו שאמרו דברו חכמים בלשון הבאי; (**ב**) וכן יש מן המדרשין שהן על דרך מעשה ניסים שמראה הקב״ה כחו לחסידיו; (**ג**) ויש מן המדרשין שכוונת חכמים בהם לדרוש המקרא בכל ענין שיכולין לדרשו — הוא מפטיר כדלקמן: "והמלגלג על דבריהם עליו נאמ׳ ויהיו מלעיגים במלאכי אלקים ומתעתעים בנביאיו, ובכמה מקומות נענשו עונש גדול על שהיו מלגלגים בדברי חכמים."[73]

הצד השווה שבעיסוק מעמיק ונמרץ זה באגדה הוא הזיקה לבעיתיות שבה; המפרשים־הסניגורים טיפלו בראש ובראשונה באותם המקורות המאפשרים למקטרגים שונים להונות בהם את ישראל או במאמרים המזקיקים מאמץ מיוחד בכדי לסלק מהם כל שמץ של הגשמה. המונח העיקרי החוזר כפזמון בהצהרות ובחוות־הדעת הוא לעג או ליגלוג. מגמה כפולה זו — פולמוס ואפולוגטיקה, כלפי חוץ וכלפי פנים — היא העוברת כחוט השני בכל מאמצי הפרשנות של חכמי ישראל. אין להתפלא אם כן שנצטבר ילקוט מסויים של מקורות שכמעט כל החכמים נזדקקו להם וניסו לפרשם ולהתרחק מן הזרות שבהם. הזרות המדומה, הנעוצה באי־הבנה, גורמת ליגלוג.

לא כן הפניני; המקורות הקלאסיים, האגדות, "המשבשות את הדעת"[74], מדרשי הפליאה אשר גאונים וחכמים לכל מחנותיהם טיפלו בהם בכדי להוציא מלבן של קראים, נוצרים ומקטרגים למיניהם, אינם זוכים לתשומת לב מיוחדת של הפניני. הכיוון כלפי חוץ המובלט ע״י הרמב״ם והמקבל ביסוס עיוני ודחיפה חדשה בפירושו לפסוק "כי היא חכמתכם ובינתכם לעיני העמים"[75] אינו עיקר

דידן, אין הבעיה כה גדולה: שכן הפניני מתעסק לא בפילוסופיה מקצועית — סודות ומה שאחר הטבע — אלא בפילוסופיה עממית — תפיסה רוחנית של הדת והכוונה רוחנית של המעשה הדתי והשאיפה הדתית. ובכל זאת הסעיר את הרוחות. מאידך, מנהל הפניני פולמוס ער נגד בעלי התלמוד המסיחים דעת מן החכמות ומתכווצים לתוך ד׳ אמות של הלכה. הוא ממציא הזדמנויות שונות בכדי להתקיף את החכמים המכלים את ימיהם בתלמוד בלבד ואינם עוסקים לא בעניני אמונה וחכמה ולא בתוכן החויתי של מעשה המצווה. לא נתקררה דעתו עד שחרץ משפט קשה: תלמודיזם בלעדי גורם ערפול או טשטוש רוחני. וזהו ״במחשכים הושיבני כמתי עולם — אמר ר׳ ירמיה זה תלמוד של בבל״. ״ובאו להורות ז״ל לכל אדם המשתדל לדעת החכמה ההיא לבדה [דהיינו תלמוד] ולא ראה חכמה אחרת כי הוא הולך חשכים.״[63] עצם עיסוקו באגדה מפגין את עמדתו ומשתזר לתוך הבקורת התרבותית-תורנית שהוא מותח על כת בעלי התלמוד. דברי התנצלותו של בעל ילקוט המכירי, תהלים (ירושלים תשכ״ד), עמ׳ ג, תואמים את מגמתו של הפניני: ״ובטרדת לבם בתלמוד, בדינין באסור ובמותר, לא ימצאו ידיהם לאלתר המדרש הנדרש בכל פסוק ופסוק כפי הצריך להם״. צר לו כי תשש כחם של חכמים וכהה מאור עיניהם בגלל העדר השכלה פילוסופית.

IV

בגישה מגמתית זו נתייחד הפניני ונבדל מכל קודמיו, מרב האי גאון ור׳ שמואל בן חפני ואילך. בדברו על האגדה ובסקרו את השתלשלות פרשנותה כתב עזרי׳ מן האדומים:[64] ״כרבנו נסים גאון והרשב״א וזולתם מאנשי לבב אשר לקחו לפניהם האגדות והספורים הנמצאים להם ז״ל שנראה בהם **איזה קושי אצל השכל** ובקשו להלום אותו כתפוחי זהב במשכיות כסף.״[65] בדברים אלה יש סיכום תמציתי וקולע על בעית האגדה בדרך כלל ועל העיסוק המיוחד בדברים קשים. אפשר לאושש ולהמחיש את הדברים ע״י גביית עדות מאת הנוגעים בדבר. ר׳ אברהם בן הרמב״ם מדגיש: ״ובזה ימלט נפשו מלהוציא על המדברים ז״ל דבות שלא כראוי כאשר יוציאו הקראים והכסילים וכיוצא בהם; או שיטבע ביון הסכלות בדברים הנמנעים ויחשוב שימצא דבר שאינו מצוי ושאירע דבר שלא היה ונברא, ויבוא לכפור בהשי״ת בהגשימו אותו וכיוצא בזה.״[66] מטרה כפולה, אם כן, למפרשי האגדה: לא ליתן פתחון פה למקטרגים וגם כענין חשוב בפני עצמו, בלתי תלוי בגירוי חיצוני, לא ליפול בפח של הגשמה ואמונות טפלות. ההדגשה הזאת חוזרת וניעורה אצל בני דורו ובני ארצו של הפניני. נזכיר אחדים מהם. ר׳ הלל מוירונה כותב: ״וכל דומה לזה שהם דברים זרים ורחוקים מאד מן הפירוש שפירשו בו, אותם בוודאי יש להם להבינם במשל והם תפוחי זהב במשכיות כסף על הדרך שפירש רבינו משה . . . וכל מי שיבינם כפשוטו הוא אצלי חסיד שוטה . . . ״.[67] ר״י אבן כספי מרחיב את הדבור בנידון דידן בצוואתו לבנו: ״ . . . עוד אזכירך דבר אחד פן תשכח בעבור היות לך גירסא דינקותא בגמרא, ובפרט במס׳ ברכות שהיא ההתחלה. ובאו בה כמה הגדות יורה פשוטם מציאת ענינים נמנעים אצל השכל או ענינים מיחסים גשמות או שינוי או היפעלות מה לשם. פן תאכל ושבעת מאלו המאכלים הרעים סמי המות, רצוני אותם הפשטים, האלקים יצילך. לכן דע בני כי רוב ההגדות הנמצאות בגמרא וביתר ספריהם אשר פשוטם יורה אלו הענינים אשר זכרתי, יש בהם תוך והסתר והם כולם משלים, הן שנבין אנחנו הנסתר הן שלא נבין. ולנו יש לדעת כי מי שהוא מזרע אברהם אבינו אשר השליך את נפשו לחלוק עם כל בני ארצו ומלכם שהיו מאמינים גשמות באל יתברך, הוא מאמין באמונתו. ומי שמאמין חילוף זה בגשמות הוא מעיד על עצמו שאינו מזרעו של אברהם אבינו אכן הוא מזרע נמרד או מיתר בני כשדים

(3) כל מאמר על תורה ודרך ארץ או חכמה ומצוות מציג את סולם הערכים של שלמות המדות ושלמות הדעות או תיקון הגוף ותיקון הנפש.
(4) תפלה או עבודה שבלב זהה עם השגה שכלית.[52]
(5) קילוס ושבח לה׳ כוונתם הלל והודאה ע״י הבנת סדרי הטבע לאשורם.[53]
(6) קדושה כוונתה שלילת החומר וחוש המשוש, ״אשר הוא חרפה לנו.״[54]
(7) הערלה הושאלה על כל דבר הנמצא באדם שמונע אותו מהשיג שלמות.[55]
(8) ״ערוה וערלה הם שמות מושאלים על כל דבר מגונה.״[56]
(9) ״דברו ז״ל הנה על המלך בדרך הסתר וקראו המלך המושל ברוחו ובחומר שלו.״[57]
(10) עם הארץ הוא ״המתנהג על סדר ישר עם זולתו ולא יפסיד ההנהגה המדינית כי כל אדם מדיני בטבע וצריך עזר מזולתו. והאיש המתנהג עם חברו להיות לו לעזר נקרא עם הארץ כי הוא יודע בהנהגת הארץ והיישוב המדיני ולא ראה לבו חכמה ודעת.״[58]

בקיצור, הפניני מפגיש מערכת רעיונות קבועה עם קורפוס ספרותי מקודש ומכובד, בעל השפעה כבירה — ובמיוחד בפרובנס היתה האגדה נפוצה מימות ר׳ משה הדרשן ואילך.[59] תקוותו ומגמתו החינוכית־דתית היא להרגיל את הקוראים להבין את האגדה על תכניה הרוחניים, רמיזותיה הפילוסופיות והנחיותיה השכלתניות. ״כבר ביארנו **דוגמתה** בחלק ב׳ בתנחומא״; ״כבר ביארנו **דוגמת** זה המאמר בתנחומא״, ״כונת זה המאמר כבר ביארנוה **בדוגמתו** בחלק ה. . . .״. בפירושו לסנהדרין, לאחר שביאר שורת המאמרים על אשתו של אדם — כגון ״כל אדם שמתה אשתו ראשונה בחייו כאילו חרב בית המקדש בימיו״, ״כל אדם שמתה אשתו בחייו עולם חשך בעדו״, ״אין אדם מוצא קורת רוח אלא מאשתו הראשונה״ — כמתארים את יחס האדם לחומר ולענינים גופניים (״ולא דברו ז״ל לפי הנגלה מדבריהם אלו אם לא בדרך הסתר ועל דרך משל ומליצה וחידות״),[60] מעיר הערה מאלפת היוצאת ללמד על הכלל כולו: ״ושאר הדבר[ים] אשר האריכו לדבר בזה על האשה כלם הולכים על הכוונה הזאת, טובה כפולה ומכפלת, **ומדבריהם אלו אשר בארנו תוציא הכוונה על האחרות** כי כלם נקשרות זו בזו וכוונה אחת להם והיתה ההזכרה והביאור עליהם ללא צורך״. הפניני מקים בניני־אב — דוגמאות — וסומך על הקורא שידע להוציא דבר מדבר ולדמות דבר לדבר, ליישם את הכללים בהקשרים ספרותיים שונים לא מאומד ומשמועה אלא בדיוק רב ובקפדנות כמעט מדעית.[61]

ישנם מוטיבים אחדים בולטים המשמשים בריח תיכון בכל כתביו. רעיון יסודי המזדקר לעיני הקורא הוא המאמץ הבלתי פוסק לזכך את דעות ההמון, להוציא מלבות ההמון, להעלותו באטיות ובהדרגה אך ללא סטיות וללא פשרות.

ההמון שקוע בחמריות ויש לחוס עליו שהוא בבחינת הולך בדרך — ״כי הם ז״ל קראו ״הולך על דרך״ בדרך משל האדם כל ימי חייו״ ומפסיק משנתו. וכאן מתגלית הסתירה הגדולה ביחס המשכילים לפשוטי העם. מצד אחד, מקפידים על סודיות ומקימים חיץ בין דעותיהם ובין אמונות העם. לא ניתנו סודות התורה אלא למלכים, מאן מלכי — חכמים־פילוסופים. יש פער עצום בין ההמון והיחידים ולא קרב זה אל זה ״ורוב השבושים והספקות קרו מדברי המערבים אותם כי ירצו להבין להמון הדברים העמוקים, שלא יסבלום שכלי רב החוקרים, כ״ש שכלי ההמון.״[62] מאידך, כל אדם שזוכה להגיע לידיעה צרופה והשגה שכלית של סודות התורה ויסודותיה רוצה, ואף חייב, לשתף אחרים בהשגתו ובידיעתו. מצוה לפרסם. כתוצאה מכך, פונה היחיד להמון ומגלה באטיות ובהדרגה מדעותיו האמתיות ושואף להשפיע — בבחינת ״יושב ודורש והאש מלהטת סביבותיו״. בקיצור, מחד גיסא, החכם עג עוגה ועומד בתוכה, מאידך גיסא, שואף לפרוץ את הגדר ולצאת לרשות הרבים. בנידון

III

סיבת ההבדל החותך בין הדברים המאופקים והממושמעים שבאגרת ההתנצלות ובין הדברים המרחיקים לכת בפירושים נראית פשוטה ומחוורת. אף לא נסתפק בזה שבאגרת יש לצפות למפרע לעמדה שמרנית ובפירושים לחרות גדולה וגמישות יתרה באלגוריזציה של פיסקאות תמוהות — כי לא בזה מדובר. כן לא נסמוך על הבחנה סבירה אחרת: באגרת כתב הפניני כנציגם של חכמי פרובנס או שאפילו ערך את האגרת יחד עם חכמי מונפלייר.[47] ידעיה הפניני יצא להפיץ את מעיינותיו חוצה. פירושו הוא מפעל חינוכי־ספרותי, נסיון רחב־ממדים להחדיר רעיונות פילוסופיים, נטיות רוחניות ודפוסי־מחשבה שכלתניים לתוך האגדה ודברי חז״ל בכלל. מן המפורסמות הוא שכל הפילוסופים האחיזו את רעיונותיהם במאמרי חז״ל. הפניני מוסיף על כך ומאחיז את השקפותיו גם בהלכה. לפניו שקדו פרשנים ויגעו יגיעות אבל לא מיצו את הענין, וברצונו להראות שדברי חז״ל מתובלים בכל מיני תבלין פילוסופיים ומושתתים על יסודות רוחניים־שכלתניים. כחה של ההצהרה הרגשית בסוף אגרת ההתנצלות יפה גם לגבי הפירושים: ״כי על כבוד הרב הגדול ז״ל וספריו הם חושבים להלחם, ועל קדושת תורתו ימסרו ממונותם ותולדותם ונפשותם עוד נשמת רוח חיים באפם״. והנה לא רק שהוא יוצא להגן על כבוד הרמב״ם ותורתו אלא שהוא מעמיק ומרחיב את עקרונות תורתו ומתאמץ להעלותם מתוך דברי חז״ל. הסתמכותו על הרמב״ם גם בנוגע לפירושים עצמם מוצהרת בראש פירושו למסכת אבות: ״ואני לא באתי לפרש מה שהוא פירשו כי המוסיף על דבריו גורע כי הוא דבר גדולות ונכבדות בפי׳ המסכת ועל דבריו הטובים אין להוסיף. ומה האדם שיבא אחרי המלך,[48] על כן על כל דברי המסכתא לא באתי אם לא לבאר את אשר לא דברו הנבי׳״. מכאן ואילך רשאי הוא להוסיף, להגביר את המתח הרוחני ולדרוש סמוכין להשקפותיו הפילוסופיות. ויותר ממה שהצהיר בפנינו כתוב כאן; רעיונות מיימוניים, שאין שמו של הרב נקרא עליהם בהדיא, מונחים ביסודו של הפירוש הזה.[49]

כיון שמצא הפניני בקעה להתגדר בה, מתייחס הוא לכל דבר הניתן להתפרש לפי שיטתו או לצורך משנתו. וממילא נפתרת שאלת הברננות בפירושיו, שכן קשה במבט ראשון להחליט מהם קווי־היסוד לבחירת החומר העומד להתבאר. הפניני אינו מפרש שיגרתי אלא מגמתי וכוונתו שקופה: שזירתם של עקרונות פילוסופיים בניסוחים המדרשיים של חז״ל. הרציפות הפרשנית אינה קובעת, ההדגשה הפילוסופית היא הנותנת. הפולמוס הרעיוני קובע את צביון החיבור, התעמולה השכלתנית מטביעה את חותמה על אופי הפירוש. מתקבל הרושם שהפניני מתהלך עם קופת רוכלין: יש לו אוצר מסויים של רעיונות־יסוד והוא מוכן לחזור עליהם חלילה ולשבצם למסגרות שונות. אם כי צריך תמיד להזהר מהכנסת שיטתיות יתרה במקום שיש רק הברקות פרשניות, הערות בודדות, ושברי רעיונות בלבוש מדרשי, אפשר כמעט לעשות מפתח ענינים ומושגים לפירושו של הפניני והקורא יוכל באופן דדוקטיבי לעמוד בעצמו על הפירוש הצפוי. שיטתו בפירוש דברי חז״ל עקיבה מאד; לפעמים הוא בעצמו מצהיר על יסודות פרשנותו ולפעמים העקביות נראית ממילא. ״כבר הקדמנו בהרבה מקומות כי הם ז״ל המשילו המדות האנושיות ללחם כי המה סועדות נפש האדם ומוליכות אותה למחוז חפצה.״[50] משפט כזה מעודדנו להכליל הכללות ולהשלים את המפתח גם בענינים שהוא לא הצביע עליהם בפירוש.

(1) כל מסורת או תורה מכוונת לפילוסופיה וסתרי תורה. תורה וחכמה שמות נרדפים הם וזהותם מופגנת תמיד.[51]

(2) כל אזהרה נגד אריכות לשון — מאמרים פשוטים כ״לא מצאתי לגוף טוב משתיקה״ או ״מרבה דברים מרבה חטא״ — מכוונת כלפי המגשימים והמשתמשים בתארים ברשלנות ובחוסר דייקנות.

הדבר תלוי אלא בי, הניח ראשו בין ברכיו וגעה בבכי׳ עד שיצתה נשמתו. יצתה בת קול ואמרה ר״א בן דורדיא מזומן לחיי העולם הבא״*[42] — יוצא הפניני להתפלמס עם בני דורו המצמידים את תפלתם לאמצעים ואינם משליכים את יהבם על ה׳ במישרין: ״אינו צריך לאמצעים אחרים בינו לבין אלקיו כי כלם עלולים ממנו . . . ״ ״וכבר טעו בזה קצת מהמוני התורה הנותנים אמצעי ביניהם לבין אלקיהם לכפר פניו . . . זה יצא להם משרש נחש ואמונה משובשת הקרובה לאמונת השניות. וזאת לפנים בישראל ועדין רשומה נכר בתוך עמנו כאשר יקומו בלילות באשמורת הבקר ימים עשרה, שנה שנה מראש השנה עד יום הכפורים, הם יתפללו ויאמרו מכניסי רחמים ומחלים פני אמצעיים שיתפללו בעדו. וזה שבוש גדול להם המביאם לאמונת השניות כי הוא ית׳ אינו צריך לאמצעי . . . ״. נתוספה לנו פה עדות חדשה, הבוטה כמדקרות חרב, על מנהג אמירת ״מכניסי רחמים״ שהסעיר את הרוחות עד לעת החדשה.[43] כאן דוגמה מובהקת לפולמוסו של הפניני עם הדתיות העממית הנותנת טעם לפגם. הוא אינו גורס ״הנח להם״ אלא — ״לך רד.״

(6) תפיסתו את הבבא הראשונה במסכת אבות מוסיפה נדבך חשוב למערכת פירושיו ורעיונותיו. קודם כל ״משה קבל תורה מסיני ומסרה ליהושע״, הכוונה ״על העלמת הדבר הנכבד ההוא המופשט מחמר שאינו מושג בחוש אם לא בשכל האדם הזך והצלול, אמרו שמסר משה האמתות ההם ליהושע . . . ״ תורה, אם כן, אינה תורה שבכתב ואף לא הלכה אלא ״החלק המיוחד ממנה בידיעת השם ומלאכיו הנבדלים מחמר . . . ״ גם סדר המסירה — יהושע לזקנים וזקנים לנביאים — אומר פרשני כי הסדר הזה הופך עליונים למטה ותחתונים למעלה, שהרי ״הנביא הוא שלם וחכם מן הזקן . . . שלמות הנביא גדול יתר מאד על הזקן ויתרונו רב עליו כיתרון האור על החשך ולרב שלמות הנביא על החכם לכל דבר, יתרון הכשר חכמה ויתרון מעלה במדות אנושיות, הוא ית׳ משרה שכינתו על הנביא יותר מן הזקן שקנה חכמה . . . .״ הוא מותיב ליה והוא מפרק ליה בתשובה נועזת הנעוצה בתפיסה מיימונית אשר יש לה תהודה ניכרת בתקופה זאת. ״ובהקדימם הנה הזקן לנביא לא אמרו ז״ל אלא לפי דעת המוני התורה החושבים שהנבואה שורה על איש שוגה או פתי ואם לא ראה לבו חכמה ודעת יוכל להנבא אם בחרו השם על זה.[44] וזה ידוע ומפורסם ומושכל ראשון שנמנעת הנבואה בחוק כל אדם שלא קדמתו חכמה כי איך יתראה פנים ית׳ לאיש אשר לא הכירו ולא ידע מה הוא . . . אך שמו הנה הזקן לפני הנביא לפי סברת המוני התורה, ואם ידיעתם משובשת בזה הם שמו הזקן ראשונה לפי סברת ההמון״. הפניני מסתמך פה על הנחה פרשנית־הרמנוטית הנותנת הרמנא לפירושים מפתיעים והפותחת שער לסברות שונות ומשונות. חז״ל מתחשבים בדעה המונית אעפ״י שהיא מוטעית וחסרת־שחר. במלים אחרות, דעות משובשות ומסולפות נרשמו ונשמרו ע״י חז״ל בגלל תפוצתן הרבה; קול ההמון הטועה בוקע ועולה. נדמה כי בנין אב לתפיסה זאת הוא הסברו של הרמב״ם לאיסור קללה; למה חייבים עליו מלקות אם כי הוא לאו שאין בו מעשה, והרי כל מצוות לא תעשה ״שאין בהן מעשה, ההפסד שבא מאתם הוא מעט ואי אפשר ג״כ להשמר ממנו מפני שהם דברים לבד״ ומשום כך אין לוקין עליהן. שלשה יוצאים מן הכלל, כידוע: נשבע, מימר, ומקלל — והרמב״ם מנמק כדרכו. נשבע — ״בעבור מה שהוא חייב להאמינו מהגדלת השם״, מימר — ״שלא יביא זה לבזות בקרבנות המיוחסות לשם״, מקלל — ״להיות היזק הקללה להמון יותר גדולה מהיזק שנופל בגוף,״[45] בעצם, אין הקללה מזיקה כלל — דבורים בעלמא; רק בדמיונו של ההמון היא הרת סכנות.[46] לפי הרמב״ם, אם כן, התורה מזדקקת לנתונים פסיכולוגיים ומתחשבת בדעות המוניות אם כי מוטעות. לפי הפניני, חז״ל המשיכו בדרך זו ולעתים ניסחו את מאמריהם בהתאם לדעות המוניות אם כי מוטעות הנה. לאור זה אפשר על נקלה להשתחרר ממאמרים קשים, בלתי־נוחים. אפשר להניף את מקל הקסמים ולומר — דעה המונית שנקבעה בכתובים.

הפניני: "ואמרו בעלי קומה, ר"ל שהשלימו עצמם וזכו את ארחם לעלות במעלות הסלם להשיג את בוראם נצב עליו. ועל זה קראו בעלי קומה שהם עליונים במדרגה ובמעלה להשיג הדבר המופשט מחמר". ולא נתקררה דעתו עד שהוציא מלבם של הפשטנים בפירוש: "ולא קראם ז"ל בעלי קומה מצד גבהות קומתם כבני ענקים כי הוא ית' אינו בוחר בבני אדם מצד החמר..."

(4) לעתים נדמה כי הפניני מסתבך ומפליג בניסוחו לרגל המגמה הפילוסופית־ספיריטואליסטית אשר לפניו. בקשר למשנה במסכת אבות "חביבין ישראל שנקראו בנים למקום, חבה יתרה נודעת להם שנ' בנים אתם לה' אלקיכם" מציע הפניני הסבר מוזר, מגומגם קצת, המשחיל את היחס הפילוסופי למות לתוך הלכות אבלות. "ראינו כונת התורה שחמל[ה] על הכהן והנזיר **וכל איש ישראל הנוטה להתנהג כמותם להיות קדוש** שבאה הצואה עליהם שלא יבאו על נפש מת... ואל יראה במותם ולא יבכה ויתאונן עליהם כי יזיקנו וימנע ממנו טובה הרבה וכל שלמות אמתי, ולא יוכל להשיג את בוראו מתוך כאב לב ועצבון רוח וחמל השם על נפשם לבלתי השחיתה אם יתעצב אל לבו והמס ימס בקרבו מתוך הדאגה. ולא מנע לכל העם בכלל כי לא יוכלו להתאפק במות המת, האב והאם, אם יראו במותם, לאח ולאחות, שלא יבכו ויתאוננו עליהם... **אך באה הערה להם על הכהן והנזיר שאם ירצו להתנהג כמוהם על האבל ולעשות עצמם כתלמיד חכם הרשות בידם לבלתי יתאוננו על נפש מת.** ואמר רבן של נביאים לכל העם בכלל לא תתגודדו ולא תשימו קרחה בין עיניכם למת. ולא הזהירם לבלתי יבכו כלל. ואם ירצה למנוע את עצמו הרשות בידו שאין הכונה במין האדם ממנו ית' על החמר הנפסד בהכרח ולא יועילנו אבלו עליו ולא יצילנו ממות... ועל זה הורה רבן של נביאים והזהירם על ענין האבלות ואמר בנים אתם לה' אלקיכם, הורה להם כי האב ההוא המוליד הצורה לא ימות לעולם והצורה אם השלימה חיו תחיה לא תמות. ולא ידאג על פרידת נפשו מן החמר שלו כי שם ינוח לה ואז תתענג על ה'". תיארתי את הדברים כמוזרים שכן ההשקפה הפילוסופית, כמעט דואליסטית, מתנגשת עם החיובים ההלכתיים. קודם כל, איסור טומאת מת לכהן ולנזיר מתבסס פה לא על יסוד הקדושה אלא על הרעיון הפילוסופי המאדיר את המיתה ע"י שלילת החומר והדגשת המטרה הבלעדית שהיא השגת המושכלות והאמתות.[39] יתר מיכן, הרשות נתונה כאן לכל אדם להפקיע את עצמו מניהוג אבלות. כל אדם יכול לעשות את עצמו כתלמיד חכם — היינו כהן ונזיר, היינו פילוסוף הפורש מחשבונות העולם והבליו — ולבטל הלכות אבלות. אתמהה! הרי אפילו כהן מתאבל; מוזהר הוא רק על טומאת מת. הרמב"ם כידוע הבחין בין שתי הרשויות: מיתה כנשיקה, תכלית החיים ושיאם, ומיתה כמאורע טרגי־הרסני הגורר בעקבותיו יאוש ועצבות ואנינות הלב. יש מיתה "אשר הוא המלט מן המות עד האמת" וקראוה חכמים "על דרך מליצת השיר המפורסמת... נשיקה."[40] מאידך קבע הרמב"ם מסמרות להלכה כי "כל מי שאינו מתאבל כמו שצוו חכמים הרי זה אכזרי", אעפ"י שאסור להתאבל יותר מדי — כי כך מנהגו של עולם — חובת האבלות אינה זזה ממקומה.[41]

יש לשער כי הפניני הפריז פה על מדותיו ובהתלהבות עצומה הרחיב את תוקפם וחלותם של דברי הרמב"ם הקובעים, בתחום אחר וללא עימות כלשהו עם ההלכה, כי **כל אדם** השואף לעולם שכולו טוב יכול להתעלות ולהתקדש ככהנים וכלוים: "ולא שבט לוי בלבד אלא כל איש ואיש מכל באי העולם אשר נדבה רוחו אותו והבינו מדעו להבדל לעמוד לפני ה' לשרתו ולעובדו לדעה את ה' והלך ישר כמו שעשהו האלקים ופרק מעל צוארו עול החשבונות הרבים אשר בקשו בני האדם, הרי זה נתקדש קדש קדשים ויהיה ה' חלקו ונחלתו לעולם ולעולמי עולמים ויזכה לו בעה"ז דבר המספיק לו כמו שזכה לכהנים ללוים."[42]

(5) מהמסופר על אלעזר בן דורדיא — החוטא הגדול אשר פנה להרים וגבעות, שמים וארץ, חמה ולבנה, שיבקשו עליו רחמים עד שהסיק את המסקנה כי "אין

להקריב הקרבן לאשר בחרו. ונצטווה רבן של נביאים אז על הבנין ההוא להורות לעם ולהמציא להם מציאותם בכללו ואחר השיגם המציאות ישיגו המחוייב מהם... ולהורות להם על החדוש ולהרחיק הקדמות בא להם הבנין הנכבד ההוא... ואמרו ז״ל על הבנין (!) שעשה משה שמשיחתן בשמנים מקדשתן. כבר ידעת שבאה בתורה ובנביאים המשיחה והשאילוה על רכוך הלבב, אם הוא ערל והכניע לבבו כמו שידוע על המשוחים בשמן מחוץ שירכך הבשר המשיחה ההיא, כן הושאלה על רכוך הלבב אם היה ערל... ״ היוצא מדברים אלה הוא כי שמן משחה נותן טעם לפגם, לא לשבח; משה רבן של נביאים הוכרח להשתמש בו לא כסגולה מיוחדת אלא בגלל המצב הירוד של העם, אמונותיו ודעותיו. בניגוד לכך הגיעה האמונה הטהורה למצב של גאות בימי שלמה; הפניני משתמש פה ב־*topos* ספרותי הנפוץ במיוחד בין חכמי פרובאנס[32] בתארו את תקופת שלמה כתקופה מזהירה של חכמה ועיון: ״שנפקחו עיניהם... וראה לבם כל חכמה אמתית, הם לא היו צריכים אז למשיחה ההיא כי הם היו רכי הלבב מצד עצמם... ובאו ז״ל להורות על העם אשר יצא ממצרים על ידי משה במלאכות השם כי הם היו קטני אמונה והיו סכלים מן הידיעה האמתית ממנו ית׳ ועל זה היו צריכים אל המשיחה בשמן לרכך לבבם הערל. ובימי שלמה וכל חכם לב בעם, אחר שנתנה להם התורה... אז לא היו צריכים למשיחה ההיא כי היו רכי הלבב.״[33]

(2) ההבדל בין בעלי העיון האמתי ובין ההמון העלוב, אנשים מקופחי הבנה שכלית וחסרי רגישות, מבלי עולם רוחני מזוקק, משתקף לפי הפניני בהלכה הקובעת כי במקדש שם נאמר שם הויה בפירוש ובמדינה בכנוי — הלכה יסודית בקשר לסדר העבודה ביום הכפורים, ברכת כהנים וכיוצא באלו.[34] והנה במדרש תהלים (פז:ג) על הפסוק ״נכבדות מדובר בך״, אמר רב הונא אמר רב אידי למה היו ישראל מזכירין את השם במקדש בפירוש, ובמדינה בכינוי, דכתיב ליראה את השם הנכבד והנורא הזה את ה׳ אלוהיך (דברים כח נח), הוי נכבדות מדובר בך, ואין מתאמר בקרייתא דאלהא, בקרייתא דציון, ואיכן עיר האלהים סלה״ (הוצ׳ באבער). שוב מצא הפניני בקעה הלכתית להתגדר בה: ״לכן ראוי שיתרחק כל שלם מלבאר ולגלות האמתות להמון מפני שהשגתן לא תסבלם וזאת היא החומרא החזקה אשר החמירו בהוראת מעשה בראשית ומעשה מרכבה ודרשתן להמון אלא ליחיד אשר יראו בו אותות ההצלחה בעיון ויהיה שלם במדותיו בעזיבת המדינות וצרכי הגופות. אבל להמון ימסרו קצת האמתות בקבלה והן אותן ההכרחיות[35] בסדור קבוצן בהאמנת מציאות האלוה, כל מעיין בגמול ועונש בפרטיהן, כדי שייראו האל ויפחדו ממנו. שכל אלו הענינים יובנו מהאל אשר בתארים יתארוהו בהם הנביאים **והם הכינויין**. ולכן אמרו שבכינויין יזכר ה׳ במדינה שהיא מלאת ההמון ורבת העם להעיר על זאת הכוונה והוא היראה מהאל ושיזכר במקדש בלי כינוי מפני שהוא מקום ההתבודדות והוראת כל תיקון וששוכניו היו יחידי האומה רבי ההשגה... ראוי שימסרו להם האמתות בלי הסתר וחידה אבל במופתים העיוניים המשוללים מכל דמיון...״. במקדש, שם נמצאים ״נקיי האמונה וזכי הדעות״[36] מבטאים שם הויה בפירוש ואילו במדינה, שם ״מפרסמים האמת בשפלים ומדברים בזה עם ההמון... ואי אפשר שידובר אלא בדיבורים אשר יסבלום דמיונותן כדי לקרבן אל האמת קירוב הקבלה,״[37] משתמשים רק בכינוי, כי המרחק בין ההמון והיחידים הוא עצום.

(3) ״אין מושיבין בסנהדרין אלא בעלי חכמה ובעלי קומה ובעלי מראה... ״ (סנהדרין יז ע״א). ההלכה כפשוטה באה להדגיש את ערך החיצוניות, כלשונו של הרמב״ם: ״כשם שבית דין מנוקין בצדק כך צריכין להיות מנוקין מכל מומי הגוף וצריך להשתדל ולבדוק ולחפש שיהיו כולן בעלי שיבה, בעלי קומה, בעלי מראה, נבוני לחש... ״.[38] הדגשה גופנית זו לא נתקבלה על דעתו השכלתנית־רוחנית של

ע״א).[27] (ג) מאמרים הסותרים את חוקי הטבע ואינם תורמים מאומה לחיזוק האמונה — כגון אגדות רבה בר בר חנא — מצווים אנו להסיע את עצמנו מהפשט (״מגלויו״) וליישבם יישוב אלגורי. אמנם, מוסיף ידעיה, משוכנע הוא כי אגדות אלו נאמרו לכתחלה כמילי דבדיחותא, לשעשע את התלמידים ו״להניח מכובד העיון ועמל הגרסא״. בכל זאת, על אף המסקנה הברורה שאין לדברים אלה תוכן רציני, שומה עלינו להתאמץ ולפרשם פירוש אליגורי בגלל סבה משולשת: (1) בכדי להרחיק זרויות מדברי חז״ל ו״שמירת המעיינים שלא נביאם לחשוב רע עליהם״; (2) בכדי לשמור על האופי הסגולי והמיוחד של נסים — שלא יהא לבנו גס בהם כבדברים שגרתיים; (3) בכדי להדגיש כי המופת יהא תמיד למטרה מוגדרת ולא סתם לראווה. סוג שלישי זה אומר דרשני. מצד אחד קובע ידעיה — בעקבות אבן עזרא[28] והרמב״ם[29] — כי אין כל משמעות רצינית לאימרות אלו; ומצד שני, במקום להרשות לכל אחד לדחותן בקש, תובע ליצור עבורם תכן הראוי להתכבד בו. בשעה שהמפרש בדרך כלל מתמודד עם המאמר ומתאמץ לגלות את כוונתו הטמירה של בעל המאמר, בנידון זה מתמודד המפרש עם עצמו, עם מערכת מושגיו ואמונותיו, ויוצא ליצור פירוש שמעולם לא עלה על דעת המחבר. (ד) דברי אגדה שהם נמנעים — כגון ״כל היודע שעורו של יוצר בראשית מובטח לו שהוא בן העולם הבא״ (ברכות ג׳ ע״א) או ״הקב״ה מניח תפלין״ (ברכות ו ע״א)[30] — אעפ״י שעשויים להועיל בעניני דת ולחזק את אמונתם של פשוטי העם, בשום אופן אין לקיימם אלא אם נוציאם מפשטיהם ונעמיד אותם בפירוש אלגורי התואם את שרשי האמונה ״בתכלית הנקיות והברור״. כאן תפקידו של הפרשן ברור: עליו לפענח את הצפון ולהעלות משמעות סבירה ומאירת עינים. במקרים כאלה אין המדובר בהוספת נדבך פרשני. הפרשן חייב לקלוע לפירוש המכוון המסותר כגרעין מתחת לקליפה עבה. הנוקט בפשט הנראה לעין מחטיא את המטרה, כי הפשט משולל מלכתחלה.

II

מי שעובר מקווי־יסוד אלה לעצם פירושו של הפניני רואה תיכף ומיד את הפער העצום ביניהם: התכנית המתווה קווי־יסוד היא בבחינת כל הדבר הקשה יביאו אל הפירוש האליגורי, ואילו בפירושים גופם מצודת הפירוש החפשי והדרשנות הפילוסופית פרושה על הכל, לא רק על הדברים הקשים, הזרים והרחוקים, אלא גם על מאמרים אשר דוקא הפשט יפה להם והאליגוריה אונסת אותם. יתר מיכן, אפילו מאמרים פשוטים המושתתים על ענינים הלכתיים הופכים בידו חומר לדרשנות פילוסופית־שכלתנית. כפי שנראה, מוצעים הפירושים מתוך תפיסה אחידה, מתוך ראות מיוחדת של מאמרי חז״ל, הלכה ואגדה גם יחד. דוגמאות מספר ימחישו את הדבר וידגימו את החידוש שבדברים ומגמתם.

(1) ״כל הכלים שעשה משה משיחתן מקדשתן מכאן ואילך עבודתן מחנכתן״ (סנהדרין ט״ז ע״ב). אמנם, ענין שמן המשחה הוא מסובך ובעיתי אך ההלכה פשוטה וברורה. הרמב״ם סיכם את ההלכה בניסוח זה:[31] ״כל כלי המקדש שעשה משה במדבר לא נתקדשו אלא במשיחתן בשמן המשחה שנאמר ״וימשחם ויקדש אותם״, ודבר זה אינו נוהג לדורות, אלא הכלים כולן כיון שנשתמשו בהם במקדש במלאכתן נתקדשו שנאמר: ״אשר ישרתו בם בקודש״, בשירות הם מתקדשין״, ידעיה מפרש כדרכו כי הכל תלוי בהשגה שכלית, והלכות כלי המקדש כאן משקפות את רמת החכמה והתפיסה הפילוסופית של בני הדור. שמן המשחה אינו אלא סמל להכשרת הלבבות וטיהורן לאמונה זכה ומופתית, לתיקון הדעות. ״באו ז״ל להורות על זה שבימי משה היה העם והגוי כלו מאמיני הקדמות ולא היו משיגים סבה ראשונה למציאות למעלה מן הגלגל ועל זה היו עושים מן הגלגלים אלוה ובונים להם במות

והזיקה המתמדת אליו על מנת "להועילם ולהשכילם לדעת דעת עליון."[19] בעצם, הקוטביות המחודדת המאפיינת את עמדתם של השכלתנים בתקופה זו משתקפת בשלמותה: אין דעתה נוחה מעם הארץ השקוע בחומריות ואף לא מן תלמיד החכם הפונה עורף להתעסקות רוחנית. השכלתן — קרי ר' י' הפניני — נאבק על ייחודו הדתי ויעודו הרוחני של העם. ייעודם החינוכי של הפירושים בולט, והוא מאיר מעמדת תצפית מיוחדת את המתיחויות והפילוגים בצבור היהודי בפרובנס ובספרד.

מטרת מאמרי זה היא לאפיין את החיבור הגדול הזה באופן כללי, ספרותי־עניני, לקבוע את מקומו במערכת הפרשנות המדרשית של ימי הבינים, ולהעריכו מבחינה היסטורית. אין בדעתי לשרטט את השקפת עולמו של הפניני[20] ואין צורך לעת עתה לחזור ולתאר את תפקידו בפרשת הויכוח והחרם נגד לימוד הפילוסופיה.[21]

I

בסוף אגרת ההתנצלות דוחה הפניני לחלוטין, ללא כחל וללא שרק, את הקטרוג כי חכמי פרובנס נוטים אחר פירושים אלגוריים המבטלים פשוטו של מקרא,[22] ובחדא מחתא מקיים, בגאוה ובסיפוק נפש, את טענתו של הרשב"א כי חכמה יונית נפוצה בין חכמי פרובנס. כלפי לישנא אחרינא מלמד הוא סנגוריה איתנה על חכמה זו והולך ומונה את מעלותיה והישגיה, את השפעותיה והשלכותיה העיוניות — בבחינת "דברי חכמים כדרבנות וכמשמרות נטועים". הוא מגלה חוש היסטורי מפותח בהעריכו את תרומתו המכרעת והמדרבנת של הרמב"ם לשיקום הפילוסופיה והחזרת עטרה זו ליושנה בתולדות האמונה היהודית.[23] ידיעת הפילוסופיה ויסודותיה מדרבנת ומדריכה את החכמים להבנה אמתית ומעמיקה של פסוקי המקרא ומאמרי האגדה ומבערת דעות משובשות מקרב העם.[24] בהקשר זה מתאר הפניני תכנית רעיונית־שיטתית המתווה קווי־יסוד לפרשנות האגדה וקובעת בבהירות מירבית מתי מותר ואף נחוץ להזדקק לפרשנות אלגורית ולדרשנות פילוסופית. הוא טוען, ובזה גם מתגונן נגד הבקורת החריפה של הרשב"א, כי סיפורי התורה צריכים כולם להתפרש לפי פשוטם של מקראות אפילו במקרים שהם נמנעים בטבע[25], כל זמן שאינם נמנעים בחק יכולת ה'. היות וכל הנסים נכללים בסוג זה אין צורך להכזיבם או להוציאם מפשוטם — ושלום על ישראל. יש רק סוג אחד שהוא יוצא מן הכלל: במקרים שתפיסת ענין או סיפור פשוטו כמשמעו נמנעת אפילו בחק ה' — היינו כל מה שנוגע לשיבושי אמונות או קיבוץ שני הפכים בנושא אחד — אז יש לפתוח את שערי הפירוש לרוחה. הדברים בכללם הם מדודים ומאופקים.

בנוגע לאגדות — ובניגוד לנזכר לעיל — הולך הפניני ומונה ארבעה סוגים: **(א)** יש לקיים מאמרים שאינם נוגדים את חוקי הטבע כפשוטם, אם כי שיח ושיג להם עם דברים רחוקים ("מיני האפשרים הרחוקים"). הנימוק לזה ראוי לתשומת לב, שכן הוא מבצבץ ועולה בהקשרים אחרים: "כדאי אותו השלם בעל המאמר המעיד בו לסמוך עליו בעונתו."[26] **(ב)** מאמרים הנוגדים את חוקי הטבע (חורגים "ממנהג הטבעי וסדורו ההקשי") אבל מאוששים פנות התורה ויסודות האמונה — גם אותם יש לקיים כפשוטם כל זמן שאינם סותרים או הורסים אמונה מוסכמת ויסודית. והיה, אם פרט וכלל מתנגשים ומתרוצצים, יש לדחות את הפרט מפני הכלל. למשל, פירוש פשטני, בלתי אלגורי של מאמרים על שכר גופני ושינוי מערכות הטבע כגון "עתידה א"י שתוציא גלוסקאות וכלי מילת" (שבת, ל' ע"ב) יכחיש ויערער את העקרון המקיף והיסודי "שאין בין העולם הזה לימות המשיח אלא שעבוד מלכויות בלבד" (ברכות, ל"ד ע"ב) או "שאין בעולם הבא לא אכילה ולא שתיה" (ברכות, י"ז

ר׳ ידעיה הפניני ופירושו לאגדה*

יצחק טברסקי

פירוש האגדות לר׳ ידעיה בדרשי הפניני,[1] חבור גדול לפי קני מדה איכותיים וכמותיים גם יחד, מוזנח כמעט לגמרי ומונח כאבן שאין לה הופכין; אין דורש ואין מבקש אותו. בדורות הסמוכים לו — כנראה עד למאה הט״ז — נשאו ונתנו בדבריו, העתיקו אותם והתוכחו עליהם. יש מצטט ומשבח[2] ויש מצטט ומגנה.[3] היו כאלה שהכירו בראשוניותו[4] ואחרים עברו עליו ועל מפעלו בשתיקה.[5] מספר ניכר של כתבי יד מעיד על תפוצתם של פירושיו שהקיפו את כל התלמוד, מדרש רבה, תנחומא, פרקי דר׳ אליעזר, וכו׳ — אוצר אגדה בלום.[6] בדורות אחרונים לא נתמזל מזלו. אין לנו מחקרים לא על שיטתו בפרשנות האגדה ולא על מגמתו,[7] ובררי כי אין לנו הוצאות מדעיות מדוייקות.[8] מצב זה הוא מעוות שיוכל לתקון, וכדאי להזדרז בתיקונו, כי אין ספק שעיון מקיף ומעמיק בפירוש האגדות מחזיק ברכה וחזקה שיניב פירות משובחים בתחומים שונים.

(1) קודם כל, ניתוח הפירוש ועמידה על תכנו, עיקרו ותכליתו, יאפשר שרטוט שלם של דמות דיוקנו של ידעיה הפניני, אותו ״חכם כולל״[9] הנידון ומתואר כמשורר,[10] פילוסוף,[11] ואף כראש המדברים בכל מקום בכבוד השכלתנות הפילוסופית[12] אבל לא כאישיות שלמה ואחידה, עתירת גוונים ורבת הישגים. החכם הכולל נדחק לעלמא דפירודא ויצירתו הספרותית המסונפת נתפצלה מגלות מגלות, קטעים קטעים.[13] מצווים אנו לשחזר את האחדות ולשלב עד כמה שאפשר את כל התחומים השונים ובלי הכרת הפירושים ייבצר מאתנו להגיע להערכה כנה ומאוזנת.[14]

(2) על יסוד בדיקה ראשונה, נדמה כי לא נגזים אם נוסיף ונקבע כי פירושים אלה מהווים את גולת הכותרת — ההישג המקורי ביותר — של מפעלו הספרותי. חכמים למיניהם ימצאו בהם ענין רב אם רק יהפכו בהם. בעלי אגדה ודאי ישתעשעו בהם. בעלי הלכה יבואו על שכרם וימצאו סוג חדש של פירושי הלכה ואנשי הפילוסופיה יגלו בהם מימדים חשובים.

אף חומר היסטורי, אם כי במדה צנועה למדי, שקוע בו.[15] בעקיפין, אף הזיקה בין שירה ופילוסופיה בתקופה זו תתברר; הפניני התחיל כילד שעשועים של השירה העברית — בקשת המְמין, ספר הפרדס, אוהב נשים, והכל מגיל ארבע עשרה עד שמונה עשרה — ואז פרש לפילוסופיה, עממית ומקצועית גם יחד.[16] תופעה זו של פרישה או התנזרות משירה, המוכרת לנו היטב, היא בעלת משמעות רבה ומשקפת את המתיחות שביצירה הספרותית הטרום־מודרנית. בעקבות הרמב״ם תפס את האגדה כ״דמות מליצת השיר״,[17] וזיהוי זה בין אגדה ושירה חשוב ומאלף. בקיצור, זהו עולם קטן המשמש בבואה נאמנת לעולמו הגדול של הפניני על הרפתקאותיו ולבטיו, הישגיו ומחדליו, שאיפותיו ותסכוליו.

(3) הפירושים הללו ישלימו את התיאור ההיסטורי של פרשנות האגדה לזרמיה ובתי מדרשיה, שיטותיה וגישותיה, בימי הבינים. מהרבה בחינות ניתן לומר כי תקופה זו — שלהי המאה הי״ג וראשית המאה הי״ד — היא תקופת גיאות לפרשנות האגדה[18] — טיפול פילוסופי, פולמוסי, פרשני — וידעיה הפניני מוסיף נדבך חשוב הקובע ברכה לעצמו ורשות לעצמו.

(4) לבסוף, הכרת החיבור הפרשני תסייע להבנת האינטלקטואליזם בראשית המאה הי״ד (ובימי הבינים בכלל), מגמותיו ובעיותיו, תודעת ההתבדלות מן ההמון

מתאר את תהליך ההאצלה כתהליך של השפעת אור מן המקור העליון לעולם הספירות ודרכן לשאר העולמות תוך כדי המעטת כמות האור ואיכותו, המצויים בכ״י מנטובה מס׳ 66 ובכ״י אוקספורד מס׳ 40, אני דנה במקום אחר תוך הקבלה למשלים קבליים בעלי אופי דומה (של ר׳ אשר, של מאיר ן׳ גבאי, של אלחנן סגי נהור, מספר הזהר ומ״ספר אהל מועד״). ברור שבספרות הקבלה בצפת, שבה ספר הזהר מקודש כל כך, קיימת נטיה לפנות אל סמלי האור והזהר. על סמלים אלה בספרות הזהר ראה: י. תשבי, ״משנת הזהר״, ירושלים תש״ט, כרך א׳ עמ׳ קנ״א–קנ״ג.

43. עריסת הרעיון עוד בעולם ההלניסטי. ראה: (למעלה, הע' 36) A. Altmann, *Studies* . . . וראה: "A Note on the Rabbinic Doctrine of Creation", p. 136. A.H. Armstrong, *Plotinus,* London 1953, Introduction, pp. 24–25.

44. ראה למשל: שלמה אבן גבירול, כתר מלכות: "אתה אור עליון . . . אתה אור עולם . . .". בניאופלטוניות היהודית הרבו להשוות בין ישויות רוחניות עלאיות ובין אור השמש. למשל: יצחק ישראלי (ראה בספרם של A. Altmann and S.M. Stern, *Isaac Israeli,* Oxford University Press, 1958 וראה את הדיון בתורתו ביחוד בעמ' 160, וגם את ההשוואות בין דעותיו של יצחק ישראלי ובין אלו המובאות בחבור "בן המלך והנזיר", שם (בעמ' 95–117) או שלמה אבן גבירול (ראה: "מקור חיים", שער שלישי, נ"ב וליקוטי מקור חיים בתרגום של שם טוב אבן פלקירה, ליקוטי המאמר השלישי, 10).

45. על מקורו הארסיטוטלי של המשל ראה: (למעלה, הע' 36) A. Altmann, *Studies* . . . "Ibn *Bajja* . . ." השוה: שלמה אבן גבירול, מקור חיים, שער רביעי, י"ד, וליקוטי המאמר הרביעי, 22. וראה גם: Sara O. Heller Wilensky, "Isaac Ibn Latif", in *Jewish Medieval and Renaissance Studies,* ed. A. Altmann, Cambridge, Mass. 1967, p. 208 n. 163.

46. יהודה הלוי, "ספר הכוזרי", מאמר רביעי, ט"ו.

47. על המשל ועל שמות האל אצל יהודה הלוי ראה: (למעלה דף נט, הע' 33) D. Kaufmann, "Die Lehre vom hochsten Gottesnamen" pp. 165–240; H.A. Wolfson, "Maimonides and Halevi, A Study in Typical Attitudes towards Greek Philosophy in the Middle Ages, *JQR,* N.S. 2, iii (1912), pp. 316–337.

48. משה הנרבוני, "ביאור לספר מורה נבוכים", וינא תרי"ג, דף ד' עמ' ב'. וראה: D. Kaufmann, *Ibid.,* pp. 208–209, n. 186. ראה שם גם הערתו בענין דברי משה אבן עזרא: "ומליצי הערב ממשלים הבורא לאור הנר", המכוונים נגד המשוררים הצופיים. יצחק אברבנאל (בפירושו לתורה, פרשת פקודי) מעמיד זו לעומת זו את דעתו של אבן רושד האומרת שהאל הוא אור רק "על צד הדמוי", מפני שהאור הוא רק הגשם הטהור ביותר, ואת דעת קודמו, גזאלי, האומרת שהאל הוא אור מוחלט המשפיע אור לזולתו ושרק לו נאות השם אור. דעתו של גזאלי מובאת על פי "ספר האורות האלהיות" שלו (משכאת אלאנואר). אברבנאל מציין שהמקובלים, בתורת הצחצחות שלהם, תומכים בדעתו של גזאלי. על תורת הצחצחות בקבלה ראה: ג. שלום, ראשית הקבלה (הוצאת שוקן, תש"ח) עמ' 170–175. (יצחק אברבנאל מציין כמקור לזהוי אור ואל את "ס' העצמים העליונים". אברבנאל עצמו מבחין בין אור שהוא למעלה מן הטבעי ובין אור טבעי).

49. יוסף אלבו (למעלה, דף נט, הע' 33), שם.

50. המקור בתורת אריסטו. בספרו על הנפש (ספר שלישי, פרק ו') מתיחס אריסטו להוצאת הצבעים הנמצאים בכח לצבעים ניכרים בפועל. השוה דברי הלל מוירונה בספר "תגמולי הנפש", ליק, תרל"ד, דף ז' עמ' ב', על השמש הגורמת לרואה בכח להיהפך רואה בפועל ועל האור המוציא את המראים (הגוונים) מן הכח אל הפועל. (הוא מסתמך על אלפרבי). על עמדת אלפרבי ראה: A. Altmann (למעלה, דף נט, הע' 36), שם. אצל אלבו כאן נושא ההשואה הוא אחר.

51. יוסף אלבו (למעלה, דף נט, הע' 33), שם. והשוה למשל עם אברהם בר חייא, "מגלת המגלה" (ברלין, תרפ"ד, עמ' 27) המבחין בין אור ובין מאור בלשון זו: "יהי אור מפני שלא היה האור ההוא גוף ולא נתפס בגוף ולא נפרש על גוף וביום הרביעי קראו מאור . . . ואין האור אלא אור דבוק בגוף . . ."

52. "ברית הלוי" (למעלה, דף נט, הע' 27), שם.

53. על תאורי ההאצלה כהארה בספרות הניאופלטונית ראה בספרם של א. אלטמאן וש.מ. שטרן על יצחק ישראלי (למעלה, הע' 44) ביחוד בעמ' 119–20, 176, וראה: שלמה אבן גבירול במקור חיים במקומות שהזכרנו. על שפיעת האור "האמתי הנאצל מאת הבורא ית' בלי אמצעות", ראה: יוסף אבן צדיק, "ספר העולם הקטן" ב"מאמר באמתת השכר והענש", ברסלאו, 1903, עמ' 76 ועל ענין זה בספרם של א. אלטמאן וש.מ. שטרן, שם. תאורים כאלה נקלטו בקבלה. ראה למשל את משל מראות הזכוכית בפירוש האגדות לר' עזריאל, מהדורת תשבי, עמ' 83. על חדירת התאורים לחוג המקובלים של גרונה ראה ג. שלום, "עקבותיו של גבירול בקבלה", "מאסף סופרי א"י", ת"ש, עמ' 171–173, וכן בספרם של א. אלטמאן וש.מ. שטרן, שם עמ' 130–132. על ההבחנה בין ההאצלה הקבלית לבין ההאצלה הניאופלטונית ראה: ג. שלום, "ראשית הקבלה", עמ' 111–112. במשלים אחרים של אלקבץ, שבהם הוא

25. אברהם ביבאגו, "דרך אמונה", קושטא רפ"ב, דף י"ג, עמ' א'.

26. יצחק אברבנאל, פרוש על התורה, ירושלים תשכ"ד, על בראשית א, דף לא. וראה: שם טוב אבן פלקירא, "ספר הנפש", ורשה תרפ"ד, דף י"ב.

27. "ברית הלוי", ירושלים תש"ל, ט, ב.

28. "ברית הלוי", שם. המשל והנמשל בעלי אופי ניאופלטוני. נשוב לדון בכך כשנסביר את הנמשל. בענין הכאת הניצוץ במים השוה יצחק אברבנאל, שם, שם.

29. "לקוטי הקדמות לחכמת הקבלה", כ"י אוקספורד מס' 40, 175א. ענין זה נדון על ידי י. בן שלמה בספרו "תורת האלהות של ר' משה קורדוברו", ירושלים, תשכ"ה, עמ' 268–270.

30. "אילת אהבים", ד, א.

31. השוה: שם טוב אבן פלקירא, שם עמ' יא: "... ואין האור דבר אחר אלא שלמות הגוף הזך במה שהוא זך".

32. השוה דעתו של גרוסטסט: האור, בנתינתו אחדות, פרופורציה וזכות לגופים הוא גם המהות של היופי. A.C. Crombie, (למעלה דף נח, הע' 12) p. 109, n.3. וראה: יהודה אברבנאל, "ויכוח על האהבה", ליק, 1871, דף מ"ב עמ' ב': "השמש... מיפה ומאיר כל המציאות". יהודה אברבנאל מרבה לעסוק ב"אור".

33. השוה דעתו של אגוסטינוס ב"על הרצון החפשי", ספר II, 36 (Migne, *P.L.* 32, 1260): בעלי העינים הבריאות והחזקות אוהבים להביט בשמש עצמה בזמן שחלשי העינים מביטים רק בדברים המוארים ע"י השמש. השוה: משל העטלף והנשר אצל יוסף אלבו, "ספר העיקרים", מאמר שני, פרקים כ"ט-ל'. ראה: D. Kaufmann, *Geschchte der Attributenlehre in der jüdischen Religionsphilosophie des Mittelalters von Saadja bis Maimuni,* Gotha, 1877, p. 187, n. 153.

34. השוה: יצחק עראמה, "עקידת יצחק", פרעסבורג תר"ט, שערים כט, חלק א, רכו, ב. סח, חלק ג', קכח, ב. וראה להלן את המשל של יהודה הלוי.

35. השוה: רמב"ם: פתיחת "מורה נבוכים". (הניסוחים של הרמב"ם אינם מונחים ביסוד המיון הזה של טאיטאצאק ושל אלקבץ. טאיטאצאק מפתח את דבריו בעקבות מה שלמד מתומאס אקוינאס).

36. יוסף טאיטאצאק, "פורת יוסף", שם. וראה י. סרמוניטה (למעלה, הע' 2), עמ' קעט. על שלש דרגות השגה המשולות לשלשה סוגים של ראיית מראות, ראה: A. Altmann, *Studies in Religious Philosophy and Mysticism,* "Ibn Bajja on Man's Ultimate Felicity", chap. 2. The similes of Light and Sun, pp. 84–88. מינים שונים של ראייה קשורים לעתים קרובות לשאלת הנבואה. על ראייה נבואית בפלוסופיה היהודית ראה: Colette Sirat, *Les Théories des Visions Surnaturelles dans la Pensée juive du Moyen-Age,* Leiden, 1969.

37. "אילת אהבים", ב, ב.

38. יצחק עראמה, שם, כרך שני, דף קג, עמ' א.

39. יצחק עראמה, שם, כרך שלישי, דף קלב, עמ' א. פסוקים השגורים בדיונים ב"אור" נמנים ע"י יצחק אברבנאל בפירושו לתורה, פרשת פקודי.

40. אפרים א. אורבך, "חז"ל אמונות ודעות", ירושלים 1971. פרק שלישי עמ' 36.

41. מדרש תנחומא, מהדורת בובר, וילנא תרמ"ה, תצוה ו'.

42. ראה: p. 105 (למעלה, דף נח הע' 12) A.C. Crombie, וראה דיונו של C. Baeumker במטפיסיקה של האור בפלוסופיה היונית, בגנוסטיקה, בפלוסופיה הניאופלטונית ובקבלה בעמ' 357–467 של ספרו על Witelo (למעלה, דף נח, הע' 15). וכמו כן בתורת האור של ויטלי בעמ' 8–16 ובהסברם, במיוחד בעמ' 357–358. V. Ronchi בספרו *The Nature of Light* (למעלה, דף נח, הע' 3), עמ' 62–63, מצביע על שלש תקופות בהתפתחות המטפיסיקה של האור בפלוסופיה הנוצרית של ימי הבינים: (א) התקופה בה זיהו את האור עם האל. (ב) התקופה בה נחשב האור כהאצלה אלהית. (ג) התקופה בה נתקיים ויכוח בשאלה האם האור הוא ישות גשמית או רוחנית. על ויכוח זה שבין תומאס אקוינאס ובין אגידיוס הרומי, ועל עמדתו של ר' יהודה רומאנו בשאלה זו, ראה: י. סרמוניטה (למעלה, דף נח, הע' 2), עמ' קמח–קמט. ר' יהודה רומאנו (בעקבות אלברטוס הגדול) היה בדעתו של אגידיוס. בפרק ג' של מאמרו (עמ' קמז–קנא) מפנה י. סרמוניטה את תשומת לבנו לכך שבכלל שהפלוסופים העוסקים במהות האור מבליטים את רוחניותו, הם קרובים יותר לניאופלטוניות ופותחים דרך

הכוכבים, משתלשל אפוא מן האור העליון, אבל רב המרחק בין האור העליון ובין האור התחתון. אלקבץ מדגיש את הריחוק בין שני האורות באמרו שאין בין האור העליון ובין האור התחתון "כי אם שתוף השם בלבד."[53] יהיה עלינו לדייק אפוא ולקרוא: "כי ג' קני מנורה אלה נמצאם הכנה ודרך להשגת האל ית' **הנקרא** אור" תוך כדי הטעמת המלה 'הנקרא'. המלה 'אור', המובנת לנו על פי האור המוחשי, באה להסביר דברים מופשטים ולהקל על הבנתם. האל שהוא מין "אור" רוחני ועילאי, הוא אין־סופי ונסתר, והתורה, המשולה לאור הישר, היא העשויה להביא את האדם להשגה הבהירה ביותר האפשרית לו.

הערות

* מתוך עבודת מחקר שנעשתה בהדרכתו של פרופ' א. אלטמאן.

1. שלמה אלקבץ, "אילת אהבים", ונציאה שי"ב, דף ב', עמ' ב'.
2. "ספונות" ספר י"א, מכון בן צבי, תשי"ז–תשל"ג, עמ' קלה–קפה.
3. דברי המבוא הללו על התפתחות תורת האור ביון נשענים על הפרק "Optics in the Graeco-Roman Age" מתוך ספרו של Vasco Ronchi, *The Nature of Light*, Harvard University Press, 1970.
4. טימאוס 45b, "כתבי אפלטון" (בתרגום י.ג. ליבס), הוצאת שוקן, תשכ"ט, כרך ג' עמ' 548.
5. תיאיטיטוס 156de, שם עמ' 94.
6. על הנפש, ספר שני, פרק ז' 418b. תרגום אנונימי לבאור הארוך על ספר הנפש של אריסטו למוחמד אבן רושד. כ"י בודפשט — קאופמן 283, עמ' 180.
7. ש. פינס, מבוא לפרק "ימי הבינים" בתוך האנתולוגיה "המחשבה הפיסיקאלית בהתהוותה" בעריכת ש. סמבורסקי, מוסד ביאליק, 1972 עמ' 173.
8. ראה: Ibn Al-Haitam, Light, in: *Proceedings of the Celebrations of 1000th Anniversary of Ibn-Haitam*, Pakistan, 1969, p. 217.
9. אבן אל היתֿ'ם, אור. השתמשתי בתרגום אשר באנתולוגיה שערך ש. סמבורסקי, שם, עמ' 149–148.
10. Ibn Al-Haitam, Light, p. 216.
11. י. סרמוניטה (למעלה, הע' 2), עמ' קמח.
12. A.C. Crombie, *Robert Grosseteste*, Oxford, 1953, p. 120 n. 5.
13. שם, עמ' 159.
14. שם, עמ' 215.
15. C. Baeumker, *Witelo, ein Philosoph und Naturforscher des XIII. Jahrhunderts* (B.G.P.M. iii.2), Münster, 1908, Aus Witelo's Perspectiva, p. 131 וראה גם עמ' 640–606.
16. ראה: י. סרמוניטה, שם (למעלה, הע' 2), עמ' קלח, הערה 2.
17. יוסף טאיטאצאק, "פורת יוסף", ונציאה שנ"ט, דף סז עמ' ב.
18. י. סרמוניטה, שם, עמ' קעח–קעט. י. סרמוניטה מביא את דברי טאיטאצאק בהשואה למקור הלטיני שלהם.
19. יוסף טאיטאצאק, "לחם סתרים", ונציאה שס"ח, דף י"ז עמ' ב'.
20. יוסף טאיטאצאק, שם, שם. השוה אברהם בן דאוד הלוי, "האמונה הרמה", המאמר הראשון, הפרק הששי, פרנקפורט 1852, עמ' 28. עמ' 28. לוי בן גרשון, "מלחמות השם", המאמר הראשון, הפרק הששי, ריווא די טרינטו, ש"ך, דף ח' עמ' א.
21. Abraham Bar Hiyya, *La Obra Enciclopédica, Yesodé Ha-Tebuná U-Migdal Ha-Emuná*, Jose M. Millás Vallicrosa, Madrid-Barcelona, 1952, עמ' מ"ז.
22. שם, עמ' מח. בתרגום הספרדי שבהוצאה הזאת נמצאות בהערות הדרכות למקורותיו של בר חייא (בעמ' 88–80).
23. שם טוב אבן פלקירא, "ראשית חכמה", ברלין, תרס"ב, עמ' 44.
24. משה די ריאטי, "מקדש מעט", וינה, 1851, דף ט"ו עמ' ב'. ראה: י. אפרת, "הפלוסופיה היהודית בימי הבינים מונחים ומושגים", תל אביב דביר, תשכ"ט, עמ' 119 (בפרק מונחים פלוסופיים בכתבי ר' אברהם בר חייא הנשיא, במונח אור).

נרו מיד יוכל לקום לאור באור ה׳ הזורח עליו תמיד.״[38] בשער הששים ושמונה חוזר עראמה לענין הנר: ״ירצה כי נשמת האדם היא נר ה׳ בידו, באורו יראה אור.״[39] יתכן מאד שאלקבץ, שאת כתבי עראמה הכיר, זכר דיון זה בשעה שהעלה את דבריו שלו על הכתב. מכל מקום שינה אלקבץ את נוסח המשל ובמקום ג׳ מיני אורות העדיף לציין ג׳ קני מנורה.

אנו מוצאים שבספרות חז״ל נתכנה האל בשם אור. אפרים א. אורבך טוען שכאשר אמרו חז״ל ״הקב״ה שכולו אורה״ או ״אומה זו שאלהיה של אור״ (תנחומא, בהעלותך ז, מדרש תהלים כב, יא) הם ״לא התכוונו לומר שהוא חומר של אור אלא שהאור הוא שלו ואינו צריך לאור אחר.״[40] לפי דעתו האור לא בא לציין את מהות האל כי אם את העובדה שהאל הוא מקור האור וכך הוא מסביר גם את מגמת הכתוב במדרש תנחומא (על דניאל ב, כב, ״ונהורא עמה שרא״): ״מי שנתון בחשך רואה מה שבאור, ומי שנתון באור אינו רואה מה שבחשך אבל הקב״ה רואה מה שבחשך ומה שבאור.״[41] בין הפלוסופים היו שזיהו את האל עם האור. אגוסטינוס דבר על האל כעל אור בלתי גשמי ואין־סופי שהוא המקור גם לאור הרוחני וגם לאור הגשמי הנברא, כשהאור הגשמי הנברא הוא הזך שבגופים.[42] האור הגשמי עומד בגבול שבין רוח וחומר,[43] וזאת הסבה אשר בגללה מרבים חכמים להשתמש במשלי אור כאשר הם רוצים להסביר תופעות מטאפיסיות ובכללן מהות האל ודרכיו.[44] יהודה הלוי למשל, כשרצה להבחין בין שמות שונים של האלוהות, דימה אותם להיקלטות שונה של אור בגופים שונים: ״ואוסיף לך באור בדמיון מהשמש, שהיא אחת אך מתחלפים מערכות הגשמים המקבלים אותה[45] ואשר יקבל אורה קבול שלם יותר — הפנינים והשהם על הדמיון, והאויר הצח והמים, ויקרא בזה, ׳אור נוקב׳ ויקרא באבנים הזכות והשטחים הקלליים אור בהיר על הדמיון ובעצים ובארץ וזולתם אור נראה ובכל הדברים . . . אור סתם בלתי שם מיחד. והאור הסתם הוא כמו אמרנו אלהים . . . והאור הנוקב הוא כמו ה׳.״[46] יהודה הלוי מציין שהשם ה׳ מורה על היחס בין האלוה ובין הנביאים. נפשותיהם הזכות של הנביאים קולטות את האור האלהי כמו שאבני הפנינים והשוהם קולטות את אור השמש.[47] בין הפלוסופים היהודיים יש המביאים את הלבטים בשאלה האם לכנות את האל בשם אור ע״פ ההגות המוסלמית. בפירושו של שם טוב למורה נבוכים חלק א׳, פרק ל״ה, מביא שם טוב את דברי משה הנרבוני מפירושו לאותו פרק. משה הנרבוני עצמו מסתמך על אבן רושד: ״ואמנם החכם אבן רש״ד אמר כי אין ראוי לומר להמון שאיננו גשם כי יבטל מציאותו אצלם, גם איננו ראוי לומר כי הוא גשם כי הוא חלוף האמת, אבל ראוי שנבחר היותר נכבד ממשיגי הגשם ושנאמר כי הוא אור כי נמלט אותם מאמונת ההגשמה ויהיה נמצא אצלם ונכבד שבנמצאים עד שיכלול זה מן הצדק כמו שהאור סבת מציאות הגוונים בפעל וסבת ראותינו אותם כן האל ית׳ סבת הנמצאות כלם וסבת השכלתם . . . ״[48] יוסף אלבו, שאלקבץ מסתמך על דבריו כמה פעמים, מצביע על שורה של ענינים אשר להם הושאל השם אור והוא גם עורך אנלוגיה בין האור ובין האל. האל, כאור, ״אי אפשר להכחיש מציאותו ואינו גשם . . . [49] ומוציא דברים מן הכח אל הפעל״.[50] ההשגה בו גורמת תענוג, אך היא מוגבלת. מסתבר שיוסף אלבו מבחין בין האור העליון הרוחני ובין האור המוחש. הוא טוען שיש הבדל בין האור הרוחני (השכלי) ובין האור המוחש. כאשר הוא מסביר את הפסוק ״ונגה כאור תהיה . . . ״ (חבקוק, ג, ד) הוא כותב: ״האור המוחש נמשך מן הגשם והנגה ההוא לא היה נמשך מדבר גשמי וע״כ אמר כאור עם כ״ף הדמיון ולא אמר כאור בשילוח.״[51] בדרך זו נוקט גם אלקבץ כאשר הוא מסביר ב״ברית הלוי״[52] את הירידה תוך העלמה של האור העליון. האור העליון יורד כלפי מטה דרך הספירות עד ספירת מלכות ומשם ״אל כוחות הטומאה וחיילותיהן״ ואח״כ ״אל צבא השמים ואל הכוכבים״. האור המוחש, זה הנובע מן השמש ומן

ענינים...״[21] ג׳ ענינים אלה נקראים בפי אברהם בר חייא: אור נשבר, אור פושט ואור נזור. קוי האור מיניהם ארבעה: ישרים, נשברים, פושטים ונזורים.[22] בספר ״ראשית חכמה״ של שם טוב אבן פלקירא נמנים ארבעה מיני שביבי אור ״העוברים בגופים הזכים אל המעיין אליו או שיהיו ישרים או מתעקלים או מתהפכים או משתברים... השביבים הישרים הם אשר כשיצאו מהראות הם נמשכים על יושר נגד הראות...״[23] ובספר ״מקדש מעט״ לר׳ משה די ריאטי חוזר המנין הזה: ״ישר, נזור, מתהפך ונשבר.״[24] כאשר אברהם ביבאגו ויצחק אברבנאל מציינים מה בין תליית המאורות בשמים ובין האור שנברא במאמר ראשון הם מזכירים שביום הרביעי לבריאת העולם כבר היתה יבשה, לפיכך היה ״מקום להתהפכות הניצוץ... האור אשר יאצל מן הגשם המאיר, שמש וגשם שמימי וזולתו... לא היה יכול להמצא קודם היום הד׳ למה שלא נמצא מקום וגשם יבש ממנו תתהפך האורה לכל חלקי המציאות.״[25] ועוד: ״כי כבר התבאר בחכמה הטבעית שהניצוץ יאיר בהכותו בגשם קשה....״[26] אלקבץ עצמו בספרו ״ברית הלוי״ ממשל ״משל יפה לקרב הדברים אל השכל והוא מהאור הזה המורגש אצלנו.״[27] במשל, שתפקידו להסביר את האצלת האור האלהי והשתלשלותו מלמעלה למטה, מתאר אלקבץ גם את הכאת ניצוץ האור במים: ״ואם יכה הניצוץ ההוא במים עכורים מתעוות האור ההוא עד שיאמר האומר כי נחשך האור ההוא.״[28] תחת הכותרת ״דרוש אחר בענין האצילות״, מביא אלקבץ משל המתאר התהפכות וחזרה של אור: ״וביאור ענין זה דמיון אור המכה בכתל מלוטשת ומסוידת כי יראה לעין כל התהפכות וחזרת האור ההוא לאחור ונצוצות מתהפכות ממקום הכאת הכתל ההוא...״ באמצעות משל זה מסביר אלקבץ את התהפכות האור בעולם הספירות, וכשהוא מסביר את ההתרחשות הפנימית בתוך כל ספירה הוא מזכיר ״אור ישר״ ו״אור מתהפך״: ״בכל ספירה וספירה נכללות העשר, אשר בה אור ישר ואור מתהפך.״[29] בשעה שאלקבץ כבר מפרש את הנמשל,[30] כשהוא מסביר את מעלת האור הישר, חוזר הוא ומעלה פרטים השייכים לתורת האור: אור השמש ״הוא שלמות האויר ומכל גשם בהיר ספיריי[31]... נותן יופי לכל התמונות הנראות[32]... משמח חוש הראות לבריאים ומכאיבו לחלושים.״[33] אור השמש ״מעורר הב״ח מהשינה הלילית״. ״ניצוץ השמש הנה הוא מטביע התמונות במראות״. ״ניצוץ השמש יתנועע כפי הכנת החמר אשר אליו יגיע כי אם הגשם יהיה ספיריי יזהירהו ויבהקהו וההפך בהפך״ (ובלשון אחרת: ״האור הזה נתוסף בעצמים הבהירים ומתמעט בחשוכים״).[34]

ג׳ מיני האורות אצל טאיטאצאק מציינים ג׳ דרגות של ראיית האל והכרתו:[35] ״המין הראשון, רוצה לומר לראות האל יתב׳ במהות, הוא טבעי לאל ית׳ והמלאך והאדם יזכו לראות האל ית׳ במהותו למעלה מן הטבע ברצונו של הב״ה. המין הב׳ בראיית האל ית׳ הוא טבעי למלאך. המין הג׳ שהוא הראייה באספקלריאה הוא טבעי לאדם באלו החיים במה שמכיר את האל ית׳ ממה שנראה כוחו וחכמתו וגדלותו במעשיו.״[36] אם הראייה במהות מקבילה לאור התורה, הראייה במין לאור העולם הבא, והראייה באספקלריאה לאור הגשמי, הרי שלפנינו דרוג דומה מאד לדרוג שמעמיד אלקבץ. אצל אלקבץ האור הישר הוא אור התורה, האור החוזר הוא אור חדרי גן עדן והוא אור הטבע המעולה שישרור בימות הגאולה, והאור הנשבר במים ומתעוות בהם הוא אור חדרי שמים, והוא אור הטבע הקיים בעוה״ז. שלשה מהלכי האור הנם כנגד שלש דרכים להשגת האל: דרך התורה, דרך הנסים והנפלאות, ודרך החקירה השכלתנית. ״ג׳ קני מנורה אלה נמצאם הכנה ודרך להשגת האל ית׳ הנקרא אור, כמאמר לאור באור ה׳, באורך נראה אור.״[37] בספרו ״עקידת יצחק״, בשער ארבעים ותשעה המוקדש למעשה המנורה, מביא יצחק עראמה מדברי המדרש על ״בהעלותך את הנרות״ (במד״ר, פרשה ט״ו) ומעיר: ״והכתוב, שהביא ראיה גדולה: קומי אורי כי בא אורך, כי כשיקדים האדם להאיר

גרוסטסט (1253–1175 בערך).[12] גרוסטסט הבחין בג׳ "radii principales", (א) "linea recta", (ב) "linea reflexa" (ג) "fractio radii". רוג׳ר בייקון (1214 בערך — 1294 בערך) אף הוא מדבר על שלשה מינים של קרני אור ראשיות: ישרות, מוחזרות ונשברות.[13] ויטלו (נולד בערך ב־1230), כמו רוברט גרוסטסט ורוג׳ר בייקון, מזכיר שלש צורות של ראייה. כוונתו לקרני אור ישרות, לקרני אור מוחזרות ולקרני אור נשברות.[14] "Patet itaque ex praemissis quia triplex est modus videndi; quidam per unum tantum medium, qui est visio directa; quidam vero per reflexionem formarum visibilium a corporibus politis: quidam vero per refractionem formaum visibilium propter diversitatem mediorum".[15] יתכן מאד שאלה הם החכמים שאליהם מתכוון אלקבץ.

בספר "פורת יוסף" מסתמך טאיטאצאק לא אחת על תורות מדעיות של "חכמים" מבלי שהוא נוקב בשמותיהם.[16] בפירוש לפסוק "ומתוק האור וטוב לעינים לראות את השמש" (קהלת יא, ז) נזקק אף הוא לברור מציאותם של "ג׳ מיני אור" או "ג׳ מיני ראות". בספר "פורת יוסף", שהוא ספר פירושים לפסוקי מגילת קהלת, הוא כותב: "הנה כפי זה המאמר יש להבחין ג׳ מיני אור. האור הגשמי אשר הוא מניצוצי השמש ואור התורה ואור עולם הבא. ולהבין ג׳ מיני האור הנזכר ראוי להבחין הקדמה אחת אשר נזכרה ב"ספר האמת" בחומר הח׳, פרק ג׳. כי באחד מג׳ פנים יראה הדבר במהות, במין, באספקלריאה. ראייה ב"מהותו", וזה כשהדבר הנראה יתחבר ויתדבק לראות כמו שהעין רואה האור. ראייה "במין" הוא כשדמיון הדבר הנראה מצטייר כראות מהדבר הנראה בעצמו כמו שהאדם רואה את האבן, כי דמיון האבן ההיא מצטייר בראות והדמיון לקוח מהאבן עצמה. הפן הג׳ שהוא ראייה ב"אספקלריאה" הוא כאשר דמיון הדבר הנראה אינו לקוח מהדבר הנראה בעצמו רק דמות הדבר הנראה מצטייר באספקלריאה ומהדמות אשר באספקלריאה לוקח הראות מוחשו..."[17] טאיטאצאק בחר להסתמך על דברי תומאס אקוינאס ב"ספר האמת".[18] גם החלוקה לראייה במהות, במין ובאספקלריאה קשורה למחקרים בתורת האור. בספר "לחם סתרים", שהוא אוסף פירושים של טאיטאצאק על ספר דניאל ועל המגילות, נמצא גם כן פירוש לפסוק ובו מבחין טאיטאצאק באופן דומה ב"ג׳ מיני ראות."[19]

המשל של אלקבץ שונה מהמשל של רבו. הרקע התרבותי של המשלים הוא אחד. במשל של אלקבץ משוקעות מלים וקבועים בטויים, שאפשר למצוא כמותם אצל טאיטאצאק ואצל החכמים היהודיים הקודמים לו. בפירוש לקהלת יא, ז, אשר ב"לחם סתרים", ישנו דיון ע"פ התורה האריסטוטלית באמצעי שהוא "האויר ספיריי שהוא עומד בין הרואה והנראה... אותו האויר שעומד בין הרואה והנראה... ספיריי וזך ויעבור בו הראות הדבר..."[20] בחבורי פלוסופים יהודיים ביה"ב מצויים תאורי מהלכי אור בעולם הגשמי כמו למשל בחבורו האינציקלופדי של אברהם בר חייא, או בספר "ראשית חכמה" של שם טוב אבן פלקירא. אם כי את הפלוסופים האלה העסיקו בעיות אור אחרות (כגון האור היוצא מן העין ותורת המראות), יתכן שמונחים אחדים שלהם מצאו דרכם אל המשל של אלקבץ (לאו דוקא בהקבלה). בספר "יסודי התבונה ומגדל האמונה" של אברהם בר חייא כתוב:

"וכל הדברים הם נראים... על ידי אור הנפרש באויר או בגולם זהיר באויר עד שיגיע אל הנראה, והאור הזה נמצא בקוים ההולכים אל העין או היוצאים מהעין, ואלו הקוים יש מהם על יושר דרכו עד שהוא מגיע אל הנראה או עד שיכלה כחו ויסוף אורו ואלו נקראים אורות ישרים".

יש קוים הנתקלים "קודם הגעתם אל הנראה" ב"מונעות וכלים נזהרים... והם משיבים אותם מדרכם אחורנית" והם "שונים מן המקרה הזה הקרה אותם על ג׳

להיות גופו המיוחד של כל יום ויום. שכן האש הטהורה שבקרבנו אחות היא לאש הזאת, והם גרמו לה שתזרום דרך העינים, בעשותם את העין כולה חלקה וסמיכה.... כשאור היום נמצא... משתפך זרם הראייה חוצה, שהרי הדומה נמשך אל דומהו; וזרם הראייה מתלכד עם האור לגוף אחד ואחיד המתמשך בקו ישר מן העינים לכל מקום בו נתקל הזרם המשתפך מבפנים בדבר הפוגשו מבחוץ..."[4] וב"תאיטיטוס": "כשבמקום שבין זוג המולידים נעה הראייה היוצאת מהעיניים ונע הלובן היוצא מהדבר ההוא המשתתף בהולדת הצבע — כי אז תתמלא העין ראייה..."[5] אריסטו, שהתנגד לדעות של קודמיו, פרש את הראייה כתנועה הנעה בחומר המתווך (השקוף) שבין הגוף הנראה ובין העין. בספרו "על הנפש" כתב כך: "...האור הוא שלמות מזה רצוני הספיריי מצד היותו ספירי. אמנם בכח הוא אותו אשר הוא בו נמצא עם זה חשך. והאור כמעט מראה הספיריי כאשר היה ספיריי כפי השלמות מפני האש והדומה לו כמו הגשם העליון ובזה נמצא הדבר ההוא בעינו. וכבר נאמר מהו הספיריי ומהו האור ושאינו אש ולא גשם כלל ולא דבר נגר מהגשם כלל לפי שאם היה הדבר כן היה כפי זה האופן גשם מה אבן הוא המצא האש או הדומה לו בספירי כי הוא מבואר שהוא בלתי אפשר שיהיו שני גשמים במקום אחד."[6] אוקלידס תמך בדעה שהאור נפלט מן העין. הוא חבר שני ספרים העוסקים בתורת האור — את ה־"Optica" ואת ה־"Catroptica" (דהיינו תורת ההשתקפות). בספרים אלה ניתן למצוא, מלבד סכום של תוצאות נסיונותיו, כמה הנחות על מהות האור ועל תכונותיו. אוקלידס הגדיר את קרן האור כ"חוט" דמיוני דק של אור, קבע שקרני האור מתפשטות בקוים ישרים וניסח את חוק ההחזרה של קרני האור. קלאודיוס פטולמיאוס (תלמי) התענין במיוחד בשבירת קרני האור ואף ניסח חוק שבירה. אמנם הניסוח של פטולמיאוס נתגלה במרוצת הזמן כבלתי מדויק אך נסיונותיו קידמו מאד את המחקר בתורת האור.

לפני המאה השלוש־עשרה שלט בימי הבינים המדע הערבי. טקסטים מדעיים יוניים היו מצויים בתרגומים ערביים (והיו גם נוסחים ערביים של כתבים בסאנסקריט). "ויכוחים מדעיים ערים התנהלו בכל העולם המוסלמי, ובשטחים מסוימים התקדמו הערבים אף מעבר ליונים. האופטיקה, כפי שפותחה ע"י אבן אל הית'ם, היא דוגמה לכך."[7] אבן הית'ם דחה את הרעיון שהראייה נוצרת ע"י יציאת קרני אור מן העין ופגיעתן בגוף הנראה. הוא טען שקרני האור המתפשטות בקוים ישרים מוחזרות אל העין מן הגופים הנראים ומעניקות לאדם את תחושת הראייה.[8] לפי דבריו: "הגופים המאירים בעצמם אשר החוש משיגם הם משני סוגים דהיינו הכוכבים והאש... בכל הגופים הטבעיים, השקופים והאטומים, יש כח לקבל אור, כח זה מקבל את האורות מן הגופים המאירים. בגופים השקופים יש נוסף לכח המקבל את האור כח המעביר את האור... האור נמשך בגופים השקופים בקוים ישרים בלבד... כאשר מתפשט האור בגוף השקוף ומגיע אל גוף שקוף אחר אשר שקיפותו שונה מזו של הגוף הראשון אשר בו התפשט כשהוא נוטה אל שטח הגוף השני נשבר האור ואינו חודר ישר."[9] אבן הית'ם מציין ש"אם נניח גוף מוצק מול נר, או כל גוף מאיר אחר, ואין כל חיץ בין שניהם, האור יוחזר מן הגוף המוצק בתנאי שהגוף הזה אינו מונח בריחוק רב מדי מאיתנו או מן הגוף המאיר."[10] אבן הית'ם מזכיר גופים מאירים, גופים שקופים המעבירים אור בקוים ישרים, החזרת אור מגופים מוצקים, וסוקר נסיונות רבים הקשורים בתופעת השבירה.

במאות הי"ג והי"ד תפס מדע האופטיקה מקום מרכזי בפלוסופיה הנוצרית. אמנם הפלוסופים אשר עסקו באופטיקה היו מעונינים יותר בשאלות המטפיסיות מאשר בבעיות הטכניות מדעיות של תורת האור, אך "העסוק ב"הארה" בשדה המטפיסיקה הביא עמו בהכרח דיונים מעמיקים במהות האור בשדה הפיסיקה ובמיוחד באופטיקה."[11] החשוב בין חוקרי תורת האור הנוצריים היה הבישוף האנגלי רוברט

משל ג' האורות בספר "אילת אהבים" לר' שלמה הלוי אלקבץ*

ברכה זק

ספרו של אלקבץ, "אילת אהבים", הוא פירוש בדרך הקבלה למגילת שיר השירים. כתיבת הספר נסתיימה בשנת רצ"ו. אלקבץ רואה בשיר השירים דו־שיח בין השלם העוסק בתורה ובין התורה. העוסק בתורה יודע את מעלתה, מבין אותה על כל רבדיה הגלויים והנסתרים, לומד אותה ומלמדה לתלמידיו ומקיים את מצוותיה כראוי. התורה מזככת את העוסק בה ומביאה אותו לאמונה אמיתית ולדבקות באל. בראשית הספר, בפירוש לפסוק הראשון של המגילה, כאשר בא אלקבץ להציג לפנינו את מעלתה של התורה הוא ממשל משל הלקוח מתורת האור של ימי הביניים. המשל מובא בשם "חכמים":

> "הן אמת חכמים יגידו אשר יש ג' מיני אורות במציאות השפל, מושפעים מהאור העליון אשר הוא הארה מה נמשכת מעצם האור המקובל באויר, שהוא האמצעי או בגשם אחר בהיר ספיריי. הא' האור הנשבר כמו הניצוץ המכה במים שתתעות ההארה להשבת הניצוץ בתוך גוף המים לרפיונם. השני היא רפה והיא מתהפכת מהגשם אשר תפול עליו להתחלתה, דרך משל כשיפול הניצוץ על אבן לבן קשה מחובר החלקים לא יוכל לעבור בגשמו והניצוץ מתהפך למקורו. השלישי הוא ישר יען כי הניצוץ נופל על יושר מבלי מניעה בשום אופן מהגשם המקבל אותו להיותו מוכן ונכנע אל הקבול".[1]

מי הם החכמים אליהם מתכוון אלקבץ ומהי תורתם הנרמזת כאן? יוסף ב. סרמוניטה, במאמרו "הספרות הסכולאסטית בספר "פורת יוסף" לר' יוסף טאיטאצאק",[2] מציין שתי עובדות: (א) שבפזורה היהודית באיטליה במאות הי"ד–ט"ז התפשטה פרשנות סכולאסטית, ו(ב) שיוסף טאיטאצאק הכיר ספרות סכולאסטית והשתמש בה להכנת דרשותיו. לא מן הנמנע איפוא שגם תלמידיו של טאיטאצאק ובכללם אלקבץ הכירו הגות סכולאסטית, אם בשל האוירה התרבותית הכללית שהיו שרויים בה, אם בשל השפעת רבם. ראוי אפוא לבדוק תפיסות של "מיני האורות" בכתבים שהכיר אלקבץ במישרין וגם לעיין בתפיסות שונות של "מיני אורות", מאלו שרווחו בימי הבינים בין הוגי דעות יהודיים ובסביבתם התרבותית.

התופעה ששמה "אור" העסיקה הרבה את החכמים מאז קיומן של התרבויות הקדומות,[3] ביון העתיקה התענינו הפלוסופים יותר במהות הראיה מאשר במהות האור, מפני שהאדם עמד במרכז החקירה וחוש הראיה נחשב לחוש החשוב ביותר שלו. חכמי יון העמידו כמה תיאוריות ששמשו בסיס לחקירות שנערכו בימי הבינים. הראשונה, שאומצה ע"י הפיתגוראים, אומרת שהעין מוציאה "משהו" כלפי הגוף הנראה. השניה, שהאטומיסטים, ובראשם דמוקריטוס גרסו, טוענת שהגופים הנראים פולטים "משהו" כלפי העין. השלישית, של אמפדוקלס, שלבה את שתי השיטות; לפיה יוצאות קרני אור מן העין אל הגופים הנראים ובעת ובעונה אחת מן הגופים הנראים אל העין. אפלטון הניח שקיים אמצעי חיצוני, בהירות השופעת מן הגוף הנראה ונקלטת בעין, והיא האור, ושקיים כח פנימי בעין, מעין אש פנימית, השופעת מן העין ומשלימה את פעולת הראיה. וכך כותב אפלטון ב"טימיאוס": "אותה אש שאין בה כדי לשרוף, אבל יש בה כדי להעלות אור נוח, — אותה זימנו

58. ש׳ פוזנאנסקי, *REJ*, xlv (1902), עמ׳ 193–194.

59. ע׳ (NS) *JQR*, xv (1925), 4/הע׳ 15–20/10; ועי״ש פירושי א״ב במובאות 3/4–הע׳ 10.

60. עי׳ אלוני, ״בן זוטא הוא בן עטא הקראי״, ״תרביץ״, מה (תשל״ו), עמ׳ 76–78.

61. עי׳ הרכבי, ״חדשים גם ישנים״, 17–23/128, ושם נזכרים פירושים אנטי־קראיים ליחזקאל לב, כז; מה, לא. ועי׳ א׳ נויבואיר, *Notice sur la lexicographie Hébraique*, פאריס 1863, 165/הע׳ 2, על פי כ״י אוקספורד 316 (Hunt. 155), שבו נמצאות הערות א״ב בשוליים; ז׳ באכר, *Abraham ibn Esra als Grammatiker* בודפשט 1881, 186/סע׳ 14, המביא את א״ב בפירושיו; יש להוסיף עליהם: ישראלסון, הנ״ל (הע׳ 57), 273/הע׳ 2, את הרשום אצל פרידלנדר, פירוש ראב״ע הארוך, לונדון 1877, עמ׳ 28 (ולא מצאתי).

62. א״ב המשורר והפייטן יתפרסם בבמה אחרת, כי רב מדי היה היקף המאמר. כאן עלי להביע את תודתי לידידיי י׳ בלאו ומ״י קיסטר, שדנו אתי על השם וביאורו. תודתי נתונה למר יוסף דרורי, שקרא את המאמר לפני מסירתו לפרסום ובדק את מוה״מ. ערך מאמר זה לדפוס ידידי יהושע שטיין, שהעיר הערות חשובות, וחן חן לו.

31. עי׳ א׳ אשתור, ״קורות היהודים בספרד המוסלמית״, א, ירושלים תש״ך, עמ׳ 151–146; נ׳ אלוני, ״שירים לדונש בן לבראט״, מבוא, ירושלים תש״ז, עמ׳ כא-ל.

32. עי׳ תג׳ניס מהד׳ אברמסון[1], ערך מרי; פוקס, עמ׳ 20, 26/הע׳ 46; ישראלסון, פירוש ירמיה, ״ספר היובל לא״א הרכבי״, לנינגראד תרס״ט, 12–15/276 (רז״ל בפירוש ירמיהו) — 15 פעם.

33. רמב״ע[1], 40/ע״א/7–ע״ב/12; מ׳ שטיינשניידר, *CB*, אוקספורד 1859, עמודה 1293.

34. הרכבי, ״חדשים גם ישנים״, מהד׳ כרמיאל, ירושלים תש״ל, 19–21/129; אברמסון[1], עמ׳ 51.

35. לפי זה היה חסר גם בסופו פירוש אבן בלעם, אף על פי שהוא מביא מלים רק מנוסח הגמרא וחסר עמוד אחד אחרון בערך, יבמות קכב ע״א/31 — קכב ע״ב (סוף).

36. אלוני[2], 74–79/542; אלוני־שייבר, 69–72/164; בשתי הרשימות קטע זהה מפירוש יבמות, ואין באחד יותר מאשר בחברו, ויש בו שתי מובאות סמוכות זו לזו, וההבדל הוא רק בתוספת כסיום המובאה השנייה. מן הראוי להזכיר את פירוש יבמות לבן יהבוי, אברמסון[2], 83 עמודה ב/4; ועי״ש, 86/הע׳ 26. ולא זוהה פירוש חכם זה (דרך אגב, מה פירוש השם יהבוי?), ועי׳ גם פירוש שבת לרב יוסף בן יהבוי, שייבר[2], 1–2/547; פירוש כתובות לרב יוסף בן יהבוי, שייבר[1] 36/548.

37. הש׳ למובא לעיל, אלוני[2], 51–52/540, ושם נזכר, כי חסרים שלושת פרקים אלה.

38. יבמות נג ע״ב/28 — נד ע״א/33.

39. וחבל שעיקר הפירוש חסר כאן, כי לדעתי זו מובאה מפירושו הבלשני לאבן בלעם.

40. מסתבר בעיני, כי אף כתוב זה מפירוש א״ב, ולא עלה בידי לזהותו. הש׳ נדה מו ע״א.

41. עי׳ פוזנאנסקי, 15–20/22.

42. יבמות כא ע״א/13.

43. בנדפס: דרב, ותיקנתי.

44. עי׳ י׳ בן צבי, ״מקדשיה הירושלמי וכתרי התורה שבבתי הקראים בקושטא ובמצרים״, ״קרית ספר״, לב (תשי״ז), עמ׳ 366–374; ועי״ש, 7–8/368: ״גם השם ד׳אלבורנש מעיד על מוצא ספרדי, ואין לנו כל זכר לקהלה קראית בספרד״. על מקדשיה עי׳ נ׳ וידר, *JJS*, viii, (1957), עמ׳ 165–175.

45. מ׳ שטיינשניידר, *Jüdische Literatur*, האנציקלופדיה אירש וגרובר (Ersch und Gruber), מחלקה ב, xxvii, לייפציג 1850, עמ׳ 406–407.

46. עי׳ מאמרי ״השקפות קראיות במחברת מנחם״, ״אוצר יהודי ספרד״, ה (תשכ״ב), עמ׳ 21–54.

47. עי׳ ״ספר הזכרון לקורנגרין״, תל אביב תשכ״ד, עמ׳ 324–363.

48. כך הוא מכנה את הקראים. עי׳ א״א הרכבי, ״חדשים גם ישנים״, 127/סי׳ ב; פוזנאנסקי, עמ׳ 17; פוזנאנסקי, *REJ*, xiv (1920), 3/193; וזה בפירושו לויקרא טו, כה; ירמיה יז, כז; יחזקאל מד, לא.

49. עי׳ אלוני, ״גניזה וכתבי יד עבריים בספריות קמבריג׳״, ארשת, ג, ירושלים תשכ״א, עמ׳ 395–425; ״ספרות חז״ל בניקוד ארץ ישראלי״, ירושלים תשל״ד, מבוא, עמ׳ 1 והערות 2–3.

50. עי׳ אברמסון, עמ׳ 107–108.

51. עי׳ אברמסון, 1–9/60; ועי״ש, הערות 13–14. השתמשו בכתוב זה כל המתפלמסים על קידוש החודש על פי הראייה: רס״ג, אבן משיח, בן זוטא, יעקב אלקרקסאני, שמואל בן חפני, עלי בן ישראל אלוף, ראב״ע ועוד.

52. פוזנאנסקי, 9–20/20. פוזנאנסקי ציין שם כי זהו בראשית כתב היד 1 ע״א — 2 ע״ב.

53. נדה סו ע״א. גם בשריד מפירושו ליבמות דן בעניין מתוך צירוף הכתוב במסכת נדה (עי״ל).

54. בנדפס: ואתמאנהא (?), ותיקנתי על פי ההשערה ולא על סמך בדיקת כה״י, כי לדאבוני הרב אין כה״י עומד לרשותנו.

55. פוזנאנסקי, 9–20/22.

56. מסתבר, כי דן בפירושו ליבמות גם בקטע זה ובכתובים אלה. עי״ל.

57. י׳ ישראלסון, ״פירוש על ספר ירמיהו לרבי יהודה בן אבן בלעם״, ״ספר היובל להרכבי״, לנינגראד תרס״ט, עמ׳ 291–292. הש׳ הרכבי, עמ׳ 19–20.

5. על שם זה כתמורה ליוחנן וליהודה, שנשארה חידה בעיני עד עצם היום הזה, עי׳ נ׳ אלוני, ״יהודה בן דויד ויהודה חיוג׳״, ״מנחה ליהודה״, ירושלים תש״י, עמ׳ 68 והערות 16–14.

6. תענית כ ע״א/10; סנהדרין קו ע״ב/12; אבות פ״ה מכ״ב; ועוד.

7. עי׳ ד׳, ב׳, 296 (מו״מ רבים), וזהו הפיוט הראשון שנודע לנו (עי׳ הע׳ 14–13 להלן); צונץ, Literaturgeschichte der synagogalen Poesie, Berlin 1865 עמ׳ 201–200; שירמן[3], עמ׳ 300–299.

8. עי׳ שירמן[2], עמ׳ 329–328, סי׳ 157. עי׳ להלן בירור הכתובת הקשה לקרא בראש שיר זה בכתב היד.

9. עי׳ ד׳, ב׳, 500 (מו״מ מעטים); צונץ הנ״ל, עמ׳ 201–200.

10. עי׳ ד׳, י, 1729; צונץ הנ״ל, עמ׳ 201–200 (לפיו מסופק הוא), על פי מחזור רומניא.

11. ח׳ שירמן[1], עמ׳ קמה–קמו.

12. עי׳ ד׳, צ, 180 (מחזור ארם צובה ועוד); צונץ, עמ׳ 201–200 (לפיו מסופק הוא) על פי מחזור טריפולי. המלה ״צובה״ באקרוסטיכון רומזת למחזור ארם צובה ושוללת את הפיוט מאבן בלעם.

13. י׳ רייפמן, ״תולדות רבנו זרחיה הלוי״, פראג תרי״ג, 69/הע׳ 117. כבר רשם פיוט זה מקלנבורג (Meklenburg), *Israelitische Annalen*, א (1839), עמ׳ 340.

14. א״א הרכבי, ״המגיד״, תרל״ז (1877), 134 עמודה ב. אף הוא קשר סברתו, כי לפנינו אב ובנו, בסיפור האגדה על התפלה בבית הכנסת ודברי ר׳ משה הכהן אבן ג׳קטילה באותה הזדמנות: ״ר׳ בלעם אבי ר׳ יהודה היה החזן, וכאשר אחר לבוא התפלל בנו תחתיו . . .״; א״א הרכבי, ״חדשים גם ישנים״, מס׳ 7, עמ׳ 129–128.

15. עי׳ הע׳ 8; ועי״ש, 299/הע׳ 8. להלן נשוב לדון בשיר ובכתיבת השיר.

16. אלחנן נתן אדלר ור״י ברוידה, *JQR*, xiii (1900/01), עמ׳ 56–52; והעירו: חיבורים בדקדוק. לאחר שנים אחדות פרסם אדלר שנית את הרשימה בספרו: *About Hebrew Manuscripts*, אוקספורד 1905, עמ׳ 48–35, ולא הזכיר את שם שותפו לפרסום הראשון.

17. ש׳ פוזנאנסקי, *JQR* xiii (1900/01), 327/סי׳ 49, 50.

18. אברמסון[2], 83 עמודה ב׳ 18–17, והעיר שם הע׳ 44: ״וקיצור (קרע בכה״י)״.

19. עי׳ נ׳ אלוני, ״קרית ספר״, ל (תשט״ו), עמ׳ 446–445, סי׳ ו, ז. לחיבור מכ׳תצר חיוג׳ עי׳ וורמן, *JQR* xx (1908), 461/36–35: ״מכ׳תצר חיוג׳״.

20. עי׳ נספח, שבו רשימה מיוחדת לסוברים, כי השם בלעם.

21. עי׳ למעלה, הע׳ 13. לדעה זו לא נצטרף הרכבי (עי׳ הע׳ 14), אף כי סבר כמוהו שלפנינו אב ובן.

22. עי׳ M.L. Fleischer, *Literaturblatt des Orients*, vii, (1846), p. 451. זה מובא במאמרו של י׳ פירסט בביקורת על הספר Ewald-Dukes, *Beiträge der ältesten Austegung und Spracherklärung des Alten Testaments*, Stuttgart, 1844.

23. עי׳ נספח: השם בלעם, בלעאם.

24. א״א הרכבי, ״המגיד״, תרל״ז (1877), עמ׳ 181.

25. שטיינשניידר, מבוא, x (1898–1897), 136/סע׳ 77.

26. Marcelin Beaussier, *Dictionnaire Pratique Arabe Français Nouvelle*, édition par M. Mohammed Ben Cheneb, Alger 1958, p. 70, col. 1. המהדורה הקודמת של המילון הופיעה בשנה 1931. שמות עצם פרטיים כאלה נשמעים בשנים האחרונות באמצעי התקשורת.

27. שטיינשניידר, מבוא, x (1898–1897), 134/סע׳ 62–50.

28. ניו יורק, בית המדרש לרבנים באמריקה, וסימונו: ENA 1290, שנתפרסמה על ידי ז׳ באכר, *REJ*, xxxii (1896), עמ׳ 129–126.

29. M.S. Howell, *A Grammar of the Classical Arabic Language*, Allahabad, 1911, d. IV; fasc. I, 1842; II, 1843, 1845. רמז לספר זה מסר לידי ידידי י׳ בלאו, ועלי לספר בשבחו, שתחלה התנגד לזיהוי שהצעתי לשמות אבן אלעם ואבן בלעם, אולם אחרי ימים אחדים נתקשר בטלפון לביתי, ומסר את המקור הזה שהוא חשוב ביותר בזיהוי שני שמות אלה, אף על פי שהיה בו סיוע לדעתי והתנגדות לדעתו.

*29. A. Gonzalez Palencia, *Los Mozarabes de Toledo*, i, Madrid 1926, pp. 280–281, 338.

30. על המלה אבן בשע״פ עי׳ ב׳ קלאר, ״מחקרים ועיונים״, תל־אביב תשי״ד, עמ׳ 281–276; שטיינשניידר, מבוא x, עמ׳ 121–120/סע׳ 15; ix 228/סע׳ 12; שם, 606–605/סע׳ 6; 618–613/סע׳ 10–9; נ׳ אלוני, ״לשוננו״, יג (תש״ד–תש״ה), עמ׳ 162–159.

וארבע משאלות שואל הלב בסוף דיוננו זה:
(1) כינוס פירושי א״ב והכנת מהדורה מדעית.
(2) גילוי פירושיו של א״ב בתלמוד.
(3) גילוי החיבור נגד הקראים לא״ב.
(4) גילוי שירים ופיוטים נוספים מדיואן א״ב.[62]

הערות

1. במאמר זה אשתמש בקיצורים הבאים:
א״ב = אבן בלעם, אבן אלעם = יהודה בן שמואל אבן בלעם.
אברמסון[1] = ש׳ אברמסון, ״התג׳ניס (הצימוד) לרב יהודה בן בלעם״, ״ספר ילון״, ירושלים תשכ״ג, עמ׳ 149–51.
אברמסון[2] = ש׳ אברמסון, ״רב יוסף ראש הסדר״, ״קרית ספר״, כו (תש״י), עמ׳ 95–72.
אלוני[1] = נ׳ אלוני, ״שלושה קטעים חדשים מחיבורי א״ב״, ״בית מקרא״, כ–כא (תשכ״ד), עמ׳ 122–87.
אלוני[2] = נ׳ אלוני, ״שתי רשימות ספרים אוטוגרפים של ר״י ראש הסדר״, ״קרית ספר״, לח (תשכ״ג), עמ׳ 557–531.
אלוני־שייבר = נ׳ אלוני וא׳ שייבר, ״רשימת ספרים אוטוגרף לרב יוסף ראש הסדר״, ״קרית ספר״, מח (תשל״ג), עמ׳ 172–152.
ד[וידזון] = י׳ דוידזון, ״אוצר השירה והפיוט״, ד כרכים, ניו יורק תרפ״ט–תרצ״ג.
הרכבי = א״א הרכבי, ״חדשים גם ישנים״, מהד׳ כרמיאל, ירושלים תש״ל.
פוזנאנסקי = S. Poznánski, "Fragment eines Commentars zu Leviticus", *ZfHB* iv (1900), pp. 17–22.
פוקס = S. Fuchs, *Studien über Abu Zakaria Jachja (R. Jehuda) Ibn Balām*, Berlin 1893.
רמב״ע[1] = משה אבן עזרא, כתאב אלמחאצ׳רה ואלמד׳אכרה (ספר העיונים והדיונים), כ״י, אוקספורד Hunt.559 (קטלוג נויבאיר מס׳ 1974.) עתה יצא לאור בצירוף מבוא, הערות ותרגום עברי על ידי א.ש. הלקין, ירושלים, תשל״ה.
רמב״ע[2] = משה אבן עזרא, הספר הנ״ל, תרגום בן ציון הלפר, שירת ישראל, לייפציג, תרפ״ד.
שטיינשניידר, מבוא = M. Steinschneider, "Introduction to the Arabic Literature of the Jews", *JQR* ix–xiii (1896–1901).
שטיינשניידר *CB* = M. Steinschneider, *Catalogus . . . Bodleiana*, Oxford 1859, cols. 1292–1297.
שטיינשניידר *HÜ* = M. Steinschneider, *Hebraïsche Übersetzungen des Mittelalters*, Berlin 1893. pp. 913ff.
שטיינשניידר = *Die arabische Literatur der Juden*, Frandfurt a. M., 1902, pp. 138–143.
שירמן[1] = ח׳ שירמן, ״ידיעות המכון לחקר השירה העברית״, ב, ברלין תרצ״ו.
שירמן[2] = ח׳ שירמן, ״שירים חדשים מן הגניזה״, ירושלים תשכ״ו.
שירמן[3] = ח׳ שירמן, ״השירה העברית בספרד ובפרובאנס״, ב חלקים, תל אביב תשט״ו, תשכ״ה.

2. ספרות עליו עי׳ *EJ* (הגרמנית) viii, ברלין 1931, עמ׳ 321–320; ויצויינו כאן כנוספות אברמסון[1] ואלוני[1].

3. ראב״ע, ״מאזנים״, מהד׳ ראשונה, ויניציאה ש״ו (1545), קצז ע״ב/6–5. על פי פתיחתו זו ודברי ראב״ע בפירושיו, כגון: תהלים פד, ד נודע אבן בלעם כבלשן וכפרשן. ראב״ע שאב דבריו על אבן בלעם בפתיחתו לספר ״מאזנים״ מספרי רמב״ע, ״כתאב אלמחאצ׳רה ואלמד׳אכרה״ (עי׳ להלן מקורות השם אבן בלעם).

4. הראשון שגילה שם אביו הוא ש׳ פוזנאנסקי *Zur jüdisch-arabischen Literatur*, ברלין 1904, עמ׳ 64, על פי קטע הגניזה Ms. Heb. d. 68 [2836/11]: ׳בש[מא רחמנא] שרח מגילת אסתר לפט׳ ומעני למרינו יהודה ביר׳ שמואל בן בלעם הספרדי ת[היה?] זכ[ר] צד[יק] לבר[כה]׳; קטע זה נזכר גם על ידי אברמסון[1], 51/הע׳ 3, אחרי ששים שנים (מסתבר, כי נעלמו מאברמסון דברי פוזנאנסקי); פוקס שכתב את מחקרו עשר שנים לפני מאמר פוזנאנסקי, עדיין לא ידע שם אביו: שמואל. אולם בספרותנו ידוע שם אביו לכותבים על אבן בלעם ועי׳ *EJ* (גרמנית) הנ״ל, הע׳ 2.

המקור

אל ההרים לא אכל,[59] יריד אכל ד׳באיח אלאצנאם ומא אצ״ל ענן ואשיאעה פי מנעהם ען נכאח אלחבאלי ויג׳עלון דלילהם מן הד׳א אלפסוק ולקד תפטן אבו סרי בן זוטא למא עליהם פי הד׳א ואנכרה ואסתדל בקול אללה נקי יהיה לביתו שנה אחת ושמח את אשתו אשר לקח. קאל ופי אלאמכאן אן תחבל אלמראה דון אלסנה פיא לך ממן יזעם אן אללה יכלף מא לא יטאק פאנה לו כאן הד׳א חקא לוג׳ב עלי גאשי זוג׳ה אול מרה אן ינעזל ענהא חתי תסתברי אלחבל ויעוד עליהא והד׳א כלה הד׳יאן ובדעה יקול אללה פיהא אשר לא צויתי ולא דברתי ולא עלתה על לבי.

התרגום

כוונתו אכילת זבחי האלילים. ואין טועה גדול יותר מענן ותומכיו בענין איסור חיי אישות עם נשים הרות. והם מביאים מפסוק זה ראיה. ואבו סרי בן זוטא[60] כבר הבין את טענתם בענין זה וגינה אותה. והביא ראיה מהפסוק ״נקי יהיה לביתו שנה אחת ושמח את אשתו אשר לקח״ (דברים כד ה). אמר: אפשר שהאשה תהרה לפני חלוף השנה? ואיזה איש הוא זה אשר טוען, שאלוהים מטיל דבר אשר אי אפשר לשאתו? אילו היה אמת, כי אז היה מוטל על האיש הבא אל אשה בפעם הראשונה לפרוש ממנה, עד אשר תדע בודאות שאינה הרה, ואז יוכל לשוב אליה. וכל אלה הם דברי הבל וחידוש מגונה. ובעניין זה אמר אלהים ״אשר לא צויתי ולא דברתי ולא עלתה על לבי״ (ירמיהו ט, ה).

אף ידועים לנו מקומות נוספים במקרא בפירושיו המכוונים נגד הקראים,[61] ויש להצטער שאין בידנו להביאם כאן בגלל חוסר שיתוף הפעולה בין ספריות ישראל לספריות רוסיה בברית המועצות.

(י). **סיכום וסיום:**

(1) במאמר זה נתבררה לראשונה משמעות השם ״בלעם״, הרכבו וגלגוליו אבן אלעם — בלעם — אבן בלעם.

(2) משמעות השם הוא אפוא אבן אלעם (בן הדוד מצד האב).

(3) המחבר חתם רק בלעם, ואילו אחרים רשמו שמו גם אבן אלעם וגם אבן בלעם.

(4) זהו שם המשפחה, וזה אפוא כינוי משפחתו ולא שם עצם פרטי.

(5) אין השם קשור בשם הנמצא במקרא בלעם בן בעור.

(6) אין כל מקום לחשוב, כי לפנינו שם האב בלעם ושם הבן אבן בלעם.

(7) א״ב היה גם בעל הלכה חשוב מאוד ונשארו רק פירורים מפירוש יבמות בלבד, כמובאות ברשימות ספריו של ר׳ יוסף ראש הסדר ובפירוש ויקרא לא״ב.

(8) א״ב היה לוחם גדול בקראים, ונלחם בהם לא רק בחיבוריו הבלשניים והפרשניים אלא גם בחיבור מיוחד בשם ״כתאב אלרד עלי אלקראיין״ (ספר התשובות על הקראים). הובאו רק קטעים אחדים מפרשנות המקרא נגד הקראים, שיהיו לעזר בזיהוי קטעי גניזה מחיבורו.

(9) א״ב היה גם משורר ופייטן חשוב וכונסו במאמר מיוחד רק ארבעה פיוטים ושלושה שירי איזור, ושיר אחד שקול רגיל.

(10) חשוב הוא ביותר שנודע לנו, כי אבן בלעם הבלשן והפרשן הוא אבן אלעם בעל ההלכה והפולמוסן והוא בלעם המשורר והפייטן.

יח, ט), ואין זאת חזרה, שכן זה היה בלתי מועיל, ואילו הקב״ה מטרה נעלה יותר מכך. אין טועה גדול יותר מזה, אשר אסר את בת האח ובת האחות בדרך ההיקש מענין גברים לענין נשים. אמר: כמו שאסר הכתוב את אחות האב ואת אחות האם כך אסורה בת האח ובת האחות, וזהו חידוש מגונה שאין בו ראיה. וכאשר אנו הולכים בדרך ההיקש... הכתוב מורה שהאיש... עריות מן התורה מספרם עשרים והוסיפו הקדמונים, שמונה איסורי עריות נוספים בדבריהם, ואמרו (יבמות כא ע״א):[56] תנו רבנן מה הם שניות [אם אמו] ואם אביו ואשת אבי אביו [ואשת אבי אמו] ואשת אחי האב ואשת אחי האם בין מן האם ובין מן האב, וכלת בנו וכלת בתו... והנכון הוא בעניין זה תשעה איסורי עריות נוספים עליהם, והם בת בן הבן ובת בן ה[בת?] בן בת אשתו ובת בן... אם אם חמיו ואם אם חמותו. והביא את הנדה בסוג העריות בגלל חומרת טומאתה.

4) פירוש ירמיהו יז, כז: ולבלתי שאת משא ובא בשערי ירושלים.[57]

המקור

ט̃ן בעץ׳ מן ידעי אלפהם אן פי הד׳א קלאול רד̃אעלי אלכ׳וארג׳ פי אנדארהם אלנקל ולקד כנת חאצ׳רא והו יתבג̃ח אנה קאטע בהם קאל לא יכ׳לו הד׳א אלמעני אן יכון ענד אלקום מן עצר מוסי לאנ̃א אן לם נקל כד׳לך וקענא פי באב אלזיאדה פי אלשרע פלא שך̃ אנ̃ה כאן מנקולא ענד אלקום ולם יד׳כרה אלי אן פשת פיה אלמעציה פד׳כרהם במא פי ד׳לך עליהם, ולם יזר הד׳א אלקאיל אנה דאכ׳ל תחת קול אללה תעאלי שבו איש תחתיו אל יצא איש ממקומו ביום השביעי, ומן לם יבח להו אלכ׳רוג׳ פלא פאידה אן יקאל לה לא תכ׳רג׳ שיא מן מוצ׳עך. פאד׳א כאן הד׳א אלמעני פי טי הד׳א אלקול פלא פאידה אן יקאל לה לא תכ׳רג׳ שיא מן מוצ׳עך. פאד׳א כאן הד׳א אלמעני פי הד׳א אלקול פלא חג̃ה פיה למחתג̃, ונחן נקול אן אכת׳ר אלחדוד פי אלסבת וג׳ורהא וכמיאת אלשראיע וכיפיאתהא מנקולה ען אלרסול אכ׳ד׳וא ד׳לך ענה פי מדה מקאמהם פי אלבריה. ומן עט׳ם אלסבת ג׳על ג׳זא חפט׳הא בקו אלדולה ועקובה בד׳להא כ׳ראב אלבלד וזואל אלמלך והד׳א עט׳ים ונחן כת׳ירא מא נבד׳להא סר̃א ועלאניה.

תרגום

אחד המתימרים להיות מן המבינים חשב, שבפסוק הזה יש תשובה לקראים בענין כפירתם בתורה שבע״פ. והייתי נוכח בעת שהתפאר שהוא פוסק להם פסק, אמר: המשמעות הזאת בהכרח נמצאת אצל העם מזמן משה, זאת משום שאם לא נאמר כך נעבור על ״בל תוסיף״ בחוק. ולכן אין ספק, שזה היה מסור אצל העם ולא זכרו אותו עד אשר התפשט אי קיום המצוות בעם, ואז הזכיר להם מה שמוטל עליהם בענין זה. ולא הרגיש הדובר שהוא [האיסור] מצוי בדברי האלוהים יתעלה: ״שבו איש תחתיו אל יצא איש ממקומו ביום השביעי״, ומי שאסורה עליו היציאה, אין תועלת לומר לו, אל תוציא דבר ממקומך. ואם המשמעות הזאת מצויה בתוך הפסוק הזה, אין בכך משום טענה לטוענים. ואנו אומרים, שרוב הסייגים בענין השבת וזולתם וכמות החוקים ודרך ביצועם נמסרה מפי הנביא [משה], והם קיבלו זאת ממנו בזמן שהותם במדבר. ובגלל חשיבות השבת קבע ששכר שמירתה קיום השושלת והעונש על חילולה חורבן הארץ ואבדן המלוכה, ולעתים קרובות אנו מחללים בסתר ובגלוי.[58]

5) פירוש יחזקאל, יח, ו: אל ההרים לא אכל.

אלא במי מקוה אד׳ ליס ענדנא אלאן את׳קל נג׳אסה מנהא פאלויל למן סהל עלי נפסה פי אתמאמוהא.[54] בעד אלגסל פי אלחמאם או מת׳לה פליעלם אנהא לו צבת אלפראת עלי ג׳סמהא שי בעד שי לם תטהר בד׳לך לאנ֗הא טמאה מטמאה פמא מן ג׳ז יצל אלי ג׳סמהא מן אלמא אלמצבוב וקד נג׳סתה הי פכיף יטהרהא מא נג׳ס אנ֗מא תטהר במא הו פי ענצרה והו אלד׳י נץ֗ אללה עליה פי כתאבה ״אך מעין ובור מקוה מים יהיה טהור״ ואקל֗ מא עלי מצ׳אג׳עהא כרת ואלולד בן נדה. וסנדכ׳ר לך בעד הד׳א וג׳וה פי אלנדה יעתבר בהא אלמסאמחון פי אמרהא ויעלמון קדר נג׳אסתהא.

תרגום

וכבר נבוכו הקראים בענין זה ולא הגיעו לאמת בעניין זה בשום אופן, כי אינם מודים בדברי הקדמונים אשר כללו בדבריהם, שהיא מיטהרת במים, ספירה וקורבן. ובימינו אלה, בתקופת הגלות קבענו שהנדה זבה ותספור שבעה נקיים על כל דם. ואין היא צריכה לשמור שבעה ימים בשלמות אלא מזמן הפסקת [זיבת] הדם בין אם זה היה יום אחד ובין אם יומים או יותר, תספור אחרי כן שבעה ימים נקיים ותטבול במי מקוה, כלומר מים **לא עומדים** ובכך תהיה מותרת לבעלה. וכך אמרו הקדמונים:[53] אמר רב זירא בנות ישראל החמירו על עצמן אפילו רואות טיפת דם כחרדל יושבת עליה שבעה ימים נקיים. ואין היא מיטהרת אלא בטבילה במי מקוה. גם אם תשאר כך שנים, לא תצא מידי טומאה בשום אופן אלא במי מקוה, משום שלפי דעתנו כעת אין טומאה יותר כבדה ממנה. ואוי לו למי שמקל לעצמו להשלימה [הטהרה] אחרי הרחצה בבית מרחץ או בדומה לו. עליו לדעת שאילו שפכה את כל מי הפרת כולם על גופה לא תטהר על ידי כך, משום שהיא טמאה ומטמאה. ואין שום כמות מן המים הנשפכים המגיעה אל גופה מבלי שתטמא אותה היא. וכיצד יטהרו אותה מים טמאים. אין היא מטהרת אלא במים במקורם, והוא אשר קבע אותו אלהים בספרו ״אך מעין ובור מקוה מים יהיה טהור״ (ויקרא יא, לו), והעונש הקל ביותר על השוכב עמה הוא כרת, והילד הוא בן נדה. ונביא לפניך אחרי כן עניינים שונים בעניין הנדה, אשר באמצעותם ילמדו לקח אלה המבקשים להקל בנידון וידעו את מדת טומאתה.

3) פירוש ויקרא יח, יא: ערות בת אשת אביך מולדת אביך אחותך היא לא תגלה ערותן.

מקור

פלאוזר[55] עליה קו׳ פי אלעריות ערות בת אשת אביך הו עלי סביל אלביאן לקו׳ פוק הד׳א ערות אחותך בת אביך וליס עלי סביל אלתכריר פאנה כאן יכון גיר מפיד ואלוחי ארפע מן הד׳ה ומא אצ׳ל֗ מן חרם בנת אלאך׳ ובנת אלאכ׳ת בקיאס אלאנאת׳ עלי אלד׳כור קאל כמא חרם אלנץ֗ אלעמ֗ה ואלכ׳אלה כד׳לך תחרם בנת אלאך׳ ובנת אלאכ׳ת והד׳ה בדעה לא דליל לה פיה ומתי תאבענא עלי קיאסה... אלנץ֗ ידל אן אלרג׳ל... עריות מן אלנץ֗ עשרון וזאד אלאו֗לון ת׳מאן שניות [נאידה]... פי אקואלהם וקאלוא תנו׳ רבנן מה הם שניות [אם אמו] ואם אביו ואשת אבי אביו [ואשת אבי אמו] ואשת אחי האב ואשת אחי האם בין מן האם ובין מן האב וכלת בנו וכלת בתו... ואלחק בהד׳א טת שניות זאיד עליהן והי אבנה ולד אלאבן ואבנה ולד אלא... ולד אבנה אלזוג׳ה ואבנה ולד... וואלדה ואלדה חמוה וואלדה חמאתה ואדכ׳ל אלנדה פי צ׳רב אלעריות לת׳קל נג׳אסתהא.

תרגום

החטא הגדול ביותר עליו הוא דעתו בענין עריות: ״ערות בת אשת אביך״ (ויקרא יח, יא), (אשר) בא להבהיר את הפסוק שנאמר לעיל: ״ערות אחותך בת אביך״ (ויקרא

2) כת׳ אלרד̇ עלי אלקראיין לבן אלעם.
קמבריג׳, T-S. K 6/170 (אלוני, ר״י רה״ס, בהכנה לדפוס, ג, ע/10–9).
3) כת׳ אלרד̇ עלי אלקראין לבן אלעם.
קמבריג׳, T-S. K 6/170 (אלוני, ר״י רה״ס, בהכנה לדפוס, ג, ע/30).
4) ז׳ כראריס אלרד̇ עלי אלקראיין.
(שבע מחברות — התשובות על הקראים).
קמבריג׳, T-S. K 20/9 (מאן[1], 92/655).
5) רד̇ עלי אלקראיין.
(התשובות על הקראים).
קמבריג׳, T-S. 10 K 10 20/7 (מאן[2], 180/סי׳ א).
6) כתאב אלרד̇ עלי אלכ׳וארג׳[45].
(ספר התשובות על הכופרים).
קמבריג׳, T-S. 10 K 20/8 (מאן[2], 178/סי׳ 9).

נמצא, כי בשלוש מובאות המחבר הוא בן אלעם (בלעם), ואילו ביתר השלוש בלי שם מחבר, ובאחת מהן אף שם החיבור שונה. אולם אין ספק, כי היה חיבור לבן בלעם נגד הקראים.

לדאבוננו הרב, לא הגיע לידינו מחיבורו זה נגד הקראים מאומה, אף כי ייתכן שיתגלו שרידים הימנו בגניזת קהיר, אם יסודר החומר בו ויירשם כהלכה.[49] על כרחנו יובאו כאן רק דוגמאות מחיבוריו הבלשניים הנמצאים בידינו ומפירושיו למקרא בנדון.

מקור

1) כתאב אלתג׳ניס (ספר הצימוד).[50]

הנה חדש מחר (שמ״א כ, ה): חדש חדש אלאול ואכלו חדש ימים וקד וקע על ראס אלשהר פקט פיקולה הנה חדש מחר ויתבי̇ן מן קצה שאול אן אלאו̇לין מעו̇להם כאן עלי אלחסאב אלא תרי אלי קולה ויהי ממחרת החדש השני ולא ד׳לך אלא בטריק אלחסאב לא באלרויה ואלב מן חדש אסם אמראה.

תרגום

המשמעות הראשונה... (במ׳ יא, כא); ויהיה גם במשמעות ראש החודש בלבד בפסוק... (שמ״א כ, ה); ומתברר מסיפור שאול כי הקדמונים היו נעזרים בחישובי החשבון. הלא תראה את הכתוב: (שמ״א כ, כז).. ואין זה אפשרי אלא בשיטת החישוב ולא בראיית הירח. המשמעות השנייה שם עצם פרטי לאשה (דה״א ח, ט)).

אין ספק, כי נהגו בני ישראל לקדש את החודש על פי הראיה, כפי שמוכיחה המשנה בראש השנה לא רק בתקופת המקרא אלא גם אחרי בית שני, אלא שאבן בלעם מתנגד כאן לקראים והרבו הרבנים להשתמש בכתוב זה כנגד הקראים.[51]

2) פירוש ויקרא טו, כה: ואשה כי יזוב זוב דמה ימים רבים.

מקור

פקד[52] תחי̇יר אלכ׳וארג׳ פיה ולם יציבוא אלחק פי ד׳לך ביג׳ה אד׳ לם יקרוא בקו׳ אלקדמא אלד׳ין תצ׳מ̇נוא אנ̇הא תטהר במים וספירה וקרבן ופי זמאננא הד׳א פי עצר אלגלות ג׳עלנא אלנדה זבה ותספור שבעה נקיים עלי כל דם ולא תראעי תמאם סבעה איאם בל מן וקת אנקטאע אלדם פי יום כאן ד׳לך או פי יומין או פי מא זאד תחצי בעד ד׳לך שבע׳ ימי נקיים ותטבל במי מקוה אעני מאא גיר מסתקריאן ובד׳לך תחל לזוג׳הא וכד׳א קאל אלקדמא[53] אמ׳ ר׳ זירא בנות ישראל החמירו על עצמן אפילו רואות טפת דם כחרדל יושבת עליה שבעת ימי נקיים ולא טהארה להא אלא באנגמאם פי מא מקוה ולו בקית כד׳לך אעואמא לם תכ׳רג׳ מידי טומאה בוג׳ה

שומה הן פיר׳ שומה שהלכה כמה שפסק ראבא ענדי ומן הנא נאקץ״. (ותרגומו: מפירוש יבמות חסרים שלושת הפרקים הראשונים,[37] וחסר לי מראש פרק הבא על יבמתו (יבמות פרק ו) עד והטיח ביבמתו ביאה כינוי לבעילה,[38] ומן כינוי לבעילה עד אם הביאה שתי שערות שומה הן פי׳ שומה[39] שהלכה כמו שפסק רבא (נמצא אצלי[40], ומכאן ואילך חסר).

(2) ״אלעאיז[35] מן גמר יבמות מן בבואה אית להו בבואה דבבואה לית להו אלי אכ׳ר אלמסכתא״. (ותרגומו: החסר מגמרא יבמות . . . עד סוף המסכת [יבמות]).

(3) בפירוש ספר ויקרא[41] הובא קטע מפירוש יבמות, ושמא אף זה מפירושו הביא, ואף יעזור לזיהוי פירושו כשיתגלה:[42]

״וזאד אלאולון ת׳מאן שניות [. . .] פי אקואלהם וקאלוא תנו רבנן מה הם שניות [אם אמו] ואם אביו ואשת אבי אביו [ואשת אבי אמו] ואשת אחי האב ואשת אחי האם בין מן האם בין מן האב וכלת בנו וכלת בתו . . . ואלחק בהד׳א טת שניות זאיד עליהן והי אבנה ולד אלאבן ואבנה ולד אלא . . . ולד אבנה אלזוג׳ה ואבנה ולד . . . וואלדה ואלדה חמוה וואלדה ואלדה המאתה ואדכ׳ל אלנדה פי צ׳רב[43] אלעריות לת׳קל נג׳אסתהא״. (ותרגומו: והוסיפו הקדמונים שמונה אחרות . . . בדבריהם, ואמרו: תנו רבנן מה הם שניות ואם אמו ואם אביו ואם אבי אביו ואשת אבי אמו ואשת אחי האב ואשת אחי האם בין מן האם בין מן האב וכלת בנו וכלת בתו . . . והנכון בענין זה תשעה איסורי עריות נוספים עליהם והם בת בן הבן ובנו מן [הבת?] . . . ילד בן אשתו ובנו ילד . . . ואב אבי חמיו ואבי אבי חמותו והנדה הביא בסוגי העריות בגלל חומרת הטומאה).

לפי מובאות מעטות אלה נוכל לומר רק דברים מעטים על פירושו:

(1) הפירוש הכיל פירושים בלשניים כמו בפירושיו למקרא:
הטיח ביבמתו — כינוי לבעילה.
שומה — ?

(2) דברי פולמוס נגד הקראים בדיני העריות.

(ט). **ספר התשובות נגד הקראים לא״ב.** מתוך חוסר ידיעות מדויקות או מתוך רצון לראות את בני ישראל מאוחדים איחוד מלא, יש מעלימים עין ממחלוקת שהיתה בעבר בין כיתות שונות בישראל. מתוך שבאו בני ישראל לכבות את הדליקה שפרצה בעמנו במחלוקת עם הקראים, ביקשו גם לטשטש את שרידי הזכרונות על מחלוקת זו; אף נמצאו חכמים שהכריזו, כי לא היתה מחלוקת בין קראים לרבנים בתוך ספרד כלל וכלל.[44] אף שטיינשניידר סבור היה,[45] כי רק באמצע המאה השתים עשרה פרצה המחלוקת בין שתי כיתות אלה. אולם בימינו נתרבו הידיעות על המחלוקת בין שתי כיתות אלה ועל סמך אלה סבורני, כי הקראות נתפשטה בארץ ספרד כבר במאה העשירית ונמשכה עד המאה החמש עשרה, עד גירוש בני ישראל מארץ ספרד. בא הכוח הרציני של דעות הקראים בארץ ספרד במחצית הראשונה של המאה העשירית הוא מנחם בן סרוק, וזו היתה סיבת המחלוקת בינו לבין דונש בן לבראט,[46] וזו היתה הסיבה לעונשים שהענישו קשה חסדאי אבן שפרוט הרבני. עדות לקראות בארץ ספרד אני מוצא במצחפי המקרא שבהם נמצאת ״רשימת המונחים הקראית העתיקה מהמאה השמינית״.[47] והנה נתגלה לנו לאחרונה, כי היה ר׳ יהודה אבן בלעם לוחם גדול בקראים לא רק בפירושיו למקרא, אלא אף כתב חיבורי פולמוס מיוחדים נגד הקראים.

החיבור נגד הקראים לר״י אבן בלעם. ואלה הן העדויות ברשימות הספרים:

1) כת׳ רד̈ עלי אלקראיין לבן אלעם ז״ל.
(ספר התשובות על הקראים לבן אלעם ז״ל).
T-S. C. 2/146 (שייבר^2, 8/73/מס׳ 38).

(ז). **פירוש יבמות לאבן בלעם**. א״ב היה בקי בהלכה, וזה ניכר גם בדיוניו בענייני הלשון אף בחיבוריו הבלשניים.[32] בידנו אף עדות מפורשת מפי בן דור סמוך לא״ב, רמב״ע, וזו לשונו.[33] ״ומן ד׳וי אלאחסאב אלכרימה ונביאת אלנבאהה ומן קלילי אלקול אלאסתאד׳ אלמאהר אלחאפט׳ אלד׳אכר אלמתפקّה פי אכ׳ר עמרה אבו זכריא יחיי בן בלעם אלטליטלי ת׳ם אלאשבילי רחמה אללה״. (ותרגומו: ומבעלי החשיבות הנכבדים ואצילי האצילות וממעיטי הדיבור המורה הזריז הזוכר בטבעו והזוכר על סמך הניסיון, בעל ההלכה בסוף ימיו, אבו זכריה יהודה בן בלעם יליד טולידו, ולאחר זמן איש סביליה ירחמהו ה׳).

משנתפרסמו דברי רמב״ע, ולא מצאו החכמים התאמה לידוע להם, ביקשו לכוון משמעות למלים של רמב״ע, ובמקום לומר איש ההלכה איש בקי בהלכה או מחבר דברי הלכה עשאוהו בעל משרה של דיין.[34] אולם בשנים האחרונות נתפרסמו רשימות ספרים לר״י ראש הסדר, ובהם נמצא אישור לדברי רמב״ע בהתאם למשמעותן הנכונה של המלים:

1) קמבריג׳, T–S. NS. J94/126 (אלוני[2], 34/540):
אלעאיז מן פי׳ יבמות (החסר מפירוש של מסכת יבמות).

2) הנ״ל (אלוני[2], 36/540):
תמאם פי׳ יבמות (השלמת הפירוש של מסכת יבמות).

3) הנ״ל (אלוני[2] 51–52/540):
אלעאיז מן גמר יבמות פיה אלג׳ פרוק אלאולה מן יבמות
(החסר ממסכת יבמות פירוש שלושת הפרקים הראשונים של מסכת יבמות).

4) הנ״ל (אלוני[2], 68–69/540):
אלעאיז מן פי׳ יבמות אסתערהא
(החסר מן הפירוש של מסכת יבמות אשאלנו).

5) קמבריג׳, T-S. Misc. 36/148 (אלוני־שייבר, 97/166):
פיר׳ יבמות לבן אלעם נאקץ (פירוש מסכת יבמות לבן אלעם חסר).

6) קמבריג׳, T-S. Misc. 136/150 (אסף, 274/ סי׳ 61: לאבי, אולם לפי כה״י: לאבן).
ג׳זוין פי׳ יבמות לאבן אלעם (שני חלקים פירוש יבמות לאבן אלעם).

7) קמבריג׳, T-S. Misc. 36/148 (אלוני־שייבר, 70–71/164):
אלעאיז מן גמר יבמות מן בבואה אית להו בבואה דבבואה לית להו אלי אכ׳ר אלמסכתא (החסר ממסכת יבמות מן . . . עד סוף המסכת).[35]

משבע המובאות כאן מתברר, כי היה פירוש יבמות לאבן בלעם, ובידי ר״י ראש הסדר היה הפירוש חסר. השאלה היא: אם יש בידנו למצוא שרידי פירוש זה? אף נודע לנו כאן, כי היה זה פירוש רב היקף, והיה בן שני כרכים.

(ח). **שרידי פירוש יבמות לר״י אבן בלעם (אבן אלעם)**. לא נודע פירוש יבמות לא״ב לא בצורת חיבור מיוחד ולא בצורת מובאות, אולם נדמה לי, כי יש מקום ליחס לא״ב את הקטעים הקצרצרים המובאים בתוך רשימות הספרים לר״י ראש הסדר, על פי מהלך ראיות זה:

(1) אבן אלעם חיבר פירוש מסכת יבמות, והוא אבן בלעם, שתי מובאות;
(2) באחת מן המובאות עדות כי פירוש אבן אלעם היה חסר.
(3) בארבעה עיולים ברשימותיו רשם ר״י ראש הסדר פירוש יבמות חסר (עאיז) בלא שם המחבר.

יש אפוא מקום ליחס את המובאות מפירוש כזה ברשימות ר״י ראש הסדר לר״י אבן בלעם, ואלה הם:[36]

(1) ״פירוש יבמות יעווני אלג׳ פרוק אלאולה ויעוזני מן אול פרק הבא על יבמתו אלי והטיח ביבמתו פיר כינוי לבעילה ומן כינוי לבעילה אלי אם הביאה שתי שערות

משפחה זו, ותהליך השם הזה ככינוי היוחסין היה: (1) אבן אלעם> (2) בלעם> (3) אבן בלעם.

סיכומו של בירור: יש שמות עצם פרטיים שהם מורכבים משלושה רכיבים: (1) המילה אבו או אבן; (2) סימן היידוע: אל; (3) שם העצם הפרטי. התמזגותם של שלושת הרכיבים נמצא בספרות הערבית הקלאסית, והיא נמצאת וקיימת בלשונות הערבים עד עצם היום הזה. שמות עצם פרטיים מסוג זה נמצאים גם בספרות הערבית היהודית מהמאה האחת עשרה, ואף ייתכן כי כבר היו בין בני ישראל אף קודם למאה זו. מכיוון שש״פ מסוג זה נתגלו בין העמים המוסלמים באפריקה הצפונית, יש אולי להסיק, כי גם משפחת אבן בלעם היתה בין המשפחות שהגרו מאפריקה הצפונית לספרד בימי רב חסדאי אבן שפרוט ורב שמואל הנגיד.[31]

(ו). **קיצור ספרי חיוג׳ לא״ב**. על קיצור ספרי חיוג׳ לא״ב ידוע לנו מרשימות ספרים בגניזת קהיר מאה שנים בערך:

1) מכ׳תצר חיוג׳... ורקא ח דר׳ (קיצור ספרי חיוג׳... נייר. שמונה דרהם).
וורמן, 36–37/461

2) מכ׳תצר חיוג׳ ומכ׳תצרין פי אללג[ה].
וורמן, שם שם; ועי׳ פוזנאנסקי[2], 13/113: כאן אנו מוצאים קיצור לא ידוע ממקור אחר.

3) כתאב אלתג׳ניס... ומכת׳צר ח[יוג׳ לבן] אלעם מג׳לד. (ספר הצימוד... וקיצור חיוג׳ לאבן אלעם מכורך)
אברמסון[2], 83 עמודה ב/17; ועי׳ נ׳ אלוני, ״קרית ספר״, ל (תשט״ו), 445/סי׳ ז.

4) ומכ׳תצר חיוג׳ לבן ג׳קטילה רחמה אללה (בכה״י: מכתצאר!)
קמבריג׳, T-S. NS. 312/84 (נ׳ אלוני, הע׳ 165/43, *SBB*, vi (1964)).

נמצא, כי מקור אחד מיחס את הקיצור לא״ב, ואילו השני לבן ג׳יקטילה, וסבורני, כי היה זה א״ב המקצר, ואילו בן ג׳יקטילה היה המתרגם חיבורי חיוג׳ בשלמותם.

קטעי הגניזה, שהם כנראה ״מכ׳תצר חיוג׳״, והם ידועים לי כיום, הם:

1) אוקספורד, MS. Heb. e. 75, דף 3837 [2828/18] — שני דפים.
התוכן: הנחים: הש׳ Morris Jastrow, *Weak and Geminative Verbs by Abu Zakariyya.. Ḥayyuj*, Leiden 1897 עמ׳ 132–135; 142–145 נל״ה וחסרי הקצוות.

2) ניו יורק, ENA 2713, דף 21–22.
התוכן: הכפולים. הש׳ יאסטרוב, שם, עמ׳ 243–244.

3) ניו יורק, ENA 2753, דף 6 ע״א (כ״י שונה).
התוכן: הכפולים. הש׳ יאסטרוב, שם, עמ׳ 227–230.

4) קמבריג׳, T-S. K 9/7, שני דפים.
התוכן: הנחים. הש׳ יאסטרוב, שם, עמ׳ 75–84.

5) קמבריג׳, T-S. Ar. 31/172, דף אחד.
התוכן: הנחים. הש׳ יאסטרוב, שם, עמ׳ 84–85.

6) קמבריג׳, T-S. Ar. 31/217, דף אחד.
התוכן: הכפולים. הש׳ יאסטרוב, שם, עמ׳ 222–224.

7) קמבריג׳, T-S. NS. 301/7, דף אחד (כ״י שונה).
התוכן: הנחים נפעל. הש׳ יאסטרוב, שם, עמ׳ 80–82.

חמישה מהם הם חלקים של כ״י אחד (1, 2, 4, 5, 6), ויתר השנים (3, 7) כל אחד מהם הוא קטע מכתב יד אחר. קיצור זה לא הוצא לאור, ואף לא ידוע לי מאמר העוסק בנושא זה.

בלשון הערבית מצאנו שמות עצם פרטיים כאלה בלשון אלג׳יר ובתקופה האחרונה במאתים השנים האחרונות. השאלה היא: הנמצאים בלשון הערבית שמות עצם פרטיים שנתמזג בהם הרכיב אבו או אבן בימי הבינים או בהעתיקה?

איננו מוצאים את הסוג הזה של שע״פ במילונים הקלאסיים הערביים כמות ״לסאן אלערב״ וה״צחאח״ ואף לא במילונים האירופיים הערביים המבוססים על הספרות הלקסיקוגרפית הערבית או הספרות הערבית הקלאסית כמות דוזי, האבה, ליין, ועוד. יש להעיר, כי אין המילונים מביאים שמות עצם פרטיים, ואין מחקרים מיוחדים לאונומסטיקון הערבי. אין ספק בעיני, כי היו שמות עצם פרטיים בצירוף הרכיב אבו או אבן בימי הביניים. למזלנו הטוב נתגלו שמות מסוג זה בספרות הערבית הקלאסית, ומהם נוכל ללמוד בנקל קל וחומר ביחס לימי הבינים. ואלה הם השמות שהובאו בספר הדקדוק רב ההיקף המבוסס על הספרות הקלאסית:[29]

בלענבר — אבו אלענבר (بالعَنبَر)

בלעדויה — בנו אלעדויה (بالعدوية)

בלחארת׳ — בנו אלחארת׳ (بالحارث) — שם זה מובא לעיל בלשון האלג׳ירית.

בלעם — בנו אלעם (بَالعَمّ)

לפנינו לא רק שמות העצם הפרטיים בצירוף הרכיב אבו או אבן, אלא שאותו שם עצמו ״בלעם״ כשם עצם פרטי ומוזכר בדיוק כמוהו, המתאים התאמה מלאה לענייננו. אף הוא מביא שם את בית השיר כששם זה שלוב בתוכו וארוג בו:

אד׳א גאב גדוא, ענך בלעם לם יכן / ג׳לידא ולם תעטף עליך אלעואטף

إذا غاب غدواً عنكَ بَالعَمْ لَم يَكن / جليداً ولم تعطف عليك ألعواطف

(כאשר בני הדוד מצד האב נעדרו ממך ביום המחר / יהיה כקרח ולא יחוסו עליך רגשי הרחמים.)

ונמצא השם גם בתעודה שהגיעה לידנו מטולידו:[29]

على إعتراف الثقَة المذكور من ابن سمرة بن عزرى وأبن هارون بن بَالعَم اليهودين البائعين عنهما وعن سائر يهود مدينة طلبيرة

עלי אעתראף אלת׳קה אלמד׳כור מן אבן סמרה בן עזרא ואבן הרון בן בלעם אליהודין אלבאיען ענהמא וען סאיר יהוד מדינה טלבירה

וכך תורגם באותו ספר לספרדית, ותרגומו טעון תיקון:

otorgada por . . . ben azri y Abuharun ben Balaam judios en representacion de los judios de Talavera.

אף על פי שכבר נתברר לנו כי השם בלעם הוא שם עצם פרטי מורכב משלושה רכיבים, עדיין לא נתפרש לנו, אם הרכיב הראשון בו הוא אבו או אבן (בנו).

1) אבו — באופן כללי לפי מילון בוסיי הרכיב הראשון הוא אבו, כלומר השם הנוסף לאב אחרי שנולד לו הבן הבכור או הבן הראשון במשפחתו, וכך נקרא האיש בל (או באל) קאסם — אבו אלקאסם וכד׳. אולם קשה לגרוס כך ביחס ל״בלעם״, כי בשמו אנו מוצאים אבו זכריא יחיי אבן בלעם.

2) אבן[30] — בתקופה הקלאסית מדובר בעיקר בצירוף הרכיב אבן לשם עצם פרטי ונמצא כי השם בלעם הוא אבן אלעם, וזה מה שמתאים לשם שלפנינו בלעם, כפי שחותם המחבר עצמו בשירו באקרוסטיכון, וזה מתאים לכל אותם המקורות שרשמו את שם מחברנו: אבן אלעם. אולם השאלה היא: אם בלעם הוא אבן אלעם, איך נתגלה השם ״אבן בלעם״, שאם נפרקנו לרכיביו יהיה: אבן אבן אלעם?

מסתבר אפוא, כי השם ״אבן בלעם״ בצורתו המאוחרת הוא לכינוי היוחסין של

הפתרון החדש מבוסס על הסברה, כי לפנינו שם מורכב משלושה רכיבים: (1) אבו או אבן; (2) סימן היידוע אל, שנתמזג עם הקידומת: אבו אל בל או אבן אל בל: (3) השם עםּ (عم), ומשמעותו: הדוד מצד האב. ונתרכבו אבו אלעם בלעם; אבן אלעם בלעם. ביאור זה של השם הוא פשוט מאוד, בהיר וברור, זהור וצהור, אולם הוא נתאפשר לי בעזרת חומר חדש מגניזת קהיר בימים האחרונים ובעזרת ספרות חדשה של מזרחנים בשנים האחרונות, שלא היו ברשותם של חכמי ישראל שקדמו לי.

הרכיב ״אבו״ או ״אבן״ כמתרכב בשמות עצם פרטיים הוא כיום ידוע ומפורסם באפריקה הצפונית, ואף מובאים השמות המורכבים ברכיב זה במילונים, וזו לשון מחבר מילון ללשון הערבית בארץ אלג׳יר:[26]

״בל (بل) או באל (بال) בתור קיצור של אבו אל או אבי אל, ולפעמים במקום אבן אל, כגון:

באלאכ׳צ׳ר — אבו אלאכ׳צ׳ר.
באלחאג׳ או בלחאג׳, במקום אבן אלחאג׳ — Bel Ḥadj.
בלגית׳ — אבו אלגית׳.
בלחארת׳ — אבו אלחארת׳.
בליל, במקום: אבן אלליל.
בלעבאס — אבו אלעבאס.
בלעין — אבו אלעין.
בלצ׳יאף — אבו אלצ׳יאף.
ובימינו: בלקאסם — אבו אלקאסם; ועוד״.

גם בספרות הערבית היהודית ידועים שמות עצם פרטיים לא מעטים, שיש בהם הרכיב אבו או אבן שנתרכב בהם ונתמזג עמם. אף שטיינשניידר עצמו מביא שמות עצם פרטיים לא מעטים מסוג זה:[27]

בוג׳נאח — אבו ג׳נאח (והעיר: אולי במקום אבן ג׳נאח).
בוזאגלו — אבו זאגלו.
בוזיד — אבו זיד.
בומנדל — אבו מנדל.
בומרדכי — אבו מרדכי.
בנאים — אבן נאים (והעיר: קרא — בו נאים).
בועזיז — אבו עזיז.
בורגיל — אבו רגיל.
בושערה — אבו שערה.

ברשימת ספרים אחת בלבד נמצאים ארבעה שמות עצם פרטיים בצירוף הרכיב אבו, והרשימה היא בת המאה השתים עשרה, כי הספריה היתה שייכת לאבו אלעז, ואלה הם השמות:[28]

בומנצור — אבו אלמנצור — אבו מנצור.
בואלעז — אבו אלעז.
בועלי — אבו עלי.
בואלפרג — אבו אלפרג׳.

תהיה זו מסקנה נכונה, אם נאמר כי לפנינו שמות עצם פרטיים לא מעטים, ויש בהם הרכיב אבו או אבן, ובספרות הערבית היהודית היו שמות עצם פרטיים מסוג זה בימי הבינים.

ויש להוסיף עליהם שע״פ בימי הבינים, שלא נתפרשו עד היום: בחיי — אבן יחיי או אבליחיי: בן זכריה או בן יהודה. ברון — אבן הרון או אבלהרון: בן אהרן.

6) כאן נתברר לראשונה, שיהודה אבן בלעם הוא לא רק הבלשן והפרשן אלא גם בעל הלכה ופולמוסן.

(ה). **מוצא השם וקריאתו.** היו דעות שונות ביחס למוצא השם. הדעה הראשונה והתמימה היא זו שסבורה, כי השם הוא מקראי, ואף נמצא לה מבסס שם זה ומפרש מקורו בתקופה הערבית. דעה זו היתה מהלכת בחכמת ישראל במשך מאה וחמישים שנים ובין חסידיה יש למנות: וולף, די רוסי, ביזנטל ולבריכט, דירנבורג, ויעקב רייפמן.[20] השם הוא מקראי כמו בלעם בן בעור (במדבר, דברים, יהושע ומיכה). האחרון אף סבור היה, כי שם מקראי זה תואם לכת הקראים, ועל כן היו שניהם, אבן בלעם הבן ובלעם האב קראים:[21] "ובלעם זה היה בלי ספק מהקראים, כי הרבנים לא מסקי בשמייהו דרשיעי, ככתיב ביומא (לח ע"ב/16) . . . ואגב גררא אחוה דעי על ר' יהודה בן בלעם המובא בפתיחת מאזנים להראב"ע, כי גם הוא היה קראי מהראיה הנ"ל, ואולי היה בנו של בלעם הנזכר". לאמתו של דבר אין אב ובנו לפנינו אלא איש אחד, שהיה רבני והיה אחד הלוחמים הגדולים והחשובים ביותר שנלחמו בקראות בארץ ספרד וכל הדעות־ההפוכות האלה באו לתלמיד חכם חריף זה, כי סבור היה שזהו השם המקראי, בלעם בן בעור.

פליישר המזרחן הדגול היה האיש שביסס דעה זו, ולפיו זהו בלעם בן בעור בכתיבו הערבי המקביל ללקמאן, וזו לשונו:[22] "השם הוא השם הכפול לשם החכם האגדי לקמאן בן באעורא בספרות הערבית, ואפשר לכתבו כתיב מלא בלעאם או בלעם בכתיב חסר. אף הוא מצא בית שיר, ובו השם בכתיב מלא:

ומא ד'א אפאד אלעלם בלעאם והו מן / בני אדם למא אלי אלארץ' אכ'לדא

(מה הועילה לבלעם החכמה, שהרי היה / מבני אדם כאשר פנה לארץ ונצטרף לבני אדם)"

ואף סימן מובהק לפליישר בזיהוי זה: בלעם בן בעור — לקמאן בן באעורא, ומשמעות השם לקמאן הוא כמו בלעם — לבלוע, ללגום.

זהו המקור לתעתיק הכפול של השם בלעם — בלעאם.

החלק הנכון בדעה זו הוא, כי מקור השם הוא בלשון הערבית. אולם אין זה נכון, כי השם אבן בלעם קשור בשם בלעם בן בעור, וממילא אינו קשור בלקמאן בן באעורא. ועוד נוסף כאן כתיב לא נכון, שלא נתגלה אפילו פעם אחת במקורותינו: בלעאם, אולם רבו לו החסידים בין חכמינו.[23]

הדעה השלישית היא, כי השם הוא ברברי. דעה זו העלה הרכבי:[24] "כי בודאי לא נקרא בניקוד בִּלְעָם, כי אם בַּלְעַם (או בַּלְעָם), והוראת המלה בערבית כמו בלע, ר"ל נתחשק, נתאוה. גם נקראו בני ישראל בימים הקדמונים האלה בשמות בשפת ברבר [Berber] כאשר מצאתי עתה כי בשם ברהון . . . נקרא אחד ממשרתי המלך באדיס (אדון ר' שמואל הנגיד), אשר היה מבני הברברים הנקראים בשם פלשתים אצל סופרי ספרד . . . ואולי גם השם בלעם לקוח משפת הברברים אשר משלו אז בדרום ספרד . . . " לא נודע לנו איש אחר, שיהיה סבור כמו הרכבי, ונשארה דעתו דעת יחיד.

הצד השווה לכל בעלי הדעות הנ"ל, שכולם סברו, כי זוהי מלה אחת ושם בן מלה אחת, ולא העלה איש על דעתו, כי זהו שם מורכב משלושה רכיבים. האיש הפינומינלי והביבליוגרף המובהק שטיינשניידר נבוך בביאור שם זה, והוא אומר:[25] "אין השם ידוע כשם נוצרי ולא כשם ערבי", ויחד עם זה קיבל את דעת הסוברים, כי יש לקראו כמו Balám בערבית, ובכתיב מלא דווקה: Ibn Balám.

כת׳ אלרּד עלי אלקראיין **לבן אלעם**.
כנ״ל (אלוני, שם, ש/30).

6) פירוש שמות, אנונימי:
ויכון מעני אלרפואה עאפיה ותבעה פי ד׳לך **אבן אלעם** ז״ל.
קמבריג׳, T-S. Ar. 25/103, דף 4 ע״א/2– (מו״מ זה מסר לי ד״ר חגי בן שמאי, וחן חן לו).

אולם כבר לפני שבעים שנים ומעלה[16] נתפרסמה רשימת הספרים הראשונה לרב יוסף ראש הסדר (בגדאד, המחצית השנייה של המאה השתים עשרה — פוסטאט, המחצית הראשונה של המאה השלוש עשרה), ובה היה רשום השם "אבן אלעם", אולם מכיון שהיה כתה״י מחורר לא נתפענח השם כל צרכו עד עצם היום הזה, וזו לשון הרשימה (במהדורה א):

ש׳. 49. כת׳ אלת׳גניס ות[ערי]ף אלמאן ואלאפעאל אלמשתרך.
ש׳. 50. מן לאם . . . ומכ׳תצרה . . . מג׳לד.

(א) פוזנאנסקי טיפל בשורות אלה ופרסם שנית בתיקוניו, וזו לשונה:[17]
כת׳ אלת׳גניס וחרוף אלמעאן ואלאפעאל אלמשתקה
מן אלאס[מא] (ולא המשיך יותר).
בפעם השלישית נתפרסמו שתי שורות אלה על ידי אברמסון, ואף הוא קידם את קריאתן:[18]
כת׳ אלתג׳ניס וכת׳ [חר]וף אלמעאן ואלאפעאל אלמשתקה
מן אלאס[מא] ומכתצר ח . . . פרם מג׳לד.
והרי קריאתן, כפי שנתפענחו בשלימותן כיום:[19]
כת׳ אלתג׳ניס וכת׳ [חר]וף אלמעאן ואלאפעאל אלמשתקה
מן אלאס[מא] ומכ׳תצר ח[יוג׳ לבן] אלעם מג׳לד.

ותרגומו: ספר הצימוד וספר המלות וספר הפעלים הנגזרים
מן השמות וקיצור [ספרי הדקדוק ל] חיוג׳ לבן אלעם מכורך

כל כתבי אבן אלעם ביחד, ולא רק קיצור כתבי חיוג׳, כי אין לחשוב שהשם אבן אלעם מתייחס לחיבור האחרון בלבד. לפנינו אפוא כל כתבי אבן בלעם ביחד.

הסיכום:

1) עשרות רבות של מקורות לשם "אבן בלעם", ואילו לשם אבן אלעם רק שש פעמים בלבד.

2) החיבורים הקשורים בשם "אבן בלעם": ספרי הבלשנות ופירושי המקרא, ואילו לשם "אבן אלעם" קשורים החיבורים: פירוש יבמות והתשובות על הקראים. אמנם ידוע לנו, כי היה אבן בלעם איש הלכה בסוף ימיו, אולם לא ידענו את שם חיבורו ואת תכנו. וכן ידענו, כי נלחם אבן בלעם בקראים, אולם לא ידענו שהקדיש לנושא זה חיבור מסויים.

3) מובאה אחת בלבד לעת עתה, ואף היא לקויה בחסר ומחוררת, שהיא מעידה שספרים שידועים לאבן בלעם נתייחסו בה לאבן אלעם, ואלה הם ספרי הבלשנות בלבד, ואף נמנים בה לא רק שלושת החיבורים, הצימוד, הפעלים הנגזרים מן השמות והמלות, אלא גם קיצור שלושה ספרי הדקדוק לר׳ יהודה חיוג׳ הוא לאבן בלעם.

4) כאן נודע לנו לראשונה, כי קיצור חיבורי חיוג׳ הוא לאבן בלעם.

5) כאן נתברר לראשונה, שאבן בלעם הוא בעל פירוש יבמות ובעל החיבור תשובות על הקראים.

11) שער לשלושת החיבורים בגניזת קהיר:
כתאב אלתג׳ניס . . . לר׳ [יהודה **בן**] **בלעם** ז״ל.
קמבריג׳, T–S. Ar. 31/73, שער החיבורים בבלשנות.

12) רשימת ספרים: עי׳ לוח הקיצורים של רשימות ספרים, קרית ספר, מח, תשל״ג, עמ׳ 156–157.
כתאב אלתג׳ניס **לאבן בלעם.**
קמבריג׳, T–S. NS. J94/53 (אלוני[3], 2/400).

13) קולופון לפירוש ספר עזרא:
כמל בחמד אללה ועונה תלכ׳יץ שרח ספר עזרא ממא עני בתאליפה ר״י **בן בלעם.**
קמבריג׳, T-S. NS. 310/9 (אברמסון[1], 9/55): תלכיץ; אברמסון: אלכוף (?).

14) תפסיר אלנביאים אלח׳ **לאבן בלעם.**
בודפשט, כ״י קויפמן, 123/3 (שייבר[1], 14–16/547) לאבן, שייבר: אלא בן (תיקון יתיר).

15) כנ״ל:
תפסיר כתובים **לבן בלעם.**
שם, שם (שייבר[1], 8–9/547).

16) כנ״ל:
ואלפאט׳ אלארבעה אלאכ׳ירה לר׳ יהודה **בן בלעם** ז״ל.
קמבריג׳, T-S. NS. 312/84 (אלוני, *SBB*, vi (1964) p. 169).

17) כנ״ל:
מג׳לד תפסיר ד׳ אכ׳יר **לבן בלעם.**
ניו יורק, ENA 2539 (אברמסון[2], 28/83).

18) כנ״ל:
תפסיר . . . **לבן בלעם** או **לאבן בלעם** (פעמיים) לכל חלקי המקרא בערך.
קמבריג׳, T-S. K20/10 (מאן[2]; *REJ*, lxxii (1921) p. 164).

(ד). **המקורות לשם "אבן אלעם".** זה למעלה משלושים שנים שידוע לנו בבירור השם "אבן אלעם" כתלמיד חכם, וחכמינו מהלכים תוהים ותמהים על איש תלמיד חכם שלא זוהה ואיננו ידוע לנו; והרי המקורות הידועים לנו כיום:

1) רשימת ספרים:
ג׳זוין פר׳ יבמות **לאבן אלעם.**
קמבריג׳, T-S. Misc. /150 (אסף, 274/סי׳ 61): לאבי, אולם בכה״י: לאבן (!).

2) כנ״ל:
פיר׳ יבמות **לבן אלעם** נאקץ.
קמבריג׳, T-S. Misc. 36/148 (אלוני-שייבר, 97/166).

3) כנ״ל:
כת׳ כד עלי אלקראיין **לבן אלעם** ז״ל.
קמבריג׳, T-S. C. 2/146 (שייבר[1], *JJS*, xxii (1971) p. 73; **המהדיר העיר: אולי זהה עם כתאב אלתרג׳יח. אלעם, שייבר תיקן: בלעם, ואינו זהה, ויפה נוסח כה״י.**

4) כנ״ל:
כת׳ אלרד̇ עלי אלקראיין **לבן אלעם.**
קמבריג׳, T-S. K. 6/170 (אלוני, ר״י רה״ס ורשימותיו, ש׳, 9–10 ועומד להתפרסם).

היו חכמים חשובים ונכבדים שסבורים היו, כי אלה הם לאב, ואילו הידוע לנו בשם "אבן בלעם" הוא לבן. מתוך חתימות וחריזות גם יחד האמינו בזה. רייפמן אמר:[13] "בסדר סליחות לספרדים נמצאה תחנה אחת המתחלת בזכרי על משכבי, וחתום בה בלעם חזק . . . ואולי היה בנו של בלעם הנזכר". הרכבי אמר כמוהו:[14] "מצאתי סליחה אחת (סימן נח) אשר בראשי הבתים נרשם בלעם חזק, ואולי הוא אבו יהודה בן בלעם, וזה תארה: בזכרי על משכבי". אולם מוזר הוא שלפנינו יהיה פייטן ומשורר בלבד, ומאידך יהיה לנו בן שאין לנו מידו מאומה בשירה ובפיוט, בשעה שידוע לנו, כי מעידים עליו שהיה משורר ופייטן. שניהם לא הסבירו את השם "בלעם", ושניהם גם יחד לא קלעו למטרה. לאחרונה ביקש שירמן[2] לשלול מאבן בלעם את הפיוטים ואת השירים בגלל כתובת בלתי קריאה.[15]

(ג). **מקורות השם "אבן בלעם"**. לשם בכתיב זה רבים המקורות ויובאו כאן מעטים מהם, מחיבורי חכמים בני הדור הסמוך לאבן בלעם ומרשימות ספרים מגניזת קהיר:

1) רמב"ע (גראנאדה, 1065 — אסטיליה (Estella), 1135): אבו זכריא יחיי **בן בלעם** אלטליטלי ת׳ם אלאשבילי.
רמב"ע[1], 40 ע"א/7 — ע"ב/2.

2) הנ"ל:
ופי צדר כתאב אלארשאד לאבי זכריא **בן בלעם**.
שם, 73 ע"א/2–1.

3) הנ"ל:
ופי הד׳ה אלחרוף אלמשתקֿה מן אלאסמא מולף אבו זכריא **בן בלעם** ז"ל.
שם, 73 ע"א/2–1.

4) הנ"ל:
ולאבי זכריא **בן בלעם** רח׳ אללה תאליף . . .
שם, 139 ע"א/17–14.

5) יצחק אבן ברוך הספרדי (סאראגוסה ומאלקה, המאה ה־11–ה־12):
ואשאר מ׳ יהודה **בן בלעם** אלאן מענאהא כ׳וף אלסיף (אבח־אבחת חרב).
כתאב אלמואזנה, לנינגרד 1890, עמ׳ 26.

6) יצחק בן שמואל הספרדי (ספרד, המאה ה־12 — מצרים, המאה ה־12):
ווג׳דת בעד ד׳לך לר׳ יהודה **בן בלעם** זכר׳ לבר׳ פי נכת אלארבעה ועשרין אלתי לה.
מובא במאן, *Texts and Studies,* Cincinnati, 1931, p. 391

7) ראב"ע:
ור׳ יהודה הנקרא **בן בלעם** ספרדי ממדינת טליטלה.
מאזנים, עי׳ הערה 3.

8) הנ"ל:
ואז קם ר׳ יהודה **בן בלעם** וילעג עליו (על ר׳ משה הכהן אבן ג׳יקטילה).
שפת יתר, מס׳ לח (תשובות על דונש בן לבראט), מהד׳ ג׳ ליפמן, פרנקפורט 1843, יד, ע"א.

9) הנ"ל:
לעג עליו **בן בלעם**.
פירוש תהלים פד, ד.

10) יצחק בן אלעזר הלוי (בגדאד, המאה ה־12), הרקמה (כ"י):
אמר ר׳ יהודה **בן בלעם**.
כתב יד פריס — hébreu 1225, 20 ע"ב; 28 ע"א.

בלעם ואבן בלעם הבלשן והפרשן והוא המשורר והפייטן והוא בעל ההלכה והפולמוסן

נחמיה אלוני

(א). **פתיחה:**[1] השם אבן בלעם ידוע הוא בספרותנו כל הימים, והוא שם הבלשן והפרשן המפורסם בארץ ספרד[2] (טולידו, ע׳ 1030 — סביליה, ע׳ 1080) הודות לראב״ע שהרבה להזכירו בפירושיו בשם אבן בלעם ובפתיחתו ל״ספר מאזנים״, כשהוא מונהו בין זקני הלשון:[3] ״ור׳ יהודה הנקרא בן בלעם ספרדי ממדינת טוליטולה אסף ספרים קטנים״. ראב״ע לא הכיר את אבן בלעם פנים אל פנים, כי נולד במרחק רב מהעיר סביליה (טודילה, 1092 — רומא, 1167), וקרוב לאמת, כי נולד ראב״ע לכל הפחות עשר שנים אחרי שנסתלק אבן בלעם לעולמו. השם המלא של האיש הנפלא הזה הוא: יהודה בן שמואל[4] אבן בלעם (הוא אבן אלעם־בלעם), ובערבית: אבו זכריא יחיי[5] אבן בלעם, אלטוליטלי ת׳ם אלאשבילי.

החלק האחרון של השם ״בלעם״ טומן בחובו סודות רבים, ועל כן עורר את סקרנותם של חכמינו, ומראשיתה של חכמת ישראל שימש נושא לויכוחיהם, כי לא ידעו את קריאתו בדיוק, וממילא לא ידעו גם את משמעותו. הקריאה הקלה הייתה לבני ישראל ״אבן בלעם״ — השם השגור על פיהם במקרא, והכול בא על מקומו בשלום. אולם היו חכמים שלא נחה דעתם מקריאה זו, כי לא יכנה איש מישראל את עצמו בשם[6] ״בִּלְעָם הרשע״, ועל כן קראו ״בלעם״ בתעתיקים ובקריאות שונים ״בַּלְעָם״ או ״בִּלְעָאם״, בַּלְעָאם. כל החכמים סבורים היו, כי לפנינו מלה אחת, והיא שאולה מן הערבית. אף היו נסיונות שונים להסבירה כמלה אחת כפי שנראה להלן. נמצאנו למדים, כי היה השם ״בלעם״ מהלך בספרות חכמת ישראל במשך מאה וחמישים שנים לא ברור ולא בהיר, לא זהור ולא צהור.

(ב). **מקורות לשם ״בלעם״ בלי הקידומת לייחוס משפחה ״אבן״.** ואלה הם:

1. בזוכרי על משכבי[7] — אקרוסטיכון: בלעם חזק.
2. בי אהובי אלי השכיל[8] — אקרוסטיכון: בלעם.
3. ביום עשור[9] — אקרוסטיכון: בלעם ח[זק].
4. יום זה למרום[10] — אקרוסטיכון: לבלעם.
5. צבי יין הרקח[11] — אקרוסטיכון: בלעם.
6. צועקה מים[12] — אקרוסטיכון: צובה בלע[ם].

הסיכום הוא:

(1) בסך הכול ידועים חמישה מקורות, שבהם השם ״בלעם״ בלבד באקרוסטיכון. המקור השישי מפוקפק הוא גם באקרוסטיכון וגם בתכנו.

(2) כל המקורות הם שירים (2, 5) ופיוטים (1, 3, 4, 6).

(3) במקורות אלה חתם המחבר עצמו, ומן הראוי היה לשים לב לצורת חתימה זו, כי זוהי חתימתו.

אנגלי של C.E. Rolt, London, 1920)); *The Cloud of Unknowing*, בעריכת E. Underhill, London, 1934, עמ׳ 64, 73–72, 90–86, 114.

73. על זמן אמירת תורה זו, ר׳ ״חיי מוהר״ן״ ח״א, ״שיחות השייכים להתורות״ עמ׳ 13 ס׳ י״ח. התורה נרשמה בידי ר׳ נחמן עצמו ולא בידי ר׳ נתן הסופר. היא מופיעה ב״ליקוטי מוהר״ן״ תחת הכותרת ״לשון רבינו ז״ל״, ור׳ נתן מספר, שרבו אמר תורה זו בהתלהבות כה רבה, עד כי אי אפשר היה לו עצמו ולשאר הנוכחים להבין את דבריו.

74. ר׳ י. תשבי, ״משנת הזוהר״ ח״א עמ׳ קע״ו-קע״ז.

75. ״ליקוטי מוהר״ן״ ח״א, תורה כ״ד ס׳ ח׳.

76. ״חיי מוהר״ן״ ח״ב, ״גדולת השגתו״ עמ׳ 15 ס׳ מ״ג.

77. ראוי לציין, שאמר אז לר׳ נתן ״שאין יודעין כלל כלל לא. והפליג מאד בגדולת הבורא ית׳ אשר א״א לבאר ואמר שאין יודעין כלל״ (שם, שם) ולא השתמש בנוסחה הרגילה, שבה התיחס כנראה לנסיונות ׳איני יודע׳ האישיים שלו, כפי שמסרה ר׳ נתן משמו: ״אמר שאינו יודע כלל״ וכו׳. תאורים מפורטים של אותה הנסיעה מברסלב לאומאן, ושל התישבות ר׳ נחמן באומאן, מופיעים ב״חיי מוהר״ן״ ח״א, ״נסיעתו וישיבתו באומין״ עמ׳ 76 ס׳ א׳-ו׳, וכן ב״ימי מוהרנ״ת״ ח״א, דף ל׳ ע״א-ע״ב. בשני התאורים אין כל זכר למצב ״איני יודע״ של ר׳ נחמן, וברור שלא נתנסה בו אז, אם כי ימים אחדים קודם לכן, כשביתו בברסלב עלה באש, נראה שהיה שרוי במצב זה. ר׳ נתן כותב על כך באוטוביוגרפיה שלו: ״ואח״כ ביום ג׳ נתגלגל מאת ה׳ שחזרתי ונסעתי לפה, ונתעכבתי עד ש״ק שהוא ר״ח אייר [תק״ע]. בליל ש״ק ענה ואמר שאינו יודע כלל, כדרכו כל פעם, כנדפס מזה קצת. בתוך כך נעשה רעש של השריפה שהיתה ברחוב הסמוכה לביתו . . . ״ (״ימי מוהרנ״ת״ ח״א, דף ל״ט ע״א).

78. ר׳ לעיל, עמ׳ כ״א-כ״ב.

79. ב״ליקוטי מוהר״ן״ ח״א.

80. ״חיי מוהר״ן״ ח״א, ״שיחות השייכים להתורות״ עמ׳ 15–14 ס׳ כ״ד.

81. ״לפרש שיחתו לפני הקב״ה״ או ״לפרש שיחו בינו לבין קונו״ הם מן המונחים המציינים בספרות ברסלב את המוסד המיוחד לחוג זה, של השתפכות בפני הבורא ביחידות ובלשון יידיש, בנוסף, ולא כתחליף, לתפילה הפורמלית בעברית. ר׳ נחמן נהג כך מאז ילדותו, והמליץ פעמים רבות לכל תלמידיו שינהגו בכך כמוהו, ואכן המנהג נשתרש.

82. ר׳ המובאה לעיל.

83. ״שיחות הר״ן״ (עם ״שבחי הר״ן״) דף נ״ח ע״ב ס׳ קנ״ד.

84. ר׳ לעיל עמ׳ כ׳.

85. ״חיי מוהר״ן״ ח״ב, ״מעלת תורתו״, עמ׳ 24 ס׳ ב׳.

86. ר׳ ״חיי מוהר״ן״ ח״א, ״ספורים חדשים״, עמ׳ 42 ס׳ י״א.

87. ר׳ לעיל, עמ׳ ט״ז.

88. י. וייס, ״ר׳ נחמן מברסלב על המחלוקת עליו״, בספר ״מחקרים בקבלה ובתולדות הדתות מוגשים לג.ג. שלום״ (ירושלים, תשכ״ז) עמ׳ 114–101.

89. על יחסו של ר׳ נחמן להשכלה, ועל מגעיו עם משכילים באומאן, ר׳ מ. פייקאז׳, ״חסידות ברסלב״, פרק שני, עמ׳ 55–21.

90. ר׳ וייס, במאמר הנ״ל, עמ׳ 111–106.

91. יש להזהר בקביעה זו, שכן העדויות שבידינו, הקשורות בתקופת חייו הראשונה של ר׳ נחמן, מועטות ביותר. רוב המסורות הקיימות שייכות לתקופה שאחרי הצטרפותו של ר׳ נתן הסופר לחוג ברסלב.

92. ישעיהו מ״ג, ב׳.

93. ״חיי מוהר״ן״ ח״א, ״נסיעתו לא״י״, עמ׳ 65 ס׳ י״ט.

94. שם, שם.

והדברים משתמעים גם מתאור מצב "איני יודע" ב"חיי מוהר"ן", שהובא לעיל, על פיו מטעים ר' נחמן מיד בהתנערו ממצב זה, "שהוא עתה ירא, שקורין פרום", מה שלא כן בעודו שרוי ב"איני יודע", שאז מן הסתם אין הוא בחזקת "פרום" כלל.

70. "שבחי הר"ן", "סדר הנסיעה..." דף כ' ע"א–ע"ב ס' ל"ג.

71. שם, כ' ע"ב ס' ל"ד–ל"ה. לא ברור איזהו הטקסט אליו שולח ר' נתן את הקורא באמרו "וע' עוד מזה במקום אחר". אמנם תאורי מצב 'איני יודע' של ר' נחמן נמצאים בכל ספריו של ר' נתן, והנוסחה הפרדוכסאלית "תכלית הידיעה היא אשר לא נדע" מופיעה כמה פעמים ב"חיי מוהר"ן" ופעם אחת, בדיון קצר ביותר בנושא, גם ב"לקוטי מוהר"ן" ח"א, תורה כ"ד (ר' להלן). אבל כל שאר ספריו של ר' נתן נתחברו זמן רב אחרי צאתו לאור בתקע"ה/תקע"ו של "סדר הנסיעה", שנכלל במהדורה הראשונה של ה"ספורי מעשיות" (ר' ג. שלום, "אלה שמות", עמ' 28 ס' 99; נ.צ. קעניג, "נוה צדיקים", בני־ברק, תשכ"ט, עמ' מ"ה). אם, כבר בזמן כתיבת "סדר הנסיעה" סמוך למותו של ר' נחמן בתקע"א (השוה לעיל, הע' 44), יכול היה ר' נתן להתיחס למקום אחר הנמצא בכתובים, שבו נדון ענין "איני יודע" ביתר הרחבה, נראה שהיו בידיו רשימות מפרי עטו, ששמשו לו אחר כך כחומר גלם לכתיבת "חיי מוהר"ן", "שיחות הר"ן" ו"ימי מוהרנ"ת", ויתכן שרשימות אלה הופצו בין אנשי ברסלב עוד זמן רב לפני שנדפסו בספריו. ידוע שהפצת כתבי יד טרם צאתם לאור היתה נהוגה. (על הפצת "הספר הנשרף" של ר' נחמן עם ס' "לקוטי מוהר"ן" טרם הדפסתו, ר' י. וייס, "הספר הנשרף..." עמ' 264–266; על הפצתן בכתב יד של התפילות שחבר ר' נתן, שהפכו אח"כ לספר "לקוטי תפילות", ר' "ימי מוהרנ"ת" ח"א, דף מ"ח ע"ב, ח"ב ס' ה'.) לעומת זאת, הערתו של ר' נתן בסוף הקטע המובא, "ויתבאר במ"א אי"ה", קלה לזהוי. תאור הנסיבות בהן השיג ר' נחמן לראשונה את משמעותו האמיתית של "איני יודע" שלו, אחרי פסח תקס"ה, מופיע ב"חיי מוהר"ן" ח"ב, "גדולת השגתו" עמ' 15 ס' מ"ב. בקטע שלפנינו מודיע ר' נתן על כוונתו לכתוב תאור זה בעתיד, ואכן, אין כל ספק ש"חיי מוהר"ן" נכתב בתקופה מאוחרת יותר, שנים מספר אחרי צאתו לאור של "סדר הנסיעה".

72. "חיי מוהר"ן" ח"ב, "גדולת השגתו" עמ' 15 ס' מ"ב. להשגת "תכלית הידיעה" כאי ידיעה יש, כמובן, שושלת יוחסין מכובדת במקורות, והיא מופיעה כהכרת מוגבלות הידיעה הפילוסופית־שכלית של האל (ר' על כך ברכה זק, "יחסו של ר' שלמה אלקבץ לחקירה הפילוסופית", "אשל באר שבע", כרך א', תשל"ו, עמ' 289 והע' 6). אף בספרות החסידית הסמוכה לזמנו של ר' נחמן מופיע הניסוח לא פעם. ר' מ"מ מוויטבסק, למשל (ר' "ליקוטי אמרים", לעמברג תרע"א, מכתב י"ח, דף כ"ד ע"א) מביא את המאמר (כפי הנראה לפי ניסוחו ב"ספר העיקרים" של אלבו, ורשא, תרל"ו, מאמר שני, סוף פרק ל') בהטעימו את כוחה של אמונה, "שהיא גבוהה מהשגת השכל בלי גבול", ואשר רק באמצעותה מתאפשרת השגת האל, מה שאין בכוח הידיעה השכלית־פילוסופית להשיג. ר מ"מ מפרש, אם כן, את "תכלית הידיעה שלא נדע" כידיעה פילוסופית, שאינה ידיעה אמיתית, אך הוא טוען לאפשרות ידיעה אמיתית של האל, או לתחליפה, באמצעות אמונה. הבעש"ט, לעומת זאת, מקבל את העקרון של "תכלית הידיעה שלא נדע", מבלי לפרש אם כוונתו לידיעה — אי ידיעה פילוסופית או מיסטית, אך הוא מבחין בה בשני סוגים אחרים: האחד, שאותו הוא דוחה, הרי הוא אי ידיעתם של אותם אנשים המוותרים מלכתחילה על כל נסיון לדעת. הסוג השני, שעליו הוא ממליץ, הוא אי הידיעה של אותם שניסו בכל מאודם לדעת את האל, ואגב כך התקרבו אליו במידת האפשר (ר' "כתר שם טוב", ירושלים תשכ"ח, עמ' 5). ר' משולם פייבוש מזבארז' ("דרך אמת", ירושלים, תש"ד, חלק שני, עמ' ע"ד) אף הוא משתמש במאמר לצורך פולמוסי, ואת חיציו הוא יורה בלמדנים הגאים, המתנשאים על הצדיקים וטוענים לידיעת האל. ידיעתם, לדבריו, אינה ידיעה, שכן "תכלית שנדע שלא נדע". להבדיל מכל הנ"ל, ניסוח הרעיון בכתבי ר' נחמן אינו מופיע בקונטקסט פולמוסי, ואף אין הוא מבחין כלל בין סוגי ידיעה שונים. ברור שכוונתו לידיעה המיסטית של האל, כלומר, להתמזגות עמו, שאותה הוא רואה כתהליך בלתי פוסק, כעליה במדרגות גבוהות יותר ויותר של ידיעה בלתי אפשרית זו. תפיסה דומה יותר לזו של ר' נחמן ניתן לשייך לר' אברהם קאליסקר (ר' "חסד לאברהם", ירושלים, תשל"ג, חלק שני, הפטרת כי תצא, דף מ"ח ע"א). על היות מדרגות גבוהות והולכות של "אי־ידיעה" תכלית כל הידיעה הדתית, כתופעה בחיי הדת המיסטיים בכלל, ר' למשל, Rudolf Otto, *Mysticism East and West*, London, 1932, pp. 185–187; Dionysius Areopagita, *de Divinis Nominibus, de Mystica Theologia*, Migne, *P.G.L.* 3, 586f., 997f. (תרגום

50. ״לקוטי מוהר״ן״ ח״ב, תורה ע״ח.

51. שם, שם. והשוה עם המקור המדרשי, שמות רבה, ״כי תשא״, מ״ה.

52. ע״פ תורה זו, הצדיק בשעת קטנותו כמוהו כרשע גמור ולא רק כאיש פשוט, המוני, העלול לחטוא אבל אינו בהכרח רשע אלא שאין הוא מסוגל לשלימותו המוסרית־דתית של הצדיק. על זהות תודעת הצדיק בשעת ירידתו עם הרשע, ר׳ י. וייס, ״ראשית צמיחתה של הדרך החסידית״, ״ציון״ ט״ז, תשי״א, עמ׳ 95. אבל יש לציין, שבניגוד לתורה זו, ממנה משתמעת תודעת הרשעה המופשטת של הצדיק — ר׳ נחמן — בשעת פשיטותו, מבלי שמהותה תתורגם ללשון מעשים מפורשת, יש בידינו כמה תאורים קונקרטיים של מעשי ר׳ נחמן במצבי פשיטות או בזמני ״הנהגת פראסטיק״ שלו, שתכנם תמים לחלוטין. השוה להלן, עמ׳ כ״ד–כ״ה.

53. ״לקוטי מוהר״ן״ ח״ב, תורה ע״ח.

54. על מסורת חז״ל בדבר טרומיותה של התורה וקיום כל מצוותיה דורות רבים קודם שנתנה למשה בהר סיני, ר׳ למשל, סוטה י״ד ע״א; בראשית רבה א׳, ד׳–ה׳; ויקרא רבה ב׳, י׳.

55. ר׳ א. אורבך, ״חז״ל, אמונות ודעות״, ירושלים, תשכ״ט, עמ׳ 316–320. לוי גינצבורג, ״אגדות היהודים״, רמת־גן, תשכ״ח, ח׳ י״א (״משה במדבר״), עמ׳ 58.

56. ״לקוטי מוהר״ן״ ח״ב, תורה ע״ח.

57. צבאות נפוליון הגיעו לעכו ב־20 במרץ, 1799 והחלו במצור על העיר שעות ספורות בלבד אחרי הפלגת ר׳ נחמן ובן לויתו ממנה. ר׳ הערה 58.

58. ״שבחי הר״ן״, ״סדר הנסיעה . . . ״ דף ט״ז ע״ב, ס׳ כ״ג.

59. ״חיי מוהר״ן״ ח״א, ״נסיעתו לא״י״ עמ׳ 64, ס׳ י״ד.

60. ר׳ מדרש ויקרא רבה, סדר צו, פ׳ ט׳.

61. ר׳ נחמן נזקק כאן לפרוש רש״י הידוע על בראשית, א׳, א׳, על פיו פותחת התורה דווקא בספור הבריאה, ולא בפרשת מתן תורה, מתוך צפייה מראש של התנחלות ב״י בארץ כנען, כדי לקבוע מיד את זכותו של הקב״ה, בורא העולם כולו, להנחיל את הארץ לעם בחירתו. השוה בראשית רבה, א׳, ב׳.

62. ״לקוטי מוהר״ן״ ח״ב, תורה ע״ח.

*62. מ. פייקאז׳ בספרו מקשר אל נכון את הנסיבות הקונקרטיות שבהן נאמרה תורה ע״ח, היינו, השתכנותו של ר׳ נחמן בבית המשכיל נחמן נתן רפפורט באומאן, עם תכנה של התורה (ר׳ ״חסידות ברסלב״, עמ׳ 46–42), וקרוב לוודאי שהוא צודק בראותו ב״כבוש א״י״ שבתורה רמז לתחושת ה״כבוש לקדושה״ של ר׳ נחמן, בבואו לגור דווקא בביתו של משכיל. אך פייקאז׳ אינו עומד על מהות הקשר העקרוני שבין זכר חווית הנסיעה לא״י של ר׳ נחמן לבין מצב ה״פשיטות״ שלו הנידון בתורה ע״ח, והוא פוטר את ענין הנסיעה לא״י, הנזכר שם הרבה, כזכרון מעודד סתם, ״שהיה בו כדי לפזר את העננים הקודרים שכסו על לבו ומוחו [של ר׳ נחמן] ולזכותו ברגע של חסד . . . ״ (שם, עמ׳ 43).

63. ר׳ לעיל, הע׳ 58, 59. אבל מן המובאה השנייה משתמע, שר׳ נחמן נסה את כוחו בקיום מצוות התורה בדרך זו כבר בזמן המסע לא״י, שהרי הוא מכריז בשובו: ״בדרך הזה קיימתי כל התורה בכל האופנים״, וזאת על אף שהוא מציג את השגו החדש כסגולה נגד המצב המשוער של גלות כפויה בלבד.

*63. הדירה היתה שייכת למשכיל נחמן נתן רפפורט. ר׳ על כך, פייקאז׳, ״חסידות ברסלב״ עמ׳ 29–27.

64. ״שיחות הר״ן״ (עם ״שבחי הר״ן״), נ״ז ע״ב–נ״ח ע״א, ס׳ קנ״ג.

65. על היות הנפילה למצב זה מסממניה המובהקים של החויה המיסטית בכלל, ר׳ למשל, E. Underhill, *Mysticism* בפרק "The Dark Night of the Soul" עמ׳ 380–412. לענין תודעת החטא המיסרת את המתנסים במצב הנפשי של ריחוק מן האל ו״אי־ידיעה״, ר׳ עמ׳ 390–391.

66. יש לשער, שתקופות ׳איני יודע׳ של ר׳ נחמן, שלא היו צפויות מראש וחלו לעתים דוקא במועדי ההתקבצות הקבועים של החוג, שבהם נהג ר׳ נחמן ״לומר תורה״, גרעו ממידת הפופולריות שלו והפחיתו את מספר חסידיו. יש בידינו כמה עדויות על כך, שמחלקן נכרת התמרמרות מה מצד החסידים על התנכרות רבם אליהם. ר׳ למשל, ״ס׳ כוכבי אור״, ״שיחות וספורים״, ״כת״י הרב מטשעהרין״ עמ׳ קס״ז; ״חיי מוהר״ן״ ח״א, עמ׳ 65 ס׳ י״ט.

67. ״ימי מוהרנ״ת״ ח״א, דף ל״א ע״א–ע״ב.

68. ״חיי מוהר״ן״ ח״א, עמ׳ 85 ס׳ ל״א. ור׳ מ. פייקאז׳, ״חסידות ברסלב״, עמ׳ 44–45.

69. על זהות תודעתו בשעת פשיטות עם רשעים גמורים, השוה לעיל, עמ׳ ט״ו והע׳ 52.

34. ר׳ מ. ליטינסקי, ״קורות פאדאליא וקדמוניות היהודים שם״, אודסה, תרנ״ה, עמ׳ 32–33, 62; ובהסתמך על עדות זו, ש.א. הורודצקי, ״החסידות והחסידים״, תל־אביב, תרפ״ח, כרך ג׳ עמ׳ 28; מ. פייקאז, ״חסידות ברסלב״ עמ׳ 75; 211; י. וייס, ״מחקרים בחסידות ברסלב״, עמ׳ 35–26.

35. מ. פייקאז (בספרו הנ״ל, עמ׳ 75) מקבל את עדותו של ליטינסקי כמהימנה ומוסיף לה כמה עדויות ברסלביות פנימיות, שהוא מפרשן כמשקפות את קיומן של האשמות אלה נגד קבוצת ברסלב. אין הוא מטיל ספק בכך, שר׳ נחמן וחסידיו אכן האשמו בפרנקיזם ע״י הסבא משפאלי ועדתו, ואח״כ גם ע״י הרב משה צבי מסאווראן. אך פייקאז אינו מציג את השאלה, ק״ו את התשובה לה, מה גרם לצמיחתן של האשמות אלה? אפילו אם נטיל ספק במהימנות המקור, שעליו מסתמך ליטינסקי בהעידו, שחסידי ברסלב האשמו בפרנקיזם, (וייס בספרו הנ״ל רואה באותו מסמך זיוף, אך אין הוא שולל את האפשרות שהזיוף נתבסס על ידיעות אותנתיות) עצם קיומן של השמועות על כך דיו לעורר תמיהה. ואם נניח, שאכן הושמעו הטענות נגד ברסלב, קשה לבטל את חשיבותן ולראות בהן נשק לוחמה בין־חסידי גרידא, שהרי מריבות פנימיות הרבה חלו בתנועה החסידית כמעט מראשית הווסדה, והאשמות מסוג זה לא היו שכיחות.

36. ר׳ להלן, עמ׳ י״ד ואילך.

37. וייס, שלא נמנע מהצגת השאלות, הטעים, שההאשמות חלו לא רק על דעותיו של ר׳ נחמן אלא גם על כמה ממעשיו. ר׳ ״מחקרים בחסידות ברסלב״ עמ׳ 23–21.

38. ר׳ שם, עמ׳ 108–96.

39. ר׳ שם, עמ׳ 26–23; 35–34.

40. על אורח כתיבתו של ״לקוטי מוהר״ן״ ר׳ ״ימי מוהרנ״ת״ ח״א, דף ה׳ ע״ב; דף כ״ב ע״ב; ההקדמה ל״לקוטי מוהר״ן״, לקראת הסוף.

41. על מקורותיו של ר׳ נתן בכתיבת שני ספורי הנסיעה, ר׳ ע. רפפורט, ״שני מקורות . . .״ עמ׳ 150–148.

42. ״שבחי הר״ן״, ״סדר הנסיעה . . .״ דף י׳ ע״ב ס׳ י״ד.

43. ר׳ למשל, ״חיי מוהר״ן״ ח״ב, עמ׳ 30 ס׳ ל״ט; עמ׳ 29–28 ס׳ כ״ח־ל״א; ההקדמה ל״לקוטי מוהר״ן״, לקראת הסוף, ששם ר׳ נתן מעיד על עצמו: ״. . . כי אני דקדקתי לכתוב כפי מה ששמעתי מפיו הק׳ בלי גרעון ותוספת . . .״

44. על זמן הכתיבה של כל אחד משני ספורי הנסיעה לא״י ע״י ר׳ נתן, ר׳ ע. רפפורט, ״שני מקורות . . .״ עמ׳ 153–150.

45. על זמן אמירת התורה, ר׳ ״חיי מוהר״ן״ ח״א, עמ׳ 85 ס׳ ל״א; שם, ״שיחות השייכים להתורות״ (ברשימת הזמנים שבהם נאמרו רוב התורות שבס׳ ״לקוטי מוהר״ן״), עמ׳ 30 ס׳ נ״ט.

46. בכתבי ברסלב מתיחס המונח ״צדיק האמת״ לר׳ נחמן עצמו, לצדם של מונחים סופרלטיביים אחרים כגון ״צדיק הדור״, ״צדיק אחד״ ולעתים גם ״הצדיק״ סתם. מפתח זה להבנת כתבי החוג נקבע לראשונה ע״י י. וייס ז״ל, והשמוש בו להלן יחשב כמובן מאליו.

47. ״לקוטי מוהר״ן״ ח״ב, תורה ע״ח, בהתחלה.

48. שם, שם. הסבר מקביל לזה, על צורך הלמדן בהפסקה מתלמודו, מופיע ב״חיי מוהר״ן״, שם כותב ר׳ נתן: ״אמר, כשהמוח נתייגע מהלימוד אז צריכין לשוח ולדבר שיחות חולין עם בני אדם כדי לפקח דעתו. והשיחה הזאת היא כמו שינה שהיא נייחא להמוחין. ושיחה כזו אינה בכלל דברים בטלים ח״ו כלל. אדרבא, היא מצווה גדולה. וע״ז ארז״ל, ביטולה של תורה זהו קיומה, כ״ש, עת לעשות לה׳ הפרו תורתך [תהל׳ קי״ט, קכ״ו]. כי אם לא יתבטל קצת לפקח דעתו בשיחה אזי ח״ו יתבטל מכל וכל.״ (״חיי מוהר״ן ח״ב, ״עבודת ה׳״ עמ׳ 62 ס׳ פ״ז). המובאה התלמודית של ר׳ נחמן: ״ביטולה של תורה זהו קיומה״ אינה מדויקת. במקור נאמר: ״פעמים שביטולה של תורה זהו יסודה״ (מנחות צ״ט ע״א־ב.) ראוי לציין, שגרסתו של ר׳ נתן זהה עם הנוסח השבתאי של אותה אמרה (ר׳ ג. שלום, ״מצווה הבאה בעבירה״, בכרך ״מחקרים ומקורות . . .״ עמ׳ 37, 43). אך אין להסיק מכאן, שר׳ נחמן או ר׳ נתן סופרו השתמשו ביודעין ובכוונה הנוסח השבתאי. קרוב יותר לוודאי, שלקחוהו מאותו מקור (ג. שלום משער, שהנוסח לקוח מס׳ חסידים. ר׳ שם, עמ׳ 37).

49. על זהות התורה עם הקבה״ה, ר׳ ג. שלום, *On The Kabbalah and its Symbolism* (London, 1965), 'The Meaning of the Torah in Jewish Mysticism' עמ׳ 44–45; י. תשבי, ״משנת הזוהר״, ח״א, ירושלים, תשי״ז, עמ׳ קמ״ה; ח״ב, ירושלים, תשכ״א, עמ׳ שע״ב.

19. "חיי מוהר"ן" ח"א, "נסיעתו לא"י" עמ' 61 ס' ג'.

20. פרשת כתיבתו של "הספר הנשרף", הנסיון להפיצו ושריפתו נדונו בהרחבה במאמרו של י. וייס, "הספר הנשרף לר' נחמן מברסלב", "קרית ספר" מ"ה, תש"ל, עמ' 253–270.

21. "חיי מוהר"ן" ח"א, "נסיעתו לנאווריץ", עמ' 73 ס' ג'.

22. אותם שני אנשים היו ר' יודיל ור' שמואל־אייזיק, מתלמידיו הותיקים של ר' נחמן, שאת שמותיהם ואת חשיבות מעמדם בברסלב, מטשטש ר' נתן בשטחיות, כנראה משום שהתנגדו למנהיגותו אחרי מות ר' נחמן. המקור לזהויים עם ב' האנשים שבתאורו של ר' נתן הוא "ס' כוכבי אור", ירושלים תשכ"א, עמ' נ"ב ס' כ"ה.

23. "חיי מוהר"ן" ח"א, "נסיעתו ללעמברג" עמ' 74 ס' ט'–י"א. ראה גם הקטע המקביל ב"ימי מוהרנ"ת" ח"א, לעמברג, תרס"ג, דף ט' ע"ב.

24. לענין זה ר' מ. בניהו "ספר תולדות האר"י", ירושלים, תשכ"ז, עמ' 99–98, 197–198, 200–202.

25. "שיחות הר"ן" (עם "שבחי הר"ן") דף ס"ה ע"ב ס' קפ"ח.

26. ר' "ימי מוהרנ"ת" ח"א, דף י"א ע"ב, שם כותב ר' נתן על ענין ביאת המשיח: "ואמר [ר' נחמן] שכבר היה מוכן שיבוא בעוד איזה שנים, וידע באיזה שנה ובאיזה חודש ובאיזה יום יבוא, אך עכשיו בוודאי לא יבוא באותו הזמן. וכפי המובן מדבריו היה שהעכוב הי' מחמת שנפטר אצלו בנו." על תפיסתו המשיחית של ר' נחמן ועל המשבר שחל בה כתוצאה ממות בנו יורחב הדבור במקום אחר.

*26. רח"ו, המדווח על פרשת מות בן האר"י בכמה מקומות בכתביו, מוסר שאותו סוד שגילה האר"י היה מ"סודות זמן הקטנות", ודוקא משום כך נענש, שכן "בהיות האדם מתעסק בסודות התורה, אם יהיה בענין זמן הגדלות העליון . . . אין לאדם כל כך סכנה כמו בזמן שעוסק בסודות זמן הקטנות. כי בהתעסקו בהם הנה החיצונים מתעוררים בהם ומתאחזין שם, ומזכירים עוונותיו של האדם המתעסק בהם" ("שער הכוונות", ענין ספירת העומר, דרוש י"ב). על אף שהמדובר כאן בסודות הקטנות האלוהית, לא מן הנמנע הוא שר' נחמן שאב מכך, ולו גם באורח אסוציאטיבי בלבד, את קישור סוד קטנות עם עונש חמור ויישמו על סוד הקטנות הצדיקית שלו.

27. "קלי עולם" הם משכילים. השוה מ. פייקאז, "חסידות ברסלב", עמ' 24; 36–34.

28. "חיי מוהר"ן" ח"א, עמ' 64 ס' י"ז.

29. זאת בעיקר בשעת מגעיו עם מנהיגי הקהילה החסידית בא"י, שהתיחסו אליו בכבוד רב. אין בתיאורי פגישותיו עמם כל רמז להתנהגות התמוהה, שהיתה אפינית למצבי קטנותו של ר' נחמן. ר' למשל, "שבחי הר"ן", "סדר הנסיעה . . . " דף י"ב ע"א–י"ג ע"ב ס' י"ט–כ'.

30. ר' ג. שלום, בספרו האנגלי הנזכר, *The Messianic Idea in Judaism* בפרק "Devekut or Communion with God" pp. 221–222; רבקה ש"ץ, "למהותו של הצדיק בחסידות" עמ' 372; י. וייס, "מחקרים בחסידות ברסלב", ירושלים, תשל"ה, עמ' 103–104.

31. ר' רבקה ש"ץ, במאמר הנ"ל, עמ' 372, ביחס לר' אלימלך מליזנסק; ש. דרזנר, *The Zaddik* (London–New-York–Toronto), עמ' 192, ביחס לר' יעקב יוסף.

32. ר' דרזנר, שם, עמ' 207–200. ג. נגאל בספרו "מנהיג ועדה", ירושלים, תשכ"ב, עמ' 76 ואילך אף הוא מטעים, שבכתבי ר' יעקב יוסף המדובר לא פעם במעשה עבירה בפועל, אלא שנכרת בהם ההתלבטות בבעיה בתוקף זכרון פתרונה השבתאי. ר' יעקב יוסף נזהר להדגיש את ההבדל בין חטאי הצדיק, שהם "בשוגג", "כביכול" או שחומרתם זעומה, לבין חטאי "אנשי החמר" ההמוניים. למרות הגבלות אלה, הממתנות את מהות חטאו של הצדיק, אם כי ללא עקביות, סבור נגאל, שהכוונה היא לחטא ממשי ומסוים: חטא הגאווה, החנופה והשקר המוצא את בטויו בזמן הדרשה (ר', שם, עמ' 95–82). ומוקד ירידת הצדיק בשעת הדרשה הוא "הפשט החריף", המכשילו בגאווה. הגדרה זו של חטא הצדיק נראית צרה מכפי הצורך, ואין היא מתישבת עם התביעה להתחברות עם המוני העם דווקא, ע"י השתוות עמם בזמן הירידה. בכל המשלים העוסקים בירידת הצדיק מצטיירת דמותם של אנשי החמר החוטאים כבורים, גסי הליכות, אכרים המוניים, ולאו דווקא כאותם תלמידי חכמים מתנשאים המצטיינים ב"פשט חריף" ומתגאים בתלמודם. אמנם יש בכתבי ר' יעקב יוסף בקורת חריפה כלפי אלה, אך ודאי שאין הלמדן הגאה משמש לו כאב־טפוס של החוטא ההמוני, ואין תכלית ירידתו של הצדיק ההזדהות דווקא עמו.

33. ר' למשל, "לקוטי מוהר"ן" ח"א, תורה ס"ד ("בא אל פרעה") ס' ג'; "חיי מוהר"ן" ח"ב, "להתרחק מחקירות . . . " עמ' 39–38 ס' ו'; "לקוטי מוהר"ן" ח"ב, תורה י"ט; שם, תורה קט"ז.

על מה אתם מתאנחים. והשיב לו רבינו זצוק״ל, שאני מתגעגע לבוא למדריגתו. ואמר לו הר״ר ברוך, הלא אתם כבר כצדיק פלוני. השיב לו, כבר הגעתי למדריגתו. ויחשוב לו כמה מדריגות של צדיקים, עד שבא למדריגת הבעש״ט ז״ל. ואמר רבינו זצוק״ל שגם למדריגתו הגיע, ושהגיע לזה בעת שהיה י״ג שנים. (ואז דחף אותו הר״ר ברוך עד שכמעט נפל מן העליה...) ומאז התחיל המחלוקת ביניהם.״ (״אבניה ברזל״, בתוך הכרך ״ספר כוכבי אור״, ירושלים, תשכ״א, עמ׳ י״ז ס׳ ט״ו). ר׳ נחמן רמז שוב לעליונותו על הבעש״ט, המגיד ממיזריטש וכל שאר צדיקי ישראל שקדמו לו, בקטע הבא: ״אמר שיודע כל הצדיקים שהיו מאדם הראשון עד עכשיו מאיזה מקום היו ומאיזה מקום הם אומרים תורה ובאיזה מקום נשארו בשעת הסתלקותם. והתחיל לחשוב. הבעש״ט ז״ל מבינה, והמגיד ז״ל מחכמה, אע״פ שבינה למטה מחכמה אעפי״כ היה אומר תורה מאותה הבינה שהיא למעלה מאותה החכמה. ר׳ ברוך ז״ל מבינה שהיא למטה מאותה החכמה. אבל אני אומר תורה וכו׳.״ (״חיי מוהר״ן״ ח״ב, ״מעלות תורתו וספריו...״ עמ׳ 26 ס׳ י״ד); אמנם ר׳ נתן הסופר, כדרכו, קוטע את הדברים ומפסיק ב״וכו׳״, ואין בידינו הצהרתו המפורשת של ר׳ נחמן בדבר מקורה הנעלה מכל של תורתו (אין, כמובן, לבטל האפשרות שר׳ נחמן עצמו הפסיק כאן ולא פירש). אבל בהמשך הדברים רושם ר׳ נתן, ומנוסח דבריו נראה, שאכן ר׳ נחמן הוא זה שנמנע מלפרש את הענין: ״שמעתי פ״א שהתפאר בשבח גדולת תורתו ואמר אז בתוך דברי התפארותו, הלא אני יודע מהיכן אני לוקח אותם. והמובן מדבריו ומתנועותיו הק׳ אז היה שהוא לוקח תורתו ממקום גבוה ועליון מאד.״ (שם. שם). בין הסברות שפשטו בקרב חסידי ברסלב על סיבות נסיעתו המסתורית של ר׳ נחמן לקאמיניץ, סמוך לצאתו לא״י, היתה הדעה, שנסע כדי למצוא שם את כתבי הבעש״ט הנעלמים. ר׳ נתן רושם: ״... קצת אמרו שנס׳ כדי למצוא שם את הכתבים של הבעש״ט שסגרם באבן ואומרים קצת שהם טמונים שם בקאמיניץ ואמרו שנסע לשם בשביל זה. והוא ז״ל התלוצץ מזה ואמר שלא נסע כלל בשביל זה כי אינו צריך להם כלל ואמר, אלו היה רוצה אותן הכתבים הי׳ מביאים אותם לביתו. אך הוא א״צ להם כלל.״ (״שבחי הר״ן״, ״סדר הנסיעה שלו לא״י״, דף ז׳ ע״ב ס׳ ד׳); ר׳ גם ״שיחות הר״ן״ (עם ״שבחי הר״ן״) דף ע״ג ע״ב, ס׳ רל״ט. ברור, שאת הערכתו זו של ר׳ נחמן את מעלת הבעש״ט ומעמדו יש לשבץ בקונטקסט של בטולו, במישור תודעה מסוים, את ערך כל מנהיגי ישראל שקדמו לו (ר׳ למשל ״חיי מוהר״ן״ ח״ב, ״גדולת השגתו״ עמ׳ 16 ס׳ נ׳), וכל מנהיגי החסידות בני זמנו, ואף אמונתו, שצדיק כמותו לא יקום גם בעתיד. תפיסתו זו, והקשר בינה לבין אמונתו ביעודו המשיחי, ידונו במקום אחר.

10. ר׳ לעיל, עמ׳ ח׳.

11. ״שבחי הר״ן״, ״סדר הנסיעה...״ דף ט׳ ע״ב ס׳ י׳.

12. שם, דף י״ח ע״ב — י״ט ע״א, ס׳ ל׳.

13. נראה שביסודה של הקביעה ״הבושה חשובה כמו מיתה״ מונח המאמר הידוע, ״כל המלבין פני חבירו ברבים כאילו שופך דמים״ (בבא מציעא נ״ח ע״ב). אבל ר׳ נחמן מעקמה במקצת בהחליפו את נקודת המבט של המבייש, שהוא בחזקת שופך דמים, בנקודת המבט של המבוייש, שהוא בחזקת מי שנהרג, כביכול. פשט הגמרא מתכוון להדגיש את חומרתו השלילית של מעשה הביוש ברבים, וודאי שאין הוא משווה באורח מיכני את כובד משקלן של בושה ומיתה כעונשים.

14. על פרשת אותה נסיעה ר׳ ״שבחי הר״ן״, ״סדר הנסיעה...״ דף ז׳ ע״א-ע״ב ס׳ א׳. בן לויתו לא היה ר׳ שמעון, שנתלוה אליו ברוב נסיעותיו האחרות ואף בראשית דרכו לקאמיניץ, אלא חסיד אחר, ששמו לא נשתמר. ר׳ רשימתי הנ״ל, ״קרית ספר״ מ״ו, עמ׳ 147 הע׳ 3.

15. בין השנים 1789 ו־1797 נאסר על היהודים לגור בעיר קאמיניץ, ורובם התרכזו בערים ובכפרים שמסביב לה. ב־1797 בוטל האיסור. ר׳ למשל, R. Mahler, *A History of Modern Jewry 1780–1815* (London, 1971) p. 381; B.D. Weinryb, *The Jews of Poland* (Philadelphia) p. 354 n. 23, p. 137.

16. ״שבחי הר״ן״, ״סדר הנסיעה...״ דף ז׳ ע״א.

17. על פעילות הפרנקיסטים בקאמיניץ־פודולסק, ר׳ למשל ספרו הנ״ל של ווינריב עמ׳ 245–248; א. יערי, ״שריפת התלמוד בקאמניץ־פודולסק״, ״סיני״ מ״ב, תשי״ח, עמ׳ רצ״ד–ש״ו.

18. ר׳ ״שבחי הר״ן״, ״סדר הנסיעה...״ דף ז׳ ע״ב.

בעולם הזה, כשלון שיתוקן רק ב״עלמא דקשוט״. רק בתקופה מאוחרת יותר, בסביבות תקס״ג וסמוך להשתקעותו בברסלב, נוסף לחווית ״איני יודע״ של ר׳ נחמן המימד החדש של היותה גם השגתו הגדולה ביותר. רק אז הבין, שדווקא בזמנים בהם חדל לכאורה לפעול כצדיק, הגיע למדרגתו הצדיקית הגבוהה ביותר. וכך, הנסיון שהיה בראשיתו אפשרות רחוקה אך מאיימת, ונעשה בהדרגה לחובה יזומה ולאמצעי, הפך בסופו למטרה הנעלה ולהשג הגדול כשלעצמו.

הערות

1. ר׳ ג. שלום, "Devekut or Communion with God" בספר *The Messianic Idea in Judaism* (London, 1971) עמ׳ 222–219.

2. ר׳ רבקה ש״ץ, ״למהותו של הצדיק בחסידות״, מולד 144–145, עמ׳ 368–370.

3. מלת יידיש ממקור סלאבי שמובנה ״איש פשוט״. ראוי לציין, שיעקב פרנק קרא לעצמו ״פרוסטאק״ (ר׳ ג. שלום, ״התנועה השבתאית בפולין״, בספר מחקרים ומקורות לתולדות השבתאות ולגלגוליה, ירושלים, תשל״ד, עמ׳ 119) אבל אין להסיק מכך, שר׳ נחמן שאב את הכנוי דווקא וביודעין מן המסורת הפרנקיסטית. אף הבעש״ט נתכנה ״פראסטאק״ בגרסת יידיש של ״שבחי הבעש״ט״ (ר׳ א. יערי, ״שתי מהדורות יסוד של ״שבחי הבעש״ט״״, ״קרית ספר״ ל״ט, תשכ״ד, עמ׳ 255; 261. ד״ר י. שחר המנוח העיר את תשומת לבי לכך.) אמנם הקטע שבו מופיע הכנוי לא נכלל במהדורה העברית, ולפי דברי יערי, קרוב לוודאי שמחבר המהדורה העברית השמיטו בכוונה (ר׳ שם, עמ׳ 261) אבל הקטע המושמט כולו מתיחס אל הבעש״ט כאל איש פשוט ועם הארץ, ויתכן שהסבה להשמטתו היתה הרתיעה מהטעמת תדמיתו ההמונית של הבעש״ט לפני התגלותו, ולאו דווקא החשש מפני ההד הפרנקיסטי, שעלול היה להשתמע מן הכנוי פראסטאק. עצם השמוש החסידי במונח זה ביחס אל הבעש״ט מורה שלא הוכתם בפרנקיזם. ד״ר ח. טורניאנסקי אף היא מאשרת, שהמונח היה נפוץ ומשולל קונוטציות פרנקיסטיות מיוחדות.

4. התאור הארוך, שנכתב ראשון, מופיע בס׳ ״שבחי הר״ן״ (עם ״שיחות הר״ן״) ביחידה נפרדת הנקראת ״סדר הנסיעה שלו לארץ ישראל״. התאור המאוחר יותר נדפס ב״חיי מוהר״ן״ ח״א, ״נסיעתו לארץ ישראל״. על יחסם של שני התאורים זה לזה ועל מחברותם, ר׳ רשימתי, ״שני מקורות לתאור נסיעתו של ר׳ נחמן מברסלב לארץ ישראל״, ״קרית ספר״ מ״ו, תשל״א, עמ׳ 153–147.

5. ״שבחי הר״ן״ (עם ״שיחות הר״ן״), לעמברג, 1901, דף ט״ז ע״א ס׳ כ״ב.

6. מגפת הדבר.

7. ״חיי מוהר״ן״ ירושלים, תש״ו, ח״א, ״נסיעתו לא״י״, עמ׳ 63 סי׳ י״א. השוה עם הנוסח הארוך יותר ב״שבחי הר״ן״, ״סדר הנסיעה...״ דף ח׳ ע״ב — דף ט׳ ע״ב.

8. ״חיי מוהר״ן״ ח״א, ״נסיעתו לא״י״ עמ׳ 64–63 ס׳ י״ב.

9. אין כל ספק, שבניגוד לעקרון המסורתי של ״פוחת והולך״ וליחס הכבוד שרחשו החסידים בדורות המאוחרים יותר אל הבעש״ט ובני דורו (ראה בענין זה, מ. פייקאז׳, ״חסידות ברסלב״, ירושלים תשל״ב, עמ׳ 104–102), ראה ר׳ נחמן את עצמו כגדול במעלה מאביו זקנו ומכל שאר קודמיו בחסידות. כך, למשל, רמז להיותו מסוגל להשלמת שליחות התיקון העולמית, שהבעש״ט ואחרים נכשלו בה: ״אמר, הבעש״ט ז״ל וכמה צדיקים עשו ותקנו בעולם מה שתקנו. ואח״כ כשנפטרו ונסתלקו נפסק הדבר. היינו ההארה שהאירו בתלמידיהם והחזירום להשי״ת לא נמשך מדור לדור רק נפסק. ע״כ צריכין לעשות דבר שיהיה לו קיום לעד״ (״חיי מוהר״ן״ ח״ב, ״מעלות תורתו וספריו...״ עמ׳ 29 ס׳ ל״ד). כנגד זאת אמר על פעולתו שלו בעולם: ״מיין פיעריל ווט שוין טלאין ביז משיח וועט קומן. האש שלי תוקד עד שיבוא משיח.״ (שם, ״גדולת השגתו״ עמ׳ 18 ס׳ ס״ו). אף המריבה בין ר׳ נחמן לבין דודו ר׳ ברוך ממדזיבוז החלה כנראה על רקע התנשאות ר׳ נחמן הצעיר מעל למדריגת הבעש״ט, התנשאות שהיה בה משום רמז גם ליחס הבטול שלו כלפי ר׳ ברוך עצמו, שכן ר׳ ברוך החזיק בעקרון גדולתו המוחלטת של הבעש״ט ובסס עליו את תביעתו למנהיגות חסידית בתוקף היותו נכד הבעש״ט. ר׳ נתן מדוח כך על ראשית המחלוקת ביניהם: ״ובא רבינו ז״ל אל הר״ר ברוך. וכאשר ישב רבינו זצוק״ל אצלו היה מתאנח. ויאמר לו הר׳ ברוך,

ללא כל לחץ חיצוני וכתוצאה מחטא חמור ולא ידוע, "שוכח" את תכנן, ובהכרח, אין הוא יכול לקיימן אפילו באותה דרך שנפתחה בפניו בזמן הנסיעה לא"י. ר' נחמן הגולה והמנודה מתקשה בתחילה להשיג "ספר", אך משעולה סוף סוף הדבר בידו הוא מגלה ששכח לא רק כיצד לקרוא בו, אלא אף כיצד להניחו לפניו ולפתחו. במאמרו "ר' נחמן מברסלב על המחלוקת עליו"[88] נתח יוסף וייס את מושג ה"שכחה" בחלום בלהות זה, לאור השמוש בו בכמה תורות בספר "לקוטי מוהר"ן". וייס הראה, שמשמעות ה"שכחה" היא נכור מוחלט מן המסורת היהודית, שנציגה בחלום הוא ה"ספר". ע"פ נתוחו נובע נכור זה משני מקורות: הכפירה הפילוסופית־ראציונליסטית מצד אחד, (ידוע שר' נחמן קרא בספרות פלוסופית ואף התקרב ל"אפיקורסים"־משכילים יהודים באומאן,[89] על אף שאסר על חסידיו בתכלית האסור להגות בספרות זו ולחקות אותו במעשיו). ומצד שני, שתי הכפירות הדתיות שהעיבו על שמי יהדות דורו של ר' נחמן, השבתאות, ובעיקר הפרנקיזם.[90] אם כן, נראה ש"שכחה", בחלום הבלהות כבמצב "איני יודע", אינה רק התרוקנות מתוכן, התרחקות ממסורת מסוימת אל תוך חלל ריק, אלא היא אף משיכה מסוכנת אל תוכן אחר, המתחזה כ"ידיעה" אלטרנטיבית.

על אף שכל מאמרי ר' נחמן ותורותיו על "קטנות", "פשיטות" ו"איני יודע", שהגיעו לידינו, נוסחו בתקופה שלאחר נסיעתו לא"י בתקנ"ח והיו קשורים בתודעתו קשר הדוק עם אותה נסיעה, ועל אף שגם לשונות "איני יודע" שלו נראה שנטבעו רק בתקופה זו בחייו,[91] אין כל ספק, שהחויה הנפשית־דתית של "איני יודע" כשלעצמה לותה אותו משך כל חייו. בין התאורים הבודדים ששרדו מן התקופה שקדמה לנסיעה לא"י מופיע הקטע שלהלן, בו מתואר ר' נחמן במצב זה, אע"פ שאף אחד מן המונחים "קטנות" "פשיטות" ו"איני יודע" אינו מופיע בו:

> "קודם שנסע לא"י בסמוך שאל לו אחד, מפני מה אינו מקרבם ואינו מדבר עמם. אמר לו שאין לו עתה דבורים. ואמר, שנודע לו עכשיו כי תעבור במים אתך אני,[92] איך יכולין לראות מתי שרוצין את האבות אברהם יצחק ויעקב. וגם ה' חידוש אצלי מפני מה ע"פ זה דווקא. אך אני חושב מחמת שאני צריך לעבור על הים. אך למה לכם זאת, מה צורך לכם בזה. ואפילו אם הייתי יכול להלביש זאת במוסר, שיהיה צורך לכל, אך עתה אין לי דבורים...."[93]

מצב "אין לי עתה דבורים" ודאי שאינו אלא גלגול מוקדם של "איני יודע". אפינית לו אי היכולת לומר תורה, שלוותה את מצבי "קטנות", "פשיטות" ו"איני יודע" בשנים המאוחרות יותר. ברור, מכל מקום, שלפני נסיעתו לא"י ואף בשנים הראשונות לאחריה, לא מצא ר' נחמן כל צד לחיוב בתקופות השתיקה וההתרחקות שלו כשלעצמן, ששמשו לו כאמצעי פרדוכסלי לעליותיו למצבי גדלות. אדרבא, הוא עמד על כך, שתקופות הסתגרותו ריחקו ממנו תלמידים ותרמו לכשלונו היחסי כמנהיג חסידי. מיד בהמשך הקטע המובא לעיל, ובהקשר ישיר עם "אין לי דיבורים" כותב ר' נתן:

> "אח"כ הי' הולך ושב בבית, וענה ואמר, אני עני ואביון יותר מכל הגדולים. זה יש לו ממון, זה יש לו כסף וזה יש לו עיירות, ואני אין לי כלום. אך זאת כל נחמתי, כשאני מזכיר שבעלמא דקשוט יהיו כולם צריכין לי וישתוקקו כולם לשמוע החידושים שאני מחדש בכל עת ובכל רגע, מהו אני רק מה שהנשמה שלי מחדש. (גם זה קודם ארץ ישראל)".[94]

אמנם הודאתו של ר' נחמן בהיותו "עני ואביון יותר מכל הגדולים" מעידה על מידה ניכרת של גאוה ותחושת יחוד, אך יש בה גם משום הכרת כשלונו כצדיק

״שמעתי בשמו שאמר שעיקר מה שהגיע למדריגתו הוא רק ע״י ענין פראסטיק שהיה מדבר הרבה ומשיח הרבה בינו לבין קונו ואמר תהילים הרבה בפשיטות ועי״ז דייקא הגיע למה שהגיע. ואמר אם הייתי יודע שהש״י יעשה ממני מה שאני עתה דהיינו חידוש כזה הייתי עושה ביום אחד מה שעשיתי בשנה כולה (כלומר שהיה מזרדז כ״כ בעבודתו עד שמה שהיה עושה ועובד הש״י בשנה כולה היה עושה ביום אחד. והיה מתגעגע מאד מאד אחר מעלת העבודה בבחי׳ פראסטיק באמת, ואמר איי איי פראסטיק. גם אמר שדבר עם כמה צדיקים גדולים ואמרו ג״כ שלא הגיעו למדרגתם כ״א ע״י ענין פראסטיק שעסקו בעבודתם בפשיטות גמור בהתבודדות ושמחה בינו לבין קונו וכו׳. ועי״ז הגיעו למה שהגיעו אשרי להם.)״[83]

בולט כאן יצוגו של ״ענין פראסטיק״ או ״פשיטות״ של ר׳ נחמן כאמצעי לעליה אל מדרגתו הגבוהה, ולא כמדרגה הגבוהה עצמה, כפי שהוגדרה אי־הידיעה בקטעים שהובאו לעיל. מבחינה זו אין המושגים ״איני יודע״ מכאן, ו״פשיטות״ ו״קטנות״ מכאן, חופפים זה את זה אלא באורח חלקי.

כמו כן אין כאן כל זכר לאפשרות החטא, או אפילו לתודעת החטא, שהדהדה מדברי ר׳ נחמן על ״איני יודע״, ״פשיטות״ ו״קטנות״ במקומות אחרים. אין כאן זהות תודעה עם הרשע, שעבר על כל מצוות התורה כולן ושאינו יודע כיצד מתחילים להיות יהודי, אלא עם היהודי הפשוט, שכשרות מעשיו אינה מוטלת בכל ספק. המדובר בירידה עד לנקודת אבדן המעלה הצדיקית המיוחדת, ולא בשקיעה לתהומות התודעה החוטאת, קל וחומר לחטא בפועל.

אך כנגד תמונת ״פשיטות״ ו״איני יודע״ התמימה, כפי שנצטיירה בשתי המובאות האחרונות, מופיעים בכתבי ר׳ נתן תאורים אחרים, המאשרים את נוכחותם של רמזים אנטינומיים בדברי ר׳ נחמן על מצבי אי־הידיעה שלו.

בקטע שכבר צוטט לעיל[84] נאמר על ר׳ נחמן, שבשעות ״איני יודע״ ראה בעצמו ״מי שעבר על כל התורה כולה ח״ו כמה וכמה פעמים״ ו״אמר בלשון השתוקקות וכסופין איך זוכין להיות יהודי . . . כאילו לא התחיל עדיין כלל.״ כלומר, במצבים אלה, לא זו בלבד שאבד את תחושת מעלתו המיוחדת, אלא אף נתנסה בתודעת נכור מוחלט מדת ישראל ומסורתו. צד זה של ״איני יודע״ בולט יותר בקטע הבא:

״אמר, מה שאין יכול לומר תורה לפרקים זהו חדוש יותר, שכבר מוכן ומזומן אצלי כמה חידושים גדולים ובתוך כך הכל נשכח מאתי, ואינו זוכר כלום ואינו יודע כלל משום ספר בעולם, ואפילו ניגון אינו יודע, רק הכל באשר לכל נשכח ונעלם ממני. וזה פלא גדול באמת. וכמה פעמים שמעתי מפיו הק׳ ענין זה, כי רגיל אצלו שכמה פעמים הוא אומר, עתה איני יודע כלל, כלל לא, אע״פ שבשעה הקודמת גילה חידושים נפלאים ונוראים.״[85]

מוטיב ה״שכחה״, בעקר ביחס ל״ספר״ או ״הספר״, חוזר ומופיע בדברי ר׳ נחמן פעמים אחדות. הוא תופס מקום מרכזי בכמה מתורותיו, וכן למשל בחלום הבלהות שספר בכסלו תק״ע, סמוך למותו, באומאן.[86] בחלום זה מופיע ר׳ נחמן כאיש מוחרם ומנודה ע״י הכל, בשל מעשה חטא שעל טיבו ומהותו אין הוא עצמו מודע. למרות זאת הוא מקבל עליו את האשמה ובורח לארץ נכר בתקוה שעד שם לא הגיע שמע חטאו, אך בגלותו מיסרהו פחד נורא, שמא ישכח את כל תלמודו. פחד זה בחלום בתק״ע מזכיר את חששו של ר׳ נחמן, בזמן נסיעתו לא״י בתקנ״ח, שהוא עלול להמכר לעבדות בארץ נכר, בה יבצר ממנו לקיים את מצוות התורה, החשש שהביאו לראשונה לידי הכרת אפשרות קיום המצוות כפי שנתקיימו לפני מתן תורה.[87] אך בחלום הבלהות הופך מצב משוער זה למציאות מחרידה ונואשת עוד יותר, שהרי בחלומו אין איש מונע ממנו את קיום המצוות כפשוטן, אלא הוא עצמו,

מזמן צאתו מברסלב לאומאן בתק״ע ועד לאותו רגע בשעת הנסיעה, שבו הודיע לר׳ נתן כי השגתו בתקס״ה בטלה זה מכבר, השיג ר׳ נחמן מדרגה גבוהה יותר של ״איני יודע״ מזו שעמד בה בראשית הנסיעה. מכאן, שהשגת כל מדרגה חדשה לא נבעה ישירות מירידותיו של ר׳ נחמן למצבי ״איני יודע״ או ״פשיטות״ המוגדרים. ידוע, למשל, שבאותה נסיעה עצמה לא היה שרוי במצב ״איני יודע״.[77]

בזמנים אחרים, לעומת זאת, בהם ברור שהתנסה ב״איני יודע״, לא דבר כלל על היות ״איני יודע״ תכלית הידיעה עצמה. כך, למשל, סמוך לחג השבועות תקס״ה, שבועות אחדים אחרי הכרזתו, שהשיג כי ״תכלית הידיעה היא אשר לא נדע״,[78] התנסה ר׳ נחמן בירידה קשה אל מצב ״איני יודע״. ר׳ נתן מוסר על בקורו אז בברסלב, בחברת ידידו ר׳ נפתלי. הוא מתאר בפרטי פרטים את התנהגות ר׳ נחמן במשך שהותם עמו. בכל התאור כולו אין אף זכר לעניין היות ירידתו ״תכלית הידיעה״ של ר׳ נחמן. אדרבא, הנסיון נתפס על ידי ר׳ נתן, וכנראה גם ע״י ר׳ נחמן עצמו, כנסיון שלילי לחלוטין, שבו הוא ״רחוק בתכלית הרחוק מהשי״ת:

״פ״א באנו אליו אני וחבירי ר׳ נפתלי סמוך לשבועות תקס״ה. ואמר לנו שעתה אינו יודע כלל, רק זאת נודע לי בעתים הללו, שע״י לשון הרע שבעולם אין הצדיקים יכולין להיות ענווים וכו׳, כמבואר בסימן קצ״ז[79] ויתר מזה אינו יודע. ואמר בפירוש, כמו שאתה אינך יודע כך ממש אני איני יודע עכשיו כלום. ואמר שעכשיו הוא מתנהג בפשיטות, שעומד בבוקר ומתפלל תפלתו, ואח״כ הוא לומד קצת, ואח״כ הוא אומר תהילים, ואח״כ אוכל אכילתו ומניח עצמו לישון קצת, ואח״כ הוא עומד ומפרש שיחתו קצת לפני השי״ת ברחמים ותחנונים, ויש לי רחמנות עלי (און איך האב אויף מיר רחמנות) ואלו הדבורים שיש לו רחמנות על עצמו אמר בתמימות ובלב נשבר עד שכל מי ששמע אלו הדבורים והבין גודל הרחמנות העצום שיש לו ע״ע, כאילו הי׳ רחוק בתכלית הריחוק מהשי״ת ח״ו, וכו׳. וסיפר לנו אז שחלם לו שהיה שבועות, והיינו כולנו כדרכנו בכל שנה להתקבל אליו על חג השבועות. ולא הי׳ יכול לומר תורה כלל והי׳ מבזה ומיסר אותנו מאד, ואמר כי הכל בשבילנו, שמחמת טוביותנו וכו׳ אינו יכול לומר תורה. (כמבואר אצלינו שהתורה של הצדיק נעשית מהאנשים הבאים ומתקבצים אליו.) והוכיח אותנו מאד, ועי״ז נתעוררנו כולנו בתשובה גדולה . . .״[80]

כפי שהיא מתוארת כאן, התנהגות ר׳ נחמן במשך מצב ״איני יודע״ זה כמוה כהתנהגותו בעת ״פשיטות״ — מונח שהוא נרדף ל״איני יודע״ בלשונו של ר׳ נתן לאורך כל הקטע. סדר יומו כולל תפילה, ״קצת״ למוד, אכילה ושתיה לספוק צרכי הגוף ו״שיחה״ עם הקב״ה.[81] חלומו של ר׳ נחמן כפי שספרו אז לר׳ נתן ולר׳ נפתלי, אף הוא משקף את אחד מאותותיה המובהקים של חוית ה״פשיטות״ או ״איני יודע״, היינו, אי היכולת ״לומר תורה״. ״איני יודע״ מתואר כאן כמצב דפרסיבי: בהיותו מנותק לחלוטין מן האל, ר׳ נחמן שרוי בדכאון קשה שאין בו אף שמץ מן ההתעלות הכרוכה בהשגת ״תכלית הידיעה״. אדרבא, אי ידיעתו היא חד־משמעית ומשפילה, וודאי שאינה מוצגת כהשגו הגדול ביותר. כל זאת, על אף שרק שבועות ספורים קודם לכן חגג ר׳ נחמן לראשונה את השגתו, שאי הידיעה הריהי תכלית הידיעה.

מענין לציין, שבאותו מצב ״איני יודע״ שבו נתנסה ר׳ נחמן בזמן בקורם של ר׳ נתן ור׳ נפתלי, דמה את עצמו, כל עוד הוא שרוי ב״איני יודע״, לתלמידו וסופרו ר׳ נתן, באמרו: ״כמו שאתה אינך יודע כך ממש אני איני יודע עכשיו כלום״.[82] אם יכלה ״פשיטותו״ הטבעית של ר׳ נתן לשמש את ר׳ נחמן כדוגמת פשיטותו המכוונת שלו, הרי שירידתו ל״פשיטות״ או למצבי ״איני יודע״ היתה תמימה לחלוטין וחסרה כל מימד אנטינומי. תמונה זו של מצב ״איני יודע״ מתישבת יפה עם תאור סדר יומו של ר׳ נחמן באותו מצב, כפי שהובא לעיל, וכן עם דבריו של ר׳ נתן על כך במקום אחר:

פריסא ברדיפא דהאי מחשבה, מטי ולא מטי, **ופריסא**, זה המסדר והמיישב, שהוא בחי׳ כתר, שהוא פרוס בין הנאצלים ובין המאציל **ואיתעבידו תשע היכלין דלאו** אינון נהורין, ולא רוחין ולא נשמתין, ולית מאן דקיימא בהו, ולא מתדבקין, ולא מתידעין ודע, שזה תכלית הידיעה, כי תכלית הידיעה דלא ידע.״

ור׳ נתן מפרש:

״...כי הכתר הוא המיישב והמסדר את המוחין. דהיינו, הכוח שיש בהשכל של אדם לישב ולסדר את המוח והדעת לבל יהרוס לצאת חוץ מן הגבול. זה הכוח הוא בחינת כתר כנ״ל. וזה הכוח הוא כמו מחיצה המפסקת בין המוחין ובין האור א״ס. כי זה הכוח שהוא מיישב והמסדר הוא מעכב את המוחין בעת מרוצתם ורדיפתם, לבל יהרסו לעלות אל ה׳ למעלה ממחיצתם... כי אם לא היה המעכב הנ״ל כלל, ולא היה מי שיעכב את המוחין מרדיפתם ומרוצתם, היו מתבטלין המוחין לגמרי. כי היה האדם מתבטל במציאות. כי אור הא״ס א״א להשיג. אך ע״י שני הבחינות שהם הרדיפה והמעכב, עי״ז נעשין בחי׳ מחיצות והיכלין הנ״ל שעל ידם משיגין אור הא״ס רק בבחי׳ מטי ולא מטי. ופירוש מטי ולא מטי ידוע למבינים. דהיינו שמגיע ואינו מגיע, שרודף ומשיג להשיג, ואעפ״כ אינו משיג ומשיג שזה נעשה ע״י הרדיפה והמעכב. ואע״פ שנעשין אילו ההיכלין הנ״ל, אעפ״כ לא ידיע ולא אתידע ולית מאן דקיימא בהו, ולא מתדבקין ולא ידעין וכו׳ כנ״ל. כי א״א לצייר בשכל אלו ההיכלות הנ״ל, כי הם למעלה מנפשין רוחין ונשמתין, למעלה מכל השכליות, כי הם למעלה מהספירות וכו׳ כמבואר לעיל בלשון רבינו ז״ל.״[75]

אם כן, כבר בקיץ תקס״ג השיג ר׳ נחמן ש״תכלית הידיעה היא אשר לא נדע״. אך מתוך הכרתו בדרגות השונות של השגה זו, ובהתאם עם תפיסת עצמו כמי שנמצא כל ימיו בתהליך של עליה למדרגות ידיעה והשגה גבוהות יותר ויותר, יכול היה, שנתיים לאחר מכן, אחרי פסח תקס״ה, לבטל את ערך השגתו הקודמת ולטעון, שרק עכשיו השיג את ״תכלית הידיעה״ לאמיתה. כעבור חמש שנים נוספות, בקיץ תק״ע, שוב שלל את אמיתות ידיעתו האחרונה בתקס״ה, והודיע, שמאז התקדם והשיגה במדרגה גבוהה עוד יותר. ר׳ נתן רושם ב״חיי מוהר״ן״:

״אחר זמן רב, בקיץ תק״ע, בעת שנסע לאומין חזר וסיפר קצת מענין הנ״ל ואמר שאין יודעים כלל כלל לא. והפליג מאד בגדולת הבורא ית׳ אשר א״א לבאר, ואמר שאין יודעים כלל. ושאלתי אותו, הלא כבר אמרתם זאת, וספרת׳ מזה מענין תכלית הידיעה אשר לא נדע, וכבר ביארתם כל זה, שאע״פ שזוכים לזה הידיעה אשר לא נדע, אעפ״כ עדיין אין יודעים כלום. כי כבר נדמה לכם שזכית׳ לזה התכלית וכו׳ וכנ״ל. ענה ואמר, מי יודע באיזה ידיעה היה זה התכלית, היינו, כי גם אז, בעת שסיפר זאת אחר פסח, לא זכה לבחינת לא נדע ממש, כ״א באיזה ידיעה, היינו שבאותו הידיעה זכה להתכלית אשר לא נדע. וכוונתו, כי יש ידיעה למעלה מידיעה, השגה למעלה מהשגה, גבוה מעל גבוה. ואצל כל ידיעה והשגה עד למעלה למעלה התכלית היא אשר לא נדע. ואמר אז, גם מעת שיצא מברסלב עד עכשיו (שהיה באותו היום, ולא שהה רק בערך איזה שעות, כי אז לא נסע עדיין רק בערך ג׳ פרסאות) שוב אינו יודע. היינו שגם באילו השעות זכה לבחינת אינו יודע. והבן דברים אלו, כי הם הדברים עמוקים ועליונים וגבוהים מאד, אשרי ילוד אשה שזוכה להשגות כאלו, לתכלית האמת.״[76]

לא ברור כיצד קשורה היתה השגת כל מדרגה חדשה של ״תכלית הידיעה היא אשר לא נדע״ עם ירידתו של ר׳ נחמן למצבי ״איני יודע״ — ״פשיטות״ או, בראשית דרכו — ״קטנות״. בקטע המצוטט לעיל טוען ר׳ נחמן, שהשגת ״תכלית הידיעה״ לא היתה אלא תהליך, שנמשך משעה לשעה כל חייו. אפילו בשעות הספורות שחלפו

שעכשיו יודע שתכלית הידיעה היא אשר שלא נדע לא נדע ממש, א״כ הוא יודע, מאחר שזכה לתכלית הידיעה. אך אעפ״כ אינו יודע כלום, כי הלא כבר נדמה לי שאני אצל זה התכלית הידיעה אשר לא נדע. ועכשיו אני רואה איך הייתי רחוק מזה התכלית. (ואמר אז בלשון גנאי על עצמו, כי החזיק עכשיו לכסילות זה התכלית של הזמן הקודם, שנדמה לו אז שזכה לתכלית הידיעה אשר לא נדע) כי עכשיו נודע לו שתכלית הידיעה אשר לא נדע ממש. ודבר זה ג״כ אינו יכול לאומרו ולבארו כי נראה כפשוטו. אך באמת רק עכשיו נודע לו זאת, וכן הדבר הראשון.״[72]

ע״פ ר׳ נתן, בהתגלות זו, שחלה בתקס״ה, בדבר היות תכלית הידיעה אי הידיעה עצמה, העלה ר׳ נחמן את הנושא בפני תלמידיו לראשונה. אך מדברי ר׳ נחמן עצמו משתמע שהדברים לא נתחדשו בתקס״ה. לפחות פעם אחת בעבר נראה היה לר׳ נחמן שהשיג ידיעה זו לאמיתה, אלא שעתה, בתקס״ה, בטל ערך אותה השגה נוכח השגתו החדשה שהשיג את אי־ידיעתו. ואמנם הנוסחה ״תכלית הידיעה דלא נדע״ מופיעה כבר בתורה ״אמצעותא דעלמא״ — תורה כ״ד ב״לקוטי מוהר״ן״ ח״א, שנאמרה בקיץ תקס״ג, כמעט שנתיים קודם להתגלות שעליה דוח ר׳ נתן.[73] קרוב לודאי, שהשגת ״איני יודע״ של ר׳ נחמן באותה עת היא זו שלה נתכוון בבטלו את תקפה אחרי פסח תקס״ה.

בתורה כ״ד, ״אמצעותא דעלמא״, דן ר׳ נחמן במאמצי השכל האנושי לרדוף ולהשיג את ״אור אין סוף״ הנמצא מעל לכל הספירות ומאציל עליהן. ביסודה של התורה מונח הקטע מן הזוהר (בראשית ״נח״ ס״ה ע״א) העוסק במאמצי הספירה ״חכמה״־״מחשבה״ להשיג את מקורה, הספירה ״כתר״ (״רעותא דלא אתידע ולא אתפס כלל לעולם״ — הרצון שאי אפשר לדעתו או לתפסו לעולם) בעת נוח האור האלוהי עליה. ״מחשבה״ יכולה להשיג את אור אין סוף רק באורח בלתי ישיר, שכן מסך (״פריסא״) קם ועומד בינה לבין ״כתר״, הנאצלת הראשונה. רק מבעד למסך זה זורח האור האלוהי על ״מחשבה״, הספירה השניה, וכך היא משיגה אותו בדרך של השגה־לא־השגה, של ״מגיע ואינו מגיע״ (מטי ולא מטי). בזמן זרוח אור אין סוף על המסך המפריד בין ״כתר״ ל״חכמה״, ״חכמה״ מקרינה על המסך את אורה שלה. כתוצאה מהתנגשות שני גופי האורות האלה נוצרים תשעה היכלות, שאינם ספירות, (״לא אינון נהורין ולא אינון רוחין ולא אינון נשמתין״) אבל הם מסמלים את תשע הספירות מ״כתר״ ומטה. אף היכלות אלה מתאמצים להשיג את ״הוריהם״ — ״כתר״ ו״חכמה״ אבל גם הם אינם יכולים להשיגם אלא בדרך ״מטי ולא מטי״.[74]

ר׳ נחמן מעתיק מרדף זה אחר האור האלוהי מתחום הספירות בינן לבין עצמן אל התחום האנושי. השכל האנושי מתאמץ בלי הרף להשיג את אור אין סוף, אך אין הוא מסוגל לכך אלא בדרך ״מטי ולא מטי״. ע״פ ר׳ נחמן, מגבלה זו של השכל האנושי נועדה להגן עליו. ה״פריסא״, אותו הוא מפרש כספירה ״כתר״ עצמה, ולא כמסך המפריד בינה לבין ״חכמה״, כפי שהוגדר ב״זוהר״, אינו מאפשר לשכל האנושי כל מגע ישיר עם האור האלוהי, וכך הוא מונע מן השכל הסופי, המוגבל, את השמדת עצמו בהתאחדות עם האור, שהוא אין סופי ובלתי נתן להשגה. אם כך, השגתו הגבוהה ביותר של השכל האנושי היא השגה־לא־השגה זו של האור האלוהי. זוהי הנקודה שבה הוא משיג את גבול יכולתו, את אי יכולתו להשיג. מכאן — ״תכלית הידיעה היא אשר לא נדע״. ר׳ נחמן כותב:

״וכשעושה ומתקן את המיישב והמסדר שהוא הכתר כראוי, והמוחין רודפין להשיג את האור אין סוף, והכתר מעכב את השכל, כדי ליישב את השכל. וע״י הרדיפה והמעכב, אזי מכה המוחין בהמיישב והמסדר, ונעשין היכלות לאור אין סוף. ואעפ״כ לא ידיע ולא אתידע, כמובא בזוהר פ׳ נח (דף סה ע״א) ומגו האי

עד כאן מתישב תאור "איני יודע" זה, שנכתב ע"י ר' נתן, עם כל הידוע לנו על חויות "קטנות" ו"פשטות" של ר' נחמן בזמנים שונים. אך בהמשך הדברים מופיעה נימה חדשה; על אף שנסיונות "איני יודע" שלו נראו לעין כ"נפילות" או "ירידות" למדרגת קטנות הנמוכה ביותר ממדרגתו הטבעית, מדרגה שבה הוא בחזקת "איש פשוט" — "פראסטיק" או אפילו רשע שעבר על כל מצוות התורה כולן, למעשה אין נסיונות אלה אלא "חידוש גדול ביותר" — עליות שהן מופלאות ונשגבות עוד יותר ממצבי גדלותו הגלויים, שבהם הוא "אומר תורה" ונוהג כצדיק. לאמיתו של דבר, ה"איני יודע" של ר' נחמן הוא כשלעצמו השגתו הגדולה מכל, שכן השגת אי־הידיעה היא היא "תכלית הידיעה" — הידיעה האופטימאלית:

"ואמר בפירוש על עצמו שהתורה שלו היא חידוש גדול מאד, אבל האינו יודע שלו הוא חידוש גדול ביותר. היינו ענין הנ"ל, כי בכל פעם היה דרכו לומר שעכשיו אינו יודע כלל. ועי' עוד מזה במקום אחר . . . . ובענין תכלית הידיעה אשר לא נדע סיפר ג"כ קצת עמנו איזה פעמים איך בכל ידיעה יש זה התכלית וע"כ אע"פ שזוכים לבוא לזה התכלית אשר לא נדע, אעפ"כ עדיין אין זה התכלית האחרון, כי עדיין אין זה תכלית הידיעה, כי אם בידיעה זו. וצריכים אח"כ לטרוח לזכות בתכלית גבוה יותר, לזכות למדריגת התכלית אשר לא נדע בידיעה הגבוה יותר. וכן לעולם. נמצא שלעולם אין יודעים כלל. ואעפ"כ לא התחיל עדיין להשיג התכלית. (וכבר מבואר מזה קצת בדברינו במקום אחר). וענין זה עמוק ונסתר מאד מאד. ועוד יש בענין זה מה ששמענו פ"א אחר פסח, ויתבאר במ"א אי"ה."[71]

ירידת ר' נחמן ל"פשיטות" הוצגה בתורה ע"ח כרע הכרחי, גם משום מגבלות הטבע האנושי, שאינו מתיר לשום אדם להתקיים בגדלות מתמדת, וגם משום החובה המוטלת על הצדיק להשתוות עם אנשים "פשוטים" על מנת להעלותם. פשיטותו של ר' נחמן ע"פ תורה ע"ח היא הנקודה, שבה הוא מרוחק בתכלית הרחוק ממטרתו הטבעית: דבקות עם האל או, כפי שנוסחו הדברים שם, עם התורה. בדומה לכך, קטנותו של ר' נחמן בנסיעה לא"י הוצגה כשלב נמוך ביותר בסולם, שראשו גדלות. שני קצוות הסולם הקיצוניים הופרדו בבירור, על אף שהודגש גם הקשר הפרדוכסאלי ביניהם: העליה אל האחד מצריכה ירידה אל השני, וחוזר חלילה. אבל בקטע שלפנינו מתחדד הפרדוכס בזהוי שני קצוות הסולם זה עם זה: הירידה לתחתית הסולם אינה רק המסלול המכשיר את הצדיק לעליה, שזהותה עצמאית ונפרדת, אלא היא כשלעצמה גם העליה למדרגה הגבוהה ביותר. הצדיק המתנסה במצבי "אי ידיעה", משיג בכך (ולא ע"י כך) את "תכלית הידיעה" שהיא אי־הידיעה כשלעצמה. כל אחת מירידותיו הנמוכות והולכות אל מצבי אי־ידיעה הרי היא גם עליה למדרגה גבוהה עוד יותר של ידיעה, המבטלת את השגת ידיעתו־אי־ידיעתו הקודמת. התהליך נמשך ללא הרף, ומכאן, שידיעה אמיתית, סופית ומוחלטת היא מטבעה בלתי נתנת להשגה. לכן, "נמצא שלעולם אין יודעין כלל". ר' נחמן השיג לראשונה, ש"תכלית הידיעה היא אשר לא נדע" אחרי פסח תקס"ה. ר' נתן מדווח על כך:

"אחר פסח תקס"ה סיפר עמנו ואמר שנודע לו עכשיו שני דברים, אך איני יכול לאומרם כי נראים כפשוטים. כי גם פשוטו של דבר היא כך לכאורה. אך אעפ"כ נודע לו עכשיו אלו הדברים. היינו כי נודע לו מה שארז"ל אדם עובר עביר' אומר שלא יראני אדם. ולא אמר כלום, רק דחק בתיבות שלא יראני אדם, ולא ביאר כלום מה נודע לו בזה, כי כבר הקדים שאינו יכול לבאר בדברים כי נראה פשוטו של דבר כך. אך אעפ"כ רק עכשיו נודע לו זה הסוד. והב' נודע לו מה שאיתא תכלית הידיעה אשר לא נדע. אשר לא נדע ממש. (ולא ביאר ג"כ כלום רק דחק ג"כ התיבות אשר לא נדע ממש) ואף על פי שפשוטו של דבר כך, אעפ"כ רק עכשיו נודע לי זה הדבר, שתכלית הידיעה היא אשר לא נדע. לא נדע ממש. ואמר מאחר

שעושין בשביל איזה עובדא שבקדושה, אין שום תנועה ולא שום מחשבה נאבדת כלל. והכל נרשם למעלה לטובה, אשרי כשזוכין לקפץ ולדלג על כל המניעות וזוכין לגמור ולעשות איזה עובדא טובה. והיה אז בשמחה גדולה, וגער בר׳ נפתלי על שהי׳ בוש קצת לנגן אז, ואמר מה יש לנו להתבייש, כל העולם לא נברא אלא בשבילנו נפתלי. וואס האבין מיר זיך צו שעמין. בשבילנו נברא העולם. והיה אז בשמחה מאד.״[68]

הקשר בין ״איני יודע״ ופשיטות מצד אחד, וזכרון נסיעתו של ר׳ נחמן לא״י מצד שני, מפורש גם כאן. חוית קטנותו בשעת אותה הנסיעה, והבנתו אז את דרך קיום התורה כפי שנתקיימה לפני מתן תורה, הן שעצבו את תפיסתו המאוחרת יותר של ״פשיטות״, והן שאפשרו את המשך קיומו בזמן מצבי ״אי ידיעה״ שלו.

בסוף ספור פרשת הנסיעה לא״י ב״שבחי הר״ן״ סוטה ר׳ נתן מנושא חיבורו העיקרי ומעיר הערה כללית על יכולתו המופלאה של ר׳ נחמן בכל הזמנים, כבזמן הנסיעה, לעלות למדרגות גבוהות ביותר של ״השגת האלוהות״ בגדלות, דוקא מתוך ירידות מופלגות והשפלות עצמו בקטנות. בעוד שבגוף הסיפור ר׳ נתן נמנע, כאמור, מלכנות ירידות אלה בכל שם אחר מלבד ״קטנות״, בקטע המסים הוא מתארן במונחים השאובים מתוך הכרותו שלו, המאוחרת יותר, עם מצבי ״איני יודע״ של ר׳ נחמן. תאורים אלה חזקים ביותר: במצבי איני יודע שלו אין ר׳ נחמן יודע ״איך זוכין להיות יהודי״, כמוהו ״כמי שעבר על כל התורה כולה ח״ו וכמה וכמה פעמים״, והוא סובל ומתחרט ומכניע עצמו ממש כבעל־תשובה שכזה.[69] הירידות והעליות תלויות זו בזו, והן מתרחשות בקצביות מחזורית. ר׳ נתן כותב:

״...כפי ששמענו מפיו הקדוש וראינו בעינינו כי בכל פעם היה דרכו שהיה מתגעגע להש״י והיה שפל בעיני עצמו באמת, והיה לו רחמנות גדול על עצמו, כאילו לא הריח עדיין מעולם שום ריח של עבודת ה׳, וכמי שלא התחיל עדיין כלל ובאמת אפילו מי שעבר על כל התורה כולה ח״ו כמה וכמה פעמים. וכשזה האיש נתעורר בתשובה באמת, שאז בודאי כשמסתכל על עצמו היכן הוא בעולם, בודאי יש לו לב נשבר מאד, ויש לו רחמנות גדול מאד על עצמו בהכנעה גדולה וכו׳, וא״צ להאריך בזה בדבר המובן מעצמו, אעפ״כ אפילו זאת הרחמנות והלב נשבר של הבעל התשובה הנ״ל לא יגיע לחלק מאלף ורבבה של גודל הרחמנות והלב נשבר בהכנעה גדולה וכו׳ שהיה לרבינו ז״ל בכל פעם ופעם קודם שבא לאיזה השגה. והכלל כי לעולם לא נח ולא שקט אפילו בימי גדולתו, אע״פ שכבר זכה למה שזכה, להשגת אלוקות במדריגה גבוה עצומה ונוראה מאד, אעפ״כ לא היה מסתפק עצמו בזה, וטרח ויגע בכל עת ובכל שעה, וקיבל יסורין על עצמו יסורים קשים ומרים אשר כמעט אין דוגמתם בעולם, והרבה בתפילות ותחנונים ובהפצרות ובקשות רבות בגעגועים וכיסופין גדולים ונוראים מאד, עד שבא להשגה ומדריגה יותר עליונה. ואח״כ תיכף שזכה לזאת ההשגה, ואז הי׳ קצת בשמחה, ולפעמים זכינו לשמוע מפיו שהודיע לנו שכעת נודע לו חדשות וכו׳, ואז הי׳ שמח קצת, ואח״כ תיכף שזכה לזה, אח״כ התחיל עוד מחדש, ושכח כל העבר, כאילו לא התחיל עדיין כלל. וחזר והתחיל מחדש כמי שמתחיל לילך ולכנוס בקדושת ישראל. ולפעמים היינו שומעים מפיו הק׳ בפירוש שאמר בלשון השתוקקות וכיסופין, איך זוכין להיות יהודי. ואמר זאת באמת ובתמימות גדול, כאילו לא התחיל עדיין כלל. וכן היה כמה כמה פעמים. והי׳ תמיד הולך ועולה ממדריגה למדריגה. אע״פ שזכה למדריגות גבוהות ונוראות מאד למעלה למעלה וכו׳, אעפ״כ מעולם לא ה׳ מקרר דעתו בזה כלל. ותיכף אח״כ הי׳ לו לב נשבר והיה לו רחמנות גדול על עצמו בהכנעה גדולה וכו׳ כנ״ל. עד שזכה למדריגה יותר גבוהה... וכמה פעמים היה דרכו שאמר שעתה אינו יודע כלל. כלל וכלל לא. ופעמים נשבע על זה שבאמת אינו יודע כלל, אע״פ שביום הקודם ובשעה הקודמת גילה דברים עתיקים, אעפ״כ אח״כ אמר שאינו יודע כלל.״[70]

האל שרוי ב״העלמה והסתירה״ מפני ר׳ נחמן.[65] בתקופות ״איני יודע״ ר׳ נחמן אינו יכול לומר תורה, הוא מרחק את חסידיו, הממשיכים להתדפק על דלתו, בהצהירו ש״אינו יודע כלל״ ממש כמותם.[66] כל עוד הוא שרוי במצב זה, ר׳ נחמן ״מחיה את עצמו״ רק ״מהדרך של ארץ ישראל״ או ״במה שהיה בארץ ישראל״. והרי לפנינו נסוח מפורש על משמעותה האישית של הדרך לא״י בתורה ע״ח, שהיא דרכו של ר׳ נדומן עצמו לא״י בשנת תקנ״ח, בה התנסה ב״קטנות דקטנות״ והשיג לראשונה את אפשרות קיום המצוות בכוח, ולא בפועל.

ברור שר׳ נתן התרשם עמוקות מאותו ״איני יודע״ של ר׳ נחמן בתק״ע, שנסתיים באמירת תורת הפשיטות ע״ח, שכן רשם את נסיבות אמירתה של התורה פעם נוספת, ובהרחבה, באוטוביוגרפיה שלו, ״ימי מוהרנ״ת״:

״בשבת נחמו נתקבצו אצלו כמה אורחים על שבת הנ״ל. ונכנס מחדרו להבית שאכלו שם, וקידש על היין בחלישות כוח, כי כבר הי׳ חלוש מאד, כי הי׳ סמוך להסתלקותו. וישב על השולחן אחר שקידש, קודם שנטל ידיו לסעודה, והתחיל לדבר עם העולם. ענה ואמר. על מה באו העולם לכאן, הלא עתה איני יודע כלל. כשאני אומר תורה בוודאי כדאי לבוא, אבל עתה באמת שאיני יודע כלל, כי אני עכשיו איש פשוט לגמרי, שקורין פראסטיק, ואיני יודע כלל, ועל מה באו העולם. והאריך בשיחה זו קצת שהוא עתה פראסטיק גמור ואינו יודע כלל באמת, ואמר שהוא מחייה את עצמו עתה רק בדרך שהלך לא״י. והאריך בשיחה זו קצת ג״כ, עד שמתוך השיחה הקדוש׳ הזאת, שסיפר שאינו יודע כלל ושהוא פראסטיק גמור, ושהוא מחייה א״ע רק בהנסיעה לא״י, מתוך דברים אלו נכנס בדברים עד שגילה לנו תורה נפלאה איך דייקא ע״י הדרך של נסיעת א״י מחייה א״ע הצדיק בעת פשיטותו וכו׳, כנדפס כבר. אך א״א לבאר בכתב כל הענין איך נתגלה ונמשכה התורה הזאת יש מאין באמת. כי מתחילה לא הי׳ יודע כלל באמת, כי בכל עת שאמר שאינו יודע, לא הי׳ יודע כלל באמת, כאשר פעם אחד נשבע על זה בשבת קודש ואמר בזה״ל (דא שווער איך בייא שבת) על ענין זה שאינו יודע כלל. ובאמת אמר על עצמו שהאינו יודע שלו הוא חידוש נפלא וכו׳. ועתה סיפר הרבה איך שאינו יודע עתה כלל. ובתוך זה נכנס לשיחה נפלאה עד שעי״ז בעצמו גילה תורה נפלאה ע״ז בעצמו, שמחי׳ א״ע בעת פשיטותו בהדרך שנסע לא״י. ואח״כ בא לשמחה גדולה, וצוה לנגן הרבה, וזמרנו לפניו אזמר בשבחין . . .״[67]

כל פרטי המאורע מופיעים כאן שוב, ובנוסף עליהם מסתבר מן הקטע בעקיפין, שנסיון ״איני יודע״ זה לא היה הראשון או היחיד בחיי ר׳ נחמן, אלא אדרבא, מצבי ״איני יודע״ חזרו ונשנו, שהרי ר׳ נתן מטעים: ״כי **בכל עת** שאמר, שאינו יודע, לא היה יודע כלל באמת״.

גרסה נוספת של פרשת אמירת התורה ע״ח מופיעה ב״חיי מוהר״ן״, שם כותב ר׳ נתן:

״ליל שבת נחמו תק״ע באומין, אחר קידוש אמר תורה מענין פשיטותו, היינו מה שהוא לפעמים איש פשוט שקורין פראסטיק, שהוא מחייה עצמו אז בעת פשיטותו מהדרך שנסע לא״י. וביאר הענין כמובא בספרינו בסימן ע״ח בלק״ת ע״ש. ואמר שאינו יודע כלל ונשבע בשבת קודש ואמר בזה״ל: אני נשבע בש״ק, היינו על ענין הנ״ל שהוא אינו יודע כלל עכשיו. ואח״כ אמר שהוא עתה ירא, שקורין פרום, ושמח, ואמר אשרינו שהשי״ת הטיב עמנו מאד, שזכינו לקדושת ישראל. ואמר שיש לו שמחה גדולה על שזכה להיות בא״י. כי כמה מניעות וכמה בלבולים וכמה מחשבות וכמה עכובים וסכסוכים הי׳ לו על ענין הנסיעה לא״י, ומניעות מחמת ממון. והוא קפץ על כולם וגמר העובדא בשלימות, שהי׳ בא״י. ואמר זה אני מאמין גם אני יודע הרבה בענין זה, שכל התנועות וכל המחשבות וכל מיני העובדות

עצם קיומו של קשר הדוק בין ירידות ר׳ נחמן למצבי ״פשיטות״ לבין נסיונות ״איני יודע״ שלו אינו מוטל בספק, אם כי מהותו של הקשר אינה ברורה כל צרכה. ר׳ נחמן ״אמר״ את תורת הפשיטות החשובה שלו (ע״ח ב״לקוטי מוהר״ן״ ח״ב מיד אחרי יציאתו ממצב, שר׳ נתן, המשתמש כנראה בבטוי שטבע ר׳ נחמן עצמו, קראו ״איני יודע״ שלו. ר׳ נתן תאר את נסיבות אמירת התורה ע״ח פעמים אחדות בכמה מספריו, ובכל אחד מתאוריו המקבילים השתאה על כך שר׳ נחמן, בעודו בשלבי התנערות האחרונים ממצב של אי־ידיעה מוחלטת, מצב, שאחד מסימניו האופיניים היה אי היכולת ״לומר תורה״, מסוגל היה לגלות לחסידיו הנוכחים בבהירות כה רבה את מהות נסיונו בפרשו לפניהם את תורת הפשיטות ע״ח. ב״שיחות הר״ן״ ר׳ נתן כותב על כך:

״בליקוטי תנינא סי׳ ע״ח בענין הנהגת הפשיטות וכו׳, כי לפעמים הצדיק איש פשוט לגמרי, שקורין פראסטיק וכו׳ ע״ש, יש בזה הרבה לספר. איך ובאיזה ענין נאמרה זאת התורה. אך א״א לצייר בכתב כל מה שעבר בענין זה אך אעפ״י כן ארשום מה שאפשר: דע כי זאת התורה נאמרה בשבת נחמו באומאן סמוך להסתלקותו. ומעשה שהי׳ כך הי׳. באותה העת בסמוך נכנס לדירה אחרת שנסתלק שם. ואותה דירה היתה טובה לפניו מאד לישב בה. כי הי׳ לו שם רחבת ידים ואויר יפה, כי הי׳ שם גן לפני החלונות. אך הדירה היתה של וכו׳.*[63] וסמוך לשבת נחמו נכנס לשם. ועל אותו השבת נתקבצו כמה אנשים חדשים וגם ישנים שבאו אליו על שבת ק׳, והי׳ קיבוץ גדול. ובליל שבת ק׳ נכנס מחדרו לבית שהי׳ העולם מקובצים שם. והי׳ חלוש מאד מאד, כמעט לא הי׳ לו כח לדבר ותיכף קדש על הכוס. ואחר הקידוש ישב אצל השולחן ולא חזר לחדרו תיכף, כדרכו תמיד בעת הקיבוץ. וישב בחלישות גדול, והתחיל לשיח ולדבר מעט בחלישות ובעייפות גדול. ענה ואמר. מה אתם נוסעים אלי. הלא אני איני יודע כלל. כשאני אומר תורה יש לכם על מה לנסוע ולבוא אלי, אבל עתה על מה באתם. הלא אני איני יודע עתה כלל. כי אני עתה רק פראסטיק לגמרי. והאריך בשיחה זאת, וכפל ושלש כמה פעמים שאינו יודע כלל ושהוא רק איש פשוט לגמרי ושהוא פראסטיק. ואז אמר שהוא מחייה א״ע עתה רק במה שהי׳ בארץ ישראל. והאריך בשיחה זאת, שבאמת לאמיתו אינו יודע כלל כלל לא, ושהוא רק פראסטיק לגמרי, רק שהוא מחייה א״ע במה שהי׳ בא״י. ומתוך שיחה זאת התחיל לדבר ולבאר כל ענין הנורא ההוא, איך מחיה א״ע בעת הפשיטות מהדרך של א״י, ושבזה מחיין את כל הפשוטים שבעולם (שקורין פראסטקים), הן לומדים בעלי תורה שבטלים מן התורה, הן אנשים פשוטים שהם פראסטקים גמורים, אפילו או״ה צריכים לקבל חיות וכו׳ וכו׳, כמבואר כל זה בסי׳ הנ״ל ע״ש היטב... וגמר כל ענין התורה הזאת. ואח״כ בא בשמחה גדולה וצוה לזמר אזמר בשבחין תיכף קודם נט״י (נטילת ידים) לסעודה (מה שדרכו הי׳ תמיד לזמר אחרי ברכת המוציא) וגם בעיתים הללו שהי׳ חלוש מאד ע״פ רוב לא היו מזמרים כלל. אך עכשיו מגודל השמחה צוה לזמר תיכף, וגם הוא בעצמו הי׳ מזמר עמנו יחד. ואח״כ הי׳ מדבר ומשיח עמנו הרבה בשמחה גדולה ובחן אמיתי נפלא ונורא מאד מאד... והתפאר בעצמו שהוא עתה בשמחה גדולה, ואמר שהוא ביראה ובשמחה.... ואז ראינו ישועת ה׳ ונפלאותיו ונוראותיו העצומים, שהוא חומל על עמו ישראל בכל עת, שמתוך העלמה והסתירה כזאת נתהפך לרצון כזה שבתחילה לא היה יודע כלל באמת. ומתוך אינו יודע כזה בא לידי התגלות כזה. ואם באמת אין אנו יודעין כלל בענינו הק׳, בפרט בענין האינו יודע שלו, שהוא ענין עמוק עמוק ונסתר מאד. ואמר בעצמו שהאינו יודע שלו הוא חידוש יותר מידיעה שלו, כמבואר במ״א. אך אעפ״כ במה שמתנוצץ בדעתינו ראינו אז נפלאות ונוראות אשר א״א לבאר ולספר...״[64]

ככל הנראה לעין, מצב ״איני יודע״ אינו אלא חוית הקיום כ״איש פשוט״ או ״פראסטיק״. זהו מצב של רחוק מן האל, או, כפי שהדברים מנוסחים כאן, מצב שבו

אם כן, דרך קיום מצוות התורה ע״י הפרתן, האפינית למצבי ״פשיטות״, נפתחה בפני ר׳ נחמן לראשונה (ובפני ר׳ נחמן בלבד — ברור שאין כאן הכשרת בטול המצוות כפשוטן לגבי איש מלבדו) דוקא בשעת מסעו לא״י, המסע שעמד, מראשיתו ועד סופו, בסימן קטנות דקטנות.

הקשר שבין תורת ה״פשיטות״ של ר׳ נחמן, שנאמרה בשנת תק״ע, כלומר, קשר בין חוית קיום מצוות התורה בשעת פשיטות אפילו או דוקא בדרך ביטולן, כפי שנתקיימו קודם מתן־תורה, לבין חויות ה״קטנות״ הממשיות והמשוערות שלו בנסיעתו לא״י בתקנ״ח–תקנ״ט, מסתבר לא רק משני הקטעים בספורי פרשת הנסיעה, שהובאו לעיל, אלא הוא נרמז אף בתורה ע״ח עצמה. אין כל ספק, שנסוחה הרעיוני של תורת הפשיטות, כפי שקבעו ר׳ נחמן סמוך למותו, ראשיתו באירועי הנסיעה לא״י, כשתים עשרה שנה קודם לכן, וההשגות הגדולות והחדשות שהשיג על ידם. ר׳ נחמן רומז על כך בדרשו את ״דרך ארץ״, שע״פ המדרש קדמה למתן תורה בכ״ו דורות,[60] ושעל פיה נהגו יושבי העולם דאז בהעלם התורה מהם, כ״דרך לארץ ישראל״, היינו, כבוש א״י ע״י ב״י מידי עמי כנען, שאף הוא לא חל אלא דורות רבים לאחר בריאת העולם, ובכל זאת תוכנן, והיה קיים בכוח, אם לא בפועל, כבר בשעת הבריאה.[61]

״. . . כי אז לא הי׳ שום תורה, והיו עוסקין רק בישוב העולם ובדרך ארץ, כשארז״ל במדרש (רבה צו פ׳ ט׳) גדולה דרך ארץ, שקדמה לתורה כ״ו דורות. . . ובכל הדיבורים של העולם, ובכל העובדות והעשיות, הן מי שחוטב עצים או כל עובדא שיהיה, בכולם נעלם התורה . . . והצדיק בשעה שפורש מן התורה והוא בחי׳ איש פשוט, הוא מקבל חיות מבחינה זו של קודם מתן תורה. וזהו בחי׳ הדרך של ארץ ישראל . . . נמצא שעשרה מאמרות, שהם מלובשין בדרך ארץ, היינו בישוב העולם, כי בהם נברא העולם, הם דרך לארץ ישראל. כי ע״י בחי׳ העשרה מאמרות יכולין לכבוש את ארץ ישראל כנ״ל. וזהו בחי׳ דרך ארץ, היינו שהוא דרך ונתיב לארץ, היינו לארץ ישראל. כי דרך ארץ, שהוא ישוב עולם, שנברא בעשרה מאמרות, זה זה בעצמו הוא נתיב ודרך לארץ ישראל כנ״ל. וזהו דרך ארץ, היינו דרך לארץ ישראל. ובזה הדרך, היינו הדרך של ארץ ישראל, שהוא בחי׳ עשרה מאמרות שבהם נברא העולם, ששם נעלמת התורה, שבזה היה העולם מתקיים בחסדו כ״ו דורות שקודם מתן תורה, בזה בעצמו הצדיק מחייה עצמו בעת פשיטותו, שאינו עוסק בתורה.״[62]

המשואה ״תורה נעלמה״ — ״עשרה מאמרות״ — ״דרך ארץ״ — ״הדרך לארץ ישראל״ הורכבה על דרך הדרש, באורח אסוציאטיבי, ואין כל ספק ש״דרך לארץ ישראל״, המופיעה כאן כדוגמא הסטורית לקיום רצון האל בכוח טרם הוצאתו לפועל, נבחרה לשמש בתפקיד זה דווקא משום שנשאה עמה מטען של אסוציאציות אישיות, שנבעו מנסיעתו של ר׳ נחמן לא״י, בה נתגלה לו לראשונה אורח קיום המצוות בכוח, מתוך הפרתן בפועל.

מעניין לציין, שבזמן מסעו לא״י השיג ר׳ נחמן, לפי דבריו, את **אפשרות** קיום המצוות בדרך הפרתן, אפשרות שהגשמתה היתה תלויה בצרוף נסיבות שמחוץ לתחום שליטתו, ואשר נועדה לשמש לו בשעת דחק בלבד.[63] אבל כשבא לנסח את הדברים בתורת הפשיטות שלו, שתים עשרה שנה לאחר מסעו לא״י, הפכה אפשרות מאיימת זו **לחובה קבועה** המוטלת עליו, ליצור נסיבות שכאלה במו ידיו, ע״י ירידתו הרצונית והמווסתת אל מצבי ״פשיטות״. ואף נוסף לה לירידה זו, שבתקנ״ח–תקנ״ט נראתה לו כהכרח השעה להמשך קיומו שלו בלבד, מימד האחריות כלפי ה״פשוטים״, אשר לצרך העלאתם הוא מקבלה על עצמו.

העולם בעשרה המאמרות, שבהן ברא האל את העולם.[55] אם כן, בעת פשיטותו אין הצדיק מתנסה בעולם שהוא חפשי לחלוטין מן התורה ומעול מצוותיה, אלא בעולם שבו המצוות חבויות, קיימות בכוח, אך לא בפועל:

"...ובאמת גם קודם קבלת התורה, בוודאי גם אז היתה התורה במציאות כי התורה היא נצחיית. אמנם אז קודם מתן תורה הייתה התורה בהעלם ובהסתר. היינו כי כל התורה כלולה בעשרת הדברות. ואז קודם מתן תורה היו העשרת הדברות נעלמין בעשרה מאמרות שבהם נברא העולם. נמצא שהיתה התורה כולה נעלמת ונסתרת בתוך יישוב העולם שנברא בעשרה מאמרות. ובכל הדיבורים של העולם ובכל העובדות והעשיות, הן מי שחוטב עצים או איזה עובדא שיהיה, בכולם נעלם התורה. כי הכל נברא בעשרה מאמרות. אשר שם התורה נעלמה ונסתרה קודם מתן תורה. והצדיק בשעה שפורש מן התורה והוא בחי׳ איש פשוט הוא מקבל חיות מבחינה זו של קודם מתן תורה."[56]

מהי משמעותו למעשה של הקיום בעולם, שבו המצוות נעלמות ואינן נגלות? מהו ההבדל הקונקרטי בין שמירת המצוות כפשוטן לבין שמירת מהותן הנסתרת? נראה שהבדל זה כמוהו כהבדל שבין שמירת המצוות כפשוטן להפרתן כפשוטן. ר׳ נחמן ממחיש את הדברים היטב בהקשר אחר: בשני התאורים המקבילים של נסיעת רבו לא״י מדווח ר׳ נתן, כפי הנראה ע״פ עדותו של ר׳ שמעון, שדווקא בזמן אותה הנסיעה נסתברה לר׳ נחמן לראשונה אפשרות קיום כל המצוות אפילו בדרך הפרתן, כפי שקיימון האבות וכל שאר יושבי העולם בתקופה שקדמה למתן תורה. ר׳ נחמן הגיע לידי הבנת הדבר בזמן הפלגתו חזרה מא״י באנית מלחמה טורקית, בעצומם של הקרבות בין צרפת וטורקיה בשערי א״י.[57] שרוי היה אז בפחד גדול, שמא יתפסוהו החיילים המוסלמים שבספינה וימכרו אותו ואת ר׳ שמעון בן לויתו לעבדות בארץ נכר. בתחילה נראה היה לר׳ נחמן, שאם אכן ייגזר עליו לחיות כעבד בארץ זרה, לא יוכל לקיים את המצוות כלל. אך לאחר זמן מה הבין, שאפילו אם יאלץ להפר את כל המצוות כולן, יוכל לצאת ידי חובת קיומן בדרך קיום המצוות לפני מתן תורה. והרי דרך זו היא דרך השאיבה מ"אוצר מתנת חינם" של חסד האל, עליה דבר שנים רבות לאחר מכן, בתורת הפשיטות ע״ח שהובאה לעיל. ר׳ נתן כותב:

"וגודל עוצם הסכנות שהי׳ להם בחזירתם א״א לספר. כי היו על הספינה זו של מלחמה שהיתה מלאה ישמעאלים. והם היו רק שני יהודים לבד. ודרך הישמעאלים, בפרט אנשי מלחמה, לתפוס יהודים ולמכרם במרחקים לעבדים. והי׳ לרבינו ז״ל פחד גדול מזה. ואמר שהתחיל לחשוב בעצמו מה יעשה אם יוליכו אותו לאיזה מקום על הים שאין שם יהודי וימכרו אותו שם, ומי ידע מזה. והי׳ לו צער גדול איך יוכל לקים שם את מצות התורה. והתחיל לחשוב בדעתו מענין זה, עד שזכה ובא על השגה, שיוכל לעבוד את הש״י אפילו כשלא יוכל ח״ו לקיים המצות. כי השיג את העבודה של אבות העולם שהי׳ להם קודם מתן תורה, שקיימו כל המצוות אע״פ שלא עשו אז המצוות כפשוטן. כמו יעקוב אבינו שקיים מצוות תפילין ע״י המקלות אשר פצל כידוע, וכיוצא בזה. עד שהשיג איך לקיים את כל המצוות בדרך זה כשיהי׳ אנוס שם במקום שימכרו אותו ח״ו."[58]

ובתאור הנסיעה המקביל והמאוחר יותר, ב"חיי מוהר״ן", שוב כותב ר׳ נתן:

"כשבא מא״י אמר, בדרך הזה קיימתי כל התורה בכל האופנים. כי השגתי קיום כל התורה, שאפילו אם היו מוכרים אותי לישמעאל במדינות רחוקות שאין שם שום יהודי, והוא ישלח אותי לרעות בהמות, ואפילו אם לא אדע מתי שבת ויו״ט, ולא יהי׳ לי טו״ת ולא סוכה ולא שום מצוה וכו׳ וכו׳ אעפ״כ הייתי יכול לקיים כל התורה כולה. וכבר מבואר מזה במ״א."[59]

פשיטותו הצדיק מנוכר מחוקי התורה. דוקא את מובנה זה של המלה מדגיש ר׳ נחמן בקבעו, שבמצב פשיטות, מצב ״פרישות״ או ״הבדלות״ מן התורה, הצדיק מקיים את עצמו בדרך, שבה נתקיים העולם קודם למתן תורה, בתקופה שקדמה להגבלת סדרי העולם ע״י אסורים והתרים, מצוות התורה וחוקיה, ע״י מידת הדין של הקב״ה, ואשר בה נתקיים העולם בכוח חסדו בלבד:

״כי דע כי כל הפשוטים הנ״ל, הן למדן שהוא עוסק בתורה לשם שמים . . . כשמבטל מלימודו, שאז הוא בחי׳ איש פשוט ממש כנ״ל, הן שאר הפשוטים, כ״א וא׳ כפי אחיזתו בהתורה כן הוא מחיה עצמו בעת פשיטותו מבחי׳ קיום העולם קודם קבלת התורה. כי קודם קבלת התורה הי׳ העולם מתקיים רק בחסדו. כי לא היה עדיין תורה ושום עשיה של מצווה שעל ידו יתקיים העולם. והיה עיקר קיום העולם ע״י חסדו לבד. והצדיק בעת פשיטותו, בשעה שבודל מן התורה, הוא מקבל חיות מבחינה זו.״[50]

אם הבדלות מן התורה מובנה הבדלות מן החוקים והמצוות משמע, שבשעת פשיטותו, כשהוא מובדל מן התורה, הצדיק מתנסה בחויית הקיום בעולם שהוא חפשי מעול המצוות. מן הסתם, אין הוא מודע את קיומן, אין הוא חייב בהן כפשוטן, אין הוא מתקיים על פיהן, אלא הוא שואב את כוח חיותו ממדת החסד של האל, אשר בתחומה אין אפשרות הרע, בצועו וענשו, קיימת כלל, וכל מעשה הוא בבחינת טוב. למדת חסד זו, שהיא מקור חיותו הבלעדי של הצדיק בשעת פשיטותו, קורא ר׳ נחמן ״אוצר מתנת חינם״, אשר ממנו יונקים את חיותם אותם רשעים גמורים שאינם, למעשה, זכאים לה כלל, ובכל זאת הם שואבים מאוצר זה ומתקיימים בחסדו של האל בחינם:

״. . . וזה [כלומר, קיום העולם ב״חסד״ בלבד] . . . בחינת אוצר מתנת חינם . . . כי יש אוצר של מתנת חינם, שמי שאין לו שום זכות כלל מקבל משם . . .״[51]

לכאורה, ממשיך ר׳ נחמן, ״אוצר מתנת חינם״ מיועד לרשעים גמורים, שלא קיימו אפילו מצוה אחת. הצדיק, שהוא כאחד מהם בשעת פשיטותו (שהרי קיומו באותה שעה משולל תוקף המצוות) מתחלק עמם במתנת חינם זו.[52] אך למעשה, לא כן הדבר. הצדיק הוא איש, שמידותיו לאמיתן מושלמות. רק בתקופות ירידתו לפשיטות הוא הופך לרשע, שמידותיו מושחתות. לו היה הרשע מקבל ״מתנת חינם״ כצדיק, היה בכך משום העדפתו על פני הצדיק, שהרי שכרו של הרשע היה זהה עם שכר הצדיק, בעוד שמידותיו של זה, שעל פיהן נקבע שכרו, פחותות לאין ערוך ממידותיו של זה. לכן, מסכם ר׳ נחמן, אין ״אוצר מתנת חינם״ עומד לרשותם של רשעים ממש, אלא אך ורק לרשותם של אותם הרשעים, שהם למעשה צדיקים השרויים במצב של פשיטות:

״. . . ובוודאי אין זה האוצר מוכן בשביל רשעים. כי א״כ הרשע הוא גדול מן הצדיק. כי הרשע בוודאי אין לו שום זכות כלל, וכי יזכה בשביל זה לקבל מהאוצר מתנת חינם. אך באמת הרשע בוודאי אינו מקבל משם. רק זה האוצר מתנת חינם הוא בשביל הצדיק לבד. היינו, בשעה שהצדיק הוא איש פשוט כנ״ל, אז הוא מקבל מזה האוצר מתנת חינם.״[53]

ר׳ נחמן ממהר להגביל את דבריו, על חויית הפשיטות של הצדיק בעולם טרום־תורתי, בהצביעו על כך, שהתורה ומצוותיה קדמו לבריאת העולם והתקיימו בו בכוח ובנסתר עד זמן התגלותן בפועל, במתן־התורה לבני ישראל.[54] שהרי התורה כולה כלולה בעשרת הדברות, ועשרת הדברות טמונות היו בזמן בריאת

"הנהגת פשיטות" של "הצדיק האמת"[46] בפתיחת התורה נכר, שפשיטותו של ר' נחמן כללה את כל יסודותיה של "קטנות". פשיטות היא מצב של נפילה מדביקות, שבו הצדיק הוא איש פשוט לכל דבר:

"בענין הנהגת פשיטות של הצדיק האמת. היינו כי לפעמים הצדיק האמת הוא איש פשוט ממש (שקורין פראסטיק), שמתנהג עצמו בדרכי הפשיטות ואינו מגלה שום תורה, ועוסק בשיחת חולין וכיוצא. והוא אז בחינת איש פשוט ממש."[47]

ממש כבמאמריהם של קודמיו בחסידות על ענין "קטנות", מבחין ר' נחמן בשני פנים לצורך הצדיק בפשיטות: (א) אין הצדיק עצמו יכול להתקיים בדבקות מתמדת. (ב) אנשים פשוטים, שאינם מסוגלים לדביקות ישירה עם האל, מקבלים את כוח חיותם, הנאצל עליהם ממנו, אך ורק דרך הצדיק, ע"י הפכו זמנית לאחד מהם:

"דע כי עיקר החיים היא התורה... וכל הפורש מן התורה כפורש מן החיים... וע"כ לכאורה הדבר תמוה ונפלא. איך אפשר לפרוש עצמו מן התורה אפי' שעה קלה. ובאמת זהו מן הנמנע ובלתי אפשר להיות דבוק בהתורה תמיד יומם ולילה בלי הפסק רגע. וכל בעל תורה, הן למדן שעוסק בלימוד התורה בגמפ"ת וכיוצא, כ"א כפי ערכו, כפי עסק למודו, בהכרח שיבטל מהתורה איזה שעה ביום. וכן אפי' בעל השגה ואפי' מי שהוא גבוה יותר ויותר למעלה למעלה, אעפ"כ בהכרח שיפסיק ויבטל מהשגתו איזה זמן, כי א"א להיות דבוק תמיד בתורה והשגה בלי הפסק. כי צריכין בהכרח להפסיק איזה שעה, אם לעשות איזה מו"מ או כיוצא בזה. כי צריכין לעסוק בצרכי הגוף ג"כ... כי דע כי כל אלה הפשוטים, דהיינו זה הלמדן בשעה שבטל מן התורה שאז הוא איש פשוט כנ"ל, וכן יש איש פשוט ממש, שאינו למדן כלל ואעפ"כ הוא איש כשר וירא שמים ובוודאי מקבל חיות מן התורה, וכן אפילו הנמוכים למטה יותר, ואפילו או"ה גם הם מקבלים בודאי ג"כ חיות מן התורה. וכל אלה הפשוטים צריכין שיהיה עליהם איש פשוט גדול, שכולם יקבלו על ידו חיות. כי כל הפשוטים הנ"ל כולם צריכין לקבל איזה חיות מהתורה שהיא עיקר החיים. ובאמת הם רחוקים מהתורה, כי הם אנשים פשוטים (שקורין פראסטאקים) ע"כ צריכין שיהי' עליהם איש פשוט גדול שעל ידו הם מקבלים חיות מן התורה."[48]

מעניין לציין שבהיותו שרוי במצב קטנות, בשעת נסיעתו לא"י, התיחס ר' נחמן לנסיונו כלהתרחקות **מן האל** ("... מחמת מוחין דקטנות אני מרוחק מהשי"ת...") אך כאן, בעסקו בפשיטות, שהיא מעיקרה, כפי שראינו, נסיון זהה, בחר לתארה כהתרחקות או פרישה **מן התורה** ("לפרוש עצמו מן התורה"). למעשה, תורה ע"ח כולה עוסקת בדבקות מכאן ובפרישות מכאן ביחס לתורת משה ולא אל האל. יתכן שהסבה המיידית לכך היא, שבתורה ע"ח ר' נחמן מסביר את הכרחיות נפילתו הזמנית של הצדיק — המיסטיקן — מדבקותו עם האל לידי פשיטות, בדרך המשלתה להפסקה הזמנית, ההכרחית לא פחות, בריכוזו האינטלקטואלי של הלמדן, העוסק בלמוד תורה בשטה המסורתית. מכל מקום, העברת מרכז הכובד בתורה זו מן האל אל תורתו, ככל הנראה אינה משקפת הבדל מהותי בין מושגי קטנות ופשיטות של ר' נחמן. שהרי אין הפרישה מן התורה אלא הבט מסוים של הפרישה מן האל.[49] קרוב לודאי שר' נחמן התכוון לכל שכבות מובניה של המלה "תורה" בתארו כאן את מצב "פשיטות" כפרישה דוקא ממנה. אך מעל לכל, הגדרת פשיטות כמצב של פרישה מן התורה פתחה לו פתח להטעמת המימד החדש, שבו נבדלה פשיטותו מ"קטנות": מובנה הראשוני של "תורה" בתורה ע"ח שב"לקוטי מוהר"ן" ח"ב הרי הוא מערכת החוקים והמצוות שנצטוו בהם ישראל. בשעת

זאת יש לזכור, שתאורי מעשיו של ר׳ נחמן בשעות קטנותו מקוטעים במכוון. אם נביא בחשבון את העובדה, שלמרות ה״טיהור״ הפנימי היסודי של כתבי ברסלב מכל זכר לענין, נראה שר׳ נחמן ותלמידיו האשמו בשבתאות ובפרנקיזם ע״י אויביהם במחנה החסידי,[34] יש מקום לשאול, מדוע האשמו בכך, והאם יש ממש בהאשמות?[35] האם נבעו מהבנת הנימות האנטינומיות־משיחיות המהדהדות מתוך כמה מתורותיו של ר׳ נחמן ומאמריו,[36] או שמא נמצא פסול בהנהגתו האישית, שניתן היה לדמותו לכפירה הפרנקיסטית או לשייכו לה?[37] למותר לציין, שר׳ נחמן לא היה פרנקיסט, וודאי שחסידיו היו יהודים כשרים מן השורה. אך, כפי שהראה וייס, רגישותו של ר׳ נחמן לבעיית הכפירה של דורו היתה חדה, אולי יותר מזו של כל דמות אחרת בתנועה החסידית.[38] חטא יעקב פרנק העסיק אותו, והוא ראה צורך לעצמו לפעול לתיקונו.[39] כיצד? דווקא ההבחנה החמורה בין מהות הצדיק (ר׳ נחמן), אורח הנהגתו ותפקידו, לבין מהותם של ״הפשוטים״, התלויים בו, המוטעמת הטעמת יתר בתורת ברסלב, עשויה היתה לפתוח פתח בפני ר׳ נחמן ל״ירידות״ מופלגות ומסוכנות ביותר, בשעה שחסידיו הורחקו מהן בתכלית הריחוק, וברוב המקרים לא ידעו כלל את תכנן. מחוסר כל עדויות ישירות על כך במקורות, אין לפי שעה כל אפשרות להשיב על שאלות אלה בתוך תחומי החקירה ההסטורית.

המונח ״קטנות״ כמעט שאינו מופיע בכתבי ברסלב מחוץ לשני תאוריו של ר׳ נתן את מסע רבו לא״י. בהתיחסו בתורותיו למצב, שנראה שהוא קשור קשר הדוק עם מצב קטנות, משתמש ר׳ נחמן בבטויים ״פשיטות״, ״הנהגת פשיטות״ או ״בחינת פרוסטיק״. גם ספר התורות ״לקוטי מוהר״ן״ וגם ספורי הנסיעה לא״י יצאו מתחת קולמוסו של ר׳ נתן הסופר — האחד על יסוד הכתבות ישירות מפי ר׳ נחמן ובפקוחו,[40] והאחרים בהסתמך בעיקר על עדות הראיה של ר׳ שמעון, בן לויתו של ר׳ נחמן בנסיעה לא״י.[41] אעפ״כ, ההבחנה בין המונחים ״קטנות״ ו״פשיטות״ בשני גופי המקורות הללו היא עקבית. רק פעם אחת, בתאור הארוך יותר של המסע לא״י ב״שבחי הר״ן״ נזקק ר׳ נתן למושג ״פשיטות״ לשם הגדרת מצב ״קטנות״ של רבו. וכך הוא מגשר בין המושגים:

״כי זה ידוע, שקודם שיוצאים מדרגא לדרגא צריך שיהיה ירידה קודם העליה, ואז צריכים לעניני קטנות, להיות איש פשוט לגמרי. . .״[42]

נראה שההבחנה בין ״קטנות״ ל״פשיטות״ בלשונו של ר׳ נחמן, כפי שהגיעה אלינו מיד ר׳ נתן, היתה בשעתה הבחנה כרונולוגית ולא קונספטואלית. במונח ״קטנות״ השתמש במשך הנסיעה לא״י ומיד לאחריה, בתקס״ח–תקס״ט. באותה תקופה עמד ר׳ נחמן הצעיר בראשית דרכו כצדיק, ונראה שעדיין לא השתחרר מן הטרמינולוגיה החסידית הקלאסית. בתקופה מאוחרת יותר טבע את המונח ״פשיטות״, ובו השתמש בעקביות, אולי כדי להבדיל את פשיטותו מקטנות קודמיו. ר׳ נתן הסופר היה מודע את הצורך להנציח את דברי רבו במדת הדיוק האפשרית ואף התגאה ביכולתו לעשות זאת.[43] וכך, על אף שבשעת כתיבתו את ספורי הנסיעה לא״י שנים רבות לאחר התרחשותם,[44] כבר הכיר ר׳ נתן את המונח ״פשיטות״ ואת קרבתו ל״קטנות״, נזהר שלא להקדים את המאוחר ומסר דברים כפי ששמעם, בקראו לקטנותו דאז של ר׳ נחמן בשמה.

המקור העקרי לתורת הפשיטות של ר׳ נחמן הוא תורה ע״ח ב״לקוטי מוהר״ן״ ח״ב. זוהי תורה מאוחרת, אותה ״אמר״ ר׳ נחמן באומאן בתק״ע, חדשים ספורים לפני מותו.[45] על אף שהמונח ״קטנות״ אינו מופיע בה אפילו פעם אחת, מהגדרת

"בחזירתם מא"י בנסיעתם מנהר דניעסטער והוכרחו לשנות מלבושיהן ונדמו כדרך הסוחרים בני הנעורים הנהוגים עכשיו וכו׳, ומחמת זה טעו בהם כמה אנשים וסברו בהם שהם מהקלי עולם וכו׳[27] ובבואו לאומין הי׳ להם נסיון וכו׳. ואז בנסיעתם משם בזריזות מיד לימד זכות על העולם ואמר, תדעו שכל דרכינו הוא לידע שיש נסיונות בעולם. ובקל יכולים ליכשל ח"ו. ואמר אוי ואבוי וכו׳. והתאנח ע"ז מאד. כי באותו הבית שעמד שם הבע"ג הבינו וראו שיש שם זנות וניאוף גדול ר"ל וכו׳. אבל אמר שבעזה"י יהי טובה מה שהי׳ שם, שמעתה לא ימצא שם זנות עוד בבית הזה. ואז נתקררה דעתו. גם בטעפליק לא ידעו ממנו. ונכנס אצל מלמד אחד, ושיחר פנים לקבלו על שבת, ולא רצה המלמד, מחמת שנדמה לו כאילו הוא ח"ו מהגנבים. ובא אל האיש שהי׳ עמו וסיפר לו וכו׳."[28]

נסיעת ר׳ נחמן לא"י כולה, מרגע צאתו עד שובו לביתו, עמדה בסימן "קטנות" או "קטנות דקטנות". אמנם ברור, שהיו גם בה תקופות, בהן לא חפפה התנהגותו את "הנהגת קטנותו" המובהקת.[29] אבל אין כל ספק, שבנסיעה חזרה, המתוארת בקטע המצוטט לעיל, היה ר׳ נחמן שרוי במצב של קטנות קיצונית, כפי שהגדירה ר׳ נתן במקומות אחרים. שהרי שוב נסע בעלום שם, לבוש בגדים לא־יהודיים, ואף נחשב ע"י מלמד בעיר טעפליק לגנב; ומדוע יחשדהו הלה בכך אלא אם כן העידו עליו חזותו, ובעיקר אורח התנהגותו, שאכן "הוא ח"ו מהגנבים".

לא ברור מה עשה ר׳ נחמן בטעפליק, או באותו בית באומאן, שבו מצא "זנות וניאוף גדול", ממש כפי שאין אנו יודעים מה עשה בשעת ביקורו בקאמיניץ. אך תוצאת שהותו שם נהירה לפחות לו: "מעתה לא ימצא שם זנות עוד בבית הזה". אין לפרש את פעולת ר׳ נחמן במקרה זה אלא כירידה מופלגת, במצב של "קטנות דקטנות", לתחומו של החטא על מנת לתקנו, כפי שעשה במקרים אחרים, אגב סכון עצמו ועצם הצלחת המבצע כולו. החל מראשית נסוחיו בספרות החסידית קשור מושג הקטנות קשר הדוק עם תורת הירידה של הצדיק. רק בהיותו שרוי בקטנות מסוגל הצדיק ל"ירידתו" או "נפילתו" אל מישור קיומם של "ההמוניים", שהוא המישור בו מתאפשרת מציאותו של החטא. שהרי בעת גדלותו, כשהוא מגשים את דבקותו עם האל, חודר הצדיק אל התחום שבו כלה הניגוד בין טוב לרע והחטא חדל מלהיות. אך כתגובה לתורת הירידה הרדיקאלית של השבתאות, שתבעה מן המשיח (ובכמה חוגים שבתאיים קיצוניים, אף מכל מאמיניו) בצוע כל חטא שאל תוכו "ירד" על מנת לתקנו, הקהתה החסידות את חודו של הרעיון בהגדירה את מהות ירידת הצדיק כתרגיל מחשבתי בלבד: אין הצדיק מתנסה בעבירה אלא בהרהור של עבירה.[30] אמנם הדברים אינם חד־משמעיים, ובנסוחי תורת הירידה מודגש, מצד אחד, הצורך לחטא ממש ולא להסתפק במראית עין, ומצד שני נאסר זימונו המכוון של החטא, מחמת החשש פן תחסם אפשרות העליה ממנו. אך לפחות מחלקם של המאמרים העוסקים בכך משתמע, שעל הצדיק לבצע עבירה בפועל, ותהא זו קלה ככל שתהיה, על מנת לאפשר את "ירידתו" ואת הזדהות תודעתו עם תודעת הרשע בשלמות.[31] מהותה של העבירה מוגדרת לפעמים כמעשה, שהצדיק לוקה בו בשוגג או בכורח נסיבות שמחוץ לתחום שלטונו, ולעתים אין היא אלא תודעת אשמה פיקטיבית, וכל חטאו אינו אלא "כביכול".[32] אין בכתבי ברסלב כל ראיה לכך, שבמצבי קטנות עבר ר׳ נחמן עבירות על מנת לתקן את הטומאה, החטא והכפירה עמן בה במגע, אם כי ברור שהתמודד עמן ישירות. אפילו ראיתו את עצמו כחייב ענשים שונים וחמורים על פעולות התיקון הנועזות שלו, אין בה בהכרח משום רמז לכך שסטה כמלוא הנימה משטת התיקון החסידית הממותנת. שהרי על פי דרכו, הנהגת הצדיק שונה במהותה מהנהגתם של אנשים פשוטים: במה שהוא לאו חמור לגביהם עשוי הוא להיות מצווה,[33] ומן הסתם, להפך: מה שנחשב להם כהנהגה טבעית ונסבלת נחשב לו כסטיה חמורה מנורמה צדיקית עליונה. יחד עם

"הספר הנשרף אנו מכנים בשם ספר הב׳. כי כל אלו הספרים שנדפסו הם בחינת ספר הראשון, כי כולם הם בחינת נגלה שלו... והספר שצווה לשרוף כשהיה בלעמברג זה הוא ספר הב׳ והוא בחינת רזין שלו. וזה ספר הב׳ העתקתי לפניו בשנת תקס״ו. והעתק שלי נתן בידי ב׳ אנשים[22] להוליך בעיירות ולומר בכל עיר מעט מהספר הזה כנ״ל. והשביע אותם אז שלא יגלו הדבר לשום אדם... אח״כ באתי לפניו בתחילת קיץ תקס״ו. והזהיר אותי להתפלל על הולד היקר שלמה אפריים ז״ל, כי היה לו חולי ההוסט אז. והזהיר אותי מאד להרבות בתפילה עבורו ואמר, ידעתי כשמסרתי זה הספר לידי האנשים הנ״ל שיקחו עצמם ויתגברו על התינוק הזה (היינו המקטרגים) וגם האיש שמסרתי הספר הנ״ל לידו (היינו אחד מב׳ האנשים הנ״ל) הזהרתיו מאד בעת שמסרתי לידו הספר למע״ה שיהיה נזהר להתפלל ולהעתיר על התינוק הנ״ל, ובעו״ה התגבר הקטרוג עד שנסתלק באותו הקיץ התינוק הנ״ל".[23]

ובעוד שבקטע זה מבואר מות התינוק שלמה אפרים באורח סתמי, כתוצאה של "התגברות המקטרגים" בגלל פרסום "הספר הנשרף", באחת מ"שיחות הר״ן" מופיע הסבר אחר המורה בפרוש כיצד ראה ר׳ נחמן במות זה את ענשו:

"פ״א היה נכדו ז״ל מוטל על ערש מחולי הפאקין ר״ל. והיה קובל לפני מאד שיש לו צער גדול מזה. וספר לי אז ואמר שיש דרכי ה׳ שא״א להבינם כי איתא שאצל האר״י ז״ל נסתלק בן אחד. ואמר שנסתלק בשביל הסוד שגילה לתלמידו ר׳ חיים ויטאל ז״ל. והלא באמת האר״י היה מוכרח לגלות לו, כי אמר שלא בא לעולם כי אם לתקן נשמתו של רח״ו ז״ל. נמצא שהי׳ מוכרח מן השמים לגלות לו הסוד. ואעפ״כ נענש ע״ז כנ״ל.[24] וזה דרכי ה׳ שאי אפשר להבין בשכל בשום אופן. והמובן מדבריו לענין עצמו, שכל צערו ויסוריו וצער בניו שי׳ הכל הוא רק מחמת שעוסק עמנו לקרבנו להשי״ת. ואע״פ שהוא מוכרח לזה, כי בודאי הש״י רוצה בזה... ואעפ״י כן הי׳ לו יסורים קשים וגדולים מאד ע״ז, כי הוא דרכי ה׳ כנ״ל... שוב שמעתי מאיש אחד מאנשים שנשמע ג״כ מרבינו ז״ל ענין זה בעת שנסתלק אצלו בנו הקטן שלמה אפריים ז״ל, שאמר שיש לו יסורים בשבילנו. הלא האר״י ז״ל לא גילה כ״א סוד אחד היה לו עונש. מכ״ש שאני גיליתי לכם כ״כ סודות רבות כאלה".[25]

מלבד הסבל והצער האישי שגרם לו מות בנו היחיד, נענש ר׳ נחמן בכשלון תכניתו להשלמת מלאכת התיקון העולמית ולהבאת הגאולה. דוקא גילוי אותם סודות, שבו הוכרח לשם הגשמת תכנית הגאולה, הוא הוא שהכשילה. עקב מות שלמה אפריים נדחתה הגאולה, שבכוח עצמו להביאה במהרה ובימיו האמין עד יום מותו של הבן בתקס״ו, ועתה לא תחול אלא בעתיד הרחוק ובמועד בלתי ידוע.[26]

אם כן, ר׳ נחמן ראה עצמו חייב עונש על מעשים שונים, שהוכרח לבצעם ונאסרו עליו בעת ובעונה אחת, בלחץ שני מרכזי הכובד המנוגדים של צדיקותו. מות בתו, מות בנו ואפילו מות אשתו, בכולם שלם על "חטאיו". אך נראה, שעל מעשה חמור אחר נגזר עליו לשלם במותו הוא עצמו באסטנבול. רק הבזיונות שנתנסה בהם ברדתו ל"קטנות דקטנות"[26*] הצילוהו מענשו זה, והמות נתחלף לו בבושה.

ר׳ נתן אינו מפרש את טיבו של המעשה, שבגללו נחשב ר׳ נחמן כחייב מיתה. לא ברור אף אם הכוונה היא למאורע אחד, לפעילות ממושכת בזמן מסוים או לתודעת חטא ואשמה בלבד, ללא קשר לבצוע מעשה כל שהוא.

אך בשני ספורי הנסיעה לא״י מופיעים כמה רמזים מעורפלים ומקוטעים על מהות "נסיונותיו" של ר׳ נחמן במשך המסע, שחוית "קטנות" היתה מאותותיו הבולטים ביותר. לא מן הנמנע הוא, שיש לשבץ "נסיונות" אלה בקונטקסט של תפיסת ר׳ נחמן את עצמו כבר עונש מות, שנצל רק בזכות "בושה" ו"בזיונות". ר׳ נתן מספר:

בשביל זה ג״כ לא ניחא קמיה, כי גם ענוש צדיק לא טוב. ע״כ הוא ית׳ מסיבות מתהפך ומעמיד על הצדיק איש כזה שהוא חייב מיתה ועונש מכבר, ומזמנם שניהם לפונדק אחד, וזה מבזה את הצדיק, והצדיק נפטר בזה מן דינו כנ״ל. וזה האיש נענש אח״כ ונתקדש ש״ש שבשביל כבוד הצדיק נענש. ובאמת גברא קטילא קטיל, כי כבר הוא חייב עונשו מקודם; ודרכי ה׳ ישרים ולא עולתה בו.״[12]

התשובה לשאלתו של ר׳ שמעון ברורה ואינה חשובה לענייננו כאן. אך בדרך אגב אנו למדים ממנה פרט חשוב: ממש כאותו בן־שררות שבמשל, שעבר עבירה חמורה נגד המלך אוהבו, אשר בגללה נגזר עליו למות בהתאם לחוקי המדינה, כן ראה ר׳ נחמן את עצמו כעובר עבירה חמורה נגד מלכו־אלוהיו, שענשה מות ע״פ חוקי התורה. רק הבושה הנוראה בה נתנסה, כחביב־המלך שבמשל, בשל בזיונותיו וקטנותו, היא שהצילה אותו מן העונש הראוי לו, שכן כוחה של בושה יפה ככוח מיתה לכפר על עוונות שענשם מות.[13]

מה היה חטאו החמור של ר׳ נחמן, שבעטיו נגזר עליו למות באסטנבול? ר׳ נתן אינו נוגע בשאלה זו, ואין לדעת אם ידע את התשובה לה. אך מתוך הגיונה הפנימי של תפיסת ר׳ נחמן את צדיקותו ברור, שכל ״חטאיו״ של ר׳ נחמן, שעליהם, כפי הבנתו, נענש כמה פעמים בחייו, קודם נסיעתו לא״י ולאחריה, היו למעשה ״ירידות״ — מעשים שהוכרח לבצעם בתוקף חוקיותה הפרדוכסאלית של צדיקותו עצמה: הדרך היחידה שבה יכול היה למלא את תפקידו כצדיק בשלמותו היתה הדרך, שדווקא בה אסור היה לו לנקוט. הוא הקריב את עצמו למען חסידיו בבצעו לשמם מעשים שנאסרו עליו, ושעל בצועם ההכרחי נענש קשות. כך, למשל, נענש על נסיעתו המסתורית לקאמיניץ־פודולסק סמוך לצאתו לא״י בתקנ״ח. ר׳ נחמן נסע לקאמינץ בלווית אחד מחסידיו.[14] באותה עת אסור היה על היהודים ללון בין חומות העיר.[15] לעת ערב שלח ר׳ נחמן את בן לויתו אל מחוץ לעיר, והוא עצמו ״. . . לן שם לבדו בתוך העיר, ואין שום בריה יודעת מה עשה שם.״[16] אין אנו למדים ישירות מה היתה מטרת בקורו של ר׳ נחמן בעיר, שלא זו בלבד שהיתה אסורה אז על היהודים, אלא אף נודעה כקן פרנקיסטי מובהק.[17] מכל מקום, זמן קצר לאחר מכן נפתחו שערי קאמינץ בפני היהודים, וחסידי ר׳ נחמן ראו בכך תוצאה ישירה של בקורו שם.[18] אך ר׳ נחמן לא נשכר על פעילותו בקאמיניץ. אדרבא, את מות בתו מיד אחרי שובו לביתו פרש הוא כתוצאת בקורו בעיר:

״כשבא מקאמיניץ נפטרה אצלו ילדה אחת ע״ה. ענה ואמר, כהנה וכהנה ח״ו ימות אצלי בשביל תנועה אחת. שיש חילוק ביני בין קודם היותי בקאמיניץ בין לאחר היותי שם.״[19]

בדומה לזה נענש ר׳ נחמן ענש חמור ביותר, שהשלכותיו היו עצומות ומרחיקות לכת, על נסיונו להעלות על הכתב וכך לגלות לתלמידיו את סודות ״הספר הנשרף״ שלו:[20]

״בלעמברג, בין פורים לפסח בשנת תקס״ח הלך לחדר מיוחד ובכה הרבה מאד שם. וקרא לר׳ שמעון . . . וספר לו אז מעניין אשר יש לו ספר בביתו שאבד את אשתו ובניו בשביל זה. ומסר נפשו על זה. ועכשיו אינו יודע מה לעשות. והענין היה כי ראה רבינו מסופק ולא ידע לתת עצה בנפשו מה לעשות. כי היה לו צר מאד לשרוף זה הספר הק׳ והנורא מאד אשר מסר נפשו ע״ז וכו׳. ועוצם קדושת ונוראות של זה הספר א״א לדבר מזה כלל. ואם היה נשאר הספר בעולם היינו רואים גדולת רבינו ז״ל עין בעין וכו׳.״[21]

הקשר הסיבתי, שבין הנסיון להפיץ את כתב־יד ״הספר הנשרף״ לבין מות בנו של ר׳ נחמן, מפורש בקטע הבא:

דוקא ע״י ירידתו המופלגת ל״קטנות דקטנות״ במשך הנסיעה. הוא מתנצל ואומר, שכל נסיון לבטא גדלותו זו במלים עלול להפחית מגדלותה ומגדולת השגו של ר׳ נחמן. אך למרות שתיקתו טעונת הרמזים של ר׳ נתן, דומה שנתן להבחין בשני תאורי הנסיעה מפרי עטו בכמה פרטים נוספים העשויים ללמד על טיבה של ירידת ר׳ נחמן למצב ״קטנות דקטנות״.

ר׳ נתן מדוח, שבשעת קטנותו היה ר׳ נחמן משתדל להביא על עצמו השפלה ובזיונות. אכן, באיסטנבול תעתע בשני התיירים היהודים מפודוליה, שקר להם והכעיסם על מנת שישפילוהו.[10]

בתאור הנסיעה הארוך שב״שבחי הר״ן״ ר׳ נתן מספר על ״בזיונות״ אלה בפרוט יתר, וטוען שבלעדיהם לא היה רבו משלים את נסיעתו לא״י אלא היה מת באסטנבול. בענין זה הוא רושם מפי ר׳ שמעון הערה שהעיר ר׳ נחמן בשעתו:

״כלל הדבר כי הוא ז״ל עשה בכוונה והניח עצמו לבזות בכל מיני בזיונות. ואמר להאיש שהי׳ עמו, שאלה הבזיונות יהי׳ לו לטובה גדולה בהליכה ובחזרה. כי גודל עצם המניעות הגדולות שהי׳ לו לבוא לא״י א״א לשער ולהעריך ולספר. ולא הי׳ לו באפשרי לבוא לא״י כ״א ע״י קטנות זאת, כאשר נשמע אח״כ מפיו בפירוש. ואמר שאם לא הי׳ לו אלו הבזיונות והקטנות לא הי׳ לו באפשרי לבוא לשם בשום אופן. ואמר שראה שהוא מוכרח לישאר שם בסטאנבול, דהיינו למות שם. אך זאת הקטנות והבזיונות הצילו אותו. כי קודם שבאין לא״י וכו׳ כנ״ל״[11]

בקטע זה אין ר׳ נתן מסביר מדוע היה על ר׳ נחמן למות באיסטנבול וכיצד נצל ממות ע״י קטנותו ובזיונותיו. אך בסוף תאור הנסיעה לא״י שב״שבחי הר״ן״ הוא חוזר לאותו ענין: בשוב ר׳ נחמן ובן לויתו מא״י נודע להם, שאחד משני היהודים ״מסביבותינו״ בהם פגשו באיסטנבולי האיש שהעליב את ר׳ נחמן וגרם לו ל״בזיונות״ מרובים שם, מת סמוך לבואו לביתו. בהניחו שמות האיש לא היה אלא ענשו על שבזה את ר׳ נחמן באיסטנבול, תמה ר׳ שמעון מדוע נענש, שהרי ״בזיונות״ אלה לא הזיקו לר׳ נחמן אלא אדרבא, הצילוהו ממות וסיעו בידו להשלים את נסיעתו. ר׳ נחמן יישב את תמיהת תלמידו במשל:

״שהיה מלך א׳, ואהב א׳ מבני השררות. וחיבב אותו וקרבו בכל מיני אהבה וחיבוב. ואח״כ כשהגדיל העיז נגד המלך. ואמר המלך, תדע שאע״פ שאני אוהב אותך מאד, אעפ״כ א״א לי לעבור על דת ומשפט המלכות, ומשפטיך חרוץ למיתה. ותיכף ציוה המלך לסוגרו בכבלי ברזל ונתנו בבית הסוהר. והתחיל זה הבן לצייר בדעתו היסורים שלו שיהיו לו מן המיתה. וראה שצערו לא יומשך זמן הרבה כ״א עד שייהרג. אבל כשהתחיל לצייר בדעתו צער המלך ראה שצער המלך יגדל מאד, כי צער המלך יהי׳ תמיד. כי הוא יודע שהמלך אוהב אותו מאד, ויהיה לו געגועים גדולים אחריו וצער גדול מאד לעולם. והיה לו רחמנות על צער של המלך יותר מצערו, וחשב מחשבות איך להציל את המלך מצערו, ונתישב כך. הלא בושה חשובה כמו מיתה. וצוה להשר של התפיסה להכניסו לפני המלך, ואמר אל המלך. האמת ידעתי כי צערך גדול מצערי, אך א״א לך לעבור על חק ודת מלכות. בכל זאת העצה היעוצה, שתסבב תחבולות שיבייש אחד אותי ברבים. והבושה חשובה כמו מיתה. ע״כ תראה להוציא מהשבויים גזלן א׳ שדינו הריגה, ואני אתגרה בו עד שיכעס עלי ויבזה אותי ויכה אותי ברבים, ויגיע לי מזה בושה גדולה, ויהיה נחשב כמו מיתה. ואח״כ יקחו את הגזלן החייב מיתה בלא זה, וימיתוהו כדינו. והעולם יהיו סוברים שבשביל שביזה עבד המלך החביב נהרג, ולא יתחלל כבוד המלכות והעבד שלו. כך לפעמים א׳ מבזה את הצדיק, ובאמת הוא עושה טובה גדולה להצדיק, כי מכפר לו על זה מה שהיה חַיָב להסתלק, ונתחלף לו על בושה. אך אעפ״כ אין זה כבוד שמים שלא ליקח נקמה מזה שביזה עבד המלך החביב לו מאד, ולענוש את זה שביזה את הצדיק

״ובסטאנביל השליך עצמו לתוך קטנות מופלג מאד אשר אין לשער. והלביש עצמו במלבוש קרוע, והלך יחף ובלא כובע עליון, והלך בחוץ והלך כאחד מן הפחותים שבפחותים. וכיוצא באלה ענינים רבים כאלה מעניני קטנות ופחיתות שעשה שם איזה זמן. ועשה מלחמה עם שאר אנשים בדרך צחוק, כדרך הנערים שמצחקים זה עם זה וכו׳. וכיוצא בזה שאר עניני צחוק וקטנות אשר א״א לבאר ולספר. גם נזדמן שהי׳ שם בסטאנביל מסביבותינו שני אנשים שהיו תחילה בא״י וחזרו אז בעת שהי׳ רבינו ז״ל בסטאנביל בדרך הילוכו לא״י. ופגעו עמו ולא הכירו אותו. ועשה בחכמתו ונדמה להם כאילו הוא איש מרמה ח״ו, והיו מבזים אותו בכל מיני בזיונות כמה ימים רצופים, והוא הי׳ מקבל ע״ע כל הבזיונות, ואדרבא עשה תחבולות לזה שהם יבזו אותו. ואמר רבינו ז״ל שאילו לא הי׳ עליו זאת, היינו הקטנות, שהשליך עצמו לקטנות גדול הנ״ל, לא הי׳ באפשרי לבוא מחמת המניעות שהי׳ לו. כי בכל מקום שבא לשם הי׳ שם עיפוש[6] ר״ל ומלחמות גדולות היו אז בעולם, ואנשי צרפת היו אז בסביבות א״י, ורוב המניעות שהיו לו א״א לספר. ואמר שהבעש״ט ז״ל והגאון ר׳ ר׳ נפתלי ז״ל לא יכלו לבוא לא״י מחמת המניעות שהי׳ להם, והוא ז״ל הי׳ עליו כל המניעות שהי׳ להם, ועבר על כולם. והקטנות הנ״ל הועיל לו מאד, ובלא זה לא הי׳ יכול לבוא לשם.״[7]

במצבי קטנות היה ר׳ נחמן מתראה כבור ועם הארץ, משולל נמוסים, רמאי ושוטה גמור. היה עושה כמיטב יכולתו כדי להביא על עצמו השפלות ובזיונות לרוב. בהתאם עם התפיסה לפיה מצבי קטנות וגדלות שניהם מצבים יחסיים, ויש להבחין בהם דרגות שכלול רבות ושונות, העמיד ר׳ נחמן את מדת קטנותו ביחס ישיר עם עוצם גדלותו. ככל שהיתה גדלותו ״קטנה״ יותר, כלומר, ככל שהיתה מדת קטנותו רבה יותר והסבל וההשפלה שסבל בעטיה גדולים עד לעין שעור, כן גברה ״גדלותו״ והגיעה לממדים, שאף אותם אי אפשר לשער:

״ושמעתי בשם רבינו ז״ל שאמר כי קודם שבאין לגדלות צריכין ליפול בתחילה לקטנות. וא״י הוא גדלות דגדלות, ע״כ צריכין ליפול בתחילה בקטנות דקטנות, וע״כ לא הי׳ יכול הבעש״ט ז״ל לבוא לא״י, כי לא הי׳ יכול לירד לתוך קטנות כזה. והוא ז״ל זכה לבוא לא״י ע״י גודל הקטנות שירד לשם בחכמתו העצומה לקטנות מופלג, קטנות דקטנות, עד שזכה לבוא לא״י שהוא גדלות דגדלות. ועוצם ההשגה שזכה בא״י אלו כל הימים דיו וכו׳. אין מספיק לבאר אשר לא נשמע ולא נראה מי שיזכה ע״י כניסה לא״י להשגה מופלגת עצומה ועליונה כזו, עד שעלה למעלה ומדריגה עליונה גבוה מאד. וחלילה לנו לדבר מזה. שלא לפגום ולמעט בכבודו ח״ו. כי אין לנו כלים ודיבורים לכנוס בהם עוצם השגתו ומעלתו . . .״[8]

מה משמעותה של אותה ירידה (שהבעש״ט עצמו לא היה מסוגל לה)[9] לדרגת קטנות הנמוכה ביותר, ל״קטנות דקטנות״? אם קטנות סתם תובעת מן הצדיק ירידה לדרגת התנהגות מוסרית־דתית של אנשים פשוטים, שהיא נמוכה לאין ערוך מדרגתו הטבעית הצדיקית, כלום אין ״קטנות דקטנות״ שלו מצריכה את ירידתו לדרגה, שהיא כעין הפוכה של דרגתו הטבעית, אל מצב שבו אין הוא שרוי במישור פעולתם של אנשים פשוטים סתם, אלא הוא מתנסה בקיומם משולל־החוק ואולי אף מהופך־החוק של רשעים גמורים?

בשני תאוריו את נסיעת רבו לא״י חוזר ר׳ נתן ומצהיר ש״אי אפשר לשער״ או ש״אי אפשר לבאר ולספר״ את כל מדת קטנותו של ר׳ נחמן באותה נסיעה. כשהוא מתאר בפרוטרוט כמה ממעשי הקטנות של ר׳ נחמן באסטנבול הוא רומז לקורא, שאין תאורו ממצה, ושאין ביכולתו לכתוב על הנושא יותר מן הנדפס. כמו כן מודיע ר׳ נתן, שאי אפשר לתאר במילים את גדלותו העצומה של ר׳ נחמן, אותה השיג

"קטנות", "פשיטות" ו"איני יודע" של ר׳ נחמן מברסלב

עדה רפפורט־אלברט

בקבלת האר"י מתיחסים שני ההפכים, "קטנות" ו"גדלות" למצבים מסוימים של האלוהות בתחום מערכת הספירות. החסידות, כדרכה, "הורידה" מושגים אלה אל המישור האנושי ונזקקה להם כלמגדירי תפיסת ה"דבקות" שלה. "גדלות" הפכה בחסידות למצב שבו הגשים האדם את אידיאל הדבקות במלואו, ו"קטנות" למצבו בעת נפילה מדבקות. שני המושגים נתפסו כיחסיים: לכל אדם מדת גדלות ומדת קטנות משלו.

הצדיק בחסידות שואף תמיד ואף מסוגל להגיע למצב של גדלות. אך משום שתי סבות עליו לרדת לפרקים למצבי קטנות: (**א**) אין האדם, ואפילו הוא צדיק גמור, יכול לשאת במתח הגבוה של דבקות מתמדת. הירידה לקטנות היא התפרקותו הנפשית מדבקות, המאפשרת את המשך קיומו הארצי ומשמשת לו כהכנה הכרחית לעליתו הבאה והגבוהה יותר לגדלות. (**ב**) ע"י ירידתו המכוונת ממצב דבקות לקטנות הצדיק מתחבר עם אנשים פשוטים, "המוניים", השקועים תמיד בקטנות יחסית ואינם מסוגלים לעליה כשלו, וזאת על מנת להעלות אף אותם לדבקות.[1]

קטנותו של הצדיק מתבטאת בהתנהגות האפינית לאנשים פשוטים: שיחה בטלה, עסוק במשא ומתן ובענינים חילוניים כיוצאים באלה. רק במצב זה, כשהוא משים את עצמו לאיש פשוט, מסוגל הצדיק לבוא בדברים עם חסידיו ולצאת ידי חובתו כלפי עדתו, שהוא משמש כמרכזה הדתי והחברתי. שכן, כשהוא שרוי במצב של גדלות, הרי הוא בדבקות מבודדת עם האל, הרחק מעבר לתחום השגם של חסידיו.[2]

אף על פי שמושג "קטנות" תופס מקום חשוב בתורתו של ר׳ נחמן מברסלב, ולמרות שללא ספק התנסה בנפילות מגדלות לרוב, אין המונח עצמו שכיח בכתבי החוג. בספרי ברסלב מופיעים כמה מונחים אחרים: "פשיטות" או "הנהגת פשיטות", "בחינת פרוסטיק"[3] ומעל לכל "בחינת איני יודע", שכולם נראה כי הם מיצגים ניסוחים נבדלים אך קשורים זה לזה ולמושג החסידי המסורתי של "קטנות". מאמר זה הוא נסיון לעמוד על מהותם, על היחס ביניהם ועל יחסם למושג "קטנות" במשנת ר׳ נחמן.

המונח "קטנות" מופיע פעמים מספר בשני תאוריו של הסופר ר׳ נתן שטרנהרץ את נסיעת רבו לא"י בתקנ"ח.[4] במבט ראשון נראה, שמצבי ה"קטנות" בהם, ע"פ שני התאורים, נתנסה ר׳ נחמן במשך כל אותה נסיעה, לא נשתנו כלל ועיקר מ"קטנות" כפי שהגדירוה בדור מיסדי החסידות: במצבי קטנות אלה הופרע ר׳ נחמן מדבקותו. כך, למשל, לא היה מסוגל להתפלל על הצלתו והצלת חברו לנסיעה — ר׳ שמעון — בשעת סערה בים, משום רחוקו מן האל באותה שעה:

"וישאל אותו האיש ואמר לו, אני איני יודע להתפלל אפילו תפילה שסדורה מאנשי כנה"ג, מכ"ש עכשיו בעת הצרה הזאת. אבל כת"ר יודע להתפלל בעד כלליות ופרטיות, מפני מה אין אתם מתפללים עכשיו? והשיב שעכשיו מחמת המוחין דקטנות אני מרוחק מהש"י."[5] באין לאל ידו להתפלל או לעסוק בכל פעולה רוחנית אחרת הצריכה דבקות, התנהג ר׳ נחמן משך אותה נסיעה באופן, שאותו כנה ר׳ נתן "הנהגת קטנות שלו". התאור הבא להלן של מעשיו בעת שהותו באסטנבול, בדרך לא"י, עשוי להדגים את "הנהגת קטנות" של ר׳ נחמן:

דבר העורכים

מקצת שבחו של אדם אומרים בפניו וכלו שלא בפניו, ואע״פ שדברי הקדמה לספר יובל נכתבים בסתר נראים הם בעיני בעל היובל כאילו נאמרו לפניו. בכל זאת אינו מן הראוי לוותר על הבעת תודה והוקרה בפומבי כלפי מורנו ורבנו פרופסור אלטמאן, שממימי תורתו שאבו רבים ומאור משנתו הוארו עיני חבריו תלמידיו וידידיו. וכיצד מוסיפים על גודל זכויותיו ומדותיו של מי שבכל מגוריו יסד מוסדות להפיץ תורה וחכמה? מכאן כלולים בקובץ זה מאמרים ממאמרים שונים העוסקים בקורותיהם ובדעותיהם של עם ישראל, הן בדברי אמונה ועיון הן בעניני מדינה מזמן המקרא עד ימינו אנו.

לפיכך באים מגישי המאמרים הללו ועורכיהם בדברי איחול וברכה לבעל היובל שיזכה לשנים רבות, ויהי רצון שיוסיפו מוקיריו ליהנות מלקחי חכמתו שעתיד הוא להעניק להם. ברוך המלמד תורה לעמו ישראל.

יהושע שטיין
רפאל הלוי לוועוע

תוכן

מאמרים כתובים עברית

מאמרים כתובים לועזיות

ראה סידורם בסוף הספר